Theoretical Approaches to Disharmonic Word Order

Theoretical Approaches to Disharmonic Word Order

Edited by
THERESA BIBERAUER AND
MICHELLE SHEEHAN

OXFORD
UNIVERSITY PRESS

OXFORD
UNIVERSITY PRESS

Great Clarendon Street, Oxford, OX2 6DP,
United Kingdom

Oxford University Press is a department of the University of Oxford.
It furthers the University's objective of excellence in research, scholarship,
and education by publishing worldwide. Oxford is a registered trade mark of
Oxford University Press in the UK and in certain other countries

First published in 2013

Impression: 1

Published in the United States of America by Oxford University Press
198 Madison Avenue, New York, NY 10016, United States of America

British Library Cataloguing in Publication Data
Data available

Library of Congress Control Number: 2013948770

ISBN 978-0-19-968435-9

As printed and bound by
CPI Group (UK) Ltd, Croydon, CR0 4YY

Contents

Acknowledgments

This volume takes its name from the eponymous conference held at Newcastle University in 2009, organized by Anders Holmberg, Michelle Sheehan, and Laura Bailey. All but one of the chapters originated as a paper presented at this conference, which was held under the auspices of the Arts and Humanities Research Council (AHRC)-funded project, *Structure and Linearization in Disharmonic Word Orders* (AHRC Grant No. AH/E009239/1; Principal Investigator: Professor Anders Holmberg).

In addition to the authors, without whose co-operation this volume would, of course, never have been possible, we would like to thank the following for their reviewing assistance: Klaus Abels, Edith Aldridge, Linda Badan, Lawrence Cheung, Silvio Cruschina, Maximiliano Guimarães, Bill Haddican, S. J. Hannahs, Roland Hinterhölzl, Anders Holmberg, Jaklin Kornfilt, Iain Mobbs, Neil Myler, Johan Oosthuizen, Matt Pearson, Marc Richards, Norvin Richards, Ian Roberts, Kirill Shklovsky, Andrew Simpson, Luis Vicente, Irene Vogel, George Walkden, Wim van der Wurff, and Maria Luisa Zubizarreta. Additionally, we are very grateful indeed to the two anonymous OUP reviewers who reviewed the entire manuscript, not only for their very positive evaluations, but also for their extremely helpful suggestions. Thanks too to Jessica Brown for her help with various formatting tasks; to Leston Buell for his phenomenal copyediting; and to Anna Asbury and Jess Smith for their meticulous work at the proofs stage. Last, but certainly not least, our grateful thanks to OUP's Julia Steer for her immensely efficient, but always friendly and, where necessary, patient support; and to Kate Gilks for having overseen the final stages of the project.

Theresa Biberauer and Michelle Sheehan

Cambridge, July 2013

The Contributors

Michael Barrie is an Assistant Professor of linguistics at Sogang University in Korea. His main research interests are in generative syntactic theory, phrase structure, Antisymmetry, Distributed Morphology, and the Minimalist Program. He is interested in noun incorporation, Control, *wh*-movement, Northern Iroquoian, Algonquian, Romance, and Chinese. He is also interested in on-going language revitalization efforts of Iroquoian languages in the Six Nations community in Canada.

Theresa Biberauer is a Senior Research Associate at the University of Cambridge, where she is also a Fellow of Churchill College, and an Associate Professor Extraordinary at her South African *alma mater*, Stellenbosch University. Her research interests are principally in theoretical and comparative (synchronic and diachronic) morphosyntax, with Germanic generally and Afrikaans in particular being areas of specific interest. Her past work has focused on word-order variation, (null) subject phenomena, negation, information structure, and the larger question of the nature of parametric variation.

Brian Hok-Shing Chan is currently an Associate Professor at the University of Macau. He obtained his PhD in Linguistics at University College London, where he completed his PhD thesis entitled *Aspects of the Syntax, Production and Pragmatics of Code-Switching—With Special Reference to Cantonese and English*. A revised version of the thesis was published subsequently by Peter Lang in 2003. Since then he has continued his research on code-switching, while retaining an interest in the syntax of Cantonese. More recent publications can be found in *Lingua* (2008) and *The Cambridge Handbook of Linguistic Code-Switching* (2009) and *World Englishes* (2009).

Guglielmo Cinque is Professor of General Linguistics at the University of Venice, with interests in syntactic theory, typological linguistics and Romance linguistics. He has been involved in teaching and administration at the University of Venice and has taught at various universities abroad (Paris VIII, Vienna, Geneva, Harvard, UCLA, Ecole Normale, Paris, Brussels).

Since receiving her PhD in Linguistics in 2010 from the University of Padova, Federica Cognola has been working at the University of Trento as a Post-doctoral Research Fellow and a Contract Lecturer in German linguistics. Her research interests are syntax, monolingual and bilingual language acquisition, language variation and change, and the history of German and its dialects. She is the author of several articles on the syntax of the German dialect Mòcheno and of two monographs: *Acquisizione plurilingue e bilinguismo sbilanciato: uno studio sulla sintassi dei bambini mocheni in età prescolare* (Padova: Unipress, 2011) and *Syntactic Variation and Verb Second: A German Dialect in Northern Italy* (Amsterdam: John Benjamins, 2013).

REDOUANE DJAMOURI is a Researcher at the Centre national de la recherche scientifique (CNRS) and affiliated to the Centre de recherches linguistiques sur l'Asie orientale (CRLAO) at the École des hautes études en sciences sociales (EHESS) and the Institut des langues et civilisations orientales (INALCO) in Paris. His main interest is the syntax of Early Archaic Chinese. He has published articles on various subjects concerning the language of the Shang and Zhou dynasties (13th–2nd c. BC): negation, deictics, focus clefts, prepositional phrases, and so on.

ARANTZAZU ELORDIETA is Associate Professor in the Department of Linguistics and Basque Studies at the University of the Basque Country. Her major areas of research interest include word order, null arguments, the syntactic and phonological realization of topic and focus, and syntactic microvariation within Basque. She is a research member of HITT (Basque Research Group of Theoretical Linguistics) and is also involved in the projects and activities organized by Basdisyn, a research group which brings together syntacticians, dialectologists, and computational linguists and studies syntactic variation phenomena across Basque dialects.

JOSEPH EMONDS has published four books and numerous articles on syntactic and morphological analysis: *The Transformational Approach to English Syntax, Unified Theory of Syntactic Categories, Lexicon and Grammar: the English Syntacticon,* and *Discovering Syntax.* He is American, but moved to England in 1992. He has also taught in France, the Netherlands, Japan, Austria, and Spain, and now teaches and does research in the Czech Republic. His research focuses on how Universal Grammar interacts with formalized grammatical lexicons.

JOHN A. HAWKINS is Professor of Linguistics at the University of California Davis and Emeritus Professor of English and Applied Linguistics at the University of Cambridge. He has held previous positions at the University of Essex, the Max Planck Institute for Psycholinguistics in Nijmegen, and the University of Southern California, and visiting appointments at institutions including UC Berkeley, the Free University of Berlin, and the Max Planck Institute for Evolutionary Anthropology in Leipzig. He has broad interests in the language sciences and has publications in language typology, psycholinguistics, pragmatics, applied linguistics and second language learning, English and the Germanic language family, and historical linguistics.

ROLAND HINTERHÖLZL is Professor of German Linguistics at the University of Venice, Ca' Foscari. He has done research in comparative and diachronic German syntax. He has published an OUP monograph on scrambling, remnant movement, and restructuring in West Germanic (2006) and co-edited (with S. Petrova) a volume on information structure and language change with Mouton de Gruyter (2009). He is currently working on issues of the interfaces between syntax, prosody, and information structure. His most recent publications include a comparative study of word-order regularities in German and English (*Syntax* 12, 2009), a paper on the development of V2 in Germanic (*Lingua* 120, 2011), and a lead paper (written with Ans van Kemenade) in the *Handbook of the History of English* (OUP 2012).

RICHARD S. KAYNE has a PhD from MIT, a Doctorat ès Lettres from the University of Paris VIII, and honorary doctorates from the University of Leiden and the University of Bucharest. Currently Silver Professor at NYU, he is the author of *French Syntax: The Transformational Cycle*, *Connectedness and Binary Branching*, *The Antisymmetry of Syntax*, *Parameters and Universals*, *Movement and Silence*, and *Comparisons and Contrasts*.

YASUTOMO KUWANA is a Senior English Teacher in charge of curriculum and instruction at Asahikawa Jitsugyo High School. He finished his master courses at Sapporo University and Ball State University in 2003 and 2005, and respectively obtained his Master's degrees in English Linguistics and Teaching English to Speakers of Other Languages (TESOL). He has contributed chapters in collected volumes published by Mouton de Gruyter. His research interests include phonology, typology, and second language acquisition.

BALKIZ ÖZTÜRK is an Assistant Professor of Linguistics at Boğaziçi University, Department of Western Languages and Literatures. She received her Ph.D. degree from Harvard University in 2004. She has mainly worked on issues related to the syntax of Turkic Languages, such as relativization, incorporation, DP-structure, word order, EPP, case, and agreement systems. Her most recent research involves the interaction between event structure and argument structure in Laz, an endangered South-Caucasian Language spoken in Turkey.

WALTRAUD PAUL is a researcher at the French Centre national de la recherche scientifique (CNRS) and affiliated to the Centre de recherches linguistiques sur l'Asie orientale (CRLAO) at the École des hautes études en sciences sociales (EHESS) in Paris. Her main interest is the syntax of modern Mandarin, with occasional excursions into the diachronic syntax of Chinese. She has published articles on a large variety of subjects: topic, focus, clefts, split CP, double object constructions, adjectival modification, serial verb constructions, and so on.

MICHELLE SHEEHAN is a Research Associate at the University of Cambridge specializing in comparative syntax with a particular interest in the Romance languages. She has worked on null arguments, Control, word-order variation, extraposition, clausal-nominal parallels, and case/alignment. She is co-author of the CUP volume *Parametric*

Variation: Null Subjects in Minimalist Theory and the forthcoming volumes *The Final-over-Final Constraint* (MIT Press) and *The Philosophy of Universal Grammar* (OUP).

HISAO TOKIZAKI is Professor of English Linguistics at Sapporo University. He finished the doctoral course at Hokkaido University in 1988 and received his PhD from Tsukuba University in 2007. A revised version of his dissertation was published in 2008 by Hituzi Syobo Publishers as *Syntactic Structure and Silence: A Minimalist Theory of Syntax–Phonology Interface*. He has published articles in journals including *English Linguistics* and *Phonological Studies* and contributed chapters in collected volumes published by Mouton de Gruyter and Equinox. His research interests include phonology, morphology, syntax, and typology.

TAKASHI TOYOSHIMA received his doctoral degree from Cornell University in 2000. He is now an Associate Professor at Kyushu Institute of Technology, Japan. He is interested in the mathematical foundations of Minimalist syntax and has worked on the issues of computational complexity, derivational economy, phrase structure, and head movement, among other things. He has also co-authored a few papers in artificial intelligence and neural computation about induction of formal grammars with algorithms and in a self-organizing map.

MARK DE VOS is a Senior Lecturer at Rhodes University in South Africa. He obtained an MPhil at Tromsø University in Norway before obtaining his PhD from the University of Leiden Center for Linguistics in the Netherlands. His research interests include the role of Dependency and Relational Theory in syntax, the interaction between syntax and PF output conditions, Agreement, pseudo-coordination, language variation, and, more recently, how linguistic-theoretical insights can be applied to indigenous-language literacies in South Africa.

JOHN WHITMAN is Director of the Division of Crosslinguistic Studies at the National Institute for Japanese Language and Linguistics (NINJAL) in Tokyo and Professor of Linguistics at Cornell University. He works on historical/comparative linguistics, language typology, and syntactic theory, with a primary focus on the languages of East Asia.

List of Abbreviations

A	declension class in Urarina
ACC	accusative
ACT	active
AF	affective
AGR	agreement
AH	Accessibility Hierarchy
ALL	allative
AP	Adjective Phrase
ART	article
ASP	aspectual marker
AT	actor
AUX	Auxiliary (verb)
AuxP	Auxiliary Phrase
BBC	Basic Branching Constraint
BDT	Branching Direction Theory
BHR	Biberauer, Holmberg, and Roberts
BPS	Bare Phrase Structure
CCH	Cross-Category Harmony
CED	Condition on Extraction Domain
CL	clitic
CLF	classifier
CND	conditional/temporal
CNT	continuous aspect
COLL	collective
COMP/C	complementizer
CONJ	conjunction
CONT	continuative
COP	copula verb
CP	Complementizer Phrase
CRD	Constituent Recognition Domain
D	clension class in Urarina
DAT	dative

DEM	demonstrative
DET	determiner
DEVLD	devalued
DP	Determiner Phrase
DUR	durative aspect
E	declension class in Urarina
EIC	Early Immediate Constituents
EMPH	emphatic marker
EPP	Extended Projection Principle
ERG	ergative
EVID	evidential
EXP	experiential aspect
F	feminine
FD	functional dependency
FOC	focus
FOFC	Final-over-Final Constraint
FUT	future
FV	final vowel (Bantu)
GB	Government and Binding
GEN	genitive
H	head
HAB	habitual
HDT	Head Dependent Theory
HFF	Head-Final Filter
HRS	hearsay
IC	immediate constituent
iF	interpretable feature
IMPF	imperfective
IMPST	immediate past
IND	indicative
INDOBJ	indirect object
INGR	ingressive
IRR	irrealis
ITER	iterative
LCA	Linear Correspondence Axiom
LF	Logical Form

LOC	locative (verb)
M	masculine
MaOP	Maximize On-line Processing
MiD	Minimize Domains
N	neuter
NC	noun class
NEG	negation marker
NM	noun marker
NOM	nominative
NP	Noun Phrase
NSP	Natural Serialization Principle
NUM	Number
NUMCL	numeral classifier
NZLR	nominalizer
O	object
OSV	Object–Subject–Verb
OV	Object–Verb
OVS	Object–Verb–Subject
P	adposition (postposition/preposition)
p	light P
PART	particle
PASS	passive
PAST.HEARSAY	past evidential marking
PathP	Path Phrase
p^{DIR}	directional adposition
PFV	perfective aspect
PRF	perfect
PF	Phonological Form
PFV	perfective
PGCH	Performance–Grammar Correspondence Hypothesis
PL	plural
PLD	Primary Linguistic Data
p^{LOC}	locative adposition
POL	Polarity
POSS	possessive

POSSD	possessed
POST	postposition
PP	Adposition Phrase
PREP	preposition
PRES	present
PRET	preterite
PRO	pronoun
PROG	progressive
PTCP	participle
PST	past
PURP	purpose
PVC	postverbal constituent
Q	question particle/interrogative
QUAN	quantifier
REL	relativizer
Rel cl	relative clause
REM	remote past/future
S	subject
SFP	sentence-final particle
SG	singular
SOV	Subject–Object–Verb
SS	same subject marker
STR	strong
SUB	subordinating marker/subordinator
SUBJ	subject
SUP	superessive
SVO	Subject–Verb–Object
TOP	topic
TP	Tense Phrase (= IP– Inflectional Phrase)
uF	uninterpretable feature
UG	Universal Grammar
v	light verb
V	verb
V2	Verb Second
VO	Verb–Object

VOS	Verb–Object–Subject
VP	Verb Phrase
*v*P	light verb Phrase
VSO	Verb–Subject–Object
WALS	*World Atlas of Language Structures*
WI	Word Interpretation
1	first person
2	second person
3	third person

1

Theoretical Approaches to Disharmonic Word Order

THERESA BIBERAUER AND MICHELLE SHEEHAN

1.1 Introduction

Word order has not always been of great interest to grammarians. In ancient times, when the study of grammar meant the study of what we would today identify as the phonology, morphology, and syntax of a particular language,[1] word order was typically a minor syntactic concern, with largely morphologically based categorization considerations taking centre stage. As Henri Weil (1818–1909) notes, by the mid 19th century, grammarians had 'very carefully studied isolated words, as also their syntactical concatenation; but most of them [had] given no attention to the order in which words may follow each other' (1879 [1844]: 11). To the extent that they were concerned with word order, ancient grammarians were interested only in providing some rationale for the order of constituents. Thus Priscian (*floruit* 500 AD), drawing on the work of his contemporaries, proposed an abstract OV order for Latin based on the idea that 'the noun precedes the verb because the substance expressed by the noun precedes the accidents expressed by the verb' (Seuren 1998: 29, citing Luhtala 1994: 1467).

This pursuit continued into the 17th and 18th century, with grammarians being famously interested in word order as an indicator of the order of thought. Thus 18th-century linguists in the *grammaire générale* tradition compared the word orders of different languages in search of the *ordre naturel*. Some, including Nicolas Beauzée (1717–89), afforded SVO this status, making French 'analogical' in that its words tracked the order of thought, as opposed to Greek, Latin, and German, which were 'transpositive' as the correlation was indirect (Graffi 2001: 84). Others, including the

---

[1] As Seuren (1998: 29) notes: 'The Greeks and Romans were not directly concerned with universal properties of human language, their linguistic horizon being extremely restricted.'

philosopher Denis Diderot (1713–84), rejected the idea that the word order of a particular language could achieve such a status (cf. Graffi 2001: 17, citing Jellinek 1913–14 II: 425–64). The idea of a natural order nonetheless retained currency and is also observed in the work of Wilhelm von Humboldt (1767–1835) in the 19th century. Weil himself proposed a more nuanced status for word order, and he is perhaps most famous for noting that 'the syntactic march is not the march of ideas' (Weil 1879 [1844]: 21). This quote is misleading, however, as he nonetheless maintained that 'to treat of the order of words is then, in a measure, to treat of the order of ideas' (Weil 1879 [1844]: 11). Weil was principally interested in the reason why the modern European languages (French, German, English) had such little freedom in their word order compared with the Ancient languages (Latin and Greek). His claim in this connection is that, to the extent that word order is free, it reveals pragmatic meaning, an idea which later became central to the work of the Prague School and to which we return below.

Twentieth-century thinking about word order was initially strongly influenced by the views of Ferdinand de Saussure (1857–1913).[2] Given that the Father of Structuralism is often criticized for the relatively limited attention he paid to syntax as a component of language structure—certainly when compared to his consideration of phonology and morphology (cf. i.a. Joseph 2012: 540 ff. for discussion)—this may at first seem surprising. Saussure did, however, explicitly consider the nature of syntax generally and word order in particular in relation to his seminal distinction between *langue* and *parole* (see Belletti and Rizzi 2002: 1–4 for overview and Joseph 2012 for detailed discussion). For Saussure, the regularities of phrase construction clearly fell into the domain of *langue*; the freedom with which speakers are able to combine elements taking into account the discourse situation in which they find themselves, on the other hand, was for him *le propre de la parole* (Saussure 1916: 172, cited in Belletti and Rizzi 2002: 3), i.e. the domain of *parole*. Since word-order choices within a given language are to such a large extent conditioned by communicative considerations which individual speakers must weigh up, it is not difficult to see why following generations of linguists would have interpreted the minimal discussion in Saussure's *Cours*[3] as (further) justification for investigating word order primarily from a functional perspective. As such, Saussure's syntactic legacy contrasts sharply, and in a way that is not always recognized, with the influence his work had on phonology and morphology.

A major factor in Saussure's sparse discussion of word order having the influence it did within the domain of early 20th-century word-order research is undoubtedly

---

[2] We thank an anonymous OUP reviewer for drawing our attention to Saussure's influence on the direction that word-order studies took in the first half of the 20th century.

[3] As the OUP reviewer mentioned in the previous footnote points out, Saussure himself did no syntactic analysis.

also the work of Vilém Mathesius (1882–1945). Independently of Saussure, the founder of the Prague Linguistic Circle had also in his (1911) paper, *O potenciálnosti jevů jazykových* ('On the potentiality of language phenomena'), pointed to the distinction between the two forms of language that Saussure made famous as *langue* (cf. the *potenciálnosti* of Mathesius's 1911 title) and *parole*. Further, influenced by Masaryk (1885), he had also discussed the importance of a distinction betweeen 'static' and 'dynamic' aspects of language, one which he later related to Saussure's synchrony/diachrony dichotomy (cf. Mathesius 1927/1983). Unlike Saussure and the first generations of structuralists more generally, Mathesius, however, had firmly comparative linguistic interests, and his own work on Czech, German, and English reinforced in him the view that the appropriate *tertium comparationis* in comparative linguistics should be language function. More specifically, Mathesius's view was that languages differ in the structural means (word order, intonation, use of specific constructions, etc.) via which they permit speakers to communicate successfully, with the extent to which they draw on these structural possibilities defining their 'linguistic characterology' (cf. Mathesius 1928). He introduced to functionalist linguistics and the study of word order more generally the notion of 'functional sentence perspective',[4] in terms of which utterances can be divided into what is today referred to as a *theme* or *topic* (roughly, what the utterance is about) and *rheme* or *focus* (approximately, what is said about the theme/topic). Crucially, he also highlighted the way in which these notions correlate with what is today referred to as *information structure*: typically, the theme/topic maps onto discourse-old/salient information, while the *rheme/focus* corresponds to discourse-new/non-salient information. Importantly, this comparatively inspired work naturally connected with research, also being completed during the first decades of the 20th century, that was clearly inspired by Weil's earlier ideas. Based on his meticulous study of the history of German, Otto Behaghel, in his monumental four-volume *Deutsche Syntax: Eine geschichtliche Darstellung* ('German syntax: a historical account', published between 1923 and 1932), postulates a number of information-structure-sensitive word-order principles or Laws, which he assumed to be cross-linguistically valid. These include the following:

(1)   a. **Behaghel's Second Law**: That which is less important (or already known to the listener) is placed before that which is more important (or unknown).

   b. **Behaghel's Law of Increasing Terms** (*Gesetz der wachsenden Glieder*):[5] Given two phrases, the shorter precedes the longer where possible.

---

[4] More accurately, Mathesius himself employed the Czech term *aktuální členění větné* (literally 'actual division of sentence'), and it was Firbas (1957) who, building on Mathesius's own German translation (*funktionale Satzperspektive*), proposed the term *functional sentence perspective*.

[5] Following Cooper and Ross (1975), this Law is also often referred to as *Pāṇini's Law*.

During the early decades of the 20th century, then, various strands of European linguistic research were converging on the centrality of what would today be labelled 'functional' considerations in the study of word order, while simultaneously emphasizing the value of comparative work.

Strikingly, contemporaneous American structuralism was very different in its orientation, focusing on the purely synchronic structural description of individual languages and, in line with Bloomfield's (1934: 36) sentiments, avoiding the 'larger synthesis' or 'General Grammar, which will register the similarities between languages' until more was known about languages, non-Indo-European ones in particular (cf. also Bloomfield 1933: 46). As DeLancey (2001) notes, American structuralism's strong description-first/explanation-later orientation and the wider intellectual influence of behaviourism in psychology and logical positivism in philosophy created an intellectual climate within which comparative research received little attention. Thus early 20th-century European works such as those mentioned above, Wilhelm Schmidt's ground-breaking (1926) study of cross-linguistic variation in word-order patterns and their significance for language classification,[6] and even Sapir's (1929) pioneering classification of the indigenous languages of the Americas aroused little immediate interest in mainstream linguistics. It would take the work of Joseph Greenberg, student of both Sapir's teacher, Franz Boas, and, later, the Prague Circle's Roman Jakobson to unite the European and American research traditions and truly ignite 20th-century research in cross-linguistic word-order variation. In what follows, we review Greenberg's work and the influential typological tradition to which it gave rise before considering the status of word order in the generative tradition and future prospects in this domain more generally.

1.2 Harmony and disharmony from Greenberg to the present

1.2.1 *Greenberg's correlation pairs and the notion of harmony*

Greenberg (1963: 60) notes that 'linguists are in general familiar with the notion that certain languages tend consistently to put modifying or limiting elements before modified or limited, while others just as consistently do the opposite'. This is the basis of the notion of 'harmony' which lies at the heart of this volume. Thus, in English, modifiers tend to follow modified elements like verbs and adpositions, whereas the opposite is true in Hindi:

---

[6] In relation to Schmidt's work, it is worth noting that, despite its systematic treatment of word-order phenomena, its author's objective was not primarily linguistic; instead, it was intended as a vehicle for the interpretation of cultural history. Greenberg (1963: 105, note 4), who acknowledges the value of Schmidt's contribution, says of this 'applied' component of the work, 'His results there verge on the fantastic.'

(2) John [is [at [school]]]   V P O

(3) Raam [[[skuul] par] hai]   O P V
     Raam school at   is
     'Ram is at school'

The basic word-order phenomena discussed by Greenberg are the following (based on Greenberg 1963: Appendices I–II):

(4)   i. verb-initial/medial/final
      ii. adposition–noun order
     iii. noun–adjective order
      iv. noun–genitive order
       v. noun–demonstrative order
      vi. noun–numeral order
     vii. pronominal–verb order

For Greenberg, though, the term 'harmony' actually has a more technical definition, relying crucially on his notion of 'dominance'. A particular order is dominant over another order, where it is less constrained in the following terms:

A dominant order may always occur, but its opposite, the recessive, occurs only when a harmonic construction is likewise present.   (Greenberg 1963: 62)

This is effectively illustrated by a tetrachoric table, as shown in Figure 1. 1:

	V-DP	DP-V
pro-V	Y	Y
V-pro	Y	N

FIGURE 1.1 Positioning of lexical nominal and pronominal complements in relation to the verb

Figure 1. 1 indicates that three of four potential word-order combinations involving verbs and lexical/pronominal complements are attested. Crucially, the fourth, whereby pronominals follow, but full lexical complements precede the verb, is unattested. This means that V–DP is dominant over DP–V, as the latter order is more constrained than the former, occurring only where the order of pronominal and verb is harmonic with the order of full nominal (DP) and the verb.[7] Greenberg claims that harmony between two correlation pairs arises wherever we see this

---

[7] Note that this distributional fact might be viewed as support for Kayne's influential Antisymmetry hypothesis, discussed below and in several of the papers in the volume. Kayne (this volume) himself cites this universal in support of Antisymmetry.

particular pattern in a tetrachoric table. Note that for Greenberg, then, harmony is a notion which is defined across languages based on patterns of attested cross-linguistic variation (in this case a core sample of 30 and an expanded sample of 142 languages, but ideally the sum of all attested languages).[8] Interestingly, although the focus of his (1963) work was not primarily on explanation, his concluding speculations on this point did clearly indicate that harmony seemed to him 'very obviously connected with the psychological concept of generalization' (Greenberg 1963: 62; see also Hawkins 1980, 1982, and 1983 for further discussion and elaboration).

Many of the papers in this book adopt a slightly different notion of harmony, defined in relation to a specific language, but drawing on the cross-linguistic patterns first identified by Greenberg. In these terms, two phrases are harmonic if and only if their respective 'modifying or limiting elements' pattern together in *uniformly* occurring at the right or left edge of the phrase concerned. Thus VP and PP can be said to be 'harmonic' in this sense in the English and Hindi examples above: in both cases, the 'modified' V/P systematically occurs to the left/right of its 'modifier'. Likewise, in a specific language with pro–V and V–DP orders, the order of pronominals and verbs can be said to be disharmonic with the order of full DPs and the verb, as pronominals and full DPs (the 'modifiers' in this case) do not uniformly align left/right. This perspective on harmony naturally lends itself to interpretation in terms of a Head Parameter, as we shall see in section 1.2.2 below; more generally, it is also obviously compatible with Greenberg's (1963: 62) psychological generalization proposal, with Hawkins' much-discussed (1983) Principle of Crosscategorial Harmony, and with Roberts' (2007b) Input Generalization (see again section 1.2.2, and also section 1.3.1 below). Worth noting here, however, is that proposals to relate typological harmony and typological patterns more generally to Universal Grammar (UG) have been strongly challenged by both generativists and non-generativists (see i.a. Newmeyer 2005a, Haspelmath 2008b, Whitman 2008, and Boeckx 2010 for discussion). Non-generativists typically point to the paucity of genuinely exceptionless cross-linguistic patterns, calling into the question the role of uniformity-imposing UG. The typical generativist objection, in turn, is formulated by Newmeyer (2005a: 105) as follows:

---

[8] Greenberg's (1963) paper also arguably contains the roots of Cartography (cf. Cinque 1999, 2005a amongst many others). Consider the following:

Another type of relation than those that have just been considered is illustrated by Universals 20 and 29. These may be called proximity hierarchies. What we have is a rule that certain elements must be closer to some central element than some other satellite. The central element may be the root morpheme or base of a word or the head-word of an endocentric construction. (Greenberg 1963: 104)

He goes on to add that '[t]hese hierarchies are presumably related to degrees of logical and psychological remoteness from the center, but no analysis is attempted here.'

Our minds/brains, after all, have no clue as to the typological status of any aspect of any element of our mental grammars. The relationship between typological generalizations and I-language is therefore necessarily quite indirect.[9]

And to this, we can also add Odden's (1988: 461) caveat that '[i]t is misguided to attribute every accidentally true statement about human language to UG, for doing so trivializes the theory of UG itself'.

We return to the issue of the relationship between (dis)harmonic word orders and mental grammars below (see the discussion in sections 1.3 and 1.4 in particular). Our immediate concern, however, is a more detailed consideration of the notion of 'harmony' and the theoretical ideas it has given rise to.

1.2.2 *Harmony and the Head Parameter*

Building on Greenberg's landmark paper, Vennemann (1972, 1974a,b) proposed an assimilation of the various word-order correlation pairs to a single operator/operand template. This in turn allowed him to posit a *Natural Serialization Principle* (NSP) whereby an unordered set {operator {operand}} is universally 'serialized' or linearized as either operator–operand or operand–operator in a given language. In later work (Vennemann 1976; Vennemann and Harlow 1977), Vennemann explicitly refers to operands as *Heads* and operators as *Specifiers*. As Dryer (1992a: 88) notes, however, it is important not to equate this use of *Specifier* with the generative notion 'specifier', as it is clear that Vennemann's intention here was to refer to dependent elements. The pairs in (5) illustrate the types of elements Vennemann was concerned with:

(5) | **Operand/Head** | **Operator/Dependent ('Specifier')** |
|---|---|
| Verb | Object |
| Verb | Adpositional Phrase |
| Verb | Manner Adverb |
| Noun | Relative Clause |
| Noun | Genitive |
| Noun | Adjective |

In a sense, the NSP can be considered a precursor of the Head Parameter, the idea that in a given language L, a head universally precedes/follows its complement. Consider this in relation to Chomsky (1970) and Jackendoff's (1977) X-bar theory:

---

[9] Lightfoot's oft-cited (1979) objection to the Sapirian notion of 'drift' makes the same point in relation to diachronic typology:

Languages are learned and grammars constructed by the individuals of each generation. They do not have racial memories such that they know in some sense that their language has gradually been developing from, say, an SOV and towards an SVO type, and that it must continue along that path. After all, if there were a prescribed hierarchy of changes to be performed, how could a child, confronted with a language exactly half-way along this hierarchy, know whether the language was changing from type *x* to type *y*, or vice versa? (Lightfoot 1979: 391)

(6)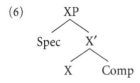

Here, Vennemann's operand could be seen as equivalent to the Head X, while a relevant subset of his operators are equivalent to Comp.

Hawkins (1980) offers an eloquent critique of the NSP, based partly on the observation that only 47.89% of the languages in Greenberg's sample actually have consistent operator–operand/operand–operator order across all the categories he considered. These are given below:

(7)   i. verb-initial/-medial/-final (collapsed to verb–object order by Vennemann— see (5) above)
      ii. adposition–noun order
      iii. noun–adjective order
      iv. noun–genitive order[10]

The lack of ordering consistency across pairs of elements means that very few languages are consistently 'harmonic' in the second, consistent left/right alignment sense discussed in section 1.2.1, i.e. for a given system, the modified X systematically occurs in a fixed position—left/right—in relation to its modifier. As Hawkins notes, then, what might be termed *disharmonic languages* actually outnumber their consistently harmonic counterparts, and the NSP's inability to account for the former is thus a major failing.[11] Vennemann (1975) had in fact proposed that languages which fail to conform to either word-order type are in a state of flux, being in the process of undergoing a diachronic change, but, as Hawkins notes, this is a problematic claim. Of the 24 logically possible word-order combinations, eight remain unattested (cf. Hawkins 1980: 198).[12] There is thus a second sense in which the NSP is problematic, as it fails to provide an account of these eight unattested types. All orders diverging from the consistently harmonic orders (again, in the second, non-Greenbergian sense) have the dubious status of intermediary stages of diachronic change for Vennemann, and, unless independent considerations are identified as to why the unattested systems fail to surface as intermediary systems, they cannot be ruled out by his approach. It is also worth noting that many attested disharmonic systems do not obviously appear to be in the process of change in the direction of harmony, i.e. a

---

[10] Given Greenberg's original three-way distinction for (i), this gives 3×2^3 (24) potential combinations.
[11] As Hawkins puts it (1980: 198), a scientific theory which accounts for less that 50% of the data is not a good theory.
[12] Vennemann proposes the merging of SVO and VSO languages to give the single type VO, but Hawkins takes issue with this move, mainly because, as Greenberg (1963) showed, VSO languages display much stronger correlations than SVO languages.

stable system. English, for example, has retained its disharmonic Saxon genitive over many centuries, with this structure in modern English being significantly more productive than the postnominal PP option (consider: *my friend's house* and *the house of my friend*). Sapirian 'drift'-oriented interpretations of Vennemann's NSP therefore do not appear to hold up (cf. Sapir 1921 on 'drift' and Roberts 2007b: 340–57 for discussion of potential theoretical interpretations of this notion). Finally, Hawkins points out that the NSP posits a series of bilateral relations between correlation pairs which in turn prevents one from capturing Greenberg's notions of dominance and harmony in their original sense: unilateral implicational universals lie at the heart of the Greenbergian notion of dominance and, in eliminating them, Vennemann again detracts from the viability of the NSP.[13]

There is thus a sense in which the Head Parameter (in the form of the NSP) was proposed early in the typological literature and quickly rejected. In a slightly later paper, though, Hawkins (1982) returns to the issue and discusses the notion of harmony more explicitly in relation to X-bar theory and potential 'spec' and 'head parameters'. He observes that X-bar theory, with its three-way head/specifier/complement distinction, might provide a finer-grained distinction than the two-way modifier/modified or operator/operand distinctions used by Greenberg and Vennemann, respectively. Once again, though, he notes that there is no evidence that specifiers, heads, and complements are systematically ordered (albeit in potentially different ways) across a given language. Even once we allow for the specifier/complement distinction, he argues, 'languages will vary according to the degree of cross-categorial generalization which their grammars incorporate' (Hawkins 1982: 9). Translating into a generative perspective, then, Hawkins (1982) concludes that word order cannot be regulated by a single parameter; it might, however, be regulated by a series of spec and head parameters which are psychologically related. In fact, Hawkins argues explicitly that '[g]rammars with more cross-categorial generalizations will be simpler than, and hence preferred over, those with fewer'. This is essentially a formalization of Greenberg's intuition that harmony is connected to generalization. In the modern generative context, specifically, Chomsky's 'three-factors' framework (cf. Chomsky 2005), this can very naturally be understood as the consequence of an intuitively plausible 'third factor'[14]—something like Roberts'

---

[13] Hawkins goes on to propose his own theory of the Greenbergian word-order correlations based on the combination of four absolute implicational universals and his relative principle of 'Cross-Category Harmony' (CCH), which aims to predict the relative frequencies between the 18 permitted word orders. We return to this principle in section 1.3.1.

[14] In the context of Chomsky's 'three-factors' approach, the factors assumed to play a role in determining the form of adult grammars are specified as UG (Factor 1), the PLD (Factor 2), and, additionally, rather vaguely specified 'third factors' or non-language-specific considerations, which include principles of efficient computation and principles of data analysis employed in acquisition (see Mobbs 2008, in progress for further discussion).

(2007b) Input Generalization, a strategy acquirers are assumed to employ in analysing the Primary Linguistic Data (PLD) they are exposed to. Importantly, this 'third-factor' take on the source of harmonic patterns removes the need to appeal (stipulatively) to (first-factor) UG, while also potentially addressing generative concerns (such as those of Newmeyer (2005a) and Lightfoot (1979), highlighted in the previous section) about the feasibility of understanding typological patterns (here: consistent left/right alignment harmony). Particularly worth noting in the present context, though, is the fact, typically overlooked by generativists, that, as early as the early 1980s, Hawkins rejected the idea that a single word-order parameter (e.g. the Head Parameter) could account for attested word-order variation and also that this variation could be understood as a direct reflex of UG alone.

Dryer (199-2a) tests Greenberg's word-order correlations on a much larger, more balanced 625-language sample. One of the theoretical objectives of his research is to test the feasibility of what he calls *Head Dependent Theory* (*HDT*), stated in (9):

(9) **The Head Dependent Theory (HDT)**
     Verb patterners are heads and object patterners are dependents, i.e. a pair of elements X and Y will employ the order XY significantly more often among VO languages than among OV languages if and only if X is a head and Y is a dependent (Dryer 1992a: 87).

In the context of a Head Parameter-based approach, the HDT, then, predicts that heads will be verb patterners, while complements are object patterners. Thirteen of the verb–object patterners identified by Dryer arguably involve head–complement relations. Consider (10):

(10) **Head–complement correlation pairs** (taken from Dryer 1992a: Table 39, 108)
      (i)   verb–object
      (ii)   adposition–DP
      (iii) copula verb–predicate
      (iv)   want–VP
      (v)   auxiliary verb–VP
      (vi)   negative auxiliary–VP
      (vii) complementizer–S(entence)
      (viii) article–noun
      (ix)   plural word–noun
      (x)   noun–genitive
      (xi)   adjective–standard of comparison
      (xii) verb–PP
      (xiii) adverbial subordinator–S(entence)

The remaining four, however, are less obviously head–complement relations:

(11)   **Other correlation pairs** (taken from Dryer 1992a: Table 39, 108)
     (i)   question particle–S(entence)
     (ii)   noun–relative clause
     (iii)   verb–manner adverb
     (iv)   verb–subject

Question particles are often taken to be heads selecting clausal complements (cf. Cable 2010 for recent discussion), but some problems for this are raised by Biberauer, Holmberg, and Roberts (in press) and Sheehan (this volume). In traditional analyses, relative clauses are taken to be adjuncts, but on Kayne's (1994) raising account, they are complements of the determiner, and so might arguably pattern with complements for this reason, as articles are verb patterners. Manner adverbs are generally assumed to involve either adjunction (cf. Ernst 2002) or, from a Cinque (1999) perspective, a specifier relation, and so are more problematic. Likewise, subjects are accepted to occupy a specifier position in X-bar theory, and so also present a potential problem. Evidently, then, Dryer's findings empirically reinforce Hawkins' observation that it cannot be a single Head Parameter which determines the observed harmonic patterns.

This point is also suggested by the potential correlation pairs (posited by Greenberg or others) which fail to pattern with verb–object order in Dryer's larger sample. Consider (12) in this connection:

(12)   **Non-correlation pairs** (Dryer 1992a: 108, Table 40)
     (i)   adjective–noun
     (ii)   demonstrative–noun
     (iii)   adverbial intensifier–adjective
     (iv)   negative particle–verb
     (v)   aspect/tense particle–verb

Worth noting about these pairs is that none of the non-correlation pairs involve clear head–complement relations: (i) is generally taken to involve adjunction or a spec–head relation in the extended nominal projection (Svenonius 1993), but not usually complementation (although see Abney 1987); (ii) is commonly thought to involve a spec–head relation (see i.a. Cinque 1995; Bernstein 1997 and 2008, and Giusti 2002); (iii) is taken to involve either adjunction or a spec–head relation (Bresnan 1973; Jackendoff 1977; though see Corver 1997 for a head analysis of a subset of degree words). The status of (iv) and (v) is unclear, as is made manifest by several of the papers in this volume (cf. Chan and Sheehan, and see also Biberauer and Sheehan 2011 on the problems posed by particles in the generative context). It is therefore not immediately clear that the non-correlating behaviour of the elements in (12) constitutes a challenge to the HDT. Dryer (1992a: 108–18), however, rejects

HDT-type, and thereby also Head Parameter-based, approaches, proposing the Branching Direction Theory instead:

(13)   **The Branching Direction Theory (BDT)** (Dryer 1992a: 109)
Verb patterners are non-phrasal (non-branching, lexical) categories and object patterners are phrasal (branching) categories, i.e. a pair of elements X and Y will employ the order XY significantly more often among VO languages than among OV languages if and only if X is a non-phrasal category and Y is a phrasal category.

In terms of BDT, the non-correlation pairs in (12) can be understood as cases involving pairs of items which do not consistently exhibit an identifiable branching direction because (a) each of the two items in question can readily be represented by single words, e.g. *blue skies* (i), *this weekend* (ii), *very tall* (iii), *not leave* (iv), and *repeatedly coughing* (v), and (b) the modifying element in each case is not fully recursive in the sense that it can embed other XPs (e.g. PPs, NPs, or clauses). The difficulty with the non-correlation pairs in (12), then, is that the modifying element does not exhibit the expected phrasal properties. What is predicted, however, is that, where an optionally branching modifier is fully recursively phrasal in the above sense, it will exhibit the behaviour of an object patterner. This prediction is borne out in cases such as those illustrated in (14–15) below:[15]

(14)   a. **blue** skies

b. **skies **blue***

c. skies [$_{AP}$ **blue** [$_{CP}$ **as the most brilliant sapphire**]]

d. ****blue as the most brilliant sapphire** sky*

(15)   a. J'   admire   **souvent**   le   courage de mon   père
I   admire   often   the   courage of my   father
'I often admire the courage of my father.'

b. **J' admire le   courage de mon père   **souvent***

c. J' admire le   courage de mon père   **quand je regarde à la   télé des**
I   admire the courage of my   father when I   look   at the TV of
films sur   la   Deuxième Guerre mondiale
films over   the second   war   world
'I admire the courage of my father when I watch TV programmes about the Second World War.'

d. **J'admire **quand je regarde à la télé des films sur la Deuxième Guerre mondiale** le courage de mon père*

---

[15] Thanks to an anonymous reviewer for the examples in (15).

A clear difference between BDT and HDT, then, is that the former, but not the latter—and, by extension, therefore, also not Head Parameter-based approaches more generally—can account for the fact that harmony affects not only heads and their complements (defined in terms of subcategorization), but also potentially branching adverbial modifiers: in BDT terms, all 'fully recursive phrasal dependents' are expected to exhibit harmonic behaviour in relation to verb patterners (Dryer 1992a: 116). An anonymous reviewer suggests that BDT's ability to account for the placement difference between fully recursive and non-fully recursive modifiers renders it superior to accounts referring only to grammar-internal considerations. While we do not dispute this point (see below), we do, however, wish to note that there are data which pose a challenge to Dryer's BDT proposal (rejected in Dryer 2009).[16] These include phenomena such as that illustrated in (16):

(16) a. den över sin dotter   stolt- a   mamma-n   [Swedish]
        the of   her daughter proud-DEF mother-DEF
        'the mother who is proud of her daughter'   (Cabredo Hofherr 2010: 15)

    b. ett sedan i går   välkänt   faktum
        a   since yesterday well.known fact
        'a fact well-known since yesterday'   (Delsing 1992: 25)

Here a fully recursive AP modifier precedes the modifiee, despite the fact that object patterners in Swedish should follow their modifiees. Similar patterns are observed in a range of languages with otherwise head-initial nominals, i.e. nominals in which (fully recursive) dependents should, in BDT terms, follow their modifiee (see Sheehan 2012 for overview discussion and references). Dryer's processing-oriented account, then, also does not straightforwardly account for the observed harmonies and disharmonies. Importantly, Dryer's (1992a) and subsequent research finds that the preference for harmony (i.e. consistent patterning across verb and object patterners) is statistical rather than absolute, with very few languages emerging as fully harmonic in Dryer's terms (cf. Dryer 1992a: 109, note 17). To the extent that parameters can play a role in the understanding of harmony and disharmony, then, what seems to be required is a series of semi-independent parameters and, addition-ally, some overarching and quite possibly 'externally' (i.e. non-UG-imposed) prefer-ence for harmony (of the second, consistent left/right alignment type discussed above). In what follows, we will mostly restrict our focus to the disharmonic word

---

[16] Dryer's (2009) rejection of BDT is motivated by his rejection of the hierarchical constituents it assumes; in place of the BDT, he argues that the observed word-order patterns—some of which he shows, on the basis of a further enlarged sample, to hold even more strongly than was possible in the (1992a) paper—can be ascribed to more general processing considerations, the nature of which is, however, largely left to future research.

orders that are this volume's main concern and that Dryer's research in particular has shown to be cross-linguistically very common.

1.2.3 *Disharmony*

Today, there is recognition in both the typological and the generative literature that very many and possibly even the majority of languages fail to be fully harmonic in the sense that all head–complement pairs pattern alike (this point is once again picked up on by Cinque, this volume).[17] As an across-the-board Head Parameter, set once for all categories, clearly cannot account for the observed variation, generative grammarians have proposed interacting parameters designed to account for disharmonic word orders. Li (1990: 41), for example, proposes the following constraint to account for word-order patterns in Mandarin:

(17) **The Chinese Word-Order Constraint**
    a. Chinese is head-final except under the requirements of Case assignment.
    b. Case is assigned from left to right in Chinese.
    c. A Case assigner assigns at most one Case.

This constraint has the advantage of accounting for the unusual word-order properties of Mandarin (e.g. the initial position of Case-assigning verbs and adpositions in a language where the nominal domain appears to be head-final and relatives also precede their associated nominal), whilst maintaining a single setting for the Head Parameter in that language. Analysis of V2 effects in West Germanic languages (Travis 1984) and of OV orders in Vata (Koopman 1984) can be seen to do essentially the same thing in relation to the behaviour of clausal XPs. In all cases, transformations, motivated by Case or other features, serve to interrupt a harmonic underlying head-initial or head-final word order.

While these approaches were highly constrained and empirically successful, they implied a notion of linear order at the narrow syntactic level, which came to be viewed as problematic by some. The reason for this was the increasing evidence that grammar is sensitive only to constituent structure and not to linear order. Thus children apparently fail to posit syntactic operations which are non-structure-dependent (Crain and Nakayama 1987), and modules such as Binding Theory seem to be sensitive only to hierarchical notions such as c-command and not to linear precedence. This was coupled with a renewed interest in something highlighted by Hawkins (1980, 1982): the observation that there are robust gaps in attested word orders. Kayne (1994) brings these various concerns to the fore, and proposes a

---

[17] Moreover, as Emonds (this volume) points out, the behaviour of specifiers, which might be considered the complements of phrasal projections, means that many so-called head-initial languages are, in a certain sense, really disharmonic (cf. also Hawkins 1980 on this).

theory whereby two asymmetric structural relations (dominance and asymmetric c-command) come together to determine linear order. The following section briefly considers this proposal and relates it to our principal concern: disharmonic word orders.

1.2.4 *Antisymmetry*

In a certain (controversial) sense, antisymmetry can be viewed as a return to the *grammaire générale* idea that there is a natural order of language (see section 1.1 above), though it is less clear in the generative paradigm that this is in any way connected to the order of thought. Kayne's (1994) Linear Correspondence Axiom (LCA) proposes the following direct connection between hierarchical structure and linear order:

(18) **Linear Correspondence Axiom** (Kayne 1994: 6)
      [For a given phrase marker P, where d is the non-terminal to terminal dominance relation, T the set of terminals, and A the set of ordered pairs <X_j, Y_j> such that for each j, X_j asymmetrically c-commands Y_j—TB/MS], d(A) is a linear ordering of T.

The LCA states that the dominance relation applied to the set of ordered pairs determined by asymmetric c-command relations gives a linear order of the set of terminals in a given phrase marker. Kayne argues, largely on an empirical basis, that the relevant linear order is precedence rather than subsequence so that the following holds:

(19) **Implication of the LCA**
      A terminal X precedes a terminal Y iff a category dominating X asymmetrically c-commands a category dominating Y.

Given the further assumptions in Kayne 1994 (discussed by Kayne, this volume and Toyoshima, this volume), Kayne's proposal that (18) is a principle of grammar (UG) and that the relevant relation is universal precedence leads to what has become known as the Universal Base hypothesis. This refers to the fact that, in the absence of any movement, a phrase will have default spec–head–comp linear order, based on its inherent c-command relations.[18] It follows that all other surface word orders must be derived from this basic order via movement. This might, in a sense, be considered an extreme version of the proposals in Li, Travis, and Koopman (cited above in section 1. 2. 3), whereby disharmony arises via transformations from a harmonic base. In the case of the LCA, all orders diverging from consistent head-initial order must be movement-derived, even harmonic head finality. Importantly, though, independent

---

[18] This is assuming Kayne's (1994) category-based definition of c-command.

considerations (e.g. V-raising, the presence of a canonical subject position, the presence of a canonical topic position, and the activation of the left periphery more generally) entail that harmonically head-initial systems also require movement (compare standard generative analyses of English, French, Swedish, and Niuean[19] in this regard, for example). To the best of our knowledge, no language features only structures directly reflecting the Universal Base (see section 1.2.5 of this introduction, and Cinque, this volume, for further discussion).

One of the conceptual attractions of the LCA is that it apparently permits the eradication of linearity from Narrow Syntax (especially under Chomsky's 1995b reappraisal (p. 340)).[20] Kayne (this volume), however, claims that 'order' is still required at the narrow syntactic level, calling into question this apparent advantage. Its main empirical advantage, and the one that is of central importance here, is that it provides a potential explanation for several word-order asymmetries. Firstly, as Kayne notes, movement is very generally to the left in natural languages, and not the right. Rightward 'movement', where it occurs, has very different properties to its leftward counterpart, being subject to numerous restrictions (e.g. the Right Roof Constraint; cf. Ross 1967 for discussion). The LCA provides an immediate explanation for this fact, given Chomsky's (1993) Extension Condition: if movement is only possible to the root of the tree, and the root of the tree is the highest position in c-command terms (i.e. it c-commands all other nodes), then it follows that movement will always be leftwards (see Sheehan 2010 for an LCA-compatible account of extraposition). Kayne also notes other word-order asymmetries which similarly derive from the lack of rightward movement, such as the apparent lack of verb-penultimate languages and penultimate position effects more generally (cf. Kayne 1994 for further examples). A final example which is worthy of note concerns the apparent lack of *wh*-movement in OV languages. Kayne attributes this to the ban on multiple specifiers imposed by the LCA.[21] If head finality is derived via roll-up movement, then it follows that *wh*-movement to Spec-LCP will be banned where TP-to-spec-CP movement has taken place.

In its initial form, then, the LCA appears to be a restrictive theory of word order with the potential to account for a number of word-order gaps and asymmetries of the kind observed by typologists.[22] As Roberts (2007a: 13–14) notes, from the

---

[19] Cf. Pollock (1989), Holmberg and Platzack (1995), and Massam (2000, 2001, 2005) for discussion. Cf. also Alexiadou and Anagnostopoulou (2001, 2007) on the so-called *Subject in Situ Generalization* and its proposed universal consequences. For Chomsky (2013), who also specifically cites this Generalization, movement is very generally required in language systems, regardless of their head initiality or head finality, to facilitate labelling.

[20] Chomsky (1995a,b) takes the LCA to function as a linearization algorithm, applying only at the mapping to PF. See also Moro (2000).

[21] This stems from the category-based version of c-command which Kayne posits. In such a system, multiple specifiers of the same category mutually c-command each other and so cannot be linearized.

[22] The hypothesis, however, is not without its critics and we return to this matter in section 1.4.2 below.

perspective of the LCA, the notion of harmony reduces to a preference for either all or no heads to trigger comp-to-spec movement, a preference that may result from Input Generalization, the third-factor acquisition bias mentioned above. Mixed systems, by this standard, are then more difficult to acquire, and hence are predicted to be less frequent. Given Hawkins' and Dryer's findings that the majority of languages are actually disharmonic, however, it is not so clear that this is straightforwardly correct. Worth bearing in mind here, though, is undoubtedly Dryer's (1992a: 109, note 17) observation that 'the majority of inconsistencies among inconsistent [i.e. disharmonic—TB/MS] languages can be attributed to a small number of pairs of elements for which there is a skewed distribution, such as the general preferences for NRel order'. Also relevant is the extent to which individual disharmonic elements instantiate high-frequency items in the systems in question, as it is well known that high-frequency elements may exhibit irregular properties in relation to the more general system and it also seems to be the case that high-frequency irregulars are represented differently from regular forms (cf. i.a. Pinker and Prince 1991, 1994, and Marcus, Brinkmann, Clahsen, Wiese, and Pinker 1995 on the Dual Mechanism model).

1.2.5 *Remaining questions*

As already noted, the existence of harmony and of both harmonic and disharmonic orders creates particular difficulties for Principles and Parameters approaches to word-order typology, which predict that, all things being equal, any grammatical system must fall on one side or another of any cross-linguistic dichotomy. From this perspective, the fact that disharmonic languages are so prevalent is apparently positive for Kayne's LCA, which takes word order to be tied to language-specific movement operations. There is also a sense, though, in which the Universal Base Hypothesis is deeply surprising in the light of typological research. According to Greenberg (1963) and Hawkins (1980), the purest harmonic word-order types are VSO and SOV, with SVO being a mixed type with much less clear correlations. From Kayne's perspective, there is a sense in which SVO is the underlying order of all languages. Of course, whether this is a problem depends on what status is afforded to this universal base. If Cinque (this volume) is right, for example, then even head-initial surface orders are derived, in which case, there is clearly no sense in which SVO is predicted to be the most frequent order (contra Newmeyer 2005a). Nevertheless, as an anonymous reviewer observes, there is also no immediately evident sense in which a Kaynian approach, taken on its own, predicts the head initiality/head finality distribution facts thrown up by Dryer's (1989c, 1992a) genera[23]-based studies,

---

[23] In Dryer's (1989c) terms, a *genus* is a group of languages that are clearly closely related, with a time depth of 3500–4000 years. As indicated in Dryer's (2011e) genealogical language list contribution to the

in terms of which head-final systems consistently emerge as the most common cross-linguistically. Dryer (1989c) shows that in 111 genera (58% of the total at the time), OV order predominates,[24] giving a cross-linguistic tendency for objects to precede verbs, while Dryer (1992a) shows that postpositions are found in 119 genera out of 196, with the predicate preceding the copula in 76 out of 127 genera. Worth noting in relation to the distribution of head finality, however, is the constraint to which it appears to be subject, the Final-over-Final Constraint (FOFC), discussed in section 1.4 below, which Biberauer, Holmberg, and Roberts (2008a *et seq.*) have argued to follow from a version of Kayne's theory interacting with more general and, in part, possibly non-language-specific principles (see also the discussion in section 1.3.1 below of Hawkins' findings regarding constraints on the internal make-up of left-branching phrases).

What remains indisputable about the current theoretical situation, however, is that many questions remain unanswered. These include: Is there any evidence for the movement required to derive head-finality from a universal base? How are word-order generalizations to be captured, by movement or base-generation or a combination of the two? Given the attested variation, are word-order parameters to be stated for each (lexical/functional) category, for classes of categories, or for all categories subject to some defeasibility constraint? Is it then true that, in fact, anything goes, beyond, possibly, each category having to have a fixed internal order? If not, what generalizations can be made aside from the simple observation that most languages are tendentially head-initial or head-final? Is word order connected to other aspects of grammar, such as prosody? How stable are disharmonic systems and how are they acquired and thus preserved? Are there alternative linearization mechanisms which should be considered alongside the LCA and Head Parameter-based approaches? What role do extragrammatical factors play in the determination of word order, particularly in frequency-based terms? The papers in this volume aim to answer questions such as these, throwing new light on the nature of the relation between surface order and Narrow Syntax. In the following sections, we consider some of these issues in more detail.

World Atlas of Language Structures Online (*WALS Online*)—a list which distinguishes 510 genera and 212 language families, taking 2,678 languages into account—the choice of term is guided by the general idea of 'genus' in biological classification, where a genus is 'a set of species that are clearly closely related to one another'; thus his genealogical classification of languages is intended to be such that 'even a conservative "splitter" would accept [it]'.

[24] Considering the distribution of SOV, SVO, and VSO orders by genera, Dryer (1989c) obtains the following areal breakdown:

	Africa	Eurasia	Aust-NewG	NAmer	SAmer	Total
SOV	22	26	19	26	18	111
SVO	21	19	6	6	5	57
VSO	5	3	0	12	2	22

1.3 Word order and linguistic theory

1.3.1 *Frequency*

As noted repeatedly above, the preference for harmony across head–complement pairs is statistical rather than absolute (the question of whether absolute implicational universals also exist is separate and we leave it aside here; see i.a. Whitman 2008 and Biberauer, Holmberg, and Roberts in press for discussion). In recent years, there has been much debate as to the relevance of frequency skewings for theoretical linguistics. Hawkins (1980: 193) first proposed that 'the theory of Universal Grammar must include both implicational universals and universals of language distribution in the description and explanation of word order'. Hawkins objects to Greenberg's use of statistical universals where absolute implicational universals are empirically and theoretically superior, but he also notes that the preference for harmony is statistical rather than absolute. His point, then, is that while gaps can be attributed to UG principles, statistical trends must have a different kind of explanation. In his 1980 paper, he posits Cross-Categorial Harmony (CCH) to address the statistical nature of harmony in the word-order domain:

(20) **Cross-Categorial Harmony (CCH)**
      The more similar the position of operands relative to their operators across different operand categories considered pairwise (verb in relation to adposition order, noun in relation to adposition order, verb in relation to noun order), the greater are the percentage numbers of exemplifying languages.

      (Hawkins 1980: 98)[25]

---

[25] Hawkins thus draws a connection between markedness and frequency. This connection was also discussed by Lightfoot (1979: 77), who claimed that languages with more marked grammars will be less frequent than languages with less marked grammars, with diachronic changes being expected to involve changes from more to less marked (see also McCarthy and Prince 1994 on the Emergence of the Unmarked effects conceived of in Optimality-Theoretic terms, and Roberts 2007b for recent minimalistically oriented discussion). Evidently, statements of this type rest heavily on the interpretation assigned to the notion 'marked'.

A very different and, for a time, very influential approach to markedness considerations determining the cross-linguistic frequency of word-order patterns is found in Tomlin (1986). In terms of this approach, three interacting functionally motivated principles determine the observed frequencies: Theme First (more thematic information tends to precede less thematic information), Verb–Object Bonding (in a transitive clause, the object is more tightly 'bound' to the verb than it is to the subject—cf. also Baker 2009, 2010 for further discussion in a generative framework), and Animate First (Animate NPs tend to precede other NPs). Since SOV and SVO languages are consistent with all three of these principles, they are the most frequent, followed by VSO languages, which violate only Verb–Object Bonding, and then VOS and OVS languages, which violate the other two principles, but respect Verb–Object Bonding; since OSV languages violate every one of these principles, they are expected to be the least common. The difficulties with this type of functionalist markedness approach are well known (see Song 2012 for overview discussion and references), and, since it does not relate very directly to the question of (dis)harmony, we leave it aside here.

The reasoning here is that 'by reserving implicational statements for the task of distinguishing attested from non-attested co-occurrences, we can, therefore, formulate just one supplementary distributional regularity [i.e. CCH—TB/MS] ... which captures generalizations which [statistical implications—TB/MS] are intrinsically unable to state' (Hawkins 1980: 232). This distributional regularity is arguably not a principle of UG, but rather a generalization over E-languages (see Chomsky (1986) for discussion of this term and how it differs from 'I-language').

Recently, this position has been endorsed by Newmeyer (2003, 2005b) and others (e.g. Whitman 2008). Newmeyer (2005b: ch. 3) has famously proposed that theoretical linguistics should concern itself only with possible and not probable languages. The frequency of a certain word order, he claims, is to be explained by external factors, such as patterns of diachronic change (as influenced by acquisition), functional pressures, or even arbitrary social pressures and language contact. Most specifically, he has endorsed Hawkins' (1994, 2004) processing-based account of the preference for harmony (cf. also Hawkins this volume). In this more recent work, Hawkins has moved towards an explicitly functional explanation for the CCH, based on his Performance–Grammar Correspondence Hypothesis (PGCH), which claims that languages have grammaticalized word orders which are efficient from a processing perspective. From this perspective, principles of processing efficiency such as Minimize Domains (MiD) (Hawkins 2004: 31, this volume) favour head adjacency as well as optional processes such as extraposition. Hawkins also argues that other more nuanced typological trends can be traced back to the PGCH: for example, the tendency for rigid VO languages to develop initial articles. This is because initial articles serve to construct NP and this is more efficient at the left edge in VO but not OV languages. A final asymmetry of this kind is that '[l]eft-branching phrases [...] are often more reduced and constrained in comparison with their right-branching counterparts [...]' (Hawkins this volume, p. 405). Thus prenominal relatives are often reduced compared to their postnominal equivalents.

The authors in this volume take different positions in this debate. Cinque's approach might lead us to expect that unmarked systems (i.e. those featuring fewer deviations from the 'ideal harmonic derivations' he postulates; see also discussion in section 1.3.2 below) should (all else being equal) be more frequent than more marked systems. This is not to say, however, that frequency cannot be affected by extragrammatical factors; hence his discussion of the relative scarcity of VOS orders in natural languages, despite the fact that the latter is one of the two abstract harmonic orders proposed by Cinque. In other papers, too, infrequent orders are taken to be ruled out by Universal Grammar or at least made difficult to generate by it. Thus, one of the reported benefits of Toyoshima's graph-theoretical linearization approach is that it 'accounts for the rarity of the other three logically possible [word-order] variations (VOS, OVS, OSV)' (Toyoshima, this volume: 360). Djamouri, Paul, and Whitman, on the other hand, argue explicitly against the approach taken by Cinque whereby frequency is indicative of markedness. Instead, they attribute the rarity of head-final PPs in VO languages to diachronic factors. To the extent that diachrony is a reflex of acquisitional considerations, however, it could still be the case that markedness plays a role in determining the frequency of systems of different types.

Even if one accepts that third-factor pressures of the type alluded to in Chomsky (2005; see section 1.2.2 above) can interact with UG to give the Greenbergian correlations, it remains to be decided at what level this interaction takes place. Kiparsky (2008) seems to imply that the interaction operates at quite a deep level:

The generative program opens up the possibility that [third factors—TB/MS] might have become biologized within UG itself... (Kiparsky 2008: 25)

Abels and Neeleman (2009) likewise speculate (as one possibility) that the requirement that a filler precede a gap might act 'as motivation for a grammatical principle stating that a moved constituent must be linearized at PF as preceding its sister' (cf. Ackema and Neeleman 2002 for the original discussion and motivation of these ideas). Once again, the implication appears to be that third-factor considerations could shape the very nature of UG. It is difficult to see how such a thing could be possible unless one adopts the evolutionary scenario put forth by Pinker and Bloom (1990), whereby UG evolved gradually via natural selection. The familiar objections to such an approach remain (see Fitch 2010 for overview discussion). A different perspective on the interaction of UG and third factors takes the latter to exert an influence only at the point of acquisition (parameter-setting in some models; cf. Biberauer, Holmberg, Roberts, and Sheehan 2010; Biberauer, Roberts, and Sheehan 2013 for more detailed discussion). The advantage to such a view is that third factors are not themselves 'biologized', but they rather serve only to constrain variation within a biologically determined variation space. If this speculation is on the right track, Newmeyer's (2005a: 105) conviction that '[t]he relationship between typological generalizations and I-language is therefore necessarily quite indirect' (cf. section 1.2.1 above) may not be so well-founded: our minds/brains may not *need* to 'know' about the typological status of components of mental grammars, as envisaged by Newmeyer, if typological facts can be shown to fall out as the consequence of the interaction between UG and suitably clearly formulated third-factor considerations.[26] As should be clear from this discussion, much work remains to be done to clarify the role of third factors in accounting for empirical skewings, and, more generally, to gain a better understanding of the significance or otherwise of frequency facts in the linguistic domain.

---

[26] As an anonymous reviewer points out, the question of how third-factor explanations relate to functional explanations of the kind proposed by Hawkins, Givón, Croft, Haspelmath, and others is just one of the issues that requires clarification. See Mobbs (2008, in progress) for partial discussion.

1.3.2 *On the nature of disharmony*

In relation to disharmonic word orders, Cinque opens the discussion by noting, as we have in this introduction, that extensive empirical research has undeniably reduced Greenberg's word-order correlations to statistical tendencies. He goes on to suggest that the search for *surface* word-order universals is arguably misplaced and that what Greenberg's generalizations really reveal is the order of Merge—the abstract universal hierarchical order of natural language.[27] The extent to which the linear order of categories in a given language departs from this abstract order can then be measured, yielding a finer-grained word-order typology. From this perspective the 'harmonic' orders are 'epiphenomenal', rather than basic, in that they represent cases in which the hierarchical order is systematically reflected at the linear level. Importantly, Cinque proposes that when word-order patterns are reconsidered from this perspective, a pervasive generalization nonetheless emerges:

(21)   [W]hatever precedes the VP/NP reflects the order of Merge, and whatever follows is in the mirror-image of the order of Merge.   (Cinque, p. 54)

The status of (21) is open to interpretation. If one assumes, as Cinque does, that surface word orders result directly from c-command relations, as proposed by Kayne (1994), and that there is a universal order of Merge, then word-order variation must be indicative of differences in movement operations between languages. As such, (21) can be taken to be a restriction on movement, as argued in Cinque (2005a, 2009a). Importantly, Abels (2007) and Abels and Neeleman (2009, 2012) suggest a different perspective: for them, processing considerations such as the filler–gap-related one discussed in the preceding section motivate leftward rather than rightward movement, but this consideration plays no role in determining base generation; consequently, c-command relations need not play any role in this domain, leaving open the possibility that First Merge could deliver both head-initial and head-final structures (cf. also Richards 2004 for a different argument for leaving open this possibility at the bottoms of projections, building on Epstein et al. 1998).

Other papers in the volume approach the topic of disharmony by considering a specific disharmonic language. Djamouri, Paul, and Whitman discuss evidence from Mandarin, which, they argue, represents a stable disharmonic system with both prepositions and postpositions, raising problems for the classical Head Parameter. In a careful empirical study, they show clearly that both prepositional and postpositional phrases can occur in postverbal argument position, but that there are restrictions governing the possibility of PPs in adjunct and subject positions: whereas certain kinds of postpositional phrases are banned from preverbal adjunct positions, prepositional phrases are systematically banned from subject position. Crucially, DPs

---

[27] What Greenberg (1963: 104) called the *proximity hierarchies*; cf. note 8.

are also banned from the subject position of existential sentences, suggesting that the distinction is not simply connected to the purported 'nominal status' of postpositional phrases (contra i.a. Li 1990; McCawley 1992; Huang, Li, and Li 2009). Inside DP, they show that, whereas prepositional phrases can modify only relational nouns, postpositional phrases can modify any kind of noun. These differences in distribution, they argue, serve as a cue to learners that postpositional phrases are pPs, whereas prepositional phrases are pure lexical projections, lacking a pP layer. pPs are analysed as being headed by a light preposition which attracts the complement of P to its specifier, yielding a surface head-final order. Prepositional phrases, on the other hand, are reduced PPs, without p, which therefore have a different distribution from full pPs. Strikingly, Djamouri et al. show that this system has remained reasonably stable from the first century BCE onwards. It must therefore be straightforwardly acquirable, potentially on the basis of specific distributional cues such as those mentioned above.

The same is arguably true in Basque, as Elordieta (this volume) discusses in a later section. Monolingual and bilingual Basque speakers acquire the disharmonic structures of Basque very early on without producing non-target-like orders at any stage of the acquisition process. The same has been shown to be true even in languages with complex V2 patterns (cf. Westergaard 2009a). More generally, it is well known that children acquire the word-order facts of their target language very early, at least as soon as they begin combining words (Bloom 1970; Brown 1973; and see Wexler 1998 on so-called *Very Early Parameter Setting* more generally). In fact, recent research suggests that prosodic cues have an effect on language-acquiring children at the *prelexical* stage already (cf. i.a. Christophe, Nespor, Guasti, and van Ooyen 2003; Bion, Höhle, and Schmitz 2007; May, Byers-Heinlein, Gervain, and Werker 2011). The theoretical implications of this fact are unclear, as Christophe et al. note. Elordieta (this volume), however, claims that the fact that Basque children acquire disharmonic structures as early as they do undermines the Universal Base Hypothesis in terms of which Kaynean Spec–Head–Comp structures are universal. She therefore interprets this acquisitional fact as support for the Head Parameter. Djamouri et al., on the other hand, claim that the stable disharmony in Chinese arises in a system which is underlyingly head-initial. Now, if head finality involves movement of a complement to some higher functional head, as i.a. Cinque, Djamouri et al., and de Vos propose in this volume, and children at the two-word utterance stage operate with truncated tree structures, lacking functional heads, as Rizzi (1993/1994) has suggested, then the data would appear to be problematic for the Universal Base Hypothesis. However, given that the truncation model is not uncontroversial (see i.a. Wexler 1998 for discussion; Guasti 2000 is a response) and that, according to Cinque, head-initial orders also involve the obligatory presence of functional heads, the data might rather be taken as evidence against that model of acquisition.

Cinque and Djamouri et al. focus on instances of disharmony where the same language contains some categories or even lexical items which are consistently head-initial and others which are consistently head-final. A different kind of disharmony is observed in languages with variable word order, where one and the same category or lexical item either precedes or follows its complement, depending on context. Thus Cognola discusses Mócheno (German: *Fersentalerisch*), a Tyrolean variety spoken in the speech island *Valle dei Mócheni* (German: *Fersental*), in Northern Italy (Eastern Trentino). This variety displays mixed VO/OV orders, and Cognola focuses her discussion on the complex ways in which the VO/OV alternation interacts with the language's V2 property. Taking particular note of this latter feature of the Mócheno CP, Cognola argues that a similar V2 constraint regulates the structure of the VP, and that this is what is responsible for the observed VO/OV alternations. As such, wherever an XP is extracted via A-bar movement from VP, the lower V2 constraint forces the past participle to raise to a position high in the VP edge, triggering VO word order in an otherwise OV language. This analysis has important implications for our understanding of the V2 effect, and its potential explanation. It also provides empirical evidence for the existence of a VP periphery of the kind proposed by Belletti (2004).

1.3.3 *The connection to prosody*

Ancient rhetoricians such as Dionysius (60 BCE–7 CE) proposed that the order of words was determined by 'the rhythmic movement produced by the succession of long and short syllables' (Weil 1878 [1844]: 11–12). This position is not so far removed from recent claims in the generative literature that there is a close connection between prosody and word order. The original proposal for this connection came from Nespor and Vogel's (1982, 1986) Complement Law:

(22) **Complement Law** (Nespor and Vogel 1982)
      Complements rather than heads are preferred locations for stress in all types of domains.

This has the following effect (as spelled out by Nespor, Guasti, and Christophe 1996; cf. also i.a. Cinque 1993).

(23) **Relative prominence in a prosodic phrase**
      In languages whose syntactic trees are right-branching, the rightmost node of [a prosodic phrase—TB/MS] is labelled *strong*. In languages whose syntactic trees are left-branching, the leftmost node of [a prosodic phrase—TB/MS] is labelled *strong*. All sister nodes of *strong* nodes are labelled *weak*.

This idea is explored by Emonds (this volume) in relation to the syntax and morphology of French and English.

As Emonds points out, it has long been assumed that ordering in the morphological component proceeds on a different basis to ordering in syntax. Thus, conventional wisdom has it that the Right-hand Head Rule applies in the morphology of many languages which are otherwise head-initial (Williams 1981; Hoeksema 1985, 1992; Scalise 1988; Lieber 1992). Emonds questions this widely-held belief, claiming that 'no head ordering statements pick out a domain coinciding with "Morphology" [in his terms—TB/MS]'. In particular, he takes issue with the commonly held claim that English is head-final in the morphological component and head-initial elsewhere. In the context of a Lieber (1992)-style approach to morphology, this is because a 'morphological component' cannot be meaningfully distinguished from a 'syntactic component'. Building on Lieber, Emonds' argument in this volume is that the properties that are typically ascribed to 'affixes' (and, thus, morphology) are such that it is impossible to distinguish 'morphological' elements from functional elements more generally. Specifically, affixes are typically said to (a) lack semantically interpretable features of the encyclopaedic type, beyond those which are syntactically active (cf. Chomsky 1965 for the original generative distinction between what Minimalists today call *semantic* and *formal* features), and (b) fail to contribute their own stress to word stress. Functional elements, according to Emonds, exhibit exactly the same properties. Against this background, he considers the headedness of English and French, both above and below what is traditionally taken to be 'the morphological level'. Emonds' central claim is that the universal default word order of natural language requires complements (and specifiers, which he views as a kind of complement) to precede heads. This is, in some respects, reminiscent of proposals by Haider, whose *Basic Branching Constraint* (BBC) also establishes head-final structures as the default option (cf. i.a. Haider 2000b for discussion and references). For Emonds, exceptions to the complement–head pattern are, however, possible, subject to UG principles and only in 'free' domains, defined as follows:

(24)　**Free domain**
　　　Domain Y is free if (i) no daughter of Y is an obligatorily bound morpheme and (ii) at least one daughter is an X^j that can further project, where X = N, V, A, P *and j = 0 or 1*.

This serves to force specifiers to be initial, as long as there is a single-specifier condition, so that no further projection of the phrasal head is possible. It also means that in the morphological component, only head-final structures are possible, as long as a bound morpheme is involved. Where morphemes are not bound, however, they can diverge from the universal default word order, as is the case in French. Thus Emonds shows that French compounds are head-initial only where they contain free morphemes, which can project further. He gives an extensive list of compounds of this type, including:

(25)   **English right-headed compounds**   **French left-headed compounds**
    tanker **truck**   **camion** citerne
    video **cassette**   **cassette** vidéo
    bedroom **suburb**   **ville** dortoir

The relevant trigger for head–complement order in such domains is, of course, stress, which is uniformly on the right in French. This, combined with Nespor and Vogel's (1982) Complement Law (22), means that French is as left-headed as is permitted by UG. The reason why English is comparatively less left-headed stems from the fact that it exhibits left-hand stress, and so having left-hand heads would 'decrease compliance with the Complement Law'.[28]

While there is undeniable evidence for a connection between headedness and stress, as pointed out by Cinque's (1993) discussion of the Nuclear Stress Rule, it is not clear what the direction of causality is. Is it that the requirement for initial stress forces head-finality or is it rather that stress is sensitive to hierarchy rather than word order, and so tracks the position of complements? Emonds' contribution suggests that the former is true, and that, as Christophe et al. (2003) have proposed, stress is essentially an acquisition device which the child uses to set the word-order parameters of her language (arguably by the end of the first year of life[29]).

Hinterhölzl (this volume) proposes that the tendency towards harmony derives from a prosodic constraint of the following kind:

(26)   **Mapping Condition to PF (prosodic transparency)**
    A heavy syntactic constituent must appear on a dominant branch in prosodic phrasing if its containing phase is weight-sensitive. (Hinterhölzl this volume: 163)

This constraint ensures that, all else being equal, heavy (branching/recursive) constituents will align harmonically in a given language. In this system, disharmonic orders arise, then, (and can be preserved over time) where an optional and interfering constraint of the following kind applies:

(27)   **Mapping Condition to LF (scope transparency)**
    If *a* scopes over *b*, the Spell-Out copy of *a* should c-command the Spell-Out copy of *b*.   (Hinterhölzl this volume: 163)

This less straightforward constraint appears to apply at the mapping to PF at the imposition of LF, in a way that is not possible within the standard Y-model. It forces

---

[28] Emonds discusses apparent counterexamples to this generalization from compounds involving prepositions.

[29] Worth noting here is that this statement should only be taken to refer to basic word-order parameters; the acquisition of discourse-sensitive word-order options like West Germanic scrambling is known to be delayed (cf. i.a. Schaeffer 1997, 2000 for discussion).

the object to be spelled out in its derived VP-external position in OV languages. Where it fails to apply, it follows that the lower VP-internal copy of the object is spelled out, yielding VO order in the context of the Kaynean model Hinterhölzl adopts, in compliance with (26). Importantly, this condition goes beyond the stipulation that German is OV whereas English is not, as it ties the OV order in German to the fact that it is scope-rigid, something which is apparently also true of other OV languages (cf. also Öztürk this volume).[30]

The applicability of (27) in German but not English also serves to explain the following contrast, first discussed by Haider (2000b): that (some) OV languages permit right-branching preverbal adverbials in apparent violation of the Head-Final Filter (HFF), whereas VO languages do not:

(28) a. John (more) often (* than Peter) read the book

     b. Hans hat öfter   (als der Peter) das Buch gelesen
       Hans has more-often than the Peter the book read
       'Hans read the book more often than Peter.' (Hinterhölzl this volume: 164)

In fact, German actually disallows extrapositon of these adverbials, something which is obligatory in English:

(29) a. John read the book more often than Peter

     b. *Hans hat das Buch gelesen öfter   (als Peter)
       Hans has the book read   more-often than Peter
                             (Hinterhölzl this volume: 164)

As Hinterhölzl notes, following Haider, this difference cannot be captured by a Head Parameter alone, as the relation between adverbial and *v*P is not one of complementation (cf. parallel difficulties for Head Parameter-based approaches already raised in relation to Dryer's 1992a non-correlation pairs in section 1.2.2 above). Adopting the Universal Base Hypothesis, Hinterhölzl proposes that the differences between VO and OV languages of this kind stem not from the fact that one involves movement whereas the other does not, but rather from the different sizes of the moved constituents, as motivated by the differing 'mapping conditions' (26) and (27) in the two kinds of languages (cf. also Cinque 2004, this volume for a similar proposal).[31]

---

[30] The VO/OV word-order variation attested in Old High German, he claims, stems from the at the time stronger force of the condition on scope transparency in conjunction with the weaker force of the condition on prosodic transparency. This OT-like model can thus potentially offer a prosodic explanation for harmony, a description of synchronic disharmonic systems and an account of diachronic word-order change.

[31] Hinterhölzl argues that movement of the *v*P to a pre-adverbial position (which he terms *intraposition*) is semantically motivated by the need for the adverbial to become a predicate of *v*P. As the moved *v*P functions effectively as a subject after movement, this is A-movement. The ability of *v*P to function first as a predicate and then as an argument is linked to the phase-based model which Hinterhölzl adopts.

In a VO language, *v*P intraposition will give rise to an optimal prosodic unit where the adverbial, which is heavy (in his terms), occupies a right branch (in his terms) and receives stress. This also favours pied-piping of the PP if subsequent *v*P movement is required (e.g. in the presence of another adverbial modifier), correctly yielding the following (unmarked) word order:

(30)   [$_{IP}$ John$_i$ [[[$_{vP}$ t$_i$ visited them] $_k$ in Vienna t $_k$]$_j$ on Friday t$_j$]]

In German, on the other hand, event-related (time, manner, and place) adjuncts can either precede or follow the verb, with the difference crucially correlating with a scope-related interpretive difference (see (31)). Significantly, in both languages, adverbials surface in the unmarked preverbal order T>P>M, with M>P>T being the unmarked order postverbally.

(31)   a. weil   Hans   oft   im   Kaffeehaus   sitzt
          since   Hans   often   in-the coffee-house sits
          'as Hans often sits in the coffee house'

       b. weil   Hans   oft   sitzt   im   Kaffeehaus
          since   Hans   often   sits   in-the coffee-house
          'as Hans, when he is in the coffee house, often sits'

On Hinterhölzl's proposal, this is explained because 'placement of adjuncts is weight-insensitive' in German (p. 181) because of (27): adverbials scope over *v*P and so must precede them, even if this violates (20). If further adverbials are present, then it follows that pied-piping of the adverbial will be optional.

Tokizaki and Kuwana (this volume), in turn, attempt to provide a different explanation for the connection between stress and word order. They first observe that the juncture between terminals in right-branching structures is longer than the juncture between those in left-branching structures. They take this as evidence that left-branching structures are actually compounds (an idea which Zwart 2009b has also explored). The repercussion of this is that stress patterns in left-branching structures must adhere to the word-stress pattern of a language. Right-branching structures, on the other hand, need not mirror the word-stress rules of a given language. This fact, it is argued, serves to explain the close connection between word stress and word order first noted by Nespor and Vogel (1982) and also explored by Emonds (this volume). Although left-branching structures are 'compounds', they nonetheless receive their stress derivationally, rather than lexically, presumably via the Nuclear Stress Rule (this idea is, of course, also compatible with Lexical Morphology models such as that of Halle and Mohanan 1985, which assign compounds to a third stratum of stress assignment, following irregular inflection and derivation, and regular derivation respectively). This means that stress falls on the most embedded constituent in a given structure. In the case of VO/OV orders, they claim, O is always more embedded than V, as it is potentially branching (and this is true even where it has moved to Spec-VP). In a language with initial stress, it follows that OV order will be permitted and arguably required, as this movement serves to re-establish initial stress at the level of the compound. Where a language has right-edge stress, on the other hand, movement is blocked, as it would move the stress too far to the left, violating the word-stress rules of the language. Matters are more complex with other stress patterns, but Tokizaki and Kuwana nonetheless claim that the attested word-order patterns are roughly as predicted by the proposal.

It is interesting to note that while these three approaches are similar in spirit, they differ substantially as to the relationship they posit between grammar and linear order. Hinterhölzl, and Tokizaki and Kuwana both adopt a version of the LCA whereby head finality is derived via movement (albeit of different kinds). Emonds, on the other hand, argues against the LCA and proposes an alternative whereby SOV is the universal base (see again Haider 2002 for another OV base-order proposal). That proponents of both types of proposal are able to appeal to (22) reinforces the fact noted by Christophe et al. (2003) that Nespor and Vogel's Complement Law is consistent with both movement-derived and base-generated approaches to head finality.

In the following section, we consider movement-derived head finality in more detail.

1.4 The question of Antisymmetry

1.4.1 *Head-Complement order, movement, and the derivation of OV languages*

Whether one accepts the LCA in its strongest form or not, it seems reasonably clear that the surface word order in many languages is derived via movement. OV languages, for example, come in at least three guises:[32]

(32) i. DP-V-X (Nupe, Mande (Niger-Congo) (postpositional) and Päri (Nilo-Saharan, Nilotic, Sudan), Tobelo (West Papuan, North Halmaheran, Indonesia), Iraqw (Afro-Asiatic, Southern Cushitic, Tanzania), and Neo-Aramaic (Afro-Asiatic, Semitic, Israel) (prepositional))

---

[32] Worth noting here is that the OV languages discussed here can, in generative terms, be thought of as differing in relation to the extent to which they are head-final in the clausal context: type I is only minimally head-final, while type III is maximally head-final, with type II occupying quite a broad spectrum in between. Not discussed here, but also relevant to more fine-grained consideration of the typological question we raise here is the matter of the headedness of non-clausal categories (e.g. nominal and adpositional heads).

ii. DP/PP-V-CP   (West Germanic, Turkish, Persian, Hindi, plus Lokaa and
Vata with added complications[33])

iii. rigid OV   (Japanese, Malayalam, Sinhala, Korean, Kannada)

Movement-based approaches to head finality are highly plausible for Type I
languages, where only DP direct objects surface in a preverbal position (cf. Roberts
2007a: 14 for discussion). Kandybowicz and Baker (2003) (henceforth K&B) discuss
one relevant language, Nupe, which displays this word order in perfect clauses. In all
cases, only a single argument can and must precede V:

(33) Musa   á   etsu   yà   èwò.
      Musa   PRF   chief   give garment
      'Musa has given the chief a shirt.'

Manner adverbs can follow V (but cf. Mous 1993 on Iraqw, Cushitic, another Type I
language):

(34) Musa   á   nakàn   ba   sanyin.
      Musa   PRF   meat   cut   quietly
      'Musa has cut the meat quietly.'   [Nupe, K&B (2003: 123)]

Given that DP direct objects, unlike PP/CP arguments and adverbials, enter into an
Agree relation with a higher functional head (v in Chomsky 1995a), which assigns
them Accusative Case, it seems highly plausible that OV order in this language (and
others like it) is derived via A-movement, as K&B propose.

In Type II languages, it is less immediately clear that the movement-based
approach has any immediate empirical advantages over a base-generation account,
but advantages arguably emerge upon closer consideration, given certain assumptions. In Dutch, which might be considered a canonical Type II language, DPs,
predicative PPs and APs, and non-sentential adverbs *must* precede V. CP arguments
must and certain (phrasal and sentential) adverbials *can* also follow V (cf. Zwart
1997a,b on Dutch, and Baker 2005 on Lokaa, which is SOVCP only in negative
clauses). The traditional account of this pattern takes these languages to be base-
generated OV languages (cf. i.a. Koster 1975 and den Besten 1977/1983 for Germanic,
Kural 1997 for Turkish, and Karimi 2005 for Persian). Stowell's 'Case Resistance
Principle' (stating that Case may not be assigned to a category bearing a Case-
assigning feature, Stowell 1981: 146) then forces CPs to be extraposed to avoid Case
assignment. Certain problems arise for such an account, however, notably the fact
that it seems to wrongly predict that PPs should pattern with CP rather than DPs.
A further problem stems from the fact that extraposition should move the CPs to a
non-argument position, predicting they will be strong islands, but they actually
appear to permit subextraction in a number of Type II languages (cf. i.a. Zwart

---

[33] See Baker (2005) for discussion.

1997a,b on Dutch, Mahajan 1990 on Hindi, Aghaei 2006 on Persian, and Biberauer and Sheehan 2012 for overview discussion):

(35) Hoe heeft   Piet gezegd   dat Jan   zich   t gedragen   heeft?
      how has   Piet said   that Jan   himself   behaved   has
      'How did Piet say that Jan behaved himself?'   [Dutch Zwart 1997a: 66]

Zwart (1997a,b) proposes a movement-based analysis of Dutch, which accounts for these facts and might plausibly extend to all Type II languages. DP direct objects raise to a Case position above V, giving DP–V order. PP/AP predicates, however, move to Spec-PredP, a distinct preverbal position, while CPs simply remain *in situ*. Zwart provides evidence that material can intervene between V and a small clause complement, strongly suggesting that the latter at least *can* move (Zwart 1997a: 103):

(36) De kwast waar   Jan de deur   rood [PP mee t]   verft
      the brush where   Jan the door red   with   paints
      'The brush that Jan paints the door red with'

More generally, the Germanic languages appear to conform to a 'size'-based generalization, which can, following Wurmbrand (2001: 294), be stated as 'the "bigger" a complement..., the more likely it is to extrapose; the "smaller" the complement..., the more likely it is to occur in intraposed position' (cf. also i.a. Hinterhölzl 2006: 15). Biberauer and Roberts (2008) relate this pattern to the Final-over-Final Constraint (see section 1.4.4 below), predicting its occurrence to extend beyond Germanic (see also Biberauer and Sheehan 2012). For present purposes, the important point is that structures like (36) are, like those involving nominal and adpositional complements, clearly amenable to a leftward movement analysis of the sort an antisymmetric analysis would lead us to expect.

   An alternative movement-based account of Type II languages is provided by i.a. Hinterhölzl (2006, this volume) for German, Haegeman (1998) for West Flemish, Baker (2005) for Lokaa, Biberauer (2003) for Afrikaans, and Biberauer and Roberts (2008) for West Germanic generally. These approaches basically derive head finality via X-movement followed by remnant XP movement, which serves to carry X's complement to a pre-head position (cf. Roberts 2007a: 15–16 for a simple overview):

(37)

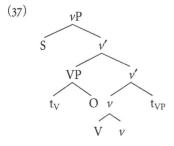

This captures the fact that in Type II languages, everything except CP (and some adverbials) precedes V, even elements that cannot move independently (e.g. particles). It also avoids the positing of distinct functional projections to house DP and predicate arguments. The question remains, though, why CP fails to move to a preverbal position with the VP-remnant. In his discussion of Lokaa, Baker (2005) simply proposes that CPs are extraposed before VP movement. Biberauer and Roberts (2008), on the other hand, propose that CPs are radically spelled out when the vP phase is complete: this entails that the CP is removed from the syntactic computation prior to vP movement, being linearized immediately, with the result that it is, as the first constituent to be sent to the interfaces, spelled out in final position. While these accounts are not implausible, the fact that postverbal CPs remain transparent for subextraction remains potentially problematic, to the extent that it holds in all Type II languages.[34] The remaining problem is that, from a movement perspective, there is no deep explanation why PPs/APs pattern with DP in being preverbal, whereas CPs do not. From a remnant movement perspective, there is no clear explanation why CP remains postverbal, though proposals exist. The pattern might, for example, potentially be explained by the Final-over-Final Constraint/FOFC (in some formulation) if DP/PP/AP are not subject to FOFC (at least in some languages), whereas CP *is* (cf. Biberauer and Sheehan 2012 for an account along these lines and see section 1.4.4 below for discussion of FOFC).

In the case of Type III languages, the evidence for movement is somewhat scarcer. In rigid OV languages, all arguments and adverbials precede V. While a remnant movement account of the kind proposed by Biberauer and Roberts (2008) and Baker (2005) can clearly replicate this fact, it is not clear that there is any evidence in favour of such movement. These languages remain, then, from an Antisymmetry perspective, the most controversial in status, and the arguments for deriving their surface orders via movement are largely conceptual, stemming from the desire for a uniform approach to word order. Öztürk (this volume) discusses a number of Turkic languages, which might be classed as Type III languages, in relation to the LCA, Similarly, Elordieta (this volume) discusses Basque, a language which is predominantly head-final, but which displays some degree of variability and disharmony.

More generally, a number of the papers in this volume contribute to the ongoing debate surrounding Antisymmetry. Kayne (this volume) can be considered a reassertion of the LCA in its strongest form, rejecting Chomsky's (1995a) influential reappraisal of this axiom as a linearization algorithm. Barrie (this volume) further shows that it is possible to analyse the OVS language Hixkaryana in LCA-compatible terms. In earlier sections, Cognola proposes an LCA-compatible account of OV/VO alternations in Mochenò, and Hinterhölzl of basic word order in German. The other

---

[34] If Huang's (1982) Condition on Extraction Domain is correct, the possibility of subextraction necessarily means that the postverbal CPs under discussion here were base-generated in that position.

papers in the section under discussion here are, however, more critical of the LCA: Öztürk and Elordieta question the validity of the LCA for Turkic languages and Basque respectively. In addition, Toyoshima, who offers a novel alternative to the LCA (see section 1.4.3 below), raises conceptual objections to the version of the LCA adopted in many discussions of word order. He notes that the SVO 'universal base' is largely an artefact of (i) the definition of c-command adopted by Kayne and (ii) the arbitrary choice of precedence over subsequence, which is a primitive of the axiom. These challenges are acknowledged and addressed by Kayne in his contribution.

Kayne's chapter can be divided into three distinct parts. Firstly, he reviews the evidence that OV order must be derived in many languages, drawing on a wealth of research since Kayne (1994). For this reason, there must be more to word order than the Head Parameter. Secondly, he reviews further empirical evidence that syntax is not symmetrical, drawing on work from generative and typological studies: the predominance of left-dislocation over right-dislocation, the fact that clitics often surface further to the left than full DPs, the fact that agreement on X is often suspended where DP follows X, but not where DP precedes X, certain asymmetries in relative clause formation, the fact that serial verbs surface in the same order in so-called head-initial and head-final languages (Carstens 2002, also discussed in Kayne 2003a), and the fact, observed by Zwart (2009a), that coordination always requires a coordinator between the two coordinates, which follows if the coordinator is always a head and the basic linear order of a coordinate phrase is Spec–Head–Comp. The final asymmetry discussed is of a different order to the others and indeed to those discussed previously by Kayne (1994, 2003a), though. Kayne notes that while some languages disallow backwards pronominalization (38), no language is known to block forwards pronominalization (39):

(38)   The fact that he's here means that John is well again.

(39)   The fact that John is here means that he's well again.

This asymmetry, he notes, cannot be stated purely in terms of c-command, as the R-expression and pronominal enter into no c-command relation in either (38) or (39). This cross-linguistic asymmetry Kayne, then, takes to suggest that precedence itself is syntactically encoded, contra Chomsky (1995a,b) and much subsequent work on the LCA.

The remainder of his chapter addresses the more fundamental question of why natural language is antisymmetric. The argument can be deconstructed roughly as follows:

(40)   a. Probe–Goal search shares the directionality of parsing and of production.

    b. Production proceeds from left to right.

    c. Therefore, Probe–Goal search proceeds from left to right.

    d. Probes are heads and Goals are contained in their complement domain.

    e. Therefore, heads must precede complements.

In essence, this means that 'FL has incorporated an abstract counterpart of temporality' (Kayne this volume: 234). The validity of this argument hinges on the acceptance of (40a), which Kayne proposes without any specific justification. If Probe–Goal directionality is merely stated in hierarchical terms, then it is consistent with either Comp>Head or Head>Comp linear order (at least for non-head complements, i.e. those that do not fall foul of the much discussed 'bottommost pair' problem—see i.a. Chomsky 1995b: 418; Richards 2004 for discussion). In a sense, the argument in (40a–e) is a means of reducing (e) to (a), but it is by no means a justification of (e). The discussion of Specifier>Head order is more opaque. Here Kayne rejects Abels and Neeleman's (2009, 2012) claim that leftwards movement be elevated to the status of an axiom, and maintains the idea that it should derive from the more general fact that specifiers precede heads. His proposal is that specifiers merge with heads directly, rather than phrases (cf. Sheehan in press for a similar proposal). The problem is that even in instances of internal Merge, the head probes the (derived) specifier prior to movement under standard assumptions, so that the predicted order is actually Head>Specifier according to Kayne's assumptions. Kayne denies this probing relation, the implication being apparently that Specifier probes Head. The fact that pair-Merge must lead to immediate precedence is also invoked, so that the only way for H to pair-Merge with two distinct phrases is if they surface on different sides of H. The need for immediate precedence also serves to rule out multiple specifiers (given that the merger of two phrases is banned). Note, though, that, as was the case in previous versions of antisymmetry theory, a non-projecting specifier (head) should still be able to merge with a phrase without projecting, giving rise to multiple non-branching specifiers (cf. Guimarães 2000). Ultimately, then, the fact that specifiers must precede heads also follows from (a). If (a) is rejected, it follows that neither conclusion can be maintained. At the end of his contribution, Kayne makes the radical proposal that the Specifier/Complement distinction may not be reflected structurally, so that branching is ternary rather than binary. Among other things, this has the effect that binding theory can no longer be stated in terms of c-command (unless the definition of c-command is amended).

Barrie's contribution considers the properties of Hixkaryana, an OVS language. He proposes a smuggling analysis (cf. Collins 2005) whereby the object is carried past the subject via VP-fronting. This serves to derive the fact that OVS languages appear to disallow scrambling, as the object must remain low enough to be carried along via VP-fronting. He contends that this correlation provides empirical support for the LCA, as Head Parameter-based analyses of OVS orders fail to capture the correlation of these two properties. As an anonymous reviewer pointed out, though, this is not necessarily the case as, however OV order is derived, a ban on fronting anything larger than VP will also serve to rule out OXVS order. The generalization, then, while it provides strong evidence that OVS order is derived via VP movement, for the reason Barrie outlines, does not necessarily bear on the derivation of OV order. In fact, given anti-locality (cf. Abels 2003), it could even be argued that the ban on OXVS order is an empirical challenge for his analysis. In the same way that the general availability of scrambling in SOV languages is taken as crucial evidence that OV is a derived order, it could also be concluded that the ban on OXVS is evidence that OV order is *not* derived via movement. This issue is partially addressed by Barrie via his discussion of Japanese vs Germanic OV. He claims that in the former case, a ghost or proxy (cf. Nash and Rouveret 2002) projection gives rise to rigid OV order, irrespective of Case, whereas in the latter, OV order results from (presumably Case-related) object shift. An alternative interpretation (consistent with the retention of a more restricted Head Parameter) would be that Germanic OV languages derive OV order via movement, whereas Japanese base-generates it.[35] Evidently, then, there are still a great many open questions relating to the structural analysis of different types of OV order, and the role that Antisymmetry has to play in increasing our understanding of it.

1.4.2 *Problems with the LCA*

The chapters by Öztürk and Elordieta argue that the LCA is not suited to enhancing our understanding of languages exhibiting a considerable amount of head finality. Öztürk's contribution focuses on some empirical challenges from the syntax and semantics of postverbal constituents (PVCs) in two lesser-studied OV languages, Khalkha and Uyghur. Building on Kural's (1997) challenge to the LCA, Öztürk claims that postverbal constituents in Turkish and Uyghur pose recalcitrant difficulties for the idea that asymmetric c-command maps to precedence. She argues at length that PVCs in these languages display the properties of movement, displaying island sensitivity of the same kind as constituents that have undergone leftward movement and failing to co-occur with resumptive pronouns. Importantly, this is different from what is observed in other OV Altaic languages such as Japanese and Khalkha, where PVCs are clearly base-generated. Any attempt to account for the Uyghur facts via leftwards movement, she argues, will prove problematic, as these languages are otherwise scope-rigid, meaning that scope tracks surface c-command relations (cf. Hinterhölzl's (27), discussed above). As PVCs can take either wide or narrow scope

---

[35] As Biberauer (2008b) notes, third-factor considerations—specifically, representational economy at the level of the child's stored grammar (I-language)—could plausibly lead the child to 'reanalyse' a grammar for which all heads are associated with a linearization-related movement diacritic (*EPP-feature* in Barrie's terms) as one in which all heads simply take their complements to the left, i.e. in which these heads are diacriticless and PF imposes across-the-board head finality (cf. Richards 2004, 2009 for discussion of the mechanics of a PF Head Parameter). What seems crucial to approaches seeking to combine antisymmetric derivations of head-final orders with Head Parameter-based ones is that there be a principled basis on which we (and language acquirers) are able to determine which of the available options (movement or 'base generation'/a PF parameter) underlies input from different types of head-final languages. In the absence of a principled distinction of this type, the acquisition task arguably becomes intractable, while the syntactician's task of unambiguously characterizing what underlies the head finality of specific systems is also compromised.

with respect to preverbal quantifiers, rightward movement would seem to be required in order to capture these facts straightforwardly. Öztürk claims that, in the absence of rightward movement, the facts elude explanation, forcing one to abandon scope rigidity and to posit unmotivated ad hoc movements. According to Öztürk, the reason why Turkish/Uyghur pattern differently from Japanese/Khalkha (and other familiar languages such as English, German, French, etc.) is that the former, but not the latter, have an EPP requirement. She argues that the presence of a left-hand specifier blocks the possibility of a right-hand specifier, and hence right-ward movement. To ensure that rightward movement is not possible at any structural level (vP, TP, CP, etc.), the proposal seems to require that all clausal heads bear an EPP feature: this is what is necessary to trigger the projection of a leftward specifier, which then suppresses the projection of a rightward specifier. It is not, however, clear that this prediction holds up. The correlation between a lack of subject-related EPP (i.e. an EPP feature on T) and rightward movement which Öztürk's paper highlights seems to hold in a number of languages, but why this should be the case remains opaque.

The discussion of Basque in Elordieta (this volume) also touches on this subject, as Basque is another language which displays both VO and OV orders, depending on context. In her contribution, Elordieta argues against Haddican's (2004) anti-symmetric approach to this alternation. Her main claim is that a non-antisymmetric (Head Parameter-based) account of the facts is possible, so that the Basque OV/VO facts cannot be interpreted as specifically lending support to the Universal Base Hypothesis, contrary to what has previously been claimed. In fact, what emerges from Elordieta's discussion is that it is very difficult to construct robust empirical evidence against either approach in the Basque case: without a prin-cipled basis for distinguishing between movement- vs Head Parameter-imposed OV and VO orders and without constraints on what may move where, both approaches can derive the attested orders (cf. note 35 and also the discussion in Abels 2007). From an acquisitional perspective, we might expect the child to opt for simpler rather than more complex representations of the available input, an expectation which might initially seem to favour non-antisymmetric approaches. This is true, though, only if such simple representations are made possible by UG. Among other considerations, such approaches, however, appear to offer no insight into cross-linguistically unattested word orders (such as those ruled out by the Final-over-Final Constraint, which we turn to in section 1.4.4, for example), and it is also not so clear that a Head Parameter-only approach to the types of OV languages discussed in section 1.4.1 will facilitate insight into this instance of attested variation. Taking this into account, it becomes clear that the (in some cases) greater representational simplicity associated with Head Parameter-oriented interpretations of OV/VO word-order variation cannot be taken, in isolation, to signify the superiority of approaches of this type.

1.4.3 *Novel approaches to disharmonic word order*

Aside from papers highlighting difficulties with Head Parameter- and Antisymmetry-based analyses, the volume also contains two papers proposing novel analyses of disharmonic word-order phenomena. De Vos (this volume) discusses the various kinds of adpositional phrases attested in Afrikaans and Dutch. Building on previous work by Oosthuizen (2000), Biberauer and Folli (2004), and Biberauer (2008a), he shows that, whereas prepositional phrases in these languages receive a locative interpretation, postpositional and circumpositional phrases are always directional, encoding directed motion:

(41)   Disharmonic word orders in the Afrikaans adpositional domain

    a. Ek loop **in** die kamer
        I   walk in the room
        'I walk around inside the room.'   [head-initial adposition]

    b. Ek loop die kamer **in**
        I   walk the room in
        'I walk into the room.'   [head-final adposition]

    c. Ek loop **in** die kamer **in**
        I   walk in the room in
        'I walk into the room.'   [circumpositional adposition]

He further argues that postpositions, unlike prepositions, Agree with the DP which they select. It is this Agreement dependency, he argues, which gives rise to either (i) postpositions or (ii) circumpositions. There is a sense in which de Vos's proposal appears to be a notational variant of existing approaches to movement. Landau (2007), for example, proposes that the EPP feature is essentially the need to realize a certain narrow syntactic Agree dependency overtly at PF (via displacement of the Goal), and more generally, it is typically assumed that A-movement at least is a PF effect which is parasitic on existing Agreement dependencies. De Vos's account, however, differs from existing approaches in that it proposes that *circumpositional* structures fall out from the same PF requirement. Essentially, faced with the paradoxical need to realize both P→DP (selection) and DP→P (Agree) dependencies linearly, the PF component has two options: (i) DP–P–DP or (ii) P–DP–P. If option (i) is chosen, a language-specific requirement forces deletion of the rightmost DP, yielding a postpositional phrase.[36] If option (ii) is chosen, then in Afrikaans, no chain reduction is required and both copies of P are retained, yielding a circumpositional phrase. This approach provides an elegant PF account of the variation in Afrikaans, which makes no allusion to the Head Parameter. Despite its elegance,

---

[36] Exactly why or how this linear deletion operation applies remains unclear, however.

however, it raises certain questions, the most obvious being: given the pervasive existence of agreement dependencies in natural language; for example, why is it that doubling is not more common?

Toyoshima develops a graph-theoretic linearization proposal originally made by Kural (2005). In terms of this proposal, the major word orders, defined in relation to S, O, and V, all result from PF undertaking different tree traversals of the same underlying structures. In particular, Toyoshima's version of Kural's algorithm derives the three commonest word-order variants (SOV, SVO, and VSO) from a single structure. Furthermore, it is also argued to account for the rarity of the other three logically possible variations (VOS, OVS, OSV) and for disharmonic word-order patterns of the type found in Vata and German. The general approach addresses some of the challenges facing Kural's approach, notably its reliance on notions such as 'right' and 'left' at the narrow syntactic level, which Toyoshima replaces with the notions 'consanguineous' (i.e. dominated node of which the label is non-distinct from that of the parent node) and 'adopted' (i.e. dominated node of which the label is distinct from that of the parent node). Challenges to this approach would seem to include its ability to capture *wh-* and head movement. Of greatest relevance to the concerns in this volume, however, is what needs to be said about disharmonic word orders. In the German case, for example, it is necessary to stipulate a 'parametric feature' on phase heads that is visible at PF, specifying the order of traversal for specific phrases. Additionally, like Head Parameter- and Antisymmetry-based approaches to disharmonic word orders, the traversal approach, however, seems to fall short when it comes to being able to account for a striking gap in the attestation of such word orders: those ruled out by the Final-over-Final Constraint, to which we now turn.

1.4.4 *The Final-over-Final Constraint*

Recently, it has been pointed out in several places that the empirical evidence given in favour of the LCA is incomplete. While Kayne and others have provided strong empirical support for the lack of right-hand specifiers, it is claimed that the lack of lefth-hand complements is less well evidenced (cf. Richards 2004, 2009; Abels and Neeleman 2009, 2012). Some of the data discussed in this volume provide potential evidence of the required kind. Firstly, there is Barrie's claim that *OXVS order is banned, for principled reasons. Unfortunately, it is not clear (i) that this bears on the lack of a Head Parameter or (ii) that this follows necessarily from Antisymmetry. Even if OV order were derived via a Head Parameter, it would be sufficient to ban movement of any constituent larger than VP in order to rule out OXVS, as long as specifiers are always to the left so that OVS order is necessarily derived via movement. The crucial evidence that the order of heads and complements is regulated in some way by the LCA comes only, it seems, from the Final-over-Final Constraint

(FOFC; cf. Biberauer, Holmberg, and Roberts/BHR 2008a, in press), discussed in the final three papers of the volume.

In basic terms, FOFC as formulated by BHR rules out head-initial phrases dominated by head-final phrases which are part of the same extended projection, where 'extended projection' is understood in essentially the same sense as Grimshaw's original (1991) notion. The relevant definition of 'extended projection' is given in (42), while the basic configuration ruled out by FOFC is schematized in (43):

(42)   X is a *head* of YP, and YP is a *projection* of X iff:

    a. YP dominates X;

    b. the categorial features of YP and X are consistent;

    c. there is no inconsistency in the categorial features of all nodes intervening between X and Y (where a node N *intervenes* between X and YP if YP dominates X and N, N dominates X, and N does not dominate YP); and

    d. no node intervening between X and YP is lexical.

(43)   *

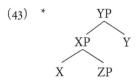

where X is the head of an extended projection which YP is also part of, by virtue of its bearing the same categorial features as X and its not being a lexical category (i.e. the type of category that defines the bottom of an extended projection).

Among other patterns, FOFC rules out VOAux and VOC orders in the clausal domain. Where *Aux* is an 'inflecting' element and C is a subordinating complementizer, the literature—generative and typological—is clear about the fact that these patterns are indeed practically always ruled out (cf. i.a. Greenberg 1963 on VOAux patterns, and Hawkins 1994, Kayne 1994, Dryer 2009 on the VOC gap; Biberauer and Sheehan 2012 observe that Harar Oromo (Cushitic) and Akkadian (Semitic) superficially appear to constitute counterexamples to the latter generalization). That the generalization does not hold of the large inventory of discourse-related C-particles found in languages like Chinese is immediately clear if one considers the data discussed in Chan (this volume; cf. also Paul to appear, and see Biberauer and Sheehan 2011 for more general discussion of C-particles). Similarly, it does not hold for (a class of) auxiliary particles in languages like Chinese, some of the Karen languages (e.g. Bwe-Karen; cf. Dryer 2008), and many Central African VO languages (cf. Dryer 2009). Consideration of even a subset of the apparently FOFC-violating elements suggests that they are unlikely to share a single property that makes them immune to FOFC, a point also highlighted in Sheehan (this volume). If FOFC is really a constraint on headedness within an extended projection, however, it is clear what sorts of properties might allow C- and auxiliary elements to surface finally without violating the constraint: acategorial (or syncategorematic) elements, and lexical elements entirely lacking formal features, which cannot therefore project, would be two cases in point (cf. Biberauer, Holmberg, and Roberts 2009, in press for discussion).

The papers in the final section of this volume are all in one way or another concerned with FOFC as a constraint on permissible disharmonic word orders, defined in terms of mixed headedness. Hawkins considers harmonic and disharmonic word orders from a typological, grammatical, and processing-efficiency perspective. He argues, in keeping with Hawkins (1994, 2004), that the most readily processed structures are the ones that become grammaticalized as components of competence grammars. In relation to FOFC specifically, he argues that (43), viewed from a typological perspective, appears to be both too strong and too weak. It is too strong in that it rules out actually attested structures: as noted above, we do find surface VOAux and VOC structures. It is too weak in that we see patterns involving 'cross-projection' structures, like Noun-Possessive PP inside PP (e.g. *with soldiers of the king*) where *both* disharmonic orders appear to be dispreferred equally to the corresponding harmonic orders. Worse, it appears to be the case that postnominal head-final relative clauses (i.e. N [$_{CP}$ TP C]) are unattested; (43), however, addresses neither the relation between XPs associated with different extended projections nor that between adjuncts and the XPs they modify, thereby apparently missing a significant empirical gap.[37] From a processing-efficiency perspective, these gaps can be understood as the consequence of structures that constitute a processing challenge being dispreferred. Thus a centre-embedded CP of the type found in [$_{VP}$ [$_{CP}$ C TP] V] and [$_{NP}$ [$_{CP}$ C TP] N] is expected to be harder to process than a likewise centre-embedded 'lighter' NP or PossPP. Consequently, we expect to find instances of [$_{NP}$ [$_{PossPP}$ [P NP]] N] and [$_{VP}$ [$_{NP}$ N PP] V], but not of the above-mentioned CP structures, which is indeed what typological frequency suggests. Ultimately, Hawkins' contention is that the best characterization of word-order generalizations like FOFC will need to follow from combined consideration of what we know about formal grammatical principles, cross-linguistic surface typology, and online processing.

---

[37] Hawkins also highlights the absence of head-final postverbal complement clauses (i.e. V [$_{CP}$ TP C]) in relation to the inventory of structures that cannot be accounted for by (43). As Biberauer and Sheehan (2012) and Sheehan (this volume: p. 414) note, however, this structure is in fact ruled out by (43) for cases where any XP dominated by final C is head-initial; as Bayer (1999, 2001) observes, cases where a consistently head-final CP surfaces in postverbal position do seem to be marginally possible in languages like Bengali. Crucially, structures in these languages in which C is head-initial (i.e. where C is derived from a *wh*-element) cannot surface preverbally, however, i.e. [$_{CP}$ C TP] V is ruled out, as predicted by (43).

Sheehan's paper specifically aims to compare and contrast the success with which Hawkins' (1994) processing-efficiency proposal can account for attested skewings and gaps in the disharmonic domain with how a formal, phonological (PF) interface account like that of Sheehan (in press) would fare. Like Hawkins, she adopts a definition of FOFC in terms of which any head-final XP dominating a head-initial XP is ruled out, regardless of extended-projection considerations (cf. Holmberg 2000). In terms of the PF interface account, such structures are ruled out because they cannot be linearized on the basis of the linearization algorithm that Sheehan argues usually to be in play, namely (44):

(44) **Revised LCA**
  (i) If a category A c-selects a category B, then A PRECEDES/FOLLOWS B at PF.
  (ii) If no order is specified between A and B by the sum of all precedence pairs defined by (i), then A PRECEDES B at PF if A asymmetrically c-commands B.

In terms of (44), Kayne's LCA emerges as a Last Resort linearization mechanism in only those cases where c-selection-based ordering, as outlined in (i), cannot be established. That asymmetric c-command should, as Kayne has always stipulated, result in precedence rather than subsequence is justified on the grounds that the choice between the two actually amounts to what Biberauer, Holmberg, Roberts, and Sheehan (2010) and Biberauer, Roberts, and Scheehan (2013) designate a 'no-choice parameter', one which is always set to PRECEDE on account of processing consider-ations not dissimilar to those considered by Hawkins in his contribution. More specifically, the proposal is that parsing preferences such as i.a. Filler precedes Gap (cf. Ackema and Neeleman 2002; Wagers and Phillips 2009) favour the precedence setting in relation to less local ordering phenomena. The same pressure arguably does not come into play in the local Head–Complement domain because, as Hawkins has convincingly shown in this volume and also in earlier work, head-final and head-initial orders are equally optimal in parsing terms. Importantly, then, Sheehan's proposed PF account of linearization generally and FOFC specifically follows from a combination of the asymmetry imposed by Narrow Syntax (the fact that asymmet-ric c-command relations exist between elements in a hierarchically constructed phrase-structure tree) and, crucially, processing pressures.

Her chapter shows that a Hawkins-style processing-efficiency account and the PF interface account which she proposes are, in many cases, equally capable of account-ing for attested empirical skewing in the disharmonic domain. A major prediction made by the former, but not the latter, however, relates to contexts in which there is harmony between two categories and an FOFC effect obtains: as the principle which gives rise to harmony for Hawkins (Early Immediate Constituents (EIC) in Hawkins 1994 or Minimize Domains (MiD) in Hawkins 2004) is also the one that underlies FOFC, the prediction is that FOFC effects should always affect the same categories that exhibit a preference for harmony, with these effects correspondingly being absent where categories do not exhibit a harmony preference. As Sheehan shows, this does not, however, seem to be straightforwardly true: articles are verb-patterners (cf. Dryer 1992a), meaning that there is harmony between V and (simplifying somewhat[38]) D, but there does not appear to be any FOFC effect between V and D; similarly, looking at the bidirectional implication of Hawkins' approach from the opposite perspective, it appears that Polarity Heads and C-complementizers respect FOFC (cf. Biberauer, Sheehan, and Newton 2010; Sheehan this volume), whereas it does not seem to be the case that they exhibit any preference for harmony (see again Sheehan this volume: 438 ff.). What emerges from both Sheehan and Hawkins' papers, then, is the need to look very closely—much more so than has been possible at present—at attested disharmonic word-order data: a suitably detailed, grammatically informed characterization of the data is clearly essential to facilitate insight into the merits and demerits of analyses proposed to date.

Sheehan's paper ends with consideration of the particle question highlighted above, which is also the sole focus of Chan's contribution. Sheehan highlights the need for an explicit characterization of the notion 'particle', proposing one possibility, namely that these elements be thought of as functional heads lacking uninterpretable formal features other than c-selection features, which therefore have to be merged with an atomized[39] phrase (as noted above, alternative characterizations are also suggested in Biberauer, Holmberg, and Roberts 2009, in press). The Chinese and, in particular, Cantonese particles considered by Chan have previously been said to behave in the manner suggested by Sheehan (cf. Hsieh and Sybesma 2007), but this is not the approach Chan himself endorses. Instead, he questions the mainstream view that sentence-final particles (SFPs) in Chinese varieties are C-heads which are merged with TP. Distributional considerations constitute the key argument in favour of this proposal as it is so strikingly the case that canonical C-heads, instantiated by *that*-type complementizers, cannot occur in VOC structures (cf. the references cited at the start of this section). To further support his argument, Chan considers a specific context in Cantonese which is compatible with a range of SFPs: the Dislocation Focus Construction. In relation to Cantonese SFPs, he observes (p. 463) that they are often polysemous, a property that we typically associate with lexical (in the sense of contentful, open-class) elements rather than functional categories; functional polysemy might best be thought of as entailing radical semantic and possibly also syntactic underspecification, with the result that the element in question is able to

---

[38] That elements functioning as articles do not always instantiate D-heads is, of course, well known (cf. i.a. Alexiadou, Haegeman, and Stavrou 2007 for overview discussion).

[39] 'Atomization' here is understood in the sense of Hsieh and Sybesma (2007) and Fowlie (2013), i.e. as entailing the conversion, at a specified point (e.g. completion of a phasal domain), of a portion of hierarchical structure to an atomic head, where there is no active phase edge. Johnson's (2002) 'renumeration' has the same effect.

surface in a range of contexts, with its very general meaning interacting with the specific meanings of other sentence components in such a way that the particle appears to have a range of slightly differing meanings. Both hypotheses seem plausible in relation to the data discussed by Chan; as noted at the beginning of this section, both can also potentially provide an explanation as to why (superficial) FOFC compliance is not required. Chan's own interpretation of the Cantonese data is that the SFPs in question are affixed to focused constituents in the Dislocation and Clause-Internal Focus Constructions respectively and, as such, do not represent Cs.[40] If it is more generally the case that SFPs may combine with a range of constituents, in the manner of focus particles more generally (cf. i.a. Barbiers 2010 for recent discussion), for example, then we may understand these elements as syncategorematic elements, which do not violate FOFC on account of the fact that they either do not project at all (Chan's proposal here and the interpretation could extend to particles with very specific lexical content; cf. Cardinaletti 2011 for one formal account of the syntax of particles of this type) or because they project category-neutral structure (cf. Biberauer 2008b and Bayer and Obenauer 2011 for two recent proposals along these lines). More than anything, what is evident from Chan's discussion, however, is how much we still have to learn about particles as a cross-linguistically seemingly particularly disharmonic category.

1.5 Conclusion

Word order has become of interest in the generative paradigm only fairly recently (cf. Hawkins 1980; Kayne 1994) and even now its theoretical status remains somewhat controversial (cf. Berwick and Chomsky 2011 for an apparently extreme view, relegating word order to the PF interface). The reason for this is fairly clear: the word orders of different languages vary in puzzling and complicated ways, so much so that it is often claimed that word order tracks syntax only in arbitrary and language-specific ways (see even Chomsky 2001: 7). Relegating word order to the PF component or 'externalization' more generally is permissible inasmuch as we have an elaborated theory of PF/externalization which can account for word-order correlations, asymmetries, and gaps, or inasmuch as some other third-factor pressure can

---

[40] Interestingly, Chan's discussion of Cantonese focus constructions appears to highlight the existence of two left-peripheral focus domains in this system: one at the *v*P edge (Clause-Internal Focus) and the other at the CP edge (Dislocation Focus). This calls to mind the phasal peripheries discussed in Cognola's contribution, and, more generally, adds to the growing body of literature highlighting the variously information-structure-related nature of phasal peripheries. Given the well-established link between information structure and word-order variation, with the former typically being seen to perturb aspects of basic word order, this consideration is clearly an important one in the context of studies of disharmonic word order.

be shown to account for these skewings. The papers in this volume make a valuable contribution to this complex issue and introduce new relevant data to the debate, which, it is hoped, will instruct future research. What will hopefully become clear during the following pages is the extent to which disharmonic word orders specifically deserve to be the focus of intensive research in the years to come.

Part I

On the Nature of Disharmony

2

Word-Order Typology: A Change of Perspective*

GUGLIELMO CINQUE

2.1 Introduction

In much work stemming from Greenberg (1963), the order of the direct object with respect to the verb has been claimed to correlate (to varying degrees) with the relative order of many other pairs of elements, among which those in (1):

(1) VO   OV

    a. P > DP (Prepositional Phrases)   DP >P (Postpositional Phrases)

    b. Aux > V   V > Aux

    c. copula > predicate   predicate > copula

    d. V > manner adverb   manner adverb >V

    e. (more) A (than) 'Standard of   'Standard of Comparison' (than)
       Comparison'   A (more)

    f. A > PP   PP > A

    g. V > complement/adjunct PP   adjunct/complement PP > V

Despite the feeling that we are confronting some *great underlying ground plan*, to borrow one of Sapir's (1949: 144) expressions, and despite the numerous attempts to uncover the principle(s) governing it,[1] the concomitant demand of empirical

* I wish to thank the audiences of the workshop on 'Theoretical Approaches to Disharmonic Word Orders' (Newcastle, 30 May –1 June, 2009) and of the Département de linguistique of Paris VII (25 January, 2010), where versions of this paper were presented. I also thank Theresa Biberauer, Richard Kayne, Michelle Sheehan, and two anonymous reviewers for their comments on a previous draft.

[1] Cf. Greenberg's (1963) *modifier > modified vs modified > modifier tendency* (as well as his notion of *harmonic relations*) (p. 100); Lehmann's (1973) *Fundamental Principle of Placement*; Vennemann's (1973) *Principle of Natural Serialization*; Sanders' (1975) *Invariant ordering Hypothesis*; Antinucci's (1977: ch. 1) *Principle of Left- vs Rightward Linearization*; Keenan's (1978b: 188) *Serialization and Dissimilation Principles*; Hawkins' (1983) *Principle of Cross-Category Harmony*; Chomsky's (1964: 123, fn. 9, 1995a: 35) and Dryer's (1992a) *left vs right branching*; Dryer's (2007) and others' *'head-finality' vs 'head-initiality'*.

accuracy with respect to actual languages has reduced all of the correlations proposed to the state of mere tendencies. In particular, with the increase of the number of languages studied, the neat mirror-image picture emerging from some of the works mentioned in note 1 has come to be drastically redressed.[2]

As shown in Dryer (1991, 1992a, 2007), virtually all *bidirectional* correlations, like those in (1), have exceptions. For example, the existence of OV languages with prepositions and VO languages with postpositions (Dryer 1991: 448 and 452, 2007: 87f.) is an exception to (1a).[3] Mande languages (Kastenholz 2003; Nikitina 2009) and some Chibchan languages (Ngäbére—Young and Givón 1990), with the order SAux-OVX, are an exception to (1b), as is VSO Island Carib (Northern Maipuran—Heine 1993: 133, note 4) with inflected auxiliaries following the main verb.[4] OV Ngäbére, with the copula preceding the predicate, is also an exception to (1c), as is VO Wembawemba (Pama-Nyungan) with the copula following the predicate (Dryer 1992a: 94). Angami, an OV Tibeto-Burman language, with manner adverbs following the V (Giridhar 1980: 85, cited in Dryer 2007: §2.2; Patnaik 1996: 72) is an exception to (1d). Chinese (VO with Standard > Adjective) is an exception to (1e). And so on.

Even the second type of correlation, *unidirectional* ones, like that in (2),[5] are not exempt from exceptions. Mandarin, Cantonese, Hakka, Bai (Sinitic), Amis (Formosan—Austronesian) (Dryer 2005a), and Asia Minor Greek (Campbell, Bubenik, and Saxon 1988: 215), are VO and RelN.

---

[2] Greenberg's (1963) decision to resort to finer distinctions than VO vs OV (such as VSO, SVO, rigid SOV and non-rigid SOV), and Hawkins' formulation of complex implicational statements (e.g., Postp ⊃ (NAdj ⊃ NGen), of the type of Greenberg's Universal 5) were attempts to achieve exceptionless universals by narrowing down the number of languages to be checked for conformity to some statement. These too, however, have turned out to have exceptions. See Dryer (2007: §9) for an exception to Greenberg's Universal 5, which was given as absolute, and Payne (1985), Campbell, Bubenik, and Saxon (1988), Dryer (1997: 141), and LaPolla (2002: §2) for exceptions to Hawkins' (1983) absolute complex implicational universals. Despite their non-universality and their more restricted scope, such complex implicational universals may nonetheless provide important clues as to which harmonic properties are more stable, and which more prone to be relaxed.

[3] Also see the Konstanz Universals Archive, no. 55, Whitman (2008: 238), and references cited there. Postpositions are even attested in a number of VSO languages: Guajajara, Nomatsiguenga, and Yagua (Payne 1985: 465; Campbell, Bubenik, and Saxon 1988: 212ff.), Cora and Tepehuán (Pickett 1983: 549).

[4] To judge from Taylor (1952: 162) the order is V Aux O. Also see the Konstanz Universals Archive <http://typo.uni-konstanz.de/archive/>, no. 501, where it is reported that 'the only VO language in Dryer's sample from Australia–New Guinea area has V Aux order'. Greenberg (1963: Appendix I and note 15) gives Guaraní as SVO and as having postverbal auxiliaries (although they may be particles, intervening between the V and the object—Tonhauser 2006: 273).

[5] (2) cannot be strengthened to a bidirectional correlation, by adding NRel ⊃ VO and OV ⊃ RelN, because OV languages distribute evenly between RelN and NRel (Dryer 2005a gives 111 languages as OV and RelN and 95 languages as OV and NRel). Similarly, the implications in (i.a–b) concerning complement (and adverbial) clauses and subordinators cannot be strengthened to a bidirectional correlation by adding those in (ii.a–b) as [IP C] V and V [C IP] are equally represented in OV languages (Dryer 1980; Hawkins 1990: 225, 256; Dryer 1992a: §§4.3 and 4.5, 1992b; Diessel 2001; Kayne 2005b: 227):

(i) a. VO ⊃ C IP   b.   IP C ⊃ OV
(ii) a. C IP ⊃ VO   b.   OV ⊃ IP C

Exceptions to (i) are mentioned below in note 31 and in section 2.7.

(2) N(P) and Relative clause (Dryer 1992a: 86; Cinque 2005a)

    a. VO ⊃ NRel

    b. RelN ⊃ OV

Finally, other word-order pairs have seemingly turned out to be *no correlation pairs* at all; for example, those in (3):

(3)   a. Adjectives with respect to N (Dryer 1988a, 1992a: §3.1)

     b. Numerals with respect to N (Dryer 2007: §7.3)

     c. Demonstratives with respect to N (Dryer 1992a: §3.2, 2007: §7.2)

     d. Intensifiers with respect to Adjectives (Dryer 1992a: §3.3, 2007: §7.6; Patnaik 1996: 70)

     e. Negative particles with respect to Verbs (Dahl 1979; Dryer 1988b, 1992a: §3.4, 2007: §7.4; LaPolla 2002: 209)

     f. Tense/aspect particles with respect to Verbs (Dryer 1992a: §3.5, 2007: §7.5)

So, this viewpoint (which strives for absolute formulations that may capture the underlying ground-plan and avoid at the same time being falsified by actual languages) leads at best to the scarcely enlightening picture of the three cases just seen (non-exceptionless bidirectional correlations, non-exceptionless unidirectional correlations, and no correlations at all); in other words, to statistical tendencies at most (however important they may be).

2.2 A change of perspective

We may wonder whether something would change if we reversed this perspective; not by asking what the *predominant* correlates of OV and VO orders in actual languages are, but by asking what precisely the harmonic word-order types are that we can theoretically reconstruct, and to what extent each language (or subset of languages) departs from them.

This change of perspective entails viewing the 'harmonic' orders as abstract and exceptionless, and independent of actual languages, though no less real[6] (below I will suggest that these harmonic orders should not be regarded as primitives, but rather as derived from a universal structure of Merge reflecting the relative scope relations of the elements involved, via two distinct movement options, with actual languages departing to varying degrees from the 'ideal' derivations).

---

[6] This perspective is closer to Vennemann's later (1976) interpretation of his Natural Serialization Principle than to his earlier one (1973). For discussion of the evolution of Vennemann's thought, see Hawkins' (1983: §§2.3–2.6).

This way of looking at things has a number of implications, some apparently undesirable (under the strongest interpretation):

(4) a. Every word-order pair belongs to one or the other of the harmonic word-order types. In other words, *there are no non-correlation pairs.*

b. Each correlation pair is related *bidirectionally* to every other correlation pair of its harmonic type (Dem N ⊃ DP P and DP P ⊃ Dem N. Dem N ⊃ V Aux and V Aux ⊃ Dem N, etc.). In other words, *there are no merely unidirectional correlations.*

c. It should in principle be possible to measure the distance of a certain language (or group of languages) from one of the abstract harmonic types (how much it 'leaks', in another of Sapir's expressions[7]), thus leading to a finer-grained typology than just VO and OV.[8]

d. More interestingly, perhaps, such measuring should lead one to try to determine which correlation pairs are more stable and which more prone to be relaxed, possibly along a markedness scale, which in turn should correlate with the number of the languages belonging to that (sub)type (though it is not to be excluded that each language will ultimately represent a subtype of its own, of some higher order (sub)type).[9]

---

[7] '[...] no language is tyrannically consistent. All grammars leak.' (Sapir 1949: 40).

[8] The word-order types are indefinitely more numerous than the VO/OV types, depending on the number of properties and subproperties taken into consideration. For example, in Greenberg's (1963) larger sample of 142 languages, the 4 word-order properties chosen (VSO/SVO/SOV; Pr/Po; NG/GN; NA/AN) yield as attested 11 VO types (with different proportions of languages). See his Appendix II. More VO types have in the meantime been documented (see, for example, Campbell, Bubenik, and Saxon 1988), and undoubtedly many more types would have to be countenanced if the number of word-order properties considered were to be augmented (Cf. Siewierska 1988: 20 for discussion of this point). The SVO variant of VO differs in certain respects from the V-initial variant of VO (i.e. VSO and VOS). But even the SVO type is not at all homogeneous. In addition to the different subtypes in Greenberg's (1963: 109) Appendix II, one finds extensive variation in virtually every word-order pair. For example, in the relatively minor word-order pair of proper noun/common noun, Bulgarian, Chinese, English, Greek, Italian, and Norwegian all differ in the way they linearize the various combinations of common nouns ('year', 'hour', 'month', 'title', 'street', 'island', 'mountain', 'river', etc.) and proper nouns (with Bulgarian, Chinese, and Norwegian displaying more 'head-final' orders than German). See Cinque (2009b).

A comparable non-homogeneity is found in the other orders: VSO (see Kaplan 1991; Lancioni 1995; Polinsky 1997; Tallerman 1998b: 628; Broadwell 2005; Macaulay 2005; Otsuka 2005; Roberts 2005: 157), VOS (see Polinsky 1997; Aldridge 2006; Holmer 2006: 103, among others), and SOV (cf. Greenberg's 1963 five classes of SOV languages in his Appendix II). Given the different subtypes existing in each of these orders, and presumably in languages with OVS and OSV orders (see Campbell, Bubenik, and Saxon 1988), to the limit one type for each language, unqualified reference to VO and OV is bound to lead to statistical tendencies at most, as noted.

Such tendencies can be seen as intermediate levels of generalization between the abstract level of the 'ideal' harmonic types and the level characterizing the typological properties of each single language.

[9] To the effect that possibly no language will prove to be fully 'harmonic', or 'consistent'. Cf. Sapir's comment in note 7, as well as Smith (1981: 40), Kroch (2001: 706), and Kayne (1994: xv, 2005b: 220).

To take one illustrative example from the literature, Table 2.1, from Hawkins (1979: 645) (adapted from Mallinson and Blake 1981: 416), shows that there is a decline in the number of attested languages (in Hawkins' sample) the more the language deviates from the word-order type:[10]

TABLE 2.1 **Actual attestation of SOV word-order types exhibiting greater and lesser consistency**

SOV	Postposition	AN	GN	(consistent)	80 languages
SOV	Postposition	*NA*	GN	(one deviation)	50 languages
SOV	Postposition	*NA*	*NG*	(two deviations)	11 languages

If we take this general perspective, then the first task should consist in determining precisely what the abstract harmonic orders are.

2.3 The two abstract harmonic orders

A complete reconstruction of the two abstract harmonic orders is out of the question here. I will present a fragment of these orders merely to illustrate the logic of the approach. The harmonic orders can to a large extent be gathered from the correlation pairs attributed in the literature to OV and VO languages (in the Appendix, I list a number of such pairs, with an indication of their source, forcing, as noted, their bidirectionality even when this flies in the face of the empirical data, as with the order of noun and adjective in 'head-final' languages). These orders should be seen as ideal mirror-image orders drawn from the most polarized language types (rigid SOV and rigid VOS languages, which are the best approximations to the ideal orders, but mostly still not quite coincident with the ideal orders).[11]

---

[10] It is not really important if samples larger than Hawkins' were to redress, or even subvert, some of the figures of Table 2.1 (see for example the figures of these correlations in Dryer 1988a, 1992a: §3.1, 2005b). What matters here is the spirit of the approach suggested by Hawkins.

[11] Even Japanese, one of the most 'rigid' SOV languages, displays some non-'head-final' characteristics. For example, one postnominal numeral classifier modification (see (i), and Tsunoda 1990, Choi 2005 for the same property in Korean), head-medial complex numbers (Bender 2002), and the arguably initial heads *wa* and *ga* (Kayne 1994: 143, 2005b: 220; Whitman 2001: §2):

(i) Neko   ni   hiki   wo   kau   (Siegel and Bender 2004: §3.1.4)
     cat   two   NUMCL   ACC   raise
     '(I) am raising two cats.'

Japanese also has one *common noun > proper noun* order which is typical of 'head-initial' languages (Cinque 2009b): *number > name of number* instead of *name of number > number*: *bangoo roku* (number six) (example provided by Yoshio Endo, p.c.). Lehmann (1978b: 400) and Smith (1981: 40) mention additional non 'head-final' characteristics of Japanese.

A fairly rigid VOS language like Seediq (Formosan—Austronesian) also displays some non-head-initial' characteristics (among which a final subordinator: *han* 'when/while'—Holmer 1996: 59f. see the example (42b) below).

What renders the task more difficult is the fact that correlation pairs, though important, do not suffice to reconstruct the 'ideal' harmonic orders. They fall short of giving the *total* order of functional heads, arguments, circumstantials, and modifiers of the clause, and of the other major phrases in 'head-initial' and 'head-final' languages.[12] Exclusive focus on correlation pairs can even mislead one into attributing to the same type word-order types that should be kept distinct. To take one example, if one considers only the orders of *pairs* of elements like NA/AN, NNum/NumN, NDem/DemN, without considering their *total* order, one is led to put three languages like Lalo (Tibeto-Burman—Björverud 1998: 116ff.), which has N A Dem Num, Luo (Nilotic—Heine 1981), which has N Num A Dem, and Gungbe (Niger-Congo—Aboh 2004: ch. 3), which has N A Num Dem, in one and the same class, as all of them are: NA, NNum, NDem. Yet, while the order found in Gungbe is the overwhelmingly prevalent postnominal order of these elements, the orders found in Lalo and Luo are quite rare in the languages of the world (cf. Cinque 2005b: 319f.). Thus, one runs the risk of not singling out the correct subtypes and of misrepresenting the number of languages belonging to each. Cases like this, where attention is limited to lists of word-order pairs of elements, rather than to the complete sequence of these elements in each phrase, are unfortunately the norm. For the two abstract harmonic types I will use the widespread terms of 'head-initial' and 'head-final' even though these are, strictly speaking, misnomers; in many cases it is a projection of a head rather than a head which is initial or final. This appears to be the case with the head of a relative clause, which may (arguably, must) contain more than just the head N (cf. Kayne 1994: 154, fn. 13, 2005b: 119f. Cinque 2005a: note 11):

(5)   the [two or three recently arrived sick immigrants] that each doctor had to visit

And the same may be true of the verb in relation to subordinate clauses. It too can, possibly must, head a phrase containing more than just the lexical V:

(6)   a. He [convinced us] that he was the right person

       b. I [went home] before they arrived

       c. They [doubt (it)] that you will go

Nonetheless, as we will see, phrases containing the lexical nucleus (NP, VP, . . .) and the (X-bar) functional heads of the extended projections of the lexical nucleus align similarly.

---

[12] This is one aspect of traditional word-order typology which appears particularly wanting. Among the rare exceptions which consider more than just pairs of elements are, for the nominal phrase, Greenberg's (1963) Universals 18 and 20 on the order of demonstratives, numerals, adjectives, and noun, Hetzron (1978), Plank (2006), and Lahiri and Plank (2009: §7.2) on the order of various classes of adjectives, and, for the clause, Boisson's (1981) discussion of the relative order of Manner, Place, and Time adverbials. Needless to say, the elements to be taken into consideration for the clause and the other phrases are considerably more numerous.

2.3.1 *The 'head-initial' type*

The generalization concerning the harmonic 'head-initial' word-order type appears to be that *all higher (functional) heads precede VP/NP in their order of Merge, and phrasal specifiers (arguments, circumstantials, and modifiers) follow, in an order which is the reverse of their order of Merge.* See (7) and (8), which contain some suggestive examples (I postpone consideration of arguments and circumstantials):

(7)   a.   C° T° Asp° V(P) AdvP$_3$ AdvP$_2$ AdvP$_1$[13]

      b.   **Tsy**   manasa   tsara foana intsony   mihitsy   Rakoto[14]
           NEG   PRES.AT.wash well   always no.longer at.all   Rakoto
           'Rakoto does not wash at all any longer always well.'

      c.   **Mae**   hi   **wedi** bod **yn**   socian   am dridiau
           be:PRES 3FSG   PFV   be   PROG soak   for three.days
           'It's already been soaking for three days.'

                              (Welsh—Celtic, VSO—Cf. Tallerman 1998a: 31)

      d.   **N`jẹ́** Adé **yóò** **máa** wá   ní   ìrọ̀lẹ́?
           Q   Ade FUT HAB come in   evening
           'Will Ade be coming in the evenings?'

                            (Yoruba—Niger-Congo—SVO, O. Ajíbóyè, p.c.)

      e.   **ye**   uxe   dheya **wada**   gmeeguy di
           Yes/No NEG 3PL   **AUX$_{Past}$** steal.AF PART
           'Have/Had they stolen (the basket of pears)?'

                   (Seediq—Austronesian, Formosan, VOS—Lin 2005: 116)

(8)   a.   Art° PL° N(P) AP$_2$ AP$_1$ NumP DemP[15]

      b.   **àwon** okùnrin méta yĭ
           PL   man   three this
           'these three men'   (Yoruba—Niger-Congo, SVO—Dryer 1989a: 875)[16]

---

[13] See sections 1 and 2 of Rackowski and Travis (2000) on Malagasy (VOS) and Niuean (VSO), respectively: 'there [...] seems to be a correlation between preverbal elements which appear in their hierarchical order and postverbal elements which are in the reverse order' (p. 127).
    On what appears preverbally in 'verb-initial languages' see the first part of Greenberg's (1963) Universal 16: 'In languages with dominant order VSO, an inflected auxiliary always precedes the main verb', and Carnie and Guilfoyle's (2000b: 10) claim that a trait of VSO languages is represented by 'preverbal tense, mood/aspect, question, and negation particles'. Also see the Konstanz Universals Archive, nos 501 and 1553, Dryer (1992a: §4.3 and §4.5), and Hendrick (2000). On the phrasal, rather than head, status of the verbal, adjectival, nominal, etc. predicate following the preverbal particles in a number of V-initial languages, see Massam (2000: §2), Lee (2000a), Cole and Hermon (2008).

[14] Malagasy (Austronesian, VOS, cf. Rackowski and Travis 2000: §1). Also see Koopman (2005a) on Maasai V adv S O.

[15] On the order **article** > N in all VOS languages (except Toba Batak) in his sample, see Keenan's (1978a: 298, G15, p.). On the order PL > N in VO languages, see Dryer (1989a, 1992a: §4.7).

[16] Yoruba postnominal modifiers are a mirror image of (English) prenominal ones: [N A$_{color}$ A$_{size}$ A$_{value}$ Num Dem]. See Ajíbóyè (2005: 258).

c. **ea**   **pi**   kaarroo   neey
  ART   PL   car   this
  'these cars'   (Yapese—Austronesian, VSO—Dryer 1989a: 868)

2.3.2 *The 'head-final' type*

The generalization concerning the 'head-final' word-order type is that *all higher (functional) heads follow the lexical VP/NP in an order which is the reverse of the order of Merge, and phrasal specifiers (arguments, circumstantials, and modifiers) precede VP/NP in their order of Merge:*

(9)   a. AdvP$_1$ AdvP$_2$ AdvP$_3$ V° Asp° T° C°

     b. [ngasā shia natu] [yingtung-tunga] ke pai **nuam hī**
         fish   fish   PURP early.in.morning I   go **want IND**
         'I want to go out early in the morning to fish.'
                        (Siyin Chin—Tibeto-Burman, SOV—Dryer 2007: 120)

     c. yer   ngeti tyapat **me**   **tu**
         tomorrow I sit   swim   **PROG** **FUT**
         'Tomorrow I shall be swimming.'
                    (Maranungku—Australian, Daly, SOV—Tryon 1970: 46)

(10) DemP NumP AP$_1$ AP$_2$ N° PL° Art°
      [Kí   tu?lu **tem** **ci**] nuŋ
        house   big   PL   the   in
      'in the big houses'   (Ao—Tibeto-Burman, SOV—Gowda 1975: 65)

2.3.3 *The overarching generalization*

The property which both the 'head-initial' and the 'head-final' word orders have in common is that whatever precedes the VP/NP reflects the order of Merge, and whatever follows is in the mirror image of the order of Merge. In actual languages the mirror-image order found postverbally and postnominally is in fact just the prevalent order (for reasons discussed in Cinque 2005b, 2009a). Also see Kiss (2008).

2.4 Deriving the two abstract harmonic types

As I said, I take the two abstract (mirror-image) harmonic types to be epiphenomenal. They are the product of the application of two different sets of movement options to one and the same structure of Merge, common to all languages, which, as noted, presumably reflects the relative scope of the elements involved.[17]

If we want to capture the fact that manner adverbs take scope over the lexical verb whether they precede it (typically in 'head-final' languages) or follow it (typically in 'head-initial' languages), and that modal (functional) verbs also take scope over the lexical verb (and the manner adverb), whether they come after (typically in 'head-final' languages) or before (typically in 'head-initial' languages) (Adv_{manner} V Mod in 'head-final' languages vs Mod V Adv_{manner} in 'head-initial' languages), neither of the two orders can be taken to be more primitive than the other. Rather, both have to derive from a common structure of Merge that reflects the relative scope of the elements involved, via two different sets of movements:

(11)

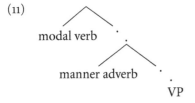

For the sake of illustration, let me take two very small fragments of the unique structures of Merge of the extended projection of VP (the clause) ((12a)), and of that of NP ((12b)):

(12)   a.   b.

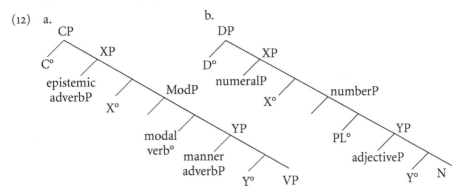

---

[17] A reviewer raised the question whether this is a departure from the position I took in Cinque (1999: ch. 6), where it was claimed that the order of functional projections is part of UG (narrow syntax) and cannot be simply reduced to semantics (understood as the conceptual–intentional interface). That the hierarchical arrangement of the functional heads of the extended projection of VP (the clause), of NP, AP, etc., is compatible with the relative scope of the elements involved was actually assumed in Cinque (1999) too, with one proviso. What should not be given up is the encoding of such heads and projections in narrow syntax, for the simple reason that many more things exist in our conceptual–intentional module than those that receive a grammatical expression in the languages of the world (in UG). As noted there (p. 136), the rigid ordering of the functional projections of the clause can apparently be reversed only if one operates across two clauses. Also see Cinque (2006: 6; 2013a), Cinque and Rizzi (2010a: 65).

I take these to be antisymmetric Spec > head > complement structures (Kayne 1994) terminating in (or rather originating from) a non-branching VP/NP, with complements of V and N merged in specifier positions above VP/NP, to the effect that nothing is merged to the right of V or N, for reasons discussed in Cinque (2009a).[18] (I will come back to complements and circumstantials.) It is not really important here to recall the evidence for quite rich ordered sequences of elements in the clause and in each of the other phrases. See, for example, the sequencing of different types of complementizers (Rizzi 1997; Benincà and Munaro 2010), that of Mood, Modal, Tense, Aspect, and Voice elements (heads and adverbial phrases) in the clause (Cinque 1999, 2006), and that of the different functional (including adjectival) projections in the nominal phrase (Cinque 1994, 2005b, 2010; Scott 2002; Svenonius 2008).

Having said that, let me return to the overly simplified structures of Merge in (12a–b) to tentatively sketch the kind of consistent types of movements which seem to lead to the two ideal 'harmonic' types. As noted, actual languages will depart from these to varying degrees, something that remains to be investigated in detail (and is likely to disclose much more variation among languages).[19]

To briefly give the basic idea, the movement is initiated by the nucleus (VP, NP, etc., 'the initial engine') and is taken over by each higher functional head endowed with the same categorial feature, so it seems (in the case of VP: auxiliaries, modals, aspectual verbs, certain particles, complementizers, . . .). If the raising takes place via pied-piping of the *whose*-picture type (Cinque 2005b), we have the 'head-initial' order; if it takes place via pied-piping of the picture-of-*whom* type, we have the 'head-final' order.

Let us consider the two cases in turn (needless to say, at this stage, any proposal can only be programmatic in character, and extremely tentative).

2.4.1 *The 'head-initial' type*

Recall the generalization concerning the 'head-initial' word-order type: *all higher (functional) heads precede VP/NP in their order of Merge, and phrasal specifiers (arguments, circumstantials, and modifiers) follow, in an order which is the reverse of their order of Merge*. See (7a) and (8a), repeated here (I postpone consideration of arguments and circumstantials):

---

[18] Also see Barbiers (2000) and Kayne (2005b: 215).

[19] I mention just one example from the distribution of attributive adjectives, for which, as noted, there is suggestive evidence that they enter a strict order (see in particular Scott 2002: 114; Cinque 2010). Again, to consider just a subset of these adjectives, the 'head-final' order appears to be 'other' > quality > size > age > colour > nationality > N, and the 'head-initial' order its mirror image. Yet, many languages show mixed orders; for example, Welsh (in Willis's 2006 description), with N A_{size} A_{colour} $A_{nationality}$ A_{age} $A_{quality}$ 'other', or, to judge from Kuiper and Oram (1991: 277), Diuxi-Tilantongo Mixtec, with N > colour > size > shape, recalling the type of derivations discussed in Cinque (2005b).

(7)   a. C° T° Asp° V(P) AdvP$_3$ AdvP$_2$ AdvP$_1$

(8)   a. Art° PL° N(P) AP$_2$ AP$_1$ NumP DemP

The orders in (7a) and (8a) can be achieved if the VP/NP rolls up around the first phrasal specifier (is attracted to the Spec of a functional head above the phrasal specifier—see (13a), after which it continues with pied-piping of the *whose*-picture type (cf. Cinque 2005b) around additional phrasal specifiers, if any (thus reversing their order of Merge). When the VP/NP crosses over a head endowed with the same categorial feature (an auxiliary, a modal, or (certain) tense/mood/aspect particles in the clause, (plural) number in the DP), it is the latter that becomes the 'engine' of the movement.[20]

(13)   a.   b.

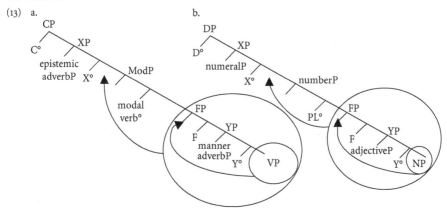

For 'head-initial' languages, I will assume, after Kayne (2005b: §9.4.5) (also see Koopman and Szabolcsi 2000; Jayaseelan 2010a, b), that aspectual verbs (but also modals, auxiliaries, and (certain) particles) are crossed over by their complement, after which the insertion of a (possibly covert) complementizer-like preposition attracts the remnant (with the effect of restoring the initial linear order), as shown in (14):

(14)   a. try leave (merger of K) →

    b. K try leave (movement of InfinP to Spec-K) →

    c. leave$_i$ K try t$_i$ (merger of P/C) →

    d. to leave$_i$ K try t$_i$ (movement of VP to Spec-P/C) →

    e. [try t$_i$]$_j$ to leave$_i$ K t$_j$

Applied to (13a), this gives (15):

---

[20] For a possible motivation for such movements, see §2.5 below.

(15)

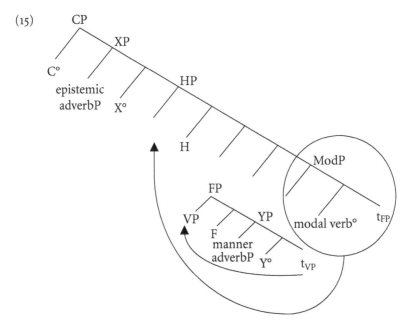

As noted, if raising continues (in the *whose*-picture mode), it is the higher ModP that becomes the 'engine' of movement, pied-piping HP around epistemic adverbP. This yields the overall order C°—modal verb°—lexical verb—manner adverb—epistemic adverbP, which appears to be the order of many verb-initial languages. Cf. the sentence in (16), from VSO Peñoles Mixtec:[21]

(16)   ní   šitu   baʔa   naʔi-dě   (Daly 1973: 15)
       COMPLETIVE   plough   well   probably-he
       'He probably ploughed well.'

Subject, complements, and circumstantial DPs, which I take to be merged above VP/ NP in the following (partial) hierarchy DP_{time} DP_{place} ... $DP_{instrument}$ ... DP_{manner} DP_{agent} DP_{goal} DP_{theme} VP (cf. Cinque 2002; Schweikert 2005a,b; Takamine 2010), and which raise to higher licensing positions, also surface, in 'head-initial' languages, in the reverse order (owing to the roll-up derivation):

---

[21] This kind of derivation allows the raising of verbal heads as phrases. This may be welcome for those languages (like Bulgarian) which can move an auxiliary over a higher one, in so-called 'Long Head Movement', with no apparent violation of the Head Movement Constraint:

(i)   Bil$_i$ săm   t$_i$ kupil   knigata
      been   am   bought   the.book
      'I have allegedly bought the book.'

(17) V(P) DP$_{theme}$ DP$_{goal}$ DP$_{agent}$ DP$_{manner}$ ... DP$_{instrument}$ ... DP$_{place}$ DP$_{time}$

This is a special case of what we have seen in (13). Here it is to the Spec of a functional head above the licensing position targeted by each DP that the (extended) VP is moved, with pied-piping of the *whose*-picture type.

The order in (17) is again tentatively reconstructed from the order of arguments and circumstantials in verb-initial languages (see, for example, Massam 2000: 98 on Niuean and Sells 2000: 124 on Pangasinan).[22] There may be more than one (specialized) licensing position for each DP, as shown by the Malagasy case in (18), from Rackowski and Travis (2000: §1.3), where the object DP may occur in different places among the adverbs (depending on the position it reaches before the reversal operated by the raising of the (extended) VP with pied-piping of the *whose picture*-type). On the position of subjects with respect to adverbs, see §6.1 below.

(18) Tsy manasa   tsara foana \<**ny lamba**\> intsony \<**ny lamba**\> mihitsy
      NEG PRES.AT.wash well always \<DET clothes\> anymore \<DET clothes\> at.all
      \<**ny lamba**\> Rakoto
      \<DET clothes\> Rakoto
      'Rakoto does not wash at all any longer always well the clothes.'

                                                      (Rackowski and Travis 2000: §1)

In case a DP has to be licensed also by a (functional) P I will assume, following Kayne (2000b, 2005b), that the P is merged not with the DP directly, but above the licensing (Case) position targeted by the DP; a merger that causes, in 'head-initial' languages, attraction of the remnant. See the illustrative derivation in (19) (similarly for IPs and complementizers—see (20)):

(19) a. [... [DP ... VP]] (merger of the licenser and attraction of DP) →
      b. [DP$_i$ [K° ... [t$_i$ ... VP]]] (merger of P and attraction of the remnant) →
      c. [[t$_i$ ... VP]$_k$ [P [DP$_i$ [K° ... t$_k$]]]]

(20) a. [... [IP ... VP]] (merger of the licenser and attraction of IP) →
      b. [IP$_i$ [K° [... t$_i$ ... VP]]] (merger of C and attraction of the remnant) →
      c. [[... t$_i$ ... VP]$_k$ [C [IP$_i$ [K° t$_k$]]]]

---

[22] To judge from Schweikert (2005b) and Takamine (2010) circumstantial PPs are actually merged in specific points within the sequence of the adverbs (V(P) ... DP$_{manner}$ AdvP$_3$ ... DP$_{place}$ AdvP$_2$ AdvP$_1$ DP$_{time}$).

2.4.2 *The 'head-final' type*

Recall the generalization concerning the 'head-final' word-order type, which has *all higher (functional) heads following the lexical VP/NP in an order which is the reverse of the order of Merge, and phrasal specifiers (arguments, circumstantials, and modifiers) preceding VP/NP in their order of Merge:*

(21)   AdvP$_1$ AdvP$_2$ AdvP$_3$ V° Asp° T° C°

(22)   DemP NumP AP$_1$ AP$_2$ N° PL° Art°

This can be achieved if (an extended projection of) VP/NP rolls up around the first auxiliary, modal, or particle head (i.e. is attracted to the Spec of a functional head above them), with pied-piping of the picture-of-*whom* type (cf. Kayne 1994: §5.5; Cinque 1999: §3.2; Julien 2002: ch. 2). See (23a–b):

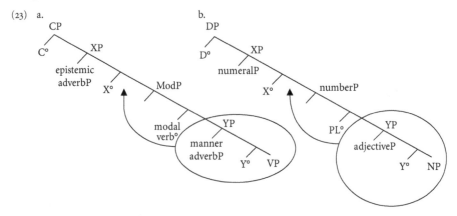

After that, if raising resumes, it is the head that is crossed over by the extended projection of VP/NP which becomes the 'engine' of movement, pied-piping all the rest (in the picture-of-*whom* mode). See (24a–b):[23]

---

[23] In Cinque (2005b) I took the order Dem Num A N not to involve movement, but if the view taken here is correct that both the 'head-initial' and the 'head-final' orders are derived by movement from a common structure of Merge ([Dem [Num [A [N]]]]), then even Dem Num A N must involve raising of NP with pied-piping of the picture-of-*whom* type. This is in fact supported by the fact, noted in Svenonius (2008: §2.5.1) for Norwegian, and in Myler (2009) for Quechua, that while the order of specifiers is Dem Num A N, the N is followed by affixes marking plurality and definiteness. This would not be easily understandable if no movement were involved, given that these heads are interspersed among the Dem Num A specifiers, but it becomes understandable under the analysis adopted here, where the plural head and the determiner head are crossed over by the NP which pied-pipes all the specifiers in the picture-of-*whom* mode (Svenonius and Myler themselves develop very similar analyses).

(24) a.   b.

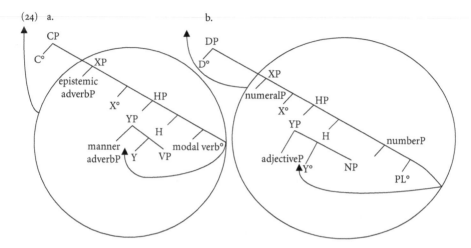

Subject, object, and circumstantial DPs, when present, raise to higher licensing positions, and surface in the same relative order in which there were merged:[24]

(25) DP_{time} DP_{place} ... $DP_{instrument}$ ... DP_{manner} ... DP_{agent} DP_{goal} DP_{theme} $V°$

In case a DP has to be licensed by a P, I will assume that it, rather than the remnant (as in 'head-initial' languages), raises to Spec-P, after raising to Spec-K to check its Case. See (26) (again the same possibly holds of C's. See (27)):[25]

(26)   a. [... [DP ... VP]] (merger of the licenser and attraction of DP) →

   b. [DP_i [K ... [t_i ... VP]]] (merger of P and attraction of DP) →

   c. [DP_i [P [t_i[K ... [t_i ... VP]]]]]

(27)   a. [... [IP ... VP]] (merger of the licenser and attraction of IP) →

   b. [IP_i [K [... t_i ... VP]]] (merger of C and attraction of IP) →

   c. [IP_i [C [t_i [K [... t_i ... VP]]]]]

Particularly telling in this regard is the distribution of PPs in nominal phrases of 'head-initial' and 'head-final' languages. In Cinque (2005b: fn. 34; also see Cinque 2010: ch. 6, note 14), it is observed that prepositional phrases are final in the DP of 'head-initial' languages, while postpositional phrases are initial in the DP of

---

[24] Order preservation may ultimately be a consequence of Relativized Minimality. See the discussion in Krapova and Cinque (2008: §7) of the analogous order preservation with multiple *wh*-phrases in Bulgarian, which develops certain suggestions of Chomsky's and Rizzi's.

[25] The fact that Case morphology typically follows the DP (DP–K–P) rather than the P (DP–P–K) (Kayne 2005b: §9.4.4) can be made compatible with (26) if the DP is merged with Case morphology, which is then checked in Spec-K. The movement of DP from Spec-K to Spec-P is not in contrast with Kayne's (2005b: §5.6) ban on raising the complement of X to Spec-X. Here it is a subpart of the complement of X that raises.

'head-final' languages (which appears to betray the higher merger of P, obscured in 'head-initial' languages by the movement of the remnant):

(28)   a. **PP** Dem Num A N (Armenian, Hindi, Malayalam, Tatar, Turkish, etc.)

vs

  b. N A Num Dem **PP** (Gungbe—Enoch Aboh, p.c.)/N Dem Num A **PP** (Kîîtharaka—Muriungi 2006: 36)/Dem Num A N **PP** (English, Bulgarian)

2.5 The movement trigger: a speculation

An important question, whose answer remains to be established, is what the force is that is responsible for such movements. In Cinque (2005b: 325f.; 2010: ch. 6, note 4) I conjectured that the movement of the lexical nucleus of DPs, the NP (and its extensions through pied-piping), could be due to the need for its extended projection to inherit the nominal feature of the nucleus, thus fully qualifying as nominal. I will tentatively hold by that conjecture (which directly extends to VP and its extended projection CP). We can think of this as effected by merging above each phrase of the extended projection of the NP/VP that is not marked categorially a functional head, F°, whose Spec ultimately comes to have such a nominal, verbal, etc., feature by movement of phrases endowed with such a feature.

2.6. Deviations from the 'ideal' derivations

2.6.1 *Some attested deviations from the ideal derivation for 'head-initial' languages*

  (a) Within VOS languages there appears to be variation as to how high subjects raise. '[A]ll postverbal adverbs are presubject in Malagasy, whereas some of them are postsubject in Seediq' (Holmer 2006: 103); in other words subjects do not raise in Seediq higher than all the adverbs (which are also in the reverse order) (Holmer 2006: note 50), so that subjects do not end up last in the clause after the raising of the remnant to their left:[26]

(29)   a. Malagasy: V AdvP$_3$ <O> AdvP$_2$ <O> AdvP$_1$ <O> S
  b. Seediq: V AdvP$_3$ <O> AdvP$_2$ <O> S AdvP$_1$

  (b) Certain 'head-initial' languages (Italian) do not reverse the order of AdvPs, thus yielding C° T° Asp° V AdvP$_1$ AdvP$_2$ AdvP$_3$ instead of (7a) (cf. Cinque 1999: chs 1 and 2). In other words, the VP (containing just the V) appears

---

[26] In many V-initial Formosan languages, some classes of 'adverbs' precede the lexical V(P). But this may not be a deviation from the harmonic derivation for 'head-initial' languages if they are actually (functional verbal) heads, as argued for in a number of works. See, for example, Holmer (1996: §3.3.3.3, 2006), Liu (2003), Tsai and Chang (2003), Hsiao (2004), Wu (2006), Chang (2006, 2009), C.-L. Li (2007), and Yu (2008). For a similar situation in VSO Maasai, see Koopman (2005a).

to raise by itself (up to a certain point), without pied-piping any other material (thus giving the impression of head movement).[27]

(30) Non   è   stato   lavato   mica   più   sempre   bene
      Not   is   been   washed   at all any longer   always   well
      'It was no longer always washed well.'

(c) Certain 'head-initial' languages show the order: V DP P

(31) a. Savíli   áánɨ   váík   ímai   [giñ-ooñí-ga   vɨɨtárɨ]
         bought   I   three   squash [my-wife-POSSD   for]
         'I bought three squash for my wife.' (Northern Tepehuan, VSO—Uto-Aztecan)[28]

Thinking of Kayne (2000b, 2005b), I take such cases to involve the derivation of postpositions as in 'head-final' languages (cf. (26)) plus the (more marked) merger of a higher (silent) P, which causes the remnant to raise to its Spec (as indicated in (32) with English glosses):

(32) a. I [my-wife-POSSD] [three squash]   raising of VP [bought] →
         [bought]

      b. [bought] I [my-wife-POSSD] [three   merger of 'for' and attraction of
         squash] t   [my-wife-POSSD] →

      c. [my-wife-POSSD] for [bought] I t   merger of silent P and attraction of
         [three squash] t   the remnant →

      d. [bought] I t [three squash] t P [my-wife-POSSD] for

In a number of languages the two attracting P heads are both pronounced. See the case of the Iranian languages in (33):

---

[27] Aspect and Tense auxiliaries can also raise on their own as (remnant) phrases, if the derivations sketched above prove correct (thus again mimicking head movement). In this connection Holmer (1996: 111f.) provides interesting evidence based on the syntax of clitics in VOS Seediq (inflected Vs, tense particles, negation) moves to CP if this is not filled by a complementizer (and no other higher verbal head is present). This evidence is compatible, as far as I can tell, with the verbal heads moving as remnant phrases. In other V-initial languages the verbal heads apparently do not raise to C. See Roberts (2005: §1.2) and references cited there.

[28] From Dryer (2007: 88). Other Uto-Aztecan VSO languages where the object of the adposition may precede it ('DP with'; 'DP from') are Papago (Tohono O'odham—Saxton 1982: 189) and Cora (Casad 1984: 238). The same V DP P order is found in certain OV languages. See (i), from Wan (Mande—Nikitina 2009: §3.2):

(i) ã   zō   [blè   yã]PP   [kōŋ   gó]PP
     they came   [quickness   with]   [village   in]
     'They quickly came to the village.'

Like Mande are some Nilo-Saharan languages (Ngiti—Lojenga 1994: 304).

(33) a. Lîstika bi   navê   'Rojnivîska Dîneki' **ji aliyê** Gogol **ve** hatiye nivîsandin
          The play named 'Rojnivîska Dîneki' **by**   Gogol **by** was   written
          'The play named "Rojnivîska Dîneki" was written by Gogol.'

(Kurmanji Kurdish)

    b. **bi**   *wan*   re
       with *them* with
       'with them'   (Kurmanji Kurdish—Thackston 2006a: 19)

    c. *lagał*   *min'*   *â*
       with   me   with
       'with me'   (Sorani Kurdish—Thackston 2006b: 20)[29]

2.6.2 *Some attested deviations from the 'ideal' derivation for 'head-final' languages*

(a) In certain 'head-final' languages (Hindi—Mahajan 1989: 225) the lexical V and the auxiliaries can be separated by the negation and (certain) adverbs (which suggests that the raising of the projection hosting the lexical verb may target a position above some AdvPs).

(b) In certain 'head-final' languages the raising is not total, with the effect that some of the highest heads remain initial (for example, in Punjabi (Indo-Aryan), the Yes/No Question head *kii* is only initial—Davison 2007: 180; as are the illocutionary force markers of SOV Nama (Khoisan)—<http://celaeno.phonetics.cornell.edu/khoisan/nama/nama.htm>).

(c) In certain 'head-final' languages there is attraction of phrases to the Spec of a (silent) C head followed by merger of another (overt) C head that fails to attract the same phrases or the remnant (see (34), from Galla (Oromo), from Mallinson and Blake 1981: 289)

(34) [**kan** [kalēsa   gale]]   C namtičča   an   arge
       REL   yesterday arrived(finite) man.DEF I   saw
       'I saw the man that arrived yesterday.'

2.6.3 *Unattested (or rare) deviations from the ideal derivations*

While there are various deviations from the ideal orders, as noted, it seems that some types of deviations are never (or almost never) found. So, for example, as Steele (1978: 42) points out, (35d) is apparently unattested,[30] in contrast to the attested 'harmonic'

---

[29] 'Certain prepositions, in particular the prepositions ba 'in, at,' da 'to, in, into' and la 'by, to, in, at' and 'from,' occur as circumpositions that envelop the complement' (Thackston 2006b: 20).

[30] 'No language with SVO or VSO basic order will have a clause final auxiliary.' The cases reported in the literature mentioned above in §2.1 appear to have a postverbal, but not clause-final, auxiliary.

orders (35a–b) and the attested disharmonic order (35c) (also see Dryer 1996: 1059, Kayne 2005b: §9.3.2, and the Konstanz Universals Archive, numbers 1382 and 1553):

(35) a. Aux [V O]

  b. [O V] Aux

  c. Aux [O V]

  d. *[V O] Aux

Similarly, as observed in Dryer (1992a: §4.3, 2009: §5), (36a–c) are all attested, but (36d) is seemingly never found (at least with complement CPs):[31]

(36) a. C [V O]

  b. [O V] C

  c. C [O V]

  d. *[V O] C

These and similar patterns have been brought in Holmberg (2000), Biberauer, Holmberg, and Roberts (2008a,b, 2009, 2010) under a general constraint, the Final-over-Final Constraint (FOFC). They correctly observe that the constraint is rigidly operative within the extended projection of a certain category, V or N (namely with heads sharing the same categorial feature), but is not as rigidly operative across the extended projections of different categories.

Whether the FOFC is an absolute constraint or only a very strong tendency (in either case an important finding) is a point that remains to be ascertained (see the discussion of certain apparent counterexamples in Biberauer, Holmberg, and Roberts 2008a,b, 2009, and Sheehan 2009a, and the VO languages with final complementizers mentioned in note 31 and below in section 2.7). Be as it may, it would in any event be interesting to derive the constraint from the general properties of the theory which tries to derive the word-order types (here the two sets of movement options for 'head-initial' and 'head-final' languages).[32] Let's consider (35) as an example.

---

[31] See Dryer's (2009: 199) table (i), and the references in note 5 above:

(i)

	Africa	Eurasia	SEAsia&Oc	Aus–NewGui	NAmer	SAmer	Total	#Lgs
a. OV&FinalComp	2	5	3	1	2	1	14	27
b. OV&InitComp	6	4	1	3	0	0	14	22
c. VO&FinalComp	0	0	0	0	0	0	0	0
d. VO&InitComp	23	9	13	4	10	4	63	140

One language apparently instantiating (i.c) (i.e. (36d) is however East !Xóõ (Khoisan). Güldemann (2004: 7), reports a sentence from Traill (1994: 17) which exemplifies this order (confirming in personal communication that the language indeed is an exception to the supposed universal SVO → initial complementizer):

(ii) ñ   ń   bà   ‡án sǎn /nǎ-e   !nǖle   tê
   1ss   ?   ?IMPF   wish:1ss   see-3   country.3   COMP
   'I want to see the country.'

[32] Biberauer, Holmberg, and Roberts (2008a,b, 2009, 2010) also propose deriving it from a constraint on the EPP features triggering movement.

(35a) and (b) are straightforwardly derived by applying consistently the movement options sketched above for the ideal 'head-initial' and 'head-final' languages (cf. (37) and (38), respectively):

(37)   derivation for [Aux [V O]]:

a. $[_{VP}$ V]   (merger of F and DP$_{object}$) $\rightarrow$

b. $[_{FP}$ DP$_{object}$ F $[_{VP}$ V]]   (merger of F' and raising of VP to Spec-F') $\rightarrow$

c. $[_{F'P}$ $[_{VP}$ V] F' $[_{FP}$ DP$_{ob-}$ (merger of Aux and raising of VP plus pied-piping
   $_{ject}$ F t$_{VP}$]]   of the *whose*-picture type across Aux) $\rightarrow$

d. $[[_{F'P}$ $[_{VP}$ V] F' [DP$_{object}$ (merger of F' and raising of the remnant [Aux t]) $\rightarrow$
   F t$_{VP}$]]][Aux t]

e. [Aux t] F' $[[_{F'P}$ $[_{VP}$ V] F' [DP$_{object}$ F t$_{VP}$]]] t

(38)   derivation for [[O V] Aux]:

a. $[_{VP}$ V]   (merger of F and DP$_{object}$) $\rightarrow$

b. $[_{FP}$DP$_{object}$ F $[_{VP}$ V]]   (merger of Aux and raising of VP plus pied-
                                        piping of the picture-of-*whom* type to a Spec
                                        higher than C) $\rightarrow$

c. $[[_{FP}$DP$_{object}$ F $[_{VP}$ V]]] [Aux t]

(35c) can also be derived as in (38) by merging Aux but not applying raising of VP (plus pied-piping of the picture-of-*whom* type) across Aux (i.e. by a *non-total* application of the consistent movement options for 'head-final' languages).

The derivation of (35d) ([V O] Aux) requires instead a movement option for the derivation of 'head-initial' languages (the raising of VP around the DP$_{object}$) followed by the raising of VP around Aux without the further raising of the remnant [Aux t] as in 'head-final' languages. Possibly, this hybrid is not available (or is extremely costly), thus accounting for the non-existence (or the exceedingly rare existence) of this order.

2.7 The apparently anomalous behaviour of particles

Particles are generally regarded as bad harmonic patterners (Dahl 1979; Dryer 1992a: §§3.4 and 3.5, 2007: §7.5; Biberauer, Holmberg, and Roberts 2009: §§2.1, 2.2, 3.3). Although in some languages they behave as run-of-the-mill functional heads like the initial question and tense and aspect particles of 'head-initial' languages or the final particles of 'head-final' languages (non-distinct from inflected auxiliaries), in other languages they appear to pattern differently. The reasons for this may vary. In some cases they may be categorially adverbs (AdvPs), like the invariant negation particles *pas* of French or *mica* of Italian. This seems to be the case, for example, of the postverbal particles of VSO Guajajara (Tupi-Guaraní), discussed in Newton

(2007), the basic meanings of which indeed are adverbial: 'in vain', 'still', 'unfortu-nate/successful action', etc. In other cases, despite being invariant free functional head morphemes, they might behave differently from the corresponding auxiliaries (i.e. dummy verbs sustaining the corresponding functional bound morphemes) for principled reasons. If it is correct to take the trigger of movement in both 'head-initial' and 'head-final' languages to be the need to mark the extended projection of a VP, or NP, with verbal or nominal features (cf. §5 above), only those particles that have such a feature will behave like verbal or nominal heads (which is possibly the case of the preverbal particles of VSO Semitic, Celtic, and Austronesian languages). But those that do not have such a feature will essentially behave like non-heads, requiring movement of (extended projections of) the VP or NP to acquire such a feature. This might be the case of some of the particles discussed in the literature as 'bad patterners' like the final modal *được* of SVO Vietnamese—see (39a); or the final aspect particle *di* of VOS Seediq—see (39b):

(39) a. Tôi [không ăn   thịt] **được**   (Duffield 1998: ex. 10a)
         I   NEG   eat meat **CAN**
         'I can't eat meat.'

      b. Wada msange   ciga   bubu   mu   **di**   (Holmer 2005: 177)
         PST   ACT.rest yesterday mother 1SG.GEN   **PFV**
         'Yesterday my mother rested (i.e. refrained from work).'

Even more problematic is the case of VO Xârâcùù and Tinrin (Melanesian—Austronesian) with two postverbal particles in the direct (rather than the reverse) order of Merge. See (40a,b):[33]

(40) a. ke   xâpârî **kae na** mûduè- nâ? (Xârâcùù—Moyse-Faurie 1995: 157)
         2SG   see   **Q   PST** brother-1SG
         'Have you seen my brother?'

      b. wiri tramwâ **ghai nrâ**   (Tinrin—Osumi 1995: 204)
         2PL   know   **Q   PST**
         'Did you know?'

Such cases may involve raising of (an extended projection of) the VP 'engine' above higher Tense and Mood heads, as shown in (41) for (40b) (with English glosses):

(41) a. Q PST [$_{FP}$ 2pl know] (raising of FP above C) →
      b. [$_{FP}$ 2pl know] Q PST t

A similar case is represented by the final subordinators of SVO East !Xóõ of note 31, of VSO Guajajara (Tupi-Guaraní—Dryer 1992b: §2) and of VOS Seediq (Formosan,

---

[33] For further discussion and other problematic cases see Cinque (forthcoming).

Austronesian—Holmer 1996) and Chol (Mayan—Coon 2010). See, for example, (43a–b), from Chol and Seediq, respectively:

(42) a. i-   muty   [chächäk-**bä**]   (Coon 2010: fn. 18)
         GEN.3- chicken [red-   REL]
         'Her chicken that is red'

     b. [Menaq ku   hini **han**]sluhe   kari   seediq rmabang malu
        [stay.AF 1S.N here **when**]learn.AF language people more   good
        'While I am staying here, I had better learn Seediq.'   (Holmer 1996: 60)

I take such cases to involve a subordinator that attracts the IP to its Spec (as in 'head-final' languages—cf. (27) above), followed by merger of a higher (silent) head, which may (42a) or not (42b) cause the remnant to raise to its Spec (as in the OV Oromo case seen in (34) above). There appear to be languages where the two heads are both pronounced, with the higher C attracting material to its Spec ((43)) or not ((44)):

(43) a. tuisi tuʔi **ke**   hu   hamut   bwika-**kai** (Yaqui—Dryer 1980: fn. 7)
         very   good COMP this woman sing-SUB
         'It is very good that this woman sings'.

     b. [[chele **je**   poR- be] **bole**] ami mon- e   kor-i ni (Bayer 1996: 263f.)
        boy COMP study-FUT3 COMP I   mind-LOC do- 1 NEG.PST
        'I haven't thought that the boy will study.'

(44) [**se**   mi- wi'é   **a**]   mí- kò   fi'e   (Fanti—Welmers 1946: 72)
      when 1SG-finish **when** 1SG-go home
      'When I'm finished, I go home.'

2.8 Conclusions

In the preceding sections, I have suggested that we should take a different look at word-order typology and that, to paraphrase Weinberg (1976), we should give a higher degree of reality to the two reconstructed harmonic types than to the observable tendencies shown by actual languages. I have also suggested that the two harmonic types should be seen as deriving from a common structure of Merge (reflecting the scope properties of the various elements involved) via two consistent movement options. In view of the fact that most (perhaps all) languages deviate from such consistent derivations to different degrees (and, as a consequence, in different proportions), the question arises how to capture the range of admitted variation, the frequency rate of the subtypes actually attested, and how the languages deviating from the ideal orders are acquired. These are empirical questions that remain to be studied. I only hint here at possible ways one could go about addressing them, starting with the acquisition problem. If we accept that the structure of Merge and the movement options that derive the two abstract orders are given by UG, then positive evidence from the primary data should be sufficient for the child to compute any deviations from the consistent application of such movement options. If so, even languages deviating more substantially from the two ideal word-order types should, perhaps, not be more difficult to acquire. Concerning variation, it would seem that intra-category variation is more constrained (cf. the 'FOFC' generalization discussed above) than cross-category variation (where, for example, DP can be 'head-initial' while IP and CP are 'head-final', as in a number of SOV languages). Nonetheless, even cross-category alignment seems to be tendentially harmonious. This is the fundamental finding of Hawkins (1983), whose Principle of Cross-Category Harmony asserts 'that there is a quantifiable preference for the ratio of preposed to postposed operators within one phrasal category (i.e., NP, VP/S, AdjP, AdpP) to generalize to the others' (p. 134).

The different attested subtypes of languages, formed by different combinations of 'consistent' and 'inconsistent' movements of the derivations that yield the ideal harmonic types, differ in the number of languages they contain, presumably as a function of the number and quality of the deviations from the ideal derivations—a calculation that remains to be done.

The points that I have tried to stress are:

(a) Virtually every single correlation pair is violated in some language.

(b) Possibly there are no fully harmonic languages.

(c) If we try to formulate word-order generalizations holding of actual languages we can at most get statistically significant tendencies.

(d) Such tendencies are nonetheless important as they allow us to glimpse the existence of two (abstract) consistent word-order types.

(e) Limiting oneself to (lists of) correlation pairs falls short of giving a full description of the two abstract order types and may be misleading.

(f) We should take seriously the task of reconstructing in detail these two consistent word-order types and try to derive them from a unique structure of Merge via two distinct sets of movements.

(g) This should provide a basis for measuring the distance of each word-order subtype (in the worst case, of each language) from the consistent word-order types.

(h) The attested tendencies can also help us single out what word orders are more stable or more prone to be relaxed.

(i) The costs associated with relaxing a certain word order can perhaps account for language frequencies (recall Hawkins' Table 2.1 above).

(j) There are innumerably more word-order types than SOV, SVO, VSO, VOS, OVS, OSV, the number being a function of the number of single word-order pairs which can differ. With 26 correlation pairs (certainly a tiny fraction of the total correlation pairs) the number of existing types risks being, if not 2^{26} (= 67,108,864), extremely high:

(i)   Languages with 'head-initial' correlation pairs except for DP P instead of P DP

(ii) Languages with 'head-initial' correlation pairs except for DP P instead of P DP and V Aux instead of Aux V

(iii) Languages with 'head-initial' correlation pairs except for DP P instead of P DP, V Aux instead of Aux V, and Num N instead of N Num

(iv) …

(v)   …

      etc.

Many more questions remain to be answered.[34] One I want to mention, venturing an answer, is: Why are there more SOV languages than VOS languages, if these are the best approximations to the two word-order types?

If SVO languages are essentially derived via a non-total application of the same sets of movements that derive VOS languages, in the sense that (projections containing) the VP do not raise all the way up as they do in VOS languages, one can expect the same non-total application of the relevant movements to be found in SOV languages. Here, however, the non-total application of the movements is not as visible, as it also yields an SOV order (cf. SOV languages with *initial* higher functional heads). The correct computation then would have to refer to the number of SOV languages compared to the number of VOS(/VSO) **plus** SVO languages; which seems roughly right. See in Table 2.2 the frequencies in the samples of Ruhlen (1975), Tomlin (1979), Mallinson and Blake (1981), as reported in Tomlin (1986: 19f.), and those of Cysouw (2008):[35]

TABLE 2.2 **Percentage of languages**

	SOV	SVO	VSO	VOS	OVS	OSV
Ruhlen (1975)	51.5%	35.6%	10.5%	2.1%	0.0%	0.2%
Tomlin (1979)	45.8%	41.5%	11.0%	1.5%	0.3%	0.0%
Mallinson and Blake (1981)	41.0%	35.0%	9.0%	2.0%	1.1%	1.0%
Cysouw (2008)	47.1%	41.2%	8.0%	2.4%	0.8%	0.4%

---

[34] I am not able to evaluate some recent work by a team of physicists, mathematicians and linguists claiming that 'each language in the world fluctuates between these two structures ['head-initial' and 'head-final', G.C.] like the Ising model for finite lattice.' (Itoh and Ueda 2004: 333) Also see Ueda and Itoh (2002) and Tsunoda, Ueda, and Itoh (1995).

[35] Also see the language numbers given in *WALS*:

(i)   SOV   SVO   VSO   VOS   OVS   OSV
      497   435   85   26   9   4

This distribution of 'head-final' and 'head-initial' languages, close to fifty–fifty, makes it plausible to take the currently existing languages to be a fairly representative sample (for word order) of all possible languages (despite the often noted fact that the currently existing ones are a tiny fraction of all the languages that were and are no longer spoken, that will be spoken in the future, and that will never be spoken).

If correct, this conjecture raises the further question why the non-total application of the movements deriving the ideal harmonic types should be less marked (yielding a larger number of languages) than the total one.

Appendix

This is a partial list of 26 regularized word-order pairs correlating with 'head-initiality' and 'head finality':[36]

'head-initial'	'head-final'
a) V > DP (VO)	DP > V (OV)
b) Aux > V(P)	V(P) > Aux[37]
c) Copula > Predicate	Predicate > Copula[38]
d) modal/functional V > V(P)	V(P) > modal/functional V[39]
e) tense/aspect/negative particle > V(P)	V(P) > tense/aspect/negative particle[40]
f) Art > N(P)	N(P) > Art[41]
g) PL > N(P)	N(P) > PL[42]
h) V(P) > PP/NP$_{adjunct}$	PP/NP$_{adjunct}$ > V(P)[43]
i) V(P) > CP	CP > V(P)[44]
j) P > DP (Prepositional Phrase)	DP > P (Postpositional Phrase)[45]
k) C > argument IP	argument IP > C[46]
l) Yes/No Q marker > IP	IP > Yes/No Q marker[47]
m) Subordinator > adverbial IP	adverbial IP > Subordinator[48]
n) marker > Standard ('than John')	Standard > marker ('John than')[49]

---

[36] Recall that these orders are to a large extent reconstructed from the most polarized types (rigid SOV and rigid VOS languages), abstracting away from the exceptions noted in the literature.

[37] Cf. Greenberg's (1963) Universal 16.

[38] Cf. Dryer (1992a: §2.5) and section 2.1 above.

[39] Cf. Greenberg's (1963) Universal 15 and Dryer (1992a: §2.6).

[40] For the possible relevance of particles in word-order generalizations, despite the problems noted in the literature, recall the discussion in section 2.7 above.

[41] Cf. Dryer (1989b, 1992a: §4.6, 2007: §5.7).

[42] Cf. Dryer (1989a, 1992a: §4.7).

[43] Cf. Dryer (1992a: §2.3, 2007: §5.2).

[44] Cf. Greenberg's (1963) Universal 13.

[45] Cf. Greenberg's (1963) Universals 3 and 4.

[46] Cf. Dryer (1992a: §4.3, 2009: §5).

[47] Cf. Greenberg's (1963) Universal 9 ('With well more than chance frequency, when question particles or affixes are specified in position by reference to the sentence as a whole, if initial, such elements are found in prepositional languages, and, if final, in postpositional'), and Dryer (1992a: §4.4). The same is presumably true of other illocutionary force markers (declarative, imperative, etc.). See the case of the initial declarative marker in N|uu (SVO Khoisan—Collins 2004), and the final declarative, interrogative, imperative, and optative markers in Sheko (SOV Omotic—Hellenthal 2007).

[48] Cf. Dryer (1992a: §4.5, 1992b); Diessel (2001).

[49] Cf. Greenberg's (1963) Universal 22.

o) A > [(marker)Standard]   [Standard (marker)] > A[50]
    (&, more generally, A > PP)   (&, more generally, PP > A)
p) A > degree word   degree word > A[51]
q) N > Gen   Gen > N[52]
r) PP-complements of an N are final in   PP-complements of an N are initial in
    the DP   the DP[53]
s) common noun > proper noun   proper noun > common noun[54]
t) V > DP > resultative > ODepictive >   SDepictive > ODepictive > DP > re-
    SDepictive   sultative > V[55]
u) V Manner (Place Time) (or Time   (Time Place) Manner V[56]
    Place Manner)

---

[50] Cf. Greenberg's (1963) Universal 22 and Lehmann (1978a: 16f.).

[51] Cf. Greenberg's (1963) Universal 21: 'If some or all adverbs follow the adjective they modify, then the language is one in which the qualifying adjective follows the noun and the verb precedes its nominal object as the dominant order'. This finds to some extent confirmation in the WALS database. Its interactive tool for combining features shows some preference for the 'harmonic' correlations (A > degree word and VO: 102 languages; degree word > A and OV: 114 languages) in opposition to the 'disharmonic' ones (degree word > A and VO: 81 languages; and A > degree word and OV: 63 languages).

[52] Cf. Dryer (1992a: §2.1).

[53] Recall the discussion at the end of section 2.4.2 above.

[54] Cf. Greenberg (1963: 89), Lehmann (1978a: §1.3), Bennett (1979), and Cinque (2009b).

[55] Compare (i)–(ii) with (iii)–(iv):

(i)   a. The smith beat the metal *flat cold*. (Simpson 1983) (V > DP > resultative > ODepictive)
      b. *The smith beat the metal cold flat.

(ii) a. He$_i$ ate the fish$_j$ *raw$_j$ drunk$_i$* (Haider 1997) (V > DP > ODepictive > SDepictive)
      b. *He$_i$ ate the fish$_j$ drunk$_i$ raw$_j$

(iii) a. Er hat das Fleisch *roh in Stücke* geschnitten (cf. Haider 1997: 10) (DP > ODepictive > resultative > V)
         he has the meat   raw to pieces cut
         'He has cut the meat to pieces raw'

      b. *Er hat das Fleisch *in Stücke roh* geschnitten

(iv) a. Daß manchmal einer   *betrunken* Fisch *roh* ißt... (cf. Haider 1997: 29)
                                                    (SDepictive > DP > ODepictive > V)
         That sometimes someone drunk   fish   raw eats.
         'That sometimes someone eats fish raw drunk...'

Also see Koizumi (1994) and Williams (2008).

[56] Cf., among others, Bartsch and Vennemann (1972: §6.2), Boisson (1981), Subbarao (1984: 18), Patnaik (1996), Haider (2000a), Cinque (2002), Schweikert (2005a,b), Hinterhölzl (2009a), Takamine (2010). All classes of adverbs precede the V in rigid SOV languages (cf. Greenberg's 1963 Universal 7). Interestingly, in a corpus study of German adverbs and adverbial PPs, Dean (1974) finds that the VO order of these elements (V > Manner > Place > Time) is only possible (alongside the OV order: Time > Place > Manner > V) in main clauses where the finite verb is in second position and no participle, infinitive, or separable prefix is found in final position. Otherwise only the OV order is possible. This seems to me to suggest that the VO order (V > Manner > Place > Time) is a function of the movement (plus pied-piping of the *whose-picture* type) of the entire VP raising to second position.

v) ascending order of temporal/locative   descending order of temporal/locative
    phrases   phrases[57]
w) NP(XP) > Rel Cl   Rel Cl > NP(XP)[58]
x) N > A   A > N[59]
y) N > Dem   Dem > N[60]
z) N > Num   Num > N[61]

---

[57] See, for example, how the sequence of temporal phrases in the complex temporal phrase 'At 8 o'clock pm of the fifteenth of January 2002' is rendered in a 'head-initial' language like Italian ((i.a)) and in a 'head-final' language like Hindi ((i.b)) from Subbarao (1984: 18, 2008: 57) (as noted there, Japanese and Telugu pattern with Hindi):

(i) a. alle (ore)   8 (di sera)   del (giorno)   quindici (del mese)   di gennaio del(l'anno)   2002
         at (hours)   8 (of evening) of the (day)   15 (of the month)   of January of (the year) 2002
     b. 2002   samvatsaram   janawari   nela   lō   padihēnō   tārīkhu   rātri-ki   enimidi   gaṇṭala-ki
         2002   year   January   month   in   fifteenth   date   night-to   eight   hours-DAT

A similar pattern is found with complex locative phrases. Compare Hindi (ii) with its English translation:

(ii) banaaras   me wiʃwanaat[h]   mandir ke   dwaar   par   (Subbarao 2008: 58)
     Benaras   in Vishwanath   temple of   gate   on
     'At the gate of the temple of Khasi Vishwanath in Benaras'

[58] See the discussion around (2) above, Cinque (2005a), and references cited there.

[59] Or, more accurately, [projections of N] > AP and AP > [projections of N]. Concerning their order w.r.t. N in relation to the basic word order of the language, the *WALS* interactive tool for combining features gives for VSO languages 56 languages (24 genera) with NA order vs 16 languages (13 genera) with AN order (thus largely confirming Greenberg's statistical Universal 17: 'With overwhelmingly more than chance frequency, languages with dominant order VSO have the adjective after the noun'), and for VOS languages 14 languages (9 genera) with NA order vs 7 languages (7 genera) with AN order. Thus, 'head-initial' languages predominantly have NA order, with certain well-known exceptions, like the Mayan languages (Campbell, Bubenik, and Saxon 1988: 213). I take AN to be the abstract order for 'head-final' languages despite the fact that SOV languages are predominantly NA (the *WALS* interactive tool gives for them 223 languages (113 genera) with NA order vs 56 languages (25 genera) with AN order. Also see Dryer 1988a, 1992a, 2007). The reason for taking this counterevidential position is that clausal modifiers (adverbs) in 'head-final' languages seem to systematically precede the head they modify. Needless to say, the high inconsistency of the adjective position in actual languages needs to be understood. Perhaps the skewing for NA order even in 'head-final' languages is tied to the existence of a relative clause source for adjectives, not always easily distinguishable from the purely attributive one (cf. Cinque's 2010 discussion), for we know that virtually half of the SOV languages have postnominal relative clauses. Relevant in this connection may be Mallison and Blake's (1981: 383) observation that '[s]ome of the examples of NA among SOV languages may reflect the verbal origin of the "adjectives"', and Greenberg's (1963) Universal 19 ('When the general rule is that the descriptive adjective follows, there may be a minority of adjectives which usually precede, ... '). But the whole question needs to be looked into more carefully.

[60] The *WALS* interactive tool for combining features gives a clear predominance of Dem N for OV languages and N Dem for VO languages.

[61] The *WALS* interactive tool for combining features give a predominance of NNum for VO languages, but it also gives a predominance of NNum for OV languages—a potential problem.

3

Postpositions vs Prepositions in Mandarin Chinese: The Articulation of Disharmony*

REDOUANE DJAMOURI, WALTRAUD PAUL,
AND JOHN WHITMAN

3.1 Introduction

Whitman (2008) divides word-order generalizations modelled on Greenberg (1963) into three types: hierarchical, derivational, and cross-categorial. The first reflect basic patterns of selection and encompass generalizations like those proposed in Cinque (1999). The second reflect constraints on syntactic derivations. The third type, cross-categorial generalizations, assert the existence of non-hierarchical, non-derivational generalizations across categories (e.g. the co-patterning of V~XP with P~NP and C~TP). In common with much recent work (e.g. Kayne 1994; Newmeyer 2005b), Whitman rejects generalizations of the latter type—that is, generalizations such as the Head Parameter—as components of Universal Grammar. He argues that alleged universals of this type are unfailingly statistical (cf. Dryer 1998), and thus should be explained as the result of diachronic processes, such as V > P and V > C reanalysis, rather than synchronic grammar.

This view predicts, contra the Head Parameter, that 'mixed' or 'disharmonic' cross-categorial word-order properties are permitted by UG. Sinitic languages contain well-known examples of both types. Mixed orders are exemplified by

* This article has its origin in a talk given at the *Conference on Theoretical Approaches to Disharmonic Word Orders*, held at the University of Newcastle in May 2009. We are grateful to Effi Georgala, Barbara Meisterernst, Victor Junnan Pan, Helmut Weiss, Zhitang Yang-Drocourt, and Zhong Chen for discussion and data, and to three anonymous reviewers for incisive comments which sharpened the theoretical focus of the paper. Last, but not least, we would like to thank the editors, Theresa Biberauer and Michelle Sheehan, for their patience and careful attention. The work of John Whitman was supported by the Academy of Korean Studies Grant funded by the Korean Government (MEST) (AKS-2011-AAA-2103).

prepositions, postpositions, and circumpositions occurring in the same language. Disharmonic orders found in Chinese languages include head-initial VP-internal order coincident with head-final NP-internal order and clause-final complementizers. Such combinations are present in Chinese languages since their earliest attestation. In this paper, we look in detail at the issue of PPs in Chinese, which are both mixed (in that they include pre-, post-, and circumpositions) and disharmonic (in that postpositions occur with head-initial VP, and prepositions with head-final NP). The basic facts are shown in (1)–(2) below. (1) shows a preverbal prepositional phrase (PrepP), (2) a preverbal postpositional phrase (PostP). (3) shows a circumpositional construction, with both preposition and postposition.

(1) Wǒ   [Prep zài jiā]   shuì wǔjiào.
     1SG   at home sleep nap
     'I take a nap at home.'

(2) Wǒ [PostP xīn-nián] yǐqián]] yào huí   jiā   yī-tàng.
     1SG   new-year before   want return home 1-time
     'I want to go home once before New Year.'

(3) Wǒ [PP zài [PostP shāfā shàng]] shuì wǔjiào.
     1SG   in/at   sofa on   sleep nap
     'I took a nap on the sofa.'

We show in this paper that both prepositions and postpositions are adpositions, contrary to the view that the latter are nouns. We argue that the structural difference between these two types of PP is readily accounted for within a cartographic approach to PP structure.

The paper is organized as follows. Section 3.2 shows that both prepositional phrases (PrePs) and postpositional phrases (PostPs) instantiate a category P, while at the same time showing certain differences. Section 3.3 takes up these differences and accounts for them within a cartographic account of PP in Chinese. Section 3.4 relates the Chinese facts to recent discussions about constituent order harmony and disharmony. Section 3.5 reviews the historical sources for postpositions.

3.2 Postpositions and prepositions in Chinese are both adpositions

A fairly comprehensive list of prepositions and postpositions in contemporary Mandarin is provided in (4):

(4) **a. Preposition**   **b. Postposition**
     cháo 'facing'   *hòu* 'behind; after'
     cóng 'from'   *lái* 'for, during'
     dāng(zhe) 'at, facing'   *lǐ* 'in(side)'

dào 'to'	*nèi* 'inside, within'
duì 'toward'	*páng* 'next to, at the side of'
duìyú 'with respect'	*qián* 'in front of, before'
gěi 'to, for'	*qiánhòu* 'around'
gēn 'with'	*shàng* 'on'
gēnjù 'according to'	*shàngxià* 'around, about'
guānyú 'concerning'	*wài* 'outside, beyond'
lí 'from, away'	*xià* 'under'
tì 'instead of, for'	*yǐhòu* 'after' (temporal)
wǎng 'in the direction of'	*yǐlái* 'since, during'
wèi(le) 'for the sake of'	*yǐnèi* 'inside, within'
xiàng 'in the direction of'	*yǐqián* 'before, ago'
yán(zhe) 'along'	*yǐshàng* 'above, over'
zài 'in, at'	*yǐwài* 'outside, beyond'
zhìyú 'concerning'	*yǐxià* 'under, below'
zìcóng 'since, from'	*zhījiān* 'between'
. . . . . .	*zhōng* 'amidst, in'
. . . . . .	*zuǒyòu* 'around, about'

A perusal of the list in (4) shows that there are semantic differences between the prepositions in (4a) and the postpositions in (4b). Prepositions include path designators like *dào* 'to', *duì* 'toward', and *cóng* 'from'. Postpositions include no designators of path per se. Instead, postpositions denote locations, e.g. *lí* 'in(side)', *shàng* 'on', and *xià* 'under'.

The main controversy regarding category concerns postpositions, which have been claimed to be nouns (cf. Li 1990; McCawley 1992; Huang, Li, and Li 2009, among others). In this section we focus on distributional criteria showing that postpositions must be distinguished from nouns. Ernst (1988) provides evidence that *shàng* 'on', *xià* 'under', *lí* 'in(side)' are postpositions, not nouns, contrasting them with the nominal status of location nouns such as *shàngmiàn* 'top', *xiàmiàn* 'underneath'. Ernst observes that like prepositions, postpositions always require an overt complement (no stranding), and that unlike nouns (cf. (5b)), they disallow the subordinator *de* intervening between the complement and head (5a):

(5) a. Shū zài [PostP *(zhuōzi) shàng].
        book be.at   table   on
        'The books are on the table.'

     b. Shū   zài [PostP (zhuōzi) shàngmiàn].
        book be   table   top
        'The books are on the top (of the table).'

(6)   a. [$_{PostpP}$ zhuōzi (*de) shàng]
              table   SUB on
         'on the table'

      b. [$_{NP}$ zhuōzi (de) shàngmiàn]
              table   SUB surface
         'the top of the table'

Ernst thus concurs with Peyraube (1980: 78), who likewise concludes that monosyllabic morphemes such as *shàng* 'on', *xià* 'under', *lǐ* 'in(side)' are postpositions, and
distinguishes them from location nouns such as *shàngmiàn* 'top, surface'. Note that
both Ernst (1988) and Peyraube (1980) focus on postpositions referring to location in
space. Taking their work as a starting point, we provide additional evidence for the
existence of postpositions expressing spatial and temporal as well as abstract location.
This overview shows that postpositions are different from nouns expressing location
(*contra* Li 1990; McCawley 1992; Huang, Li, and Li 2009, among others). In this
discussion of PostPs, we adopt the structures assigned by Ernst. These are refined in
section 3.3.

3.2.1 *Ban on adposition stranding*

Huang (1982) shows that prepositions may not be stranded. In (7) the complement of
the preposition is recoverable from the context; in such contexts verbs allow empty
objects, but prepositions do not.

(7)   Tā   měi -tiān [$_{vP}$ [$_{PreP}$ zài jiā]   [$_{vP}$ shuì wǔjiào]],
        3SG every-day   at home   sleep nap
        wǒ yě měi -tiān [$_{vP}$ [$_{PreP}$ zài *(jiā)] [$_{vP}$ shuì wǔjiào]].
        3SG also every-day   at home   sleep nap
        'He takes a nap at home every day, and I also take a nap at home every day.'

Likewise preposition stranding is impossible with relativization (8) and topicalization (9).

(8)   *[$_{DP}$ [$_{TP}$ wǒ [$_{PreP}$ gēn [e]] bù shóu]   de nèi-ge rén]
              1SG   with   NEG familiar SUB that CLF person
        ('the person I'm not familiar with')

(9)   *Zhāngsān$_i$ [$_{TP}$ wǒ [$_{PreP}$ gēn [e]] bù shóu]
        Zhangsan   1SG   with   NEG familiar
        ('Zhangsan, I'm not familiar with.')   (Huang 1982: 499, (109a–b))

We find the same ban on stranding postpositions.[1] The ban on postposition stranding observed for the spatial locative with *shàng* 'on' by Ernst (cf. (5a) above) holds for postpositions in general, including disyllabic postpostions such as *yǐqián* 'before' (a temporal locative) and *yǐwài* 'beyond, besides' (an abstract locative):

(10) a. Wǒ [PostP [DP xīn -nián] [PostP° yǐqián]] yào huí jiā yī-tàng,
      1SG   new-year   before   want return home 1 -time

      tā yě yào [PostP [DP *(xīn -nián) [PostP yǐqián]] zǒu.[2]
      1SG also want   new-year   before   leave
      'I want to go home before the New Year; he also wants to leave before the New Year.'

   b. Miǎnfèi bǎoguǎn   sān-tiān, [PostP [DP *(sān-tiān)] yǐwài]
      free   storage   3-day   3-day   beyond

      zhuóshōu bǎoguǎn-fèi.
      collect storage-fee
      'The free storage is three days, beyond three days there is a storage fee.'

The complements of the postposition in the second conjunct *xīn-nián* 'New Year' (10a) and *sān-tiān* 'three days' (10b) are recoverable from the preceding context, but stranding is blocked. In contrast, both NPs and VPs in Chinese allow stranding in contexts parallel to (10).

(11) a. Wǒ bàba huílái-le,   [NP [e] māma] yě huílái -le.
      1SG father return-PFV   mother also return-PFV
      'My father returned, and my mother returned, too.'

   b. Wǒ chī-guo shéròu,   Zhāngsān yě [vP [e] chī-guo].
      1SG eat-EXP snake.meat Zhangsan also   eat-EXP
      'I have eaten snake meat, and Zhangsan has, too.'

Similarly, postpositions cannot be stranded by relativization (12a) or topicalization (12b), again in contrast to the nouns in (12c–d).

---

[1] Note that Huang, Li, and Li (2009) do not mention the ban on adposition stranding. As for the unacceptability of *de* intervening between a postposition and its complement (cf. (6a) above), it naturally presents a problem for their assumption that so-called 'localizers' are a subclass of nouns, nouns allowing *de* (6b). Huang, Li, and Li (2009: 17, (20)) thus characterize postpositions as 'deviates' of N, where '[i]n deciding the properties of a categorial deviate, anything language-specific in the original category is disfavored.' 'Interestingly, the use of *de* is also highly language-specific. [...] As a result, L[ocalizer] keeps all the syntactic properties of N except *de*.'
[2] Given the existence of the adverb *yǐqián* 'previously', the second conjunct of (10a) is acceptable without *xīn-nían* 'New Year' under the reading 'He had also wanted to leave previously', a reading not relevant here.

(12)　a. *[$_{DP}$ [$_{TP}$ [$_{PostP}$ [e] shàng] pā-zhe yī zhī māo] de [nà liàng qìchē]]
　　　　　　　　　　　on　　　 lie-DUR 1 CLF cat　SUB that CLF car

　　　b. *[$_{TopP}$ [Nà liàng qìchē], [$_{TP}$ [$_{PostP}$ [e] shàng] pā-zhe yī zhī māo]].
　　　　　　that CLF car　　　　　　　　　　 on　 lie-DUR 1 CLF cat

　　　c. [$_{DP}$ [$_{TP}$ [$_{NP}$ [e] shàngmiàn] pā-zhe yī zhī māo] de [nà liàng qìchē]]
　　　　　　　　　　　　 top　　　　 lie-DUR 1 CLF cat　SUB that CLF car
　　　　'that car on the top of which a cat is lying'

　　　d. [$_{TopP}$ [Nà liàng qìchē], [$_{TP}$ [$_{NP}$ [e] shàngmiàn] pā-zhe yī zhī māo].
　　　　　　that CLF car　　　　　　　　 top　　　 lie-DUR 1 CLF cat
　　　　'That car, a cat is lying on the top.'

These facts are exactly parallel to the properties of prepositions as demonstrated by Huang (1982) in (8–9). A possible rejoinder to this argument might be to claim that postpositions are a type of phrasal affix or clitic (Liu 1998; Zhang 2002), and cannot be stranded because they are phonologically dependent.[3] But the clitic analysis has been proposed only for monosyllabic postpositions. Disyllabic items such *yǐqián* 'before', *yǐhòu* 'behind' cannot be clitics, since they may occur independently as adverbs, just like their English counterparts:

(13)　Zhāngsān yǐqián lái -guo Bālí.
　　　Zhangsan before come-EXP Paris
　　　'Zhangsan has been to Paris before.'

Nevertheless, disyllabic postpositions are also unable to strand their complements under topicalization (cf. (14b,c)) and relativization (cf. (14d)), exactly like their prepositional and monosyllabic postpositional counterparts.

(14)　a. Tā yào [$_{PostP}$ chúxī yǐqián] huí jiā.
　　　　　3SG want　　new.year's.eve before return home
　　　　'He wants to go home before New Year's Eve.'

　　　b. *[$_{TopP}$ Chúxī [$_{TP}$ tā yào [$_{PostP}$ [e] yǐqián] huí jiā.
　　　　　　new.year's.eve 3SG want　　　 before return home
　　　　(*'New Year's Eve, she wants to go home before.')

　　　c. *[$_{TopP}$ [Nèi ge dìqū] [$_{TP}$ wǒ xiǎng [$_{PostP}$ [e] yǐwài] méi yǒu
　　　　　　that CL district　 1SG think　　　beyond NEG exist
　　　　Zhōngguórén zhù].
　　　　Chinese　　 live
　　　　('That district, I don't think there are any Chinese people living beyond.')

---

[3] Huang, Li, and Li (2009: 21–2) explicitly reject the clitic analysis of postpositions.

d. *[DP [TP [PostP [e] yǐwài] méi yǒu Zhōngguórén zhù] de nèi ge dìqū]
            beyond NEG exist Chinese live SUB that CLF district
('*that district where there are no Chinese people living beyond')

3.2.2 *Distribution of PP*

In Modern Mandarin, only arguments are allowed in postverbal position. Adjuncts occur exclusively preverbally, to the right or to the left of the subject. Previous research on postpositions focuses on PostPs expressing spatial location, but below we provide data exemplifying all three types of location: spatial, temporal, and abstract. We shall see that these differences condition the distribution of PostPs.

3.2.2.1 *Adjunct PPs* In the sentence-initial topic position to the left of the subject, PostPs and PrePs of all types are acceptable, encoding spatial, temporal, or abstract location.

Spatial location:

(15) a. [PostP Zhuōzi shàng], nǐ kěyǐ fàng shū, [PostP yǐzi shàng] nǐ
         table on   2SG can put book   chair on   2SG
         kěyǐ fàng   dàyī.
         can put   coat
        'On the table, you can put the books, and on the chair, you can put the coat.'

   b. [PreP Zài Shànghǎi] tā yǒu hěn duō péngyou.
         at Shanghai 3SG have very much friend
        'In Shanghai, she has a lot of friends.'

Temporal location:

(16) a. [PostP [Jǐ -ge   yuè]   yǐqián] tā jiù   qù Shànghǎi le.
         several-CLF month before 3SG then   go Shanghai PART
        'Several months ago, he went to Shanghai.'

   b. [PostP [Jīn -nián nián-chū   ] yǐlái], tā yǐjīng   chū -le
         this-year year-beginning since 3SG already go.out-PFV
        sān-cì   chāi.
        3 -time   errand
        'Since the beginning of this year, he has already been three times on business trips.'

(17) [PreP Zài nà ge shíhòu] wèntí   hái bù   yánzhòng.
      at that CLF time   problem still NEG serious
    'At that time, the problem was not that serious yet.'

Abstract location:

(18) [PostP Yuánzé   shàng]   nǐmen   kěyǐ   zhèyàng   zuò.
         principle   on   2PL   can   this.way   do
     'In principle you can do it this way.'   (Ernst 1988: 229, (19))

(19) [PreP Zài   zhè   fāngmiàn]   nǐ   yào   duō   bāngzhù   tā.
         at   this   respect   2SG   need   much   help   3SG
     'In this respect, you have to help him more.'

In the preverbal position to the right of the subject, temporal, or abstract location
(including abstract means) can be denoted by PostPs (20a–c) or PrepPs (21a–b):

(20) a. Tā   [PostP [jǐ   -ge   yuè]   yǐqián]   jiù   qù Shànghǎi le.
        3SG   several-CLF month   before   then   go Shanghai PART
        'He went to Shanghai several months ago.'

     b. Tā   [PostP [jīn-nián   nián-chū]   yǐlái]   yǐjīng   chū -le
        3SG   this-year   year-beginning since   already   go.out-PFV
        sān-cì   chāi.
        3 -time   errand
        'He has already been on business trips three times since the beginning of
        this year.'

     c. Nǐmen   [PostP yuánzé   shàng]   kěyǐ   zhèyàng   zuò.
        2PL   principle on   can   this.way   do
        'You can in principle do it this way.'

(21) a. Wèntí   [PreP zài nà   ge   shíhòu]   hái   bù   yánzhòng.
        problem   at that CLF   time   still NEG   serious
        'The problem was not that serious yet at that time.'

     b. Nǐ   [PreP zài   zhè   fāngmiàn]   yào   duō   bāngzhù   tā.
        2SG   at   this   respect   need   much   help   3SG
        'In this respect, you have to help him more.'

However spatial PostPs in this position are limited to a goal or directed-motion
interpretation:

(22) a. Nǐ   [PostP wòshì   lǐ]   bù   néng   fàng   diànlú.
        2SG   bedroom   in(side) NEG   can   put   electric.stove
        'You cannot put an electric stove in the bedroom.'

     b. Lái,   wǒmen   [PostP fànzhuō   shàng]   liáo.
        come   1PL   dining.table on   chat
        'Come, let's chat at the table.'

Thus non-path, locational PPs in this position require the preposition *zài* 'in, at':

(23) Tā [$_{PreP}$ zài zhuōzi xià] / *[$_{PostP}$ zhuōzi xià]   kàndào-le yī-zhī lǎoshǔ.
      3SG   at table under   table under see   -PFV 1-CLF mouse
      'He saw a mouse under the table.'

Huang, Li, and Li (2009: 13–14) notice the unacceptability of certain PostPs in the position between the subject and the verb and use this as an argument against analysing PostPs as adpositions. Instead, they set up a special category L(ocalizer), 'a deviate of N' (2009: 21). Citing the data in (24), they argue, 'If L[ocalizer] were a postposition, there would be no reason why it should not behave like one, and its presence in (11b) [= (24b)] would be enough to introduce the nominal *chéng* 'city' just like *outside* does in English.'[4]

(24) a. Tā   *(zài) nàge chéngshì jǔbàn-guo yī-ge   zhǎnlǎnhuì.
          he   P   that city   hold-GUO   a-CLF   exhibition
          'He held an exhibition *(in) that city.'

      b. Tā   *(zài) chéng wài/   lǐ   jǔbàn-guo yī-ge   zhǎnlǎnhuì.
          he   P   city outside/ inside hold-GUO   a-CLF   exhibition
          'He held an exhibition outside/inside the city.'
          (= Huang, Li, and Li's (2009: 13), (11a–b); their glosses and translation)

However the Localizer analysis is too crude to capture the complete distribution, since as we saw in (22), PostPs may indeed appear in the position between the subject and the verb, under an appropriate interpretation. We account for this fact in section 3.3.

3.2.2.2 *Argument PPs*   In postverbal position, PrePs, Circumpositional Phrases and PostPs all occur.[5]

(25) a. Tā   jì   -le   [$_{DP}$ yī-ge   diànnǎo] [$_{Prep}$ gěi Mǎlì].
          3SG   send-PFV   1 -CLF computer   to   Mary
          'He sent a computer to Mary.'

---

[4] In fact, *chéngwài* 'suburbs, city outskirts' and *chénglǐ* 'inner city, city centre' are compound nouns (that is, N⁰s), not phrases (cf. Lü Shuxiang et al. 2000: 360 for more N-*lǐ* compounds). This is shown by the fact that they can be embedded in larger compounds, e.g. *chénglǐrén* 'city inhabitant'. Furthermore, being a bound morpheme, *chéng-* cannot occur on its own, e.g. as a modifier subordinated to the head noun by *de*, in contrast to *chénglǐ*:

(i) Hé   zài   [$_{N°}$ chénglǐ]   de nánfāng.
     river be.in   city.interior SUB south
     'The river is to the south of the (inner) city.'

(i) *Hé   zài   chéng de   nánfāng.
     river be.at city SUB south

[5] Li (1990: 4) takes the possibility of PostPs to function as complements (27)–(28) as evidence for the nominal status of postpositions, because in her approach adpositional phrases are banned from case positions. This forces her to analyse the phrases headed by *gěi*, *dào*, and *zài* in contexts like (25)–(26) as VPs instead of as PrePs notwithstanding their non-verbal properties, such as incompatibility with aspectual suffixes such as *-le* PERFECTIVE and *-guo* EXPERIENTIAL.

b. Wǒ   yǐjīng   dǎ -guo   diànhuà   [_{Prep} dào   [_{DP} tā   jiā]].
   1SG   already   make-EXP   phone   to   3SG   home
   'I already phoned his home.'

(26)   Tā   xiě -le   [_{DP} jǐ   -ge   zì   ]   [_{PreP} zài   hēibǎn   shàng].
       3SG   write-PFV   several-CLF   character   at   blackboard   on
       'He wrote several characters on the blackboard.'

(27)   a. Tā [_{V°} zuò -dào] -le   [_{PostP} yǐzi   shàng] yǐhòu, yǐzi   jiù   kuàdiào-le.
          3SG   sit -arrive-PERF   chair on   after   chair then collapse-PFV
          'After he sat down on the chair, the chair collapsed.'

       b. Tā -de   gùshi   [_{V°} dēng -zài] -le   [_{PostP} bàozhǐ   shàng].
          3SG-SUB   story   publish-be.at -PFV   paper   on
          'His story got published in the newspaper.'

(28)   Tā   [_{V°} zǒu -jìn]-le   [_{PostP} jiàoshì   lǐ].
       3SG   walk-enter-PFV   classroom   in(side)
       'He entered the classroom.'

As the position of the perfective aspect suffix -*le* indicates, in (27a) and (b) the verbs *dào* and *zài*—homophonous with the prepositions *dào* and *zài*—are part of the verbal compound. Accordingly, (27a–b) indeed involve PostPs in object position, and not PrePs.

Unlike VP-internal complement position, subject position allows us to distinguish between PostPs and PrePs on the one hand, and between PostPs and DPs on the other. PostPs occur in the subject position of locative inversion sentences like (29a), existential *yǒu* 'exist' (29b),[6] and copular *shì* with an adverb of quantification (29c).

(29)   a. [_{PostP} Chēzi   shàng]   pā-zhe   yī-zhī   māo.
          car   on   lie-DUR   1-CLF   cat
          'On the car is lying a cat.'

       b. [_{PostP} Wūzi lǐ]   yǒu   hěn   duō   rén.
          room   in(side)   have   very   much   people
          'There are many people in the room.'

       c. [_{PostP} Shān -pō   shàng]   quán shì   lìzishù.
          mountain-slope   on   all   be   chestnut.tree
          'All over the mountain slope there are chestnut trees.'

---

[6] Existential *yǒu* 'exist, there is' as an unaccusative verb is distinct from the transitive verb *yǒu* 'have, possess':

(i)   Tā   yǒu   sān-liàng   qìchē.
      3SG   have   3 -CLF   car
      'He has three cars.'

Simple DP subjects are unacceptable in these positions:

(30) a. *[DP Wūzi] yǒu hěn duō rén.
         room   have very much people

     b. *[DP Chēzi] pā-zhe yī-zhī māo].
         car   lie-DUR 1 -CLF cat

     c. *[DP Shān -pō] quán shì lìzishù.
         mountain-slope all be chestnut.tree

At the same time, certain of these contexts distinguish between PostPs and PrePs. In the locative inversion context (29a), the locative preposition *zài* 'at' is unacceptable:

(31) *[PreP Zài chēzi shàng] pā-zhe yī-zhī māo.
           at car on lie-DUR 1-CLF cat

Similarly, while PostPs are acceptable as subjects of adjectival predicates, PrePs are disallowed in this position:

(32) a. [(*Zài) wūzi lǐ   ] hěn gānjìng.
           at   room in(side) very clean
        'It is very clean in the room.'

     b. [(*Zài) lúzi qián   ] hěn nuǎnhuo[7]
           at   stove in.front.of very warm
        'It is very warm in front of the stove.'

The copula *shì* enables us to distinguish between DPs, PostPs, and PrePs. DP subjects are of course completely acceptable; PostPs are of marginal or variable acceptability, depending on the speaker, while PrePs are completely unacceptable:

(33) a. [DP Bìlú] shì jiāli zuì nuǎnhuo de dìfāng.
         fire.place be home most warm SUB place
        'The fireplace is the warmest place in our home.'

---

[7] There is an alternative parsing of (32b) available for some speakers leading to its acceptability [TopP [Zài lúzi qián] [TP *pro* hěn nuǎnhuo]] 'In front of the stove, it is warm.' When embedded in a relative, however, the *zài* PP cannot be construed as occupying topic position, and the sentence is ungrammatical:

(i) [DP [(*Zài) lúzi qián] hěn nuǎnhuo de nà-jiān fángjiān shì kètīng
        at stove in.front.of very warm SUB that CLF room be living.room
    'The room where it is very warm in front of the stove is the living room.'

b. ?/√[PostP Lúzi   qián]   shì zuì nuǎnhuo de dìfāng.[8]
            stove in.front.of be   most warm   SUB place
    'In front of the stove is the warmest place.'

c. *[PreP Zài lúzi qián]   shì zuì nuǎnhuo de dìfāng.
            at stove in.front.of be   most warm   SUB place
    ('In front of the stove is the warmest place.')

Summarizing, both PrePs and PostPs may appear in complement position after the verb. PostPs may occur as the subjects of locative inversion, adjectival, and marginally of copular predicates, whereas PrePs are disallowed in these positions.

3.2.2.3 *PPs as subconstituents of DP*   Both PrepP and PostP can be embedded in DP followed by *de*, but in the case of PrePs, this possibility is limited to DPs with relational head nouns. Examples such as (34) show that Li's (1990: 5) general ban on *[PP *de* N] is too strong.[9]

(34) a. [PreP guānyú   Chomsky] de kànfǎ
                concerning Chomsky   SUB opinion
          'the opinions about Chomsky'

      b. [PreP duì   Lǐ xiānshēng] de tàidu
                towards   Li Mr   SUB attitude
          'the attitude towards Mr Li'

(35) a. *[PreP duì   Lǐ xiānshēng] de huà
                towards   Li Mr   SUB talk
          ('the words addressed to Mr Li')

      b. *[PreP cóng   Běijīng] de rén
                from   Beijing   SUB person
          ('a person from Beijing')

---

[8] More examples showing the marginal status of sentences with a PostP in the subject position of the identificational copula are given below:

(i) ?/ √Yào shuì jiào, [PostP xīngkōng xià] shì zuì hǎo de dìfāng
        want sleep sleep   star   under be most good SUB place
    'If you want to sleep, under the stars is the best place.' (=based on Li (1990: 30; (29c))

(ii) ?/ √ [PostP Wǔfàn yǐhòu] shì zuì hǎo de xiūxi shíjiān
                  lunch after   be most good SUB rest   time
    'After lunch is the best time for a rest.'

[9] Ernst (1988: 239, fnote 10) also challenges the overall ban against PP modifiers and provides the following examples, but does not notice that the pattern is limited to relational nouns:

(i) duì   guójiā de rè'ài
      towards   country SUB love
    'love of (one's) country'

(ii) guānyú zhè-jiàn shì   de wèntí
      about   this-CLF matter SUB problem
    'the problem with this matter'

(36) a. *[$_{PreP}$ gēn   gǒu]   de   xiǎohái
               with   dog   SUB child
         ('the child with the dog')

      b. gēn   Lǐ xiānshēng   de   guānxi
          with Li Mr   SUB relation
          'the relation with Mr Li'

No such restriction is observed in the case of PostP modifiers, which are compatible with non-relational (37) and relational nouns (38) alike:

(37) a. [$_{DP}$ [$_{PostP}$ Cáochǎng   shàng / wūzi lǐ]   de rén]   dōu shì
                           sports.   on/   room in(side) SUB person all   be
                           ground
               tā-de   xuéshēng.
               3SG-SUB   student
          'The people on the sports ground/in the house are all her students.'

      b. [$_{DP}$ [$_{PostP}$ Wǔ-diǎnzhōng   yǐhòu]   de   dìtiě],   rén   tài   duō.
                           5 -o'clock   after   SUB subway person too   much
          'The subway after five o'clock, there are too many people.'

      c. Wǒ bù   xǐhuān [$_{DP}$ [$_{PostP}$ bā-diǎnzhōng yǐqián] de kè]].
          1SG NEG like   8-o'clock   before SUB class
          'I don't like classes before 8 o'clock.'

      d. Zhè shì [$_{DP}$ [$_{PostP}$ luóji   shàng]   de cuòwù].
          this be   logic   on   SUB mistake
          'This is a logical error.'

(38) a. [$_{DP}$ [$_{PostP}$ xuéxiào lǐ]   de guānxi]
                           school   in(side) SUB relation
          'the relations within the school'

      b. [$_{DP}$ [$_{PostP}$ luóji shàng]   de guānxi]
                           logic on   SUB relation
          'logical relations'

      c. [$_{DP}$ [$_{PostP}$ lǐlùn   shàng]   de máodùn]
                           theory on   SUB contradiction
          'theoretical contradictions'

Note that any XP, including clauses, can function as modifier subordinated to the head noun by *de* (cf. Paul 2012 and references therein).

3.2.3 *Complements of P*

In addition to DP complements, both prepositions and postpositions may select TP. This fact again distinguishes postpositions from nouns, because the complement clause of a noun head such as *xiāoxi* 'news' in (39) must be subordinated to the latter by *de*:

(39) [DP [TP Liú Xiáobō dé   Nuòbèi'ěr jiǎng] *(de) xiāoxi].
           Liu Xiaobo obtain Nobel   prize   SUB news
      'the news that Liu Xiaobo obtained the Nobel prize'

TP complements of prepositions (40)–(41) and postpositions (42)–(43) may denote temporal or abstract location:

(40) [PreP Zìcóng [TP tā   líkāi   Běijīng]], wǒmen yīzhí   méi jiàn miàn.
            since   3SG leave   Beijing   1PL   always NEG see face
      'Since he left Beijing, we haven't met anymore.'   (Lü et al. 2000: 695)

(41) Wǒ zuò zhèi-jiàn shì   [PreP gēn [TP nǐ zuò nèi -jiàn shì]] méi yǒu guānxi.
      1SG do this-CLF matter   with   2SG do that-CLF matter NEG have relation
      'My doing this has nothing to do with your doing that.'

(42) [PostP [TP Tā kǎoshàng dàxué] (*de) yǐhòu] dàjiā   dōu hěn gāoxing.
                3SG enter   university SUB after everybody all very happy
      'After he succeeded in entering the university, everybody was very happy.'

(43) [PostP [TP *pro* Chī yào]   yǐwài] hái děi   dǎ   jǐ   zhēn.
                       eat medicine besides still must beat several needle
      'Besides taking medicine, it is also necessary to get some injections.'

However prepositions and postpositions show a crucial difference with respect to complement selection. As we have seen, prepositions may select PostPs (44), but prepositions may not select PrePs (45).[10] Postpositions do not take any kind of PP complement (46).

(44) a. [PreP zài [PostP cūnzi   lǐ   ]]
                 in   village in(side)
          'in the village'

      b. [PreP cóng [PostP zhuōzi shàng]]
                 from   table   on
          'from on the table'

---

[10] Comparatives seem to be the only possible exception to this generalization, where *bǐ* 'compared to' and *gēn* 'with, as' may select PrePs:

(i)   Tā [duì nǐ] bǐ [duì wǒ] gèng   qíguài.
      3SG towards 2SG BI towards 1SG even.more bizarre
      'He's even more bizarre to you than to me.'

(ii) Tā [duì nǐ] gēn [duì wǒ] yīyàng   qíguài.
      3SG towards 2SG GEN towards 1SG equally bizarre
      'He's as bizarre to you as to me.'

We might adopt Lin's (2009) analysis, where *bǐ* is not a preposition, but the head of a degree phrase shell which itself is adjoined to the AP. Degree° can select NPs and PPs.

(45) a. *[PreP cóng [PreP zài [cūnzi lǐ]]]
          from   in   village in(side)
       ('from in the village')

   b. *[PreP cóng [PreP zài [zhuōzi shàng]]]
          from   in   table on
       ('from on the table')

(46) a. *[PostP [PreP gēn gǒu] yǐwài]
                  with dog   except
       ('except with dogs')

   b. *[PostP [PostP [dì'èrcì shìjiè dàzhàn] yǐhòu] yǐlái]
                     second world war   after   since
       ('since after World War II')

The fact that prepositions select PostPs but not the opposite is one of the implicit reasons why postpositions have been regarded as a type of noun. But as we have seen throughout this section, the analysis of postpositions as nouns fails to account for numerous facts: the inability of postpositions of any kind to be stranded, their ability to occur as subjects in locative inversion contexts, and their ability to take TP complements without *de*. In the next section we show how an articulated PP structure accounts for the properties of both types of adposition, and also helps explain the linear order asymmetries of PrepPs and PostPs.

3.3 The internal structure of pre- and postpositional phrases

In the previous section, we argued that prepositions and postpositions both instantiate the category P, and in particular that the latter are not nouns. However, we have also seen that there are a number of specific differences between prepositions and postpositions. In this section we account for those differences within an articulated P structure.

In an insightful discussion, Svenonius (2007) observes that Chinese prepositions denote path, while postpositions denote place; in other words the same distribution that we saw in (4). Svenonius also notices that postpositions form a closer bond with their DP complement than prepositions. In the articulated PP structure developed by Svenonius (2007) and later work (e.g. the papers in Cinque and Rizzi 2010b), a projection headed by adpositions denoting path dominates a projection denoting place. We exemplify this with (44b):

(47)   PathP   (=44b)

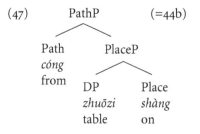

Given the generalization that prepositions denote path and postpositions denote place, this structure explains why prepositions select postpositions, but postpositions do not select prepositions. What remains to be explained is the language-particular property that path is denoted by prepositions and place by postpositions.

Two dimensions of explanation are relevant. The first is diachronic: as we show in detail in section 3.5, the historical sources for postpositions are nouns, while the historical sources for prepositions are verbs. NPs in Chinese are head-final, while VPs are head-initial, throughout the history of the Sinitic family. As we showed in section 3.2, postpositions are not nouns; the cross-categorial parallel between the constituent order properties of nouns and postpositions is a consequence of their diachronic relation.

The second dimension of explanation has to do with the derivation of head-final and head-initial order in the synchronic grammar. As noted at the outset of this article, this ordering disharmony is one of the best-known features of Chinese syntax. Unnoticed, to our knowledge, is the fact that there is a systematic difference between head-initial and head-final categories with respect to how we might expect them to interact with case. The head-initial categories are PrepP, VP, and TP (based on the clause-initial position of tense and modal auxiliaries). All three of these categories are involved in licensing case: verbs and prepositions, as we have seen, take DP complements to their right, while T licenses DP subjects in its specifier.

The head-final categories are PostP, NP, and CP.[11] The latter two are not expected to check case features. Arguments of N in Mandarin appear with *de*, labelled SUBORDI-NATOR in this article; whatever the categorical identity of *de*, its distribution indicates that it bears an EPP feature requiring its specifier to be filled; it is also reasonable to suppose that it checks the case feature of nominal arguments of N:[12]

(48)

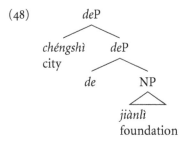

'the foundation of the city'

---

[11] Extending Lee's (1986) analysis of the sentence-final interrogative *ma* as C to all sentence-final particles in Mandarin Chinese, Paul (2009; to appear) provides extensive evidence for a three-layered head-final split CP in matrix clauses and the existence of two exclusively subordinating head-final Cs, viz. *dehuà* in conditional clauses and *de* in propositional assertion (in addition to the subordinating C *de* heading relative clauses; cf. Cheng 1986). This leaves a very narrow window for asserting, as does Dryer (2009), that subordinating clause-final Cs do not occur in VO languages. But even this circumscribed generalization does not hold up for earlier stages of Chinese such as Classical Chinese (2nd c. BC–2nd c. AD) where e.g. the interrogative C *hu* is attested in embedded questions with robust matrix VO order (cf. Djamouri et al. 2009).

[12] For a number of recent (but very divergent) proposals for *de*, cf. Cheng and Sybesma (2009), Li (2007), Paul (2012), Simpson (2001), Tang (2007), Zhang (2010), among others.

The fact that the other two head-final categories do not license case suggests an account for postpositions. Postpositions select DP arguments, but they are unable to check the case feature of their complement. Thus the complement moves to the specifier of P, where its case is checked either within the higher verbal projection or by a preposition:

(49) a. [$_{V^\circ}$ zǒu -jìn]-le [$_{PlaceP}$ jiàoshì [[$_{Place}$ lǐ] $t_{jiàoshì}$] (=28)
          walk-enter-PFV   classroom   in(side)
      'enter the classroom.'

    b. [$_{PathP}$ cóng [$_{PlaceP}$ zhuōzi [[$_{Place}$ shàng] $t_{zhuōzi}$]]] (=47)
          from   table   on
      'from on the table'

The hypothesis that postpositions fail to license case on their own explains other facts that we have observed. First, we saw in 3.2.2.2 that PostPs, but not PrePs, can appear in various types of subject position: subject of locative inversion predicates (29a), subject of *yǒu* 'exist' (29b), subject of copular *shì* with an adverb of quantification (29c), of adjectival predicates (32), and marginally of the copula (33). PreP subjects are ruled out in all of these contexts. This is because in PostP subjects, the complement of the postposition, after being raised to the specifier of PP, is available to check its case feature with T. In PrepPs the case feature of the DP complement is checked within the PP projection, and is unavailable to check the case feature of T.[13] The basic configuration for PostP subjects is shown for the locative inversion example (29a).[14]

[13] This discussion brings into focus interesting differences between Chinese and English. A full discussion of these differences is beyond the scope of this paper, but we touch on two. In English, locative inversion PP is held to check the EPP feature of T, but the case and other ϕ-features of T are checked by the postverbal associate (the notional subject) (Collins 1997). If we are right about Chinese postpositions, the PostP subject checks both the EPP, and indirectly through its complement, the case feature of T. It is tempting to speculate that this difference may be related to the absence of elaborated ϕ-features (person, number, gender, morphological case) in Chinese. This in turn may be related to a reduced role for Agree targeting ϕ-features. The second difference has to do with subjects of the copula. The possibility of PP and CP subjects of the copula in English suggests that T with copular predicates need not bear a case feature. The facts that we have discussed suggest that this is not the case in Chinese.

[14] Inherently locative nouns such as *shàngmiàn* 'top, surface' are likewise acceptable in subject position with locative inversion (cf. (12d) above); being DPs, they check the case feature of T. The unacceptability of DPs such as *wūzi* 'room', *chēzi* 'car', *shānpō* 'mountain slope' as subjects in the locative inversion structure (cf. (30a–c) above) is due to their semantics: they do not denote locations.

(50)

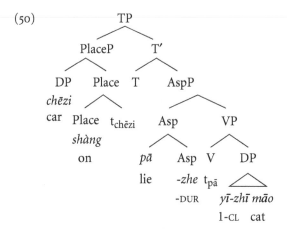

'On the car is lying a cat.'

As we saw in 3.2.2.1, bare PostPs, that is, PostPs without a preceding preposition, may appear sentence-initially or between the subject and the verb. We can specify these positions a bit more precisely: time and abstract-place PostPs, like other phrasal adjuncts, appear in three positions: sentence-initial topic position, the 'internal' topic position below the subject but above negation and auxiliaries (Paul 2002, 2005), or VP-adjoined position between auxiliaries and the verb:

(51) a. (Chúxī   yǐqián) tā   (chúxī   yǐqián) yào   (chúxī   yǐqián)
          new.year's.eve before   3SG   NY's eve   before want NY's eve   before
          huí   jiā.
          return   home
          'She wants to go home before New Year's Eve.'

     b. (Yuánzé shàng) nǐmen (yuánzé shàng) kěyǐ   zhèyàng zuò.
          principle on   2PL   principle on   can   this.way do
          'In principle, you can do it this way.'

     c. Nǐmen   bù   néng [lǐlùn   shàng] zhèyàng shuō, [shíjì shàng] què
          2PL   NEG   can   theory on   this.way speak   reality on   but
          nàyàng   zuò.
          that.way do
          'You cannot in theory speak this way but then in practice do it that way.'

Subcategorized spatial location PostPs occupy the first two of these, but not the VP-adjoined position.

(52) a. Nǐ   [_PostP_ wòshì   lǐ]   bù   néng fàng diànlú.   (=22a)
          2SG   bedroom in(side) NEG   can   put   electric.stove
          'You cannot put an electric stove in the bedroom.'

b. Nǐ   bù néng [_PreP_ *(zài) [_PostP_ wòshì   lǐ]]   fàng diànlú.
2SG   NEG can   in   bedroom in(side) put   electric.stove
'You cannot put an electric stove in the bedroom.'

This makes sense if we assume that subcategorized spatial location PostPs like *wòshì lǐ* 'in the bedroom' in (52) are moved from an underlying position inside VP. The DP complement of the PostP checks its case feature within the verbal projection, then undergoes A′ movement to one of the two topic positions. Only non-subcategorized, adjunct PostPs may be base-generated in the VP-adjoined position (51c). Thus adjunct PostPs have much the same distribution as bare NP adverbs in English (Larson 1985), and presumably are subject to the same analysis.[15]

The distribution of the preposition *zài* 'in, at' provides further support for the generalization that postpositions do not check case. *Zài* is anomalous among prepositions in that it appears to denote place, rather than path. It also is the most ubiquitous prepositional component of circumpositional patterns, as we see from examples such as (3), (23), and (44). We have seen that *zài* is disallowed in contexts where the case feature of the postpositional complement is checked (cf. (31)–(32)), such as the subject PostP examples in (29), but it is required where the case feature of the complement would not otherwise be checked, such as the VP-adjoined position in (23) and (52b). We suggest that *zài* in circumpositional PPs is a functional preposition: it checks the case features of the postpositional complement where these would not otherwise be checked. On this view, the postposition assigns the [location] thematic role to the complement; *zài* heads a functional projection *p*P and checks the case feature of the complement DP.

(53)   *p*P   (=3)

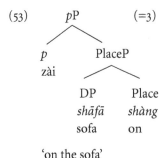

'on the sofa'

The occurrence of both PostPs and PrePs in the context ___ *de* NP can be explained by the assumption that the subordinator *de* can check the case of the item in its specifier

---

[15] In English as well, place prepositions + bare NP adverb have the same distribution as bare adverbs on their own: *(Before/After) yesterday Kim was upset*. Also like Chinese, the combination path preposition + bare adverb does not occur: **to/from yesterday*. These facts suggest that place + bare adverb is simply a subtype of bare adverb.

(cf. (48)).[16] The restriction of PP modifiers of NP to PlaceP—thus to PostP in the case of non-relational nouns—appears superficially to be a difference between Chinese and English, as shown by examples like (35)–(36a). However, PathP modifiers of NP also show distinct behaviour from PlaceP modifiers in English: in particular, they are islands for extraction:

(54) a. Who did you see a *a letter to/√a reference to? (cf. 35b)

      b. What did you encounter *a child with//√a connection with? (cf. 36a)

This contrast suggests that PathP modifiers of NP in English are embedded in additional structure, perhaps a reduced relative clause, which blocks extraction of the PathP modifier. The availability of such a structure in English, but not in Chinese, permits PathP modifiers in the former language.

Summarizing the proposals in this section, we have seen that the core property of Chinese PPs, the fact that prepositions select PostPs but postpositions do not select any kind of PP, is explained by the articulated PP structure in (47). The core property of PlaceP in Chinese, that it is postpositional, is explained by the assumption that this projection belongs to a set of categories in Chinese that do not check the case of their complements. This analysis in turn explains the ability of PostPs but not PrepPs to occur in positions where case is checked, such as a variety of subject positions, and in circumpositional constructions with the preposition *zài*.

3.4 Chinese disharmony in a harmonic world

We have shown that the disharmonic constituent-order properties of Chinese PPs follow from two independently motivated principles: the articulated structure of PP, and the generalization that the set of head-final projections in Chinese do not contain a case-checking head. According to this generalization, head-final categories are that way because their complements move to a higher position for case-driven reasons.[17] Our account made no use of cross-categorial constituent-order generalizations. Disharmonic order in Chinese PPs is the consequence of a hierarchical universal ([Path [PlaceP]]), a language-particular property (the absence of a case-checking head), and a derivational universal (uninterpretable case features must be checked).

---

[16] Note that the assumption that *de* can but need not check case is independently required in Chinese, as *de* licenses not only DP possessors (which presumably bear a case feature) but relative clauses (cf. 39) and adjectival modifiers (which presumably do not).

[17] We note here that we have not attempted to account for the head-final nature of CP. This cannot be due to case considerations, on the normal assumption that TP does not require case. Many other possible explanations come to mind, such as the possibility that transposition of TP around C is a case of pied-piping, that is, a mechanism for moving operators in TP to Spec-CP in languages such as Chinese which lack wh-movement. We leave this as a suggestion, as the issue is beyond the scope of this paper.

Current research, in particular the research collected in this volume, suggests that this approach to constituent-order generalizations—accounting for them in terms of independently motivated hierarchical and derivational generalizations—represents the future in the field of word-order typology. To take a prominent example, the Final-over-Final Constraint (FOFC) proposed by Holmberg (2000) and developed by Biberauer, Holmberg, and Roberts (2008b, 2009, 2010) rules out certain combinations of head-final and head-initial order across categories, but it is stated (and motivated) as a derivational generalization.

The FOFC rules out a specific subtype of disharmony: the case where a head-initial phrase α is immediately dominated by a head-final phrase β, where α and β are non-distinct in categorial features (Biberauer, Holmberg, and Roberts 2010):

(55)

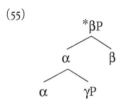

The FOFC correctly predicts the constituent-order disharmonies in Chinese PPs: a head-initial category (PrepP) may select a head-final category (PostP=PathP), but not vice versa. If we constrain ourselves to the facts of Chinese, it is not immediately clear how to choose between the account presented here, based on the hierarchical universal [Path [PlaceP]] and case-driven movement, and the FOFC (if indeed such a choice is required). As observed in footnote 11, clause-final subordinating complementizers in Chinese may raise an empirical issue for the FOFC, but we leave this issue for future research.

An assessment of the issue requires a comparison of disharmonic and circumpositional PPs in Chinese and other languages. We must verify two things: first, whether the underlying Path > PlaceP hierarchy generalizes across 'disharmonic' PPs in other languages; second, whether the derivational possibilities from underlying [Path[Place P]] in Chinese show any comparability to other languages.

The answer to the first question is yes. West Germanic PPs as studied by van Riemsdijk (1990), Koopman (2000, 2010), Oosthuizen (2000), de Vos (this volume), Biberauer (2008a), and den Dikken (2003, 2010) all confirm a basic structure where a PP whose head denotes path or direction of motion embeds a PP whose head denotes location. We illustrate with the well-known German data in (56)–(58):

(56)   unter   [DP der   Brücke]   durch
        under   the.DAT bridge.DAT through
        'through under the bridge'

(57) an [$_{DP}$ dem   Bahnhof]   vorbei
      at   the.DAT station.DAT   beyond
      'past the station'

(58) an [$_{DP}$ dem   Fluss]   entlang
      at   the.DAT river.DAT   along
      'along the river'

As van Riemsdijk shows, and other authors concur, the constituency relations in these constructions are [$_{PostP}$ [$_{PreP}$ Prep DP] PostP]:

(59) [$_{PostP}$ [$_{PreP}$ unter   der   Brücke]   durch]
                          under   the.DAT bridge.DAT   through
      'through under the bridge'

The most direct piece of evidence for this constituency is that the postpositions in these examples do not select DPs to their left; that is, *der Brücke durch, *dem Bahnhof vorbei, and similar examples are systematically disallowed. In contrast, the PPs, e.g. *unter der Brücke* 'under the bridge', occur independently. Thus, in circumpositional PPs such as (56)–(58), path-denoting postpositions select place-denoting PrepPs. The fact that the postposition *qua* Path head heads the entire circumposition is confirmed by contexts where a higher head s-selects for Path; in such contexts the postposition cannot be dropped:

(60) der Weg an dem   Bahnhof *(vorbei)/ unter der   Brücke   *(durch)[18]
      the way at the.DAT station.DAT beyond/ under the.DAT bridge.DAT through
      'the way past the station/through under the bridge'

In the German circumpositional data above, location-denoting Ps are prepositional (P-DP), while path-denoting Ps are postpositional (PrepP-P). De Vos (this volume) describes a yet more straightforward pattern in Afrikaans, where even in simplex PPs, PostPs generally denote path of directed motion, PrePs place of static location.[19] As we have seen, Chinese is the mirror image of this: in Chinese, location-denoting Ps are postpositional (DP-P), while path-denoting Ps are prepositional (P-DP). If the Chinese and West Germanic structures are mirror images of one

---

[18] Note that without *vorbei* 'beyond' and *durch* 'through', respectively, (60) is marginally acceptable under the reading: 'the way *at* the station/*under* the bridge', i.e. with 'station' and 'bridge' as Place, not Path.

[19] De Vos uses this correlation between order and meaning in Afrikaans to motivate an account based on PF linearization. According to this account, Path heads bear an uninterpretable feature checked by their DP complement, and checkers of an uninterpretable feature must precede the checkee. We are sympathetic with De Vos's attempt to develop an account of PostP ordering that does not appeal to EPP-driven movement, but the correlation between Path and an uninterpretable feature forcing 'DP-Path' order cannot be a universal parameter, as mixed languages like German have both path-denoting postpositions and prepositions (*zu* 'to', *von* 'from', *nach* 'to(wards)', *durch* 'through'), while Chinese, as we emphasize above, is the reverse of the Afrikaans situation.

another, the latter would appear to be a *bona fide* example of the structure banned in
(55): that is, a head-initial phrase immediately dominated by a head-final phrase:

(61)   (=56)

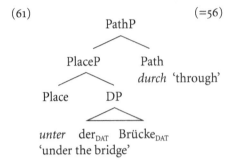

unter   der_DAT   Brücke_DAT
'under the bridge'

Whether these data from German invalidate the FOFC or not depends on the status
assigned to PlaceP. If it is analysed as distinct in categorial features from PathP, the
FOFC may be maintained. But whatever analysis that is adopted must capture the
following generalizations that hold for Chinese and German: (1) both PathP and
PlaceP (regardless of the location of their head) have the broader distribution of PPs;
(2) the relevant hierarchical universal is [Path [PlaceP]].

What about the derivation of the mirror-image orders in Chinese and West
Germanic? Previous treatments of postpositional and circumpositional orders in
West Germanic (e.g. Biberauer 2008) posit an EPP feature on the postposition to
force movement of the complement DP or PreP complement to its left.[20] It is clear
that a case-driven account of postpositional ordering such as we have developed for
Chinese does not extend to West Germanic circumpositional phrases, since in
examples like (56)–(58) dative case on the DP is checked by the preposition.

A hint about the relevant parametric difference is provided by the identity of 'light' *p*
heads in Chinese versus West Germanic circumpositional phrases. In Chinese, as we
showed in section 3.3, *prepositional* light *p* merges with *postpositional* PlaceP, as in (62):

(62)   *p*P   (=53)

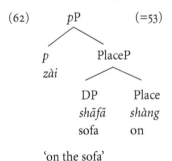

'on the sofa'

---

[20] In strict Minimalist terms, an EPP feature is required to force movement in our account of Chinese
post- and circumpositions as well. The account is not solely dependent on the EPP, however, in that a case-
checking requirement is also satisfied by the movement in question; if an EPP feature is not present, the
case feature on the DP is not checked and the derivation crashes.

In West Germanic, *postpositional* light *p* merges with *prepositional* PathP, as shown in the Afrikaans example (63) adapted from Oosthuizen (2000) (cf. de Vos (this volume, example 5)):[21]

(63)

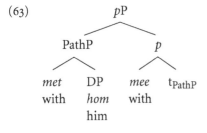

'with him'

De Vos argues for an agreement relation involving the *p* head in (63) (also cf. van Riemsdijk 1990: 240); the form *mee* is described as an 'agreeing form' of the adposition, and the relation is construed in terms of asymmetric feature checking of an uninterpretable feature on *p* by the complement DP. In versions of Minimalism (Chomsky 1995a), the relation between the fronted PathP and the postposition could be construed as a case of Spec–Head Agreement. The relevant parametric difference is an independently motivated one: presence or absence of agreement features. While agreement features play a role in West Germanic, they do not in Chinese. The light *p* *zài* 'in, at' in Chinese is merged to check the case features of the DP complement, which it does without requiring movement to its specifier. West Germanic light *p*s, in contrast, force movement, under conditions suggestive of Spec–Head Agreement.

3.5 History

As we stated in section 3.3, there are two dimensions to explaining the difference between prepositions and postpositions in Chinese languages: a synchronic dimension and a diachronic one. The objective of this section is to outline the diachronic dimension. Put simply, postpositions are diachronically derived from nouns; prepositions derive from verbs, or have always been prepositions. (Note that PrePs are attested from the earliest sources (13th c. BC), cf. Djamouri and Paul 1997, 2009.) In what follows, we briefly outline the history of postpositions, whose existence is attested from the Western Han on (1st c. BC). In contrast to previous studies focusing

---

[21] While we adopt (63) as the structure for West-Germanic circumpositional phrases, the example itself appears ill-chosen. Note that in German, the corresponding sequence 'with XP with' only arises though stranding of a separable prefix, as in *mit-kommen* 'with-come' = 'come with, accompany': Komm_i [PreP mit mir] mit-t_komm 'Come with me.' By contrast, it is unacceptable within a DP: [DP der Tanz [PrePmit mir] (*mit)] 'the dance with me'. The crucial status of NP complement position as a diagnostic site for distinguishing adpositions and homophonous separable verb prefixes was pointed out by van Riemsdijk (1990: 234).

on spatial location only, we provide data illustrating spatial and temporal location. We show that the analysis proposed above for PPs in Modern Mandarin holds for earlier stages of the language as well. In particular, no PrePs are attested in subject position, contrasting with numerous instances of existential sentences with PostP-subjects.

3.5.1 *Syntactic properties of location nouns*

Postpositions were derived via reanalysis from location nouns such as 上 *shàng* 'top', 下 *xià* 'bottom', 前 *qián* 'front, anteriority', 後 *hòu* 'posterity, posteriority; rear', etc. It is semantically unsurprising that location nouns develop into adpositions denoting place. As illustrated in the data given below, being nouns, these items could be modified, occur on their own, and be selected as complements by prepositions. Thus, in (64) 後 *hòu* 'posteri(ori)ty' is modified by the adjective *líng* 'good', while (65) and (66) show the location nouns *shàng* 'top' and *zhōng* 'middle, centre' preceded by the possessive pronoun *qí*:

(64)   霝冬霝後 (*Huang zi li* 黃子鬲 Early Springs and Autumns period, 8th–7th c. BC)
[DP líng   zhōng]   [DP líng   hòu]²²
    good   perpetuation   good   posteri(ori)ty
'[May this vessel bring his owner] a fine perpetuation and a fine posterity.'

(65)   蠶妾在其上 (*Zuozhuan* 左傳, Xi 僖 23, 4th c. BC)
Cán   qiè   zài   [DP qí   shàng].
silkworm   servant   be:at   3POSS   top
'A silkworm picker woman was located above them [i.e. up in the tree].'

(66)   立于其中 (*Liji* 禮記 chap. 13, Yuzao 玉藻, 4th–3rd c. BC)
Lì   yú   qí   zhōng.
stand   at   3POSS   middle
'[The king] stood in its middle.' (*It* refers to the half-open door.)

(67)–(70) below also involve modified NPs, with the modifier NP subordinated to the head noun by the genitive particle *zhī* (roughly corresponding to Modern Mandarin *de* discussed in section 3.3):

(67)   王用弗忘聖人之後
wáng   yòng   fú   wàng   [DP shèngrén   zhī hòu].
king   use   NEG   forget   sage   SUB posteri(ori)ty
'The king will use [this vessel] in order not to forget the descendants of the sages.'
(*Shi Wang ding* 師望鼎, Middle of the Western Zhou period, 9th c. BC)

---

²² This is one of the earliest examples attested for *hòu* as noun.

(68) 爰有寒泉，在浚之下。
    Yuán   yǒu   hán   quán   zài   [DP jùn   zhī   xià].
    then   have   cold   spring   be:at   Jun   SUB   bottom
    'And then there is a cold spring, at the bottom of the Jun river.' (*Shijing* 詩經
    32/3, *Guofeng Beifeng, Kaifeng*國風邶風, 凱風, 8th. c. BC)

(69) 帷幕之外, 目不能見十里之前 (*Huainanzi* 淮南子·9/6, 2nd c. BC)
    [Wéimù zhī wài]   mù bù néng jiàn [DP shí lǐ   zhī qián].
    curtain SUB outside eye NEG can see   ten mile SUB front
    'Outside the curtains, the eye cannot see farther than ten miles ahead.'

(70) 三月之後 (*Guanzi* 管子 85·9/3, 1st c. BC)
    [DP sān yuè   zhī hòu]...
         three month SUB posteri(ori)ty
    'After three months...'

In the examples above, *hòu* 'posteriority, rear', *qián* 'anteriority, front', *wài* 'outside', *xià* 'bottom' are clearly nouns because their modifier is subordinated by the genitive particle *zhī*. Naturally, such a complex NP 'NP *zhī* N' can also be the complement of a preposition (cf. (71)–(73)):

(71) 子姓兄弟立于主人之後...(*Yili* 儀禮, ch. 15; ca. 6th c. BC)
    Zǐxìng   xiōngdì   lì   [PP yú [DP zhǔrén zhī   hòu]]...
    sons   brothers   stand   at   host   SUB   rear...
    'The descendants and brothers stand at the rear of the host [of ceremony]...'

(72) 故加衣於君之上 (*Hanfeizi* 韓非子, ch. 7, 2/4, 3rd c. BC)
    Gù   jiā yī   [PP yú [DP jūn zhī shàng]].
    therefore add clothes   on   lord SUB top
    'And then he put some clothes on top of the lord.'
    (Context: The lord is lying drunk on the floor.)

(73) 今乃欲審堯、舜之道於三千歲之前...(*Hanfeizi* 韓非子·50, 1/4, 3rd c. BC)
    Jīn nǎi yù shěn   yáo shùn zhī dào [PP yú [sānqiān sùi
    now then want investigate Yao Shun sub way   at 3000   year
    zhī qián]]
    SUB anteriority
    'Now if one wants to investigate the Ways of Yáo and Shùn 3000 years ago...'

Bare *qián, hòu, shàng, xià* can likewise be selected as the complement of a preposition, again confirming their nominal status at this stage:

(74) 小臣二人執戈立于前，二人立于後。 (*Liji* 禮記·22·2/33, 4th c.–3rd c. BC)
Xiǎo   chén   èr   rén   zhí   gē   lì   [pp yú qián], èr   rén
little   official   two   man   hold   spear   stand   at   front   two man
lì   [pp   yú hòu].
stand   at rear
'Two assistants holding spears were standing in front [of the ruler],
and two at the rear.'

(75) 形立於上，影應於下
Xíng   lì   [pp yú   shàng]   yǐng   yìng   [pp yú   xià].
shape   stand   at   top   shadow   respond   at   bottom
'The shape stands at the top and the shadow responds at the bottom.'
(*Chunqiu Fanlu* 春秋繁露, ch. 20, Bao wei quan 保位權, 2nd c. BC)

Finally, locative NPs can occur on their own, e.g. as the subject in an existential construction:

(76) 馬知後有輿 (*Han shi waizhuan* 韓詩外傳·2·11/1, 2nd c. BC)
Mǎ   zhī   hòu   yǒu   yú.
horse   know   rear   exist   chariot
'The horse knew that behind there was a chariot.'

Since previous studies do not provide criteria for choosing between a location noun versus a postposition (that is, Place) analysis of these items, let us have a closer look at the environments where they appear. In examples (77)–(80) below, the location noun heads a complex NP where the modifying NP is simply juxtaposed with the head noun in the configuration [DP NP N], a structure generally available for nominal modification at that time.[23] As to be discussed in section 3.5.2, it is most likely this structure which permitted the reanalysis of the (location) head noun as a postposition.

(77) 馬邊縣男頭。馬後載婦女。
[DP Mǎ   biān] xuán nán tóu   [DP mǎ   hòu] zài   fùnǚ.
horse   side   hang man head   horse   rear   carry   woman
'Men's heads were hanging from the flanks of the horses, and women were carried on the croups of the horses.'
(Cai Yan 蔡琰, *Bei fen shi* 《悲憤詩》 Poem of Sorrow and Anger, 3rd c. AD)

邊 *biān* 'side' and 後 *hòu* 'rear' here clearly refer to the body parts of the horses. Thus 馬邊 *mǎ biān* 'horses' flanks' and 馬後 *mǎ hòu* 'horses' croups' are interpreted as

---

[23] The structure [DP [modifer-NP] N] is attested since the earliest sources (13th c. BC). The structure with the genitive particle *zhī* [DP [modifier-NP] *zhī* N] appears much later, i.e. around the 7th c. BC (cf. Djamouri 1999).

complex NPs, not as PostPs meaning 'at the side of the horses' and 'behind the horses', respectively.[24]

Similarly in (78) and (79), the context indicates that 馬後 *mǎ hòu* refers to the rear of the horse (and not to a general location behind the horse), and 房中 *fáng zhōng* to 'the middle of the room' (rather than to a general location inside the room).

(78) 御者執策立于馬後。

    Yùzhě   zhí   cè   lì   [PP yú [DP mǎ   hòu]].

    driver   hold   whip   stand   at   horse   rear

    'The driver was holding a whip, standing at the rear of the horse.'

    (*Yili* 儀禮, ch. 13 *Ji xi li* 既夕禮 *Obsequies of an ordinary officer*, compiled in 2nd c. BC)

(79) 夫人副褘立于房中。 (*Liji* 禮記, ch. 14, *Mingtang wei* 明堂位, 4th c.-3rd c. BC)

    Fūrén   fù   huī   lì   yú fáng   zhōng.

    wife   adorn   dress   stand   in chamber   middle

    'His wife in her adornment and dress stood in the middle of the chamber.'

Finally, in (80), the contrastive parallelism between 其下 *qí xià* 'its bottom' (in the main clause) and 山上 *shān shàng* 'top of a mountain' (in the preceding conditional clause) indicates the NP status of the latter. The fact that 上 *shàng* in the second sentence occurs on its own confirms the nominal status of *shàng* in this sentence.

(80) 山上有赭者其下有鐵, 上有鈆者其下有銀。 (*Guanzi* 管子 23, 1st c. BC)

    Shān   shàng yǒu   zhě   zhě   qí   xià   yǒu tiě

    mount   top   exist hematite NOM 3POSS bottom exist iron

---

[24] In fact, this kind of interdependence between interpretation and categorial status can be nicely illustrated using the item *zhōng* from Modern Mandarin. The location noun *zhōng* 'middle' can head a complex NP and be selected by a postposition such as *yǐlái* 'since' (cf. (i)). A PostP headed by *zhōng* 'in, during', by contrast, cannot function as the complement of another postposition (cf. (ii)), the selection of a PostP complement by a postposition being excluded:

  (i) [PostP [NP jiǔyuè   zhōng]   yǐlái]
              september middle   since
      'since mid-September'

  (ii) *[PostP [PostP jiàqī   zhōng]   yǐlái]
              holidays during   since

  (iii) [PostP jiàqī   zhōng]
           holidays during
      'during the holidays'

  (iv) [PostP jiàqī   yǐlái]
           holidays since
      'since the holidays'

shàng   yǒu   qiān   zhě   qí   xià   yǒu   yín.
top   exist lead   NOM   3POSS   bottom   exist silver
'If on the top of a mountain there is hematite, then there is iron at its bottom. If on the top there is lead, then there is silver at its bottom.'

3.5.2 *Reanalysis of location nouns as postpositions*

The reanalysis of location nouns as postpositions occurred around the 1st c. BC in the modification structure '[NP–modifier] [location noun]' without the genitive particle *zhī*. The data suggest that the complement position of prepositions favoured the reanalysis of this sequence as '[NP–complement] postposition'.

(81)   女子為自殺於房中者二人。 (*Shiji* 史記 5.16, 1st c. BC)
       Nǚzǐ   wéi   zì   shā   [Prep yú [PostP fáng   zhōng]] zhě   èr   rén.
       woman   be   self suicide   at   room   in   NOM   two person
       '[After the death of their husband] there were two women who killed themselves in their room.'

(82)   一比丘在房中臥 (*Shi song lü* 十誦律 58, 5th c. AD)
       Yī   bǐqiū   [PreP zài   [PostP fáng   zhōng] wò.
       one   monk   at   room   in   sleep
       'A monk was sleeping in the room.'

(83)   既覺洗浣於房前曬。 (*Mishasaibu* 彌沙塞部, 五分律, 5th c. AD)
       Jì   jué   xǐhuàn   yú   fáng   qián   shài.
       after arise   wash   at   room   in.front.of sun
       'After he had woken up and washed himself, he sunned himself in front of the room.'

In (81)–(83), the context indicates clearly that *zhōng* and *qián* do not refer to the 'centre' or the 'façade', but to a general location inside or in front of the room, respectively. Further research is required to confirm that the reanalysis of location nouns took place first in the complement position of prepositions, resulting in the circumpositional constructions described in section 3.2. Note, however, that the prepositions attested in (81)–(83) are *zài* 'in, at', analysed as light *p* in section 3.3, and *yú* 'in, at', a preposition with a similarly broad range of place-denoting meanings in earlier Chinese. The hypothesis that location noun > P reanalysis took place first in the complement position of these prepositions can explain why the reanalysis did not take place earlier, despite the fact that the modification structure without *zhī* [DP NP [location–N]] is attested from the earliest sources, over a millennium prior to the data in (81). Bleaching of the semantic content of *zài* and *yú* led to their reanalysis as the light *p* in (53); once this reanalysis takes place, the location thematic role is assigned by the postposition, while DP case is checked by *p*.

In the specific case of *hòu* 'posteriority, rear', temporal location 'after X' could at first only be expressed by a complex NP with the subordinator *zhī*: XP *zhī hòu* (cf. (70)), whereas for the spatial location, both structures, XP *zhī hòu* (cf. (71)) and XP *hòu* (cf. (77)) are attested. From the Western Han period on (1st c. BC), we observe that 'XP *hòu*', without the genitive *zhī*, can now denote both spatial *and* temporal location (84)–(85); we take this as an indication that the reanalysis of the noun *hòu* 'posteriority, rear' as a postposition 'behind, after' has occurred by this time.

(84)　二年後伐越，敗越於夫湫。　(*Shiji* 史記, *Wu Zixu liezhuan* 伍子胥列傳, 1st c. BC)

[$_{PostP}$ Èr　nián　hòu]　fá　yuè　bài　　yuè　yú　fúqiū.
　　　　two　year　after　fight　Yue　defeat　Yue　at　Fuqiu
'After two years, he attacked the Yue and defeated them at Fuqiu.'

(85)　閏當在十一月後 (*Hanshu* 漢書, *Lü li zhi* 律曆志, 2nd c. AD)

Rùn　　　　　dāng　zài　[$_{PostP}$ shíyī　yuè　hòu].
leap:month　must　be:at　　　eleven　month　after
'The leap month must occur after the eleventh month.'

3.5.3 *Properties of PostP in Late Han through Middle Chinese (1st c. BC–10th c. AD)*

Drawing on data from across a large time frame, from the emergence of postpositions in the 1st c. BC to the 10th century AD, this section examines the properties of PostP.[25] We show that PostPs—like PrePs—may occupy the sentence-initial topic position, may appear in preverbal adjunct position (between the subject and the verb) and be subcategorized for as an argument and hence occur in the postverbal position (reserved for arguments). Importantly, this distribution is observed up to modern times.

(86)　城河上為塞。(*Shiji* 史記, *Qin Shihuang benji* 秦始皇本紀, 1st c. BC)

[$_{TP}$ Chéng　　[$_{PostP}$ hé　shàng]　wéi　　sài.
　　　fortification　　　river　on　　make　protection
'Fortifications were built for protection along the river.'

(87)　此日山上雲氣成宮闕 … (*Ma Dibo* 馬第伯, 1st c. AD)

[$_{TopP}$ [Cǐ　rì]　[$_{TopP}$[$_{PostP}$ shān　　shàng] [$_{TP}$ yún　qì　chéng gōngquè　]]].
　　　　that day　　　　　　mountain on　　　cloud mist　form　palace.building
'That day, on the mountain, the cloud mist formed a palace […].'

(88)　和尚百年後向什摩處去？ (*Zutangji* 祖堂集 16·1·18, 10th c. AD)

Héshàng　[$_{PostP}$ bǎi　nián　hòu]　xiàng　　shénmo　chù　qù?
monk　　　　　　100　year　after　toward　what　　place　go
'After one hundred years (after your death) to which place will you go?'

---

[25] For a detailed discussion of PrePs in earlier stages of Chinese, see Djamouri and Paul (2009).

While in (86), the adjunct PostP 山上 *shān shàng* 'on the mountain' occupies the topic position to the left of the subject, the adjunct PostPs in (87) and (88) 河上 *hé shàng* 'along the river' and 百年後 *bǎi nián hòu* 'after hundred years', respectively, occur in the preverbal position to the right of the subject.

(89)   時有天即接石置山頂上。 (*Shisan seng canfa* 十三僧殘法, ch. 3, 5th c. AD)
    Shí   yǒu   tiān   jí   jiē   shí   zhì   shān -dǐng   shàng.
    once   exist   heaven   succeed   send   stone   put   mountain-summit   on
    'If one day Heaven were to send a stone, he would put it on a mountain summit.'

(90)   城在山上。 (*Shuijing zhu* 水經注 ch. 7, 6th c. AD)
    Chéng   zài   shān   shàng.
    city   be.at   mountain   on
    'The city is in the mountains.'

In (89) and (90) the PostPs 山頂上 *shān-dǐng shàng* 'on a mountain summit' and 山上 *shān shàng* 'in the mountains' are arguments subcategorized by the verb and therefore occupy the postverbal position.

So far we have illustrated the properties PostPs share with PrePs in earlier Chinese. However, there also exist a number of specific differences between them. In this respect the situation observed for post-Han Chinese resembles that described for Modern Mandarin in section 3.2 above.

The first difference is that PrePs are not attested in the subject position of existential sentences (cf. (92)), while for PostPs, this is a very common structure:

(91)   山上復有山。 (Li Ling 李陵, *Gu jueju* 古絕句, 1st c. BC)
    Shān   shàng fù   yǒu   shān.
    mountain   on   still   have   mountain
    'Beyond the mountain there are still mountains.'

(92)   *[PP 在/于(於)/自 NP] 有 NP
    zài/yú /zì   NP   yǒu   NP
    at/to/from   N   have   N
    (at/to/on/from N there is N)

Secondly, while PostPs can function as modifiers subordinated to the head noun by *zhī* 'PostP *zhī* N' (93), no corresponding structure with a PreP modifier seems to be attested (94):

(93)   宜昏飲, 此水上之樂也。 (*Guanzi* 管子·83·11/5, 1st c. BC)
    Yí   hūn   yǐn   cǐ   [DP [PostP shuǐ   shàng]   zhī   lè]   yě.
    suit   evening   drink   this   water on   SUB   pleasure   PART
    'Since it was an attractive place for drinking in the evening, this then became a popular form of amusement by the waterside.'

(94) *[$_{DP}$ PreP *zhi* N]

Last, but not least, while PostPs can be complements of PrePs (cf. (81) and (83) above), no examples of a PreP as the complement of a preposition are attested (95):

(95) *[$_{PP}$ 在/于/自 [$_{PP}$ 在/于/自   NP]]
       zài/yú /zì   zài/yú/zì   NP
       at/to/from   at/to/from NP

In this section we have described the emergence of postpositions from location nouns, and subsequent to this reanalysis, the differences between postpositions and location nouns, on the one hand, and postpositions and prepositions, on the other hand. We have seen that in earlier Chinese no PrePs are attested in subject position, contrasting with the numerous instances of existential sentences with PostP-subjects. Furthermore, PostPs can function as modifiers subordinated to the head noun by *zhi*: 'PostP *zhi* N', while no cases with PP modifiers are attested. Last, but not least, no prepositions selecting a PreP complement were found. Thus with respect to these three properties, PostPs (from the 1st c. BC onwards) and PrePs behave like their counterparts in Modern Mandarin.

3.6 Conclusion

Within the typological literature, the VO language Chinese has long been known for its 'disharmonic' and 'mixed' nature. The coexistence of Postpositional Phrases and Prepositional Phrases since the 1st c. BC is one of the numerous phenomena illustrating this property. A careful study shows that Postpositional Phrases (PostPs) and Prepositional Phrases (PrePs) instantiate the same basic category, PP; more precisely, neither type of P belongs to the category N or V, as has sometimes been suggested. The differences between these two types of PP reflect a hierarchical universal ([Path [PlaceP]]) and a language-particular property of Chinese (the absence of phrase-final heads with the ability to check case). Postpositions denote static location, that is, place. Their DP complements check case through movement to the left edge of PlaceP; case is assigned by a path-denoting preposition, the light *p zài*, or a higher verbal head. The place-denoting semantic property of postpositions and their inability to check case bear a diachronic relation to their origin as nouns, but these properties have been integrated into an articulated PP structure where postpositions function as the head of PlaceP, fully consistent with the hierarchical and derivational principles of Universal Grammar.

4

The Mixed OV/VO Syntax of Mòcheno Main Clauses: On the Interaction between High and Low Left Periphery

FEDERICA COGNOLA

4.1 Introduction[1]

In this article, I take into consideration the syntax of Mòcheno (German: *Fersenta-lerisch*), a Tyrolean variety spoken in the speech island *Valle dei Mocheni* (German: *Fersental*), in Northern Italy (Eastern Trentino).[2] This dialect is of extreme interest for the theories of linguistic change and linguistic variation since it sets itself between Romance and Germanic as far as two core syntactic phenomena are concerned: V2 and OV word orders. Focusing on OV/VO word orders, Mòcheno can be defined as a mixed OV/VO language, since in main clauses the *Satzklammerstruktur* typical of continental Germanic is possible (1a), but not obligatory (1b), and in embedded clauses, strict OV (1c) coexists with the same orders as main clauses (1d,e).

[1] I would like to thank the organizers and the participants of the TADWO conference in Newcastle, in particular Josef Bayer, Theresa Biberauer, Guglielmo Cinque, Sonia Cyrino, Roland Hinterhölzl, Richard Kayne, Susan Pintzuk, Michelle Sheehan, Ann Taylor, and Jan-Wouter Zwart for the interest they have shown in my work and for useful comments and suggestions. To Paola Benincà, Theresa Biberauer, Andrea Padovan, Cecilia Poletto, Michelle Sheehan, Chiara Zanini, and two anonymous reviewers, I want to express my gratitude for invaluable suggestions and indications that helped me to shape my ideas and to organize them in the clearest way. Finally, I would like to thank my main informant, L.T., who contributed a great deal with his keen intuitions to the analysis proposed here, Carol Morris, and the editors of this volume for checking and improving the English of this paper. All shortcomings are my own.

[2] Mòcheno is still spoken, in the villages of Palù/Palai, Fierozzo/Vlaruz, and Roveda/Oachlait, by around 580 people (as discussed by Alber 2010: 2, note 2, this is only an estimation: the exact number of speakers of Mòcheno is unknown). All data in this paper refer to the variety spoken in Palù/Palai by middle-aged speakers (see Cognola 2013a).

(1) a. Gester   hòn-e   s   puach kaft
         yesterday   have-CL.SUBJ.1SG the   book   bought
         'Yesterday I bought the book.'

     b. Gester   hòn-e   kaft   s   puach
         yesterday   have-CL.SUBJ.1SG bought the   book
         'Yesterday I bought the book.'

     c. Er   hòt mer pfrok, benn as   der Nane a puach kaft   hòt
         STR.SUBJ.3MSG has to.me asked when that the John a book   bought has
         'He asked me when John bought a book.'

     d. Er   hòt mer pfrok, benn as   der Nane hòt a puach kaft
         STR.SUBJ.3MSG has to.me asked when that the John has a book   bought
         'He asked me when John bought a book.'

     e. Er   hòt mer pfrok, benn as   der Nane hòt kaft   a puach
         STR.SUBJ.3MSG has to.me asked when that the John has bought a book
         'He asked me when John bought a book.'

The linguists who have worked on the syntax of Mòcheno (among others, Zamboni 1979: 90; Heller 1979: 119; Togni 1990: 172; Rowley 2003: 251, 289, 291) have tried to capture the facts in (1) through the idea that all orders divergent from those of standard German are the result of contact with Romance varieties. This hypothesis is fully compatible with the double-base hypothesis proposed by Kroch (1989) and applied to the syntax of mixed languages such as Old English (OE, Pintzuk 1999). According to the proponents of the hypothesis of contact for Mòcheno, the mixed character of this language is a direct consequence of the history of the settlement of the valley (Rogger 1979), in particular of the early contact of Tyrolean settlers with Romance-speaking populations. Contact with a language with different parameters led to a situation of language competition, resulting in a resetting of parameters. With respect to OV/VO word orders, the contact effect manifests itself in the possibility of having VO syntax, which is an innovation with respect to the (assumed) original grammar brought by the settlers.

In this paper, relying on the observation that the word orders in (1) are not identical with respect to information structure—which speaks against the position of constituents vis-a-vis the lexical verb being a matter of parameter setting[3]—I propose a novel account of Mòcheno syntax, which is able to capture the distribution

---

[3] I also reject an account of Mòcheno word orders that tries to connect syntax with morphology, in particular with case morphology on DPs (see Meillet 1903 and Magni 2000 for Latin and Roberts 1997 for Old English). The connection between word order and case morphology has proved to be very weak: Weerman (1997) points out that Dutch has OV base word order despite its lacking case morphology on DPs; Icelandic, on the other hand, has maintained a rich case morphology but is a VO language (Hroarsdottir 2000a). Polo (2004) shows that in all instances of VO word order in Latin, the direct object is case-marked (see, though, Magni 2000 for the opposite result for the Pompeian inscriptions). For

of OV/VO word orders within a single grammar, in which the two word orders distribute according to rules internal to the system.[4]

My account sets itself in recent research on language variation and change that has tried to make sense of the mixed OV/VO character of older stages of modern languages in terms of information structure (among others Hinterhölzl 2009c on Old High German, OHG; Taylor and Pintzuk 2012 on OE; Polo 2004 on Latin).[5] In this chapter, it is shown that the position of main sentence constituents with respect to the lexical verb (OV/VO)[6] should be connected with their information status; in particular, discourse-given XPs tend to precede the lexical verb and discourse-new XPs tend to follow it, in coherence with the observation (among others Gundel 1989) that, cross-linguistically, given information tends to appear in the higher portion of the clause, whereas new information is hosted in its lowest part. In the Old Germanic languages considered, XPs made heavy by a modification, such as a relative clause or AP and PP modifications, tend to appear after the lexical verb, in accordance with Behaghel's (1932) *Gesetz der wachsenden Glieder*, which states that light elements (pronouns and unmodified nouns) precede the finite verb, whereas heavy elements tend to follow it. According to Hinterhölzl (2009c), there is a correlation between the syntax of heavy XPs and their information status (see also Benincà 1988 for the same claim): heavy XPs appear postverbally because they are more likely to be new information foci, since they are richer in terms of the information they convey than light XPs. According to Taylor and Pintzuk (2012), in contrast, no connection between the information status of heavy XPs and their syntactic position can be detected in OE. The structure of the clause proposed for OHG and OE is sketched in (2).[7]

(2)   C background – V – presentational focus/heavy XPs   OHG/OE

Mòcheno, too, a correlation between case morphology and syntax cannot be claimed because, despite the fact that Mòcheno does not have case morphology on NPs (Rowley 2003: 133ff.), OV word order is possible.

[4] The validity of the double-base hypothesis has been challenged on both theoretical (Svenonius 2000b: 280) and empirical grounds. With respect to the role of competing grammars in language variation and change, it has been pointed out (Hinterhölzl 2009c and references cited there) that Old High German was also a language with mixed OV/VO word orders, even though this cannot be due to contact with languages with different parameters. Similar considerations hold for other languages that have undergone a shift from OV to VO, passing through a period of mixed OV/VO syntax, such as Icelandic (Hroarsdottir 2000a), Swedish (Delsing 2000), and also the Romance languages, which all stem from Latin (Magni 2000; Polo 2004).

[5] I have decided to focus mostly on these studies, leaving aside the work on modern languages with mixed OV/VO syntax such as Yiddish (Diesing 1997), Hungarian (among others Kiss 1987), or Finnish (Vilkuna 1995), because the mixed OV/VO syntax of Mòcheno is more similar to that of Old Germanic varieties, which makes the comparison with those varieties more interesting.

[6] The cited studies focus on the position of main-clause constituents with respect to the finite lexical verb, given that in the older stages of the examined languages no analytical verb forms had appeared yet. In this work, by contrast, I consider the position of the direct object (DO) with respect to the past participle in a so-called *Satzklammerstruktur* (brace construction).

[7] Hinterhölzl (2009c) also identifies a dedicated position for contrastive foci before the finite verb.

Also in the case of Latin there seems to be strong evidence in favour of the idea that the distribution of word orders in the period in which it was a mixed OV/VO language was ruled by 'pragmatically and structurally driven constraints' (Polo 2004: 92) operating at the interface between pragmatics and semantics on the one hand and syntax on the other. Polo (2004: 136ff.) convincingly shows that in the majority of sentences with VO syntax appearing in her corpus (141/188, 75%), XPs follow the lexical verb when they are either old or new information; only in a minority of cases (47/188, 25%) is the XP following the lexical verb not pragmatically marked. Interestingly, in the cases in which the XP following the verb is pragmatic- ally unmarked, it is either made heavy by a modification, or marked positively for definiteness and human features (see also Magni 2000 for similar findings for the emergence of VO syntax in the Pompeian inscriptions). The structure of the clause identified for Latin by Polo (2004) is given in (3).

(3)   V – old/new information / heavyXPs / [+definite] / [+human] XPs   Latin

The article is organized in the following way. In section 4.2, I present the relevant empirical facts concerning OV/VO word orders in Mòcheno main clauses, focusing first on the position of direct objects (DOs) in main clauses and showing that in Mòcheno there is a strong correlation between syntax and information structure, since new information foci have to appear before the past participle (OV), whereas topics have to appear either in the high left periphery or after the past participle (VO). I will also show that heaviness actually plays a role in Mòcheno, albeit one which is independent of information structure. In section 4.3, I will propose a cartographic (Cinque 1999, 2006a; Rizzi 1997, 2004b) and antisymmetric (Kayne 1994, 1998) account of the empirical facts which is able to capture the distribution of both types of information in Mòcheno main clauses and of OV/VO word orders. The core of my proposal is that the properties of Mòcheno are immediately captured if we assume that the linear word order of this language is determined by the interaction between the high left periphery (henceforth: *high periphery*) and the low left periphery (henceforth: *VP periphery*, see Jayaseelan 2001; Belletti 2001, 2004; Poletto 2006). Specifically, the proposal is that both of these peripheries (i) have the same structure and (ii) have a V2 rule, relating, respectively, to the finite verb in the higher phase and the past participle in the lower one (cf. Poletto 2006 for a similar proposal for Old Italian).

4.2 On the structure of Mòcheno main clauses

In this section, I discuss the structure of Mòcheno main clauses, focusing on (i) the position of old and new information with respect to the lexical verb (the past participle) and (ii) the effect of heaviness. For reasons of space, I only consider the syntax of main declaratives exhibiting the *Satzklammerstruktur*—i.e. the structure in which the second-position finite and finally placed non-finite verbs form a 'brace' around the principal sentence constituents—not considering the derivation of embedded clauses.

Furthermore, I only look at the syntactic distribution of DOs realized by DPs, leaving aside the syntax of object pronouns.[8] All the conclusions arrived at for DOs are also valid for all other XPs, given that they realize old or new information. The present analysis, however, does not account for the syntax of sentences in which several main-sentence constituents are present: for those cases, the analysis would need to be refined, which could not be done within the confines of this chapter (see Cognola 2010 for relevant discussion). In what follows I will make reference to the categories of topic and focus in order to refer to old/given and new/relevant information, respectively. This terminology involves a precise theoretical implementation, since it implies that constituents can be interpreted as old or new information only if they check the relevant discourse features in dedicated peripheral projections (TopicP and FocusP), as proposed among others by Belletti (2001, 2004), Benincà (2001), Benincà and Poletto (2004), and Rizzi (1997). The theoretical implementation offered by the cartographic approach, from which I will in this section only borrow the terminology without making precise reference to the syntactic derivation (see section 4.3), implies that it is possible to draw a precise map between discourse properties on the one hand and syntax on the other.

4.2.1 *On the syntax of new information focus*

In this section, I will consider the position of new information foci in Mòcheno, in order to determine whether they have a fixed position with respect to the lexical verb. In order to identify new information foci in Mòcheno, I will consider, following among others Belletti (2001, 2004) and Cruschina (2006), main declarative clauses that are answers to *wh* main interrogatives: in each case, the *wh*-element is thought to introduce the new information focus.

As can be seen in (4b), the only appropriate answer to (4a) is a main declarative clause in which the new information focus precedes the past participle (OV); the post-participial (VO, 4c) and the sentence-initial (4d) positions are ruled out for the new information focus.

(4)   a. Bos   hòs-o   kaft?
         what   have-CL.SUBJ.2SG   bought
         'What did you buy?'

---

[8] In Mòcheno object pronouns are enclitic to the finite verb and do not enter the pattern of OV/VO alternations described for DPs in this work.

b. I   hòn   a/s   puach   kaft
   STR.SUBJ.1SG   have   a/the   book   bought
   'I have bought a/the book.'

c. #I   hòn   kaft   a/s   puach
   STR.SUBJ.1SG   have   bought   a/the   book

d. #A/s   puach   hòn-e   kaft
   a/the   book   have-CL.SUBJ.1SG   bought

New information foci also have to appear before the past participle (OV) when [+human] common nouns and proper names are involved, as can be seen in the examples below (5):

(5) a. Ber   hòt-er   pakemmp?
     who   has-CL.SUBJ.M.3SG   met
     'Who did he meet?'

b. Er   hòt   der   pustin/   der   Mario   pakemmp
   STR.SUBJ.M.3SG   has   the   postman/the   Mario   met
   'He met the postman/Mario.'

c. #Er   hòt   pakemmp   der   pustin/   der   Mario
   STR.SUBJ.M.3SG   has   met   the   postman/the   Mario

d. #Der pustin/der   Mario   hòt-er   pakemmp
   the postman/the   Mario   has-CL.SUBJ.M.3SG   met
   'He met the postman/Mario.'

The data discussed so far are extremely clear: in Mòcheno new information foci, to be distinguished on the basis of the *wh* main interrogative test, have to obligatorily appear before the past participle in OV syntax.

Let us consider the position of the new information focus with respect to sentential and manner adverbs, in order to determine whether DOs in Mòcheno undergo long or short scrambling (Kratzer 1995; Diesing 1992; Hinterhölzl 2006). As shown in (6b), the unmarked position for new information focus in OV syntax is before manner adverbs and after sentential adverbs. I take this to mean that DOs undergo short scrambling and not long scrambling (6c,d), differently from German.[9]

---

[9] Following general practice in the cartographic literature (see in particular Cinque 1999), I use the low manner adverb *well* to establish the position of both the past participle and the DO. As pointed out by an anonymous reviewer, in many languages (among them English) this adverb has a particularly strange syntax. This general fact does not, however, affect the discussion in this article in any way. As shown in Cognola (2008, 2010), the manner adverb *well* behaves in the same way as manner PPs (such as *pet cura* 'carefully') and low adverbs expressing completive aspect (such as *gonz* 'completely'), in obligatorily following definite and indefinite DOs. Therefore, the syntax of *well* can be considered representative of

(6)   a. Bos   hòt-er   òlbe   schia galesn?
          what   has-CL.SUBJ.M.3SG   always well   read
          'What did he always read well?'

      b. Er   hòt   òlbe   s/a   puach schia galesn
          STR.SUBJ.M.3SG has   always the/a   book   well   read
          'He has always read the book well.'

      c. #Er   hòt   s   puach   òlbe   schia galesn
          STR.SUBJ.M.3SG has   the   book   always well   read

      d. #Er   hòt   a   puach   òlbe   schia galesn
          STR.SUBJ.M.3SG has   a   book   always well   read

The data discussed so far are summed up in the descriptive generalizations in (7).

(7)   a. New information foci have to appear in OV syntax.

      b. New information foci undergo short scrambling.

As the last topic of this subsection, I consider the syntax of new information foci made heavy by a modification, in order to determine whether heaviness (i) has a syntactic effect on the position of new information foci and (ii) whether this effect is dependent on information structure. Here, for reasons of space, I focus on modifications realized by relative clauses and I leave aside the syntactic behaviour of DOs made heavy by APs or PPs. In order to check for information structure, I consider again only main clauses that are answers to *wh* main interrogatives: on the basis of this test, the DOs modified by relative clauses can be considered unambigous new information foci.

In Mòcheno, heaviness has a different effect according to the semantic class the modified noun belongs to. As shown in (8), a new information focus realized by a [−human] common noun and modified by a relative clause can appear in both OV (8b) and VO syntax (8c); the VO position is ruled out if the new information focus is realized by a light XP (see (4) above).

(8)   a. Bos   hòs-o   kaft   en de boteig?
          what   have-CL.SUBJ.2SG bought   in the shop
          'What did you buy in the shop?'

      b. I   hòn   kaft   s/a   puach as   mer   der Mario
          STR.SUBJ.1SG   have   bought the/a   book   that to.me   the Mario
          konsigliort   hòt
          recommended   has
          'I bought the/a book that Mario recommended.'

the syntax of low adverbs in Mòcheno and a good diagnostic for detecting the syntactic position of DOs and the past participle. For an analysis of long scrambling in Mòcheno, see ognola (2013b).

c.   I   hòn   s/a   puach as   mer   der Mario konsigliort

       STR.SUBJ.1SG have the/a book   that to.me the Mario recommended

       hòt   kaft

       has   bought

       'I bought the/a book recommended by Mario.'

In (9), I consider the case in which proper names and [+human] common nouns are new information foci and are modified by a relative clause. As shown in (9b,c), with these nouns the modifying relative clause has the effect of forcing VO syntax for the new information focus;[10] again, VO syntax is ruled out when the new information focus is realized by a light XP (see (5) above).

(9) a. Ber   hòt-se   pakemmp?

         who   has-CL.SUBJ.F.3SG met

         'Who did she meet?'

    b. Si   hòt pakemmp der Mario/der pustin, as   mai kamarot ist

         STR. SUBJ.F.3SG has met   the Mario/the postman, that my friend   is

         va drai jor

         of three years

         'She met Mario/the postman, who has been a friend of mine for three years.'

    c. *Si   hòt der Mario/der pustin   as   mai kamarot ist va drai

         STR. SUBJ.F.3SG has the Mario/the postman, that my friend   is of three

         jor   pakemmp

         years   met

The data above point to the fact that heaviness has an effect on the syntax of DOs, by favouring or forcing the postverbal position; this effect is, however, independent of information structure, since all heavy DOs considered above are unambiguously new information foci. In the next subsection, I consider the syntax of topics.

4.2.2 *On the syntax of topics*

The scope of this section is to describe the syntax of topics in Mòcheno, in order to determine whether topicalized XPs have a different distribution from that of new information foci. I will consider both main declaratives and sentences with fronted operators. With the label 'topic', I refer to a constituent realizing old/given information;

---

[10] In Cognola (2010), I have pointed out that heaviness might have a different effect on the syntax of an XP according to the type of relative clause (appositive or restrictive) modifying it. This is tightly linked to the asymmetries between [−human] common nouns on the one hand and [+human] common nouns and proper names reported in this section. As far as I know, this fact has never been noticed in previous work and heaviness has been treated as a unitary phenomenon, independently of the type of relative clause involved.

following López (2009) and Cruschina (2010), I assume that the core property of all types of topics is their presuppositional character, that is, their being part of the presupposition of the speaker (D-linking in Pesetsky 1987). I further assume that topics are split into two classes according to the property of [givenness]:[11] some topics are compatible with an out-of-the-blue sentence, in which they are simply presupposed, whereas other topics are grammatical only if they have already been introduced into the linguistic context. Following the cartographic approach adopted in this chapter, I assume that all the discourse features connected to topicality are encoded in dedicated functional projections and are checked through movement in overt syntax (Rizzi 1997).[12]

As shown in (10), in Mòcheno there are two types of constructions expressing topicality: constructions with pronominal resumption, which I call clitic left dislocation (CLLD) (Benincà 1988; Cinque 1990; Rizzi 1997) and clitic right dislocation (CLRD) (Benincà 1988; Kayne 1994; Cecchetto 1999), which in Mòcheno can only realize [+given] topics, on the one hand, and constructions without pronominal resumption, such as simple preposing (SP)[13] (Benincà 1988; Cinque 1990), which in Mòcheno is compatible with [+/−given] topics, and marginalization (Antinucci and

---

[11] Cruschina (2010), following López (2009), calls this property of topics 'anaphoricity' and defines it as 'the relation with a discourse antecedent based on identity' (López 2009, in Cruschina 2010: 51). As pointed out by an anonymous reviewer, the notion of 'anaphoricity' is fully comparable with that of 'givenness'.

[12] Recent years have seen an increasing interest in the category of topic and in its syntactic realizations (see among others Frascarelli 2000; Frascarelli and Hinterhölzl 2007; Benincà and Poletto 2004). These studies have allowed us to reconstruct a precise mapping between the typology of topics identified in semantics and the phonological and syntactic properties of the different syntactic constructions through which topics are realized. Within the cartographic approach, this has led to a refinement of the projection TopicP originally proposed by Rizzi (1997), which has been shown to be an area hosting different types of topics strictly ordered one with respect to the other.

[13] Here the terminological choice has to be motivated. Benincà (1988: 142) calls the construction exemplified in (i) below 'anaphoric anteposition': this construction, which is limited to root clauses, involves a topic–comment articulation, with the topicalized XP not being doubled by a pronoun:

(i) La stessa proposta fece anche il   partito di maggioranza
     the same proposal made also the party of majority
     'The same proposal, the majority party also made.'

Rizzi (1997: 285) calls this construction 'topicalization' where the XP appearing in the left periphery is an argument and 'simple preposing' where it is an adverb (Rizzi 2004a). Cruschina (2010), citing Cinque (1990), refers to this construction as Resumptive Preposing or Simple Preposing, distinguishing between arguments and adverbs, as in Rizzi (2004a). In this chapter, I prefer to speak of 'simple preposing' (SP) for both the cases in which a verb argument and an adverb are involved. I think, in fact, that the label 'anaphoric anteposition' is misleading for Mòcheno; in this language, SP is possible with both [+/−given] (+/−anaphoric) topics, which points to the fact that it is not giveness that has to be considered the main characteristic of the construction. The label 'topicalization' is also misleading, since it may lead to confusion between the syntactic realization of a topic and the notion of topic in itself (old information), which is independent of its syntactic realization. 'Resumptive Preposing' is misleading because the core syntactic property of this construction, in contrast with CLLD, is precisely lack of pronominal resumption.

Cinque 1977; Benincà 1988; Cardinaletti 2002), which in Mòcheno is compatible only
with [−given] topics.[14]

(10) a. S puach$_j$ hòt-er-s$_j$ kaft   CLLD;[15] [+given] topics
         the book   has-CL.SUBJ.M.3SG-CL.OBJ.3NSG bought
         'The book, he bought it.'

      b. Er   hòt-s$_j$ kaft   s   puach$_j$ CLRD;[16] [+given] topics
         STR.SUBJ.3MSG has-CL.OBJ.N.3SG bought the book
         'He bought it, the book.'

      c. S puach   hòt-er   kaft   SP; [+/−given] topics
         the book   has-CL.SUBJ.M.3SG   bought
         'The book he bought'

      d. Bo   hòs -o   kaft   s puach? marginalization; [−given] topics
         where have-CL.SUBJ.2SG bought the book
         'Where did you buy the book?'

From the typology of topic constructions in Mòcheno given in (10), it can already be
inferred that topics are ruled out from the pre-participial OV position. In what
follows, I will provide evidence in favour of this claim by taking into consideration
the syntactic realization of [+/− given] topics and focusing only on the syntax of
topics lacking pronominal doubling. This choice is motivated by the fact that the
scope of this chapter is not to give a complete account of all constructions expressing
topicality in Mòcheno, but to make sense of the syntactic distribution of DOs with
respect to the past participle, defending the idea that when a connection between
information structure and syntax is missing, as in those topic constructions lacking a
pronominal doubling, it is the syntactic position of the XP that allows it to distinguish
between topic or focus.

---

[14] Here, I use for the Mòcheno constructions the labels that have been proposed for the Romance
(Italian) constructions expressing topicality. This choice rests on the formal identity between the Mòcheno
and the Romance (Italian) constructions, but it does not imply that the constructions are also functionally
identical (in fact, they are not: CLLD in Italian can introduce a new topic—see Benincà 1988; Cruschina
2010—whereas in Mòcheno it cannot). Moreover, the choice of these labels does not imply commitment
to any analysis proposed for Romance.
[15] As discussed in ognola (2013a), in main declarative clauses SP is the only available option or the
preferred option in all Mòcheno varieties, and CLLD is judged grammatical only by some of the speakers of
the Palù and Fierozzo dialects. In sentences with a fronted focus, all speakers of all dialects agree that CLLD
(or CLRD) is the only construction for realizing a topic and SP is ruled out.
[16] In Mòcheno CLRD, the dislocated XP cannot appear before the past participle, but only after it: this
hints at a correlation between post-participial position and topicality.

(i) *I hòn-en$_j$ der Mario$_j$ gester   tsechen
      I have-CL.OBJ.M.3SG the Mario yesterday   seen
(ii) *I hòn-en$_j$.   gester   der Mario$_j$ tsechen
      I have-CL OBJ.M.3SG yesterday   the Mario   seen

4.2.2.1 *On the syntax of topics in main declaratives*   Beginning with [−given] topics, in (11) I show that a [−given] topic can be realized by SP (11a) and is incompatible with the pre-participial (11b) and the post-participial (11c) positions. The constructions in which a topic without pronominal doubler follows the past participle, I take as instances of marginalization.[17]

(11)   (Context: My friend was supposed to buy a book, but was always finding an excuse for not buying it. Finally he buys the book and I can say to another friend who knows the facts:)

    a. S puach   hòt-er   gester   kaft   [−given; SP]
       the book   has-CL.SUBJ.M.3SG yesterday bought
       'The book, he bought yesterday.'

    b. #Er   hòt gester   kaft   s puach *[−given; marginalization]
       STR.SUBJ.M.3SG has yesterday bought the book

    c. #Er   hòt   gester   s puach   kaft   *[−given; OV]
       STR.SUBJ.M.3SG has   yesterday the book bought

Now, (11c) is inappropriate for a context in which the DO has a topic reading but it would be felicitous if the DO were a new information focus, as we saw above; (11b), on the other hand, would be grammatical only if the DO were modified by a relative clause, as in (12). The heavy DO in (12) can be interpreted both as a new information focus and as a topic (see below).

(12)   Er   hòt gester   kaft   s   puach
     STR.SUBJ.M.3SG has yesterday bought the book
     as-o-en   du   konsigliort   hòst
     that-CL.SUBJ.2SG-CL.INDOBJ.3SG you recommended have
     'Yesterday he bought the book that you recommended.'

The facts in (11) and (12) strongly indicate that in Mòcheno one word order corresponds to one type of information. This point is crucial in the light of the present account, since it indicates that OV and VO syntax cannot be connected to a

---

[17] In this article, I propose (see section 4.3) that the Mòcheno construction that I call marginalization has to be analysed as involving the VP periphery. Cardinaletti (2002) proposes an analysis of Italian marginalization as a construction involving *in situ* destressing. I argue that the interaction between V2 and OV/VO and the connection between the higher and the lower phase with respect to distribution of information strongly support the idea that topics without pronominal doubler appearing after the past participle (marginalization) are in the VP periphery in Mòcheno. Future research is needed in order to determine whether the analysis proposed for Mòcheno might be applied to Italian. The indications in brackets given to the right of the sentences are only meant to indicate informally what syntactic construction is compatible or incompatible with what type ([+/−given]) of topic. The asterisk indicates that the construction cannot express that type of topic; in some cases, the sentence would be acceptable if the direct object had a different information status (see above for the syntax of new information foci).

different setting of one single parameter due to contact, but rather relates to rules of information structure internal to a single grammar.

Let us now consider [+given] topics. As shown in (13), a [+given] topic can be realized through SP (13a) and cannot appear in OV syntax (13b,c) nor be marginalized (13d).

(13)   (Someone asks:

Benn	hòt-er	kaft	s	puach?
when	has-CL.SUBJ.M.3SG	bought	the	book

'When did he buy the book?')

a. S puach   hòt-er   gester   kaft   [+given; SP]

   the book   has-CL.SUBJ.M.3SG   yesterday   bought

   'The book, he bought yesterday.'

b. #Er   hòt   s   puach   gester   kaft   *[+given; OV]

   STR.SUBJ.M.3SG   has   the   book   yesterday   bought

c. #Er   hòt   gester   s   puach   kaft   *[+given; OV]

   STR.SUBJ.M.3SG   has   yesterday   the   book   bought

d. #Er   hòt   gester   kaft   s   puach   *[+given; marg.]

   STR.SUBJ.M.3SG   has   yesterday   bought   the   book

In (14), I sum up what we have seen in this subsection.

(14)   a. SP can realize both [+/−given] topics.

     b. [+/−given] topics cannot be marginalized (VO) nor appear before the past participle (OV).

The last issue to be tackled in this subsection is whether (i) heaviness has an effect on the syntax of topics and (ii) there is a connection between heaviness and information structure. In (15), I consider clear cases in which DOs are [+/−given] topics, in order to control for the information status of the DOs involved. As shown in (15a), a heavy [−given] topic can be marginalized, a possibility that is ruled out for light topics (see 11a,b above) or appear as an SP (15b); heavy [+given] topics, on the contrary, cannot appear after the past participle (15c) but only in the left periphery as SP (15d).

(15)   (Context: We know that someone was supposed to buy a book that was recommended by Mario. A friend who knows the facts can say:)

a. Schau,   as-er   hòt   gester   kaft   s   puach

   look   that-STR.SUBJ.M.3SG   has   yesterday   bought   the   book

   as-en   der Mario   konsigliort   gop hòt

   that-CL.INDOBJ.3SG   the Mario   recommended   had has   [−given; marg.]

   'Look, he yesterday bought the book that Mario had recommended to him.'

b. Schau as   s   puach as-en   der Mario konsigliort   gop hòt,
look   that the book   that-CL.INDOBJ.3SG the Mario recommended had has,
hòt-er   gester   kaft
has-CL.SUBJ.M.3SG   yesterday   bought   [−given; SP]
'Look, the book that Mario had recommended to him he bought yesterday.'
(Someone asks:
Benn hòt-er   kaft   s   puach as-en   der Mario
when has-CL.SUBJ.M.3SG bought the book   that.CL.IND.OBJ.3SG the Mario
konsigliort   gop   hòt?
recommended   had   has
'When did he buy the book that Mario recommended?')

c. #Er   hòt   gester   kaft   s   puach
STR.SUBJ.M.3SG   has   yesterday   bought   the   book
as-en   der Mario   konsigliort   gop   hòt
that-CL.INDOBJ.3SG   the Mario   recommended   had   has
*[+given; marg.]

d. S puach   as-en   der Mario   konsigliort   gop hòt,
the book   that-CL.INDOBJ.M.3SG   the Mario   recommended   had has
hòt-er   gester   kaft
has-CL.SUBJ.3.MSG   yesterday   bought   [+given; SP]
'The book recommended by Mario he bought yesterday.'

The data in (15) point to the fact that heaviness has an effect only on the syntax of
[−given] topics, which can appear after the past participle if made heavy by a relative
clause. Heavy [+given] topics, on the other hand, have to appear in the left periphery,
just like their light counterparts. Also for the case of topics, heaviness does not
interfere with information status.

4.2.2.2 Wh *main interrogatives and sentences with a fronted focus*   In this subsection, I consider the distribution of [+/−given] topics in sentences with a fronted
operator. Beginning with [−given] topics, in (16), I show that in a main interrogative
clause a [−given] topic can be realized through marginalization (16a), and that the
OV position is not only inappropriate (#) for this topic, but ungrammatical (16b).
Also SP is not only ruled out, but ungrammatical in *wh* main interrogatives (16c).

(16)   (Context: Last class I asked the students to buy the textbook; in the next class,
I ask:)
a. Ber   hòt   schua   kaft   s   puach?   [−given; marginalization]
who   has   already   bought   the   book
'Who has already bought the book?'

b. *Ber   hòt   schua   s   puach   kaft?   *[−given; OV]
   who   has   already   the   book   bought

c. *S   puach   ber   hòt   kaft?   *[−given; SP]
   the   book   who   has   bought

The fact that the examples in (16b,c) are not only inappropriate, but fully ungrammatical represents a great difference with respect to the syntax of main declarative clauses considered in the previous subsections. In those cases, different word orders were shown to be compatible with different types of information. I take this asymmetry to indicate that when an operator is present, there is less syntactic freedom.

Now let us consider [+given] topics. As illustrated in (17), it is impossible to realize a [+given] topic through SP (17a) or in the absence of pronominal doubler in an OV structure (17b): these constructions are not only inappropriate, but ungrammatical. Also marginalization is ruled out for the expression of [+given] topics (17c).[18]

(17) (My friend says: I hòn der Mario   pakemmp)
                          I have the Mario   met
                          'I have met Mario.'

a. *Der Mario   bo   hòs-o   pakemmp?   *[+given; SP]
    the Mario   where   have-CL.SUBJ.2SG   met

b. *Bo   hòs-o   der Mario   pakemmp?   *[+given; OV]
    where   have-CL.SUBJ.2SG   the Mario   met

c. #Bo   hòs-o   pakemmp   der Mario?   *[+given; marg.]
    where   have-CL.SUBJ.2SG   met   the Mario

Sentences with a focus share the syntactic behaviour of *wh* main interrogatives described above. This is fully expected given that they are both operators and are thought to appear in the same area of the left periphery (Rizzi 1997; Benincà 2001, 2006; Belletti 2001).

As was the case for *wh* main interrogatives, in (18) it can be seen that in sentences with fronted focus, a [−given] topic has to be realized through marginalization (18a) and cannot appear in OV position (18b) nor is it compatible with SP (18c).

(18) (Context: My brother says he is going out to buy a book in the bookshop, which would take him at least one hour. He is back in ten minutes because he has found the book in the village shop. My mum is amazed that he was so quick, since she thinks that he had gone to the bookshop. I say:)

---

[18] Sentences with fronted operator [+given] topics have to be realized by CLLD or CLRD.

a. EN   DE   BOTEIG   hòt-er   kaft   a/s
    in   the   shop   has-CL.SUBJ.M.3SG   bought   a/the
    puach, (ont net en de libreria)
    book,   and not in the bookshop
    'It is in the village shop where he bought the book, and not in the bookshop.'

                                                                  [−given; marg.]

b. *EN DE   BOTEIG   hòt-er   a/s   puach   kaft
    in   the   shop   has-CL.SUBJ.M.3SG   a/the   book   bought
    (ont net en de libreria)
    and not in the bookshop

                                                                  *[−given; OV]

c. *S   puach   EN   DE   BOTEIG   hòt-er   kaft
    the   book   in   the   shop   has-CL.SUBJ.M.3SG   bought
    (ont net en de libreria)
    and not in the bookshop

                                                                    *[−given; SP]

In sentences with fronted focus, [+given] topics cannot be realized through SP (19a) nor through marginalization (19b) nor appear in OV syntax (19c).

(19)   (Context: Der   Mario   hòt   s   puach   en   de   boteig   kaft
                the   Mario   has   the   book   in   the   shop   bought
                'Mario bought the book in the shop.')

a. Na,   *s puach$_j$ EN   DE   BOTEIG   hòt-er   kaft
    no,   the book   in   the   shop   has-CL.SUBJ.M.3SG   bought
    ont net en de libreria
    and not in the bookshop

                                                                    *[+given; SP]

b. #Na,   EN   DE   BOTEIG   hòt-er   kaft   s
    no,   in   the   shop   has-CL.SUBJ.M.3SG   bought   the
    puach ont net en de libreria
    book, and not in the bookshop

                                                                  *[+given; marginal]

c. *Na,   EN   DE   BOTEIG   hòt-er   s   puach
    no,   in   the   shop   has-CL.SUBJ.M.3SG   the   book
    kaft ont net en de libreria
    bought, and not in the bookshop

                                                                   *[+given; OV]

The last issue to be dealt with is the syntax of sentential and manner adverbs in sentences with VO word order. As shown in (20), all adverbs have to precede the past participle in sentences with VO syntax (for the ungrammatical sentences, see Cognola 2010).

(20) a. Ber   hòt   efter   schia   galesn   s   puach?
          who   has   often   well   read   the   book
          'Who has often read the book carefully?'

      b. DER MARIO   hòt   efter   schia   galesn   s   puach   ont net der Nane
          the Mario   has   often   well   read   the   book   (and not the John)
          'Mario has often read the book carefully (and not John).'

      c. Der Nane   hòt   efter   schia   galesn   s puach   as-en
          the John   has   often   well   read   the book   that-CL.INDOBJ.3SG
          der Mario   konsigliort   gahopt   hòt
          der Mario   recommended   had   has
          'John has often read the book that Mario recommended carefully.'

In (21), I sum up what we have seen in this subsection.

(21) a. In sentences with fronted operator, VO word order is obligatory.

      b. The XP following the past participle is a [−given] topic (marginalization).

      c. In all sentences with VO word order, adverbs have to precede the past participle.

4.2.3 *Partial conclusions*

In this section, I have described the distribution of word orders in Mòcheno main clauses, focusing on the syntax of DOs realizing new information foci and topics. For main declaratives, it can be concluded that constituents show up according to a topic–comment articulation, as in the majority of languages (Gundel 1989) including standard Italian (Benincà 1988; Rizzi 1997). Specifically, topics are realized via SP, appearing in sentence-initial position, and new information foci precede the past participle in OV syntax, as schematized in (22a). This configuration can be changed in case the new information focus is made heavy by a modification (22b). In main declaratives, marginalization is not possible for light XPs, but only for [−given] heavy topics (22c); a [+/−given] topic can never precede the past participle in OV syntax.

(22) a. topic – finite verb – new information focus – past participle

      b. topic – finite verb – past participle – new information focus+heavy

      c. topic – finite verb – past participle – [−given] topic+heavy

Sentences with a fronted operator obligatorily have VO word order and the DO following the past participle has to be analysed as a [−given] topic, realized syntactically as a marginalization (23). In sentences with a fronted operator, a topic (without doubler) cannot appear in the left periphery (SP is ruled out) nor can it appear in OV structures.

(23)　*wh*-element/focus – finite verb – past participle – [−given] topic

The description of the empirical data already allows us to take a position with respect to the results of work on language variation and change (Hinterhölzl 2009c; Taylor and Pintzuk 2012; Polo 2004) discussed in the introduction. The Mòcheno data confirm the cross-linguistic observation that in languages with mixed OV/VO syntax, heaviness favours the VO position. With respect to the competing proposals that have been set forth for OHG (heavy XPs are postverbal because they are new information foci, Hinterhöhlzl 2009c) and OE (heavy XPs are postverbal independently of their information status, Taylor and Pintzuk 2012), Mòcheno patterns with OE, where heaviness has an effect on syntax, which is, however, independent of information structure. Moreover, Mòcheno data provide support for an approach to word-order variation in terms of information structure by pointing to a connection between the position of XPs with respect to the past participle and type of information. Differently from the cited earlier work, though, the connection between syntactic position and type of information does not seem to hold universally for any sentence, but differs according to sentence type: in main declarative clauses, a [−given] topic cannot be marginalized, but has to be realized as SP in the left periphery, whereas in sentences with a fronted operator, a [−given] topic has to be marginalized (VO). In the same way, OV syntax is restricted to main declarative clauses in which the XP preceding the past participle is a new information focus and the XP in sentence-initial position is a topic. This is summed up in the descriptive generalizations in (24).

(24)　a. Word order is determined by the relations between constituents in the whole sentence.

　　　b. The XP in sentence-initial position determines the position (pre- or post-verbal) of other XPs.

In the next section, I will propose a cartographic analysis of Mòcheno main clauses able to capture the distribution of new information foci and topics in main clauses and in sentences with a fronted operator. I set forth the idea that this analysis can potentially make sense of all sentences of Mòcheno, given that—as we saw above—each order corresponds to only one type of information.

4.3　Proposed analysis

4.3.1　*On the connection between V2 and OV/VO*

We saw above that in Mòcheno word-order patterns are connected to information structure and that the position of DOs depends on the type of XP in sentence-initial position (23). Considering that Mòcheno is a V2 language (Rowley 2003; Cognola 2010, 2013a), the connection between sentence-initial position and the distribution of DOs (OV/VO) can be restated as a relation between V2 and word order, as illustrated in (25).[19]

(25)   a.   When V2 is triggered by a topic, OV is obligatory and the XP preceding the past participle is a new information focus.

b.   When V2 is triggered by an operator, VO is obligatory and the XP following the past participle is a topic (marginalization).

The fact that there is a connection between V2 and word order has been known since den Besten's (1983) classic work on German and Dutch. Den Besten's (1983) analysis draws a clear connection between the distribution of strict OV in continental Germanic and the type of constituent appearing in CP by assuming that OV is only possible in embedded clauses, where the complementizer blocks movement of the finite verb to the head of CP. Now, in Mòcheno, the connection between V2 and word order does not manifest itself in the same way as in Dutch and German, since, as we saw in (1), Mòcheno cannot be said to have a Continental West Germanic-type asymmetry between main and embedded clauses (see Cognola 2013a on this).

Even though Mòcheno cannot be compared to continental Germanic as far as the relation between V2 and word order is concerned, I think that the connection between the two phenomena also exists in this language. The remainder of this chapter is devoted precisely to showing how the relation between V2 and word order manifests itself in Mòcheno main clauses and how it can allow us to make sense of the distribution of OV/VO word orders. In the remainder of this section, I will sketch out the analysis I propose to connect Germanic-type V2 with Mòcheno-style V2.

The analysis that I propose relies on the following theoretical assumptions. Following, among others, Kayne (1994, 1998), Cinque (1999, 2006a, 2008), and Hinterhölzl (2006), I assume that the universal underlying word order is VO and that all other word orders have to be derived syntactically through leftward movements. Following Jayaseelan (2001), Belletti (2001, 2004), and Poletto (2006), I assume the presence of a VP periphery above VP. In the literature cited, it is assumed that the VP periphery has the same structure as the higher left periphery:[20] for the case of Mòcheno, I specifically assume that the VP periphery involves a TopicP–FocusP articulation.[21] Above we saw that in the high periphery both [+/−given] topics and operators can be hosted, whereas (i) new information foci and (ii) [−given] topics (in sentences with operators or with

---

[19]   Here, I use 'trigger' in an informal way, in order to refer to the requirement of the V2 rule that the EPP feature associated with Fin^0 be checked by an XP in Spec-FinP (see below).

[20]   Poletto (2006) assumes that the VP periphery lacks ForceP. Below, I will provide evidence in favour of the idea that LowForceP does in fact have to be assumed for the VP periphery and that it corresponds to the edge of the lower phase (Chomsky 2001).

[21]   In Mòcheno the order *wh*-element/focus–topic is always ruled out. In Cognola (2010), this led me to conclude that TopicPs can only precede FPs dedicated to operators, differently from what is assumed for Italian by Rizzi (1997).

heavy XPs) appear in the lower phase. Therefore, I assume that the VP periphery only hosts a TopicP for [−given] topics and a FocusP for new information foci, as in (26).[22] I assume that the VP periphery is located below sentential adverbs, given that (i) topics and foci always follow these adverbs when they appear in the lower phase and not in the high periphery, and (ii) the past participle can never precede adverbs of this class. For the moment, I leave aside the position of manner adverbs with respect to the VP periphery.

(26)   [FP **sentential adverbs** [LOW-TOPIC-P −**given topic** [LOW-FOCUS-P **new information focus** [VP]]]]

The Mòcheno facts can be captured within a theory that posits the presence of a single grammar in which OV and VO word orders are the result of the interaction between the high periphery and the VP periphery. If we assume that any XP extracted from the lower phase and moved to a TopicP or a FocusP in the high periphery has to make an in-between step in the corresponding position of the VP periphery, saturating it, we have an immediate account of the connection between the information status of the XP in sentence-initial position and of the XP appearing in the lower phase. Saturation of one of the FPs with discourse features leads to the fact that only the other LowFP is available, which gives rise to the operator–topic or topic–operator articulations. This idea, which allows us to account for the distribution of information in Mòcheno main clauses, does not, however, make sense of the fact that a new information focus has to appear in OV word order, whereas, in sentences with a fronted operator, a topic has to follow the past participle (VO, marginalization). My proposal to account for the distribution of word orders is that (i) VO has to be derived by assuming that the past participle moves (Kayne 1998; Cinque 2006a, 2008) and (ii) this movement takes place within the VP periphery in compliance with a low V2 rule comparable to the one associated with the CP periphery (cf. Poletto 2006 for a similar proposal for Old Italian).[23]

In order to illustrate how my hypothesis works, I will, in the next section, consider the syntax of the V2 rule involving the finite verb and the high periphery: the idea is that the same V2 mechanism has to be replicated for the past participle in the VP periphery.

---

[22] Here I reject an analysis that posits the presence of only the high left periphery, like that proposed for *wh* main interrogatives by Poletto and Pollock (2004). Space precludes a detailed comparison of the two analyses, but I think that my analysis is superior since (i) it allows us to make sense of the connection between V2 and OV/VO in Mòcheno and (ii) it straightforwardly captures the distribution of [+/−given] topics.

[23] I derive VO word order through head movement of the past participle, which is a consequence of the idea of the presence of a low V2 rule.

4.3.2 *Mòcheno as a V2 language*

As discussed in Cognola (2010, 2013a), the V2 system of Mòcheno is very different from that of standard V2 Germanic languages and much more similar to that of Old Romance languages (Benincà 2006), Rhaetoromance varieties (Poletto 2002), Old English (Roberts 1996), and Cimbrian (Bidese 2008; Grewendorf and Poletto 2010). All asymmetries between Mòcheno and Germanic V2 can be reduced to the fact that in Mòcheno, as in Old Romance and the other systems mentioned above, the obligatory movement of the finite verb to CP in all sentences coexists with a split CP. This can give the impression that the verb has not moved, if the DP subject is topicalized within the left periphery. In this subsection, I recall the most important properties of the Mòcheno V2 rule, focusing on two aspects of it: (i) the EPP feature and (ii) the relation between V2 and the split CP.

Following Haegeman (1997) and Roberts (2004), Cognola (2010) analyses the V2 rule as a property of the lowest projection of CP, FinP, whose head is associated with an EPP feature that forces (i) the finite verb to raise to Fin^0 and (ii) an XP to move through Spec-FinP. As in Old Romance (Benincà 2006), there are three types of constructions in Mòcheno that can check the EPP feature associated with Fin^0 in Spec-FinP: simple preposed XPs, interrogative *wh*-elements, and foci. This is illustrated in (27), where it can be seen that when one of these constituents is in sentence-initial position, subject–verb inversion is obligatory.[24]

(27) a. A puach   (*si)   hòt-se   gester   kaft   [SP]
          a book   STR.SUBJ.F.3SG has-CL.SUBJ.F.3SG yesterday bought
          'A book she bought yesterday'

      b. Bos (*si)   hòt-se   kaft   gester ?   [Wh]
          what STR.SUBJ.F.3SG   has-CL.SUBJ.F.3SG bought   yesterday
          'What did she buy yesterday?'

      c. A PUACH   (*si)   hòt-se   kaft   gester,
          a book   STR.SUBJ.F.3SG has-CL.SUBJ.F.3SG bought   yesterday,
          ont net a penna
          and not a pen
          'It was a book that she bought yesterday, not a pen.'

---

[24] Here, it is not relevant to determine whether the Spec-Head configuration between the XP in sentence-initial position is created in FinP or in a dedicated projection of the left periphery hosting the sentence-initial XP. In Cognola (2010), I provide evidence for the second hypothesis. Note that Mòcheno has three classes of subject pronouns: clitic, weak (in the sense of Cardinaletti and Starke 1999), and strong pronouns. Strong pronouns are compatible with the preverbal position, whereas clitics are obligatory in enclisis. See Cognola (2010) for a description of the Mòcheno pronominal system and its interactions with V2.

All three of these constructions are incompatible with each other: SP is incompatible with both *wh*-elements (28a) and fronted foci (28b). In (28c,d), I show that a *wh*-element and a focus cannot co-occur in the same sentence.

(28)   a. *Der Mario   bo   hòs-o   pakemmp?   *[SP–wh]
          the Mario   where   have-CL.SUBJ-2SG   met

       b. *S puach$_j$ EN DE BOTEIG hòt-er   kaft   ont net avn morkt
          the book in   the shop   has-CL.SUBJ.N.3SG bought and not at-the market
                                                                          *[SP–focus]

       c. *A PUACH   ber hòt   kaft   ont net a penna?   *[focus–wh]
          a book   who has   bought   and not a pen

       d. *Ber hòt   kaft   a puach ont net a penna?   *[*wh-in-situ* focalization]
          who has   bought   a book   and not a pen

The data in (28) above point to the fact that two XPs able to move through Spec-FinP cannot co-occur in the same sentence. For the case of *wh*-elements and foci, this is expected, since—following Rizzi (1997) and Benincà (2001)—they are both operators; the case of SP is more problematic. One way out would be to assume that SP involves *wh*-movement (as in Cinque 1990), but I reject this analysis for Mòcheno on the basis of three facts. First of all, SP expresses topicality, which, following the cartographic approach adopted in this chapter, has to be encoded in TopicPs and not in FocusPs. Then, as we saw above, when SP satisfies V2, a new information focus has to be realized before the past participle creating a topic–focus articulation, which can only be realized if the lower FocusP has not been saturated (see below). This means that SP has not been extracted as an operator from the lower phase, but as a topic. Finally, SP, unlike structures featuring fronted foci, does not give rise to weak crossover effects (Rizzi 1997). This is shown in (29):[25]

(29)   a. En Hons$_j$ hòt de   sai schbester$_{j/k}$ a puach gem
          to John   has the his sister   a book given
          'To John, his sister gave a book'

       b. EN HONS$_j$ hòt-se*$_{j/k}$ gem   a puach de sai schbester*$_{j/k}$
          to John   has-CL.SUBJ.F.3SG   given   a book   the his sister,
          ont net en Luca
          and not to Luca
          'To John, his sister gave a book, not to Luca'

---

[25] Note that in sentences with a fronted focus (thus also in *wh* main interrogatives), a DP subject has to be dislocated (the subject clitic *se* is coreferential with the DP subject *de sai schbester*), whereas in sentences with SP, the DP can follow the finite verb. Here, I cannot comment on this asymmetry in the syntax of DP subjects, and I refer the reader to Cognola (2010, 2013b).

On the basis of these considerations, I put forth the hypothesis that SP is hosted in a TopicP above FocusP and the EPP feature associated with Fin^0 is satisfied by a null operator in Spec-FinP, as proposed by Rizzi (1997) for English topicalization and by Benincà (2006) for Old Romance anaphoric anteposition. In (30), I give a simplified version of the complete structure of the Mòcheno left periphery: operators appear in the lowest part of the periphery and are preceded by other constituents that (i) are not able to move through Spec-FinP, (ii) are pragmatically topics, and (iii) are doubled by a clitic (CLLD)[26] or require a null operator (SP). CLLDs are multiple (I indicate this with the star: TopicP*).[27] The highest FP of the Mòcheno left periphery is ForceP, where complementizers are hosted:

(30) $[_{\text{FORCE-P}}$ **complementizer** $[_{\text{TOPIC-P*}}$ **CLLD** $[_{\text{TOPIC-P}}$ **SP** $[_{\text{FOCUS-P}}$ **wh-/focus** $[_{\text{FIN-P}}[_{\text{SPEC-FINP}}$ **wh-/focus**$]$ $[_{\text{F}}^{0}$ $V_{+\text{fin}}]]]]]]$

I propose that the V2 rule involving the finite verb can be replicated for the past participle in the VP periphery. As sketched in (31), I assume that the VP periphery has the same articulation as the higher one and that the past participle has to rise to the head of the lowest FP of the VP periphery—which, for the moment, I call *LowFinP* (see section 4.3.5 below)—to check the low EPP. Extracted operators and new information foci are able to move through Spec-Low FinP in the same way as in the high periphery. Topics, on the other hand, cannot move through Spec-LowFinP and are therefore compatible with operators in the order topic–operator:

(31) $[_{\text{TP}}\dots[_{\text{FP}}$ **sentential adverbs** $[_{\text{LOW-FORCE-P}}$ $[_{\text{SPEC}}$ $][_{\text{LOW-FORCE}}^{0}]$ $[_{\text{LOW-TOPIC-P}}$ $[_{\text{SPEC-LOW-TOPIC}}$ **XP**$]$ $[_{\text{LOW-TOPIC}}^{0}]$ $[_{\text{LOW-FOCUS-P}}$ $[_{\text{SPEC-LOW-FOCUS}}$ **wh-/focus**$]$ $[_{\text{LOW-FOCUS}}^{0}$ $]$ $[_{\text{LOW-FIN-P}}$ $[_{\text{SPEC}}$ **wh-/focus**$]$ $[_{\text{LOW-FIN}}^{0}$ **past participle**$][_{\text{VP}}$ $[_{\text{Spec-VP}}]$ $[_{\text{V}}^{0}$ **past participle**$]]]]]]]]]]$

In this subsection, I have introduced the core ideas of my analysis of Mòcheno main clauses as involving interaction between peripheral areas. The idea that any XP extracted from the lower phase and moved to CP has to make an intermediate stop-off in the corresponding position of the VP periphery, saturating it, allows us to make sense of the distribution of information in the sentence as a whole, while the idea of the presence of a LowV2 rule introduces a technical device in order to make sense of the syntax of the past participle. In what follows, I reconsider the syntax of main clauses in the light of this hypothesis.

---

[26] An account of the derivation of CLLD and CLRD in Mòcheno and of why CLLDs do not interfere with V2 is beyond the scope of this work. For a proposal, see Benincà (2006), Poletto (2002), and Grewendorf and Poletto (2010).

[27] In Mòcheno, multiple topics realized through CLLD are not recursive, as claimed by Rizzi (1997) for Italian topics. Therefore, this star does not indicate recursivity as in Rizzi (1997), but only multiple topics. See Cognola (2010, 2013a) on this.

4.3.3 *On the derivation of main declaratives*

In this subsection, I focus on the syntax of light DOs in main clauses and try to capture the distribution of information in main clauses and the syntax of DOs summed up in (25). In section 4.2, we saw that Mòcheno main declarative clauses have a fixed structure according to which topics are realized as SP in the left periphery, whereas light new information foci have to be realized before the past participle, as summed up in (32).

(32) a. Topic – finite verb – new information focus – past participle

   b. En de Maria   hòt-er   òlbe   a puach kaft
        to the Mary   has-CL.SUBJ.M.3SG   always   a book   bought
        'To Mary he has always bought a book'

Let us see how the hypothesis of the presence of a VP periphery connected through movement to the higher one can allow us to make sense of the syntax of a main declarative such as (32b). The idea is that in a Mòcheno sentence, the derivation starts with movement of an XP to the high left periphery (see the generalization in (25): OV/VO word order is parasitic on V2): if the XP moved to the left periphery is a topic, it moves first to LowTopicP, skipping Spec-LowFinP, since topics are not able to satisfy the EPP associated with V2. The past participle raises to the lowest head of the VP periphery, LowFinP in all sentences, in order to check the EPP feature associated with LowFin^0. An operator has to move through Spec-LowFinP as a second requirement of the V2 rule: a new information focus is realized in the VP periphery, as sketched in (33).

(33) [$_{CP}$ en de Maria . . . [$_{TP}$ . . . [$_{FP}$ òlbe [$_{LOW-FORCE}$ [$_{SPEC}$][$_{LOW-FORCE}$^{0}] [$_{LOW-TOPIC-}$
      $_P$ [$_{SPEC-LOW-TOPIC}$ en de Maria] [$_{LOW-TOPIC}$^{0}] [$_{LOW-FOCUS-P}$ [$_{SPEC-LOW-FOCUS}$ s
      puach] [$_{LOW-FOCUS}$^{0}] [$_{LOW-FIN-P}$ [$_{SPEC}$ s puach] [$_{LOW-FIN}$^{0} kaft][$_{VP}$ [$_{Spec-VP}$]
      [$_V$^{0} kaft] [$_{VP}$ [$_{Spec-VP}$ s puach] [$_V$^{0} kaft] [$_{PP}$ en de Maria]]]]]]]]]

In the next section, I will consider the derivation of sentences with a fronted operator, which constitute evidence for my account. Then, in section 4.3.5, I will come back to two issues that I have left unsolved: the nature of the lowest FP of the VP periphery (which I have informally called LowFinP) and the role of heaviness.

4.3.4 *On the derivation of sentences with a fronted operator*

I consider the syntax of sentences with a fronted operator the strongest and most convincing evidence in favour of the idea that the structure of Mòcheno clauses is the result of the interaction between the two peripheries, both of which are associated with a V2 rule.

Above we saw that sentences with a fronted operator only have VO syntax and that the XP following the past participle is a [−given] topic.

(34)   *wh*-element/focus – finite verb – past participle – [−given] topic

Following the hypothesis sketched above, it is to be expected that any XP extracted from the lower phase and moved to one of the high left periphery's FPs must first move through the corresponding projection of the VP periphery. This intermediate movement has the effect of saturating the low FP targeted by the extracted XP, blocking the movement of another XP to its Spec. This means that if a *wh*-element is extracted and moved to the high periphery, it will first move to LowFocusP, saturating it and preventing the realization of a new information focus in the lower phase. In this configuration, the only FP encoding discourse features available in the VP periphery is the TopicP dedicated to [−given] topics. However, not only does an extracted operator have an effect at the level of information structure, by saturating LowFocusP and forcing the presence of a [−given] topic in the lower phase; it also has a syntactic effect, since operators are able to satisfy the EPP feature responsible for V2. Given the properties of the V2 rule in Mòcheno, it has to be assumed that an operator (differently from a topic) can also move to the lowest Spec of the VP periphery for EPP reasons. This is illustrated in (35) for an object *wh*-element:

(35)   [$_{CP}$ **wh-** ... [$_{TP}$ ... [$_{FP}$ **sentential adverbs** [$_{LOW\text{-}TOPIC\text{-}P}$ −**given topic** [$_{LOW\text{-}}$
       $_{FOCUS\text{-}P}$ ~~**wh-**~~ [$_{LOW\text{-}FIN\text{-}P}$ [$_{SPEC}$ ~~**wh**~~] [$_{F}^{0}$ **past part**] [$_{VP}$ [$_{Spec\text{-}VP}$] [$_{V}^{0}$ ~~**past part**~~]
       [$_{NP}$ ~~**wh-**~~]]]]]]]]

The mechanism set out in (35) for Mòcheno allows us to derive in a straightforward way the ban on having two operators (*wh*-element and focus, or two foci) in the same sentence (Belletti 2001; Calabrese 1982; Rizzi 1997). It might therefore also be valid for other languages which show this restriction. The derivation in (35) does not make sense, though, of the linear word order of Mòcheno, since sentences with fronted operators are VO, whereas in the structure in (35), the past participle is in the same position (head of LowFinP) as in sentences involving a new information focus, which all have OV word order.

    In (36), I propose that the obligatory VO syntax in sentences with an extracted operator has to be made sense of by assuming that the past participle in sentences with fronted operators first moves to the head of the lowest projection of the VP periphery (LowV2), and then moves further to the head of the highest projection of the VP periphery, LowForceP. According to this hypothesis, the operator, after having satisfied V2 in LowFinP, moves to lowForceP in order to be extracted. LowForceP corresponds to the edge of the lower phase (Chomsky 2001) and functions in the same way as HighForceP, which, according to Rizzi (1997: 283), is a projection that 'faces the outside': with respect to the VP periphery, 'outside' means the higher phase:[28]

---

[28] It is plausible to assume that LowForceP has reduced properties in comparison to HighForceP. The Mòcheno data indicate, however, that the core property of ForceP at both levels is the relation with the

(36) [$_{CP}$ **wh-** ... [$_{TP}$ ... [$_{LOW\text{-}FORCE}$ [$_{SPEC}$ ~~**wh-**~~][$_{LOW\text{-}FORCE}^{0}$ past participle] [$_{LOW\text{-}}$
TOPIC-P −given topic [$_{LOW\text{-}FOCUS\text{-}P}$ [$_{SPEC}$ **wh-**] [$_{LOW\text{-}FOCUS}^{0}$ ~~past participle~~]
[$_{LOW\text{-}FIN\text{-}P}$ [$_{SPEC}$ **wh**] [$_{LOW\text{-}FIN}^{0}$ ~~past participle~~][$_{VP}$ [$_{Spec\text{-}VP}$] [$_{v}^{0}$ ~~past parti-
ciple~~] [$_{NP}$ ~~wh-~~]]]]]]]]

In the next section, I will discuss two issues that I have left unsolved: the nature of the
lowest FP of the VP periphery and the effect of heaviness.

4.3.5 *On low adverbs and LowFinP*

In this section, I discuss the nature of the lowest FP of the VP periphery, to whose
head I claim the past participle has to move in compliance with the LowV2 rule. In
order to tackle the issue of past participle movement, I have to consider the syntax of
low adverbs, which I have left aside so far. According to Cinque (1999: 101ff.), low
adverbs are hosted in the Spec position of VoiceP, which he analyses as the projection
encoding the passive voice. In Italian, active past participles have to rise above VoiceP
(after having checked the marked features in Voice^{0}), as evidenced by the fact that
the active past participle has to precede low adverbs; passive past participles, on the
other hand, can follow low adverbs (that is, remain in Voice^{0}), or move above
them, depending on the presence or the absence of a precise time reference (Cinque
1999: 103).

If the distribution of Italian low adverbs can be interpreted as signalling a
difference between active and passive structures, this does not seem to be so in
Mòcheno. As can be seen in (37), where Cinque's (1999: 102) examples are translated
into Mòcheno, both active (37a,b) and passive (37c,d) past participles in this language
obligatorily follow low adverbs:

(37) a. Sei   alua   hòn   der   spektakel   schia   uganommen
         they   only   have   the   show   well   taken
         'They alone have received the show well.'

      b. *Sei   alua   hòn   der   spektakel   uganommen   schia
          they   only   have   the   show   taken   well

      c. Der   spektakel   ist   van   olla   schia   uganommen   kemmen
         the   show   is   of   everyone   well   taken   PASS.AUX
         'The show has been received well by everybody.'

      d. *Der spektakel ist van olla   uganommen (schia) kemmen (schia)
          the show   is of   everyone   taken   well   PASS.AUX well

---

'exterior', to be understood as another sentence, in the case of HighForceP, or as the higher portion of the
same sentence, in the case of LowForceP.

In Mòcheno, both active and passive past participles remain below manner adverbs (a similar pattern is found also in French, Cinque 1999: 211, fn. 71), and it cannot be determined whether they move to two separate FPs or to the same one. For Mòcheno, I would like to propose that both active and passive past participles move to the same FP, VoiceP, and that VoiceP is the lowest FP of the VP periphery. The idea that VoiceP corresponds to the lowest head of the VP periphery has an immediate consequence for Cinque's (1999) claim that manner adverbs are hosted in Spec-VoiceP: for Mòcheno it has to be assumed that Manner adverbs are hosted in a dedicated FP and not in Spec-VoiceP, since moved operators have to check the V2-related EPP feature associated with Spec-VoiceP. The FP hosting manner adverbs necessarily has to be higher than VoiceP, given that manner adverbs in Mòcheno obligatorily precede the past participle. The derivation is given in (38):

(38) $[_{CP}$ **wh-/focus** $[_{TP} \ldots [_{FP}$ **sentential adverbs** $[_{LOW\text{-}FORCE} [_{SPEC}][_{LOW\text{-}FORCE}^0]$ $[_{LOW\text{-}TOPIC\text{-}P} [_{LOW\text{-}FOCUS\text{-}P} [_{SPEC}$ ~~**wh-/focus**~~ $] [_{LOW\text{-}FOCUS}^0] [_{FP}$ **manner adverbs** $[_{VOICE\text{-}P} [_{SPEC}$ ~~**wh/focus**~~ $] [_{VOICE}^0$ **past participle**$] [_{VP} [_{Spec\text{-}VP}] [_{V}^0$ ~~**past participle**~~$] [_{NP}]]]]]]]]]]$

There are two aspects of (38) that I want to briefly discuss. The first one regards the syntax of manner adverbs, in particular the idea that (i) manner adverbs can be hosted in a dedicated FP, and that (ii) this FP is in the VP periphery, higher than VoiceP. The idea that manner adverbs are not hosted in Spec-VoiceP is implicit in Belletti's (2006) analysis of past participle agreement in modern Italian. Belletti assumes agreement to be realized as the consequence of a Spec–Head relation between DO and past participle hosted in Spec-VoiceP and Voice^0 respectively. If Spec-VoiceP hosted manner adverbs, the Spec–Head configuration between DO and past participle could not be created in VoiceP. The Mòcheno data point to the fact that manner adverbs in this language always precede the past participle, which moves to VoiceP: they therefore have to be hosted elsewhere in the lower periphery.[29] The second issue to be dealt with is the correlation between LowV2 and past participle agreement morphology, which is missing in Mòcheno, but is present in Italian, despite the fact that for both Mòcheno and Italian (Belletti 2006) it has been claimed that the projection involved in past participle movement is VoiceP. Here, I would like to propose that lack of past participle agreement in Mòcheno is precisely what is expected in a Germanic V2 language, in light of what we find in the higher phase. Movement of the finite verb to CP in Germanic V2 languages has been connected to

---

[29] I am not in a position to decide whether this position is the base position of manner adverbs or a derived position. The idea that manner adverbs might have a dedicated position in the VP periphery might be backed up by the syntactic behaviour of manner adverbs in Romance. They are, for example, the only adverbs that can behave as QPs: *Sono ben/molto contento* 'I am very happy' (Benincà, p.c.). Moreover, in some varieties (Trentino) these adverbs have developed an aspectual value comparable to that of the German particle *wohl*. These values present in Trentino are not shared by Mòcheno *schia*.

richness of CP (den Besten 1983; Tomaselli 1990; Haegeman 1997; Roberts 2004), in particular to the fact that V2 languages have to check the finiteness feature in CP, whereas non-V2 languages check the same feature in TP. This asymmetry between V2 and non-V2 languages seems to correlate with a richness in morphology in the latter. The same facts seem to hold for the lower phase: non-V2 languages, such as modern Italian, have past participle agreement, in the same way that they have (i) rich morphology (TP) and (ii) no V2; a V2 language such as Mòcheno (i) has neither rich morphology nor past participle agreement and (ii) is V2. These facts indicate that the features connected to diathesis might be checked by the past participle in two different positions in V2 and non-V2 languages, analogously to the finiteness feature in the higher phase: in V2 languages the past participle moves to the VP periphery, in the same way the finite verb moves to CP, whereas in non-V2 languages it moves to an FP where Spec–Head agreement with DO can take place, in the same way that the finite verb moves to TP.

Now, the derivation proposed in (38) is challenged by the syntax of low adverbs in sentences with VO word order, since, as we saw in (20), VO syntax in these sentences is obligatory (the past participle is in LowForce^0) and all classes of adverbs (including manner adverbs) obligatorily precede the past participle. There are two ways out of this problem: either we propose that (i) low adverbs in sentences with fronted operators move to the edge of the lower phase, or that (ii) low adverbs move together with the past participle. Both ideas are problematic for the theoretical account proposed here, since the former implies that (i) manner adverbs can move (a departure from Cinque 1999) and (ii) an FP dedicated to manner adverbs is available above LowForceP, which could be thought of as a field (see Haegeman (2004: 168) and references there, and also Padovan (2010) for a similar idea for the higher ForceP). The latter implies that in sentences with VO syntax, low adverbs have moved together with the past participle to the edge of the lower phase, which is incompatible with my account, since movement of remnant VP is incompatible with my account of VO syntax in terms of V2. Here, I am not in a position to decide between these two hypotheses due to the lack of empirical evidence and I leave this issue open for future research.

4.3.6 *On the role of heaviness*

Having considered the derivation of unmarked main declaratives (SP–new information focus) and of sentences with a fronted focus (operator–topic), I want to reconsider the role of heaviness in the light of the derivation proposed for Mòcheno main clauses. In this subsection, I will propose that, from the point of view of syntactic derivation, the syntax of sentences involving a heavy topic or a heavy new information focus instantiate a new syntax for Mòcheno, characterized by a change in the LowV2 rule, according to which any extracted XP has to move directly to the edge of the periphery, forcing past participle movement and VO syntax. Except for new information foci realized by proper names and [+human] common nouns, which can only have the new VO syntax, all other heavy XPs examined in this chapter have both the same syntax as light XPs and an innovative syntax, which points to the fact that new and old (the one described above for light XPs) systems coexist.

4.3.6.1 *Heavy topics*   In section 4.2, we saw that heaviness does not interfere with information structure, while it does have an effect on syntax, by favouring VO word order. When realized by light XPs, [+/−given] topics have to appear in the left periphery as SPs, except for [−given] topics in sentences with fronted operators, which are obligatory postverbal (marginalization). Heaviness has the effect of allowing a [−given] topic to be marginalized in main declarative clauses, that is, the syntax of [−given] topics in sentences with fronted operators becomes grammatical in main declaratives if the topicalized XP is heavy. Yet, the fact that only heavy [−given] topics can be marginalized in main declaratives is predicted by the hypothesis of the presence of a VP periphery, in particular by the idea that it can only host a TopicP for [−given] topics and a FocusP for new information foci, whereas in the high periphery [+/− given] topics, *wh*-elements and foci are all permitted to appear. Given the proposed structure of the VP periphery, the syntactic effect of heaviness is that of allowing a [−given] topic to appear in the VP periphery, avoiding movement of the heavy XP to the high periphery.

From the point of view of the derivation proposed above, the possibility of having VO word order in a main declarative clause remains mysterious on my account, since in main declaratives the sentence-initial constituent is generally a topic, which is not supposed to interfere with LowV2 and past participle movement to LowForceP. Here, I tentatively put forward the idea that VO word order in sentences in which the XP in sentence-initial position is a topic and the post-participial XP is a heavy [−given] topic has to be made sense of by assuming that (i) the topic appearing in the high periphery has not been extracted via LowTopicP, but has moved directly to the edge of the VP periphery; (ii) since LowTopicP has not been saturated, a LowTopic can be realized as a heavy XP. This is shown in (39).

(39)   [CP **en de Maria**...[TP...[FP **sentential adverbs** [LOW-FORCE [SPEC ~~en de Maria~~][LOW-FORCE^0 **kaft**] [LOW-TOPIC-P [SPEC-LOW-TOPIC **s puach+heavy**] [LOW-TOPIC^0] [LOW-FOCUS-P [SPEC-LOW-FOCUS] [LOW-FOCUS^0] [ACTIVE-VOICEP [SPEC] [ACTIVE-VOICE^0 **kaft**][VP [Spec-VP] [V^0 **kaft**] [VP [Spec-VP **s puach+heavy**] [V^0 **kaft**] [PP ~~en de Maria~~]]]]]]]]]]

4.3.6.2 *Heavy new information foci*   With respect to the effect of heaviness on new information foci, we saw in section 4.2 that a modification realized by a relative clause (i) favours the post-participial position for a new information focus where [−human] common nouns are involved (this is ruled out when the new information focus is a light XP) and (ii) forces the post-participial position for the new information focus in the case of [+human] common nouns and proper nouns, which are OV when no modification is present. This state of affairs is completely unpredicted by the theory proposed above, since in my account, a new information focus is always able to trigger LowV2 and is in complementary distribution with a topic in the left periphery.

Starting with the derivation, the presence of VO word orders with a new information focus showing up in the lower phase has to be made sense of by assuming that (i) the topic appearing in the VP periphery has been extracted through the edge (as in (39) above), forcing past participle movement to LowForce[0]; (ii) the new information focus is in LowFocusP. It cannot be determined whether the new information focus has moved through Spec-VoiceP or not.

Why this derivation is possible only in sentences with heavy new information foci cannot be made sense of in this chapter. What has to be understood in future work is why heaviness has a different effect according to the semantics of the modified noun, which seems to point to the fact that it is not heaviness *per se* that plays a role in the syntactic position of heavy XPs, but rather the interaction between the semantics of the modified noun and the semantic contribution made by the modification. This constitutes, according to me, a main difference between the effect of heaviness on the syntax of topics and of new information foci. With topics, heaviness simply favours the realization of a topic in the VP periphery (marginalization), avoiding movement of the heavy XP to the left periphery, where all topics have to appear (as SPs) when light XPs are involved. New information foci, on the other hand, have to appear in the VP periphery, regardless of whether they are realized by light or heavy XPs. In the latter case, heaviness does not seem to play any role.

4.4 Conclusions

In this chapter, I have provided an account of the mixed OV/VO syntax of Mòcheno main clauses which allows us to make sense of variation as emanating from a single grammar in which OV and VO word orders are determined by the interaction of (i) information structure and (ii) syntactic constraints. In order to account for the interdependence of these two components, I started out from the observation that the two areas of the clause are connected, and in particular the possibility of having OV or VO orders depends on the type of XP appearing in the high periphery. This led to the descriptive generalization repeated in (40).

(40)   a. When the EPP feature is checked in Spec-FinP by a null operator, OV is obligatory and the XP preceding the past participle is a new information focus;

   b. When the EPP feature is checked in Spec-FinP by a moved operator, VO is obligatory and the XP following is a [−given] topic (marginalization).

The descriptive generalization in (40) was captured through the idea of the presence of a VP periphery (Jayaseelan 2001; Belletti 2001, 2004; Poletto 2006) that (i) is connected to the higher one through movement, representing a domain through which any XP extracted from the lower phase and moved to a TopicP or a FocusP of the high periphery has to move, and (ii) has a LowV2 rule that involves the past participle in the same way as the finite verb in the higher phase, i.e. the past participle must move to the lowest head of the VP periphery just as the finite verb does in relation to the higher periphery. Movement to the edge, which leads to VO syntax, can only take place if an operator is extracted. This hypothesis has allowed us to make sense of both the information structure facts and of the syntactic derivation. Within the proposed account the effect of heaviness has been shown (i) not to depend on information structure and (ii) to instantiate a shift in the system, according to which the past participle can rise to the edge of the VP periphery despite the XP in sentence-initial position being a topic.

In my view, the account proposed for Mòcheno is of great relevance for both the work on language variation and change and for theoretical linguistics more generally. As for the former area of research, Mòcheno provides evidence in favour of an analysis of mixed OV/VO in terms of information structure, rather than in terms of different parameter settings as a result of contact. This is even more relevant, if we consider that Mòcheno is indisputably spoken in a contact situation. Moreover, the derivation proposed for Mòcheno, which points on the one hand at a relation between V2 and OV/VO and at a connection between word orders and information structure on the other, might also turn out to be useful for other languages with mixed systems.

From the point of view of theoretical linguistics, the work on Mòcheno has led to a refinement of the cartography of the lower portion of the clause and of the VP periphery. The VP periphery has been shown to be pragmatically different from the higher one and to encode a TopicP for [−given] topics and a FocusP for new information foci, whereas the higher one allows for both [+/−given] topics, *wh*-elements and contrastive foci. The identification of clear differences between the two peripheries is a welcome result, since it speaks in favour of the hypothesis of the presence of a VP periphery, by pointing out that the VP periphery is different from and complementary to the higher one. If the two peripheries were identical, the presence of the lower one would be challenged. The second important result for the theory of the presence of a VP periphery emerging from the analysis of Mòcheno concerns the identification of a mechanism of LowV2 that affects the lowest head of the periphery, thought to be connected to Voice. Even though a lot of work remains to be done, especially on the syntax of low adverbs and on the properties of Low-ForceP in comparison to those of the ForceP of the high periphery, I think that the parallel drawn between FinP and VoiceP, on the one hand, and the identification of LowForceP, on the other, are promising areas of research and might lead to a better understanding of the VP periphery in future work.

Part II

The Role of Prosody

5

Universal Default Right-Headedness and How Stress Determines Word Order

JOSEPH EMONDS

5.1 The unity of head placement in words and phrases

Much current research involving positions of heads in syntactic domains follows Kayne's (1994) hypothesis that underlyingly they are uniformly on the left. However, most of this work fails to concern itself with unifying or even comparing head placement in phrasal and word domains.[1] Why? Perhaps because morphology specialists often propose (e.g. Lieber 1992) that particular languages order heads differently in morphological and syntactic domains, or 'components'. More generally, these components are claimed to be subject to different sets of well-formedness principles, i.e. morphology is 'autonomous' with respect to syntax, including in head placement.

As support, advocates of an autonomous morphology often focus on the ordering of heads in French and other Romance languages. In syntactic domains, which in these languages at least they take to include compounds as well as phrases, 'the heads are on the left': *camion citerne* 'truck tank' (lit. 'tanker truck'), *ville dortoir* 'city dormitory' (lit. 'bedroom suburb'), *vert foncé* 'green dark' (lit. 'dark green'). But inside a word, if a head is a bound morpheme, e.g. as in derivational morphology, it is on the right. This is interpreted as reflecting the independence of head positions in morphology and syntax, and implies that studies of head positions in syntax need not be much concerned with word-internal structure.

Once head placement in phrases is assumed to be separate from that inside words (X^0), English and French X^1 domains all seem to be essentially left-headed.

---

[1] Occasionally research of this inspiration, as pointed out by a reviewer, is concerned with head placement within words, e.g. Julien (2002) and Koopman (2005b).

Cross-linguistically however, left-headedness is not simply a symmetric counterpart to right-headedness, a fact already clear in Greenberg's (1963) original distinctions between head-initial and head-final languages (his 'non-rigid' vs 'rigid sub-types', Japanese being an example of the latter). Even in English and French, we find some obvious cases—usually not scrutinized in any detail—of right-headedness; some simple examples in syntax are subject + predicate, or measure phrase + head A or P: *three times more intelligent/trois fois plus intelligent*. These phrases in Specifiers are followed by phrasal right-hand heads X′. So not only the morphology but also the syntax of English and French exhibits some right-hand heads.[2]

More detailed investigation of several integrated morphosyntactic systems, initiated in Emonds (2009), supports a hypothesis that replaces the classical 'head-initial/final' parameter for English and French syntax and also reverses Kayne's universal underlying left-headedness. Sections 5.2–5.5 will argue that *left-hand heads result only from language-specific deviations from a universal default right-headedness*. Moreover, as part of these investigations, it becomes clear that morphology, at least as it is usually conceived, has no special principles for head placement that distinguish it from syntax.

This preliminary conclusion leads directly to new questions about the nature of head placement. If right-headedness is a universal default, (i) under which condition(s) are some subsets of a language's structures head-initial? (ii) how should these subsets be formally characterized? The key idea in my answer in sections 5.6–5.8 is a well-supported but seriously underutilized hypothesis of Nespor and Vogel (1982), namely that head placement correlates inversely with stress placement. French syntactic domains, for example, all come to have head-initial order precisely because non-contrastive stress in all these domains is on the right.

5.2 The empirical scope of 'morphology'

Prior to claiming that head placement requires no special statement in morphology, we need a relatively clear picture of what constitutes this area of 'morphology'. For English at least, it seems to focus centrally on properties of bound grammatical morphemes such as those in (1):

(1)   -al, -(a)tion, -age, -(e)d, -en, -er, -(e)s, -ess, -est, -ic, -ify, -ing, -ism, -ity, -ize, -ly, -ment, -s, -th, -ton, -ward, -y, co-, de-, ex-, mis-, non-, re-, un-, etc.

---

[2] In general, the head of X^j in both words and phrases is the immediately dominated $X^{j(-1)}$ that projects to X^j. To avoid the conclusion that Specifiers are to the left of heads, one could stipulate that (only) projecting X^k that are not 'heads' are those with Specifier sisters. But this is just an empty verbal ploy to avoid right-hand heads. Moreover, some additional statement must still say that Specifiers are on the left.

(2)   national, admiration, linkage, linked, soften, softer, edges, priestess, shortest, sarcastic, solidify, linking, criticism, nudity, stabilize, safely, resentment, links, growth, Riverton, eastward, grassy, cooperate, de-stress, ex-friend, misspeak, non-toxic, rewrap, uneasy

Linguists of an empiricist bent would like to find an 'operational test' on unanalysed data that separates out an appropriate database over which to define principles of morphology. A first proposal might be that 'bound morphemes', those defined as *not capable of standing alone as words*, constitute such a test. Formally, their lexical entries contain word-internal subcategorization features (Lieber 1980), $+X^0$___ for suffixes and $+$___X^0 for prefixes, where X characterizes the category of their host, and perhaps more information as well.

However, such a step would mean that English morphemes such as those italicized in (3) fall squarely in the domain of 'morphology'. (Hyphens are morpheme boundaries.)

(3)   *aero*-space, *astro-naut, catty* corner, *chock*-full, *cran*-berry, *criss*-cross, *e*-market, *epi-gram*, fish-*monger*, *gain*-say, *helter-skelter, iso-morph, jay* walk, low-*tech*, *luke*-warm, *multi-plex*, neat-*nik, shilly-shally*, sleep-*aholic, topsy-turvy, x*-ray, *geo-metry, gyno-phobe, micro-scopy, mono*-maniac, *necro-philia, ortho-dontic*, *phono*-graph, *sino-phile*, song-*fest, taxo-nomic, tri-lingual, were*-wolf

In practice, putative principles of morphology are not intended to explicate properties of *all* bound morphemes, for example those italicized above. These particular bound morphemes are not 'grammatical enough' to be treated in 'morphology', and seem rather to form compounds. In fact, these items exhibit *stress patterns typical of English compounds*.

On the other hand, studies of morphology do typically treat some potentially *free* morphemes, as seen in (4). Even some venerable examples of Classical Latin suffixes seem to be of this type.

(4)   able (consum-able, repeat-able), ful(l) (harm-ful; spoon-ful), like (quick-like) over (over-exert), out (out-swim), under (under-cut)
       Latin: iter 'way' (celer-iter 'quick-ly', grav-iter 'seriously')
                summus 'highest, top' (sanctis-simis 'most holy', altis-simus 'highest')

So trying to define morphology by an operational test, 'non-occurrence as a free morpheme', leads only to a contentless and inane statement: Morphology as typically understood includes the study of 'some' bound morphemes and 'some' free morphemes.[3]

---

[3] Nor does the division (1) vs (3) correlate with productivity or semi-productivity. Many items in (1) are not productive. But some compounding patterns found in (3) are fully productive (e.g. *spy store, dessert free*). Several others accept coining and certain other extensions: *e-target, fry-fest, micromanage, neophilia, screen-oholic, pornophobe, pie-monger*.

The essential difference between what tradition distinguishes as 'morphology' (1) and 'compounding' (3) does not then concern bound vs free morphemes, but rather depends on *the types of features bound morphemes express*. Chomsky (1965: ch. II) defines two types of features, giving ±ANIMATE as an example of an F of semantic content with an undeniable and in fact central role in syntax. Notice that in his system, there is *no such thing as a 'purely syntactic feature'* with no semantic content.

(5)   a. **Definition.** Semantic features F (of less specificity) with roles in both inter-pretation and syntactic derivations are called '*syntactic features*'.

     b. **Definition.** Semantic features *f* (of higher specificity) with a role in interpret-ations but no role in syntactic derivations are called '*purely semantic features*'.

In what follows, upper-case 'F' stands for features of general meaning *used in syntax* (ANIM, DEF, NEG, PAST, PATH, PLUR, WH, etc.), while lower-case 'script *f*' is used for purely semantic features. In addition an important distributional asymmetry divides the two types: *all grammatical categories* have syntactic (F) features, but *only items in the open classes* N, V, A, and P have purely semantic (*f*) features.

English suffixation in particular appears to provide a very informative diagnostic, close to an operational test, for which morphemes have purely semantic features *f* and which have only syntactic features F:

(6)   **English Morphology.** This area of study traditionally includes study of all and only bound morphemes that (i) *lack purely semantic features f,* and (ii) unlike members of compounds, *do not contribute their own stress to word stress*.

(7)   **English Vowel Reduction:** If an English suffix has no LF features except syntactic features F, *then the suffix entirely lacks stress* prior to combining in larger PF domains.

(7) is more than a definition because it claims to empirically correlate two logically independent properties (6i–ii). I use the term 'suffix' for English only for its mor-phemes μ that obey (7).[4]

---

[4] There is a division among English prefixes between those that contribute to stress and those that don't. A short appendix returns to a refinement of (7) that covers prefixes as well as suffixes.

In interesting contrast to English, French provides no phonological test that correlates with status as an affix in 'morphology' because its vowels other than unaccented *e* don't reduce, whatever the type of morpheme. French compounds and phrases (col. 1) and suffixed forms (col. 2) have *exactly the same intonations*.

[N [N rapide] [N été]]	'summer express'	[N [A rapide] [N ité]]	'quickness'
[N [a télé] [N cité]]	'TV city'	[N [a téli] [N cité]]	'telicity'
[NP un [A beau] [N thé]]	'a beautiful tea'	une [N [A beau] [N té]]	'a beauty'
[NP [N cou] [A rond]]	'round neck'	[I [V cour] [I ons]]	'let's run'
[NP son [N beau-frère] [N Roger]]	'his brother-in-law Roger'	[I sont] [A [V interrog] [A és]]	'are interrogated'

In contrast, the English combinations in (3) seem to be compounds precisely because they all participate in *compound stress*; each member has at least secondary stress. And *independently*, all morphemes in (3) also seem to have features *f* of semantic specificity and detail that don't participate in syntactic derivations; that is, none of them are 'affixes'.

We now have in (6) a definition, and additionally in English a property correlated with this definition, of what belongs in a putative morphological component. We will see as we proceed that no special 'head placement' principle applies to forms in this component, at least in the languages under scrutiny here.

5.3 Lieber's Right-Hand Head Rule in English word domains

From the perspective in (5)–(6), status as an affix (in both English and French) is entirely predictable from *the lexical feature make-up of a morpheme*. An 'affix' is simply a bound morpheme with no purely semantic features, and it has no special formal status as a category (Lieber 1992). As a consequence, we can also say that in *differently stressed* pairs as in (8), *internal category structures are identical*. Morphology and compounding don't require different types of categories or 'bar levels'.

(8)   high class, highness: $[_N [_A$ high $] [_N$ class/ -ness $]]$
      stress-free, stressful: $[_A [_N$ stress $] [_A$ free/ -ful $]]$
      deep-fry, deepen: $[_V [_A$ deep $] [_V$ fry/ -en $]]$

In these combinations, both morphemes in the left-hand compounds have some stress, while the suffixes in the right-hand words must be completely unstressed. In accord with (7), when each member of a branching X^0 category in English contributes an independent stress to the contour for X^0, as in the first of each pair above, the resulting structure is called a 'compound'. So, the factor that determines the type of English stress patterns observed in branching X^0, i.e. whether it is a compound or belongs to morphology properly speaking, is *whether a right-hand member has any purely semantic f*. In (8), the syllables -*ness*, -*ful*, and -*en* have no such feature and so do not form compounds.[5]

---

[5] A few items in English that lead to compound stress are often misclassified as suffixes. Consider the adjective-forming -*esque* and the noun-forming -*ee*. The adjectives in (i) are stressed like other compound adjectives: *cartoon-free, noise-free, riot-free, tourist-free*. The second morphemes in (ii) are stressed like some irregular heads of N–N compounds: *apple pie, Lincoln Avenue* (vs the regular *meat pie, Main Street*). Finally, the combinations in (iii) have stress identical to that in compound nouns like *steamship, battleship,* and *ferry boat*.

(i) picturesque, statuesque, carnivalesque, Romanesque
(ii) standee, recommendee, divorcee, grantee
(iii) friendship, assistantship, receivership, survivorship
     neighbourhood, knighthood, bachelorhood, maidenhood

In the perspective here, -*esque*, -*ee*, -*ship* and -*hood* are *not part of English morphology*; they aren't 'suffixes'. Rather, their features of semantic detail *f* and stress patterns are like those in other compounds. (i)–(iii) are thus compounds containing bound morphemes akin to those in (3).

The stress patterns with English prefixes transparently reflect the claim here that word-internal morphological structures and compound structures are the same, since prefixal stress patterns are like those of compounds in most cases. An appendix returns to a few cases where they are not. As can be seen in (9), in both types of combinations, the first syllables have the primary stress.

(9)   afterbirth, rebirth: [$_N$ [$_P$ after / re-] [$_N$ birth]]
      sex friend, ex-friend: [$_N$ [$_N$ sex / ex-] [$_N$ friend]]
      dry-clean, re-clean: [$_N$ [$_X$ dry / re-] [$_V$ clean]]
      speed-read, misread: [$_N$ [$_X$ speed / mis-] [$_V$ read]]

According to the extensive argument of Lieber (1980), *both* English derivational morphology and compounding patterns as in (8) are subject to a *Right-Hand Head Rule* inside words. The first lines in the following groups of examples are derivational morphology. The second lines are compounds containing bound morphemes, and the third lines are free morpheme compounds; the right-hand heads in all these types of words are in bold.[6]

(10)   a. Noun heads:
       [N [V develop] [N **ment**]]   [N [N execution] [N **er**]]   [N [A rapid] [N **ity**]]
       [N [V fry] [N **fest**]]   [N [N cran] [N **berry**]]   [N [A neat] [N **nik**]]
       [N [V think] [N **tank**]]   [N [N goose] [N **berry**]]   [N [A sour] [N **cream**]]

       b. Verb heads:[7]
       [V [V ??] [V **ate**]]   [V [N length] [V **en**]]   [V [A modern] [V **ize**]]
       [V [V gain] [V **say**]]   [V [N jay [V **walk**]]   [V [A micro] [V **manage**]]
       [V [V freeze] [V **dry**]]   [V [N vacuum [V **pack**]]   [V [A dry] [V **clean**]]

       c. Adjective heads:
       [A [V manage] [A **able**]]   [A [N stress] [A **ful**]]   [A [A blue] [A **ish**]]
       [A [V chock] [A **full**]]   [A [N water] [A **proof**]]   [A [A luke] [A **warm**]]
       [A [V stir] [A **crazy**]]   [A [N pea] [A **green**]]   [A [A bitter] [A **sweet**]]

Since syntactic studies invariably presuppose that English phrases are head-initial, the undeniable pattern in (10) leads to a dichotomy for head placement:

---

[6] The Right-Hand Head Rule applies when lexical entries underspecify word-internal structure. It thus has no effect when lexical entries fully specify internal categorial structure in e.g. exocentric compound Adjs from P–N (*anti-war, in-house, off-colour, pre-game, undersea, upbeat*) or compound Ns based on V–P such as *buyout, hangover, lay-about, put-down, stand-in, walk-on*, or *downpour, income, inlay, offspring, output, overhang*. Exocentric patterns play no role in this study.

[7] English lacks any significant class of lexical serial verbs, i.e. both V–V compounds with open-class V heads and V sequences with grammaticalized V heads. English also seems to lack V–A compounds. Though *dry* in *freeze dry* might be thought to be A, *dry* here both accepts verbal inflection (e.g. a finite past tense) and has the expected position of a V head in a larger V.

(11)   a. **Right-Hand Head Rule:** In English word domains, both compounds and morphology, open-class lexical heads N, V, and A are on the right.

    b. **Head-initial Parameter:** In English phrasal domains or 'syntax', heads are on the left.

Throughout this study, I maintain that (11a) is indeed an adequate descriptive generalization, but call into question and reinterpret the widely accepted statement (11b). After appropriate reformulations for both types of domains, I then propose a general account of these head placements. The account is based on universal principles for word order that *depend on language-particular stress patterns*.

5.4 The nature of 'head-initial structures' in syntax

For quite a time following Stowell's (1981) parametric formulation of Greenberg's (1963) word-order typology, generativists held that (11b) is a good language-particular generalization for English. But this head-initial syntax property is not uniform in English. The following patterns violate head-initial word order, since projections such as I', D', and C' (Chomsky 1986) are generally considered to be phrasal heads of the IP, DP, and CP projections respectively.[8]

(12)   a. Subjects in Spec-IP *precede their I' sister heads.*

    b. 'Possessive' noun phrases in Spec-DP *precede their D' sister heads.*

    c. In AP and PP, measure phrase NPs *precede their A' and P' sister heads.*

    d. In CPs, *wh*-phrases *precede their C' sister heads.*

The phrase-initial positions of subject and possessive DPs as in (12a–b) are too familiar to require examples. The somewhat less studied measure phrases of (12c) are exemplified in (13). Their heads (in bold) follow measure phrase modifiers (in italics).

(13)   This fence is [$_{AP}$ *two hundred meters* **long**].
     This vacation seemed [$_{AP}$ *five hundred dollars more* **expensive**].
     We should put that [$_{PP}$ *quite a bit* **beyond** (the fence)].
     The only hotel is located [$_{PP}$ *a few miles* **away**].

---

[8] Kayne and others, including myself, stipulate that Specifiers are always on the left. The definition of c-command in Kayne (1994) has this effect; in this volume he gives a different account. If one simply adopts a head-final/head-initial dichotomy for basic word orders, these Specifier-initial patterns are puzzling, as in note 2. Greenberg's (1963) ground-breaking work establishing the dichotomy in fact remarked on what he considered the non-conforming nature of pre-nominal possessive NPs in English and (a dialect of) Nahuatl. A stipulation of initial Specifiers is thus not 'natural', but is made necessary by the fact that they occur in otherwise head-initial languages.

We have in (12) four examples from phrasal syntax of head-final patterns in English, to which we can add the Right-Hand Rule for words (11a) as another example. And in view of a fact mentioned at the outset, that French treats heads in compounds and bound morphology differently, (11a) in fact amounts to two separate statements (14), making a total of six disparate patterns of right-hand heads in English.

(14) a. **English and French morphology.** In X^0 domains of derivational morphology, non-heads precede N^0, V^0, and A^0 heads.

b. **English but not French compounds.** In X^0 domains of endocentric compounding, non-heads precede N^0, V^0, and A^0 heads.

It is difficult to see how one could combine the six statements in (12) and (14) into a simple formal condition about final heads in English. We can, however, easily formulate a descriptive generalization as to when English heads *precede* non-heads. Using a concept introduced in Fukui and Speas (1986), a 'closed' projection X^j is one *which cannot further project*. The containing XPs in the configurations of (12) exemplify such closed projections. By definition, other X^j projections are 'open', and it is only in open projections above the level of the word that English allows initial heads.

(15) **English Head Placement.** Heads precede (only) maximal YP sisters (only) in *open phrasal projections X^j.*[9]

The simplicity of (15) suggests that the diverse collection in English of constructions with right-hand heads as in (12)–(14) results from an 'elsewhere' condition, rather than from language-particular stipulations. This leads to the following conjecture:

(16) **Universal Default Head-Final Order.** As a default at the syntax–PF interface, *heads are right sisters of non-heads.*

In the absence of language-particular statements, condition (16) determines a language's word and morpheme order in all syntactic domains, both those of X^0

---

[9] In addition to Specifier phrases, certain other 'short modifiers' β (in italics below) also can or must *precede heads of phrases* (in bold). Like measure phrases, these modifiers are 'short' in that they cannot contain complements (Emonds 1976: ch. I).

(i) They were drinking from some [NP *very full* (*of wine) **glasses**].
    She remained [AP *embarrassingly* (*for her husband) **defiant**] after the interview.
    Ann [VP *quite simply* (*as possible) **nodded**] when Bill asked her to marry him.
    Bill rather [VP *angrily* (*at his boss) **spoke** of resigning], and Mary did too.
    He should put that [PP *way* (*more than he did) **behind** the fence].

The pre-head modifiers in (i) and (13) have a third exceptional property. There can be *no movement of these pre-head constituents β*, according to Ross's (1967) Left Branch Constraint. Since the italicized β in (i) can't be moved and can't properly contain phrases, I conclude they are not themselves *maximal phrases*, here notated YP. This then confirms the formulation (15) in the text. For fuller analysis of the pre-head adjuncts in (i), see Emonds (2010).

and of X^1. According to (16), neither English nor Japanese have separate ordering statements for different 'components' of syntax and morphology. For example since Japanese lacks any language-particular ordering statement, *its heads are uniformly on the right* in both words and phrases. And as Greenberg (1963) notes, head-final languages like Japanese exhibit no 'mirror-image' orderings of the patterns in (13) and in (i) of note 9. As another example, English left-headed domains (15) include not all of syntax, but only *a proper subset of syntactic structures*.

Moreover, left-headed domains in other well-studied systems, rather than resulting from statements that apply 'only (or except) in morphology', seem to *cut across* any putative dividing line between syntax and morphology. The example of Chinese phrasal syntax and compounds is discussed in some detail in Emonds (2009). Based on these considerations, I claim:

(17)   No head-ordering statements pick out a domain coinciding with 'Morphology', defined as in (6) in terms of bound morphemes whose features F all have a role in grammar.

In general then, individual languages can be subject to conditions specifying 'head-initial domains' that don't conform to the Universal Default Word Order.[10] But these head-initial orders are *departures from a default* and never strictly coincide with the area of morphology or the complement of morphology. The fact that some syntactic domains share right-headedness with morphological domains indicates that the latter does not result from a 'Right-Hand Head Rule for English words', but is due rather to a Universal Default Order (16).

Section 5.9 presents some independent evidence for the claim (16) that linear order is already *determined at Spell-Out*. This conflicts with essentially theory-internal speculation that restricts linear order to PF. Although nothing in this essay requires any ordering prior to Spell-Out, a minimalist framework of bottom-up tree construction outlined in Emonds (2001) in fact provides much independent support for retaining Chomsky's (1965: 126–7) reasoning that syntactic derivations use only linearly ordered trees.

5.5 Domains where right-hand headedness is invariant

Up to this point, we have only a list of English phrasal constituents in (12) and (14) whose heads are ordered differently from those in ordinary phrases containing complements and adjuncts; something more needs to be said about these discrepancies. We must therefore ask, why does statement (15) for English stipulate head-initial order only for 'open' phrases?

---

[10] According to Lieber (1992), Tagalog presents an extreme case, since she claims that Tagalog heads always precede non-heads in both phrasal and X^0 domains. See also the last paragraph of section 5.5.

5.5.1 *Phrasal domains with uniformly right-hand heads*

The key to word order in closed projections is that they involve what are generally called Specifiers. Though this essay argues against Kayne's (1994) general hypothesis that heads are leftmost, I do adopt a stipulation that the class of Specifiers appears to the left of heads.

(18)   **Specifier Position.** A class of Specifier constituents universally appears in *fixed positions as left sisters of phrasal projections X^j.*

Based on some results in Emonds (2008), we can be more precise about what various bar notation values of X^j can accept as Specifiers, i.e. phrases that are exempt from word-order variation.[11]

(19)   **Specifier Content for all values of X^j.** When an X^j contains a functional head c-commanding its lexical head X^0, then the highest Specifier in X^j can be (i) *a subject phrase* for X = N or V or (ii) *a measure phrase* for X = A or P.

(20)   a. Subjects of predicates in English IPs and DPs:
       $[_{IP} [_{DP} That man] [_{VP} found love]]$.
       $[_{DP} [_{DP} The square wheel's] [_{NP} reinvention by Microsoft]]$.

       b. Measure phrase daughters in English PPs and APs:
       We should put that $[_{PP} [_{NP} quite a bit] [_{PP} beyond (the fence)]]$.
       That plank goes $[_{PP} [_{NP} two feet] [_{PP} under the roof]]$.
       This fence is $[_{PP} [_{NP} two hundred meters] [_{AP} long]]$.
       This vacation seemed $[_{AP} [_{NP} five hundred dollars] [_{AP} more expensive than yours]]$.

       c. French counterparts to (a) and (b):
       $[_{IP} [_{DP} Cet homme] [_{VP} recherche l'amour]]$.
       'That man   is looking for love.'
       Ces vacances semblaient $[_{AP} [_{NP} cinq cents dollars]$
       'That vacation seemed   five hundred dollars
                                 $[_{AP} plus chères que les tiennes]]$.
                                 more expensive than yours.'

More generally, a phrase with a specifier is a *closed*, not an open projection.

5.5.2 *Word domains with uniformly right-hand heads*

As we have seen, the concept of 'bound affix', central in studies that focus on morphology, is an amalgam of two factors. One factor is having a lexical entry bereft

---

[11]   In Emonds (2008) certain Specifiers are non-phrasal, notably universal quantifiers and certain degree words. However, whether or not Specifiers are always phrases does not affect (19).

of any purely semantic features. This property is shared with something like two to three hundred free morphemes *all of whose features are used in syntax.*[12] All these items together constitute the lexical component I call the 'Syntacticon', extensively described in Emonds (2000). Interestingly, this property, essential for understanding syntax, is nonetheless *irrelevant for head placement.*

The second property of bound affixes is simply that they are *bound,* i.e. they cannot appear as independent words. As established in section 5.2, this property is *independent* of any subcomponent corresponding to morphology as typically understood and is shared with many open-class members of compounds, some very far from being syntactically characterizable. The patterns of French outlined in (i)–(iii) below make clear *that this lexical property of being bound is a crucial factor for head placement.*

(21) **Bound morphemes and head placement.** Constituents immediately dominating a bound morpheme exhibit Universal Default Head-Final Order (16).

(i) *Proclitics as non-heads.* French 'clitic–X^0' order exemplifies default right-headedness inside of words. The general pattern seems to be: if a complement or adjunct is a bound morpheme in French, such as an unstressed clitic pronoun or adverbial, the heads, e.g. V or P, bold in (22), are on the right. Otherwise, these heads are on the left in the constituent containing them.

(22) a. Le chauffeur[$_{VP}$ [$_V$ *le leur* [$_V$ **apporte**]] [$_{DP}$ le   matin] [$_{PP}$ [$_P$ **avec**] [$_{DP}$ du café]]].
         the driver   it them brings   the morning   with   coffee
         'The driver brings it to them in the mornings with coffee.'

      b. Le chauffeur[$_{VP}$ [$_V$ *me* **met**] toujours [$_{PP}$ [$_P$ *là-* [$_P$ **dessus**]]] toutes les lettres].
         the driver   me puts always   there upon   all   the letters
         'The driver always puts all the letters for me on that.'

(ii) *Compounds containing bound morphemes.* When compounds contain constituents *lexically specified as necessarily bound,* French, like English, exhibits right-hand heads. I claim this is a consequence of Universal Default Word Order (16), the factor that determines that in these compounds *the right branch projects.* Hyphens in (23) show morpheme boundaries, even when spelling doesn't require them.

(23) i. English: aero-space, astro-naut, chock-full, cran-berry, criss-cross, fish-monger, gain-say, iso-morph, luke-warm, multi-plex, neat-nik, necro-philia, rasp-berry, were-wolf

---

[12] Limiting examples of such free morphemes to verbs, English *be, have, get, go, come, do, let, make, bring, take, need, want,* and perhaps a few others are fully characterized by a few features such as ±STATIVE, ±___NP, ±INCHOATIVE, ±MOTION, ±NEG, and deixis-related features.

ii. French: aéro-port, bureau-crate, choréo-graphie, grand-mère, klepto-mane, mal-heur, mi-Janvier, milli-mètre, mono-culture, pluri-disciplinaire, russo-phobie, sino-phile, télé-journal

In addition to semantic right-headedness (an *aéroport* is a kind of *port*), these French compounds all inherit their grammatical gender and number features from their right-hand members. Both semantics and syntax thus agree *the right-hand member of these compounds is the head*. We return in sections 5.6 and 5.7 to comparing these compounds containing bound morphemes with compounding patterns for free morphemes in both languages.

(iii) Bound Morphology. Combinations of stems containing grammatical suffixes lexically specified as bound on the left or the right, i.e. suffixes and prefixes, are also subject to Universal Default Word Order (16). That is, within words formed in this way it is *regularly the right branch that projects* (Lieber 1980). I give only English examples, as French morphology works the same way, and the heads are again in bold in both types of affixes.[13]

(24) a. Noun heads: [N [V develop] [N **ment**]]   [N [N execution] [N **er**]]
          Adjective heads: [A [V manage] [A **able**]]   [A [A blue] [A **ish**]]
          Verb heads: [V [N length] [V **en**]]   [V [A modern] [V **ize**]]

      b. Prefix+N = N: non-**participant**, ex-**friend**, dis-**temper**, over-**time**, counter-**spy**
          Prefix+A = A: non-**speaking**, un-**healthy**, dis-**lexic**, over-**sensitive**, counter-**productive**
          Prefix+V = V: un-**do**, un-**tie**, mis-**behave**, dis-**connect**, over-**take**, counter-**act**

Default Word Order thus yields Lieber's Right-Hand Head Rule of English words as a consequence. Her generalization depends partly, however, on a more basic and often inexplicit condition that regulates X^0 domains (Walinska de Hackbeil 1986):

(25) **Open-class projections.** The only X^0 that can project larger words are N, V, A, and P.

By (25) no functional category can be the head of a branching X^0. Therefore, if *any (non-inflectional) functional category* not itself an N, V, A, or P is a bound morpheme, it cannot be on the right, and so *must be on the left*.

(26) a. Derivational NEG items under X^0 can only be leftmost:
          de-certify, disrespect, ex-manager, inactive, non-speaking, unhealthy, untie

      b. Derivational ADV items under X^0 can only be leftmost:

---

[13] Presumably, these derivational patterns entered Middle English from French when the French-speaking upper classes of 13th- and 14th-century England abandoned that language and adopted English.

counter-attack, misinterpret, misspeak, over-react, oversleep, outrun, out-talk, re-appear

It is therefore no accident that the adverbial morphemes in (24b) are prefixes.[14] To my knowledge, only an approach incorporating the restriction (25) can make this prediction.

I now propose to conceptually unify obligatory right-headedness in word and phrasal domains. For perhaps disparate reasons related to learning of lexical words and processing of phrasal domains, the freedom in head placement allowed by Universal Grammar appears to be sometimes cancelled. That is, UG principles that depend on language-particular stress rules can have effects on head placement *only in certain X^0 and X^1 domains I call 'free':*

(27)   **Free domains.** Domains Y are free if (i) no daughter of Y is an obligatorily bound morpheme, and (ii) no daughter of Y is a specifier

Thus, the two types of domains discussed above, complex X^0 immediately dominating a bound morpheme and maximal extended projections X^1 (more familiarly XP), are not free. In these domains, the default condition (16) always prevails.

(16)   **Universal Default Head-Final Order.** As a default at the syntax–PF interface, *heads are right sisters of non-heads.*[15]

Consequently, heads can be initial in particular languages *only in domains that are free.*

A reviewer rightly observes that (16) and (27i) together prevent *obligatorily bound* derivational morphemes from being left-hand heads of words. Since this claim is incompatible with frequent statements about e.g. Tagalog and Vietnamese, the derivational morphology of these languages may require some revision or parameterization of the general framework here. For example, (27i) and/or (27ii) might be eliminated for really strongly head-initial languages. However, it is also conceivable that word-internal initial heads could result from *incorporating otherwise free grammatical morphemes* that are initial heads into following phrasal domains; something like this seems to happen with e.g. Czech grammatical Ps. Considerably more research is needed to justify taking positions among these alternatives.

---

[14] Inflections are of course typically on the right of a word, which means that Default Head-Final Order does not apply to them in any straightforward way. Section 5.9 provides more detail.

[15] The claim (16) is a one-way implication. Focus particles can be suffixes, i.e. bound on their left, without being heads, or perhaps as heads without a category they 'parasitically' receive a category from their host, along lines in Lieber (1980). Complex Qs such as *anything, someone, nobody, everywhere* are formed only in PF, alternatively realizing empty N with features ±ANIM, ±LOC, etc. This mechanism, available only in PF (see section 5.9), allows morphemes to be bound on their left without being heads of words.

5.6 Explanation of uniform French head-initial syntax

French exhibits throughout its syntax, including its compounds, a pervasive head-initial order. But its two exceptional paradigms in phrases and words are precisely those excluded from the definition of Free Domains (27). That is, *French heads are on the right in all and only domains that are not free (= 'closed')*. First, its extended projections can have initial phrasal Specifiers as in (12), though less often than in English. Their phrasal heads X^1 are thus on right branches.

Second, French compounds containing bound morphemes contrast with French's otherwise uniform head-initial order in syntax. Bound morphemes as exemplified in (23ii) are lexically specified by virtue of the word-internal subcategorization features of Lieber (1980), i.e. *aéro-* is +___N, *pluri-* is +___Y^0, *-mane* is +[...o]___, etc. As mentioned above, if either element of a French compound is a bound morpheme (those in bold below), gender and number features of the compound are the same as those of the right-hand member in isolation, which confirms that the latter is the head.

(28) **aéro**port 'airport'   bureau**crate** 'bureaucrat'
       choréo graphie 'choreography'   **franco**-allemand 'French-German'
       grand-mère 'grandmother'   **grand**-messe 'high mass'
       klepto mane 'kleptomaniac'   mal**heur** 'ill chance'
       mono culture 'monoculture'   **mi**-Janvier 'mid-January'
       pluri disciplinaire 'multi-disciplinary' **russo**phobie 'phobia of Russia'
       sino phile 'sinophile'   **télé**journal 'television news'
       téléspectateur/**télé**spectatrice
                                           'television viewer'

For the same reason, word-internal subcategorizations also force the heads of French bound morphology to be *on the right*: *-iser*, V, +A___'-ize'; *-ment*, N, +V___ '-ment'; *-ique*, A, +N___ '-ic', and similarly in English *-ness*, N, +A___; *-en*, V, +A___; *-less*, A, +N___. Because of such lexical requirements, neither derivational formations nor the compounds in (28) are Free Domains, and so both classes of words exhibit Universal Default Head-Final Order (16).

Different head positions in Romance compounds and bound morphology have been used to support a separate or 'autonomous' morphological component such as proposed in Aronoff (1976). However, this reasoning has overlooked right-headed compounds as in (28). Such compounds, outside of morphology as traditionally conceived (see again section 5.2), show that this putative division into components is spurious. Heads are placed finally in closed syntactic word domains of French, whatever the lexical nature of the bound morpheme closing the domain.

Nonetheless, in all other domains, French orders heads on the left—even inside X^0, unlike English. Gender and number inheritance show that the (bold) heads of the French compounds in (29) are on the left. Thus, if a left-hand noun is feminine plural, e.g. *Nations*, so will be the compound *Nations Unies*.

(29) English right-headed compounds: French left-headed compounds:[16]

tanker **truck**	**camion** citerne
video **cassette**	**cassette** vidéo
bedroom **suburb**	**ville** dortoir
hand**bag**	**sac** à main
ten-storey **building**	**bâtiment** à dix étages
vacuum **pack**	**emballage** à vide
steam**boat**	**bâteau** à vapeur
dark **green**	**vert** foncé
hot **dog**	**chien** chaud (Quebec French)
dry **cleaning**	**nettoyage** à sec
brand-name **product**	**produit** de marque
rail**road**	**chemin** de fer
Lincoln **Avenue**	**Avenue** Jean Jaurès
Rocky **Mountains**	**Montagnes** Rocheuses
Macy's **Store**	**Magasin** Printemps
United **States**, United **Nations**	**Etats** Unis, **Nations** Unies

(30) **French head placement** (descriptive generalization). French heads are placed on the left *in all and only free domains*.

The central hypothesis of this study, *that stress determines word order*, can now be clearly illustrated for French, because its stress system is so highly uniform. As is well-known, French stress is on the right in all domains:

(31) **French stress.** In all domains X^k, *a right hand daughter receives more stress* than its left sister(s), leaving aside any special contrastive stresses.

I now use an important universal correlation (32) largely neglected in syntactic theorizing. This principle together with (31) implies that heads in French should be *leftmost as often as UG permits*. Simply said, the language's pervasive head-initial syntax is *a consequence of its stress patterns*.

(32) **Complement Law** (Nespor and Vogel 1982). Complements rather than heads are preferred locations for stress in all types of domains.

The following statement formalizes the restriction on (31) to the effect that heads can be *ordered on the left only in the Free Domains* defined in (27).

(33) **Universal Stress Tendency** (UST). If non-emphatic stress in a set of free domains X^j (j = 0 or 1) is uniformly on the right, then to *increase compliance with the Complement Law*, heads are ordered initially in X^j at Spell-Out.

---

[16] I am grateful to S. Pourcel for constructing and discussing many French compounds.

According to (31) and (33) heads of all French phrases are correctly predicted to be initial. By the same reasoning, heads of French compounds of free morphemes, unlike in English, must be *on the left*. (Recall, this order contrasts with the order in French compounds containing bound morphemes.) In general, a language's basic stress patterns, i.e. a central aspect of its phonology, therefore determine syntactic ordering in free domains. French final stress forces it to exemplify a kind of 'pure head-initiality'.[17]

Some cross-linguistic implications. If a language has stress patterns essentially the opposite to those in French, namely its non-contrastive stresses are on the left in syntactic domains, then the UST does not sanction a departure from universal default right-hand heads. A language which systematically places its heads on the right should reflect phrase-initial stress. Thus, the careful cross-linguistic study of Nespor, van de Vijver, Schraudolf, Shukla, Avesani, and Donati (2008), showing that *a typical head-final language, Turkish, has the converse of French stress*, is firm support for the UST (33). That is, phrasal stress and word orders inversely correlate in both head-final and head-initial systems.

Japanese provides an interesting test for the UST, since it consistently exhibits right-hand heads. Informal consultations with various researchers suggest that, as expected, its *phrasal stress* is on the left. In compound X^0 domains, however, Japanese stress (taking pitch-fall as a form of word accent) sometimes falls on the left member and sometimes on the right. But for words to have left-hand heads, the UST (33) would require Japanese word stress to be *uniformly* on the right, which is not the case. Consequently, the language does not depart from Universal Default Head-Final Order (16).

As this paper's research programme is in its first stages, I chose a less than exact requirement in the UST (33), to the effect that stress be 'uniformly on the right in a given set of X^j domains'. This should allow for reformulations that maintain basic ideas while modifying their execution.

To be clear, I do not suggest that head placements are decided on the basis of stress *in each derivation*. Rather the UST uses non-contrastive stress patterns in the acquisition process to determine head placement in sets of X^j in a language, for specific values for X and j. If the stress in a certain domain is final, initial heads are considered. Otherwise they are not.

---

[17] I take it that the strongly head-initial systems of Celtic and Semitic languages reflect obligatory syntactic movements of lexical and functional heads over specifer phrases to functional head positions of C and D; French lacks these obligatory movements. Alternatively, the subject and possessive DPs of these languages don't move out of VP or NP to Spec-IP or Spec-DP.

5.7 Explanation of non-uniform English head-initial syntax

Since English Head Placement in phrases (15) is language-particular, an explanation of its word order requires relating it to *some other property of English*. I claim this property again concerns its phrasal stress contours. Observe first that in non-contrastive contexts the 'Nuclear Stress Rule' for English phrases (Chomsky and Halle 1968: section 3.8) generates stronger stress on complements. (Upper case indicates the word with strongest stress.)

(34)　[$_{VP}$ buy expensive ORANGES from time to time]
　　　[$_{NP}$ a better road IN]
　　　[$_{AP}$ so angry at her PARENTS-in-law]
　　　[$_{PP}$ right inside a vacant HOUSE]

(35)　**English (non-contrastive) 'nuclear stress'.** In phrasal domains Y^k, the right-most complement X^j receives more stress than its left sister(s) Z^i.[18]

In contrast, most English endocentric X^0 compounds are stressed on the left-hand member. This is expressed by the 'Compound Rule' in Chomsky and Halle's (1968: section 3.9). The following examples are from my speech.

(36)　N: FREE time, HANDbag, HIGH school, MEAL ticket, STEAMboat, TANKER truck
　　　V: BARtend, CHAIN-smoke, CLEARcut, DOWNload , DRY-clean, SHORTlist
　　　A: BITTERsweet, HEADstrong, HOMEsick, LUKEwarm, SUPER fine, TOP heavy

English adjectival compounding patterns are often stressed on their right-hand head, as demonstrated in Bates (1988). However, a *majority* of all English compound patterns taken together are stressed on their left member, no matter how one counts 'compounding patterns'. That is, non-contrastive stress in English compounds is not *uniformly* on the right, even if the calculation is limited to A^0 compounds.[19]

---

[18] A reviewer declares there are 'numerous robust exceptions to this generalization' of Chomsky and Halle (1968), but mentions however only one: '...more recently it has become clear that the exceptions concern unaccusative verbs.... Q: *What happened? A: A boy fell.*' Actually, stress on *boy* in this example is contrastive, but other examples with unaccusative verbs have at least optional non-contrastive stress on subjects: *The Pope just appeared.*
　This interaction of unaccusative verbs with stress is not a recent discovery. When Bresnan (1972) argued forcefully that initial stressed phrases (*What boys did the girls invite home?*) receive *nuclear stress prior to wh-movement*, a similar analysis seemed natural for the presumably moved subject in *The Pope just appeared*. These three hypotheses taken together (the nuclear stress rule, Bresnan's proposal for its cyclic nature, and movement of unaccusative subjects) then predict the reviewer's unexplained stress pattern, which is thus compatible with this paper's framework.

[19] In British speech, initial stress in compounds may be a bit less uniform than in mine. M. Sheehan gives some forms among the examples of (36) with final stress, some of them adjectives: *freeTIME, downLOAD, dryCLEAN, topHEAVY, bittterSWEET,* and *lukeWARM*.

(37) **English compound stress.** Except in certain marked patterns, English compounds are stressed on the left-hand member, contrary to the French patterns in (29).

The right-hand Nuclear Stress in phrases (35) and left-hand Compound Stress in words both conform to Nespor and Vogel's cross-linguistic Complement Law (32). In order to express this formally, I first combine (35) and (37) into (38):

(38) **Unified English stress.** In word domains $Y^k = +N^0$ or $+V^0$, a leftmost daughter receives stress. Elsewhere, stress is on the rightmost daughter of Y^k, $k = 0$ (words) or 1 (phrases).

$+N$ and $+V$ refer to Chomsky's basic lexical category features that cross-classify N, V, A, and P. The first clause of (38) determines stress inside N, V, and A compounds, but does not include $P^0 = [-N, -V]^0$. This exclusion will be justified in the next section.[20]

The implications of (38) for head placement in Free Domains (27) are straightforward. By the UST (33), the heads of words in the categories N, V, and A are rightmost daughters, while in compound Ps and all phrases, heads are leftmost.

(39) **English word-order corollaries in narrow syntax:**
   a. In free phrasal domains Z^1 English heads are on the left (initial), due to the Nuclear Stress Rule (35), i.e. the Elsewhere clause of (38).

   b. In word domains Z^0 with open-class heads N, V, or A, English heads are on the right in accord with Universal Default Head-Final Order.

   c. In word domains P^0, stress is again assigned under the Elsewhere clause of (38), i.e. on the right. The Complement Law then requires that P heads in English that project to complex Ps must be on the left.

Though heads in final position can accord with Universal Default Word Order (16), as in Turkish and Japanese, right-hand stress in French (31) and English (35) phrases *overrides* (16) so as to increase compliance with the Complement Law (32). In contrast, English compounds don't have left-hand heads because the latter would *decrease* compliance with the Complement Law.

5.8 Left-headed P^0 in English

Though Ps can project to larger words by (25), a well-justified condition (40) restricts their locations within X^0. The condition may relate to P being the X^0 category with (i)

---

[20] We can note in passing that the Elsewhere clause in (38) is simply French stress used as a default after application of the first clause. Historically, when the numerically small but socially powerful and prestigious Normans abandoned French and switched to speaking English in the late 13th and 14th centuries, they may have learned initial stress for the open classes of English words, and *otherwise simply retained French phrasal stress patterns unmodified.*

by far the smallest lexical membership, and/or (ii) no positive specification for either cross-classifying feature +N or +V.

(40)   **Open-Class Heads.** In narrow syntax (outside PF), only open-class categories (N, V, and A) can appear on right branches inside X^0.[21]

Open-Class Heads limits *derivational formations to complex Ns, Vs, and As*, as seems correct. Condition (40) excludes N–P formations such as *side-in, *doors-out, *stairs-down, *seas-over, no matter what the category of the combination. Yet it properly allows P–N compounds such as *inside, outdoors, downstairs, overseas*, etc. Such Ps realize two possible compound structures that conform to (40):

(41)   a. $N^0 = [$ complement P – head N$]$

b. $P^0 = [$ head P – complement N$]$

The structure (41a) is a standard projection of an $+N^0$ and so appears in *contexts for syntactic NPs*. In accord with (39b), derived from Unified English stress (38) and the Complement Law, stress must then be on the non-head P: dównstairs, ínside, óuthouse, úndertones.[22]

(42)   The villa's [$_{NP}$traditional [$_N$ **dówn**stairs/ **ín**side/ **óut**buildings/ **ún**dertones]] impressed us.
       She discussed [$_{NP}$ { a wooden [$_N$ **ín**lay]/ economic [$_N$ **úp**swings]/ some [$_N$ **óver**nights] }].
       He will talk about [$_{NP}$ { some old [$_N$ **óut**houses]/ the [$_N$ **óver**tones] of your speech }].

But (39b) fails to apply to the compound Ps of (41b), which means that the elsewhere case in Unified English stress (38) *must apply as a default*. In contexts for syntactic PPs, this yields stress on the complement N rather than on the head P. The data in (43), whose stresses contrast with (42), fully bear out these predicted consequences of the Complement Law (32). (I continue to abstract away from contrastive stress.)

(43)   They are going to stay [$_{PP}$ [$_P$ off **míke**/ on**líne** / over**níght**/ over**séas**]] tonight.
       Put the supplies [$_{PP}$ back [$_P$ down**stáirs**/ in**síde**/ up**stréam**/ on **boárd**]] when you can.

---

[21] Ps inserted on right branches *in PF* include *to* in *ínto* and *onto*, and those in the much-studied productive Dutch and German versions of the atrophied Modern English pattern *herewith, thereon*, etc. I further assume that *without* and *within* are not synchronic compounds.

[22] M. Sheehan observes that in her British speech, a few formations as in (42) and (43), such as *inside* and *downstairs*, are uniformly stressed on the last syllable, as is in fact the noun *outdoors* in American English. I take it that these pronunciations result from these items no longer being analysed as compounds, like *beside(s)* and *before*.

These left-hand P heads within words actually contradict Lieber's Right-Hand Head Rule, and thus show that *English has no unified position for 'X⁰-internal head'*. Rather, English heads in both Ps and PPs are on the left, exactly as predicted by this essay's stress-driven system.

5.9 Why inflectional suffixes may be orthogonal to head placement

According to the lexical theory of grammatical elements justified in Emonds (2000: Ch. 4), inflections are 'alternative realizations' of neighbouring c-commanding or c-commanded grammatical categories γ. That is, some category γ, say a plural quantifier [Q, PL], can be spelled out either in its standard 'canonical' position, say as *many, several, three*, etc. and/or 'alternatively realized' as a plural inflection on the nearest D or N that c-commands or is c-commanded by Q: $[_D$ *these*$]$ $[_Q$ *many* $]$ $[_N$ *boys* $]$. These alternative realizations enter derivations only at PF.[23] The LF interpretations of such categories crucially depend on their canonical structural positions, in the example the Q position, and not on their surface Spell-Out positions.

This bifurcation of syntactic positions associated with inflections is the same as what Embick and Noyer (2001: 558) describe with the term *dissociation*:

> These morphemes must be added postsyntactically…such inserted morphemes are called *dissociated*, since the information their signalization conveys is partly separated from the original locus of that information in the phrase marker [my 'canonical positions'—JE]…. Dissociated morphemes are not interpreted in LF, since they are *inserted only at Spell Out*. [my emphasis]

In this study, the mechanism of PF insertion is not itself really at issue; we wish rather to know how it relates to head ordering. Since this paper has claimed that stress contours and left–right order are imposed in a derivation *no later than at the syntax–PF interface*, bound morphemes spelled out on the right of words in PF (inflectional alternative realizations/dissociations) are *not* necessarily heads of words. There are then two possibilities:

(44)   **Status of inflections with respect to word-internal heads.**
   (i) Inflections might by convention inherit the category of the word they attach to, yielding a word-internal structure $[_V$ $[_V$ *wash*$]$ $[_{V, PAST}$ *ed*$]]$. Or:
   (ii) Structural items inserted in PF after Spell-Out might simply not fall under the scope of ordering principles.

---

[23] This device also accounts for many grammatical free morphemes, e.g. English infinitival *to, is/are*, etc. For example, the latter finite copulas alternatively realize under I the feature STATIVE on Vs. For details on this way to eliminate English '*be*-raising', see Emonds (2000: ch. 7).

Option (ii) seems suggested by the well-known fact, noted by a reviewer, of 'a strong overall bias in favour of suffixes, which are overrepresented even in head-initial languages'. On the other hand, inflectional prefixes, though less common than suffixes by far, disproportionately occur with head-initial syntax (noted by the same reviewer). This latter tendency may reflect (i) rather than (ii). It would be better to move beyond reiterating these well-known contrary correlations and actually analyse inflectional prefixes, so as to decide between formal alternatives such as (i) and (ii), or to propose conditions under which one might hold to the exclusion of the other.

As Lieber (1980) acknowledges, her Right-Hand Head Rule for English words, which works so well for derivational morphology, should not extend to inflections.[24] This consequence follows from the UST (33) holding at Spell-Out and PF insertion of inflections, taken together. More generally, I thus conclude that *morphemes inserted during a PF computation may appear to violate otherwise required right-hand headedness.*[25]

5.10 General conclusions of this study

This study has three main conclusions. First, left-headedness is not simply a symmetric counterpart to right-headedness. Pervasive left-headedness is in fact rare; head-initial systems are almost always partial, and in quite different ways. This asymmetry has not been recognized in generative adaptations of Greenberg's typology. But as argued here, *left-headedness always results from language-specific deviations from Universal Default Head-Final Order.*

Second, word order in both word-internal and phrasal domains is generally, perhaps always, determined by the independently defined intonation patterns of a language, rather than vice versa. It has been thought that phonology does not determine syntax, but at least *in the area of stress and intonation, phonological considerations determine head ordering.* Particularly of note is the fact that consistent final stress in French gives rise to left-headedness that is compromised only by the fixed positions of Specifiers in larger phrases and by bound morphemes inside words. English final stress, being limited as a general pattern to phrasal syntax and P^0, yields head-initial structures only in these latter domains. (Final stress in English words is more the exception than the rule.)

Third, English and French exhibit different word-order variations in the syntax of compounding, but neither *has any ordering property applying to a special construct 'morphological head'.* This study thus fits into a more general programme that no

---

[24] Hence the Right-Hand Head rule has in fact never been a candidate for belonging to a 'morphological component' or 'autonomous morphology'.

[25] For example, Japanese finite suffixes follow head Vs, even though (16) requires Vs to be the final elements in both Vs and VPs.

linguistic categories or principles belong in a special 'Morphological Component'. Even the very principle that defines 'English morphology', given in final form (48) in the Appendix, is defined entirely in terms of syntactic features and categories, and has consequences that are purely phonological. *Left–right ordering principles are independent of and more general than any putative domain of Morphology.*

Appendix on prefixes: how their stress patterns differ from suffixes

Items traditionally termed 'prefixes' in English interact with word stress in two different ways. A prefix with *an interpreted syntactic feature F*, as in (9) has at least secondary stress. In these 1–2 and 2–1 stress patterns, the prefixes are stressed like the first elements in compound patterns. Thus, corresponding to compounds with a 2–1 stress such as *spring-fresh, ice-cold, apple pie, Lincoln Avenue, iron mask*, etc. we have compositionally interpreted prefixes as in (45) with the same pattern. Hyphens again indicate morpheme boundaries.

(45)   2–1: de-plane, ex-wife, fore-tell, mis-speak, out-swim, over-cook, re-think, trans-figure, un-happy

However, prefixes with no inherent LF content at all (with no interpreted features, neither F nor *f*) are *totally unstressed* and their vowels typically reduce. This contrast is systematically remarked in grammars of Old English for ancestors of prefixes as in (46a). Modern English extends the list to other prefixes as in (46b):

(46)   0–1 stress pattern; the prefixes are unstressed:
   a. be-take, en-act, for-get, under-stand, with-hold
   b. de-tain, con-fuse, ex-hale, re-view, sub-mit

The same contrast in German distinguishes stressed, 'separable' prefixes with compositional meanings (47a) from unstressed 'inseparable' prefixes (47b), which *lack any inherent interpretable features.* The 'separable prefixes' in (47a) appear to be incorporated prepositions (Maylor 2002: ch. 1).

(47)   a. auf-stehen 'get up', ab-steigen 'dismount', teil-nehmen 'take part'
   b. ver-stehen 'understand', be-steigen 'climb', ent-nehmen 'take'

Thus, the derivational prefixes in English (45) and German (47a) lack purely semantic *f* but their syntactic F are separately interpreted in LF. The same holds of the English derivational suffixes covered by (6). Yet the grammatical prefixes contribute to stress, while the suffixes do not. Why? The only difference between unstressed but *interpreted suffixes* and *prefixes* is that the prefixes lack what we may call 'syntactic *head* features'. This term allows a reformulation of (7) that expresses the fact that these purely grammatical prefixes with interpreted F contribute to compound stress exactly as if they were open-class items with interpreted *f*.

(48)   **English Morphology and Vowel Reduction, generalized.** If a bound morpheme μ has no LF features *except syntactic head features F, then μ entirely lacks stress* prior to combining in larger PF domains.

In comparison, the 'meaningless' English prefixes (46a), like the inseparable German prefixes (47b), lack intrinsic content (= syntactic or semantic features), and so never contribute to word stress, and their vowels reduce if possible. Principle (48) thus correctly predicts that *(only) prefixes with fixed content have stress*, as in (45).[26]

---

[26] Lieber (1980) claims that a few English prefixes e.g. *be-* and *en-* are exceptionally heads. This widely cited claim has been refuted in both Walinska de Hackbeil (1985) and Maylor (2002: section 5), who argue convincingly against their special status and conclude that *no prefixes are heads*.

6

(Dis)Harmonic Word Order and Phase-Based Restrictions on Phrasing and Spell-Out

ROLAND HINTERHÖLZL

6.1 Introduction[1]

Greenberg (1963) noted that there is a strong tendency in languages to set the head–complement parameter of its various phrase types in the same direction (cf. the notion cross-categorial harmony in Hawkins (1983)). Despite this strong tendency, there are a large number of languages which are disharmonic in this respect. One of the most notable examples is German: German nominal and adpositional phrases are head-initial and its adjectival and verbal phrases are head-final. If we dispense with the head–complement parameter and adopt the Universal Base Hypothesis (Kayne 1994), the question arises which properties of the grammar (surface) word-order differences between languages can be derived from or related to. Secondly, the question arises as to which factors are responsible for the tendency towards harmony and which factors are responsible for the stable presence of disharmonic word orders of the kind found in German.

Hawkins (1994, 2004) argues that word-order properties and cross-categorial harmony derive from processing constraints on the basis that disharmonic word orders lead to centre embeddings and crossing dependencies which are dispreferred by the human parser and thus tend to be avoided. While this proposal seems fairly reasonable, it raises the question of what keeps disharmonic word orders in languages like German workably alive. In this paper, I will explore an alternative approach and propose that the tendency towards harmonic word orders derives from an interface condition on the mapping between syntactic structure and prosodic structure, as given in (1).

[1] I would like to thank the editors and Leston Buell for corrections and helpful comments.

(1) Mapping Condition to PF (prosodic transparency):
     A heavy syntactic constituent must appear on a dominant branch in prosodic
     phrasing if its containing phase is weight-sensitive.

In other words, I will argue that the placement of a syntactic constituent depends on
its prosodic weight, and since prosodic weight is argued to be determined by internal
syntactic structure, the connection between the headedness of a syntactic constituent
and its placement within the clause is derived for those languages and domains—
crucially defined in terms of phases, as will be explicated below—in which the
mapping from syntactic structure onto prosodic structure is weight-sensitive.

Secondly, I will argue that disharmonic word orders derive from the alternative
presence of an interface condition on the mapping between syntactic structure and
logical form, as given in (2).

(2) Mapping Condition to LF (scope transparency):
     If *a* scopes over *b*, the Spell-Out copy of *a* should c-command the Spell-Out
     copy of *b*.

The paper is organized in the following way. In section 6.2, I discuss the effects of the
prosodic condition in English. It is argued that the differences in the placement of
event-related adjuncts between German and English is due to the application/non-
application of the Head-Final Filter (HFF) in the I-domain of these languages.
Furthermore, it is argued that the HFF is to be derived from a weight restriction
on the mapping between syntactic structure and prosodic structure.

In section 6.3, I discuss the syntax and licensing of event-related adjuncts.
I propose a novel account of the syntax of adjuncts in which the latter do not belong
to the extended projection of the verb, in the sense of Grimshaw (1991), but constitute
separate phases. The notion of homorganic/non-homorganic phases is introduced,
which will be argued to play a crucial role in determining restrictions on prosodic
phrasing. Adjunct licensing will be argued to involve *v*P intraposition, in which the
*v*P is interpreted as subject of predication by the event-related adjunct. Evidence from
German is provided that strongly suggests that *v*P intraposition—contrary to Barb-
ier's (1995) original account—always occurs before LF.

In section 6.4, I outline the tenets of a phase-based mapping between syntactic
structure and prosodic structure within which the working of the prosodic condition
in (1) is embedded.

In section 6.5, I sketch a comparative approach in which the differences in preverbal
versus postverbal placement of these adjuncts in German and English derive from the
basic choice between *v*P pied-piping and *v*P extraction in a uniform derivation, which in
turn is argued to be determined by the (non-)application of the prosodic condition in
(1). In particular, I will argue that there are two modes of prosodic composition which
are determined by the distinction between homorganic and non-homorganic phases.

In section 6.6, I extend the comparative approach to the placement of adjuncts in German and English onto the placement of arguments in these languages. I will argue that the placement of arguments in these languages also follows from the prosodic rendition of HF effects in (1).

In section 6.7, I address the question of how it came about that German developed into a scope-transparent OV language from an older state, represented by OHG, in which it allowed for mixed OV/VO word orders, like Old English did. I argue that the variation in OHG is due to information-structural factors which strengthened the application of the condition on scopal transparency in (2) above and at the same time weakened the application of prosodic transparency in (1) in the German I-domain. Finally, section 6.8 summarizes the most important arguments of the paper.

6.2 The effects of the prosodic condition in English

One difference between VO languages like English and OV languages like German that strikes me as being essentially prosodic in nature is the fact that adjuncts that can occur between the subject and the vP in VO languages are subject to restrictions absent in OV languages (cf. Haider 2000a).

(3)   a. John (more) often (* than Peter) read the book

     b. Hans hat öfter (als der Peter) das Buch gelesen
       Hans has often than the Peter the book read

Descriptively speaking, the head of the adjunct must not have material to its right (HF effect) in VO languages. This is only possible if the adjunct appears in sentence-final position, an option that, however, is not available in OV languages, as the contrast illustrated in (4) shows. In sum, material that can remain in the middle field in a VO language must be light, while the middle field of an OV language can also contain rather heavy constituents and their heaviness alone is not a licence for post-positioning:

(4)   a.   John read the book more often than Peter

     b.* Hans hat das Buch gelesen öfter (als Peter)

Another difference between German and English that cannot possibly be subsumed under the head complement parameter is the observation that the position of event-related adverbs, that is, Time, Place, and Manner adverbs, correlates with the position of the object with respect to the position of the verb. In the unmarked case, these adverbs occur preverbally in the order $T > P > M$ in OV languages but postverbally in the exact mirror image in VO languages (cf. Haider 2000a; Hinterhölzl 2002), as is illustrated in (5).

(5)   a. C   T P M-V   OV languages

     b. C   V-M P T   VO languages

Alternative orders are found in OV as well as in VO languages. In English, manner adjuncts can also occur preverbally, if they are non-branching. As is illustrated in (5c) for German, OV languages like German and Dutch also allow for postverbal occurrences of these adjuncts. These orders are generally assumed to be derived either in terms of extraposition of the adjunct or in terms of intraposition of the vP. As will be discussed in detail in section 6.3.2, cases like (5c) represent marked orders in German, since they are connected with specific interpretations and are not possible with quantificational types of event-related adjuncts. Here we are concerned with the base-generated unmarked order of these adjuncts with respect to each other and with respect to the verb.

(5)   c. weil   der Hans   die Sabine   getroffen   hat gestern   in Wien
         since   the Hans   the Sabine   met   has yesterday in Vienna

The question that arises from a comparative point of view at this point is why it is the positioning of exactly this type of adjunct, but not the positioning of, say, higher sentential adverbs that correlates with the head—complement parameter. Secondly, the question arises how the word order in (5b) can be derived in a Cinquean approach which has adjuncts base-generated in the Specifiers of dedicated functional heads above *v*P. Various authors have argued that postverbal adjuncts derive from successive cyclic *v*P intraposition (cf. Barbiers 1995; Hinterhölzl 2004b; Cinque 2006b). In a corpus study on word-order variation in OE, it is argued in Hinterhölzl (2001) that *v*P intraposition in English came about due to a stylistic rule of light predicate raising which was induced primarily by event-related adjuncts, since they were typically realized as rather heavy NPs and PPs.

In section 6.3, I will argue that *v*P intraposition is not stylistic but constitutes an obligatory operation that occurs in OV and VO languages alike. In section 6.4, I will argue that the differences in word order in a uniform derivation in German and English follow from an elementary choice between pied-piping and subextraction that is determined by the phase-based application of the prosodic condition in (1) above.

6.2.1 *The Head-Final Filter*

The restrictions illustrated in (3) and (4) above are reminiscent of head-final effects, first discussed by Emonds (1976) and Williams (1982). The data in (3) and similar contrasts like the one illustrated in (6) can be captured by a generalized version of the Head-Final Filter (HFF), given in (8) below. On the basis of contrasts like in (7), Williams (1982) proposed a condition which requires that the head of a prenominal modifier be adjacent to the (modified) noun.

(6)   a. John very carefully read the book

      b. *John with care read the book

(7) a. a proud man

  b. * a proud of his children man

(8) (Generalized) Head-Final Filter
  A premodifier must be head-final.

It is important to note that the HFF, in contradistinction to premodifiers, does not generally apply to specifiers. As is illustrated in (9), it does not apply to subjects, that is, specifiers of I (9a) and specifiers of functional heads in the C-domain (cf. (9b,c)).

(9) a. Students of philosophy read Wittgenstein a lot

  b. On Tuesday evening I will take out Mary for dinner

  c. In which bar did John insult Mary?

In the Minimalist framework, the HFF must be treated as an output condition since notions like directionality and adjacency are taken to be irrelevant to narrow syntax. Note, however, that (8) cannot be a pure output condition either, since the difference between specifiers and modifiers is not accessible in phonology anymore. Therefore, it is argued in Hinterhölzl (2011) that HF effects should be treated as the results of a prosodic condition, given that prosody constitutes the interface between syntax and phonology and has been argued to have (limited) access to syntactic information.

6.2.2 *The prosodic rendition of HF effects*

In this section, I will summarize the arguments given for a prosodic basis of HF effects in Hinterhölzl (2011). The basic question is why prosodic weight should play a role in a condition like the HFF. A domain in which the notion of prosodic weight and its role for metrical structure building and stress assignment is relatively well understood is the domain of stress assignment at the word level.

Word-level stress is computed by virtue of foot construction parameters (left- or right-headed foot, direction left to right, or right to left, and so on), where a foot involves one dominant (strong) and at least one recessive (weak) branch. Stress systems may be quantity-insensitive, quantity-sensitive, or quantity-determined. In a quantity-sensitive stress system, a heavy syllable cannot occupy a recessive branch, as is specified in (10a), and is thus mapped onto the dominant or strong branch in metrical structure, as is illustrated for stress assignment in Hopi in (10b). In this language, stress falls on the second syllable, if the first syllable is light, but on the first syllable, if the latter is heavy. In (10b), stressed syllables are indicated with bold letters.

(10) a. weight sensitivity:
  A heavy syllable must occupy a dominant branch, i.e. must be dominated by the head of the foot.

  b. ho**na**ni (badger)   **sip**masmi (silver bracelet)

In prosody, a syllable counts as heavy if its right branch (the rhyme) is itself branching, the complexity of the left branch (the onset) being immaterial for calculating its weight. If we draw a direct parallel between syllable structure and syntactic structure, we arrive at the following conclusion: a syntactic phrase should count as (prosodically) heavy if its right branch is also branching, that is to say, if its head hosts a complement, the complexity of its specifier being immaterial for computing its weight. Upon closer inspection (cf. Hinterhölzl 2011), it turns out that a syntactic phrase counts as prosodically heavy if both its head and its complement are lexically filled. Thus, the effects of the HFF in (8) above are derived on the basis of a prosodic interpretation of the complexity of a syntactic phrase, as is illustrated again in (11).

(11)   a.   *the proud of his mother man

      b.   the very proud man

      c.   the man proud of his mother

(11a) violates the HFF filter since the head of the adjunct and the modified noun are not adjacent to each other. In the prosodic rendition of the HFF, the phrase [proud [of his mother]] counts as prosodically heavy and thus should be mapped onto a dominant branch in prosodic structure.

Now, the question arises what counts as the dominant branch in syntax and in sentence prosody. In antisymmetric syntax, the dominant branch can be identified with the right branch, the latter being the recursive branch. In sentence prosody, if matters at the sentence level are parallel to the state of affairs at the word level, the dominant branch is by default the right branch given the fact that in the normal case it is always the right branch which receives primary stress within a given domain, as is illustrated in (12).

(12)   Yesterday John visited his mother

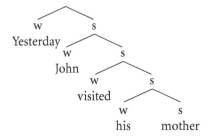

(12) shows the metrical interpretation of a simple English clause which implies that when a prosodic constituent is formed comprising the noun and its adjectival modifier in (11a), the heavy modifier should be mapped onto a right branch with respect to the modified head, as is the case in (11c).

Now, let us have a look at the prosodic status of the modifier in (11b). In syllable structure, as mentioned above, the complexity of the onset is irrelevant for computing the metrical status of a syllable. Drawing a parallel between syllable structure and syntactic structure, we can thus assume that a constituent that combines a head and a specifier (in its extended projection), even if the latter is complex, does not yield a phrase that counts as prosodically heavy. Thus, the prosodic approach provides a good motivation for the HFF.

Since in recent accounts of modification, modifiers are treated as specifiers of functional heads in the extended projection of the modified category (cf. Cinque 1999), I assume that the Head-Final Filter applies to (all) specifiers in a given domain. Thus, we arrive at the following prosodic rendition of HF effects.

(13)   Prosodic Version of the HFF:
        A Specifier within a given domain that constitutes a heavy syntactic constituent must appear on the right branch with respect to the selecting/modified head (to occupy a dominant branch in prosodic structure) if the mapping between syntax and prosody is weight-sensitive in this domain.

The condition in (13) allows the extension of head-final effects (from modifiers) to complements that have been moved into the prenominal/preverbal domain in the course of the derivation in an antisymmetric approach to the syntax of OV and VO languages to which I will turn in section 6.6. In the following section, I will discuss in more detail the syntax of event-related adjuncts in German.

6.3 The licensing of event-related adjuncts

In this section, I would like to address the question of why the syntax of adjuncts should require *v*P intraposition. To my knowledge, Barbiers (1995) was the first to propose that postverbal adjuncts in OV languages are due to *v*P intraposition. His approach is very similar to the approach that I will adopt in this paper (cf. Hinterhölzl 2009a for the details). Barbiers argues that *v*P intraposition is semantically motivated and targets a specifier position within the adjunct PP. Pearson (2000) proposed that postverbal arguments and adjuncts in Malagasy are derived via *v*P intraposition, which serves to identify the categorial nature of functional heads in the extended projection of the verb. This approach is adopted and generalized by Cinque (2006b).

6.3.1 *Superimposed predication*

My approach differs from the two approaches above in that it is assumed that adjuncts do not belong to the extended projection of the verb but constitute separate projections. *v*P intraposition is argued to serve a licensing purpose which involves the establishment of a predication relation. In this respect, my account can be seen as a version of Barbiers' original proposal, which is, however, cast in a more elaborate syntactic framework involving phases and subphases, as we will see below.

In the standard account of modification, it is assumed that adjuncts are adjoined to the maximal category of the head they modify. Thus, the attachment site of the adjunct is determined by its interpretation (it minimally has to attach to the constituent it modifies). Secondly, the syntactic operation of adjunction is interpreted as set intersection, which leads to the identification of the individual variables introduced by adjunct and modified head, as is illustrated in (14).

(14)   a. meet in the park

     b. $[_{VP} [_{VP} V(e_1)] PP (e_2)]^2$

     c. identification: $e_1 = e_2 \rightarrow$ there is an event e such that meet (e) & in the park (e)

As noted above, in Cinque's (1999) proposal adjuncts are introduced as specifiers of functional heads that are ordered according to a universal hierarchy in the extended projections of the modified head. Cinque's proposal can thus be taken to provide an alternative response to the question of how adjuncts are to be attached to the head they modify, but it fails to address the question of how the individual variables of adjunct and modified head are identified.

In other words, if we want to dispense with adjunction altogether, we must address the question of how an adjunct, being base-generated as the specifier of a functional head, is interpreted and how, for instance, the event variable of the verb is identified with the individual variable of an adjunct that sits higher up in the tree in the specifier of a functional head, possibly separated from the verb by various heads dedicated to the licensing of the arguments of the verb.

I would like to make the following proposal. The adjunct introduced as the specifier of a functional head is interpreted as a predicate on the category it is taken to modify in the standard theory. Assuming that every predicate provides a licensing domain for its arguments, introducing an adjunct in the functional skeleton of CP (or DP) will always involve two functional heads: the one that introduces the adjunct as an additional predicate (called F1 in (15)) and the other that licenses the argument of this predicate (called F2 in (15)). In the course of the derivation *v*P moves into Spec-F2 and the two individual variables are identified via predication, with the *v*P acting as subject of the predication, as is illustrated in (15). In this approach, the semantic interpretation of event-related adjuncts as predicates on the verb (phrase) is already represented in the syntax as a derived subject–predicate relation between *v*P and the adjunct.

(15)   a. $[[_{VP} V (e_1)] F2 [PP (e_2) \; F1 \ldots [t_{VP}]]]$

     b. $[[_{NP} N (y)] F2 [AP (x) \; F1 \ldots [t_{NP}]]]$

---

[2] Davidson (1967) argued that events should be treated as referential entities in the logical description of sentences (cf. also Higginbotham 1985, Parsons 1990, and Kratzer 1995 for applications of this proposal).

In this approach, the vP acts both as a predicate and as a subject. One would expect that a constituent cannot have these very different functions within the same domain. In a phase-based framework, we could assume, however, that the vP obtains these different roles in different phases in the clause. Therefore, I would like to propose that F1 and F2 in (15) constitute projections of a separate phase and are not considered as being part of the extended projection of the verb. F1 introduces an additional predicate in the clause (or DP) that has its own licensing domain, namely F2. In other words, Spec-F2 can be compared with Spec-IP in the clause. vP intraposition, therefore, has to be considered as a case of A-movement that serves to license the adjunct as a (secondary) predicate (some evidence for the assumption that vP intraposition is a case of A-movement is given in Hinterhölzl (2009a).

That the projections F1 and F2 and their respective Specifiers constitute separate phases follows from the following typology of phases. I propose that the main phases (the CP in the clausal domain and the DP in the nominal domain) comprise the following subphases: a predicate domain (roughly the vP in the clause) that intro- duces a predicate and its arguments, the I-domain, in which the (properties of the) arguments of the predicate are licensed, and a C-domain (or completing domain) that embeds the predicate in another clause or in the relevant context. I will call these sub-phases *homorganic,* since they are projected by the same phase predicate, as is illustrated in (16).

(16)   Homorganic subphases within the CP
        [CP completing domain] [IP licensing domain] [vP predicate domain]

According to this typology, adjuncts comprise a predicate domain and an I-domain but lack a completing domain, which bars them from being embedded like comple- ments. Instead of being embedded they are superimposed in the I-domain of another predicate. To be licensed event-related adjuncts must enter into a predication relation with the vP in the clause. It also follows from the above typology that the subphases of adjuncts are non-homorganic with respect to the subphases of the predicate they modify.

Since in modern approaches to temporal interpretation, Tense is analysed as a predicate that locates the event time of the vP with respect to a given reference time, I propose that this temporal predicate and its projections form their own sub-phases (which are non-homorganic with respect to the phases projected by the verb) in the I-domain of the verb (cf. (17)).

(17)   Non-homorganic subphases within IP
        [[T-domain] [Adjunct-domain] ... [Adjunct-domain]]

To summarize, vP intraposition is triggered by the licensing requirement of adjuncts. The intraposed vP acts as the subject of predication. To this end, I have proposed that the

I-domain in the clause is interspersed with non-homorganic subphases that are projected by event-related adjuncts and Tense, as is illustrated in (17).

6.3.2 *Against vP intraposition at LF*

The present proposal is similar to Barbiers' (1995) account in proposing that, (a) vP intraposition is responsible for postverbal occurrences of event-related adjuncts (cf. (18a,b)) and (b) that vP intraposition is semantically triggered. In his account, vP movement occurs to establish a qualification relation between vP and PP which requires a configuration of mutual immediate c-command between these elements. This is achieved by moving the vP into Spec-PP, as is illustrated in (18c).

(18) a. Jan heeft   [in de tuin]   gewerkt
          John has   in the garden   worked

      b. Jan heeft   gewerkt   [in de tuin]
          John has   worked   in the garden

      c. Jan heeft [$_{PP}$ gewerkt [$_{PP}$ in the tuin]] t$_{vP}$

If the vP moves into Spec-PP in covert syntax, the non-extraposed order in (18a) is derived. In short, in Barbiers' account, vP movement serves to establish a qualification relation, but this can be done in syntax or by movement at LF. I see one major problem with Barbiers' original proposal: in his account, no interpretative differences between intraposed and non-intraposed vP are to be expected.

The problem with this LF-based account is that the intraposed and non-intraposed versions are often not identical in their readings, at least in German. The postverbal PP in (19b) cannot be interpreted as being in the scope of the adverbial *often*, as it has to be interpreted in (19a), and is interpreted obligatorily as a frame adverbial (*when he is in the coffee house, Hans often sits*).

(19) a. weil Hans   oft   im Kaffeehaus   sitzt
          since Hans   often   in-the coffee.house   sits

      b. weil   Hans oft   sitzt   im Kaffeehaus
          since   Hans often   sits   in-the coffee.house

Second, non-referential adjuncts are generally bad in postverbal position in German and quantified PPs lead to ungrammaticality, as is illustrated in (20). One possible explanation for the ungrammaticality of (20b) is that the quantifier in postverbal position fails to bind the variable in the vP due to lack of c-command (cf. Haider 1993).

(20) a. weil Hans   in keinem Garten   arbeitet
          since Hans   in no   garden   works

      b. *weil Hans   arbeitet   in keinem Garten
          since Hans   works   in no   garden

Note that this explanation is not open to Barbiers (1995), since in the relevant qualification relation the PP c-commands the *v*P in his account. For sure, Barbiers' account must be revised to do justice to the German data; the question is only whether an LF-based account is appropriate for these data in the first place, since the restrictions illustrated in (19)–(20) are induced prosodically, as I will argue in section 6.4.3 below. As an alternative, I propose that *v*P intraposition always takes place in overt syntax with the different orders following from an elementary choice in the syntax, namely *v*P extraction versus *v*P pied-piping, as is discussed in detail in the section 6.5. Before that, I would like to outline some basic assumptions about the syntax–phonology interface within which the prosodic condition in (1) is embedded and which will be argued to decide whether the extraction or pied-piping option is taken in section 6.5.

6.4 Phases and modes of prosodic composition

In this section, I will outline an account of the derivation of prosodic structure from syntactic structure that is based on a metrical evaluation of the syntactic tree plus relation-based formation rules that build prosodic phrases around lexical heads, as originally proposed by Nespor and Vogel (1986), but operate independently of directionality parameters.

6.4.1 *Metrical structure and rules for prosodic domain formation*

If a syntactic tree is metrically interpreted as illustrated in (12) above and repeated for convenience in (21), the nuclear accent of the clause is correctly determined as the most prominent element in the tree, that is, main stress falls on the noun *mother* within the direct object in (21), simply by treating the right syntactic branch as the strong branch in metrical structure.

(21)   Yesterday John visited his mother

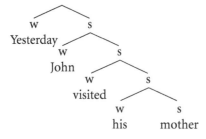

This metrical interpretation can also be used to determine the heads of prosodic constituents. For instance *mother* will be the head of the prosodic constituent (his mother) and *his mother* will be the head of the prosodic constituent (visited his mother) which constitutes the basis for assigning stress within a given prosodic domain.

But the metrical interpretation of a syntactic tree alone will not derive the correct prosodic phrasing of a sentence, since phrasing depends on distinctions that involve the relation between a head and a complement or between a head and an adjunct. For instance, in German a head and a complement form a joint phonological phrase, while a head and an adjacent adjunct are obligatorily phrased into separate phonological phrases, as is illustrated in (22).

(22) a. [(weil Hans)   (im ZELT   blieb)]
         since John   in-the tent remained
         'since John remained in the tent'

     b. [(weil Hans)   (im Zelt)   (RAUCHTE)]
         since John   in-the tent smoked
         'since John smoked in the tent'

As is also evident in (22), phrasing also has an influence on where the main accent in the clause is placed. While in (22a) main stress falls on the PP complement, main stress is placed on the verb in clause-final position in (22b), indicating that main stress in the clause falls into the last phonological phrase within the intonational phrase in German (cf. the head peripherality principle in (31) below). If prosody has access to the different syntactic status of complements, specifiers, and adjuncts, then specific mapping rules can be formulated for the prosodic composition of a head with these constituents.

Within this general approach, Wagner (2005) proposes that there are two modes of prosodic composition to account for the differences in prosodic phrasing between German and English, illustrated in (23). While in German the complement of the verb must form a joint prosodic constituent with the verb, in English, verb and complement can either form separate phonological phrases or the verb can restructure with its complement. To account for this difference, Wagner proposes two prosodic operations, namely subordination and sister-matching which are defined directionally. In his system, subordination involves obligatory restructuring of the verb into the phonological phrase of the *preceding* argument only, while sister matching applies to a verb and the argument to its right as given in (23c), allowing for optional restructuring, as indicated in (23b).

(23) a. [(weil Hans)   (das Buch las)]
         since Hans   the book read

     b. [(since John) (read   the book)]

     c. [(since John) (read) (the book)]

In the framework that I have been adopting, complements (internal arguments), subjects, and modifiers all occupy specifiers in the extended projection of the verb in OV languages, so that prosody cannot make use of these syntactic distinctions. Also, directionality parameters like those used by Wagner (2005) should be obviated in an LCA-based system.

As an alternative, I have proposed two modes of prosodic composition which are phase-based and illustrated in (24). Subordination pertains to a lexical head and its arguments—irrespective of their order—that is, to elements that belong to homorganic phases, while coordination applies to a lexical head and a modifier, that is, to elements that belong to non-homorganic phases.

(24)   Modes of prosodic composition (cf. Hinterhölzl 2009a)
      a. subordination: (DP) + V → ((DP) V)
      b. coordination: (PP) & V → (PP) (V)

(24a) is meant to indicate that if a head and an argument are combined, the result is a single phonological phrase that contains the head as prosodic word and the argument as a phonological phrase. Note that the resultant prosodic constituent is recursive. Also note that if another argument is joined with such a prosodic constituent the resultant constituent is recursive as well, as is illustrated in (24c). (24c) also indicates that subordination is taken to work independently of directionality. The only requirement is that the two elements are adjacent in the syntactic tree.

(24)   c. a subcase of subordination: combining two DP arguments with its head
        ((DP) ((DP) V)) or ((V (DP)) (DP))

(24b) is meant to indicate that if a head and an adjacent adjunct are combined, the result is two independent phonological phrases that may be joined at the next prosodic level, namely in the intonational phrase. Prosodic constituents need to be headed. I assume that there are two types of heading procedures, as is illustrated in (25). Intrinsic heading is only possible if two prosodic constituents are asymmetric, as is the case in subordination. Extrinsic heading is the default procedure and makes use of tree geometry.

(25)   a. intrinsic heading:
        In the combination of a phonological phrase with a prosodic word, the phonological phrase is metrically strong and the prosodic word is metrically weak. (This property will also be called strength sensitivity below.)

      b. extrinsic heading (default value):
        In a prosodic constituent (A B), the right-hand member is metrically strong.

For German, intrinsic heading must be assumed to derive the correct assignment of main stress in the parallel sentence, as is illustrated in (26). (26) shows the prosodic phrasing combined with a metrical evaluation after the syntactic derivation is completed. The phrasing of the complementizer is left unspecified in (26). It will restructure with the adjacent DP in a later stage of the derivation, in phonology proper. In (26), the most deeply embedded phonological phrase is intrinsically headed; all other phrases are extrinsically headed according to their position in the tree.

(26) a. weil   der Hans   das Buch   las
         since   the Hans   the book   read

      b. weil (w(der Hans) s(s(das Buch) w las))

The mapping of syntactic structure onto prosodic structure defined in (24) and (25) above, derives a recursive prosodic pattern in the case of subordination and a rather flat prosodic pattern in the case of coordination. Subordinated phrases are headed, as is indicated by the annotated metrical labels in (26b). Coordinated phrases, being in a symmetrical relationship, are not headed and require an extra mechanism that applies in prosody proper.

   In conclusion, the result of the mapping between syntax and phonology is a set of phonological phrases, some of which, namely the recursive ones, are metrically annotated.

6.4.2 *Further operations in prosody proper*

The initial prosodic structure derived by the operations of subordination and coordination in the interface needs to be further worked upon in prosody proper. First, recursive phonological phrases need to be flattened and among the coordinated phonological phrases a head for the containing intonational phrase needs to be determined to provide the basis for stress assignment within the clause. It is important to note that the recursive prosodic structures created by subordination violate the Strict Layer Hypothesis (cf. Selkirk 1984; Nespor and Vogel 1986). Note that Ladd (1986), Selkirk (1995), Peperkamp (1997), and Truckenbrodt (1999) provide arguments for the availability of recursive prosodic structures in certain languages.

   Here I propose that syntax derives an initial recursive prosodic phrasing which at phonology proper is flattened by language-specific rules that delete either outer or inner boundaries according to global prosodic parameters like rhythm, length, and branchingness of constituents and the like. In the normal case, this means that a sentence like (26a) is phrased as given in (27a). This can be achieved by deleting all the outer boundaries but the last and by restructuring of weakly marked elements with an adjacent phonological phrase. The crucial question now becomes what disallows the prosodic phrasing in (27b).

(27) a. (weil der Hans) (das Buch las)

      b. (weil der Hans) (das Buch) (las)

      c. (weil der Hans) (das Buch) las

The bracketing of (27b) is derived if all outer boundaries are deleted, as is indicated in (27c), and the prosodic word comprising the verb is included in a phonological phrase of its own, as demanded by the Strict Layer Hypothesis.

In prosody proper, every phonological phrase is assigned an accent tone (which falls on the metrically most prominent syllable in its domain) and is marked with an asterisk. Also, the head of the intonational phrase must be determined in phonology proper, if the iP contains several coordinated phonological phrases. For this purpose, I will propose a metrical version of Uhmann's (1993) rule of final accent reinforcement, which I call Rule of Strength Assignment (RSA) in (28) and illustrated in (29).

(28)   Rule of Strength Assignment within iP:
        If an intonational phrase contains several phonological phrases, the rightmost
        is assigned the metrical value s, all others are assigned the value *w*.

RSA ensures that there is a prosodic constituent within the intonational phrase that is more prominent than other coordinated constituents. Since the direct object, the locative modifier, and the verb are mapped onto separate phonological phrases according to (24) above, all these phrases contain a phrasal accent, illustrated by the beat on the third line in metrical grid representation in (29). Due to strength assignment by the RSA, main stress is correctly assigned to the most prominent element in the final phonological phrase containing the verb.

(29)   *   *   *   *
        [^{w}(Hans) ^{w}(hat die Maria) ^{w}(in Wien) ^{s}(beSUcht)]
          Hans   has the Maria   in Vienna visited

After determination of the head of the intonational phrase, we derive the following accentuation/metrical patterns for the phrasings in (27a,b), as given in (30a,b), respectively.

                    *   *   *
(30)   a. ^{w}(weil der Hans) ^{w}(der Maria) ^{s}(das Buch gab)
                    *   *   *   *
        b. ^{w}(weil der Hans) ^{w}(der Maria) ^{s}(das Buch) ^{w}(gab)

(30a) constitutes the correct accent pattern for a wide-focus sentence, since the metrical labels correctly determine that main stress falls on the last phonological phrase within the intonational phrase (iP), while in (30b), main stress falls on a constituent that does not occupy the right edge of the iP. Thus, the phrasing in (30b) can be ruled out, since it violates a natural requirement on the headedness of prosodic phrases, given in (31).

(31)   Head Peripherality Principle (HPC):
        Main stress must fall on the rightmost phonological phrase within iP.

On the other hand, no problem arises in this respect in English, since in either case main stress falls on the metrically strong complement in clause-final position. I thus conclude that subordination is not directionally constrained, but that independent factors, namely the complex interaction between prosodic phrasing, metrical structure, and stress assignment, require that the verb in clause-final position always forms a prosodic constituent with an adjacent argument.

To conclude, prosodic domain formation can be thought to proceed in a bottom-up fashion, in parallel with the syntactic derivation, starting with the lexical heads V, N, A, and adverbs, by joining arguments and adjuncts according to their phase status. In this stepwise process, guided by phases, prosodic conditions may apply to the current output of the syntactic computation, in the sense that Spell-Out options can be fixed, as we will see in section 6.6 below.

In the following section, I will discuss how prosodic constraints interact with the licensing of event-related modifiers in German and English. Here the proposal will be that prosodic conditions decide whether the pied-piping or the extraction option is taken by the operation of *v*P intraposition.

6.5 Accounting for the comparative dimension

If the account of adjunct licensing sketched in section 6.3 above is correct, then *v*P movement in the clause has to be taken to occur in OV and VO languages alike, and word-order differences in OV and VO languages should follow from an elementary choice connected to *v*P intraposition. In the following, I will argue that this basic choice involves *v*P extraction or pied-piping induced by *v*P movement.

Given the universal hierarchy of event-related adjuncts sketched in (5a), an English sentence like (32a) is derived from the base structure in (32b) in the following way. First, the *v*P containing the verb and its arguments moves into a Specifier above the locative PP (32c), then the resulting structure is moved into a Specifier above the temporal PP (32d) and in the final step the subject is extracted to be licensed in Spec-TP or an appropriate Agreement position above TP, as is indicated in (32e).

(32)   a. John visited them in Vienna on Friday

       b. [... [on Friday [in Vienna [$_{vP}$ John visited them]]]]

       c. [... [on Friday [[$_{vP}$ John visited them] in Vienna t$_{vP}$]]]

       d. [... [[$_{vP}$ John visited them] in Vienna] on Friday]

       e. [$_{IP}$ John$_i$ [[[[$_{vP}$ t$_i$ visited them]$_k$ in Vienna t$_k$]$_j$ on Friday t$_j$]]]

In this derivation, I have tacitly assumed that in a VO language like English the *v*P pied-pipes the relevant PPs at each step. However, this is just one option; the *v*P could also extract at each step. I will argue that this is generally the case in OV languages, where *v*P movement leaves the original order of adjuncts intact, and that it also occurs in VO languages, when the order of adjuncts is not permuted, as in (33).

(33)   Sue met Mary on each man's birthday at his house.

This account raises several questions. First, there is the issue of which factors decide which option is taken. This issue will be addressed in section 6.5.2. Second, if the vP extracts at each step in the process of licensing adjuncts in the middle field in OV languages, then there must be an additional step that moves the entire middle field in front of the vP again before the end of the derivation. This issue will be addressed in the following section.

6.5.1 *TP movement and vP movement into the C-domain*

In Hinterhölzl (2006), it is proposed on the basis of restructuring infinitives that the extended vP (AspP)[3] and the TP undergo licensing movement into the C-domain in German, as is illustrated in (34). These movements are argued to follow from a general theory of sentential complementation, in which the complementizer acts as a place-holder for the selectional requirements of the matrix verb. In particular, it is argued that movement of the AspP into FinP (cf. Rizzi 1997) (called Status phrase in Hinterhölzl 2006) serves to check the morphological subcategorization of the matrix verb and that movement of the TP into MoodP serves to temporally link the embedded event to the matrix event time. In (34), ForceP encodes clausal force and represents the highest head in the C-domain.

(34)   a. base structure

$[_{CP=\ FP}$ Force $[_{MP}$ Mood $[_{FinP}$ Fin $[_{TP}$ T $[_{AspP}$ V $]]]]]$

   b. finiteness

$[_{CP=\ FP}$ Force $[_{MP}$ Mood $[_{FinP}\ [_{AspP}$ V $]$ Fin $[_{TP}$ T $]]]]$

   c. temporal anchoring

$[_{CP=\ FP}$ Force $[_{MP}\ [_{TP}$ T $]$ M $[_{FinP}\ [_{AspP}$ V $]$ Fin $]]]$

In this paper, I propose that this account be extended to non-restructuring contexts. In particular, I propose that the dependency relations between C and T (cf. Chomsky 2008) and between Fin and v (cf. Rizzi 1997) are embodied via XP movement of TP and AspP into the C-domain in English and German. The rationale behind these movements is that different speech acts (forces) are connected with different verbal moods that determine the situational and temporal anchoring of the event in TP and different verbal moods select different finite and non-finite verbal forms that are expressed in the V-domain.

---

[3] In Hinterhölzl (2006) it is argued on the basis of VP topicalization data that AspP constitutes the edge of the V-domain. As will become evident below, I propose that there is an AspP in the V-domain that defines different event types (cf. Vendler 1967) and that there is an AspP in the T-domain (so-called viewpoint aspect) which together with an abstract Tense predicate defines different Tenses (cf. Smith 1991; Kratzer 1998). For example, the English simple past tense (as in *Peter ran*) expresses both past tense and perfective viewpoint.

On its way to the C-domain the extended *v*P moves into the specifier of (view-point) Aspect in the T-domain, as is illustrated in (35). I will argue in the following section that interface conditions determine that the extended *v*P pied-pipes the containing Aspect phrase in English, while in German the extended *v*P extracts from the Aspect phrase when moving on into the C-domain.

(35) $[_{\text{I-domain}} [_{\text{T-domain}}$ (Spec AgrS) [Spec PRES/PAST [vP Asp]]] $[_{\text{V-domain}} t_{vP}]]^4$

Given this scenario, we can assume that on its way to the T-domain, the extended vP moves through all the *predication* positions introduced by modifying adjuncts in the middle field. The modifying adjuncts will remain in the original order in preverbal position, if *v*P is subextracted at each step, since TP movement will then move the entire middle field anew in front of the extended *v*P in the C-domain.

On the other hand, the adjuncts will appear in the mirror order, which is typical of VO languages, if the extended vP at each step on its way up to the C-domain pied-pipes the respective functional projections containing the adjuncts. In this case, as is typical for VO languages, the entire middle field will follow the verb in the C-domain, with only the subject and possibly some higher adverbs being moved via TP movement to MoodP in front of the verb (phrase) again.

Note, however, that we must assume that pied-piping in a VO language like English is the preferred, but not the only option. To derive the correct word order in (33), in which case the original hierarchical relationship between temporal adverbial and local adverbial is preserved, we have to assume that *v*P extraction may also take place in the derivation of (33), as is illustrated in (36).

(36)   a. $[_{\text{C-domain}} [_{\text{T-domain}} [_{\text{Temp}}$ on each man's birthday $[_{\text{Loc}}$ in his house $[_{vP}$ Sue met Mary]]]]]

   b. $[_{\text{C-domain}} [_{\text{T-domain}} [_{\text{Temp}}$ on each man's BD $[_{\text{Loc}} [_{vP}$ Sue met Mary] in his house $t_{vP}]]]]$

   c. $[_{\text{C-domain}} [_{\text{T-domain}} [_{\text{Temp}} [_{vP}$ Sue met Mary] on each man's BD $[_{\text{Loc}} t_{vP}$ in his house $t_{vP}]]]]$

   d. $[_{\text{C-domain}} [_{\text{T-domain}} [_{vP}$ Sue met Mary] $[_{\text{Temp}} t_{vP}$ on each man's BD $[_{\text{Loc}} t_{vP}$ in his h. $t_{vP}]]]]$

   e. $[_{\text{C-dom}} [_{\text{T-dom}}$ Sue $][_{\text{AspP}} [_{vP}$ t met Mary] $[_{\text{Temp}} t_{vP}$ on each mans's BD $[_{\text{Loc}} t_{vP}$ in his h. $t_{vP}]]]$ $[_{\text{TP}} t_{\text{AspP}}]]$

In (36a), the base structure that is common to English and German is given. In the first step, indicated in (36b), the *v*P extracts after having moved into the licensing position of the lower locative adverbial. In the second step, indicated in (36c), the *v*P moves into the licensing position of the temporal adverbial and extracts from there to

---

[4] In (35), the specifier of the tense predicate contains a referential temporal argument (cf. Stowell 1996) with respect to which the event denoted by *v*P is situated.

move into the T-domain in the third step, illustrated in (36d). In the T-domain, not indicated in (36), the subject will extract from the *v*P and move into its licensing position in Spec-AgrP, as is illustrated in (35) above. In the final step, TP movement and *v*P movement pied-piping the containing (viewpoint) Aspect phrase will move the subject and the entire middle field into their respective licensing positions in the C-domain, as is illustrated in (36e).

To summarize, the vP in the derivation in (36) will induce pied-piping only after having moved into the T-domain. The rationale could be that extraction in this case is allowed in order to preserve the binding relation between the temporal adverbial and the locative adverbial. This implies that pied-piping is the default option in a VO language. However, this default must be taken to be ruled out by interface requirements, like the availability of certain binding relations.

In the following section, I argue that the default option of pied-piping is due to the prosodic condition introduced in the introduction which only allows for light material in the middle field of English.

6.5.2 *Prosodic restrictions on extraction/pied-piping*

Given the assumption that extraction versus pied-piping is a syntactic option at each step of the derivation, the question arises why there are not more mixed word-order patterns in the languages of the world. Why do German and English show purely inverted or purely uninverted word orders in the respective domain by default? There must be some principles that enforce uniformity within a certain domain, say in the postverbal or preverbal domain of a language.

Given that we want to dispense with the head–complement parameter and similar directionality parameters, such constraints should derive from very general interface requirements. I will argue that there are two interface requirements that enforce uniformity in applying the extraction versus pied-piping option. Also, we would like to derive why pied-piping is the default option in English, while in German the option of *v*P extraction constitutes the default. I am assuming a phase-based framework here, where interface conditions evaluate syntactic objects at specific points in the derivation. In particular, I propose that a phase is evaluated at the point of the derivation at which the respective phase has been licensed. When the extended *v*P moves into the licensing domain of an adjunct in the middle field, the adjunct is licensed and the entire phase can be prosodically evaluated. The vP and the adjunct belong to non-homorganic phases and are thus mapped onto separate phonological phrases. Given that the adjunct occupies the right branch (or is more deeply embedded) the prosodic pattern derived is as given in (37).

(37)   w   s
        [(vP) (adjunct) $_{\text{IP}}$]

In a VO language like English, where the I-domain is sensitive to prosodic weight, a heavy adjunct occupies an optimal position, giving rise to a prosodic preference for pied-piping, while no such preference is predicted for light adjuncts.

In an OV language like German, on the other hand, placement of adjuncts is weight-insensitive; thus, there is no prosodic preference for pied-piping. This may be already sufficient for ruling out pied-piping, given that it is reasonable to assume that by default the minimal phrase containing the attracted feature is targeted by further movement, resulting in a case of *v*P extraction. Note, however, that the resulting prosodic pattern in German, involving postverbal stress, violates the prosodic constraint in (40) below.

Where does the interface constraint in (40) come from, though? Note first that German does not allow for postverbal focus and hence postverbal stress in the *same* intonational phrase that contains the verb. Thus, a postverbal focus is realized in a separate intonational phrase which leads to marked structures like (38), violating the interface condition in (39).

(38) a.# Auf Gleis 5   fährt ein | der Interregio   nach Straubing
          at platform 5 comes in   the Interregio   to   Straubing

  b. [$_{iP}$ (Auf Gleis 5) (fährt ein)] [$_{iP}$ (der Interregio) (nach Straubing)]

(39) Focus constituents are mapped into the intonational phrase which contains the verb. (Nespor and Vogel 1986)

(40) Interface constraint on the syntax–prosody mapping in German:
      * [$_{iP}$ ... (V) (**XP**)]

An apparent exception to the constraint in (40) is posed by CP complements. Note that an extraposed embedded clause may provide new information, seemingly violating the condition in (40). For a given extraposed clause as in (41a), there are two phrasings possible, illustrated in (41b) and (41c), respectively. While the phrasing in (41b) is unproblematic for the condition in (40), the phrasing in (41c) involves a postverbal focus in the same intonational phrase. But the crucial point is that in (41c), there is another verb in the embedded clause that can be taken to license the focus. That this is the correct analysis, is shown by the contrast with (38). If the verb in (38) could license the postverbal focus on the subject then it would not be clear why the DP cannot be mapped into the same intonational phrase with the verb.

(41) a. Hans hat gesagt dass die Maria schwanger ist
         Hans has said   that the Maria pregnant   is

  b. [(Hans) (hat geSAgt)] [(dass die Maria) (schWAnger ist)]

  c. [(Hans) (hat gesagt) (dass die Maria) (schWAnger ist)]

In conclusion, the proposal is that the unmarked option in German is vP extraction, since pied-piping leads to a marked prosodic pattern as long as the adjunct is to receive stress.

Having derived that vP pied-piping is the default option in English and vP extraction is the default option in German, let us now focus on how ungrammatical orders can be excluded. While in English vP pied-piping constitutes the prosodically preferred option, vP extraction is still possible, if binding is at stake, as is illustrated in (34) above. The crucial point is that heavy adjuncts are pied-piped by vP movement in the last step of the derivation in English. Therefore, I propose that the prosodic condition will be checked at the end of the derivation in the C-domain (applying in the complement domain of the Force-head). As outlined above, the extended vP will move into the T-domain in the course of the derivation. Since the TP phase will be evaluated in the C-domain (as has been argued in the previous section, TP is licensed in Spec-MoodP), vP extraction results as the default option. If the vP extracts from TP, the entire middle field will be moved via TP movement into the C-domain.

In German, the result is grammatical, since the prosodic condition does not apply in the licensing domain of the verb. In English, the result will only be grammatical if the middle field does not contain heavy syntactic constituents. If the middle field contains heavy adjuncts, the extended vP in the T-domain must induce pied-piping such that the entire middle field will be moved with the verb on top of it into the C-domain, while the TP that is moved into a higher specifier (in the C-domain) will maximally contain the Subject that is exempt from the prosodic condition.

It remains to be shown how postverbal occurrences of these adjuncts can be derived in German. The descriptive generalization that emerges from the data discussed in (19) and (20) above is that German only tolerates postverbal adjuncts that are part of the background information in the clause. Note first that background material is generally part of a separate intonational phrase from the one containing the verb (see Frascarelli 2000; Kanerva 1989). Secondly, note that discourse-given information as a rule scrambles to the top of the middle field in German (see Meinunger 2000; Hinterhölzl 2006). This explains why the postverbal PP in (19) is forced to have a high reading: postverbal material must be interpreted as part of the background, since assigning stress to it, which is the prosodic correlate of non-background material, would lead to a marked prosodic output in German. In a similar vein, (20) is ungrammatical since the negatively quantified PP does not qualify as background material (it does not introduce a discourse referent nor does it qualify as a frame adverbial that defines a spatio-temporal location for the assertion of the remainder of the clause).

(42) provides a sample derivation for the example in (19). Remember that (42a) has the same interpretation as the (unmarked) variant in (42b), with wide scope of the locative modifier in a derived position. The derivation starts with the base structure given (42c). As in the case of argument scrambling for reasons of scope taking,

I assume that syntactic constituents enter the derivation equipped with scope features that need to be checked in a Spec-head configuration within the derivation (cf. Hinterhölzl 2004a). In (42), these features are marked w for wide scope and n for narrow scope, respectively.

(42) a. weil Hans oft   sitzt im   Kaffeehaus
           since Hans often sits in-the coffee house

      b. weil Hans im   Kaffeehaus oft   sitzt
          since Hans in-the coffee house often sits

      c. weil [[oft]n [[im Kaffeehaus]w [$_{vP}$ Hans sitzt]]]

      d. weil [[oft]n [[[$_{vP}$ Hans sitzt] im Kaffeehaus]w t$_{vP}$]]

      e. weil [[[$_{vP}$ Hans sitzt] [im Kaffeehaus]w] [oft]n [t$_{vP}$]]

      f. weil [[im Kaffeehaus]w [[$_{vP}$ Hans sitzt] [im Kaffeehaus][oft]n [t$_{vP}$]]

      g. weil [$_{T\text{-domain}}$ Hans [[$_{vP}$ t sitzt] [im K-haus]w] [im K-haus][oft]n [t$_{vP}$]]

      h. [$_{C\text{-domain}}$ weil [Hans im K-haus oft] [sitzt im K-haus] [t$_{TP}$ t$_{vP}$]]

In the first step, indicated in (42d) the vP is moved into its licensing position in the domain of the locative adverbial and induces pied-piping. We will see below that pied-piping is prompted by syntactic considerations: the derivation with pied-piping is more economical than the one without pied-piping, since the locative adverbial is not fully licensed at this point but needs to check its scope, necessitating further movement at a later point in the derivation. In the second step, indicated in (42e), vP and locative adverbial are moved into the licensing position of the frequentative adverbial. At this point in the derivation, the scope features of the adverbial phrases can be taken care of. Since the scope properties of the adverbials are not satisfied in their respective *in situ* positions, the derivation is extended according to (43) below (cf. Hinterhölzl 2004a for details).

In Hinterhölzl (2004a), it is proposed that non-lexical features can be assigned to any head in the course of the derivation. The enrichment of an existing structure with a non-lexical feature is defined, as given in (43).

(43) a. Assign the feature to an existing structure (the head at the root) in the course of the derivation.

      b. Assign the feature to (a copy of) a bare functional head and merge the head with the existing structure.

Thus, option (43b) is taken and a functional head annotated with a wide-scope feature is added to the root of the present tree, inducing scope movement of the locative PP *im Kaffeehaus*, as is illustrated in (42f), where both copies of the locative PP are displayed. In the next step, the *v*P pied-piping the lower copy of the locative PP is moved into the T-domain and the subject extracts to be licensed in [Spec-AgrP], as in the derivation in (36) above. This is illustrated in (42g). In the final step, the *v*P pied-piping the lower copy of the locative PP is subextracted from the T-domain moving into its licensing position in Spec-FinP in the C-domain, while the rest of the I-domain is moved into the higher licensing position in Spec-MoodP in the C-domain, as is illustrated in (42h).

If the higher copy of the locative PP is spelled out, the order in (42b) is derived. Spell-Out of the PP in its scope position constitutes the unmarked case, as will be argued in section 6.6 below. If the lower copy of locative PP is spelled out, the result is marked but grammatical since the PP constituting background information does not need to occupy the intonational phrase containing the verb.

Let us summarize: A) Since German tolerates heavy constituents in the middle field, the option of *v*P extraction yields valid prosodic output. (B) In English, the default option is pied-piping, and *v*P extraction (for scope reasons) will only be possible as long as the result at the end of the derivation does not yield heavy constituents in the I-domain.

6.6 Prosodic weight and the head–complement parameter

It is tempting to assume that the correlation in the positioning of event-related adjuncts and arguments with respect to the verb in OV and VO languages is due to the very same constraint, in our case, due to the prosodic condition in (1) above. In fact, in Hinterhölzl (2011) it is argued that the HFF and the head–complement parameter can be collapsed on the basis of the observation that HF effects appear only in head-initial projections in German and English. In other words, it is proposed that phrases in a certain domain appear as head-initial projections on the surface, since the HFF operating in this domain forces the realization of complements in the postverbal/postnominal domain. Given that DP and PP arguments, with the exception of pronominal DPs and DPs comprising only a proper name, count as prosodically heavy, the prosodic version of the HFF is sufficient to guarantee that these phrases appear on a right branch with respect to the selecting head. In such an account, one could assume that licensing movement of arguments occurs in OV and VO languages alike, but due to the (non-)application of the prosodic condition in the I-domain, these arguments are spelled out in the I-domain in German, but in the V-domain in English.

In this scenario, the question arises why licensing movement in English could not also spell out the higher copy to obey this prosodic condition, given that *v*P-movement into the T-domain moves the verb around (scrambled) arguments again anyway (cf. (35) and (36) above and (46) below). The answer to this question must be that the Spell-Out of an argument is decided before Tense is merged. In fact, there is ample empirical evidence that VO orders in English cannot be derived by object movement that spells out the higher copy plus *v*P movement around it. First note that the *v*P cannot be topicalized excluding the direct object, as is illustrated in (44). Furthermore, note that the object cannot be separated from the verb and appear in its *scope position* between adverbs, as is illustrated by the contrast between German and English in (45a–b). The intended reading of (45a) is possible in the order given in (45c), where the direct object arguably occupies its base position in the *v*P.

(44)   a. John wanted to buy something yesterday
         ...* and buy John did a book today

      b. Hans wollte gestern etwas kaufen
         Hans wanted yesterday something buy
         ...und gekauft hat er heute ein Buch
         and bought has he today a book

(45)   a. * John met every day two girls in their classrooms (Temp > DO > Loc)

      b. Hans traf jeden Tag zwei Mädchen in ihren Klassenzimmern

      c. John met two girls in their classrooms every day

      d. Hans met every day two girls in their classrooms

The contrast in (45) illustrates the working of the interface condition (2) in German: arguments and adjuncts in German are spelled out in their scope positions. I assume that the direct object in (45c) in English also moves into the relevant scope position in the middle field, but is spelled out in the *v*P. The latter fact will follow if the prosodic condition in (1) applies to arguments at an earlier point in the derivation than it does to adjuncts.

To this end, I propose that the Spell-Out of a constituent is decided at the point at which all its features have been checked, guided by the prosodic constraints that apply in the phase that contains it. Then the crucial distinction in the Spell-Out of arguments and adjuncts will follow, if we make the reasonable assumption that the prosodic condition applies to an argument or an adjunct exactly at the point in time at which this argument or this adjunct is joined with the head of the predicate domain into a single prosodic constituent. Remember that arguments in contradistinction to adjuncts are subject to subordination in prosodic domain formation, resulting in a single potentially recursive phonological phrase comprising the argument and the selecting verb.

Thus, when an argument is licensed in the I-domain, the mapping condition applies immediately, since a single prosodic constituent with the verb is computed at this point. A sample derivation is given in (47) below. For the sample derivation in (47), it is assumed that the unmarked word order in German is derived from the hierarchical order of argument and adjunct licensing heads above *v*P, as given in (46).[5]

---

[5] I propose that German has two subject positions: a lower one in the I-domain in which Nominative Case is assigned and a higher one in the T-domain which is reserved for specific DP subjects. English has lost the lower position in the course of its history (cf. van Kemenade and Los 2006; Westergaard 2009a).

(46)   [T [Temp [Subject [Loc [IO [DO [Manner [vP]]]]]]]]

(47) illustrates the case of the licensing/Spell-Out of the direct object. In (47), square brackets indicate syntactic constituents and round brackets indicate prosodic constituents. The derivation will then proceed in a strict cyclic fashion: first, the adjunct is licensed (47b), and the result is prosodically evaluated (47c). Then the argument is extracted to be Case-licensed by the higher head (47d), and prosodic evaluation creates a joint prosodic constituent of verb and argument (subordination). At this point the mapping condition in (1) applies, repeated in (48) below, with the result that the argument is spelled out in its base position.

(47)   a. $[_{IP}\dots[\dots Adjunct]\ [_{vP}\ V\ DP]]$ adjunct licensing $\rightarrow$

       b. $[_{IP}\ [\ [_{vP}\ \textbf{V\ DP}]\ Adjunct]\ t_{vP}\ ]$ coordination $\rightarrow$

       c. $[_{IP}\ [(V\ DP)\ (Adjunct)]]$ DP extracts for Case/scope checking $\rightarrow$

       d. $[_{IP}\ \textbf{DP}\ [\ (V\ DP)\ (Adjunct)]]$ subordination $\rightarrow$

       e. $[_{IP}\ (DP\ [\ V\ DP)\ (Adjunct)]]$ mapping condition $\rightarrow$ Spell-Out of the lower copy

       f. $[_{IP}\ (\text{D̶P̶}\ [\ V\ DP)\ (Adjunct)]]$

(48)   Mapping Condition to PF (prosodic transparency):
       A heavy syntactic constituent must appear on a dominant branch in prosodic phrasing if its containing phase is weight-sensitive.

When a heavy prosodic constituent that is an adjunct is licensed in the I-domain, the mapping condition does not apply immediately, since according to (24b) no single prosodic constituent is computed at this point in the derivation.

    The mapping condition in (48) will apply to it only when a single prosodic constituent is formed at the level of the C-domain that combines the verb and other elements in the I-domain. In this case, the application of (48) will ensure that only light adjuncts may remain in the middle field in English, as argued for also in section 6.5.2 above.

6.7 The diachronic dimension

In this final section, I would like to address the question of how it came about that the prosodic condition applies in the middle field of English, but fails to do so in the middle field of German. From a historical perspective, it is interesting to note that both Germanic languages started from a similar basis in their oldest accessible varieties, where they showed mixed OV/VO word orders. In the traditional literature, both stylistic and vaguely information-structural (IS) factors were held responsible for this kind of variation in Old English (OE), Old Icelandic (OI), and Old High German (OHG). A much-quoted point of view is Behaghel's (1932) observation that pronouns and unmodified nouns tend to precede the verb, while modified nouns, PPs, and other heavy material tend to follow the verb that gave rise to Behaghel's law of growing constituents, as stated in (49). The statement in (49) raises the question of which principle of grammar this tendency derives from. My take on this is, of course, that (49) does not constitute a mere stylistic principle but derives from the prosodic condition (48) in a system in which the mapping between syntax and prosody is quantity-sensitive.

(49)   Light elements precede heavy elements in OE, OI, and OHG.
        (Behaghel 1932: *Das Gesetz der wachsenden Glieder*)

Taking a closer look at OHG, there is another generalization that emerges from an IS analysis of the Tatian translation (cf. Hinterhölzl 2009b) that derives (49) as a mere corollary. Given that discourse-given elements are typically realized as light elements, while focused constituents may count as prosodically heavy elements since they receive stress, the condition in (50) also derives the tendency expressed in (49).

(50)   C   background   V   (presentational) focus   (to be revised below)

The following notions are relevant for an IS analysis of mixed word orders in OHG. (A) The discourse status of an expression denoting a discourse referent: discourse-given elements are assumed to be part of the background, that is, part of the knowledge that is assumed to be shared by speaker and hearer, while discourse-new elements are assumed to be part of the presentational focus of the clause. (B) Discourse-given elements can also be made prominent and be part of the focus domain of a clause. A typical case in question is a contrastively stressed pronoun. (C) Taking into account the prosodic properties of focused elements, we further need to distinguish between wide and narrow focus. The three different notions of focus relevant here are illustrated in (51): broad and narrow presentational focus and contrastive focus. In (51), brackets mark the focused constituents and capital letters mark a high pitch accent, which is typical for contrastively focused elements.

(51)   a. What did John do? (broad presentational focus)
            John [gave a book to Mary]

        b. What did John give to Mary? (narrow presentational focus)
            John gave [a book] to Mary

        c. John gave Mary [a BOOK], not a pen (contrastive focus)

Though the conditions in (49) and (50) partially overlap, they make slightly different predictions upon closer inspection: according to the generalization in (50), a direct object will precede the verb if it is discourse-given, but follow the verb if it is discourse-new; while according to the generalization in (49), a direct object will be placed preverbally, independently of its information-structural status if it is realized as a pronoun or a single noun, but postverbally if it is made heavy by modification.

In a corpus study (described in detail in Hinterhölzl 2009b), I investigated embedded clauses in the OHG Tatian translation which deviated in word order from the Latin original (in order to make sure to target only original OHG word-order principles). Particular attention was paid to preverbal heavy (branching) syntactic constituents and to postverbal light (non-branching) constitutents. A careful IS analysis of these cases revealed the following picture, schematized in (52): (A) a heavy syntactic constituent appears preverbally if it is either discourse-given or contrastively focused (in the latter case it appears left-adjacent to the verb); (B) a light syntactic constituent appears postverbally if it is part of the new information focus of the sentence.

(52) C   background   contrastive focus V   information focus

Now, the question arises as to which assumptions the patterning in (52) can be derived from. The pattern certainly calls for a syntactic representation of focus in OHG that distinguishes between contrastive focus and information focus. Given the Universal Base Hypothesis, arguments must be taken to move out of the vP to be licensed in (Case-)Agreement positions. If we then assume that a structural focus position is located above these licensing positions, the word-order facts in (52) follow from the following requirements on the syntax of focus: (A) The verb moves into the Focus head. (B) A contrastively focused phrase moves into Spec-FocP. (C) A constituent that represents new information focus just stays in the scope of the Focus head, while (D) background elements move out of the scope domain of the Focus head. This is illustrated in (53).

(53) Assumptions about the syntax of focus (Hinterhölzl 2004b)
      [C   Background   [$_{FocP}$ ContrastFocus V [$_{AgrP}$ InformationFocus   [$_{VP}$]]]]

The idea behind (53) is that IS interacts with syntax in terms of specific scope requirements: according to its IS interpretation a constitutent has to appear in particular scopal domains within the clause. Thus information-structural restrictions enforce the effect of the condition on scopal transparency in (2) and contribute to a weakening of the condition on prosodic transparency, repeated in (48) above, in the German middle field. It is interesting to note that Taylor and Pintzuk (2012) report that both prosodic and IS conditions also play a role in mixed word orders in OE and moreover find that the influence of IS conditions diminishes at the end of the OE period.

In conclusion, mixed OV/VO word order can be explained as the result of a complex interplay between prosodic and information-structural conditions. I have outlined the historical conditions (cf. (52)) that led German into developing into a scope-transparent OV language, while English seems to have favoured the prevalence of prosodic transparency. However, tackling this issue and investigating this development in its historic setting and progression, I have to leave for future research.

6.8 Conclusions

In this paper, I have argued that harmonic word orders are due to a prosodic condition on the mapping between syntax and PF which enforces that right-branching constituents like DPs and PPs are spelled out on a right branch with respect to the selecting head (V or A). Disharmonic word orders in German were argued to be due to a parallel interface condition on the mapping between syntax and LF which enforces that arguments and adjuncts are spelled out in their respective scope positions in the middle field preceding the selecting head (V or A). Furthermore, I have investigated the potential source of the prosodic condition and argued that it can be seen as a natural extension of the notion of quantity sensitivity, familiar from word-stress systems, into the syntactic domain. Finally, I have laid out the tenets of a phase-based derivation of OV and VO surface word orders from a common VO base in which the distinction between homorganic and non-homorganic phases provides elementary restrictions on prosodic phrasing and Spell-Out options.

7

A Stress-Based Theory of Disharmonic Word Orders*

HISAO TOKIZAKI AND YASUTOMO KUWANA

7.1 Introduction

In this paper, we argue that the location of stress in words is a crucial factor in determining morphosyntactic constituent orders in languages. It is argued that constituents consisting of a complement and head, in that order, behave like compounds. Such constituents should have the same stress location as words and compounds in the language in which they are found. We argue that the unmarked stress location determines the head–complement order of constituents from stem affix, at the lowest level, to clause-adverbial subordinator at the highest.[1] This stress-based theory of word order is set forth to explain languages with disharmonic word orders as well as those with harmonic orders.

In section 7.2, we discuss the typology of head–complement orders based on Dryer (2011a,b,c,d,e). In section 7.3, we argue that constituents with complement–head order behave like compounds because of the short juncture in left-branching structures. In section 7.4, we argue that unmarked word-stress location (Goedemans and van der Hulst 2005a,b) determines the head–complement orders in the language. Section 7.5 concludes the discussion.

* We would like to thank the organizers and participants of Theoretical Approaches to Disharmonic Word Orders, Newcastle University, 30 May–1 June 2009. Special thanks go to Theresa Biberauer, Matthew Dryer, Anders Holmberg, Ian Roberts, and Michelle Sheehan. This work is supported by Sapporo University and Grant-in-Aid for Scientific Research (C18520388, A20242010), JSPS.

[1] Dryer (2011e) defines adverbial subordinators as morphemes which mark adverbial clauses for their semantic relationship to the main clause (e.g. *because, although, when, while,* and *if* in English).

7.2 Deriving disharmonic word orders by complement movement

7.2.1 Head–complement orders

First, following Dryer (1992a), we define *head* as a non-branching category and *complement* as a branching category. We call a category 'branching' if it is made by merging two syntactic objects, with affixes counting as syntactic objects (cf. Williams 1981). For example, A is the head and B is the complement in X in (1a) and (1b), where X stands for any level of category from X^0 to XP.

(1)   a. $[_X \text{ A } [_B \ldots]]$

    b. $[_X [_B \ldots] \text{ A}]$

Then, (1a) is a head–complement order and (1b) is a complement–head order. In addition to branchingness, we must also include a standard definition of head on the basis of projection: a head is an element that projects its morphosyntactic and semantic properties onto the category made by Merging it with its complement. This is necessary to cover non-branching specifiers and categories derived by movement such as (2a) and (2b).

(2)   a. [He [likes coffee]]

    b. [*Marie*   [[*chante*+T]   [*souvent t*]]]
        Marie   sings   often

The subject *he* or *Marie* is not a head but a specifier even though it is non-branching. In (2b) *chante* is arguably branching but should be considered as the head of VP because it projects its syntactic and semantic properties to the VP.

Next, let us consider various morphosyntactic categories, each of which is illustrated with an example in (3):[2]

(3)   a. Affix–Stem (*un-[[real-ist]-ic]*)

    b. Word–Word (*chaleco salva-vidas* (vest save-lives) 'life-saving jacket' (Spanish))

    c. Noun–Genitive (*books of John*)

    d. Verb–Object (*read the books*)

    e. Adposition–Object (*in the mood*)

    f. Adverbial Subordinator–Clause (*before you go*)

In each pair of categories in (3), the left one is the head because it is non-branching. The right categories are complements because they are branching. Note that a complement

---

[2] We use examples in English dictionaries in order to show the head–complement order in all the morphosyntactic categories in (3). In fact, English is not a consistent head-initial language in that it prefers the complement–head order in a word or a compound. Thus, it is impossible to find a genuine English example of a head–complement compound, other than cases such as *spaghetti bolognese*, which is borrowed from Italian.

is branching if it is derived by merging two syntactic objects, which may be morphemes. Thus, *realistic* in (3a) is also branching in that it can be analysed as *real + istic*.

Following Kayne (1994), we assume that the head–complement orders in (3) are the universal base orders, which can be changed into complement–head orders by movement of the complements to a specifier position on the left of a head. Here we define specifier as the constituent which is merged with the resulting structure created by merging head and complement. The derivation of complement–head order from head–complement order is shown in (4):

(4) a. $[_{XP}$ X $[_{YP}$...Y...$]] \rightarrow$

    b. $[_{XP}$ $[_{YP}$...Y...$]$ X $t]$

YP moves to the specifier position of X in (4b).[3] The trace *t* in (4b) is invisible at the syntax–phonology interface because it does not have phonetic features. As Holmberg (2000) points out, from a phonological point of view the complement movement changes the right-branching structure (4a) into the left-branching structure (4b), as shown in (5) (and see section 7.3.2 below):[4]

(5) $[_{XP}$ $[_{YP}$...Y...$]$ X$]$

Then, complement movement changes the head–complement order in (3) into the complement–head order shown in (6):

(6) a. Stem–Affix (*stabiliz-ation*)

    b. Word–Word ([*red wine*] *glass*)

    c. Genitive–Noun (*John's books*)

    d. Object–Verb (*Bücher lesen* 'read books' (German))

    e. Adposition–Object (*huoneese-en* 'into room' (Finnish))

    f. Clause–Adverbial Subordinator (*anata-ga iku maeni* (you-NOM go before) 'before you go' (Japanese))

---

[3] It might also be possible for the complement YP to move to the specifier position of a higher functional head F as in (i).

(i) a. $[_{FP}$ F $[_{XP}$ ZP X $[_{YP}$...Y...$]]] \rightarrow$

    b. $[_{FP}$ $[_{YP}$...Y...$]$ F $[_{XP}$ ZP X $t]]$

This option in (i) seems to be necessary when the specifier position of X is occupied by a trace of ZP, which has moved to a higher specifier position than FP as shown in (ii).

(ii) ...ZP...$[_{FP}$ $[_{YP}$...Y...$]$ F $[_{XP}$ t_{ZP} X $t]]$

The FP in (ii) is also a left-branching structure in that only YP and X are visible at the syntax–phonology interface as shown in (iii):

(iii) ...ZP...$[_{FP}$ $[_{YP}$...Y...$]$ X$]$

[4] Holmberg (2000: 137) points out that 'Successive application of complement movement in this fashion yields a structure which is effectively left-branching except for the trace of movement left in each complement position.'

In (6a), *stabilize* can be analysed as *stable + -ize*.

7.2.2 *Universal LF hypothesis*

One question that needs to be answered is what motivates the complement movement to specifier position. We argue that complements must move to a specifier
position to check their c(ategorial) selection with their heads.

According to Kayne (1994), the base structure is universally specifier–head–
complement across languages. Kayne argues that head-final languages such as
Japanese move complements to specifier position as we have seen in the previous
section. If we assume that there is no lowering operation in syntax, including LF, then
the constituent order in LF is the same as that at Spell-Out, i.e. complement–head, in
head-final languages. Then, what kind of LF representation do head-initial languages
have for head–complement pairs?

We argue that LF is universal across languages. It seems to be plausible that
semantic representation is the same in all languages. Moreover, the idea of a universal
LF has been proposed for operator movement by Huang (1982), as shown in (7):

(7) | | English | Chinese |
|---|---|---|
| Base | $[_{IP} \ldots Op \ldots]$ | $[_{IP} \ldots Op \ldots]$ |
| Spell-Out | $[_{CP} Op [_{IP} \ldots t \ldots]]$ | $[_{IP} \ldots Op \ldots]$ |
| LF | $[_{CP} Op [_{IP} \ldots t \ldots]]$ | $[_{CP} Op [_{IP} \ldots t \ldots]]$ |

English moves *wh*-operators to the specifier of C by the time of Spell-Out, while
Chinese does so after Spell-Out. Thus, the surface orders in these two languages are
different, but the LF representations are the same. Similarly, complement movement
in head-initial and head-final languages can be illustrated as in (8):

(8) | | head-final languages | head-initial languages |
|---|---|---|
| Base | $[_{XP} X [_{YP} \ldots Y \ldots]]$ | $[_{XP} X [_{YP} \ldots Y \ldots]]$ |
| Spell-Out | $[_{XP} [_{YP} \ldots Y \ldots] X t]$ | $[_{XP} X [_{YP} \ldots Y \ldots]]$ |
| LF | $[_{XP} [_{YP} \ldots Y \ldots] X t]$ | $[_{XP} [_{YP} \ldots Y \ldots] X t]$ |

Complement movement occurs by the time of Spell-Out in head-final languages and
after Spell-Out in head-initial languages.[5]

The basic assumption behind the universal LF hypothesis is that constituents with
head–complement order are not interpretable at LF. Let us consider this point in
detail. First, it has been argued in generative syntax that the selectional relation needs
to be checked in some way. For example, Holmberg (2000) lists the three c(ategorial)-
selection mechanisms shown in (9):

---

[5] Current Minimalism assumes Agree instead of covert movement. The argument here holds if we take
agreement of features. We show a covert movement analysis here for the sake of simplicity.

(9) a. Pure f(eature)-movement (i.e. covert movement; see Chomsky 1995a: ch. 4)

   b. Head movement, i.e. f-movement pied-piping the minimal word containing the relevant feature.

   c. XP-movement, i.e. f-movement pied-piping the minimal maximal category containing the relevant feature.

The distinction between (9a), (9b), and (9c) reflects two criteria for the classification of c-selection types. First, the movement is covert (9a) or overt (9b,c). Second, the moved category is X^0 (9b) or XP (9c).

However, if we assume the universal LF hypothesis, the distinction between covert movement (9a) and overt movement (9b,c) is reduced to the order of movement and Spell-Out. Overt movement (9b,c) occurs by the time of Spell-Out. After Spell-Out, movement may apply to X^0 or XP, which has semantic features but no phonetic features. This movement after Spell-Out is equivalent to pure feature-movement. Thus, we do not have to specify pure feature-movement (9a) to check c-selection.

Let us return to the assumption that head–complement order is not interpretable while complement–head order is interpretable. This assumption is based on the observation that constituents with left-branching structure are more tightly connected to each other than constituents with right-branching structure. Put phonologically, the juncture between constituents is shorter in left-branching structures than in right-branching structures, as we will argue in section 7.3.1. Following American structuralist linguistics and Selkirk (1984), we define 'juncture' as the relations between the segments in a sequence. Juncture shows the degrees of connectedness between segments of phonological representation, which may affect the application of phonological rules.[6] We propose that constituents must be connected to each other in order to be interpreted in LF. Then, head–complement order with right-branching structure needs to have been changed into complement–head order with left-branching structure by the time the derivation reaches the LF output where semantic interpretation takes place.[7] In the next section, we show some evidence that the juncture between constituents is shorter in left-branching structures than in right-branching structures. After that, we will propose a reason for why head-initial languages defer movement until after Spell-Out while head-final languages move complements before Spell-Out.

---

[6] Selkirk (1984) proposes representing the degree of juncture in terms of the number of 'silent demi-beats', which are shown by x. For example, the examples in (ia) and (ib) are distinguished by the presence of a 'rest' or 'pause' between *man* and *eating* in (ib) (p.324).

(i) a. This is a [AP [N man-] [A eating]] fish.   [N man-] x [A eating]

   b. This is [NP a [man]] [S eating fish].   [NP a [man]] xx [S eating...]

[7] In the current Minimalist system, this is done by agreement of c-selection features instead of movement (cf. (9)). Here I show a covert movement analysis just for simplicity of explanation.

7.3 Complement–head order as compound

7.3.1 *Short juncture in left-branching structure*

Tokizaki (2008) argues that juncture between constituents is shorter in left-branching structures than in right-branching structures. Let us consider the structures in (10):

(10) a. [[X Y] Z]

    b. [X [Y Z]]

The two structures in (10a) and (10b) are symmetrical in constituency, but they differ in phonological realization. The evidence is based on phonological changes in compounds. Japanese Sequential Voicing (*Rendaku*) and Korean *n*-Insertion occur between constituents in left-branching structures but not in right-branching structures, as shown in (11) and (12) respectively (cf. Otsu 1980; Han 1994).[8]

(11) a. [[*nise*   *tanuki*]   *shiru*]   →   *nise danuki jiru*
          mock   badger   soup
         'mock-badger soup'

    b. [*nise*[[*tanuki*   *shiru*]]   →   *nise tanuki jiru (*danuki)*
          mock   badger   soup
         'mock badger-soup'

(12) a. [[*on*   *chən*]   *yok*]   →   *on chən nyok*
          hot   spring   bathe
         'bathing in a hot spring'

    b. [*kyəŋ* [*yaŋ*   *sik*]]   →   *kyəŋ yaŋ sik (*nyaŋ)*
          light   Western   food
         'a light Western meal'

The left-branching structure in (11a) and (12a) allows phonological rules to apply between constituents, and the right-branching structure in (11b) and (12b) does not. This fact can be explained by the assumption that a left-branching structure has a shorter juncture between its constituents than a right-branching structure. The long juncture between constituents blocks phonological rules in (11b) and (12b).

An alternative explanation of the contrast in (11) and (12) is to assume that phonological rules do not in fact change the phonology of the compound made by Merge. Instead, in (11a) and (12a), phonological rules apply to the third word in each example (*shiru* and *yok*), when it is merged with the result of the first Merge (of the first and the second words, i.e. *nise tanuki* and *on chən*). In (11b) and (12b), phonological

---

[8] Insertion of *n* is possible in (12b) in the Kyungsan dialect (cf. Han 1994). For discussion of this dialectal difference, see Tokizaki (2008).

rules do not apply to the second word in each example (*tanuki* and *yaŋ*), because they have been merged syntactically with the third word and become a part of a compound (*tanuki-jiru* and *yaŋ-sik*) at the time of the second Merge.[9]

This alternative idea based on the derivational cycle is an interesting one, but we will not adopt it here because of the following data. In Japanese, Accent Deletion applies to one of the two constituents when they are merged, as shown in (13):

(13)   *míso*   +   *shíru*   →   *misoshíru*
     miso   soup   'miso soup'

Accent Deletion applies to the first constituent *miso* and deletes its accent in PF. Accent Deletion applies to the first constituent in left-branching compounds as in (14a), but not in right-branching compounds as in (14b):

(14)   a. [[*nihon*   *búyoo*]   *kúrabu*]   →   *nihon buyoo kúrabu*
           Japan   dance   club
          'Japanese-dance club'

     b. [*nihón* [*hoosoo*   *kyóokai*]]→*nihón hoosoo kyóokai* (*nihon hoosoo
           Japan broadcasting association   *kyóokai*)
          'broadcasting association in Japan'

In the first constituent *nihon búyoo*, which is the result of Merging the two words, the accent is deleted in (14a). This fact cannot be explained if we assume the derivational cycle we have seen above. The derivational cycle claims that phonological rules do not change the phonology of the compound made by Merge. The derivational cycle predicts that once *nihon búyoo* is created with its accent in the first cycle, the accent on *búyoo* should not be deleted in the next cycle that makes the whole compound *nihon buyoo kurabu*. However, this is not the case: the Merge of *nihon búyoo* and *kúrabu* makes the whole compound *nihon buyoo kúrabu*, deleting the accent on *buyoo*. On the other hand, stress deletion in (14a) and non-deletion in (14b) are naturally explained with our hypothesis that juncture is shorter in left-branching structures than in right-branching structures. The constituents in the left-branching structure in (14a) are closely connected to each other and lose the left-hand stress. The constituents in (14b) are in a right-branching structure with a looser connection and thus keep their own stress. Thus, we conclude that the different phonological behaviours between left-branching compounds and right-branching compounds, shown in (11), (12), and (14), are due to junctural asymmetry, not to the derivational cycle.

The role of junctural asymmetry in compounds is further supported by data in Dutch. Krott et al. (2004) show that in Dutch the occurrence of interfixes including -*s*- in tri-constituent compounds matches the major constituent boundary better in

---

[9] We thank Kimihiro Ohno and Yoshihito Dobashi for pointing out this alternative.

right-branching compounds than in left-branching compounds. They counted the occurrences of tri-constituent compounds in the Dutch section of the CELEX lexical database, which is based on a corpus of approximately 42 million words. In (15) and (16), the number of compounds with -s- and the total number of interfixes (including -s-, -e(n)-, -er-) are shown in parentheses after the examples:[10]

(15) a. Interfixes at the constituent break in right-branching compounds (-s- 38; 60 total)
         [*arbeid-s-[vraag stuk]*]
         employment+question-issue

     b. Interfixes within the inner compound in right-branching compounds (-s- 3; 11 total)
         [*hoofd [verkeer-s-weg]*]
         main+traffic-road

(16) a. Interfixes at the constituent break in left-branching compounds (-s- 25; 39 total)
         [[*grond wet]-s-artikel*]
         ground-law+article, constitution

     b. Interfixes within the inner compound in left-branching compounds (-s- 13; 50 total)
         [[*scheep-s-bouw] maatschappij*]
         ship-building+company

Let us compare the ratios of the interfixes at the constituent break in all the cases between right-branching compounds (15) and left-branching compounds (16). In right-branching compounds (15), the ratios of the interfixes at the constituent break (15a) in all the cases ((15a) and (15b)) are 92.7% in -s- (38/(38+3)) and 84.5% in all interfixes (60/(60+11)). In left-branching compounds (16), the ratios of the interfixes at the constituent break (16a) in all the cases ((16a) and (16b)) are 65.8% in -s- (25/(25+13)) and 43.8% in all interfixes (39/(39+50)). Thus, the ratios of the interfixes at the constituent break in all the cases are higher in right-branching compounds (-s- 92.7%; all 84.5%) than in left-branching compounds (-s- 65.8%; all 43.8%). That is, interfixes occur at the constituent break more often in right-branching compounds than in left-branching compounds. This result is expected if we assume that the juncture between constituents in a right-branching structure is long enough for interfixes to intervene there. In a left-branching structure (16), the juncture between the second word and the third is about as short as the juncture between the first word and the second. Thus, marked interfixes (16b) can occur more frequently in left-branching structure (16b) than in right-branching structure (15b). This fact supports our junctural asymmetry hypothesis.

---

[10] Krott et al. (2004) give no examples of interfixes other than -s-.

Moreover, junctural asymmetry can also be seen in morphology. Hyman (2008) argues that suffixes tend to be more tightly bound to their stem than prefixes. He cites the proposals in the literature that some or all prefixes are phonological words, e.g. in Germanic, whereas suffixes are not (see Hyman 2008: 323 and the references cited there). This observation also supports the junctural asymmetry hypothesis because [$_{Word}$ prefix [$_{Stem}$ ...]] is right-branching while [$_{Word}$ [$_{Stem}$ ...] suffix] is left-branching in our terms. Thus, cross-linguistic facts show that juncture between constituents is longer in a right-branching structure than in a left-branching structure.

Furthermore, the typology of adverbial subordinators also supports the junctural asymmetry hypothesis. Investigating 660 languages in the world, Dryer (2011e) points out that all clear instances of affixal adverbial subordinators (Sb) are suffixes on the verb, with no clear instances of prefixes on the verb.[11]

(17) a. [$_{CP}$ Sb [$_{IP}$ ...]]   (399 languages)

  b. *[$_{CP}$ Sb-[$_{IP}$ ...]]   (0 languages)

(18) a. [$_{CP}$ [$_{IP}$ ...] Sb]   (96 languages)

  b. [$_{CP}$ [$_{IP}$ ...]-Sb]   (64 languages)

---

[11] In addition to the types of adverbial subordinators in (17) and (18), Dryer (2011e) lists 'clause-internal adverbial subordinators' (8 languages) and 'more than one type of adverbial subordinator with none dominant' (87 languages). Dryer (2011e) does not give the diagnostics for affixhood. As suffixal adverbial subordinators, he gives examples in Kiowa (Kiowa Tanoan; central United States) and in Hunzib (Daghestanian; eastern Caucasus, Russia):

(i) a. Kiowa
       à-dè·k'ɔ́··àl   *hɔ́n* *àn*   *à-dè·hę́·m-ô*
       1SG-lie-although   NEG   HAB   1SG-sleep-NEG
       'Although I lie down, I can't fall asleep.'

  b. Hunzib
       zaχe   *n-ex-áyd*,   *xôx-χ̓o*   *χibu* *zuq'u-r*
       wind   NC5-strike-**before**   tree-SUP   leaf   be-PRET
       'Before the wind blew, there were leaves on the tree.'

Dryer gives examples of adverbial subordinators which are separate words that appear at the end of the clause, from Kombai (Trans-New Guinea; Papua, Indonesia) and Kolyma Yukaghir (isolate; Siberia, Russia).

(ii) a. Kombai
       khe-khino   *rerakharu*   ***rofode***
       his-legs   swollen   **because**
       'because his legs are swollen'

  b. Kolyma Yukaghir
       ulum   *gud-uj-l'ie-t*   ***tit***
       mad   become-ITER-INGR-SS.IMPF   **although**
       'although he was going mad'

The verb in (ia) and (ib) has a suffixal adverbial subordinator at the right and other affixes at the left. The verb in (iib) has suffixes at the right which are followed by an adverbial subordinator. We think that this positional difference with respect to other affixes could be a diagnostic for affixhood of adverbial subordinators.

The fact that (17b) does not exist shows that clause-initial adverbial subordinators must be separated from IP as in (17a). This is because CP is right-branching in (17) with its immediate constituents—adverbial subordinator and IP—separated from each other by the long juncture between them. It is impossible to attach an adverbial subordinator to the following IP as a prefix. Clause-final adverbial subordinators can be attached to the preceding IP as a suffix as shown in (18b) because they merge with the IP on their left to make a left-branching structure. This is possible because the juncture between constituents in a left-branching structure is short enough for adverbial subordinators to attach to the preceding clause. Thus, the data in (17) and (18) support the junctural asymmetry hypothesis.[12]

7.3.2 *Complement movement as compounding*

Given that left-branching structures have a short juncture between their constituents, we can argue that complement movement results in compacting of the structure concerned. By way of illustration, complement movement changes (19a) into (19b), where the silent copy of the moved YP (formerly *trace*) is shown in italics.

(19)   a. $[_{XP} X [_{YP} \ldots Y \ldots]]$

   b. $[_{XP} [_{YP} \ldots Y \ldots] [_{X'} X [_{YP} \ldots Y \ldots]]]$

Syntactically, (19b) still has right-branching structure in X′ with YP branching. However, phonologically, XP in (19b) is left-branching, assuming that silent categories and the constituent made by merging them to another constituent are invisible at PF. Since X′ and the original copy of YP in (19b) are invisible as shown in (20a), XP in the phonological representation (20) is left-branching.

(20)   a. $[_{XP} [_{YP} \ldots Y \ldots] [_{X'} X [_{YP} \ldots Y \ldots]]]$

   b. $[_{XP} [_{YP} \ldots Y \ldots] X]$

Then, complement movement changes right-branching PF (19a) into left-branching PF (20b), which has short juncture between YP and X.[13] We expect that constituents with complement–head order (20b) will behave as compounds because of short juncture. Our proposals parallel Julien's (2002), who also claims that systematic complement-to-specifier movement creates left-branching structure in head-final agglutinating languages.

---

[12] We argue that the facts we have seen in this section can be straightforwardly explained by asymmetric juncture. We do not mean to exclude the possibility that the facts are due to factors other than juncture. However, there have been no alternative explanations for the asymmetry facts presented here.

[13] See Tokizaki (1999, 2008) for invisible categories. Holmberg (2000) also argues that complement movement creates phonological left-branching structure. However, he does not consider the compound nature of left-branching structure.

Here we assume a condition Compact PF, which prefers compounds to phrases in PF. Then, complement–head order in (20b) is preferred to head–complement order in (19a). Compact PF motivates overt complement movement unless the resulting structure violates other phonological constraints. In the next section, we argue that complement movement is cancelled by the stress constraint, which requires the main stress position in constituents with complement–head order to match the unmarked word-stress location in the language.

7.4 Typology of stress location and head–complement orders

Word-stress locations

Goedemans and van der Hulst (2011a,b) divide languages into two classes, namely languages with fixed stress location and languages with weight-sensitive stress. The two classes are divided into several subcategories according to the stress locations. The lists in (21) and (22) show the classes and subcategories and the number of corresponding languages.[14]

(21) Fixed stress location

   a. No fixed stress (mostly weight-sensitive stress, cf. (22a–g))   219

   b. Initial: stress is on the first syllable   92
      Cahuilla (Uto-Aztecan; California): *'ñaʔa̦čeh* 'sit down', *'neñukum* 'female cousins'

   c. Second: stress is on the second syllable   16
      Mapudungun (Araucanian; Chile and Argentina): *ṭi'panto* 'year', *e'lumu̦yu* 'give us'

   d. Third: stress is on the third syllable   1
      Winnebago (Siouan; Illinois): *hochi'chinik* 'boy', *waghi'ghi* 'ball'

   e. Antepenultimate: stress is on the antepenultimate (third from the right) syllable   12
      Paumarí (Arauan; Amazonas, Brazil): *ra'bodiki* 'wide', *oni'manari* 'seagull'

   f. Penultimate: stress is on the penultimate (second from the right) syllable   110
      Djingili (West Barkly; Northern Territory, Australia): *bi'aŋga* 'later', *̦ŋuru'ala* 'we all'

   g. Ultimate: stress is on the ultimate (last) syllable   51
      Weri (Trans-New Guinea; Morobe, Papua New Guinea): *u̦lua'mit* 'mist', *̦aku̦nete'pal* 'times'.
      Total   501

---

[14] The examples in (22b,f,g) are taken from van der Hulst et al. (2010: 751, 443, 577).

(22)   Weight-sensitive stress

    a. Left-edge: Stress is on the first or second syllable   37
       Malayalam (Dravidian; southern India) *'kutira* 'horse', *paṭ'ṭaaḷak̠kaaran*
       'soldier'

    b. Left-oriented: The third syllable is involved   2
       Kashaya (Hokan; California) *ʔi'mehmi* 'real fuzz', *ʔima'tahmi* 'a real woman'

    c. Right-edge: Stress on ultimate or penultimate syllable   65
       Epena Pedee (Choco; Colombia) *'warra* 'son', *wa'raa* 'flavourful'

    d. Right-oriented: The antepenultimate is involved   27
       do'mesticus 'home', *per'fectum* 'perfect' (Classical Latin)

    e. Unbounded: Stress can be anywhere in the word   54
       Dongolese (Nubian; Sudan) *'nosogid* 'old age', *kɛmiŋ'gaːr* 'all four'

    f. Combined: Both right-edge and unbounded   8
       Danish (Germanic) *'foto* 'photograph', *pe'tròːleum* 'paraffin'

    g. Not predictable   26
       Burushaski (Pakistan) *ga'li* 'he went', *'gali* 'it broke'

    h. Fixed stress (no weight sensitivity, cf. (21b–g))   282
       Total   501

Note that the number of fixed-stress languages in (21b–g: 92+16+1+12+110+51=282) corresponds to that of fixed-stress languages in (22h: 282), and the number of languages with no fixed stress in (22a–g: 37+2+65+27+54+8+26=219) corresponds to that in (21a: 219). Thus, the total number of languages listed in (21) and (22) is 501 altogether.

7.4.2 Fixed stress locations

In this and the next section, we will outline our theory of how word-stress location determines head–complement orders. First, let us consider the languages with fixed stress locations. For example, languages with penultimate stress have words with the syllable structure in (23), where the underscore represents stress:

(23) $[_{\text{Word}} \ldots \underline{\sigma} \; \sigma]$

In these languages, a phrase with head–complement order has the structure in (24), where X is the head word of the phrase and Z is the last word in the complement YP:

(24) $[_{\text{XP}} [_{\text{X}} \ldots \underline{\sigma} \; \sigma] [_{\text{YP}} \ldots [_{\text{Z}} \ldots \underline{\sigma} \; \sigma]]]$

This right-branching structure does not pose any problem in phonology: each word (e.g. X and Z) has penultimate stress in (24). However, if the complement moves to the specifier position of X, the resulting structure is (25a), which is phonologically left-branching as shown in (25b), as we have argued in section 7.3.2 above:

(25) a. $[_{XP} [_{YP} \dots [_Z \dots \underline{\sigma} \ \sigma]] [_{X'} [_X \dots \underline{\sigma} \ \sigma] \ t]]$

    b. $[_{XP} [_{YP} \dots [_Z \dots \underline{\sigma} \ \sigma]] [_X \dots \underline{\sigma} \ \sigma]]$

We expect that the left-branching XP in (25b) will have the same stress position as a (compound) word because of the short juncture between YP and X. We formulate this as a stress constraint on left-branching structures, which are derived from right-branching structures.

    We will follow Cinque's (1993) idea that the most deeply embedded element in the recursive side of a structure has the primary stress in the structure. If this is right, the primary stress goes on to Z in (24) and (25b). However, this primary stress causes a problem in (25b), because (25b) is left-branching and compound-like. If the whole XP in (25b) is considered to be a (compound) word, its main stress location, represented with bold underlining, is far back from the penultimate position in XP, as shown in (26).

(26) $[_{XP} [_{YP} \dots \underline{\sigma} \ \sigma] [_X \dots \underline{\sigma} \ \sigma]]$

This stress location deviates from the stress template (23) in this language. Thus, moving complement YP to the specifier position of the head X to make (25b) violates the phonological constraint on stress location. We expect that overt complement movement does not occur in languages with penultimate word-stress to make the complement–head order in (25b). This prediction is borne out, as we will see in section 7.4.2. The same argument applies to fixed-stress languages with ultimate and antepenultimate stress.

    On the other hand, we expect that languages with word-initial stress will allow complement movement to generate complement–head orders. The stress template of these languages can be represented as in (27):

(27) $[_{Word} \underline{\sigma} \ \sigma \dots]$

A phrase with head–complement order has the structure in (28):

(28) $[_{XP} [_X \underline{\sigma} \ \sigma \dots] [_{YP} \boldsymbol{\sigma} \ \sigma \dots]]$

The phonology of (28) does not have a problem with respect to the stress location (27) because each word has initial stress in its own domain, X and YP. However, Compact PF forces complement YP to move to the specifier position of X to make the complement–head order shown in (29):

(29) $[_{XP} [_{YP} \boldsymbol{\underline{\sigma}} \ \sigma \dots] [_X \underline{\sigma} \ \sigma \dots]]$

Assuming that YP is also left-branching, the main stress falls on the leftmost syllable in YP in the compound-like structure XP in (29). This stress location in XP matches the word-stress template (27) because the heaviest stress in XP falls on the initial syllable in XP in (29). Thus, complement–head order is the option for initial-stress languages.

    To sum up, we expect that languages with word stress fixed on the ultimate, penultimate, or antepenultimate syllable will not allow complements to move to the specifier position of the head. This is because the complement movement would make the maximal projection a left-branching compound with the primary stress on the complement. This leftward stress of the derived compound would not correspond to the righthand word-stress location in the language. In languages with word stress fixed on the initial syllable, the primary stress on the moved complement matches their word-stress template. These points are summarized in (30) and (31) with examples of compounds from Spanish and Finnish.

(30)   Languages with right-edge (penultimate or ultimate) stress: $[_{Word} \ldots \underline{\sigma} \ \sigma]$ or $[_{Word} \ldots \sigma \ \underline{\sigma}]$ (e.g. Spanish)

    a. Head–complement: $[_{XP} [_{x} \ldots \underline{\sigma} \ \sigma] [_{YP} \ldots \boldsymbol{\sigma} \ \sigma]]$ (*abre-latas* 'open cans')

    b. Complement–head:*$[_{XP} [_{YP} \ldots \boldsymbol{\sigma} \ \sigma]] [_{x} \ldots \underline{\sigma} \ \sigma]]$

(31)   Languages with initial stress: $[_{Word} \ \underline{\sigma} \ \sigma \ldots]$ (e.g. Finnish)

    a. Head–complement: *$[_{XP} [_{x} \ \underline{\sigma} \ \sigma \ldots] [_{YP} \ \boldsymbol{\sigma} \ \sigma \ldots]]$

    b. Complement–head: $[_{XP} [_{YP} \ \boldsymbol{\sigma} \ \sigma \ldots] [_{x} \ \underline{\sigma} \ \sigma \ldots]]$ (*purkin-avaaja* 'can opener')

The crucial assumption here is that constituents with complement–head order are a kind of compound which must have the same main-stress location as simple words in the language.

7.4.3 *Weight-sensitive stress*

Next, let us consider languages with weight-sensitive stress. For example, languages with right-edge stress have stress on the penultimate or ultimate syllable in a word, as shown in (32) (Goedemans and van der Hulst 2005b), where H/L stands for a heavy/light syllable and stressed syllables are in boldface:[15]

(32)   a. (**H** L)]

    b. (L **H**)]

Right-edge stress languages are different from fixed-stress languages with ultimate stress in that they allow a light syllable on the right of the stressed heavy syllable as in (32a). We argue that this flexibility of stress position allows a monosyllabic complement to move to the specifier position of the head. For example, let us consider a word with the stress pattern in (32b):

(33) $[_{Word} \ldots \sigma_L \ \underline{\sigma}_H]$

---

[15] In addition to (32a) and (32b), there are two cases for weight-sensitive stress.

(i)   a. (**H** H)]/(H **H**)]

    b. (**L** L)]/(L **L**)]

In (ia) and (ib), there are two options for stress location. These are irrelevant to our discussion here.

This word can serve as a stem when it is combined with an affix as in (34), where the affix is the head and the stem is its complement:

(34)   [$_{Word}$ [$_{Affix}$ σ] [$_{Stem}$ ··· σ_L $\underline{\sigma}_H$]]

Suppose that this affix consists of a light syllable σ_L. Then the complement, Stem, may move to the specifier position of Affix to make the complement–head order in (35):

(35)   [$_{Word}$ [$_{Stem}$ ··· σ_L $\underline{\sigma}_H$] [$_{Affix}$ σ_L] t]

In this structure, Stem and Affix are closely connected with each other to make a word as a whole. The stress falls on the penultimate syllable in the word (35). The penultimate stress in (35) may well occur in languages with weight-sensitive stress on the right edge, i.e. on the ultimate or penultimate syllable. For example, Spanish has ultimate stress and penultimate stress as shown in (36):[16]

(36)   a. inglés 'English'

        b. casa 'house'

Penultimate stress corresponds to the stress pattern of [$_{Word}$ Stem–Affix] in (35). In fact, such languages are categorized as 'strongly suffixing' languages by Dryer (2011a). Some examples of Spanish are shown in (37).[17]

(37)   a. entrar   'enter'   →   entra-da   'entrance'

        b. tardar   'delay (v.)'   →   tarda-nza   'delay (n.)'

In (37), the stem on the left has ultimate stress, and the derived word on the right has penultimate stress. Both stress locations are permitted in Spanish because it is a right-edge stress language.[18] This movement of Stem is not possible for languages with

---

[16] In fact, Spanish also has antepenultimate stress in a number of words, e.g. *bolígrafo* 'pen'. Note also that Spanish has no long vowels. Here we consider stressed syllables as 'heavy' because they may be pronounced with lengthening.

[17] Suffixes are closely connected to the stem to make a prosodic word, which is the domain of stress placement. In most cases, stress falls on the fixed stress location counting both affix and stem. Thus, stress may fall on the affix part in a word as in Spanish (i) and Italian (ii) (cf. Scalise 1984: 87, 99).

(i)   a. orar   'pray'   →   ora-ción   'prayer'
       b. barrer   'clean (v.)' →   barre-dura   'cleaning'

(ii)   a. bello   'beautiful' →   bell-ezza   'beauty'
       b. autore   'author'   →   autor-izzare 'authorize'

[18] Italian also has a variety of stress locations as shown in (i).

(i)   a. città   'city'
       b. montagna   'mountain'
       c. tavola   'table'
       d. capitano (⟨ *capitare*) 'they happen'

In Italian, most words have penultimate stress (ib), and some words have ultimate stress (ia). There are also words with antepenultimate stress (ic) and stress on the fourth to the last syllable of the word (id). However, we do not find parallel examples to Spanish (37) because most suffixes in Italian are disyllabic.

fixed stress locations such as the ultimate or penultimate syllable (e.g. Bantu), as we will see in section 7.4.5.2.

7.4.4 *Levels of complement movement*

As we saw in section 7.2.1, we assume that complement movement applies at various levels of morphosyntactic structure, from words to subordinate clauses ((3) repeated here as (38)):

(38)   a. Affix–Stem (*un-*[[*real-ist*]*-ic*])

      b. Word–Word (*chaleco salva-vidas* (vest save lives) 'life-saving jacket' (Spanish))

      c. Noun–Genitive (*books of John*)

      d. Verb–Object (*read the books*)

      e. Adposition–Object (*in the mood*)

      f. Adverbial Subordinator–Clause (*before you go*)

The head–complement orders in (38) are changed into the complement–head orders in (39) by complement movement ((6) repeated here as (39)).

(39)   a. Stem–Affix (*stabiliz-ation*)

      b. Word–Word ([*red wine*] *glass*)

      c. Genitive–Noun (*John's books*)

      d. Object–Verb (*Bücher lesen* 'read books' (German))

      e. Adposition–Object (*huoneese-en* 'into room' (Finnish))

      f. Clause–Adverbial Subordinator (*anata-ga iku maeni* (you-NOM go before) 'before you go' (Japanese))

In (39d,e,f), we showed examples from languages other than English, which does not allow complement–head order in these pairs (**books read*, **room into*, **you go before*). This is because English has right-oriented (antepenultimate, penultimate, or ultimate) stress, as we will argue in 7.4.5.4.

Examination of the data in Dryer (2011a,b,c,d,e) shows that complement movement can apply cyclically from the smallest domain (Affix–Stem → Stem–Affix) to the largest domain (Adverbial Subordinator–Clause → Clause–Adverbial Subordinator) (See Kuwana and Tokizaki 2009; Tokizaki and Kuwana (2013)). Each language has a point at which it stops complement movement. For example, Romance languages have complement–head order in Stem–Affix (39a) and head–complement order at the other levels of morphosyntactic structure: in Word (Head)–Word (Complement) (38b), Noun–Genitive (38c), Verb–Object (38d), Adposition–Object (38e), and Adverbial Subordinator–Clause (38f). Uralic languages such as Finnish and Hungarian have complement–head order in Stem–Affix (39a),

Word (Complement)–Word (Head) (39b), Genitive–Noun (39c), Object–Verb (39d), and Object–Adposition (39e), and head–complement order only in Adverbial Subordinator–Clause (38f). The table in (40) shows the complement–head orders (+) and head–complement orders (–) in a range of languages (Jap/Kor=Japanese and Korean).

(40)

		Bantu	Romance	English	Germanic	Uralic	Jap/Kor
a.	Stem–Affix	–/+	+	+	+	+	+
b.	Word (C)–Word (H)	–	–	+	+	+	+
c.	Genitive–Noun	–	–	–/+	–/+	+	+
d.	Object–Adposition	–	–	–	–/+	+	+
e.	Object–Verb	–	–	–	–/+	–/+	+
f.	Clause–Subordinator	–	–	–	–	–	+

In (40a), Bantu languages have –/+ value for Stem–Affix because Swahili is classified as a weakly prefixing language and Chichewa as a strongly prefixing language. In (40c), English and Germanic languages are assigned a –/+ value for Genitive–Noun because they show different word orders, e.g. *books of John/John's books*. Dryer (2011d) classifies English, Frisian, and Norwegian as no dominant order in the order of genitive and noun (cf. Biber et al. 1999; Rosenbach 2002 for English). He also classifies Danish and Swedish as Genitive–Noun and Dutch, German, and Icelandic as Noun–Genitive order. In (40d), the –/+ in Germanic languages indicates that they have Verb–Object order in main clauses and Object–Verb order in subordinate clauses.

Note that most languages, including English, German, and Finnish, are disharmonic with respect to head–complement orders, as shown in (40). It is implausible to argue that children need to learn the value of a head parameter for each pair listed in (40). In section 7.4.5 we argue that the stress pattern determines (dis)harmonic word orders and that children have only to learn the unmarked word-stress location in the language.[19,20]

7.4.5 *Correlation between word orders and stress location*

7.4.5.1 *Word-stress location and head–complement orders*   The order of languages in the chart in (40) is determined by Goedemans and van der Hulst's (2011a,b) classification of word-stress location.[21] This is given in (41).

---

[19] The list of weight-sensitive stress in (22) contains 26 languages with unpredictable stress location. We also need to consider how word orders are determined in tone languages without stress. We leave these matters for future research.

[20] The chart in (40) also shows a gradation of word orders among levels of morphosyntactic constituents across languages. Note that the order of the example languages in (40) corresponds to their geographical location: from Africa to Asia through Europe. The geographical distribution of word orders is an interesting topic, but we will leave it for future research (see Tokizaki 2011).

[21] Nespor and Vogel (1982) propose the Complement Law, which claims that in a head and complement pair of words, main stress falls on the complement independently of its location, i.e. both in OV and in VO languages (Nespor and Vogel 1986; Nespor et al. 2008; cf. Cinque 1993; Emonds this volume). They do not argue that word-stress location determines head–complement orders in disharmonic word orders.

(41) a. Bantu (Swahili, Chichewa): penultimate

  b. Romance (French, Italian, Spanish): right-edge (ultimate or penultimate)

  c. English: right-oriented (ultimate, penultimate, or antepenultimate)

  d. Germanic (German, Dutch): right-oriented (ultimate, penultimate, or antepenultimate)

  e. Uralic (Finnish, Hungarian): initial

  f. Japanese/Korean: no stress

Generally speaking, stress location moves from right to left as we go down the list of languages in (41). Right-edge stress languages have ultimate or penultimate stress depending on the syllable weight. Thus, strictly speaking, penultimate (41a) is not the rightmost stress in the list (41). However, penultimate-stress languages in (41a) are less flexible than right-edge languages in (41b) in not permitting an extra weak syllable to be attached to the right end of a word, as we have seen in section 7.4.2 and 7.4.3.

No-stress languages are listed at the bottom in (41f) because their word orders are all complement–head as shown in (40). Languages with no stress allow complement movement in all constituents, from words to subordinate clauses. This is possible because these languages do not have stress whose location determines whether complements can move or not.

Let us now consider why languages with right-hand stress do not allow complement movement of large constituents such as objects and clauses. The chart in (42) is a combination of (40) and (41), with the languages in order of stress location from left to right:

(42)

		Jap/Kor	Uralic	German	English	Romance	Bantu
	Word stress	no stress	initial	R-ori	R-ori	R-edge	penult
a.	Stem–Affix	+	+	+	+	+	+/–
b.	Word (C)–Word (H)	+	+	+	+	–	–
c.	Genitive–Noun	+	+	+/–	+/–	–	–
d.	Object–Adposition	+	+	+/–	–	–	–
e.	Object–Verb	+	+/–	+/–	–	–	–
f.	Clause–Subordinator	+	–	–	–	–	–

The chart in (42) shows the correlation between word-stress location and complement–head orders. As stress moves to the right end of the word (from Japanese and Korean to Bantu), the domain of complement movement, represented as +, becomes smaller (from all (a)–(f) to only (a)). The gradation of complement–head orders and its correlation with word-stress location can be explained by the size of complements and the number of syllables after the stressed syllable. We will discuss each stress type in detail below.

7.4.5.2 *Penultimate stress*   If a language has penultimate stress, it does not allow any complement to move to the specifier position. If it were to move there, a complement and the head would make a left-branching structure, which would have short juncture between the complement and the head. The whole constituent complement–head would behave like a word, and its stress location should conform to the word-stress location of the language, i.e. penultimate stress. However, complement movement would leave the head as the last unstressed element in the constituent. As a result, stress would fall on the syllable before the penultimate syllable in the constituent, as shown in (43b):

(43)   a. $[_{XP} [_X \ldots \underline{\sigma} \ \sigma] [_{YP} \ldots \pmb{\sigma} \ \sigma]]$

     b. $[_{XP} [_{YP} \ldots \pmb{\sigma} \ \sigma] [_X \ldots \underline{\sigma} \ \sigma]]$

This dislocation of stress from the fixed position would occur even if the head is a monosyllabic element such as an affix or clitic, as illustrated in (44):

(44)   a. $[_{XP} [_X \ \sigma] [_{YP} \ldots \pmb{\sigma} \ \sigma]]$

     b. $[_{XP} [_{YP} \ldots \pmb{\sigma} \ \sigma] [_X \ \sigma]]$

In (44b), derived from (44a) by complement movement, the stress would fall on the antepenultimate syllable in XP. Thus, in penultimate-stress languages, a stem cannot move to the left of an affix by complement movement to create the Stem–Affix order; these languages have the Affix–Stem (i.e. head–complement) order as shown in (45):[22,23]

(45)   a. *m-wia*   (Swahili)
       person-debt
       'debtor'

     b. *m-sungi*   (Chichewa)
       person-keep
       'keeper'

In penultimate-stress languages, moving any size complement to the specifier position results in compound-like constituent with stress on the antepenult syllable or before (e.g. *wia-m*, *sungi-m*). Thus, the complement–head order is avoided at all levels as shown in the Bantu column in (42a–f).[24]

---

[22] In (45b), the base form of *sungi* is *sunga* 'keep'. The last vowel changes from *a* to *i* for agentive nouns when a prefix is attached to the word. See Mchombo (2004: 113).

[23] Here we mainly discuss the inflectional affixes considered in Dryer (2011a), which includes four types of affix on nouns (case, plural, pronominal possessive, definite/indefinite) and six types of affix on verbs (pronominal subject, tense/aspect, pronominal object, negative, interrogative, adverbial subordinator).

[24] Penultimate stress is also seen in Welsh, in which the usual order is noun+adj, e.g. *llyfrau trwm* 'heavy books' (literally 'books heavy'), but may be adj+noun, e.g. *hen lyfrau* 'old books'. However, prenominal adjectives are limited in number (e.g. *hoff* 'favourite'; *prif* 'main'). We can consider these adjectives to be lexical exceptions.

7.4.5.3 *Right-edge stress*   Consider next languages with right-edge stress. As we saw in section 7.4.3, these languages may have complement movement in the case of Stem–Affix. These languages allow penultimate stress as well as ultimate stress. Thus, suffixing is allowed as shown in (46) (=(37)):

(46)   a. entrar   'enter'   →   entra-da   'entrance'
       b. tardar   'delay (v.)'   →   tarda-nza   'delay (n.)'

The stems *entrar* and *tardar* have ultimate stress and the derived forms *entra-da* and *tarda-nza*, made by movement of the stem to the specifier position of the affixes concerned, have penultimate stress, which is allowed in right-edge stress languages.

However, languages with right-edge stress do not allow complement–head order in compounds, NP, VP, PP, and CP as shown in the Romance column in (42b–f). For example, consider the Italian compounds in (47) where the head words are disyllabic (*capo* and *campo*):

(47)   a. *capo   stazione*   →   **stazione capo*
          head   station
          'station master'

       b. *campo   santo*   →   **santo campo*
          field   holy
          'cemetery'

Complement–head order on the right of the arrow is ruled out because stress is expected to fall on the fourth syllable from the end of the compound, which is a marked stress location for right-edge stress languages. As we saw in section 7.4.2, we assume that stress should fall on the complement, on the assumption that it falls on the most deeply embedded element on the recursive side of a tree (cf. Cinque 1993).[25]

The examples in (47) show that if the head is disyllabic, stress falls on the fourth syllable from the end of the compound. The longer the head, the earlier syllable the stress falls on, violating the constraint on stress location, right-edge. The heads listed in (42b–f), words, nouns, verbs, adpositions, and adverbial subordinators (e.g. *window, decide, into,* and *before*), are likely to be longer than monosyllables. Thus, we can correctly predict that languages with right-edge stress, such as Romance languages, do not have complement–head orders except for Stem–Affix, as shown in (42a–f).

However, what rules out complement–head orders in these languages if the head is monosyllabic? The heads listed in (42b–f), words, nouns, verbs, adpositions, and adverbial subordinators, can be monosyllabic (e.g. *desk, put, in,* and *when*).

---

[25] We have assumed that silent categories and the constituent made by merging them to another constituent are invisible at PF (see section 7.3.2). Stress is assigned to the most deeply embedded element in PF, that is, the moved complement in the specifier position in the case of complement–head order.

Monosyllabic heads add only one syllable to the resulting structure by phonologically attaching to the complement, as shown in (48):

(48)   a. [$_{PP}$ *a* [$_{DP}$ *la*   *sómbra*]]
              at   the   shade

       b. *[$_{PP}$ [$_{DP}$ *la sómbra*] *a*]

       c. *[$_{PP}$ [$_{DP}$ *sómbra-la*] *a*]

We might assume the Final-over-Final Constraint (FOFC) proposed by Holmberg (2000) and Biberauer et al. (2008b). FOFC rules out a complement–head structure whose complement has the head–complement order.[26] (48b) is ruled out by FOFC because it is a PP with the complement–head order, which dominates a DP with head–complement order (D–NP/N). Thus, the base form (48a) cannot be changed into (48b) by complement movement. Alternatively, we can claim that (48b) is ruled out because of its marked stress location. The (phrasal) compound *la sómbra-a* in (48b) has the stress on the antepenultimate syllable. This is marked in languages with right-edge stress, i.e. ultimate or penultimate stress, such as Spanish and Italian. In this view, (48b) may be constructed in syntax, but it is ruled out in the PF component. The base (48a) cannot be changed into (48c) by successive complement movement, which first moves the N *sómbra* to the specifier position of the D *la* and then moves the resulting DP *sómbra-la* to the specifier position of the adposition *a*. The harmonic complement–head structure in (48c) observes FOFC. However, its main stress falls on the fourth syllable from the end, which does not conform to the stress pattern of the languages with right-hand stress, including ultimate, penulti-mate, right-edge, and right-oriented stress. Thus, (48c) is not allowed in these languages. This is also the case with other heads. Then, languages with right-hand stress cannot have complement–head orders except for Stem–Affix even when the head is monosyllabic. They would violate FOFC or the constraint on the stress location in the language, as shown in (48b) and (48c). In this sense, our stress constraint on complement movement can be an alternative explanation for FOFC.

7.4.5.4 Right-oriented stress   Next, let us consider why languages with right-oriented stress such as English and German allow complement–head orders in compounds, as shown in (42b). Right-oriented stress differs from right-edge stress in that only the

---

[26] Biberauer et al. (2008b) formulate FOFC as (i).

(i)   If α is a head-initial phrase and β is a phrase immediately dominating α, then β must be head-initial. If α is a head-final phrase, and β is a phrase immediately dominating α, then β can be head-initial or head-final.

FOFC (i) rules out structures like that in (ii).

(ii)   * [$_{\beta P}$ [$_{\alpha P}$ γP] β] where α P is the complement of β and γP is the complement of α.

former allows antepenultimate stress. Consider the example in (49), where the head noun *rack* is monosyllabic and its complement *towel* is disyllabic:

(49)   a. rack (for) towel(s)

      b. tówel rack

The base structure in (49a) is changed into a compound (49b) by complement movement. The resulting compound (49b) has antepenultimate stress, which is allowed in English and other Germanic languages. Similarly, a monosyllabic complement (e.g. *rack*) can be moved to the specifier position of a disyllabic head (e.g. *railway*) without violating the right-oriented stress constraint, as shown in (50):

(50)   a. railway (of) rack

      b. ráck railway

Stress falls on the antepenultimate syllable in the compound (50b).

One might argue that there are compounds with more than three syllables, which violate the right-oriented stress constraint, as shown in (51):

(51)   a. towel (in) kitchen

      b. kítchen towel

In (51b), stress falls on the fourth syllable from the right end of the compound. However, English, German, and Dutch have weakening of vowels including weak vowels and vowel reduction. The example in (51b) has phonetic representations as shown in (52):

(52)   a. kɪtʃən tauəl

      b. kɪtʃn̩ taul

If the unstressed vowels are deleted, the compound has stress on the penultimate syllable (or antepenultimate if we count syllabic nasal -tʃn̩), as in (52b). Thus, Germanic languages can observe right-oriented stress in compounds even if the resulting compound has stress on the (pre-)fourth syllable from its right end.[27]

---

[27] Some compounds may consist of words lacking vowel reduction as shown in (i).

(i)   a. kɪtʃən kliːnə
      b. kɪtʃn̩ kliːnə

In this example, the main stress is on the first syllable of *kitchen*, which is the third from the last syllable (antepenultimate) in the whole compound, *kitchen cleaner*, in (ib). This is still allowed in the right-oriented stress system in Germanic, which includes antepenultimate syllable as well as penultimate and ultimate. If we count the syllabic nasal in (ib), the main stress is on the fourth from the last syllable. Then, (ib) is a marked stress location in the right-oriented stress system. A reviewer questions the perfectly pronounceable forms that are not destressed. Although there may be such exceptional examples, the majority keep the unmarked stress location in the language. The point is that as the compound word gets longer with more syllables, the weak syllables are pronounced even more weakly and are likely to be omitted. This is the factor that enables languages with a weight-sensitive stress system to have a long complement in front of the head.

Weakening of vowels is not very common in Romance languages such as Italian and Spanish, which have no vowel reduction and no weak vowels in their phonological inventories.[28,29]

West Germanic languages other than English allow complement–head order in a VP, i.e. O–V, if it occurs with an auxiliary verb or it is in a subordinate clause, as shown in (53) (taken from Dryer 2005c):

(53)   a. *Anna   trink-t   Wasser.*   [V O]
          Anna   drink-3SG   water
          'Anna is drinking water.'

       b. *Anna   ha-t   Wasser   getrunken.*   [Aux O V]
          Anna   have-3SG   water   drink.PST.PTCP
          'Anna has drunk water.'

       c. *Hans   sag-t,   dass   Anna   Wasser   trink-t.*   [C...OV]
          Hans   say-3SG   that   Anna   water   drink-3SG
          'Hans says that Anna is drinking water.'

Basically, object–verb structures are the same as the compounds we have just seen above. Objects move to the specifier position of verbs to make derived compounds. The resulting compounds may have right-oriented stress. However, complement movement is more likely to result in a marked stress location in O–V sequences than in Word (C)–Word (H) compounds because objects may well consist of more than one word. The stress position of O–V sequences can be too far to the left of the antepenultimate syllable to be rescued by vowel reduction. Thus, O–V order is not allowed in main clauses without an auxiliary in German and Dutch, and in any clauses in English.

Two questions arise here. The first is why German and Dutch allow complement movement in subordinate clauses and in main clauses with an auxiliary. The second is why English is different from German and Dutch in disallowing complement movement in subordinate clauses and in main clauses with an auxiliary. A possible answer to the second question is to assume that stress in English falls on a syllable closer to the right end of a word than in German and Dutch. This is a plausible

---

[28] Ernestus and Neijt (2008) point out that Germanic languages prefer word-initial stress. This preference seems to go well with left-hand stress in compounds.

[29] Other Romance languages such as French and Portuguese may have vowel reduction. We might expect that languages with vowel reduction have more flexible stress position, and more complement–head orders than languages without vowel reduction. One difference we have found between French and other Romance languages is the order of the adjective phrase and noun in the equivalents of the English phrase, 'a very old lady': *une très vieille dame* (French) vs *una signora molto vecchia* (Italian); *una señora muy vieja* (Spanish); *uma senhora muito velha* (Portuguese). French has the AP–N order (complement–head), similar to Germanic languages, while other Romance languages have N–AP order (head–complement). We will leave the detailed examination of word order in these languages for future study.

assumption if we consider the fact that English is influenced by language contact with French, which has right-edge stress. Thus, English has the V–O order both in main and subordinate clauses.

The first question is more difficult to answer. However, we can generalize the two cases in which German and Dutch have O–V order as follows: O–V if and only if VP is c-commanded by an overt head. Candidates for the overt head c-commanding VP are auxiliaries and complementizers. A possible explanation for the O–V order in German and Dutch is to assume that complement movement needs to occur for compacting of constituents dominated by a higher overt head. We will not go into this issue in detail here, but see Tokizaki and Kuwana (2013).

7.4.5.5 *Initial stress* Now let us consider languages with initial stress such as the Uralic languages, including Hungarian and Finnish. These languages have complement–head order from word to postpositional phrase or verb phrase level, but not to adverbial subordinator–clause level as shown in (42). Word-initial stress does not conflict with complement movement as shown in (54):

(54) a. $[_{XP} [_X \underline{\sigma} \sigma \dots] [_{YP} \mathbf{\sigma} \sigma \dots]]$

  b. $[_{XP} [_{YP} \mathbf{\sigma} \sigma \dots] [_X \underline{\sigma} \sigma \dots]]$

In the resulting compound XP in (54b), the heaviest stress falls on the first syllable because it is the most deeply embedded element in XP. This stress location in compounds matches the unmarked word-stress location in these languages. Thus, we can explain why complement movement occurs to make the complement–head orders Stem–Suffix, Word (C)–Word (H), Genitive–Noun, Object–Verb, and NP–P.[30]

The remaining question is why these languages have head–complement order only in subordinate clauses, i.e. adverbial subordinator-clauses. A possible answer is that clauses are the only type of constituent that have an overt specifier (subject). Consider the structure of subordinate clauses in SOV languages shown in (55), where AdvSub stands for an adverbial subordinator.

(55) a. $[_{CP} \text{AdvSub} [_{IP} [_{Subj} \underline{\sigma} \sigma \dots] \text{I} [_{VP} [_{Object} \mathbf{\sigma} \sigma \dots] [_V \underline{\sigma} \sigma \dots]]]]$
    Míg Péter könyvet olvas (Finnish)
    while Peter book   read
    'While Peter was reading a book'

  b. $[_{CP} [_{IP} [_{Subj} \underline{\sigma} \sigma \dots] \text{I} [_{VP} [_{Object} \mathbf{\sigma} \sigma \dots] [_V \underline{\sigma} \sigma \dots]]] \text{AdvSub}]$
    **Péter könyvet olvas míg*

---

[30] Hungarian and Finnish have variable word order. Dryer (2011b) describes the order of object and verb in Hungarian as 'no dominant order' and the order in Finnish as VO. Our theory predicts that complements must move to the specifier position of a head to satisfy Compact PF if the resulting structure observes the unmarked stress pattern. It is possible for other factors such as discourse to come into play in the case of V–O order in these discourse-configurational languages. We will leave this problem for future research.

As we have seen in (54b), (55a) is allowed in initial-stress languages. If complement movement applied to IP in (55a), the resulting structure would have the clause-adverbial subordinator order in (55b). However, the resulting compound CP in (55b) does not have initial stress: the heaviest stress falls on the object, which is the most deeply embedded element in CP, and not on the subject that is the initial element in the whole CP. CP in (55b) violates the constraints on word-stress location in initial-stress languages. Thus, initial-stress languages have head–complement order between adverbial subordinator–clause and complement–head orders with other constituents.

7.4.5.6 *No stress*   Finally, let us consider languages with no stress such as Japanese and Korean (cf. Beckman 1986; Sohn 1999: 197). These languages do not have any problems in complement movement in any of the constituents because there is no chance of stress mismatch between words and derived compounds. Complement movement applies to (56a) freely to make compounds in (56b).

(56)   a. $[_{XP} [_X \sigma \sigma \ldots] [_{YP} \sigma \sigma \ldots]]$

      b. $[_{XP} [_{YP} \sigma \sigma \ldots] [_X \sigma \sigma \ldots]]$

The presence of a subject in clauses is not a problem in deriving the clause–adverbial subordinator order in (57b) from the base order in (57a), which is unacceptable.

(57)   a. $[_{CP} \text{Sub} [_{IP} [_{Subj} \sigma \sigma \ldots] \text{I} [_{VP} [_{Object} \sigma \sigma \ldots] [_V \sigma \sigma \ldots]]]]$
         maeni anata-ga ie-o   deru
         before you- NOM home leave

      b. $[_{CP} [_{IP} [_{Subj} \sigma \sigma \ldots] \text{I} [_{VP} [_{Object} \sigma \sigma \ldots] [_V \sigma \sigma \ldots]]] \text{Sub}]$
         anata-ga ie-o   deru maeni
         you- NOM home leave before
         'before you leave home'

Thus, we correctly predict that languages with no stress have complement–head order in any kind of constituent, as shown in (42).

The remaining question is whether there are any languages without stress with head–complement pairs. Tonal languages such as Chinese and Thai might seem to be candidates. However, these languages have a light tone, which corresponds to an unstressed vowel in stress languages. Thus, we can explain the correspondence between phonology and head–complement orders by considering the position of the light tone and full tones in tonal languages. We will leave this matter for our future research.[31]

---

[31] Goedemans and van der Hulst (2011a,b) do not show whether a language has a stress system or not. At this moment, it is impossible to find languages without stress systematically.

7.5 Conclusion

We have argued that word-stress location matches the main stress position in constituents with complement–head order, which are left-branching and compound-like because of the short juncture between their elements. The complement moves to the specifier position of the head in order to be interpreted with that head at LF. This movement occurs in overt syntax (before spell-out) only if the resulting constituent with complement–head order has the same stress position as a word. We have shown that fixed stress positions and weight-sensitive stress positions allow certain kinds of complements to move to the specifier position according to the number of syllables in heads and complements.

This stress-based theory of disharmonic word orders explains a fine correlation between stress position and head–complement orders in a number of languages. The next step is to show with statistical data that this theory correctly predicts word orders in more of the world's languages (see Kuwana and Tokizaki 2009). We will leave this for another article (see Tokizaki 2011).

Part III

The Question of Antisymmetry

8

Why Are There No Directionality Parameters?

RICHARD S. KAYNE

8.1 Introduction[1]

A 'why'-question such as the one in the title can be interpreted in at least two ways. On the one hand it can be interpreted as asking for evidence that supports the assertion that there are no directionality parameters. Another interpretation, taking it for granted that it's true that there are no directionality parameters, asks why the language faculty should be put together in that fashion.

I will touch on some evidence of the standard sort in the first part of this paper (introduction and sections 8.2 and 8.3). (Subsequently, in section 8.4, I will move on to the second interpretation of the 'why'-question.)

What, then, is the evidence for saying that there are no directionality parameters?

Basically, it is that under the view that was standard in the 1980s, to the effect that there are directionality parameters, one would expect to find oneself living in a symmetric syntactic universe, with specifiers to be found on either side of their head and complements on either side of theirs. Yet if one looks at the facts of human language syntax to the extent that we know them, in search of such symmetry, one does not find it, I think.

The expectation of symmetry breaks down in a number of ways. One very simple way rests on the following observation. Nobody has ever found two languages that are mirror images of one another, i.e. nobody has ever found two languages such that for any sentence in one, the corresponding sentence in the other would be its mirror image (taken either word-by-word or morpheme-by-morpheme).

[1] This paper originally appeared in 2011 in Mary Byram Washburn, Katherine McKinney-Bock, Erika Varis, Ann Sawyer, and Barbara Tomaszewicz (eds), *Proceedings of the 28th West Coast Conference on Formal Linguistics*, Somerville, Mass.: Cascadilla Press, 1–23. I am grateful to Cascadilla Press for permission to republish it here.

Put another way, take some human language, e.g. English, and construct mirror-image English by taking the mirror image of each grammatical English sentence and then 'putting it into' mirror-image English. Though perfectly easy to imagine, such a mirror image of English has never come close to being found, and similarly for any other known language.

In a symmetric syntactic universe there should exist such pairs as English and mirror-image English (even if the question whether you would expect to chance upon them is a complicated one), but clearly nobody has ever found any. I suspect that if you ask syntacticians to make educated guesses, most would agree that we are never going to find such pairs and that it is not an accident that we have not found them yet. This, I think, is relatively uncontroversial.

The antisymmetry hypothesis that I put forth in 1994 in *The Antisymmetry of Syntax* (henceforth *AS*) leads to much stronger expectations, though, stronger than what was said in the preceding paragraphs. This is the case since, if antisymmetry holds, then for any subtree (with both hierarchical and precedence relations specified) that is well-formed in some language, the mirror image of that subtree cannot be well-formed in any language. That of course is controversial; in fact, the negation of it was standardly assumed to be correct in the 1980s.[2]

At first glance there do of course appear to be symmetrical pairs of substructures such as English VO and Japanese OV, that do give the impression that they are in a mirror-image relation. If antisymmetry is correct, though, all such cases must be misleading and must in fact involve pairs that differ in hierarchical structure.

If we assume something like Baker's (1988) UTAH principle, along with a strong interpretation of Chomsky (2001) on uniformity, then in such cases as English VO and Japanese OV this hierarchical difference will necessarily be associated with some difference in movement (internal Merge) in the corresponding derivations. Such movement differences will in turn be related, under a familiar view, to differences in the properties of functional heads.[3]

A strong position, but one that is not central to what follows and that I will not pursue here, would be:[4]

(1)   Movement differences exhaust the universe both of word-order differences and of morpheme-order differences.

8.2 Movement leading to OV order

Let us take OV as a test case. Antisymmetry as in *AS* has the following immediate consequence:

---

[2] See, for example, Chomsky and Lasnik (1993: sect in. 3.1).
[3] See, for example, Borer (1984: 29).
[4] Cf. Cinque (1999).

(2)   OV can never be associated with a structure in which O is sitting in the complement position of V.[5]

It seems completely clear and undeniable that there exist languages or subparts of languages in which OV order is produced by movement. It is hard to see how anybody could disagree with that, if it is stated as an existential. One easy example in English would be:

(3)   They're having their car washed.

in which object *their car* comes to precede via movement (of the sort found in passives) the verb *wash* that it is the object of.

Even more telling are examples of OV order involving movement of O where OV order is 'canonical' or 'neutral',[6] i.e. does not involve what one might think of as 'special' movements like the one found in (3). One such type of case is found in languages of a sort studied by Dryer (1992), with SONegV as a possible canonical order (as in Korean). As argued by Whitman (2005), on the assumption that Neg is merged outside VP, and therefore above O, the pre-Neg position of O in SONegV sentences must have been produced by movement.[7] In a SONegV sentence, O can clearly not be occupying the complement position of the pronounced V.

Whitman argues more specifically that SONegV is produced by remnant VP movement. The verb moves out of the VP by head movement; subsequently the entire (verbless) VP containing O moves past Neg, much as in Nkemnji's (1992, 1995) analysis of one word-order pattern in Nweh.[8]

A similar argument in favour of remnant movement carrying an object to the left of V is made by Baker (2005) for Lokạạ. One such case in Lokạạ is that of SONegV, matching Whitman, but Baker's argument for Lokạạ is extended to various other

---

[5] More specifically this follows from the claim in *AS* and in Kayne (2003a) that specifier, head, and complement are always found in the order S–H–C. (In Bare Phrase Structure, this translates into the order 'second-merged phrase H first-merged phrase'.)

A number of authors have jumped from S–H–C to SVO. This follows only if what we call objects are invariably complements of their verbs, which is certainly not always the case—see Kayne (1981a) and Larson (1988).

[6] Erdozia et al. (2009) argue that canonical SOV order in Basque is processed faster and more easily than non-canonical orders. They plausibly relate that to the canonical order involving less syntactic computation than non-canonical orders. At certain points, though, they seem to draw the further conclusion that canonical order involves no movement at all, which does not follow. In addition to the text discussion of canonical SOXV order in various languages, see the discussion of (6) below, as well as Pollock (1989) and Cinque (1999) on verb movement in (canonical order sentences in) French and Italian (and various other languages), and Bernstein (1991, 1997), Cinque (1994, 2005b, 2010), and Shlonsky (2004) on noun movement (in canonical order DPs).

[7] Whitman makes the same point for the S–O–Tense/Aspect–Verb languages discussed by Dryer.

[8] Cf. in part Biberauer (2008a). For a remnant movement analysis of West Germanic OV, see Haegeman (2000) and Koopman and Szabolcsi (2000). For a remnant movement analysis (in which O must move leftward first) of VO order in Malagasy and similar languages, see Pearson (2000).

such cases of canonical SOXV orders, in particular where X is a gerundive morpheme, a mood morpheme, or an auxiliary.[9]

An alternative to remnant VP movement for SOXV is to have O move past X by itself. Kandybowicz and Baker (2003) argue specifically that both options are made available by the language faculty. While remnant VP movement is appropriate for Nweh and for Lokąą, movement of O by itself is called for in Nupe. (This difference correlates with the fact that Nweh and Lokąą have S–PP–X–V, whereas Nupe does not.)[10]

The SOAuxV order found in Lokąą is, again, a clear instance in which O cannot possibly be in the complement position of the pronounced V. Such sentences are also found in (Dutch and) German in some cases, in particular in (embedded cases of) so-called IPP sentences,[11] in which the verbal complement of the auxiliary appears as an infinitive rather than as a past participle:[12]

(4)   Ich glaube dass er das Buch hätte   lesen   wollen.
      'I   believe that he the book would-have to-read to-want'
      'I believe that he would have wanted to read the book.'

In this kind of embedded sentence (strictly speaking SOAuxVV, with two Vs) in standard German, the (definite)[13] object must precede the auxiliary:

(5)   *Ich glaube dass er hätte das Buch lesen wollen.

In other words, (4) is another example of a canonical/neutral word order (this time in German) in which O (*das Buch*) and V (*lesen*) do not even form a constituent.

---

[9] Similarly, Japanese honorific *o-* looks (to me) like a functional head that precedes the (nominalized) VP, all of whose arguments move past *o-*; for recent discussion of this *o-*, see Ivana and Sakai (2007). For related proposals, see Whitman (2001).

[10] Cf. also Aboh (2004).

[11] For discussion of IPP, see, for example, Hinterhölzl (2000) and Zwart (2007).

[12] OAuxV is also found in various languages in a way limited to certain subtypes of O. In Romance languages object clitics almost always precede a finite auxiliary, e.g.:

(i)   Jean les a vus. (French 'Jean them has seen')

For a possible link to certain cases of Scandinavian object shift, see Nilsen (2005: note 7). For a possible link between object shift and passive, see Anagnostopoulou (2005) and Bobaljik (2005). In French the quantified objects *tout* ('all') and *rien* ('nothing') can precede an infinitival auxiliary (cf. Kayne 1975: ch. 1; 1981b):

(ii) Jean croit tout avoir compris. ('Jean believes all to-have understood')

(iii) Jean croit ne rien avoir compris. ('Jean believes NEG nothing to-have understood')

In Icelandic, too, negative phrases can do so—cf. Jónsson (1996) and Svenonius (2000b).

For instances of OAuxV in Finnish and further instances in Icelandic, see Holmberg (2000) and Hróarsdóttir (2000b), respectively.

[13] In German, but not in Dutch, an indefinite object to some extent can act differently—see Wurmbrand (2005: Table 7).

It should be noted that in instances of SOXV in which the O is carried to the left of X by remnant movement, it might perhaps still be the case that the pronounced O is in the complement position of the trace/copy of V. This would nonetheless be compatible with (2) as long as O, if in complement position, does not precede the trace/copy of V. On the other hand, it is by no means clear that O is allowed to remain in its Merge position, insofar as it might always have to move for Case and/or EPP reasons. (This point is strongest if, as in Kayne (1998) and Chomsky (2001), movement cannot take place at LF.) In this vein, thinking at the same time of the VP-/predicate-internal subject hypothesis[14] that is now widely held, of Kayne (2004) on prepositions as probes, and of Chomsky (2008) on the perhaps general raising of objects to Spec-V, one might well reach:

(6)   All arguments must move at least once.

Of importance both for (6) and for (2) are deverbal compounds of the English type, as in:

(7)   an avid magazine reader

(8)   that magazine-reading student over there

If we interpret (6) strongly by taking 'argument' there to cover the object in such deverbal compounds, then *magazine* must have moved at least once in both (7) and (8), in a way that would fit in straightforwardly with Baker (1988) on noun incorporation. This is important for the antisymmetric claim of (2), since (2) says that *magazine* in these examples must not be sitting in the complement position of *read*. A noun incorporation approach to (7) and (8) would, instead, have *magazine* left-adjoining to *read*, in a way compatible with (2) (and (6)).

Noun incorporation is not the only approach to (7) and (8) that is compatible with (2). An alternative would be to take *magazine* to be moving to a (low) specifier postion. That might be supported by the possibility of an intervening particle such as *down*:

(9)   an avid music downloader

(10)   that music-downloading student over there

with the pre-V position of *down* here related to the pre-V position of the particle in Swedish participial passives,[15] as well as by the possibility of having more than just a noun:

(11)   an avid (?very) old car buyer

(12)   an avid classical music downloader

---

[14] See, for example, Koopman and Sportiche (1991). For recent discussion of a canonical case of the raising of (genitive) subject and object arguments within DP, see Brattico and Leinonen (2009: 19).
[15] Cf. Holmberg (1986) and Taraldsen (2000: note 5).

8.3 Cross-linguistic gaps and asymmetries

Observationally speaking, there are apparent cross-linguistic symmetries such as VO/OV of the English/Japanese type. As discussed in the previous two sections, antisymmetry implies that the apparent symmetries are not true symmetries, when one looks more closely into hierarchical structure. In this section, I would like to touch upon some examples of cross-linguistic asymmetries that strikingly reflect the general antisymmetry of syntax. In each case, a precise explanation will of course ultimately involve other principles (e.g. locality) in addition to antisymmetry itself.

8.3.1 *Dislocations and hanging topics*

Cinque (1977) has shown that Italian has two distinct types of left-dislocation, one of which he calls 'hanging topics'.[16] Hanging topics occur at the left-hand edge of the sentence. As far as I know, there has never been a claim to the effect that there exists something exactly comparable on the right-hand edge of the sentence, in any language. If so, that is a sharp gap/asymmetry; if antisymmetry were not correct, what could we possibly attribute that to? (The core reason for the absence of right-hand hanging topics is the antisymmetric prohibition against right-hand specifiers.)

Note in particular that the other type of left dislocation that Italian has, namely CLLD (clitic left-dislocation, as discussed in more detail in Cinque 1990) does seem to have a right-hand counterpart, usually called (clitic) right-dislocation. Yet the pairing of CLLD and clitic right-dislocation (CLRD) is itself misleading. As argued by Cecchetto (1999) for Italian and by Villalba (1999) for Catalan, there are sharp asymmetries within each of those two languages between CLLD and CLRD,[17] which would be quite surprising if our linguistic universe were not antisymmetric.[18] (Again, the core reason for this asymmetry is the antisymmetric prohibition against right-hand specifiers, which forces a remnant movement analysis and/or a bi-clausal analysis of CLRD,[19] but not of CLLD.)

---

[16] Although they might appear not to involve movement, note the scope reconstruction effect for a certain kind of topicalization in Basque pointed out by Ortiz de Urbina (2002: 520). Similarly for the fairly acceptable bound-variable-type reconstruction effect in (my) English:

(i)   His youngest daughter, no man could possibly not love her. (in which *his* is bound by *no man*)

[17] Probably not related to antisymmetry, on the other hand, is the fact that, according to Villalba and Bartra-Kaufmann (2010: note 20), CLRD is 'far less common' in Spanish than in Catalan. (Similarly, I have long had the impression that French uses CLRD more than Italian.) What such differences might rest on (and how they can be made more precise) remains to be understood.

[18] It is of course logically possible that we will at some point in the future find other languages where things are the reverse of Italian and Catalan. As in any empirical science, there is no way to prove that that is never going to happen, but the weight of the evidence as of now in this sub-area of syntax clearly tilts strongly toward the antisymmetric.

[19] Relevant to the bi-clausal possibility is:

(i)   He's real smart, John is.

(ii) He's real smart, is John.

Related to this left–right asymmetry is the fact that there are SVO languages (such as Haitian creole and Gungbe)[20] that lack CLRD entirely, but apparently no SVO languages that lack left-dislocation entirely.

8.3.2 *Clitics*

Greenberg's (1963) Universal 25 states that if the pronominal object in a given language is post-V, so is the nominal object. Recast in movement terms and generalized beyond the position of V, this can plausibly be interpreted as:

(13)   No language will systematically move its lexical objects further to the left than its pronominal clitics.

Put this way, there is an immediate link to the well-known English contrast between:

(14)   I said I liked them all.

and

(15)   *I said I liked those talks all.

Here, the pronoun arguably moves further left than the lexical DP. The proposal in (13) leads to the expectation that no variety of English could reverse these judgments and reject (14) while accepting (15). From this perspective, (14)/(15) is essentially similar to the French contrast given in:[21]

(16)   Jean les voit. ('John them sees')

(17)   *Jean les chiens voit. ('John the dogs sees')

with the (correct) expectation again being that no variety of French reverses these judgments.

Both (13) and Greenberg's narrower formulation are compatible with the pattern found in Italian infinitivals:

(18)   Gianni desidera comprarli. ('G desires to-buy them')

(19)   Gianni desidera comprare i libri. ('G desires to-buy the books')

On these, cf. *AS*, section 8.3. On a bi-clausal analysis of first-conjunct agreement, cf. Aoun et al. (2010). For additional potential cases, see Kayne and Pollock (2012: note 28).

Relevant to the remnant movement possibility is Ortiz de Urbina's (2002) account of sentence-final (corrective) focus in Basque. (His observation (p. 521) that postverbal constituents are slightly marginal in some adjunct clauses in Basque recalls Vilkuna's (1998) partially similar observation on Estonian and Finnish; for a proposal, see Kayne (2003a: section 4.1).)

[20] Cf. Baker (2003) on Kinande and Torrence (2005: 70, 73, 75) on Wolof. On a possible link to the position of D, cf. Kayne (2003b: section 2).

[21] Also to some familiar cases of object shift in Scandinavian, with an important question again being whether the pronominal object in Scandinavian object shift is moving by itself, or being carried along by remnant VP movement, as in Holmberg (1999: last section), Taraldsen (2000), and Nilsen (2003).

in which both the clitic *li* and the full object *i libri* follow the infinitive. Greenberg's formulation looks wrong, though, for Basque, whose canonical order is generally taken to have the object preceding the verb, which in turn is followed by the auxiliary, so that Basque is canonically SOVAux. The term 'aux' here hides substantial complexity. As Laka (1993a) shows, the Basque auxiliary must be decomposed into (at least) three parts, each of which can be preceded by a pronominal person clitic. If so, these clitics are post-V, despite the canonical object being pre-V, in a way that goes against Greenberg's original formulation.[22]

As far as (13) is concerned, Basque highlights an ambiguity in the term 'Move', one that was touched on earlier in section 8.2 (and that is in fact relevant to the entirety of this section, too). When a lexical object moves, is it moving by itself or being carried along by the movement of a phrase containing it? One way to reconcile Basque with (13) is to say that (13) is interested only in movements affecting objects by themselves, and then to say that in Basque O comes to precede Aux (and the pronominal clitics within Aux) as the result of being carried along by some larger phrasal movement.

A second way (not mutually exclusive with the first) to reconcile Basque with (13) is to say that (13) is to be interpreted as referring to A-movement and not A-bar movement, in some sense of those terms. Clearly the French fact of (16) vs (17) is not undermined by French allowing:

(20)   Les chiens, Jean les voit. ('the dogs, J them sees')

This example of left-dislocation should not count as an exception to (13). Distinguishing between A- and A-bar movements (and taking pre-V O in Basque to be moved there by A-bar movement)[23] is one way to achieve this. (Another would be to exclude from consideration all sentences with clitic-doubling.)

Assuming that Basque is ultimately compatible with some interpretation of (13),[24] we can ask why (13) would hold in the first place. Part of the answer might lie in Cardinaletti and Starke's (1999) association of degree of movement and amount of internal structure, with pronominal clitics (and weak pronouns) being 'smaller' than strong pronouns and lexical DPs and therefore having to move further.

The other part of the answer is closer to the concerns of this paper. More specifically, the question is why 'moving further' should imply 'moving further to

---

[22] There would not be much plausibility to trying to make this problem disappear by calling all of the Basque person morphemes in question agreement morphemes and then saying that agreement morphemes don't fall under Greenberg's Universal 25 (or under (13)). Laka (1993a) sees a strong parallelism between these Basque person morphemes and Romance pronominal person clitics. (Preminger (2009) argues that the absolutive person morphemes are instances of (non-clitic) agreement, while continuing to take the ergative and dative ones to be clitics—cf. Etxepare 2006, 2009.)

[23] Much as in Jayaseelan (2001) for Malayalam. Note that A-bar movements such as topicalization typically cannot even apply to pronominal clitics.

[24] And similarly for Amharic and Persian.

the left'. An answer is given in *AS*, in particular by the conclusion drawn there that all movement must be leftward.

8.3.3 *Agreement*

Just as the 'leftness' aspect of (13) would be surprising if we lived in a symmetric linguistic universe (but is not surprising in an antisymmetric one), so would the correctness of Greenberg's (1963) Universal 33 be surprising if syntax were symmetric:

(21)   When verbal number agreement is suspended in an order-sensitive way, it's always when the verb precedes the NP.

Whereas the discussion of the preceding section concerned pronominal clitics (and weak pronouns) that in the general case convey person distinctions, Greenberg's Universal 33 as stated in (21) concerns number only and claims that number agreement in '...NP...V...' contexts is more widespread than in '...V...NP...' contexts. A controversial generalization of this would be:

(22)   Verbal number agreement always requires that the NP (or DP) in question precede the verb at some stage of the derivation.

This position has been taken (even more broadly) by Koopman (2003, 2005a),[25] who argues that Chomsky (2001) was wrong to allow for purely 'downward' agreement.

A particular proposal for the apparent counterexample to (22) constituted by:

(23)   There are books on the table.

is given in Kayne (2008) in terms of the idea that *there* in such sentences is a remnant that includes (a copy of and) the number features of *books*.[26] This proposal might carry over to Italian sentences like:

(24)   Ne sono arrivati tre. ('of-them are arrived three' = 'three of them have arrived')

if such sentences in Italian contain a silent preverbal (clitic) counterpart of *there*. On the other hand, Italian transitive sentences in which a verb seems to agree with a post-V subject:[27]

---

[25] On complementizer agreement, see Koopman (2005b: note 25).

[26] In a way akin to Moro (1997a) and especially Sabel (2000), but differently from Chomsky (2001: 7), yet in agreement with him concerning the desirability of eliminating categorial features.

Kayne (2009b) contains a proposal (differently than Marantz 1997) that makes unnecessary the use of such features to distinguish noun-like elements from verb-like elements, by taking antisymmetry to underlie the noun–verb distinction.

[27] A challenge is to extend this in a principled way to Moro's (1997a, 2000):

(i)   La causa sono io. ('the cause am I')

(25)   Lo hanno mangiato i gatti. ('it have eaten the cats' = 'the cats have eaten it')

will probably require having *lo hanno mangiato* move leftward past *i gatti*. Whether one or another of these proposals might carry over to the partially comparable Icelandic examples often discussed in the literature remains an open question.

Both (21) and (22), which is compatible with Agree necessarily being accompanied by movement, fit well with the facts of Italian past participle agreement.[28] A basic contrast is:

(26)   Li ho visti. ('them I-have seen(M.PL.)')

(27)   *Ho visti loro. ('I-have seen(M.PL.) them')

The past participle *visti* can agree with preceding *li* but not with following *loro*. Similarly for passive vs active in:

(28)   I libri saranno visti. ('the books will-be seen')

(29)   *Ho visti i libri.

In the active (29), the past participle cannot agree with the object. In the corresponding passive, the participle can (and must) agree with the preposed object (which has moved to subject position).

As with (25), large phrasal movement will in all likelihood underlie:[29]

(30)   Saranno visti i libri.

(Alternatively, (30) will contain a silent counterpart of *there*, as suggested for (24).) Either phrasal movement or head movement will underlie the partially similar:

(31)   Una volta vistili, Gianni ... ('one time seen them, G ...' = 'once he saw them, G ...')

in which the past participle *visti* agrees with the pronominal clitic *li* that it ends up preceding.[30]

It should be noted that (22) is a necessary, but not sufficient, condition for past participle agreement to hold. This is shown by the fact that *wh*-movement does not license past participle agreement in Italian:[31]

---

[28] And with French past participle agreement, relative to a gender agreement counterpart of (22). (Number agreement on French past participles is not pronounced.)

[29] Cf. Belletti (1981).

[30] Better than (29) is:

(i)   ?G si è comprata una mela. ('G REFL. is bought an apple' = 'G has bought himself an apple')

It may be that with auxiliary 'be', the object can in Italian move higher (and so precede the participle at a certain stage in the derivation) than with auxiliary 'have'.

For further discussion of French and Italian past participle agreement, see Kayne (1985, 1989, 2009a).

[31] Although it does in French. For an interesting proposal on what the underlying parametric difference might be, see Déprez (1998).

(32)   *Quali libri hai letti? ('which books have-you read(M.PL.)')

As a final remark on agreement, note that in Italian sentences like (26), (28), and (30), the finite verb shows person (and number) agreement, while the past participle shows number (and gender) agreement, but never any person agreement. Insofar as the finite verb in these cases is higher than the participle, this discrepancy between person agreement and number agreement recalls Harbour's (2008) claim that in cases of discontinuous agreement, person generally precedes number. Thinking of Shlonsky (1989), the natural proposal is that (within a given local domain) PersonP is higher than NumP, from which the ordering of person before number observed by Harbour will follow,[32] given antisymmetry.

8.3.4 *Relative clauses*

In a symmetric syntactic universe, one would expect prenominal and postnominal relatives to be similar, merely differing in their order with respect to the 'head'. However, Downing (1978) and Keenan (1985) noted substantial differences. These can be stated as follows (setting aside correlatives, and keeping to relatives that are in their canonical position for the language in question):

(33)   Prenominal relatives (as opposed to postnominal relatives) generally lack complementizers akin to English *that*.

(34)   Prenominal relatives (as opposed to postnominal relatives) usually lack relative pronouns.

(These two properties of canonically prenominal relatives are just one, if Kayne (2010b) is correct in taking English *that* and similar elements to be relative pronouns.)

(35)   Prenominal relatives (as opposed to postnominal relatives) tend to be non-finite.

These differences fed into the proposal in *AS* that prenominal relatives originate postnominally.[33] A piece of evidence in favour of that view comes from Kornfilt (2000), who observes that the Turkic languages Sakha and Uigur have prenominal relatives whose subjects trigger agreement such that the agreement morpheme actually appears following the 'head' noun. She makes the plausible proposal that this agreement is produced via leftward movement of an originally postnominal relative containing a high Agr element. Put another way, what preposes past the 'head' NP in these languages is a not quite full relative clause; in particular the preposing to prenominal position strands the high Agr element, which remains postnominal.

---

[32] Non-discontinuous agreement of the sort found in Icelandic past tense forms may involve movement of Num past Pers.

[33] For a different view, see Cinque (2003, 2010).

In an asymmetric syntactic universe, the following should turn out to be correct (as seems to be the case):

(36)   No postnominal relatives ever have their subject determining agreement that precedes the 'head' noun.

In other words, there can be no mirror image of the configuration that Kornfilt discusses for Sakha and Uigur, the reason being that the leftward (partial) relative clause movement that plays a role in Sakha and Uigur can have no rightward counterpart.

8.3.5 *Serial verbs*

According to Carstens (2002), serial verb constructions differ cross-linguistically with respect to the relative position of verb and argument, but are cross-linguistically constant with respect to the relative order of the verbs themselves with respect to one another. Put another way, the higher verb of a serial verb construction consistently precedes the lower one, contrary to what we are accustomed to seeing with other cases of higher and lower verbs. The usual case cross-linguistically seems to be that various orders are possible. For example, English and German differ (in embedded non-V2 contexts) in that English has auxiliary–participle order where German has participle–auxiliary order:[34]

(37)   We believe that John has telephoned.

(38)   Wir glauben dass Hans telefoniert hat.

with the participle in German moving leftward past the auxiliary.

   That serial verb sentences are cross-linguistically uniform in verb order must mean that for some reason (to be elucidated) the lower verb in such sentences is not able to undergo movement of the sort available in German in (38), or any other comparable movement. The fact that it is the lower verb that invariably follows the higher one in serial verb sentences will then directly reflect the antisymmetric fact that the complement of the higher verb must follow that higher verb. In effect, serial verbs, because they disallow verb movement of a certain sort, provide a transparent window on the relation between word order and hierarchical structure.[35]

---

[34] As discussed by Zwart (1996, 2007) and others, when there are more than two verbs, there are more than two possible orders cross-linguistically, in a way that is not expected from the perspective of the (vast oversimplification hidden behind the) 'head-final language' vs 'head-initial language' distinction (cf. Travis 1989), as well as Kroch's (2001: 706) observation that most languages are actually inconsistent in head-directionality, and Julien (2002, 2003). A case in point is (4) above, in which the order of verbs in German is not simply the reverse of the English order.

[35] For related discussion, see Kandybowicz and Baker (2003).

8.3.6 *Coordination*

A similarly transparent window seems to be provided by a certain type of coordination, as Zwart (2009a) shows. According to Zwart, if one looks cross-linguistically at NP/DP coordination counterparts of English *and*, and if one limits oneself to coordinations in which *and* appears only once, one finds that *and* and its counterparts invariably occur between the two conjuncts:

(39)   a. NP and NP
      b. *and NP NP[36]
      c. *NP NP and[37]

Zwart draws the reasonable conclusion that the limitation to one possible order in (39) must be reflecting absence of movement. In antisymmetric terms,[38] (39a) is telling us that *and* is a head, that the two conjuncts are specifier and complement of *and*, and that the order is as it is in (39) because S–H–C order is the only order made available by the language faculty.

8.3.7 *Forward vs backward pronominalization*

These old terms pick out configurations that are configurations of non-c-command:

(40)   The fact that John is here means that he's well again.

(41)   The fact that he's here means that John is well again.

Both (40) and (41) have the property that in them neither *John* nor *he* c-commands the other. Put another way, from a c-command perspective on pronoun and antecedent, (40) and (41) do not differ. They do, of course, differ in precedence.

English gives the impression that in such non-c-command configurations anything goes, since both (40) and (41) are possible in English. This impression fed into Lasnik's (1976) claim that pronouns could freely take antecedents subject only to conditions B and C of the binding theory.[39] Under that view of Lasnik's, the precedence distinction that holds in pairs like (40) and (41) should be irrelevant.

But English is not representative. Michel DeGraff (p.c.) tells me that in Haitian creole 'backward pronominalization' of the sort seen in (41) is systematically

---

[36] Zwart cites Haspelmath (2008a) for this observation.

[37] Here, as Zwart shows, one must be careful to distinguish *and* from *with*.

[38] Cf. *AS*, ch. 7. Munn (1993) had *and* and the following NP as head and complement, but did not take the preceding NP to be the specifier.

[39] Lasnik took these conditions to be primitives. Kayne (2002) argues that they're not, and, in a way that subsumes O'Neil (1995, 1997) and Hornstein (1999), that pronouns in fact never take antecedents 'freely' (cf. also Collins and Postal 2010). (The proposal in Kayne (2002) when applied to PRO would have PRO being the double of its antecedent, in a way that makes Landau's (2003) criticism of Hornstein not carry over.)

impossible.[40] Huang (1982) said that Chinese has much less backward pronominalization than English. Craig (1977: 150) in her grammar of Jacaltec says that Jacaltec has no backward pronominalization at all. Allan et al.'s (1995: 473) grammar of Danish says that Danish has either none or at least much less backward pronominalization than English (cf. Thráinsson et al. 2004: 331 on Faroese). Jayaseelan (1991: 76) says for Malayalam that for some speakers of Malayalam there is no backward pronominalization.

In other words, various languages completely or partially prohibit backward (as opposed to forward) pronominalization, in contrast to English. I don't know of any languages, though, that completely or partially prohibit forward (as opposed to backward) pronominalization in a parallel fashion.

There thus seems to be an asymmetry concerning antecedent–pronoun relations in contexts of non-c-command, of a sort that would be unexpected in a symmetric syntactic universe.[41] This cross-linguistic asymmetry has to do with precedence. To the extent that the backward vs forward pronominalization question is one of (narrow) syntax, precedence must be part of (narrow) syntax, in a sense to be made precise.

8.4 A more derivational antisymmetry

8.4.1 *Desiderata*

Taking all of the preceding discussion to have reinforced the correctness of antisymmetry, we can now ask specifically why it is that our faculty of language (FL) has the property of being antisymmetric and why it does not make any use at all of directionality parameters, which after all had seemed to be a perfectly reasonable subtype of parameter. *AS* in effect took the absence of directionality parameters to be axiomatic, via the LCA. There was no attempt made there to ask or answer the question, why should FL contain anything like the LCA?

Moreover, the LCA, while sufficient (in conjunction with a certain definition of c-command) to exclude the orders S–C–H, C–S–H, H–S–C, and H–C–S, could not by itself tell us why FL has as its unique order S–H–C, rather than the mirror-image order C–H–S. An attempt was made in *AS* in chapter 5 using time slots and an

---

[40] From the perspective of Kayne (2002), the absence of backwards pronominalization in Haitian might perhaps be related to its lacking heavy-NP shift (cf. Dejean 1993) and/or to its lacking CLRD (and/or to its lacking Q-float).

Lasnik's (1976) approach to pronominalization led to the expectation that there should not be languages like Haitian creole at all.

[41] In Kayne (2002), I took the pronoun in (41) to be related to its antecedent under 'reconstruction' (without c-command being necessary, only precedence), the idea being that an antecedent must always precede a corresponding pronoun at some point in the derivation (cf. in part Belletti and Rizzi 1988). This reconstruction approach to (41) is independent, strictly speaking, of the use of sideward movement in Kayne (2002); on sideward movement, see Bobaljik and Brown (1997) and Nunes (2001).

abstract node A, but was not entirely satisfactory, in particular because it did not tightly tie the S–H–C vs C–H–S question to other aspects of syntax.

I would like now to try to provide a deeper account of antisymmetry in general and simultaneously of the S–H–C vs C–H–S question than I was able to achieve in *AS*. This newer account will at the same time attempt to transpose the LCA-based ideas into the more derivational framework of Chomsky (1995a) and later work. This will require transposing into a derivational framework the LCA idea that precedence is an integral part of syntax (as is suggested for independent reasons by the backward vs forward pronominalization discussion of the previous section of this paper).

The structure of the argument will be to first show that FL has H–C order and not C–H order. The second step will be to show that S (specifier) must be on the opposite side of H from C. From those two conclusions, S–H–C will follow.

8.4.2 *Precedence is part of syntax*

Let me adopt an alternative to standard Merge that is mentioned but not pursued in Chomsky (2008), namely that Merge should always be taken to form the ordered pair <X,Y>,[42] rather than the set {X,Y}. As Chomsky notes, part of the issue is whether linear order/precedence plays a role in the mapping to C–I; in this regard the earlier discussion of section 8.3.7 concerning backward vs forward pronominalization increases the plausibility that precedence does play a role in that mapping.

Having Merge create <X,Y>, with X then taken to temporally precede Y, involves greater complexity for Merge itself, as Chomsky points out. On the other hand, Spell-Out will no longer have the burden of specifying precedence relations, which will already have been established by Merge.

If Merge creates ordered pairs, then in the case of the merger of a head and its complement (i.e. of a head and the first phrase it is merged with), there is a priori the choice between <H,C> and <C,H>, with <H,C> corresponding to 'head precedes complement' and <C,H> corresponding to 'complement precedes head'.

8.4.3 *Probes precede goals*

Let me focus initially on cases of internal Merge, where H acts as a probe relative to some goal contained within C. The question is how the probe–goal relation interacts with precedence, if precedence is part of (narrow) syntax. Assuming precedence is part of syntax, a reasonable view is that a probe, in searching a domain for its goal,

---

[42] Cf. also Zwart (2003, 2011). The idea that Merge always produces an ordered pair is to be kept distinct from the proposal in Chomsky (2004) (which I am not adopting) that pair-Merge is appropriate for adjunction and set-Merge for specifiers and complements.

Chomsky's (1995a: 204) discussion of the adjunct/complement distinction and reconstruction effects rests on the assumption that nouns like *claim* can take sentential complements, which is denied by Hale and Keyser (2002) and Kayne (2009b).

On sentential adjuncts, see Larson (1988, 1990), Cinque (1999, 2006b), and Schweikert (2005a).

must search either from left-to-right (if the probe is initial, as in H–C) or from right-to-left (if the probe is final, as in C–H). Put another way, the search starts with the probe and then moves on in a direction determined by H–C vs. C–H until it reaches the goal.[43] If H–C, the search starts at the beginning, in precedence terms. If C–H, then the search starts at the end.

The picture of search presented so far has been left–right symmetric. To distinguish H–C from C–H we need to induce an asymmetry. Let me propose:[44]

(42)   Probe–goal search shares the directionality of parsing and of production.

Both parsing and production show a beginning vs end asymmetry. The hearer hears the beginning of the sentence first and the end last. The speaker produces the beginning of the sentence first and the end last. Using the terms left and right in a familiar way, this amounts to observing that both parsing and production proceed from left to right.[45] Given (42), we therefore reach:[46]

(43)   Probe–goal search proceeds from left to right.

despite the fact that probe–goal search is not literally temporal in the way that parsing and production are. In effect, if (42) and (43) are correct, FL has incorporated an abstract counterpart of temporality.

This addresses a point raised by Chomsky (1995a: 221), who says,

If humans could communicate by telepathy, there would be no need for a phonological component, at least for the purposes of communication; and the same extends to the use of language generally. These requirements might turn out to be critical factors in determining the inner nature of C_{HL} in some deep sense, or they might turn out to be 'extraneous' to it, inducing departures from 'perfection' that are satisfied in an optimal way.

If (42) and (43) are correct, then the phonological component has indeed determined 'the inner nature of C_{HL} in some deep sense'.

Given that the probe is the head and that the goal is contained within the complement, (43) is equivalent to:

(44)   Head and complement are invariably merged as <H,C>.

---

[43] This left–right (or right–left) view of probing is compatible with the idea that the probe might skip stretches of material, e.g. previously spelled-out lower specifiers.

[44] A different kind of link between antisymmetry and parsing (though not production) was proposed in Abels and Neeleman (2006).

[45] There is no implication here that in parsing and production one cannot also 'think ahead'. The crucial point is that there is no reasonable sense in which parsing and production can be taken to go from right to left, i.e. from end to beginning.

Ultimately, we will have to clearly delineate the limits of cotemporal phenomena such as intonation and (syntactically relevant) tone.

[46] I have followed the standard assumption that there is an intrinsic asymmetry between probe and goal and that search begins with the probe.

That is, the head invariably precedes the complement.

We have thus concluded the first stage of the argument leading to S–H–C, namely that FL countenances only H–C (and never C–H). The argument has rested on the incorporation of precedence (back) into derivational syntax,[47] and specifically on the proposal in (42) that syntactic computation mimics the left–right asymmetry of parsing/production.

This conclusion sheds light on the absence of directionality parameters, for the specific case of head and complement. For there to have existed a directionality parameter affecting the relative order of H and C, there would have had to be parameterization stated in terms of the direction of probe–goal search. Such parameterization, though, could have no natural place at all in an FL for which (42) holds.

8.4.4 *External Merge*

The discussion of the preceding section focused on H–C structures involved in internal Merge, in which H probes into C in search of a goal. It was proposed that H–C order is the only order made available by FL and that the choice of H–C order was, via (42)/(43), intimately connected to the status of H as probe. What happens, though, in cases in which <H,C> is not involved in internal Merge, i.e. cases in which the subsequently added specifier arises through external Merge rather than through internal Merge? If in such cases of external Merge H does not act as a probe, then (42)/(43) would not be relevant, and it would seem as if no particular relative order would be imposed on H and C, in a way that would be appear to be incompatible with antisymmetry.

Two partially overlapping proposals exist in the literature that might eliminate this potential problem. One goes back to Chomsky (1995a: 337) and in a more general fashion Moro (2000), and says that lack of fixed order is allowed as long as one of the two elements in question is subsequently moved. From their perspective, H and C need to be ordered relative to one another only if neither moves. If one of them moves (or if both move, separately), then the question of order internal to the original constituent created by merging H and C doesn't arise, assuming order not to be part of narrow syntax. Their proposal cannot readily be melded with the preceding discussion, however, if precedence is part of narrow syntax and imposed by Merge.

The second proposal I have in mind is made by Holmberg (2000: 137), following Svenonius (1994). It has in common with the Chomsky/Moro proposal the (potential) use of head movement. More specifically, the Holmberg/Svenonius idea is that a selection relation between H and C must be mediated by movement, even in cases of external Merge. The head will have an uninterpretable selection feature that, even in

---

[47] Precedence was taken to be part of syntax in the era of phrase structure rules. The separation of precedence from syntax, which I am taking to have been a mistake, had its origins in Chomsky's (1970) X-bar theory.

the absence of internal Merge of a specifier, will act as a probe triggering either feature movement or head movement.[48]

If H is a probe in all cases in which it merges with C, then (42)/(43) is relevant to all pairings of H and C and will impose <H,C> order even in cases not involving internal Merge to specifier position.

8.4.5 *Specifiers precede probes/heads*

Let us again focus on internal Merge and for the purposes of this section on the subcase in which one phrase is internally merged to another (as opposed to head movement):

(45) $[_C \ldots S \ldots]$

Here, a phrase S (about to become a specifier of H) is contained in a larger phrase C. A lexical item H (which may be a functional head) is merged from the numeration:

(46) $H [_C \ldots S \ldots]$

S moves from within the complement C to become the specifier of H:

(47) $S \ H [_C \ldots S \ldots]$

This movement is keyed to some property or properties of H.

It might still at first glance and once clearly did seem reasonable to think of H as having an additional property of the sort:

(48)   Spell out the specifier S of H to the left/right of the phrase headed by H that S is merging with.

The parametric option 'left' in (48) would match (47); the option 'right' would match:

(49) $H [_C \ldots S \ldots] \ S$

(By the result of the preceding section, H must be to the left of C, as indicated.)

If antisymmetry is correct, FL does not provide such a choice. Only (47) is possible. The seemingly plausible option (49) is never possible.[49] Put another way, if anti-symmetry is correct, then (48) is not part of the stock of FL parameters. Why, though, would FL have turned its back on the apparently straightforward (48)?

---

[48] Holmberg allows for a third option involving movement of complement to specifier position of the same head that I no longer think is viable (cf. AS, ch. 6 vs Kayne (2004) on adpositions).

I am leaving open questions concerning the mechanics of head movement.

[49] Any apparently right-hand specifier must be a left-hand specifier whose left-hand status has been obscured by the (leftward) movement past it of the other visible pieces of the projection of which it is the specifier. One example from the sentential domain is Ordóñez (1998) on Spanish VOS sentences; for the DP domain, see, for example, Cinque (2005b).

Parallel to the preceding two sections for the case of H–C, we need to keep in mind both specifiers arising from internal Merge and specifiers arising from external Merge. For internal Merge, Abels and Neeleman (2006) have suggested taking what was a 'theorem' in *AS* to the effect that movement is always leftward and elevating it to an 'axiom'. Indeed, if movement is always leftward then any internally merged specifier will, given the extension condition, necessarily precede H–C, yielding S–H–C order. As part of their critique of Cinque (2005b), Abels and Neeleman very specifically want to limit to internal Merge the necessity for specifiers to be on the left, and propose allowing externally merged specifiers to be to the right (or to the left).

Since I feel that they have not made their case against Cinque, since I do not want to weaken antisymmetry to allow both left- and right-hand specifiers (even if limited to external Merge) and since I would like not to take leftward movement as an axiom, but rather would like to derive the leftness of all specifiers from more general considerations, I will explore a different avenue, one that is more derivational than the one followed in *AS*, with the two having in common the use of an intermediate step in the derivation of S–H–C, to the effect that specifier and complement must be on opposite sides of the head.

Returning to (48) and to the question why FL has not made use of anything like it (assuming antisymmetry to be broadly correct), a conceivable answer might be that (48) would be too complex a parameter, by virtue of containing the term 'phrase headed by H that S is merging with'. This kind of answer would not be satisfactory, however, since we lack a clear metric for parametric complexity that would yield the desired result. Nonetheless I think that it is the term 'phrase headed by H that S is merging with' that is the key, although not in a way related to parametric complexity.

What I have in mind is to instead establish a link between the exclusion of (48) from FL and the existence of a certain lack of homogeneity in our present conception of Merge. In Bare Phrase Structure, one speaks of first Merge and second Merge in lieu of complement and specifier. Neither terminology does justice to the fact that, while first Merge/complement involves merger of a phrase with a head, second Merge/specifier involves merger of a phrase with another phrase. (Put another way, classical Merge is not uniform in that first Merge with a head involves formation of a set one of whose members is the head in question, whereas second Merge involving a given head is merger with a set whose label is that head.)

This asymmetry between first and second Merge is reduced somewhat by taking second Merge (as in the transition from (46) to (47)) to depend on some property or properties of the head H. Yet the asymmetry remains.

8.4.6 *Unfamiliar derivations*

The idea that I would like to pursue is that it is at bottom the very fact that S in (47) is taken to merge with <H,C> (rather than with H) that gives the directionality parameter (48) its initial plausibility. Consequently, we can divest (48) of what plausibility it seemed to have, and thereby account for FL not countenancing it, if we are willing to take S in (47) to merge, not with <H, C>, but rather with H itself.

Taking S in (47) to merge with H itself would sharpen the sense in which heads are central to syntax, going back to Chomsky (1970). Every instance of Merge must directly involve a head, in the sense that (at least) one of the two syntactic objects merged must be a head. Merge never constructs a set consisting of two syntactic objects each of which is a phrase. From this perspective, (48) is not statable insofar as S(pecifier) is not actually merging with any phrase at all.

A way of executing this idea is as follows, with the key question remaining, why exactly is the directionality parameter (48) not countenanced by FL? Generalized pair-Merge is part of the answer, I think, but not the whole answer, since (48) could be recast in terms of ordered pairs. Thinking of the case in which the phrase S is, under standard conceptions, internally merged to the phrase {H,C} (where S originates within C), one could seemingly have a directionality parameter formulated as:

(50)   Merge produces either <S,{H,C}> or <{H,C},S>.

in conflict with antisymmetry.

What property of FL might make (50) (and (48)) unavailable? As I suggested in preliminary fashion earlier:

(51)   The merger of two phrases is unavailable.

In which case, with S a phrase, neither (50) nor (48) is formulable. What this amounts to, in the case, say, of (47), repeated here:

(52)   S H [$_C$...S...]

is the claim that when S is internally merged in (52), S is merged with the head H, rather than with the phrase <H,C>. The consequence is that, in such a derivation, H itself will have been merged both with C and (then) with S.

Taking Merge to always be pair-Merge interpreted as temporal precedence, and further taking Merge to necessarily involve (at least) one head,[50] as required by (51), leads to recasting (52) as (setting aside derivational steps leading to C):

(53)   <S,H>, <H,C>

corresponding to the precedence relations given in:

(54)   S H C

but without 'S H C' forming a standard constituent (though I return to this later).

---

[50] Departing from Zwart (2003, 2011), though remaining in agreement with him on generalized pair-Merge.

Before pursuing further the question of constituency, let me note that (53) is less symmetrical that it looks. That is so, since displayed as it is (53) fails to show the derivational steps leading to it. Derivationally speaking, S and C remain sharply distinct. C, as the phrase merged first with H, is probed by H. S is the second phrase merged with H and is not probed by H.

8.4.7 *Immediate precedence*

Precedence in (53)/(54) can and should be understood as immediate precedence (henceforth i-precede(nce)). Thus <S,H> means that S i-precedes H and <H,C> means that H i-precedes C, with the transition from (53) to (54) now clearer. Let me now use the term p-Merge as shorthand for 'pair-Merge with i-precedence'.

I-precedence is of importance in that it leads to:

(55)   H can be p-merged with at most two elements.

This holds since the (temporal) i-precedence we are interested in syntax is a total ordering that has the property that if X i-precedes Z and Y i-precedes Z then X = Y. Similarly, if Z i-precedes X and Z i-precedes Y, then X = Y.

Given (55), i-precedence yields the property that if H is separately p-merged with each of two elements X and Y (as in (53)), then X cannot i-precede Y, nor can Y i-precede X. A syntactically more perspicuous rendering is:

(56)   If H p-merges with X and also p-merges with Y, then X and Y must be on opposite sides of H.

From (55) follows in a natural way the restriction barring multiple specifiers argued for in *AS*. In effect, (53)/(54) corresponds to an ordinary instance of specifier–head–complement. By (55), nothing further can be p-merged with H. And by (51), there is no option of phrase–phrase merger. Put another way, Chomsky's (2008) point that 'Without further stipulation, the number of specifiers is unlimited' does not hold, given (51), if i-precedence is associated with pair-Merge.

From (56) it follows, more centrally to antisymmetry, that specifier and complement must invariably be on opposite sides of the head. If we now combine this conclusion that specifier and complement must invariably be on opposite sides of the head with our earlier conclusion (at the end of section 8.4.4, based on (42)/(43)) that FL consistently imposes H–C order, we reach the desired result:[51]

(57)   FL consistently imposes S–H–C order.

---

[51] Note that from the text perspective for an element to be in an i-precede relation does not imply that it must be pronounced.

Given that H–C order was argued to hold uniformly, i.e. independently of any internal vs external Merge distinction, (57) must, given (56), also hold uniformly, whether S is internally merged or externally merged.

If we return once again to the question why (48)/(50) is not a possible (directionality) parameter, the answer is again, as at the end of section 8.4.3 for H–C alone, that for there to exist a directionality parameter affecting the relative order of S and H and C, there would, given (56), have to be parameterization stated in terms of the direction of probe–goal search. Such parameterization, though, can have no natural place at all in an FL for which (42) holds.[52]

8.4.8 *Constituency*

Allowing (53), repeated here:

(58)   <S,H>, <H,C>

raises (at least) three kinds of questions concerning constituent structure. One concerns the fact that 'S H' and 'H C' in (58) both end up looking like constituents. The second concerns the fact that 'S H C' in (58) looks as if it is not a constituent. A third question concerns the relation between (58) and trees, insofar as (58) does not map to a standard tree (H would have two mothers).

Beginning with the first, we can note that the constituent status of 'H C' in (58) is unremarkable, since 'H C' there corresponds to a standard constituent (head + complement). On the other hand, the constituent status of 'S H' might appear to create a problem having to do with the potential movement of 'S H'. Notice, though, that this has been a long-standing question for 'H C', too, even though 'H C' is a standard constituent. A familiar view is that 'H C' cannot move because it is not a maximal projection. In a probe–goal framework, this amounts to saying that a probe can pick a head or the maximal projection of a head,[53] but not an intermediate-level projection. Restricting movement to heads and maximal projections would suffice to block movement of 'S H', given a suitable definition of maximal projection (which would in turn allow movement of 'S H C'), which could be, in the context of generalized p-Merge:[54]

(59)   The maximal projection of a head H is the maximal set of ordered pairs each of which immediately contains H.

By earlier discussion, this maximal set will never have more than two members.

---

[52] Nor is there any room for a (non)-configurationality parameter—cf. Legate (2001, 2003).

[53] As part of 'pied-piping'—cf. Ross (1967) and Chomsky (1995a: 262). I abstract away here from the difference between feature and lexical item. For recent discussion of pied-piping, see Cable (2010).

[54] This definition will also play a role in determining what is a possible antecedent.

8.4.9 *Speculations on trees*

Trees are not primitives in a Bare Phrase Structure derivational syntax. So one might think, since I have been attempting to achieve a deeper understanding of antisymmetry by integrating it more tightly into such a derivational syntax, that the tree question is of little interest. Yet the following may be a substantive restriction on derivational syntax:

(60)   Every syntactic object in every derivational stage[55] in a derivational syntax must be simply mappable to a tree.

The notion 'simply' would have to be made precise, but (60) might exclude (58) with the interpretation given in the first paragraph of the previous section.

Yet (58), together with (55) and (56), played a key role in deriving the prohibition against multiple specifiers and in deriving the fact that FL has the S–H–C property rather than the mirror-image *C–H–S property. Assuming (60) or something like it to be desirable, we have reached a paradox. Of course, one could take (60) itself to be paradoxical, especially if one took it to follow (in a way that would need to be made precise) from:

(61)   The correct derivational theory of FL must be simply mappable to a representational theory.

If (61) were true in a non-trivial way (that would depend on how 'simply' was defined), there would be a reason why it has been so difficult to find decisive evidence favouring a derivational over a representational theory or vice versa; (61) would be telling us that there is a level of abstraction (that we would need to find) at which the difference between derivational and representational collapses.

To make (58) compatible with (60)/(61), one could have it mapped to:

(62)   <S,H,C>

with an ordered triple replacing the two ordered pairs and then being mappable to a ternary-branching tree. This would lead to seeing my (1981a) arguments for binary branching to have two subcomponents, the first being the claim that syntax is n-ary branching with n having a single value, the second being that that value is 2. Mapping (58) to (62) would retain the first subcomponent and replace 2 by 3 in the second, arguably with no loss in restrictiveness.

This would imply that familiar relations like the binding of an anaphor by an antecedent could no longer be regulated by a tree-based notion of (asymmetric) c-command, but Chomsky (2008) had already suggested that c-command might well, in a derivational probe–goal framework, be dispensable.

---

[55] For precise definitions, see Collins and Stabler (2012).

8.4.10 *Further remarks on p-Merge*

Allowing (58), repeated again here:

(63)   <S,H>, <H,C>

leads to questions concerning restrictiveness, especially if the speculations of the preceding section were to turn out not to be on the right track. If one can p-merge two separate phrases with a given head, as in (63), why not more than two? The answer to this question has already been given, in terms of the requirement that p-Merge imply immediate precedence, combined with the fact that (in a total ordering of the temporal sort) a given head can enter into an immediate precedence relation with at most two elements. (This immediate precedence requirement will, in addition, block many other unwanted p-Merges.)

Left open, however, is the question of:

(64)   <H_2, S>, <S, H_1>

Could a specifier merged with one head subsequently be merged with a higher head? Immediate precedence would be satisfied. On the other hand, (60) would not be. This seems clear if we expand (64) to:

(65)   <H_2, S>, <S, H_1>, <H_1, C>

for which ternary branching does not suffice for compatibility with (60). An alternative would be to mimic the mapping from (58) to (62) by mapping (65) to:

(66)   <H_2, S, H_1, C>

corresponding to a tree with four branches at the highest level (there is additional branching within S and within C). This would be at the cost of giving up the idea that branching is n-ary with n restricted to a single value. (Alternatively, one could consider giving up (60) (though not necessarily (61)), i.e. abandoning the relevance of trees entirely, in which case (64)/(65) would become more plausible.)

A theoretical question is whether a theory that allows (63) would be expected to also allow (64)/(65).[56] The answer would be no if the double appearance of H in (63) were necessarily the side effect of a single application of the probe–goal mechanism,[57] which (64) could not be.

---

[56] I'm setting aside the question whether (65), if valid, is the only option, or is one of two options, the other being:

(i)   <H2, {<S, H1>, <H1, C>}>

Note that (i) illustrates the more general fact that p-Merge merges a head and a (non-singleton) set. For a proposal about first steps of derivations, see Kayne (2008).

[57] Cf. Chomsky (1995a: 233). Taking the double appearance of H in (63) to necessarily reflect a single application of the probe–goal mechanism might provide a handle on the question why (51) should hold.

A more empirical question is whether or not there are clues to the possible existence of (64) in one syntactic phenomenon or another. The answer is maybe. Insofar as (64) establishes a p-Merge relation between a higher head and the specifier of the next lower head, (64) reminds us of various ECM-type phenomena, as well as of Stowell's (1981) discussion of contrasts such as:

(67) Any question about how he could have made such a mistake must be taken seriously.

(68) *?Any question about in what sense he could have made such a mistake must be taken seriously.

In addition, (64) is reminiscent of the phenomenon of 'escape hatches', going back to Chomsky (1973, 1986) and found in Chomsky (2008), in part in terms of the PIC. Pursuing the question whether (64) is what in fact underlies the relative centrality of such head–lower Spec relations is beyond the scope of this paper.

8.5 Conclusion

In answer to one aspect of the 'why'-question in the title of this paper, there are no directionality parameters simply because the evidence against them coming from cross-linguistic gaps of all sorts is substantial.

I have given a split answer to the other aspect of the title question, which asks why it is that FL is antisymmetric to begin with. There is no C–H order, only H–C order, primarily because of (42) and (43), repeated here:

(69) Probe–goal search shares the directionality of parsing and of production.

(70) Probe–goal search proceeds from left to right.

There is no H–C–S order, only S–H–C order, primarily because of (51), namely:

(71) The merger of two phrases is unavailable.

combined with the fact that Merge imposes an immediate precedence relation.

This paper can also be read as a subcase of a type of question that we need to keep asking. Why are certain readily imaginable parameters not found in syntax?[58]

The more derivational approach to antisymmetry that I have argued for in this paper has in common with *AS* that it prohibits certain apparently (but if I'm right, mistakenly) plausible kinds of syntactic analyses, such as those involving right-adjunction or right-hand specifiers or left-hand complements. In so doing, antisymmetry will necessarily have widespread effects even in areas of syntax that have not

---

[58] Rizzi (2010) has an interesting proposal characterizing existing parameters.

played a role in the original arguments for it. Any compositional semantics closely tracking syntax will correspondingly be affected by antisymmetry.

Many of the empirical arguments for antisymmetry involve parametric variation and thereby illustrate how parametric variation can indirectly serve as a window on the principles of FL.[59]

---

[59] This point is orthogonal to the question whether some particular property of FL can or cannot ultimately be traced back to FL-external factors as in Chomsky (2004).

9

Antisymmetry and Hixkaryana*

MICHAEL BARRIE

9.1 Introduction

This paper is an examination of the properties of OVS languages and how Antisymmetry Theory (Kayne 1994) impinges on the analysis of OVS. I look principally at Hixkaryana, but also draw on some data from Urarina, another genetically unrelated OVS language. I examine whether a headedness macroparameter must be admitted in light of OVS order, or whether the properties of OVS languages in fact support an Antisymmetric view of syntax. Several questions arise from this line of inquiry. First, if OVS is the default word order, how does the object raise above the subject without violating some kind of Minimality constraint (in the sense of Rizzi 1990)? A directionality parameter (set to Complement–Head–Specifier, C–H–S) would account for OVS order in a straight-forward manner. Are there other properties of Hixkaryana and Urarina that suggest a C–H–S setting is on the right track, or are the predicted properties suspiciously absent? I will show that OVS languages impinge on Antisymmetry, and that the answers to these questions provide additional empirical support for this theory.

Antisymmetry not only imposes a strict algorithm on linearization; it also accounts for a number of otherwise puzzling asymmetries in word-order universals (Kayne 2003a). Some of these are alluded to briefly in section 9.3. In this vein, I note the following generalization, which emerges from the study of OVS languages. While SOV languages permit SOXV order (where X is any additional material such as an adverb or a PP), OVS languages do not permit OXVS order. This asymmetry is unexpected under a symmetric view of syntax, but, as we will see, receives a principled explanation under an Antisymmetric view of syntax.

* I wish to thank the participants at TADWO and other conferences where this work was presented, as well as the reviewers, for asking difficult and probing questions, thereby improving the presentation. All remaining shortcomings are my own. I gratefully acknowledge the support of the Sogang University Research Grant of 2011.

The analysis of OVS order is summed up as follows. First, I show that Hixkaryana is an OV language (in the same way that Japanese is) and that the object raises to a position to the left of the verb within the VP complex. I then propose that OV order is derived in a manner similar to Kayne's analysis for postpostional phrases. Specifically, a ghost $Agr_O'P$ attracts the object above the verb, giving rise to a VP shell with the order O–V. I also propose that the EPP in OVS languages is satisfied by VP rather than by DP (Massam 2001), thereby *smuggling* the object above the subject (Collins 2005).[1] The lack of OXVS is a result of the fact that the only way O can raise above S is for it to be smuggled together with V, thereby removing the opportunity for O to scramble above any adjoined material. Furthermore, I show that word order in embedded clauses is accounted for by the current proposal. Embedded clauses in Hixkaryana are non-finite and display ergative syntax. I argue that the TP layer is absent in these nominalized clauses, accounting for the lack of nominative Case and the ergative properties in these constructions. Given the lack of a TP, we expect there to be no VP raising, predicting SOV order in embedded clauses—a prediction that is borne out.

Kayne's (1994) Antisymmetry theory proposes a strict relationship between hierarchical structure and linear order which has yielded much fruitful research, leading to important generalizations (Aboh 2004; Bianchi 1999; Cinque 2005b; Kayne 2003a; Lee 2000b). In particular, Kayne (2003a, this volume) showed that several properties of SOV fall into place under Antisymmetry. A large portion of the forthcoming discussion is devoted to arguments against headedness in general and against any analysis of Hixkaryana (and Urarina) that relies on a Headedness Parameter. In particular, I show that a right Specifier analysis has trouble dealing with left Specifier properties, such as clause-initial *wh*-phrases.

The remainder of this paper is structured as follows. Section 9.2 describes the general properties of Hixkaryana, touching on Urarina from time to time. Section 9.3 contains a brief discussion on headedness and Antisymmetry, including a critique of some recent proposals on the return to a headedness approach to word-order variation. Section 9.4 expands on some of the ideas in Kayne (2003a) and presents the current proposal. Section 9.5 presents the analysis of the properties of OVS discussed in section 9.2. Section 9.6 is a brief conclusion.

9.2 Properties of OVS

As mentioned above, the principal language that forms the empirical foundation of this study is Hixkaryana, a Carib language with about 500 speakers in the Amazonas

---

[1] I use the term *smuggling* here loosely, as Collins originally used the term to describe an element that is carried above a potential intervener inside a larger element (as is the case here), and then subsequently sub-extracted to a higher position (which is not the case here).

region of Brazil. I also discuss to a smaller extent Urarina, a language isolate, spoken in the Peruvian Amazon Basin). Obviously, one property of these languages I wish to capture is their basic OVS order. This order should be captured with ordinary A-movements and should not involve any special fronting mechanisms or A-bar positions associated with special interpretations, such as focus. The following examples illustrate OVS order in Hixkaryana (1) and Urarina (2).[2] Note that OVS order is found regardless of whether the object is nominal or clausal.

(1) a. biryekomo y-otaha-no wosɨ
       boy   AGR-hit-PST woman
       'The woman hit the boy.' (Derbyshire 1979: 38, (85a))

   b. tɨtonɨrɨ   yokarymano
      his-own-going he-told-it
      'He told about his going.' (Derbyshire 1979: 22, (50))

   c. ɨtoko omɨn yaka,   ɨkano   ɨwya
      go   your-house to I-said-it to-him
      '"Go home," I said to him.' (Derbyshire 1979: 3, (1a))

   d. txetxa   wawo weweyomokotonɨrɨ wenyo
      forest in tree   falling.of   I.saw.it
      'I saw a tree falling in the forest.' (Derbyshire 1985, (49b))

   e. Waraka-wya   honkyo   Ø-wonɨr xe   wehxana[3]
      Waraka-by   peccary shooting-of desire   I.am
      'I want Waraka to shoot peccary.' (Derbyshire 1985, (45g))

(2) a. nitoaneĩ   hetau=te   katça lemu-e=lu   lomaj
       like.that HRS=FOC   man   sink-3SG.E=REM Lomai
       edara   ne-ĩ   kuru-a=ne   kujɲa
       water.people be-PTCP   go-PL-3SG.D=SUB   so.that
       'Lomai sank the people like that so that they would become water people.'
       (Olawsky 2006: 655, (936a))

---

[2] (1c) resembles a fronted quote, as in the English translation. Derbyshire notes, however, that direct quotes must immediately precede the verb of saying. Thus, the quotes pattern with nominal objects in Hixkaryana and not with quotes in English, which can be separated from the verb of saying by the subject. The generalization here is that all verbal complements in Hixkaryana (and in Urarina) must be immediately preverbal.

[3] Note that the embedded clause has SOV order. This is addressed later in the discussion.

b. nii   hãʉ   hetau=te   nitoaneĩ   bʉa   basihjaʉ-a
   that   because   HRS=FOC   like.that   bag   steal-3SG.D
   alau=na   hãʉ   nekajritça-he-ĩ   beree
   spider.monkey=SUB   because   suffer-CONT-PTCP   child
   ama-e   ʉnee   nʉhʉae   kʉanaj-tça
   take-3SG.E   kinkajou   mouth   inside-only
   'Therefore, because the spider monkey stole kinkajou's bag like that, the kinkajou
   carries her children in her mouth, suffering.' (Olawsky 2006: 850, (1183))

Kayne (2003a) shows that while many VO languages disallow VXO (X an adverb
or oblique of types), there is no OV language that uniformly disallows OXV (assuming O is definite). One immediate difference between OVS languages and the OV
languages Kayne refers to is that OXV is not allowed. In other words, there is no
OXVS. Hixkaryana has OVSX as its basic order (Derbyshire 1979: 40) and Urarina
has XOVS and (to a lesser extent) OVSX as its basic order (Olawsky 2007). Furthermore, WALS notes three OVS languages for which the order among verb, object, and
oblique can reliably be found: Ungarinjin, Hixkaryana, and Päri. Ungarinjin and Päri
pattern the same as Hixkaryana. That is, they have OVX order. Thus, an important
generalization[4] which must be captured is the following:

(3)   SOV → SOXV widespread
      OVS → OXVS not found

Note that the works cited for Hixkaryana and Urarina are descriptive grammars,
which typically do not contain examples of ungrammatical sentences. Nevertheless,
both authors clearly indicate that OXVS is not found in their respective languages.

The basic order of the constituents [in Hixkaryana] is OVS, with indirect object and adjunct
normally following the subject.... Any element that normally follows the verb may be fronted
to initial position in the sentence (preceding the direct object if there is one)....

(Derbyshire 1979: 40)

The most typical position for any PP is before the main verb. In transitive clause with an overt
O argument, the PP occurs before O. There are almost no attested natural examples for their
occurrence between O and the verb. One is cited in (958), where the postposition *raj* 'for' is
cliticized with a possessive proclitic; the demonstrative which functions as the object, in turn, is
realized as a proclitic attached to *itçej* 'for you'. Due to the clitic status of the elements involved, it
is questionable whether this can be characterized as a PP-insertion between O and V. Since this
example is marginal at any rate, one could conclude that generally, PPs do not occur in this position.

(Olawsky 2006: 670)

---

[4] Given the paucity of OVS languages and the fact that I have examined only two here, one may
question the validity of this generalization. Nevertheless, the fact that OXVS is not found in these languages
must still be accounted for.

Like other OV languages Hixkaryana, (4a), and Urarina, (4b), both exhibit postpositions.

(4) a. titonye   ohsamnohtoho   kom   yaka
         let.us.go   meeting.place COLL   to
         'Let's go to their meeting place.' (Derbyshire 1979: 24)

     b. nii   banaao   asae
         that   shelter   under
         'under that leaf-shelter' (Olawsky 2006: 255, (334b))

Questions in Hixkaryana obligatorily front *wh*-phrases. Hixkaryana also exhibits topicalization, which fronts the topicalized phrase to the left edge of the clause (Derbyshire 1977, 1979, 1985).

(5) a. onoki   tho   yonyetxkoni   kamara
         who   DEVLD   he.was.eating.them   jaguar
         'Whom did the jaguar used to eat?' (Derbyshire 1979: 8, (16b))

     b. onoki   biryekomo   komo   yonyetxkoni
         who   child   COLL   he.was.eating.them
         'Who used to eat children?' (Derbyshire 1979: 8, (16c))

     c. onokiwya   woto   mimno
         who to   meat   you.gave.it
         'To whom did you give the meat?' (Derbyshire 1979: 11, (22aii))

     d. Waraka   yawaka   yoheko   rohyaka   oroke
         Waraka   axe   he.sent.it to.me   yesterday
         '(It was) Waraka (who) sent the axe to me yesterday.' (Derbyshire 1977: (4b))

Similarly, focused XPs in Urarina move to the front of the clause (Olawsky 2006, 2007).

(6) raj   kalaui-**te**   fweei   bajjhja-ĩ   ama-e
     POSS   son-**FOC**   firewood   carry.on.shoulder-PTCP   take-AGR
     'Her son carries firewood on his shoulder and takes it along.' (Olawsky 2007: (8a))

Finally, I discuss word order in embedded clauses in OVS. In Hixkaryana, finite embedded clauses exist only as direct quotes under verbs of saying, while all other forms of embedded clauses are nominalized and, hence, non-finite.[5] Word order in nominalized clauses is SOV and displays ergative syntax, while matrix clauses display

---

[5] The syntax of quotes is beyond the scope of this paper. Suffice it to say that they have substantially different syntactic properties from finite complement clauses (quotative inversion, set off by heavy pauses, islands for extraction, etc.). Finite complement clauses of the English variety seem to be absent in Hixkaryana.

nominative–accusative syntax.[6] Consider the following examples (Derbyshire 1979: (60a,e)). The subject of an intransitive and the object of a transitive appear are marked with agreement on the nominalized verbal complex.[7] The subject of a transitive appears in a *by*-phrase and does not trigger agreement on the verb.

(7)   **r-amryek-nɨ-toko,**   honyko   ɨwono
      my-hunting-NZLR-when   peccary   I.shot.it.IMPST
      'When I went hunting, I shot a peccary.'

(8)   **ro-wya   Kaywana   Ø-yaryma-txhe,**   kɨkowonteko
      me-by   Kaywana   him-throwing-after   I.yell.IMPST
      'After I threw Kaywana, I cried out loudly.'

(9)   kokahtɨmno   **ro-wya   kamara   yo-nye-toko**
      I.ran.away   by-me   jaguar   AGR-seeing.of-when
      'I ran away **when I saw the jaguar.**'

(10) totke rmahaxa   natxhe   totokomo,
      having.meat very much   they.are   people
      Waraka wya   honyko   wonir   ke
      Waraka by   peccary   shooting.of   because
      'The people have a lot of meat **because Waraka shot peccary.**'

(11) **Manausɨ hona   Waraka   tonɨr   xe   wehxaha**
      Manaus to   Waraka   his.going   desire   I.am
      'I want **Waraka to go to Manaus.**' (Derbyshire 1979: 72, (72c))

In Urarina, OVS order is still found in embedded finite clauses (Olawsky 2007: 48). This is shown in the following example and in example (2b) above. Unlike the nominalized embedded clauses in Hixkaryana, embedded clauses in Urarina still exhibit a nominative–accusative pattern. These clauses are typically some kind of adjunct to the main clause.

(12) ʉnee   bʉa   basihjaʉ-a   alau=ne
      kinkajou   bag   steal-3SG   spider.monkey=SUB
      'When the spider monkey stole kinkajou's bag.'

---

[6] Derbyshire himself does not use the term *ergative* to describe the syntax of nominalized constructions in Hixkaryana. The following quote, however, makes it clear that he had already observed the ergative properties of this language (Derbyshire 1979: 26):

> The basic word order in finite clauses is OVS. In nominal constructions the NP (i.e. possessor) which is the equivalent of S in intransitives and O in transitives, always occurs preceding the derived nominal. The equivalent of S in transitives is most frequently found occurring before the derived nominal and before the possessor NP, although it can also occur after the nominal.

[7] Derbyshire (1979: 165) notes that nominalizing morphology is sometimes left off by many speakers, hence its absence in many of the examples above.

Object complement clauses in Urarina are of two types (Olawsky 2006: 758). The first type appear with the suffix /-na/. These clauses are either non-finite or nominalized, and there is an obligatory same-subject restriction between the main and the dependent clauses. Consider the following examples.

(13)   a.   **itça-na**   najɲa-a
              do-INF   finish-3SG.A
              'He finished **doing it**.' (Olawsky 2006: 764, (1066a))

        b.   **siɨra**   **ha-naa**   nɨnɨeti-a
              bag   make-INF   begin.3SG.E
              'She has begun **to make the bags**.' (Olawsky 2006: 764, (1066b))

The second type of object clause appears with the suffix (or clitic) /-ne/. These clauses may have a different subject (sometimes obligatorily), and are typically finite. Although Olawsky reports that object clauses must appear preverbally, he does give one example of a postverbal finite object clause.[8] Consider the following examples, where the subjects are obligatorily counter-indexed in the first example and co-indexed in the second example.

(14)   a.   **tɨrɨ-a=ne**   heri-ji
              arrive-3SG=SUB   want-NEG.3SG
              'He[1] does not want **him**[*1/2] to come.' (Olawsky 2006: 767, (1069b))

        b.   ruru=te   najɲe-re   **kɨraanaa ni-a=ne=ra**
              howler.monkey=FOC   be.able-IRR.3SG.E   chief   be-3SG.D=CND=EMPH
              'The howler monkey could not **be chief**.' (Olawsky 2006: 767, (1070))

To conclude, both Hixkaryana and Urarina exhibit OVS as the most natural word order. Both languages have postpositions and also have A-bar fronting movement to a position in the left periphery. These two languages differ, however, in the syntactic properties of embedded clauses. Embedded clauses in Hixkaryana are obligatorily non-finite (and nominalized) and exhibit SOV order, while embedded clauses in Urarina can be finite and exhibit OVS order. Non-finite object clauses in Hixkaryana and in Urarina both appear in canonical object position. However, finite object clauses in Urarina appear to be able to appear postverbally. Crucially, both languages prohibit OXVS order. I now move to a discussion of the theoretical background of this study.

---

[8]   Olawsky (2006: 767) argues that because the above example contains a postverbal dependent clause, it must be interpreted as an adjunct rather than as an object. (Hence, he glosses /-ne/ as SUB in (14a) and as CND in (14).) I assume Olawsky comes to this conclusion in observance of the general OVS order of this language. Below, however, I discuss the possibility that finite complement clauses do not obey the same syntactic constraints as nominal and non-finite complements.

9.3 Theoretical background

Theories of word order have traditionally piggybacked off phrase-structural models of syntax, originally designed to capture constituency effects. Notably, the Headedness Parameter (Stowell 1981; Travis 1984) proposes that word order is encoded directly in the phrase structure and makes use of relationships such as 'to the left' and 'to the right'. Arguments against headedness are found in Kayne (1994, 2003a), so I confine my remarks here to a brief summary. Recently, however, M. Richards (2008) has presented new arguments in favour of headedness. I review this proposal in more detail in section 9.3.1 and provide more substantial commentary.

Antisymmetry proposes that linear order is not encoded directly in phrase structure but rather linear order is a by-product of asymmetric c-command relations. I assume here a basic familiarity with Antisymmetry, but do introduce relevant aspects in section 9.3.2, along with a discussion on how Antisymmetry impinges on typological properties of word order.

9.3.1 *Antisymmetry*

This section briefly introduces those aspects of Antisymmetry that are important to the current study. I assume a basic familiarity with the concepts and keep the discussion necessarily brief. The reader is encouraged to consult Kayne (1994) for an in-depth discussion.[9]

The basic premise of Antisymmetry is tightly grounded in the Linear Correspondence Axiom (LCA), stated here.

(15)   LCA: $d(A)$ is a linear ordering of T.

d is a function that maps a category to the set of terminals that it dominates. A is the set of ordered pairs of categories, <X, Y> such that X c-commands Y. T is the set of all terminals. C-command is defined by category rather than by first branching node (see also May 1985). Thus, a specifier c-commands both the head of its projection and the complement, and therefore is linearized to the left of both. Furthermore, the head asymmetrically c-commands the material inside the complement (though not the complement itself) and is linearized to the left of the material inside the complement. This gives rise to Spec–Head–Complement order. As a further consequence of AS, there can be no multiple specifiers, no rightward movement, and no right adjunction.

Aside from stipulating the basic order of all XPs (namely S–H–C), the LCA captures various asymmetric typological properties of language, as described in Kayne (2003a), such as the presence of verb-second and the absence of

---

[9] There have been various attempts at bringing the LCA in line with the Minimalist Program (Uriagereka 1999a; N. Richards 2001; Barrie 2006b). I do not review these here as it does not impinge greatly on the current analysis.

'verb-second-to-last' and the rigid ordering found in serial verb constructions. As mentioned above, I also capture the lack of OXVS order.

Embedded clauses and complementizers play an important role in Kayne (2003a). Following Rosenbaum (1967), Kayne suggests that IP cannot be directly selected by V^0 unless it is first nominalized in some way. For finite clauses in English, he argues for the following derivation.

(16)

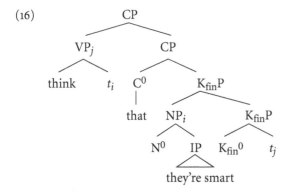

Later (his (57)), however, he conjectures that C-initial clauses are universally N–C–IP based partly on examples such as *John mentioned (the fact) that Mary was away*. This is clearly at odds with the derivation in (16) he proposes. Furthermore, the role of K_{fin}^0 is unclear. Kayne suggests it can be assimilated to one of the Rizzian split CP categories; however, the label of K suggests that it has an analysis similar to that of DPs and PPs. This is clearly not the case, however, as CP–V order does not correlate with OV order so neatly. It is also unclear how the matrix CP could be built up in this fashion since it is not selected by a higher V^0. As evidence for (16) Kayne (2003a: 226) notes that the internal word order of embedded clauses in Estonian and Finnish varies with respect to adjunct/argument status of the clause. This happens only in non-finite clauses, however. I leave the following, then, to future research. It is possible that finite clauses are introduced as complete CPs, which are selected by V^0, while non-finite clauses are built up along the lines of (16).[10] This solves the problem of how the root CP is built in the absence of a superordinate V^0 and also explains why non-finite clauses are restricted to embedded contexts.

Embedded clauses in Hixkaryana are exclusively nominalized non-finite clauses. Some of these clauses appear to have clause-final complementizer type elements; however, I analyse these as postpositions. Thus, the issues raised in the preceding paragraph do not surface.

---

[10] Kayne proposes that the *to*-infinitive is actually a PP with a bare VP (or *v*P) complement. Since IP is absent, it requires no N^0 to appear as a complement to the matrix verb.

9.3.2 *Against headedness*

Various Greenbergian properties are associated with the distinction between VO and OV word order. However, a number of languages exhibit properties of both VO and OV. For instance, prepositions are associated with VO languages, while postpositions are associated with OV languages. This correlation is not perfect, however. Many Germanic languages are typically OV, but are prepositional. Also, Persian is OV, but prepositional, and its clausal complements are postverbal. Relative clauses are also correlated with OV/VO order. Postnominal relative clauses are associated with VO languages, while prenominal relative clauses are associated with OV languages. However, Chinese languages are uniformly VO, but all typically exhibit prenominal relative clauses. English is VO, but exhibits some prenominal non-finite relative clauses (*a recently arrived letter*). Finally, *wh*-movement is associated with VO order, while lack of *wh*-movement is associated with OV order. As we have seen above, Hixkaryana has OV order, but exhibits *wh*-movement (Derbyshire 1979). Also, Chinese exhibits VO order, but *wh in situ*. Thus, many languages exhibit some or many OV properties, but no language has been shown to be completely OV, even Japanese, as suggested by Kayne (2003a) (see also Kroch 2001, who argues that most languages display head parameter inconsistencies).

Many languages appear to have some left-headed projections and some right-headed projections. Ideally, the head parameter setting should be uniform for any given language. Mixed headedness would severely overgenerate the number of possible language types. For instance, in German, the *v*P, TP, and VP (sometimes), are right-headed, while all others are left-headed. Likewise, in Kwa languages, the DP is right-headed, the PP can exhibit either order, and the VP can also exhibit either order, varying with aspect (Aboh 2004).

Finally, I point out that assuming a Headedness Parameter has obscured some generalizations that would otherwise remain unnoticed. Kayne (2003a) discusses many of these and I concentrate on the generalization in (3) in this chapter. To be sure, the asymmetry in (3) would remain mysterious under a Headedness parameter, but invites an antisymmetric analysis.[11]

---

[11] A reviewer (and a participant at a conference where this was presented) noted that the lack of OXVS under the VP fronting proposal falls out naturally from assuming a right-headed structure with no verb movement. In fact, the mechanism I propose admits the possibility of a low VP adjunct (such as a manner adverb), which the headedness approach does not admit. Note, in fact, that in Urarina at least, VP-level adverbs appear at the left edge, suggesting that something larger than a bare VP has raised (assuming a Cinquean adverbial hierarchy). The point here, however, is that the headedness approach does not predict the asymmetry in (3). If OV languages were the result of a right-headed setting, then we would expect just as frequent a ban on OXV in SOV languages as in OVS languages, which we don't. Specifically, the ban on OXVS discussed here is simply a corollary of Kayne's original observation that bans on SOXV are much rarer than bans on SVXO. The reviewer does raise an important empirical point, however. The approach presented here does predict at least some material to intervene between the verb and the object to a very limited degree. This will have to wait for further empirical investigations. This proposal also predicts that

Richards (2008) proposes a modified Headedness Parameter that includes a re-implementation of the LCA whereby parameterized deletions of certain orderings take place at PF. This is based on the notion that a head and its complement form a point of symmetric c-command (in the sense of Moro 2000), a problem that is particularly acute with pronominal objects.[12]

(17)

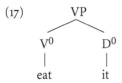

Richards states that the same problem doesn't exist for specifiers, as they asymmetric-ally c-command the head and complement. He argues that this is responsible for the universal Spec–head order (see also Oishi 2003); while much cross-linguistic vari-ation is found in head–complement order. It is not quite true, however, that specifiers fail to give rise to LCA violations. A single-headed element (such as a clitic or lexical root, say) could merge in the specifier of an XP and form a point of symmetric c-command with the next higher head up. In the following example, X^0 and Z^0 form a point of symmetric c-command.[13]

(18)

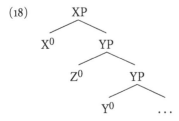

Recall that Richards observed that the point of symmetric c-command between a head on its complement (when also a head) was problematic for the LCA. This is why he proposed that the order between a head and its complement is parameterized

---

OVS should alternate with VSO if object shift out of the VP is available. That is, a remnant VP raises to Spec-TP stranding the object. It also predicts that VOS might be found for non-specific or bare objects (as in Massam's pseudo noun incorporation). These predictions will have to wait for future research.

[12] It is likely that pronouns of the English type as shown are actually DPs or ϕPs (Déchaine and Wiltschko 2002). Nevertheless, there are assumedly indisputable cases where two heads with lexical material c-command each other. Previously, I argued that this was the motivation for noun incorporation, where a verbal root merges with a nominal root (Barrie 2006a).

[13] To see how this is so, recall that Kayne's definition of c-command refers to segments of a maximal projection. X^0 c-commands Z^0 because every category that dominates X^0 (namely XP) also dominates Z^0. Note that YP does not dominate Z^0 since not all segments of YP dominate Z^0. Thus, Z^0 c-commands X^0 because every category that dominates Z^0 (only XP) also dominates X^0.

(hence stipulated). Applying the same line of reasoning leads us to posit that the order between X^0 and Z^0 in (18) is also parameterized.[14]

Another issue with Richards' proposal (though equally problematic with any headedness-based approach) concerns clausal complements. Since Richards' proposal parameterizes the order between a head and a complement, it is predicted that all complements to V^0 are uniformly to the left or right, depending on the parameter setting. Without any further refinement to the proposal, it is predicted that clausal complements appear to the left of the verb in Germanic OV languages, contrary to fact.[15] I discuss one final concern with Richards' proposal with respect to complementizers. Richards' proposal works nicely for auxiliaries in that it captures the fact that they frequently appear postverbally, from lowest to highest, (19). What the analysis fails to capture is the fact that the complementizer is consistently clause-initial. These facts about German (and other casual OV languages) could be overcome by various movement operations. However, this is exactly what Richards was trying to avoid by dismissing Antisymmetry in favour of the Headedness Parameter.

(19) ... dass   er   den Apfel   essen   sollen   hat
          that   he   the apple   eat   should   has.3SG
      '...that he has had to eat the apple.'

A reviewer has also suggested that underlying [$_{VP}$ O V] order would capture the lack of OXVS order very simply. While this of course is true, what it fails to predict is the generalization given above, namely, that SOV languages rarely disallow SOXV while OVS languages strictly disallow OXVS. If we allow underlying OV order for Hixkaryana, then we would expect to find some SOV languages with the properties of Hixkaryana reported here, which we do not.

Modifying Richards' analysis appropriately, one could argue that Hixkaryana has the following parameter setting, or that asymmetric c-command encodes linear *subsequence*, thereby parameterizing the LCA (as in Compton 2006):

(20)

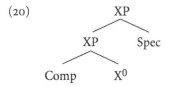

---

[14] (18) is also problematic for a strict Antisymmetric approach, of course. The point here is that Richards' approach does not completely solve the problem of symmetric c-command that Bare Phrase Structure introduces. For such approaches see Moro (2000) and Guimarães (2000).

[15] A reviewer notes the issue of clausal complements is problematic for Antisymmetry, too. If we assume, as I suggested above, that finite clausal complements are selected as fully formed CPs (while only non-finite clausal complements require the kind of treatment Kayne suggests), then this ceases to be a problem. The clause is selected and remains postverbal. DPs, on the other hand, must be licensed as described here, ending up preverbal when ghost projections are present. The presence of ghost projections does not affect finite CPs.

If OVS results from a right specifier, then the fronted *wh*-phrases and topicalized phrases in Hixkaryana are unexpected as are the fronted focused phrases that Olawsky (2007) reports for Urarina. In fact, if (20) were a possibility, then we would expect to find right-peripheral A-bar material in language more frequently; however, such phenomena are glaringly absent.[16]

Following the mirror principle (Baker 1985) the structure in (20) predicts a high degree of prefixing on the verbal complex with valence-changing morphology appearing closest to the root on the left and aspect, tense, and agreement morphology further out. We do not find this, however. Olawsky (2006: 456ff.) reports the following general order for morphemes on the verbal complex in Urarina.

(21)   V-CAUS-ASP-AGR

What is observed, then, is that the morpheme order is consistent with S–H–C order.

9.4 Antisymmetry and word order

Kayne (2003a) proposes that postpositions arise by virtue of *ghost* projections (described below), which are labelled by prime notation (X'P).[17] I assume that prepositions and postpositions are P^0 heads, while Case morphology is realized on K^0. Given that the PP/KP structure is responsible for Case, I generalize the use of ghost projections to all internal arguments with the following proposal.

(22)   Proposal: All internal arguments are assigned Case by a functional projection that either has (Japanese, Hixkaryana) or lacks (English, German) a ghost counterpart.

Thus, in OV languages such as Japanese and Hixkaryana, I propose an $Agr_OP/Agr_O'P$ shell to check Accusative Case.[18] This proposal captures the tight connection between OV and postpositions. For convenience, I distinguish between *pervasive* OV (as in SOV languages such as Japanese and Korean, as well as the OVS languages under consideration here) and *casual* OV (as in Germanic). In pervasive OV languages VO doesn't occur, clausal complements are typically preverbal, and there is the obligatory presence of postpostions. In casual OV languages VO occurs in

---

[16] The sole exception to this generalization I am aware of is *wh*-movement in ASL, where dislocated *wh*-phrases appear clause-finally. Petronio and Lillo-Martin (1997) argues that *wh*-phrases move to Spec-CP on the left with subsequent raising of the remnant clause; however, Neidle, Kegl, Maclaughlin, Bahan, and Lee (2000) refute this analysis and argue that Spec-CP is on the right.

[17] To avoid confusion, intermediate projections will not appear as X', but rather will appear as XP. Thus, X'P represents only a *ghost XP* hereafter.

[18] Although Chomsky (1995a) sought to eliminate agreement projections from UG as they were superfluous, it has been argued that there is some *v*P-internal projection that hosts objects (Johnson 1991; Rezac 2006). With regards to the subject AgrP, there are languages that show tense marking and subject agreement in distinct positions in the verbal complex (such as Northern Iraquoian, Lounsbury 1949), thus requiring a distinct Agr_SP and TP.

some circumstances, clausal complements are typically postverbal, and there is the obligatory use of prepositions. The derivation of postpostional PPs (Kayne 2003a) requires *ghost* P′P as follows.[19]

(23)

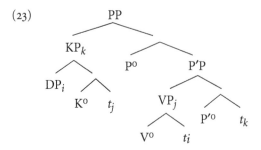

Let us posit a dummy $Agr_O'P$, a silent copy of Agr_OP, along the lines of P′P. Furthermore, I follow Koizumi (1995) and assume a split VP with an Agr_OP position for objects, in which the lower V^0 is spelled out. The derivation of pervasive OV, then, is as follows.

(24)

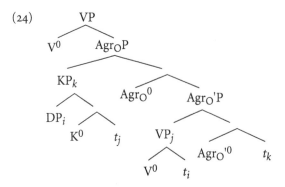

This gives rise to the strict OV adjacency observed in OVS languages. Note that the basic word order for Japanese and Korean tends to have the direct object immediately adjacent to the verb. Given that the object is in its Case-checked position, I do not expect it to move any further unless it undergoes scrambling or some (other) A-bar operation.[20]

---

[19] Kayne (2003a) assumes that the ghost is always null since it appears within the verbal complex and is never part of the nominal phrase. However, many languages require additional verbal morphology when locative expressions are present. Algonquian languages, for example, appear with *relative roots*—a morpheme inside the verbal complex—when a locative phrase is present in the clause (Rhodes 1998). Iroquoian languages also encode locative phrases with additional verbal morphology (Lounsbury 1949, 1953). Whether these morphemes are amenable to such an analysis is left to future research.

[20] Thanks to Kenji Oda and Manami Hirayama for discussing the Japanese data and to Jaehee Bak for discussing the Korean data. Their intuitions indicate that the most natural word order for these sentences has OV adjacency, but a full investigation into the matter requires further research.

Since the EPP in Korean and Japanese assumedly attracts DP rather than VP, the object can raise or scramble higher, deviating from the normal order.

(25)   Taroo-ga   Ginza-de   susi-o   tabeta
       Taro-NOM   Ginza-LOC   sushi-ACC   eat.PST
       'Taro ate sushi in Ginza.'

(26)   Moojang-i   Pusan-eyse   hoy-lul   mek-ess-ta
       Moojang-NOM   Pusan-LOC   sashimi-ACC   eat-PST-DECL
       'Moojang ate sashimi in Pusan.'

9.4.1 *Germanic OV lacks Ghost X'P*

The difference in OV/VO order in Germanic is due to object shift or similar phenomena (see the papers in Svenonius 2000a, and Aboh 2004). Given the wealth of previous work on this subject, I will confine my remarks to a few relevant observations. Note, for instance, that the direct object is never strictly adjacent to *zu*-infinitives, suggesting that OV is never a constituent in German.

(27)   ...dass   er   (Äpfel)   zu (*Äpfel)   kaufen   versprochen   hat.
       ...that   he   apples   to apples   buy   promised   has
       '...that he promised to buy apples.'

Given these differences in OV order between Germanic languages on the one hand, and Japanese, Korean, Hixkaryana, and Urarina on the other, an approach that attempts to derive a uniform (i.e. headedness) approach to OV order seems misguided.

We now turn to the derivation of multiple VP-internal elements under the Antisymmetric system that Kayne has set out.

9.4.2 *Derivation of multiple PPs/internal arguments*

To gain a full understanding of the derivation of OVS order, we must first examine how multiple internal arguments are licensed. Kayne (2003a: fn. 41) leaves open the derivation VPs with more than one PP (or a PP and DP internal object). Following Koizumi's approach, there is a VP which can serve as the base for the projection of KP and PP (and P'P in OV languages). Let us consider the derivation of SVOX (where X is a PP, say).[21,22]

---

[21] See Lasnik (2001) for arguments that objects in English raise overtly to a low functional projection in the VP domain. See also Johnson (1991).

[22] Agr$_O$P is null in English, but is possibly overt in Spanish, following Torrego (1998), where it is realized as *a*, and in Romanian, where it is realized as *pe* on definite/animate objects.

(28)   John hit the ball with a bat

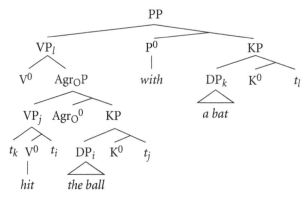

Following Kayne, the DPs are merged in the VP shell devoid of Case or prepositions. K^0 then merges with the VP and the direct object raises to Spec-KP. $Agr_O{}^0$ merges with the KP thus formed, and the remnant VP raises to Spec-Agr_OP. This gives the sequence *hit the ball* (however, with the adjunct *a bat* still attached). This is the Agr_OP shown in (28). The next segment of the VP shell merges with the Agr_OP and the process essentially repeats itself. Another K^0 merges with this larger VP and the DP 'a bat' raises to Spec-KP. Now, the preposition *with* merges with the KP and the remnant VP raises to Spec-PP. This gives the final order shown in (28). Similar derivations are possible for OV languages, as I will show below. I now turn to the derivation of OVS.

9.5 Derivation of OVS

Recall that the situation in (29) violates most any version of minimality where the two DPs are of the same type (Rizzi 1990) and are not in the same minimal domain (Chomsky 1995a).

(29) $DP_i \ldots DP_j \ldots t_i$

Collins (2005) argues such a scenario can arise by *smuggling* the higher DP inside a larger, non-DP constituent.

(30) $[_{XP} \ldots DP \ldots]_i \ldots DP_j \ldots t_i$

Consider this scenario in light of Massam's (2000) proposal on verb-initial word order in Niuean (see also Cole and Hermon 2008; Coon 2010).

(31)   Parameter: EPP satisfied by DP (French, English) or VP (Niuean, Hixkaryana)

Related to this parameter is the following contrast. Kayne (2003a) discusses the relative availabilty of OXV (X an adjunct or other VP-internal material) in OV languages, while VXO is absent in many VO languages (such as English). Surprisingly, OXV is absent in OVS languages (Derbyshire 1979; Olawsky 2007: 60). This falls out if OV is fronted as a VP-constituent in OVS as a result of EPP-VP rather than the result of object scrambling coupled with some kind of right-adjoined subject. Since OV moves as a unit, there is no opportunity for adjoined material to interpolate between the two.

We illustrate now the derivation of the following Hixkaryana sentence.

(32) bɨryekomo yotahano wosɨ (Derbyshire 1979: 38, (85a))
bɨryekomo y-otaha-no wosɨ
boy AGR-hit-PST woman
'The woman hit the boy.'

The derivation, then, proceeds as follows. The verb takes a bare DP as a complement.

(33)

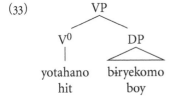

Then, the VP merges with K^0 and the DP raises to Spec-KP.

(34)

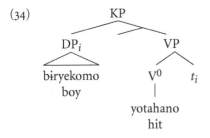

A ghost $Agr_O'^0$ subsequently merges with DP, and the remnant VP raises to Spec-Agr_O'P.

(35)

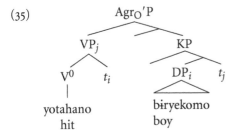

This is followed by Merge of the true $Agr_O{}^0$ with $Agr_O'P$ and raising the remnant KP to Spec-Agr_OP. Finally the VP shell is closed off by merging in the higher, empty V^0.[23]

(36)

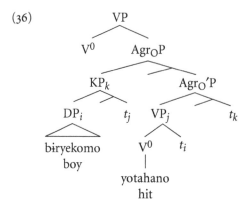

We have derived OV order for the Hixkaryana sentence above within a VP shell that will subsequently be raised. Next, we introduce the external argument and derive the rest of the clause. First, v^0 merges with the VP, and the subject merges in Spec-vP. I address the issue of Agr_SP later.[24]

(37)

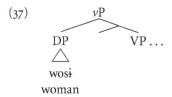

Then, TP merges in and attracts VP (rather than DP) to Spec-TP to satisfy EPP.

---

[23] A reviewer asks about the formation of the verbal complex given Pollock (1989) and much subsequent work that verb formation is syntactic. One idea is to relegate this to PF (Boeckx and Stjepanović 2001), but I leave this to future work.

[24] The other VP-fronting analyses referred to above include a VoiceP, which introduces the external argument, in addition to a vP. Closer scrutiny may reveal that such is required for the OVS languages under discussion here, too; however, the analysis presented here does not require a VoiceP, so it is left out.

(38)

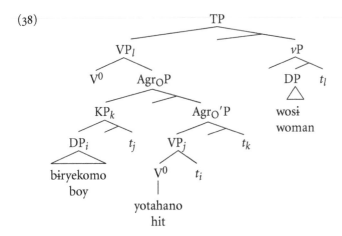

We have thus derived the basic OVS word order for Hixkaryana. Before continuing, I say a brief word about the VP fronting analysis for Niuean that Massam
proposes, in which VSO order arises by object movement out of the VP to a Case-
checking position and subsequent movement of the VP. (VOS order is derived by VP
movement with an *in situ* object.) The current analysis essentially makes use of the
same general mechanism to derive OVS order for Hixkaryana. So, why the difference
in word order between Hixkaryana and Niuean? Massam argues that full DP objects
in Niuean undergo a kind of object shift to a *v*P external projection (namely, to the
specifier of Abs(olutive)P), which is related to the ergative properties of that language
(Coon 2010 makes a similar proposal for Chol, also an ergative–absolutive language).
This movement is not found in Hixkaryana, an essentially nominative–accusative
language, rather, the object in Hixkaryana raises only as far as the left edge of the VP
and carried along when the VP/*v*P raises to Spec-TP. Furthermore, VOS order in
Niuean (and in Chol) is available only when the object nominal is impoverished—
that is, when it lacks D^0 elements and case marking, although number marking and
adjectives may be present. Massam and Coon argue that the morphologically impoverished object remains in situ (giving rise to Pseudo Noun Incorporation in Massam's terms). Thus, VP fronting in Niuean and in Chol involve raising of a V–NP
sequence rather than a DP–V sequence as in Hixkaryana.

The chart in (39) summarizes how the various word orders under discussion
arise.[25] In the next section I discuss further aspects of OVS languages with PPs.

---

[25] Absent from this chart is OSV languages. These present a problem for the current approach since
they cannot arise by the mechanisms proposed here. This is because the object raises above the subject
while the verb remains low. Thus, the object does not raise above the subject by being carried across by the
VP. Note this is also a problem for headedness approaches since there is no way to base-generate this order
with any of the four logically possible settings of such a parameter.

Specifically, I address how PPs are typically clause-final in Hixkaryana and clause-initial in Urarina.

(39)

	ghost projections present	no ghost projection
EPP–DP	Japanese-type SOV	SVO (no object shift) German-type SOV (with object shift)
EPP–VP	OVS	VOS (no object shift) VSO (with object shift)

9.5.1 *XOVS, OVSX, and *OVS*

OXVS is ruled out by VP fronting of a constituent containing only OV, which is required to smuggle the O across the S. In SOV languages such as Japanese, the O can easily undergo scrambling across an adverb (but remain below the subject), giving rise to SOXV. I must show how the OV sequence is able to move as a unit independently of the PP. Recall the derivations for a VP containing both an object DP and PP from above and consider the derivation for the following sentence. I abstract away from the position of the adverb for simplicity.

(40) biryekomo   komoyonyetxkoni
     child   COLL.he.was.eating.them
     kamara   txetxa   wawo   amnyehra
     jaguar   forest   in   long.ago
     'The jaguar used to eat children in the forest long ago.'

First, the VP is constructed as above, giving rise to OV order. Once the VP is fully formed, the P^0 and ghost P'^0 are merged in to form the post-PP. This gives rise to the derivation in (41).

(41)

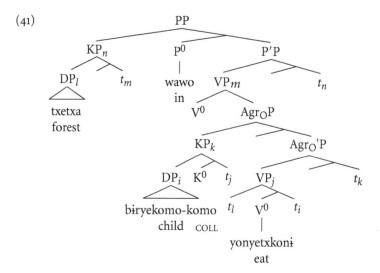

The VP (labelled VP_m) will subsequently be fronted, smuggling the object above the subject.

Next, the subject is introduced in vP. Note that v^0 is not introduced until after the Case-checking mechanisms for the internal arguments have been discharged. This results in a seemingly unconventional structure in (42), where v^0 takes PP as a complement. I argue that this is no different from other approaches that assume a variety of functional projections between v^0 and V^0 such as an inner AspP (Travis 1991) or ApplP (Pylkkännen 2008).

(42)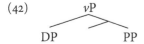

Finally, VP raises to Spec-TP, smuggling O across S and abandoning the PP in its clause-final position:

(43)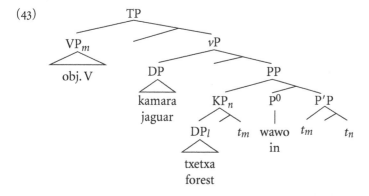

We turn now to the derivation of clause-initial PP in Urarina. Initial PPs are more common in Urarina than in Hixkaryana. Olwasky (2007) shows that PPs in Urarina can pattern both as XOVS and OVSX (with a moderate preference for clause-initial PPs).

Derbyshire (1979) shows clearly that OVSX is the unmarked order for Hixkaryana, where XOVS is possible when X is focused or emphatic. The underlying OVSX order simply results from the abandonment of the remnant PP. In Urarina, the remnant PP typically raises to a position of prominence in the left periphery, while this movement is not required in Hixkaryana. I take this to be some kind of scrambling that is not yet well understood.[26]

---

[26] It is interesting to note that Kayne (2003a) has argued that we should abandon the notion that PP is a constituent in the usual sense. While the shorter derivations do suggest this (and it is certainly true in this framework that PPs are not merged as a constituent), the derivation for Hixkaryana in (43) above shows clearly that PPs can become constituents through several applications of remnant movement.

9.5.2 *Case and the licensing of external arguments*

Let us assume that subjects are Case-marked the same way as objects—with an Agr_SP and a potential ghost equivalent. However, the agreement projections in and of themselves are not enough to define Case. As noted by Holmberg (1986), accusative Case is dependent on the presence of an external argument, which, following Kratzer (1996), is introduced by what is now known as v^0. Likewise, nominative Case is available only in the presence of finite T^0 (Chomsky 1981; Alboiu 2006), which, following Chomsky (2007, 2008), is dependent on the presence of C^0. Thus, we have the following partial derivation for the external argument. v takes VP as a complement (or PP if there are VP-internal PPs, as shown above), and the subject DP merges in Spec-vP. The process is then the same as above. K merges with vP and the subject DP raises to Spec-KP. The ghost $Agr_S'^0$ merges with KP and the vP raises to Spec-Agr_S'P. Finally, the real Agr_S^0 merges with Agr_S'P and the subject KP raises to Spec-Agr_SP.

(44)

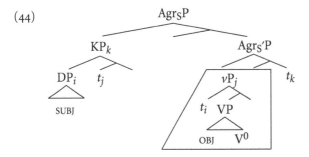

Once T^0 is merged with the Agr_SP in (44), EPP is satisfied by VP (or vP) movement (shown in the trapezoid), giving rise to OVS order. Note that both TP and CP are required for finiteness and nominative Case on the subject. This explicit mechanism for Case assignment and word order is necessary for an understanding of word order in embedded clauses, the subject of the next section.

9.5.3 *Embedded clauses*

Hixkaryana does not exhibit embedded finite clauses, except for quotes under verbs of saying. Embedded clauses (although rare) are nominalized and display ergative syntax. The unmarked word order is SOV, with the possibility of clause-final postpositions.

Following Alexiadou (2001), nominalized ergative constructions project extended verbal functional heads up to AspP.[27] Specifically, TP is absent, and so there is no EPP that triggers subject movement to Spec-TP. The consequence for OVS languages,

---

[27] It is unlikely that Agr_SP is also found in the nominalized clause. The external argument of transitives is Case marked by a postposition and does not trigger agreement on the verb. The external argument of an intransitive, however, does trigger agreement. A thorough examination of the ergative properties of embedded nominalized clauses in Hixkaryana is beyond the scope of this paper.

however, is that +the OV complex does not raise above subject, but rather remains *in situ*, thus giving rise to SOV order. Let us make the following proposal (revised from (22) above):

(45)   Case-marked arguments have uniform licensing mechanisms within one and the same language: they either have ghost X'Ps (Hixkaryana, Japanese) or lack them (English, German).

We further assume that the clause-final 'complementizer' elements are really functional adpositions (thus, a more accurate translation of *toko* would be 'during' rather than 'when'). Non-finite clauses, then, are licensed the same way PPs are. Thus, the nominalized subordinate clauses are formed as follows – derivation of (9) shown with English words in place.[28]

(46) $[_{DP}$ by.me jaguar AGR-seeing.of-when$]$ V selects DP

see $[_{DP}$ jaguar$]$ K selects VP

K $[_{VP}$ V DP$]$ DP $\rightarrow$ Spec-KP

$[_{KP}$ DP$_i$ K^0 $[_{VP}$ V^0 $t_i]]$ ghost Agr$_O$' selects KP

Agr$_O$' $[_{KP}$ DP$_i$ K^0 $[_{VP}$ V^0 $t_i]]$ VP $\rightarrow$ Spec-Agr$_O$'P

$[_{Agr_O'P}$ $[_{VP}$ V^0 $t_i]_j$ P$'^0$ $[_{KP}$ DP$_i$ K^0 $t_j]]$ Agr$_O$^{0} selects Agr$_O$'P

Agr$_O$^{0} $[_{Agr_O'P}$ $[_{VP}$ V^0 $t_i]_j$ Agr$_O$'^{0} $[_{KP}$ DP$_i$ K^0 $t_j]]$ KP $\rightarrow$ Spec-Agr$_O$P

$[_{Agr_OP}$ $[_{KP}$ DP$_i$ K^0 $t_j]_k$ Agr$_O$^{0} $[_{Agr_O'P}$ $[_{VP}$ V^0 $t_i]_j$ Agr$_O$'^{0} $t_k]]$

The structure in (46) is embedded under a VP shell as described above giving rise to the order $[_{VP}$ jaguar see$]$. At this stage, the external argument is merged in and the structure projects up to AspP (following Alexiadou). The details of the VP derived above are left out in the following derivation for space. The final tree is given below.

(47)   continuation of $[_{VP}$ jaguar see$]$

                                              v^0 selects VP

v^0 $[_{VP}$ jaguar see$]$ subject merges in

$[_{vP}$ $[_{DP}$ me$]$ v^0 $[_{VP}$ jaguar see$]]$ Asp^0 selects vP

Asp^0 $[_{vP}$ $[_{DP}$ me$]$ v^0 $[_{VP}$ jaguar see$]]$ VP $\rightarrow$ Spec-AspP

$[_{AspP}$ Asp^0 $[_{VP}$ jaguar see$]_i$ $[_{vP}$ $[_{DP}$ me$]$ v^0 $t_i]]$ K^0 selects AspP

K^0 $[_{AspP}$ $[_{VP}$ jaguar see$]_i$ $[_{vP}$ $[_{DP}$ me$]$ v^0 $t_i]]$ Subject DP $\rightarrow$ Spec-KP

$[_{KP}$ $[_{DP}$ me$]_j$ K^0 $[_{AspP}$ $[_{VP}$ jaguar see$]_i$ $[_{vP}$ t_j v^0 $t_i]]]$ ghost P$'^0$ selects KP

P$'^0$ $[_{KP}$ $[_{DP}$ me$]_j$ K^0 $[_{AspP}$ $[_{VP}$ jaguar see$]_i$ $[_{vP}$ t_j v^0 $t_i]]]$ AspP $\rightarrow$ Spec-P'P

---

[28] Evidence that the *adjunct* DP is selected directly by the verb is furnished by English examples such as the following:

(i)   I read none of the papers during/before any of lectures.

The *adjunct* in (9) is clausal in the English translation, but nominal in Hixkaryana (as in the example above). See Barrie (2009) for more details on the English examples.

$[_{P'P} [_{AspP} [_{VP} \text{jaguar see}]_i [_{vP} t_j v^0 t_i]]_k P'^0 [_{KP} [_{DP} \text{me}]_j K^0 t_k]] P^0$ ('by') selects P'P
by $[_{P'P} [_{AspP} [_{VP} \text{jaguar see}]_i [_{vP} t_j v^0 t_i]]_k P'^0 [_{KP} [_{DP} \text{me}]_j K^0 t_k]] KP \rightarrow$ SpecPP
$[_{PP} [_{KP} [_{DP} \textbf{me}]_j K^0 t_k]_l$ by $[_{P'P} [_{AspP} [_{VP} \textbf{jaguar see}]_i [_{vP} t_j v^0 t_i]]_k P'^0 t_l]]$

(48)

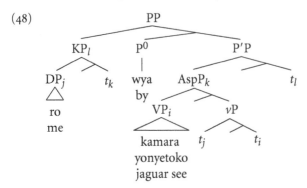

This non-finite clause undergoes nominalization before being selected by the matrix verb. Following the discussion above, the postposition (the equivalent of *when*, or *during* according to the suggestion above) is merged high, above the superordinate verb.

Recall that embedded clauses in Urarina are finite and exhibit OVS order. This is consistent with the overall approach argued for here, since the same mechanism for OVS order in matrix clauses described in the previous section can account for OVS order in the embedded clause. The analysis presented here, then, ties the difference in word order in embedded clauses in Hixkaryana and Urarina to the difference in finiteness in embedded clauses.

Finally, I discuss object complement clauses in Urarina. Olawsky (2006: 758) reports that object complement clauses regularly occupy the object position (immediately to the left of the verb with no intervening material). Recall also that such clauses are typically non-finite or nominalized (obligatorily so when the main and embedded clauses have the same subject). Again, I carry over the derivation for non-finite clauses for Hixkaryana above to Urarina to account for OVS order, when O is a non-finite clause. More interesting is the case where the object complement is a finite clause. I speculated in section 9.3 above that finite clauses are introduced differently than non-finite clauses. Specifically, I suggested that they are introduced as complete CPs without the interleaving structures found for nominal and non-finite complements. The contrast in (14) above seems to support this conclusion; however, the lack of relevant data urges us to proceed with caution and leave a fuller discussion of the syntax of finite clauses within the current framework to future research.

9.6 Conclusions

I have outlined an analysis of OVS languages within an Antisymmetric framework that hinges on two important microparameters. First, I have adopted Massam's proposal that EPP can be satisfied by VP rather than by DP in some languages. I have also proposed that the presence or absence of ghost P′Ps (and ghost Agr_O′Ps) is also subject to parametric variation, giving rise to the OV/VO distinction (and the correlated postposition/preposition distinction). The problem of raising an object DP over an intervening subject DP was solved by the notion of smuggling introduced by Collins. The object DP is smuggled across the subject DP by VP movement to satisfy the EPP. I have also seen that an Antisymmetric approach to syntax captures the *OXVS constraint in a straightforward way, while such a constraint would remain mysterious under a symmetric view of syntax. Thus, OVS languages, rather than being problematic for the theory of Antisymmetry, turn out, under closer inspection, to offer support for it.

10

Postverbal Constituents in SOV Languages*

BALKIZ ÖZTÜRK

10.1 Introduction

Khalkha Mongolian (=K) and Uyghur Turkic (=U) are two languages in the Altaic group, which exhibit the basic SOV word order and allow leftward scrambling of constituents as shown in (1) and (2), respectively. Both languages also allow their constituents to occur postverbally in colloquial speech, yielding SVO and OVS orders as given in (3) and (4):

(1) a. Bulgan ter   nom-ig   unsh-san.   (SOV)   (K)
        Bulgan this book-ACC read-PST
        'Bulgan read this book.'

     b. Ter   nom-ig$_i$ Bulgan t_i unsh-san.   (OSV)
        this book-ACC Bulgan   read-PST
        'Bulgan read this book.'

* A preliminary version of the account given here was first presented at the DGfS workshop 'Rightward Movement in a Comparative Perspective' in 2008 and appeared in Öztürk (2013). However, the current version thoroughly revises Öztürk (2013) and presents new data and argumentation. I am truly grateful to my informants Zemire Ahmed (Uyghur), Mukaddes Yadigar (Uyghur), Bulgan Ganjambal (Khalkha), Dinargul Khusphakan (Khalkha), Tsogt-Erdene Jamiyansuren (Khalkha), Said Can Umaraliev (Eastern Uzbek), Saifiddin Ibragimov (Eastern Uzbek), and Nurlan Asimov (Osh Kirghiz) for the data they shared with me.

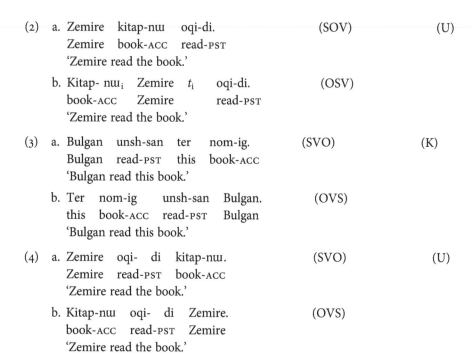

(2) a. Zemire kitap-nɯ oqi-di.   (SOV)   (U)
        Zemire book-ACC read-PST
        'Zemire read the book.'

     b. Kitap- nɯ$_i$ Zemire t_i oqi-di.   (OSV)
        book-ACC Zemire   read-PST
        'Zemire read the book.'

(3) a. Bulgan unsh-san ter nom-ig.   (SVO)   (K)
        Bulgan read-PST this book-ACC
        'Bulgan read this book.'

     b. Ter nom-ig   unsh-san Bulgan.   (OVS)
        this book-ACC read-PST Bulgan
        'Bulgan read this book.'

(4) a. Zemire oqi- di kitap-nɯ.   (SVO)   (U)
        Zemire read-PST book-ACC
        'Zemire read the book.'

     b. Kitap-nɯ oqi- di Zemire.   (OVS)
        book-ACC read-PST Zemire
        'Zemire read the book.'

Both Khalkha and Uyghur also exhibit long-distance scrambling of constituents via leftward movement as seen in (5b) and (6b) respectively. Postverbal constituents (PVCs), similar to the case of leftward-moving elements, can also adjoin across clauses as shown in (5c) and (6c):

(5) a. Bi [Bulgan-in ter nom-ig   unsh-san]-ig medne.   (K)
        I   Bulgan-GEN this book-ACC read-PST-ACC know
        'I know that Bulgan read this book.'

     b. Bulgan-in$_i$ bi [t_i ter nom-ig   unsh-san]-ig medne.
        Bulgan-GEN I   this book-ACC read-PST-ACC know
        'I know that Bulgan read this book.'

     c. Bi [___ ter nom-ig   unsh-san]-ig medne Bulgan-in$_i$.
        I   this book-ACC read-PST-ACC know   Bulgan-GEN
        'I know that Bulgan read this book.'

(6) a. Men [Zemire-niŋ kitap-nɯ oqu-gan-i]-ni   bil-i-men.   (U)
        I   Zemire-GEN book-ACC read-PST-3SG-ACC know-PRES-1SG
        'I know that Zemire read the book.'

     b. Zemire-niŋ$_i$ men [t_i kitap-nɯ oqu-gan-i]-ni   bil-i-men.
        Zemire-GEN I   book-ACC read-PST-3SG-ACC know-PRES-1SG
        'I know that Zemire read the book.'

   c. Men [___ kitap-nɯ   oqu-gan-i]-ni   bil-i-men   Zemire-niŋ$_i$
       I   book-ACC   read-PST-3SG-ACC know-PRES-1SG Zemire-GEN
       'I know that Zemire read the book.'

The aim of this study is to investigate the derivation of PVCs in two discourse-configurational languages, Khalkha and Uyghur. We will argue that the derivation of PVCs in both languages cannot be considered a uniform phenomenon. PVCs in Khalkha do not exhibit any evidence of a movement-based derivation, whereas PVCs in Uyghur behave parallel to leftward-scrambled elements, so that their derivation should involve movement. We will further argue that this movement should be to the right rather than to the left and that rightward movement should not be banned, but parameterized. In pursuit of parameterization of this type, we will argue that what enables rightward scrambling in discourse-configurational languages like Uyghur as opposed to Khalkha is the lack of EPP effects. The EPP in discourse-configurational languages is dependent on features related to information structure (Miyagawa 2005), and therefore imposes a certain degree of configurationality on the phrase structure. In relation to features such as topic and focus, it regulates the projection of specifiers specifically on the left and blocks the projection of rightward Specs hosting elements with opposing information structure features. This, it is argued, is the reason why Khalkha fails to have rightward scrambling, while Uyghur very productively allows it.

10.2 PVCs in Khalkha: movement or not?

As seen in (3) and (5c) above, Khalkha allows for PVCs in colloquial speech. Information-structure-wise, such constituents represent afterthoughts, providing or repairing missing information in the clause.[1] In the following, we will compare leftward scrambling with postposing in Khalkha to answer the question of whether postposing constructions require movement or not.

    One property of leftward scrambling in Khalkha is that nothing can occupy the base position of the scrambled element. As seen in (7a) and (7b), it is not possible to fill the base position of moved constituents with pronominal elements:

(7) a. *Bulgan-in$_i$ bi [tuni$_i$ ter   nom-ig   unsh-san]-ig   medne. (K)
       Bulgan-GEN   I   she   this book-ACC read-PTCP-ACC know

    b. *Ter   nom-ig$_i$ bi [ter-ig   Bulgan-in   unsh-san]-ig   medne.
       this book-ACC   I   this-ACC Bulgan-GEN read-PTCP-ACC know

Khalkha leftward scrambling also respects islands. While complement clauses allow for extraction of any constituent as seen in (8), syntactic islands, for example

---

[1] See Kuno (1978) for an account of Japanese PVC where he argues that PVCs express afterthoughts.

relative clauses, only allow for the extraction of genitive subjects, but not non-subjects as can be seen in (9). That is, Khalkha exhibits a certain kind of subject/non-subject asymmetry for scrambling out of syntactic islands.

(8) a. Bi [Bulgan-in   ter   nom-ig   unsh-san]-ig   medne.   (K)
      I   Bulgan-GEN this   book-ACC read-PTCP-ACC know
      'I know that Bulgan read this book.'

   b. Bulgan-in$_i$ bi [t_i ter   nom-ig   unsh-san]-ig   medne.
      Bulgan-GEN I   this   book-ACC read-PTCP-ACC know
      'I know that Bulgan read this book.'

   c. Ter nom-ig$_i$ bi   [Bulgan-in t_i unsh-san]-ig   medne.
      this book-ACC I   Bulgan-GEN   read-PTCP-ACC know
      'I know that Bulgan read this book.'

(9) a. Bi [Bulgan-in   ter   nom-ig   øg-san]   ohin-ig medne.   (K)
      I   Bulgan-GEN this   book-ACC give-PTCP girl-ACC know
      'I know the girl that Bulgan gave this book to.'

   b. Bulgan-in$_i$ bi [t_i ter   nom-ig   øg-san]   n   ohin-ig medne.
      Bulgan-GEN I   this   book-ACC give-PTCP 3SG girl-ACC know
      'I know the girl that Bulgan gave this book to.'

   c. *Ter nom-ig$_i$ bi [Bulgan-in t_i øg-san]   ohin-ig medne.
      this book-ACC I   Bulgan-GEN   give-PTCP girl-ACC know

Now if we turn to PVCs in Khalkha, we see that right-dislocated elements exhibit different properties than leftward-scrambled constituents. First, it is possible to fill the base position of PVCs with pronominals as in (10). Even in monoclausal constructions it is possible to introduce pronominal elements for the sentence-final elements as in (11b), while it is again strictly prohibited for leftward scrambled constituents in (11c):

(10) a. Bi [tuni$_i$ ter   nom-ig   unsh-san]-ig   medne Bulgan-in$_i$. (K)
      I   she   this   book-ACC read-PTCP-ACC know   Bulgan-GEN
      'I know that she read this book, Bulgan.'

   b. Bi [ter-ig   Bulgan-in   unsh-san]-ig   medne ter   nom-ig$_i$.
      I   this-ACC Bulgan-GEN read-PTCP-ACC know this book-ACC
      'I know that Bulgan read this, the book.'

(11) a. Bulgan ter   nom-ig   unsh-san.   (K)
      Bulgan this   book-ACC read-PST
      'Bulgan read this book.'

   b. Bulgan ter-ig   unsh-san, ter   nom-ig.
      Bulgan this-ACC read-PST this book-ACC
      'Bulgan read this, this book.'

    c. *Ter   nom-ig   Bulgan ter-ig   unsh-san.
       this   book-ACC Bulgan this-ACC read-PST

Second, when islands are considered, postposing again behaves differently. The subject vs non-subject asymmetry that is observed in the case of leftward scrambling out of relative clause islands disappears for PVCs. Neither subjects nor non-subjects associated with relative clause islands can occur sentence-finally:

(12) a. *Bi [__i ter nom-ig   øg-san]   ohin-ig medne Bulgan-in_i. (K)
        I   this book-ACC give-PTCP girl-ACC know   Bulgan-GEN

     b. *Bi [Bulgan-in   __i øg-san]   ohin-ig medne ter   nom-ig_i.
        I   Bulgan-GEN   give-PTCP girl-ACC know   this book-ACC

Further evidence for the difference between leftward scrambling and postposing comes from idiomatic expressions. When parts of idioms are scrambled leftward, it is possible to retain the idiomatic reading as in (13b). When they appear postverbally, however, it is not possible to retain the idiomatic reading as in (13c). This implies that *narma-ig* 'nose-ACC' and *nee* 'burst' do not form an idiomatic constituent at any point in the derivation under postposing:

(13) a. Bulgan tuunii narma-ig nee-sen.   (K)
       Bulgan his   nose-ACC burst-PTCP
       Literally: 'Bulgan burst his nose.'
       Intended meaning: 'Bulgan beat him.'

     b. Tuunii narma-ig Bulgan nee-sen.
       his   nose-ACC Bulgan burst-PTCP
       Literally: 'Bulgan burst his nose.'
       Intended meaning: 'Bulgan beat him.'

     c. Bulgan __i nee-sen   tuunii narma-ig_i.
       Bulgan   burst-PTCP his   nose-ACC
       Literally: 'Bulgan burst his nose.'
       No figurative meaning: '*Bulgan beat him.'

Furthermore, if quantifiers appear as PVCs, then they cannot interact with other scopally relevant elements in the sentence, as they necessarily get a wide-scope reading. This also implies the absence of a trace linking the PVC to a position below other scope-bearing elements:

(14) __i nom-ig   unsh-a-gy   byh huuhduud_j.   (K)
      book-ACC read-NEG-PAST all   children
      'All children did not read the book.'   (all > not, *not > all)

The discussion above clearly indicates that PVCs do not behave as parts of the sentence they adjoin to. The fact that they cannot form idioms or interact scopally with other elements in the sentence shows that they adjoin to the sentence as independent constituents. Their behaviour with respect to islands and the co-occurrence with pronominal elements imply that they are not derived in the same way as leftward-scrambled elements.

One property of Khalkha PVCs is that when postposing targets an NP, the N head cannot be postposed at the expense of leaving behind other N-bar levels as in (15c). Note that since the head noun already bears agreement morphology for the possessor, depending on the discourse conditions, it is possible to delete the possessor. This is indicated by the parenthesized possessor in (15a). If the possessor in (15a) is deleted, then *nom-ig-n* will be interpreted as 'his/her book'.

(15)   a. Bi [$_{NP}$ (Bulgan-in)   [$_N$ nom-ig-n]]   unsh-san.   (K)
        I   Bulgan-GEN   book-ACC-3SG   read-PTCP
        'I read Bulgan's book.'

       b. Bi [$_{NP}$ __$_i$[$_N$ nom-ig-n]]   unsh-san   Bulgan-in$_i$.
        I   book-ACC-3SG   read-PTCP   Bulgan-GEN
        'I read Bulgan's book.'

       c. *Bi [$_{NP}$ Bulgan-in   [$_N$ __$_i$]] unsh-san   nom-ig-n$_i$.
        I   Bulgan-GEN   read-PTCP   book-ACC-3SG

Note that Khalkha allows for discourse-bound null pronouns, as seen in (16b). However, the counterpart of (15c) without the postverbal N head given in (16c) is also ungrammatical. In order to have a fully grammatical sentence *pro* has to replace the whole NP without stranding the possessor:

(16)   a. Bi   Bulgan-in   nom-ig-n   unsh-san.   (K)
        I   Bulgan-GEN   book-ACC-3SG   read-PTCP
        'I read Bulgan's book.'

       b. Bi *pro*   unsh-san.
        I   read-PTCP
        'I read it.'

       c. *Bi   Bulgan-in   *pro*   unsh-san.
        I   Bulgan-GEN   read-PTCP

What (15c) implies is that PVCs in Khalkha are available only if the sentence that the PVC adjoins to is a grammatical sentence on its own. The reason for this requirement is that the right-adjoined element does not belong to the main sentence, and hence cannot amend the sentence if the sentence violates any of the requirements of the sentence structure of Khalkha.

The next question is how PVCs in Khalkha are derived. Are they simply base-generated independent constituents, or is it possible to assume some other type of movement for their derivation? In the literature on Japanese, which also has PVCs in colloquial speech, it has been proposed that postposing constructions are bi-clausal in nature. PVCs are assumed to appear at the left edge of a second clause, which undergoes phonological deletion under identity to the first clause (Kuno 1978; Tanaka 2001; Abe 2004; Kato 2007) as illustrated in (17):

(17) $[pro_i \text{ OV}][S_i \text{ } \overline{\text{OV}}] \rightarrow \text{OVS}$

Such a derivation explains the island effects observed in the case of Japanese postposing. As seen in (18b), it is not possible to have the object of a relative clause appear postverbally in Japanese. What is interesting is that the same construction still retains its ungrammaticality even if the base position within the relative clause is filled as in (18c), unlike in (18b). This is taken to be evidence for a bi-clausal derivation of postposing in Japanese. The ungrammaticality of (18c) is assumed to result from leftward movement of the object out of the relative clause within the second clause. This is taken to be independent from the first clause, which is grammatically well-formed, as illustrated in (18d). The illicit leftward movement in the second clause is what is causing the ungrammaticality:

(18)   a. John-ga   [Mary-ga   Bill-ni   ageta hon-o]   nusunda yo.[2] (Jp)
          John-NOM   Mary-NOM   Bill-DAT gave   book-ACC   stole
          'John stole the book that Mary gave to Bill.'

       b. ?*John-ga   [Mary-ga pro_i ageta hon-o]   nusunda yo, Bill-ni$_i$.
          John-NOM   Mary-NOM   gave   book-ACC   stole   Bill-DAT
          'John stole the book that Mary gave to him, to Bill.'   (Tanaka 2001: 555)

       c. ?*John-ga   [Mary-ga   Bill-ni   ageta hon-o]   nusunda yo, Bill-ni.
          John-NOM   Mary-NOM Bill-DAT gave book-ACC   stole   Bill-DAT
                                                                                                (Tanaka 2001: 556)

       d. John-ga [Mary-ga Bill-ni ageta hon-o] nusunda yo. ?*[Bill-ni$_i$ [~~John-ga~~
          ~~[Mary-ga~~ t_i ~~ageta hon -o]nusunda yo~~]

Note that it is not possible to argue for such a derivation for Khalkha. Compare (9b) with (12a) above. As seen in (9b), in the case of leftward scrambling it is possible to extract the genitive subject, but not in the case of postposing, as in (12a). If Khalkha postposing constructions were bi-clausal like the ones in Japanese, then the ungrammaticality of (12a) would be unexpected. Given that genitive subjects can undergo leftward scrambling out of relative clauses, (12a) should also be grammatical when

---

[2] The particle *yo* signifies that the structure in question belongs to a colloquial register; following Tanaka (2001: 551, note 3), it is left unglossed here.

leftward scrambling applies in the second clause. Furthermore, again unlike Japanese, when the (putative) base position of the postposed genitive subject is filled overtly, the ungrammaticality disappears, as seen in (19). Based on this, we argue that the derivation of PVCs in Khalkha does not involve a second clause which is subject to phonological deletion. PVCs are simply base-generated and derivationally independent of the clause they seem to adjoin to.

(19)   Bi [Bulgan-in$_i$ ter   nom-ig   øg-san]   ohin-ig   medne, Bulgan-in$_i$.   (K)
       I   Bulgan-GEN this book-ACC give-PTCP girl-ACC know   Bulgan-GEN
       'I know the girl that Bulgan gave this book to.'

The next question is why (12a) is ungrammatical, given that Khalkha allows for *pro*. If the ungrammaticality does not result from an illicit movement within a second clause and if *pro* can fill the gap, the sentence should be well-formed regardless of the PVC. We assume the ungrammaticality results from interpretational constraints. Verbs in Khalkha do not bear overt agreement markers, and, out of context, the embedded clause subject and the matrix subject are interpreted as being identical. In order to disassociate the two subjects, overt pronominal clitics need to be used, as seen in (20b). That is why (12a) is taken to be ungrammatical. Given that the gap for the subject of the relative clause is interpreted as associated with the matrix clause subject, the postverbal subject simply cannot be interpreted as related to the main clause. However, if a pronominal clitic is introduced, as in (20c), then the sentence becomes interpretable even in the presence of a postverbal genitive subject extracted out of a relative clause:[3]

(20)   a. Bi [*pro* ter   nom-ig   øg-san]   ohin-ig   medne.   (K)
          I   this   book-ACC give-PTCP girl-ACC know
          'I know the girl that I gave this book to.'

       b. Bi [*pro* ter   nom-ig   øg-san]   ohin-ig   n   medne.
          I   this   book-ACC give-PTCP girl-ACC   3SG know
          'I know the girl that s/he gave this book to.'

       c. Bi [__$_i$ ter   nom-ig   øg-san]   ohin-ig   n   medne Bulgan-in$_i$.
          I   this   book-ACC give-PTCP girl-ACC 3SG know   Bulgan-GEN
          'I know the girl that Bulgan gave this book to.'

Given the discussion above we conclude that PVCs in Khalkha cannot be derived via movement. They neither move out of the clause they adjoin to nor undergo leftward scrambling out of a second clause, but are simply base-generated

---

[3] Note that the ungrammaticality of (12b) might also be linked to constraints on interpretation, where the postverbal object simply cannot be associated with a gap within a relative clause. See Sells (1999) for such a proposal for Japanese postposing.

independent constituents, presenting afterthoughts. They can only be taken to be extra information emphasizing or clarifying the referent of the empty elements in the clause they seem to adjoin to. Their availability in the postverbal position is fully dependent on the grammatical conditions of the first clause, such as whether a clitic is available or not as in (20c). In Japanese, on the other hand, the use of PVCs is not dependent on the grammaticality of the first clause, as seen in (18c), as their derivation is dependent on a second clause phonologically identical to the first one. What could be the source of this asymmetry between Japanese and Khalkha requires further investigation.

10.3 PVCs in Uyghur: is it movement?

Now we will turn to Uyghur and investigate whether the derivation of PVCs involves movement in parallel to leftward scrambled constituents.

In Uyghur, leftward scrambling shows island sensitivity for non-subjects, since it is possible for genitive subjects to move out of islands without causing any ungrammaticality, as in (21). Thus, the same subject/non-subject asymmetry that we observed in Khalkha, illustrated in (9), is also available in Uyghur.[4] However, this asymmetry disappears in complement clauses, where both subjects and objects can undergo leftward scrambling as in (22):

---

[4] One possible explanation for the subject/non-subject asymmetry in Uyghur could be that subjects might be raising out of relative clauses into the DP the head noun projects. This is supported by the presence of the agreement morphology associated with the subject on the head noun regardless of its syntactic function in the relative clause. If subjects raise out of relative clauses into the Spec of the outer DP, they can trigger Spec–Head agreement with the head noun. The genitive that appears on the subject might also be a result of this as in (i). Possessor DPs marked with genitive also trigger agreement with nouns in whose specifiers they occur and can scramble out of the DP as in (ii). The similarity of genitive subjects to genitive possessor DPs might be the reason for the freedom of extraction exhibited by such subjects:

(i) [$_{DP}$ Zemire-niŋ$_i$ [$_{CP}$ t$_i$ kitap-nɯ   ber-gen]   qɯz-ɯ].   (U)
      Zemire-GEN   book-ACC   give-PTCP   girl-3SG
      'The girl to whom Zemire gave the book.'

(ii) a. [$_{DP}$ Zemire-niŋ   qɯz-ɯ?
          Zemire-GEN   girl-3SG

          'Zemire's girl (daughter)'

      b. Zemire-niŋ$_i$ men [$_{DP}$ t$_i$ qɯz-ɯn]-ɯ   bil-i-men.
          Zemire-GEN   I   girl- 3SG-ACC know-PRES-1SG

          'I know Zemire's daughter.'

Note that we have exactly the same type of subject/non-subject asymmetry in Khalkha as shown in (9). Head nouns in relative clauses in Khalkha can also optionally take a clitic agreeing with the subject of the relative clause. This might tentatively suggest that genitive subjects in relative clauses might also be raising to Spec-DP in Khalkha in parallel to what we have suggested for Uyghur. This might again be the source for the freedom of genitive subjects. However, this requires a thorough analysis of the relative clause constructions in Khalkha, which does not fall within the scope of this paper. See Hale (2002) for relative clauses in Dagur Mongolian.

(21) a. Men [Zemire-niŋ kitap-nʉ ber-gen   qʉz-ʉɪn]-ʉ bil-i-men.   (U)
          I   Zemire-GEN book-ACC give-PTCP girl-3SG-ACC know-PRES-1SG
          'I know the girl to whom Zemire gave the book.'

      b. Zemire-niŋᵢ men [tᵢ kitap-nʉ ber-gen   qʉz-ʉn]-ʉ bil-i-men.
          Zemire-GEN I   book-ACC give-PTCP girl-3SG-ACC know-PRES-1SG
          'I know the girl to whom Zemire gave the book.'

      c. *Kitap-nʉᵢ men [Zemire-niŋ tᵢ ber-gen   qʉz-ʉn]-ʉ bil-i-men.
          book-ACC I   Zemire-GEN   give-PTCP girl-3SG-ACC know-PRES-1SG

(22) a. Men   [Zemire-niŋ kitap-nʉ oqu-gain-in]-i   bil-i-men.   (U)
          I   Zemire-GEN book-ACC read-PTCP-3SG-ACC know-PRES-1SG
          'I know that Zemire read the book.'

      b. Zemire-niŋᵢ   men [tᵢ kitap-nʉ oqu-gain-in]-i   bil-i-men.
          Zemire-GEN I   book-ACC read-PTCP-3SG-ACC know-PRES-1SG
          'I know that Zemire read the book.'

      c. Kitap-nʉᵢ men [Zemire-niŋ tᵢ oqu-gain-in]-i   bil-i-men.
          book-ACC   I   Zemire-GEN   read-PTCP-3SG-ACC know-PRES-1SG
          'I know that Zemire read the book.'

If we return to PVCs in Uyghur, we see that, unlike the situation in Khalkha, they behave identically to leftward-scrambled elements. As such, in (23a), similar to the case in (21), genitive subjects can be extracted out of relative clauses postverbally, whereas objects cannot, as shown in (23b):

(23) a. Men [__ᵢkitap-nʉ ber-gen   qʉz-ʉn]-ʉ bil-i-men   Zemire-niŋᵢ.(U)
          I   book-ACCgive-PTCPgirl-3SG-ACC know-PRES-1SG Zemire-GEN
          'I know the girl to whom Zemire gave the book.'

      b. *Men[Zemire-niŋ __ᵢ ber-gen   qʉz-ʉn]-ʉ bil-i-men   kitap-nʉᵢ.
          I   Zemire-GEN   give-PTCP girl-3SG-ACC know-PRES-1SG book-ACC

Also the subject/non-subject asymmetry disappears when constituents are extracted rightward out of complement clauses as in (24):

(24) a. Men [__ᵢ kitap-nʉ oqu-gain-in]-i   bil-i-men   Zemire-niŋᵢ. (U)
          I   book-ACC read-PTCP-3SG-ACC know-PRES-1SG Zemire-GEN
          'I know that Zemire read the book.'

      b. Men [Zemire-niŋ __ᵢ oqu-gain-in]-i   bil-i-men   kitap-nʉᵢ.
          I   Zemire-GEN   read-PTCP-3SG-ACC know-PRES-1SG book-ACC
          'I know that Zemire read the book.'

Again unlike Khalkha, neither leftward scrambling nor postposing allow for pronominal elements to occur in the position of dislocated elements in Uyghur:

(25) a. Zemire   kitap-nɯ   oqi-di.   (U)
   Zemire   book-ACC   read-PST
   'Zemire read the book.'

  b. *Zemire   un-i   oqi-di,   kitap-nɯ.
   Zemire   it/that-ACC   read-PST   book-ACC
   'Zemire read it/that, the book.'

  c. *Kitap-nɯ   Zemire   un-i   oqi-di.
   book-ACC   Zemire   it/that-ACC   read-PST
   'Zemire read it/that, the book.'

As seen above, PVCs in Uyghur exhibit the same behaviour as leftward-scrambled elements. This implies that PVCs can also be derived via movement. Idiomatic expressions also argue for a movement-based derivation for PVCs. Parts of idioms can be scrambled leftward as well as rightward, retaining the idiomatic reading as in (26b) and (26c). That is, under both derivations parts of idioms form a syntactic unit. Only under long-distance leftward or rightward extraction does the idiomatic reading disappear, as shown in (27b) and (27c):

(26) a. Zemire   hichqachan   til-in-i   tart-ma-j-du.   (U)
   Zemire   never   tongue-3SG-ACC   weigh-NEG-PRES-3SG
   Literally: 'Zemire never weighs her tongue.'
   Intended meaning: 'Zemire never knows how to speak properly.'

  b. Til-in-i   Zemire   hichqachan   tart-ma-j-du.
   tongue-3SG-ACC   Zemire   never   weigh-NEG-PRES-3SG
   Intended meaning: 'Zemire never knows how to speak properly.'

  c. Zemire   hichqachan   tart-ma-y-du   til-in-i.
   Zemire   never   weigh-NEG-PRES-3SG   tongue-3SG-ACC
   Intended meaning: 'Zemire never knows how to speak properly.'

(27) a. Men [Zemire-niŋ   hichqachan   til-in-i.
   I   Zemire-GEN   ever   tongue-3SG-ACC
   tart-mɯ-ɣɯn-ɯn]-ɯ   bil-i-men   (U)
   weigh-NEG-PTCP-3SG-ACC   know-PRES-1SG
   Literally: 'I know that Zemire never weighs her tongue.'
   Intended meaning: 'I know that Zemire never knows how to speak properly.'

  b. Til-in-i   men [Zemire-niŋ   hichqachan tart-mɯ-ɣɯn-ɯn]-ɯ.
   tongue-3SG-ACC I   Zemire-GEN never   weigh-NEG-PTCP-3SG-ACC
   bil-i-men.
   know-PRES-1SG
   Only the literal reading: 'I know that Zemire never weighs her tongue.'
   No figurative meaning: '*I know that Zemire never knows how to speak properly.'

    c. Men [Zemire-niŋ hichqachan tart-mɯ-ɣɯn-ɯn]-ɯ   bil-i-men.
      I   Zemire-GEN never   weigh-NEG-PTCP-3SG-ACC know-PRES-1SG
      til-in-i
      tongue-3SG-ACC
      Only the literal reading: 'I know that Zemire never weighs her tongue.'
      No figurative meaning: '*I know that Zemire never knows how to speak
      properly.'

If PVCs in Uyghur are derived via movement, then we predict that they should be able to interact scopally with other elements in the clause. We see that PVCs can take scope below or above other scope-bearing elements in the clause, unlike the cases observed in Khalkha:

(28) Kitap-nɯ   oqɯ-ma-di   hemme balɯ-lar.   (U)
       book-ACC   read-NEG-PST all   child-PL
       'All children did not read the book.'   (not > all, all > not)

Moreover, in possessor constructions in Uyghur heads of NPs can be postposed, leaving behind the possessor, again unlike in Khalkha above. The counterpart of the Khalkha example in (15c), given in (29c), is grammatical in Uyghur:

(29) a. Men   [$_{NP}$ Zemire-niŋ [$_N$ kitap-ɯn]-ɯ]   oqi-di-m.   (U)
       I   Zemire-GEN   book-3SG-ACC read-PST-1SG
       'I read Zemire's book.'

      b. Men [$_{NP}$ t_i [$_N$ kitap-ɯn]-ɯ]   oqi-di-m   Zemire-niŋ$_i$.
       I   book-3SG-ACC read-PST-1SG Zemire-GEN
       'I read Zemire's book.'

      c. Men [$_{NP}$ Zemire-niŋ [$_N$ t_i]]   oqi-di-m   kitap-ɯn-ɯ$_i$.
       I   Zemire-GEN   read-PST-1SG book-3SG-ACC
       'I read Zemire's book.'

      d. Men *pro* oqi-di-m.
       I   read-PST-1SG
       'I read it.'

      e. *Men Zemire-niŋ *pro*   oqi-di-m.
        I   Zemire-GEN   read-PST-1SG

Similar to Khalkha, Uyghur allows for discourse-bound null arguments and *pro* also has to replace the whole NP without leaving behind possessors, as shown in the parallel between (16c) and (29e). However, postposing of the head noun, leaving behind the possessor, is only an option in Uyghur. The contrast between (29c) and (29e) indicates that the postverbal N head improves the sentence, unlike the Khalkha example in (15c). This implies that in Uyghur PVCs belong to the sentence they adjoin to and that this is why the sentence in (29c) is grammatical in contrast to (29e).

To summarize, the data in (21) through (29) indicate that the derivation of PVCs in Uyghur is clearly different from those in Khalkha. Therefore, PVCs in both languages cannot be handled as a uniform phenomenon: while Khalkha requires a movement-free derivation for PVCs, Uyghur appears to be a language which makes use of movement for its PVCs. Then the next question is what kind of movement this is. Could this really be rightward movement of the sort that has been claimed to exist in other Turkic languages such as Turkish (Kural 1997; Kornfilt 2005; Şener 2005)? Or could the appearance of these elements in postverbal position be handled as a case of scrambling leftward into higher specifiers as would be the case under Kayne's (1994) approach? These questions form the focus of the following section.

10.4 Directionality of movement

As shown above, PVCs in Uyghur exhibit properties that are typically associated with moved constituents. If we assume that the postverbal clause in (30b) reaches that position via movement, then we would predict that material cannot be extracted out of it. This prediction is borne out. The fact that material cannot be moved out of already postposed material also suggests that they do indeed occur in a derived position, as illustrated in (30c) below. Note that (30a) with the SOV order is identical to (22a) above, and it allows for extraction as shown in (22b) and (22c):

(30)   a. Men [Zemire-niŋ   kitap-nɯ   oqɯ-gan-i]-ni   bil-i-men.SOV   (U)
           I   Zemire-GEN   book-ACC   read-PST-3SG-ACC   know-PRES-1SG
           'I know that Zemire read the book.'

     b. Men t_i bil-i-men   [[Zemire-niŋ   kitap-nɯ   oqɯ-gan-i]-ni]$_i$.   SVO
           I   know-PRES-1SG   Zemire-GEN   book-ACC   read-PST-3SG-ACC
           'I know that Zemire read the book.'

     c. *Kitap-nɯ$_j$ men t_i bil-i-men   [[Zemire-niŋ t_j oqɯ-gan-i]-ni]$_i$.
           book-ACC I   know-PRES-1SG   Zemire-GEN   read-PST-3SG-ACC

The data in (30c) imply that PVC reach their postverbal position via movement. The next question to be answered is whether PVCs reach their position via leftward or rightward movement. Even if rightward movement is not theoretically favoured in certain accounts such as Kayne (1994, 2003a), in the following we will show that the rightward movement option presents a more elegant and straightforward account of PVCs in Uyghur. Thus, following what Kural (1997), Kornfilt (2005), and Şener (2005) proposed for Turkish, we will argue for a rightward-movement-based derivation of Uyghur PVCs.

Considering the fact that Turkish is a language exhibiting scope rigidity, where scope relations are interpreted based on surface c-command relations, Kural (1997) observes that PVCs in Turkish, which have a backgrounded interpretation, unambigously take wide scope over other scopally relevant constituents in the clause, as seen in the contrast between (31a) and (31b).[5] Based on this observation, he concludes that PVCs must be derived via rightward adjunction to the CP domain.[6]

(31) a. Herkes   [üç   kişi]-yi   dün   ara-mış.   SOV (Tk)
          everyone three person-ACC yesterday   call-PST.HEARSAY
          'Everyone called three people yesterday.'   (everyone > three people)
          only 'Everyone called three arbitrary people yesterday.'

     b. Herkes   dün   ara-mış   [üç   kişi]-yi.   SVO
          everyone yesterday   call-PST.HEARSAY   three person-ACC
          'Everyone called three people yesterday.'   (three people > everyone)
          only 'A group of three people received calls from everyone yesterday.'

Zwart (2002), however, claims that the fact that PVCs always take wide scope in Turkish does not necessarily follow from the surface c-command condition, but is due to their backgrounded status. In Dutch, for example, all tensed complement clauses appear in postverbal position and do not necessarily imply backgrounding. They can, however, acquire a backgrounded interpretation by deaccenting the postverbal material and by stressing the verb as shown in (32).

(32) ...omdat   hij niet WIST   [dat het regen-de.ø]   (D)
          because   he   not know.PST.SG   that it   rain-PST.SG
          '...because he was not aware of the fact it was raining.'   (Zwart 2002: 25)

Postverbal material in Dutch, when backgrounded, also requires a wide-scope interpretation, even though it is not necessarily in a c-commanding position. Based on this, Zwart concludes that what is crucial for the wide-scope interpretation is backgrounding (deaccenting), not right-adjunction to a high c-commanding position as argued by Kural.

Uyghur is also a language which exhibits scope rigidity, as seen in (33), where surface c-command determines the scope relations:

(33) a. Her   bala   ikki kitap-nɯ   oqu-di.   SOV (U)
          every   child two   book-ACC   read-PST
          'Every child read two books.'   ($\forall > \exists$, *$\exists > \forall$)

     b. İkki   kitap-nɯ   her   bala   oqu-di.   OSV
          two   book-ACC   every   child read-PST
          'Every child read two books.'   (*$\forall > \exists$, $\exists > \forall$)

[5] Taylan (1984) defines backgrounding in Turkish as a way of presenting material that is supplementary to the discourse. Material that is given, predictable, or recoverable from previous discourse can occupy the postverbal position. See Taylan (1984) on the properties of backgrounding exhibited by PVCs in Turkish.

[6] See Göksel (2011) for a base-generation account of Turkish PVCs.

However, Zwart's claim regarding the wide-scope interpretation of PVCs cannot be maintained for Uyghur, where PVCs also have a backgrounded interpretation. Unlike what is claimed for Turkish by Kural (1997), PVCs in Uyghur can also take narrow scope even if they are backgrounded, as illustrated in (34).[7] Therefore, we still assume that surface c-command is a crucial factor in determining the scope relations in Uyghur, which implies that PVCs can occupy different positions depending on what scope they take:

(34) a. Her   bala   oqu-di   ikki   kitap-nuɪ.   SVO (U)
         every   child   read-PST two   book-ACC
         'Every child read two books.'   ($\forall > \exists, \exists > \forall$)

      b. İkki   kitap-nuɪ   oqu-di   her   bala.   OVS
         two   book-ACC   read-PST every child
         'Every child read two books.'   ($\forall > \exists, \exists > \forall$)

Before discussing the derivation of the sentences above, a few clarifications are in order here with respect to our assumptions about the phrase structure of Uyghur. As extensively discussed in Öztürk (2004, 2005, 2008), the T head in some Turkic languages is not associated with an obligatory EPP feature, so Spec-TP does not have to be projected all the time. But when Spec-TP is projected, it behaves as a criterial position associated with scope–discourse properties in the sense of Rizzi and Shlonsky (2007). As we will discuss in detail in the next section, TP in Uyghur is not associated with an obligatory EPP feature; Spec-TP is projected only to host scope-discourse-related material. This is in accordance with Miyagawa (2005), who proposes that EPP in discourse-configurational languages is related to a focus/topic feature. Note that Uyghur is also discourse-configurational, meaning that word order is closely related to information structure. As illustrated above, PVCs denote backgrounding, i.e. they express supplementary and given information recoverable from discourse. Topic- or focus-related elements, on the other hand, typically appear in the preverbal domain. In (35), for example, where *Zemire* is presented as the topic denoting aboutness in the question, it cannot occur postverbally (35B′), but preverbally (35B), given that it is presented as a contrastive topic in the answer.

(35) A: Zemire   kitap-nuɪ   oqu-di   mi?   (U)
         Zemire   book-ACC   read-PST Q
         'Did Zemire read the book?'

      B: Bulgan   oqu-di   amma   Zemire   oqu-ma-di.
         Bulgan   read-PST but   Zemire   read-NEG-PST
         'Bulgan read it but Zemire did not read it.'

      B′: ??*Bulgan oqu-di amma oqu-ma-di Zemire.

---

[7] See Kornfilt (2005) and Şener (2005) on PVCs taking narrow scope in Turkish.

However, when *Zemire* is not used as a contrastive topic, as in (36), it can either be deleted (B) or backgrounded (B′) in the answer, along with other given material in the discourse, i.e. with *kitap-nuɪ*. Thus, the preverbal and postverbal domains are clearly reserved to encode material associated with different information-structure-related features.

(36)   A: Zemire   kitap-nuɪ   oquɪ-di   mi?   (U)
          Zemire   book-ACC   read-PST   Q
          'Did Zemire read the book?'

      B: *pro*zemire *pro*book oquɪ-ma-di.
                        read-NEG-PST
          'She did not read it.'

      B′: Oquɪ-ma-di   Zemire   kitap-nuɪ.
          read-NEG-PST   Zemire   book-ACC
          'Zemire did not read it.'

Now let us briefly consider how the scope facts in (33)–(34) can be accounted for by allowing a rightward movement option. Note that given the lack of scope ambiguity in (33), we aim to capture the scope facts via surface c-command without recourse to the reconstruction option. As Uyghur is strictly a head-final language, we also assume that the basic word order is SOV, and all other orders are derived from it.

Given these assumptions, let us consider the scope facts in (33)–(34). In (33a), given that the subject strictly takes wide scope in the SOV order, we assume that it is in an A-position. We also assume that in order to take wide scope or to be interpreted as specific, material has to leave the *v*P domain in Uyghur (Diesing 1992). As Spec-TP is reserved for scope–discourse-related material, the subject moves into this position and scopes over the object as seen in (37a). As the object denotes any arbitrary two books under the narrow-scope reading, it is expected to remain *v*P-internal as illustrated below. In the OSV order in (33b), on the other hand, the object, which is interpreted as two specific books, moves into Spec-TP—a criterial freezing position, and takes wide scope over the subject in Spec-*v*P as illustrated in (37b).

(37)   a.   b.

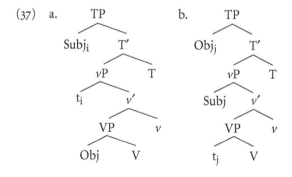

In the ambiguous example in (34a) with the SVO order, for the subject to take wide scope over the object, it again moves into Spec-TP. As the object is non-specific, we assume that it remains *v*P-internally and right-adjoins to *v*P. This is shown in (38a). For the narrow-scope reading of the subject, on the other hand, the object this time right-adjoins to the TP level. It gets interpreted as two specific books and c-commands the subject, which remains in Spec-*v*P as seen in (38b). This way, the surface c-command requirement can be fulfilled. Note that, as will become clear in the following section, we assume that the *v*P/VP, TP and CP levels all allow for right-adjunction.

(38)   a.   b.

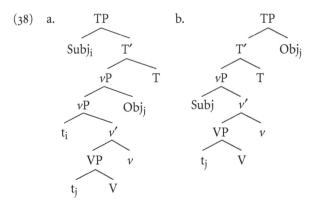

Under the OVS order in (34b), the ambiguity is again handled by a similar mechanism. When the subject takes wide scope, it right-adjoins to TP and scopes over the *v*P-internal non-specific object via surface c-command as in (39a). When it is the object which takes wide scope and is interpreted as specific, then it moves to TP and takes wide scope c-commanding the subject right-adjoined to *v*P as shown in (39b). Given the representation in (39b), the subject starts off from Spec-*v*P then adjoins to another *v*P-related position, an unfavoured operation (Ko 2005). There are several alternatives we can entertain here instead. Note that, as discussed above, backgrounded elements match with phonologically deleted material in the preverbal domain. We can either assume that overt XPs which bear the feature [+background] cannot be merged in leftward Specs and need to be introduced in rightward Specs. That is, it is possible to assume that the subject in (39b) does not undergo right-adjunction at all, but is directly merged into the structure as a rightward *v*P-Spec. Thus, this would be an example of a base-generated rightward Spec. Another alternative would be to assume that what Dyakonova (2009) proposes also holds for Uyghur. She argues that all phases have an information-structure-related edge. If we take *v*P to be a phase in Uyghur, then we can assume there to be a functional projection above *v*P, but below TP, which hosts backgrounded elements, still allowing them to have an existential reading.

(39) a.   b.

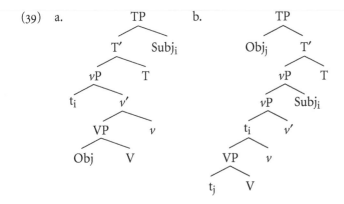

As can be seen above, rightward movement can handle the scope facts in Uyghur in a consistent and straightforward way. If rightward movement is assumed, we can still maintain the empirically supported condition of surface c-command. We do not have to assume reconstruction. Assuming that PVCs get there via rightward movement also explains why the postverbal domain behaves like an island for extraction as illustrated in (30c).

Let us very briefly discuss how the sentences in (33)–(34) can be handled under a leftward movement account. We do not aim to exhaust all the possible derivations here, due to space limitations, but try to sketch what kind of assumptions one needs to make in order to cover the data in (33)–(34) assuming the LCA. Note that given the unambiguous data in (33), we should try to accommodate the scope facts by using surface c-command relations without recourse to reconstruction. We should also assume that non-specific arguments remain *v*P-internal and that Spec-TP does not need to be filled because of the EPP, but for scope–discourse purposes.

To derive the unambiguous example (33a) with SOV order, the subject moves into Spec-TP and takes wide scope. To get the word order right, the object also needs to move from the complement position of V into some specifier position. Since the object is interpreted as non-specific, this has to be a Spec within the *v*P domain or at its edge. Note that under the specific definition of c-command by Kayne (1994) an XP projection cannot have multiple specifiers. Therefore, Spec-*v*P cannot be an option for the object to land in, since the subject already starts out from Spec-*v*P. Therefore, we are leaving this position as undefined in (40a). It can be right on top of VP, or in between TP and *v*P. In (33b), on the other hand, in order to get the unambiguous OSV order, we have to assume that this time the object moves into an A-position above the subject. Since the object has to be interpreted as specific, this would be Spec-TP and the subject can remain *in situ* as in (40b):

(40) a.

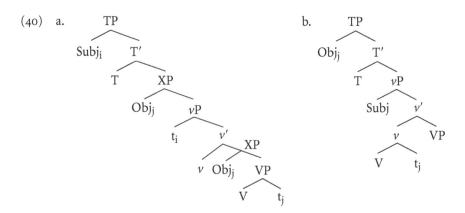

In example (34a) with SVO word order, the subject again has to move into Spec-TP to get the wide-scope reading, while the object and the verb can remain *in situ* as shown in (41a). Up to this point, the LCA account fares as well as the rightward movement account. However, we face a problem when we want to derive the narrow-scope reading of the subject below the object under the SVO order. We have to assume that both the object and the verb move to some higher positions above the *v*P-internal base position of the subject. Then the subject has to move to an A-bar position so that it can reconstruct below the object as shown in (41b). This means that we have to give up the surface scope requirement and make recourse to reconstruction, allowing an A-bar position like Spec-CP for the subject. Why this A-bar option was not available for the subject in (33a), while it is available here needs to be accounted for. In addition, we have to motivate verb movement to a position higher than the surface position of the object, which was also not needed in the examples in (33).

(41) a.

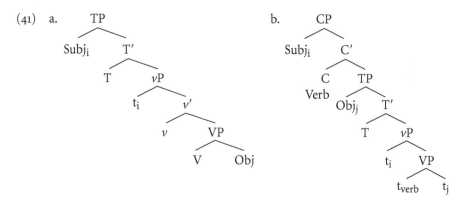

In example (34b) with OVS order, for the wide-scope reading of the object, we again have to assume that both the object and the verb move to positions above the base position of the subject in Spec-*v*P to get the word order right, as shown in (42a). For the narrow-scope reading of the object, on the other hand, we have to make recourse to reconstruction from an A-bar position into a *v*P-internal position below the subject again, as in (42b). Note again that this A-bar position was not available for the object in (33b).

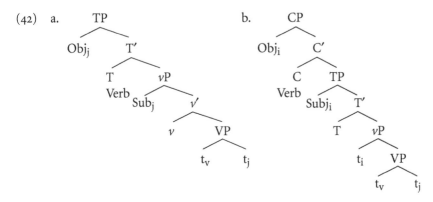

Another way to implement narrow scope for the object in (34b) could be through remnant movement. First, the subject moves into Spec-TP and then *v*P (including the object and the verb) moves into Spec-CP and reconstructs back into its position below the subject. As discussed in Müller (2000), in order for this kind of remnant construction to arise, *v*P/VP-fronting should be independently available in the language. However, Turkic languages do not exhibit any evidence for this type of *v*P/VP-fronting as discussed in detail in Öztürk (2004, 2005). Example (43) illustrates the unavailability of *v*P/VP-fronting in Uyghur example:

(43) *Kitap oquı, Zemire esla   quıl-ma-j-du.   (U)
       book read,   Zemire never   do-NEG-PRES-3SG
      'Read books, Zemire never does.'

Comparing the rightward and leftward derivations, we see that the rightward option gives us a more elegant and straightforward account of the scope facts in Uyghur. With the rightward movement account, we can retain the surface c-command requirement and do not need reconstruction at LF. Verb movement or remnant *v*P/VP movement, which cannot be independently motivated, will not be required. As reconstruction from an A-bar position will not be needed under the rightward account, we can easily predict whether there will be scope ambiguity (34) or not (33). Given these considerations, the rightward movement option clearly comes across as a better choice for explaining the Uyghur scope facts under different word orders and will be specifically assumed for the derivation of PVCs in the following.

10.5 EPP: towards a parameter for rightward movement

In section 10.4, we specifically claimed that the kind of movement used in the derivation of PVCs in Uyghur is rightward movement creating rightward Specs. Then the question arises as to why rightward Spec formation is possible in Uyghur, whereas it is disfavoured in Khalkha.

When the two languages are considered, we find another asymmetry in addition to the derivation of PVCs regarding their behaviour in relation to the EPP: Khalkha, but not Uyghur, exhibits EPP effects. First, Khalkha, but not Uyghur, obligatorily requires movement of the subject into the matrix Spec-TP in raising constructions; compare Khalkha (44) and Uyghur (45) in this connection. Thus, Spec-TP does not always have to be projected in Uyghur:

(44) a. [$_{TP}$ Bulgan$_i$ yaq   nadaa [$_{TP}$ t_i uil-san] yum shiq haragdaj
          Bulgan certainly to.me   cry-PST as   if   seem
          baina]   (K)
          AUX
       'Bulgan certainly seems to me to have cried.'

      b. *[$_{TP}$ ____ yaq   nadaa [$_{TP}$ Bulgan uil-san] yum shiq haragdaj baina]
            certainly to.me   Bulgan cry-PST as   if   seem   AUX

(45) a. [$_{TP}$ Zemire$_i$ inuqla maɣa [$_{TP}$ t_i juɣluː-ɣan] dek køryn-dy] (U)
          Zemire certainly to.me   cry-PRF   as.if seem-PST
       'Zemire certainly seemed to me to have cried.'

      b. [$_{TP}$ ____ inuqla   maɣa [$_{TP}$ sen juɣluː-ɣan-suːn] dek køryn-dy-ŋ]
            certainly to.me   you cry-PRF-2SG   as.if seem-PST-2SG
       'You certainly seemed to me to have cried.'

Second, quantified subjects in Khalkha unambiguously take wide scope over negation in the SOV word order, and thus they occur in Spec-TP (46a). Only under the OSV order can they take narrow scope as in (46b). Note that Khalkha also exhibits scope rigidity.

(46) a. Byh   huuhduud nom-ig   unsh-a-gy.   SOV   (K)
          all   children   book-ACC   read-PRF-NEG
       'All children did not read the book.'   (all > not, *not > all)

      b. Nom-ig   byh   huuhduud unsh-a-gy.   OSV
          book-ACC all   children   read-PRF-NEG
       'All children did not read the book.'   (not > all, *all > not)

However, as discussed in section 10.4, quantified subjects in SOV structures in Uyghur can take narrow scope, as shown in (47):

(47) Hemme balɯ-lar kitap-nɯ oqɯ-ma-di.   (U)
      all   child-PL   book-ACC   read-NEG-PST
      'All children did not read the book.'   (not > all, all > not)

Thus, Khalkha is a language with EPP effects and does not allow for rightward movement, whereas Uyghur lacks EPP effects and employs rightward adjunction. This raises the question whether there is indeed a correlation between having EPP effects and disallowing rightward movement and if so, what role the EPP plays in banning rightward movement?

In Uyghur, we see that example (47) is two-ways ambiguous, with the subject being able to take either narrow or wide scope with respect to negation. However, when a TP adverb is introduced, then (47) can get disambiguated based on the position of the subject with respect to the adverb. This fact also supports the surface c-command analysis that we proposed in section 10.4, rather than the LF reconstruction account that has to be assumed under a Kaynian approach. When the subject precedes the adverb, it takes wide scope (48a), but when it follows it, it takes narrow scope (48b).[8] If the TP adverb is postposed, however, the reading where the subject takes wide scope by virtue of being in Spec-TP, becomes unavailable. In other words, if we assume that the adverb right-adjoins to TP, then the subject cannot move to TP, projecting another Spec on the left, as seen in (48c):

(48) a. Hemme balɯ-lar **tynygyn** kitap-nɯ oqɯ-ma-di.   (U)
         all   child-PL yesterday book-ACC read-NEG-PST
         'All children did not read the book yesterday.'   (*not > all, all > not)

      b. **Tynygyn** hemme balɯ-lar kitap-nɯ oqɯ-ma-di.
         yesterday all   child-PL book-ACC read-NEG-PST
         'All children did not read the book yesterday.'   (not > all, *all > not)

---

[8] The implication of (48b) is that both the subject and the object can remain vP-internal below NegP, which is taken to be the position associated with the scopal properties of negation (Miyagawa 2001; Kelepir 2001; Aygen 2002; Öztürk 2004, 2005). Alexiadou and Anagnostopoulou (2007) argue that by Spell-Out a vP/VP cannot contain more than one argument with an unchecked case feature. This constraint, which blocks the simultaneous occurrence of both the subject and the object vP/VP-internally in languages like French, relies on the assumption that there is a structural case-checking relation between the object and the vP. Öztürk (2005), however, shows that this constraint is not operative in languages like Turkish. We observe the same pattern in Uyghur in (48b). Öztürk (2005) proposes that if what Alexiadou and Anagnostopoulou suggested is a cross-linguistically valid constraint, then what it implies is that there cannot be a structural case-checking relation between the object and vP in languages like Turkish. In Öztürk (2005), the object in Turkish checks its case *in situ* against a Neo-Davidsonian theta-role-introducing functional head, but not with vP. See Öztürk (2005) for details. A similar proposal has been made for accusative case in Japanese by Fukui and Takano (1998), who argue that object case assignment in Japanese is not parallel to structural case assignment but happens in a manner similar to inherent case assignment. Object case checking in Uyghur can be of the same nature as the one in Turkish or Japanese, therefore (48b) does not posit a counterexample to the constraint defined by Alexiadou and Anagnostopoulou (2007). However, the true nature of case-checking in Uyghur requires further investigation.

c. Hemme balɯ-lar kitap-nɯ oqu-ma-di   **tynygyn.**
all   child-PL book-ACC read-NEG-PST yesterday
All children did not read the book yesterday.   (not > all, *all > not)

If there is a *leftward* Spec at the TP-level, then no *rightward* Spec formation is allowed, as no bi-directional Spec formation is allowed at TP. Movement to Spec-TP is optional and not forced by the EPP feature. In languages like Khalkha, on the other hand, Spec-TP has to be filled all the time due to the EPP, so we predict no rightward Specs at the level of TP. Thus, if we interpret EPP as a feature-enforcing obligatory leftward Spec projection, then in languages with EPP effects, it will block rightward Spec formation, at least at the TP level. In section 10.7, we will come back to this blocking effect of the EPP in relation to the discourse-configurational nature of Uyghur and Khalkha.

Furthermore, in Uyghur this restriction on the projection of bi-directional Specs is not limited to TP, but also holds for the CP and *v*P domains. Consider (49). In Uyghur, just as in Turkish, embedded nominalized clauses with genitive subjects cannot host PVCs, as in (49a) (see Kural 1997 for Turkish). By contrast, embedded finite clauses with nominative subjects can, as in (49b). As discussed in the literature, genitive subjects in Turkic are in Spec-CP and higher than nominative subjects, which can occupy Spec-TP (Aygen 2002; Kornfilt 2007; Öztürk 2004, 2005). However, if nominative subjects are topicalized via a topic marker as in (50c) and thus raise into Spec-CP, then rightward adjunction to CP is blocked, as no bi-directional Specs are allowed. Note that at the matrix level, nominative subjects are compatible with the topic marker as shown in (49d); hence the ungrammaticality of (49c) does not follow from the incompatibility of nominative subjects with topic markers:[9]

(49)   a. *Men [$_{CP}$ Zemire-niŋ$_j$ (bolsa) [$_{TP}$ t_j t_i oqu-gun-in- i]   **kitap-nɯ$_i$**]
        I   Zemire-GEN (as.for)   read-PST-3SG-ACC book-ACC
        bil-i-men.   (U)
        know-PRES-1SG

<hr>

[9] One reviewer highlights the parallel example (i) from Turkish where the genitive subject is scrambled to a postverbal position within the embedded clause and argues it to be ungrammatical:

(i) Herkes   [[___ sınav-ı   kazan-dığ-ın-ı]   Ali-nin]   bil-iyor.   (Tk)
    everybody   exam-ACC   pass-NOM-3SG-ACC   Ali-GEN   know-PROG
    'Everybody knows that Ali pass the exam.'

(ii) *Herkes   [[Ali-nin ___   kazan-dığ-ın-ı]   sınav-ı]   bil-iyor.
     everybody   Ali-GEN   pass-NOM-3SG-ACC   exam-ACC   know-PROG

However, this example is not judged to be ungrammatical by my informants and is in sharp contrast with the case of postverbal object scrambling within the embedded clause illustrated in (ii). Therefore, it does not challenge the account here, but rather supports it given that when there is a genitive subject, rightward adjunction to the CP layer is blocked. As genitive subjects typically appear in Spec-CP in Turkish, it will not be possible to right-adjoin the object to the CP layer. The only implication of this data is that PVCs within an embedded clause can only adjoin to the embedded CP layer but not lower. This might result from processing difficulties, which need to be further investigated.

b. Men [$_{CP}$ [$_{TP}$ Zemire t_i oqu-di] **kitap-nɯ$_i$** dep kap-ti-men.
   I   Zemire   read-PST book-ACC as   think-PST-1SG
   'I thought that Zemire read the book.'

c. *Men [$_{CP}$ Zemire$_j$ bolsa [$_{TP}$ t_j t_i oqu-di] **kitap-nɯ$_i$** dep kap-ti-men.
   I   Zemire   as for   read-PST book-ACC as   think-PST-1SG

d. Zemire   bolsa   kitap-nɯ   oqu-di.
   Zemire   as.for book-ACC   read-PST
   'As for Zemire, she read the book.'

The same restriction is observed in relation to *v*P. Consider the scope of the adverb *peqet* 'only' in Uyghur. In (50a) and (50b) we have an unaccusative and an unergative predicate, respectively. In (50a), where we have an unaccusative predicate without any agentive subject in Spec-*v*P, we see that the postverbal adverb *peqet* can scope over the whole VP, or over the whole proposition. Note that given that there is a topicalized NP bearing the topic marker *bolsa* in Spec-CP and the adverb *tynygyn* yesterday in Spec-TP, we cannot assume that *peqet* is attached to CP or TP. The propositional reading is derived by attaching *peqet* to *v*P. In (50b) with an unergative predicate and an agentive subject in Spec-*v*P, on the other hand, the scope of *peqet* can only be the VP but never the whole proposition. This indicates that the adverb cannot right-adjoin to the *v*P level, where the agent is introduced as a leftward Spec.[10] Note that given that the subject follows the TP adverb we assume it to be in its base-generated position in Spec-*v*P. Thus, we encounter the same restriction in terms of bi-directional Spec formation. If there is an obligatorily projected leftward Spec at *v*P, then the scope of *peqet* must be established lower than the *v*P layer, since it cannot adjoin rightward to *v*P, which has a leftward projected Spec:

(50) a. Musabiqi-ler-de bolsa tynygyn   Zemire jɯɪqɯl-ɯp chush-ti **peqet.** (U)
         race-PL-LOC   as.for yesterday Zemire drop-CONJ fall-PST only

      i. 'As for in the races yesterday Zemire only fell down (and did nothing
          else)'   *VP*

      ii. 'As for in the races yesterday it is just that Zemire fell down (and
          nothing else happened)'   *Proposition*

---

[10] Even if we assume that *peqet* adjoins to *v*P as a rightward Spec, we see that the agentive subject has to escape its scope domain and be dislocated from Spec-*v*P. Given that Spec-CP and Spec-TP are filled in (50b), one potential position for the subject can be the information-structure-related edge, which is proposed to be on top of *v*P by Dyakonova (2009). Thus, (50b) can be taken to provide evidence for the availability of such a position. However, why it is not possible for *peqet* to right-adjoin to this information-structure-related edge and take the agentive subject in Spec-*v*P in its scope still remains as a question to be answered.

b. Musabiqi-ler-de   bolsa   tynygyn   Zemire   jygyr-dy   **peqet.**
race-PL-LOC   as.for   yesterday   Zemire   run-PST   only

i. 'As for in the races yesterday Zemire only ran (and did nothing else)'   *VP*

ii. NOT: 'As for in the races yesterday it is just that Zemire ran (nothing else happened)'   **Proposition*

Given the data in (50b), the question is whether it would never be possible to right-adjoin to a *v*P, in whose Spec we find a base-generated agent, e.g. in unergative and transitive constructions with agentive subjects. The relation between EPP and rightward adjunction comes to the fore again at this point. We interpret the EPP as a requirement for an *overtly* filled Spec. As long as the agentive subject does not remain *in situ* in its base position in Spec-*v*P but moves higher, right-adjunction to *v*P would be possible. The scope facts that we discussed in the preceding section are also in accordance with this. If a subject is to remain in Spec-*v*P, thus creating an overtly filled Spec in the *v*P domain, rightward adjunction should target higher domains such as TP and CP, or the lower VP domain.

To summarize, Spec formation in Uyghur is subject to certain restrictions. If there is already a leftward Spec in a given XP projection, then that XP cannot host a rightward Spec at the same time. That is, no simultaneous bi-directional Specs can be projected in a given XP projection. It is possible to have multiple Specs on the left as illustrated by the configuration in (51a). Alternatively, in the absence of a leftward Spec, projecting only a rightward Spec is also allowed, as in (51b). But what is not allowed is to have multiple Specs which are bi-directionally projected, as in (51c). Thus a single XP projection cannot simultaneously host one Spec projected on the left and one on the right:[11]

---

[11] Note that it is also possible to have multiple Specs on the right in a given XP projection as long as there is no leftward Spec. As discussed for Turkish in Kornfilt (2005), in Uyghur, too, it is possible to have more than one element postverbally. As seen in (i), it is possible for the postverbal subject to take narrow scope below negation:

(i) Yygyr-me- di   hemme   baluu-lar   ittik   ittik   (U)
    run-NEG-PST   all   child-PL   quick   quick

'All children did not run quickly.'   (not > all)

This implies that the subject is within the *v*P domain, which is modified by a manner adverb. Note that how linearization happens in such constructions does not fall within the scope of this paper. As observed for Turkish by Kornfilt (2005), even though in terms of scope relations PVCs imply a hierarchical relation at the level of interpretation, their ordering with respect to one another at the level of PF can be assumed to be non-hierarchical. However, this requires further investigation, which we leave for a future study.

(51) a.   XP   b.   XP   c.   *XP

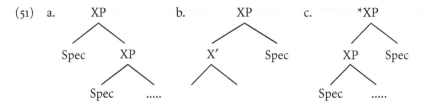

We correlate this restriction on bi-directional Spec formation with the EPP. If we reinterpret EPP as a feature regulating Spec formation specifically on the *left*, then if there are obligatory EPP effects associated with a phrasal projection in a given language, no right adjunction will be predicted, in accordance with the constraint on bi-directional Spec formation. Thus, any obligatory leftward Spec formation will block the projection of Specs on the right. We propose that this is the reason why in Khalkha, a language which exhibits EPP effects, rightward movement is banned, in contrast to Uyghur—a language with no obligatory EPP effects.

The question is why the EPP has such a blocking effect on rightward movement in discourse-configurational languages. As we will show below, the correlation between the EPP and rightward movement that we observe in Khalkha and Uyghur is also operative in other Altaic languages. In the following we will first discuss how the ban on bi-directional Spec formation works in Japanese, Turkish, Eastern Uzbek, and Osh Kirghiz, and then discuss why the presence or absence of EPP effects has such an effect on rightward movement in these languages in section 10.7.

10.6 EPP and rightward movement: cross-Altaic facts

Japanese and Turkish are two well-studied representatives of the Altaic group, which both exhibit the basic SOV word order and allow PVCs. However, PVCs in Japanese, similar to those in Khalkha, fail to exhibit any movement-based derivation (Sells 1999; Tanaka 2001; Abe 2004; Kato 2007). Turkish, on the other hand, is assumed to derive its PVCs via rightward movement (Kural 1997; Kornfilt 2005; Şener 2005). Consider the contrast between Japanese and Turkish in terms of the use of resumptive pronouns in place of PVCs, as illustrated in (53). While both Turkish and Japanese strictly ban resumption for leftward scrambling as in (52), Japanese but not Turkish allows resumption for PVCs as in (53). Given this asymmetry between the two languages, can the correlation between lacking EPP effects and having rightward movement also be extended to Japanese and Turkish? Japanese has been described as an EPP language (Miyagawa 2001, 2003), whereas Turkish has been shown to lack EPP effects (Öztürk 2008):[12]

---

[12] If T bears an EPP feature in Turkish, this is not checked via Merge/Move XP to [Spec-TP]. If such a feature is to be assumed for Turkish, then it is checked via head movement along the lines of Alexiadou and Anagnostopoulou (1998) (see Öztürk 2001, 2004, 2005, 2009 for discussion).

(52) a. *Mary-o_i   John-ga   [*pro* kanozyo-o_i nagutta to]   itta.   (Jp)

      Mary-ACC   John-NOM   she-ACC   hit   COMP said

      'Mary, John said that he hit her.'   (Abe 2004)

  b. *Mary-i   John   [*pro* o-nu   döv-düğ-ün]-ü   söyle-di.   (Tk)

      Mary-ACC   John   she-ACC   beat-PTCP-3SG-ACC   say-PST

(53) a. Watasi-wa   [John-ga   (kanozyo-ni)   sono   hon- o   kureta   to]

      I-TOP   John-NOM   her-DAT   that   book-ACC   gave   COMP

      itta,   watasi-no   musume-ni.

      said   I-GEN   daughter-DAT

      'I said that John gave that book to my daughter.' (Abe 2004)   (Jp)

  b. *Ben [John-un   on-u   oku-duğ-un]-u   söyle-di-m, bu kitab-ı   (Tk)

      I   John-GEN it-ACC read-PART-3PS-ACC tell-PST-1SG this book-ACC

Let us consider how the two languages behave in terms of EPP effects. The first piece of evidence against the obligatory projection of Spec-TP in Turkish comes from scope facts. Both under SOV and OSV orders quantified subjects can unambiguously take narrow scope with respect to negation, as seen in (54a) and (55a). Only in the presence of verbal agreement can subjects take wide scope, which implies that they are in Spec-TP in (54b) and (55b):

(54) a. Bütün   çocuklar   o   test-e   gir-me-di.[13]   SOV   (Tk)

      all   children   that   test-DAT   take-NEG-PST

      'All children did not take that test.'   (not > all)

  b. Bütün çocuklar_i t_i o   test-e   gir-me-di-ler   SOV+Agr

      all   children   that test-DAT take-NEG-PST-PL

      'All children did not take that test.'   (all > not)

(55) a. O   test-e   bütün   çocuklar   gir-me-di.   OSV   (Tk)

      that test-DAT all   children   take-NEG-PST

      'All children did not take that test.'   (not > all, *all > not)

  b. O   test-e   bütün   çocuklar_i t_i gir-me-di-ler   OSV+Agr

      that test-DAT all   children   take-NEG-PST-PL

      'All children did not take that test.'   (not > all, *all > not)

In Japanese, however, quantified subjects obligatorily take wide scope over negation under SOV word order as shown in (56a). Ambiguity only arises under OSV word order in Japanese as shown in (56b), which Miyagawa (2001) explains by appealing to the position of the object: if the object checks EPP in Spec-TP, then

---

[13] These examples have been adapted from Miyagawa (2001).

the subject remains VP-internal and takes narrow scope. But if what satisfies EPP is the subject, then the object must be in an A-bar position above TP.

(56) a. Zen'in-ga$_i$ t_i sono tesuto-o uke-nakat-ta.   SOV (Jp)
          all-NOM   that   test-ACC take-NEG-PST
          'All did not take that test.'   (all > not , *not > all)

     b. Sono tesuto-o zen'in-ga uke- nakat-ta.   OSV
        that   test-ACC all-NOM   take-NEG-PST
        'That test, all did not take.'   (not > all, all > not) (Miyagawa 2001)

Second, there is no obligatory raising in Turkish. Subject positions of clauses formed with raising verbs can be left empty in parallel to what we observe in Uyghur. This again implies that Spec-TP does not have to be filled for EPP purposes in Turkish. Note that there are no corresponding Japanese examples that we can provide here, as there are no such raising constructions in Japanese.

(57) a. [$_{TP}$ _____ bana [(sen)$_i$ yarışma-yı   kazan-acak-sın] gibi
                          to.me you   competition-ACC win-FUT-2SG   like
          gel-iyor]   (Tk)
          come-PROG
          'It seems to me that you will win the competition.'

     b. [(Sen$_i$)   bana   [t_i yarışma-yı   kazan-acak-(sın)] gibi gel-
        you   to.me   competition-ACC win-FUT-2SG   like come-
        iyor-sun]
        PROG-2SG
        'It seems to me that you will win the competition.'   (Uygun 2006: 4)

Thus, the correlation between having EPP effects and disallowing rightward movement in Uyghur and Khalkha seems to hold for Turkish and Japanese too: Turkish lacks EPP effects and allows for rightward movement (Kural 1997; Şener 2005; and Kornfilt 2005); Japanese, on the other hand, exhibits EPP effects and bans rightward movement. Note that in the literature both properties have been independently established for Japanese. Miyagawa (2001, 2003) has shown that Japanese has EPP effects, while Kuno (1978), Sells (1999), Tanaka (2001), Abe (2004), and Kato (2007) have argued that PVCs cannot be derived via rightward movement.

The correlation between the lack of EPP effects and the availability of rightward movement discussed in section 10.5 is further supported by other Turkic languages like Eastern Uzbek and Osh Kirghiz. Note that allowing rightward movement is not a common pattern observed in Turkic languages. Eastern Uzbek and Osh Kirghiz show EPP effects and disallow PVCs, unlike Turkish and Uyghur. Thus, they pattern with Japanese and Khalkha.

First, consider Eastern Uzbek, which requires an overtly filled Spec-TP due to the EPP. In Eastern Uzbek, subjects unambigously take wide scope over negation under the SOV order. This is so regardless of whether there is agreement morphology on the verb or not, as shown in (58a). Only under the OSV order, when the object checks the EPP and verbal agreement morphology is absent as in (58b), can the subject take narrow scope. Note that the presence of agreement implies that the subject is in Spec-TP, checking the EPP. That is why the subject obligatorily takes wide scope in the OSV order with agreement, while the object occupies an A-bar position in (58c), in parallel to the case of Japanese given above:

(58) a. Hamma bola-lar   kitab-ni   oki-(**sh**)-ma-di. (SOV+Agr) (EU)
          all   child-PL   book-ACC   read-PL-NEG-PST
          'All children did not read the book.'   (all > not, *not > all)

      b. Kitab-ni   hamma bola-lar *t*   oki-ma-di. OSV
          book-ACC all   child-PL   read-NEG-PST
          'All children did not read the book.'   (*all > not, not > all)

      c. Kitab-ni   hamma bola-lar *t*   oki-**sh**-ma-di.   OSV+Agr
          book-ACC all   child-PL   read-PL-NEG-PST
          'All children did not read the book.'   (all > not, *not > all)

Furthermore, there is obligatory raising in Eastern Uzbek, as seen in (59). When the embedded subject fails to move into matrix Spec-TP, the sentence in (59a) becomes ungrammatical, as shown in (59b). This contrasts with what we observe in Uyghur and Turkish:

(59) a. Sen$_i$ men-ga t_i jigla-gan kørin-di-ŋ   (EU)
          you I-DAT   cry-PST   seem-PST-2SG
          'You seem to me to have cried.'

      b. *___ men-ga   sen   yigla-gan-suɪn kørin-di
             I-DAT   you   cry-PST-2SG   seem-PST

Given that Eastern Uzbek is an EPP language, under the current account the prediction is that it should not allow for PVCs derived via rightward movement. Informants fully reject constructions with PVCs, which is even a stricter case than what we observe in Khalkha and Japanese, both of which permit PVCs. Such examples are taken to be ungrammatical in Eastern Uzbek as seen in (60):

(60) *___ men-ga t_i jigla-gan-suɪn kørin-di   sen$_i$ (EU)
           I-DAT   cry-PST-2SG   seem-PST   you

Osh Kirghiz, which is in close contact with Eastern Uzbek, also exhibits EPP effects and obligatorily projects a leftward Spec-TP. This is evident from scope facts. Quantified subjects obligatorily take wide scope over negation under SOV word order, whether or not there is verbal agreement, as illustrated in (61a). Only with OSV word order and without verbal agreement can the subject take narrow scope, which implies that the object checks the EPP in (61b). When agreement is present under the OSV word order, then the subject again takes wide scope in (61c). And finally, raising is obligatory, in parallel to Khalkha and Eastern Uzbek (62):

(61) a. Bardɯk   bal-dar   kitep-ti   oku-(sh)-ba- dɯ. SOV+(Agr)   (OK)
        all   child-PL book-ACC   read-PL-NEG-PST
        'All children did not read the book.'   (all > not, *not > all)

     b. Kitep-ti   bardɯk   bal-dar   oku-ba-dɯ.   OSV
        book-ACC   all   child-PL   read-NEG-PST
        'All children did not read the book.'   (*all > not, not > all)

     c. Kitep-ti   bardɯk   bal-dar   oku-sh-ba-dɯ.   OSV+Agr
        book-ACC   all   child-PL   read-PL-NEG-PST
        'All children did not read the book.'   (all > not, *not > all)

(62) a. Sen$_i$ ma-ɣa t_i ɯjla-gan- (sɯn) sɯyaktuu køryn-dy-n.   (OK)
        you   I-DAT   cry-PST-2SG   like   seem-PST-2SG
        'You seem to me to be cried.'

     b. *___   ma-ɣa   sen   ɯjla-gan-sɯn   sɯyaktuu   køryn-dy.
                  I-DAT   you   cry-PST-2SG   like   seem-PST

Being an EPP language like Japanese, Khalkha, and Eastern Uzbek, Osh Kirghiz also does not allow for PVCs. My informants find such examples unacceptable:[14]

(63) *Men t_i kitap-ti   oku-jtur-gan-in-i   bil-e-min   Ahmet-in$_i$. (OK)
      I   book-ACC   read-PST-PTCP-3SG-ACC know-PRES-1SG Ahmet-GEN
      'I know that Ahmet read the book.'

Thus, cross-Altaic facts also point to the same conclusion reached on the basis of our discussion of Uyghur and Khalkha, namely that there is a correlation between EPP

[14] As seen in the case of Eastern Uzbek and Osh Kirghiz, some languages with EPP effects are even more conservative than Japanese and completely disallow PVCs. This has also been observed for some speakers of Khalkha. I thank Dolgor Guntsetseg for bringing this to my attention. The question of why some languages with EPP effects totally ban PVCs, unlike Japanese, needs attention. This might follow from a difference observed in how they encode various discourse-related materials, such as topic, focus, after-thoughts, backgrounding, etc. in their syntax. Hypothetically, whatever discourse-related function PVCs serve in languages like Japanese can be handled in the preverbal domain in these languages. Thus, the difference might reside in the different discourse-related tools they have. This definitely requires a thorough comparison of these languages in terms of their information structure relations, which we leave to a future study.

effects and rightward movement. Table 10.1 summarizes what we observe cross-Altaic with respect to this correlation. As can be seen in the table, Altaic languages that exhibit EPP effects systematically ban rightward movement, whereas those lacking EPP effects allow it.

TABLE 10.1 **Cross-Altaic facts regarding EPP and rightward movement**

	Obligatory wide scope for the subject under SOV	Obligatory raising	EPP	Rightward movement
Japanese	+	Not available	+	−
Khalkha	+	+	+	−
Osh Kirghiz	+	+	+	−
Eastern Uzbek	+	+	+	−
Turkish	−	−	−	+
Uyghur	−	−	−	+

10.7 EPP, discourse configurationality, and phrase structure

Let us now turn to the question we raised at the end of section 10.5. Why does the EPP have such an effect on rightward movement in the languages discussed above? The languages given above are all discourse-configurational, where the word order is strictly correlated with information structure. Miyagawa (2005) proposes that the EPP in discourse-configurational languages like Japanese or Turkish is related to a focus/topic feature, unlike the agreement-based EPP in languages like English. He specifically claims that focus/topic features percolate down to T from C and result in EPP effects. Thus, if we adopt Miyagawa's (2005) definition of the EPP, then this means that in languages like Japanese, Khalkha, Eastern Uzbek, and Osh Kirghiz the EPP will *always* be associated with a focus/topic feature. If a given head is associated with a topic- or focus-related EPP feature, then its Spec should be filled with an XP which checks these features. This, then, will block the same head from checking the feature [+background] with another XP in its Spec, as this would lead to an ambiguous construction in terms of information structure due to the mutually exclusive nature of these features.[15] Thus, if a head overtly checks focus or topic with a constituent in its Spec, then it will not be able to project a rightward Spec to

---

[15] We foresee the same type of mutual exclusivity for focus and topic. That is, if a head checks topic, it will not be able to check focus, but it would be possible to check multiple topic or multiple background features at a given XP.

host a constituent which is to be interpreted as backgrounded. In such languages, backgrounding will be *in situ* and reserved to the preverbal domain and achieved via *deaccenting* as shown for Japanese by Ishihara (2001), but not via postposing.

In languages like Uyghur and Turkish, on the other hand, there is no EPP, that is, topic and focus can be checked *in situ* via Agree. This has been extensively discussed for Turkish in Göksel and Özsoy (2000), who argue that there is a preverbal focus field in Turkish rather than fixed focus positions. Thus, if a head in Uyghur and Turkish can check topic or focus via *in situ* Agree, this does not block that head from hosting a backgrounded element as a rightward Spec. What is blocked is to have two bi-directional Specs bearing XPs with different information-related features. As we have seen above, whenever the leftward Spec is filled in Uyghur, rightward Spec projection is blocked.

As discussed above, this ban on bi-directional Spec formation in Uyghur is not reserved to the TP domain, but is also operative in the CP and *v*P domains. Given that rightward movement is not possible in languages like Khalkha, Japanese, Eastern Uzbek, and Osh Kirghiz, then, we need to assume that, in addition to TP, CP and *v*P should also be endowed with an EPP feature. This will then block rightward adjunction to these levels as well. If we assume that all phases should have an information-structure-related edge as proposed by Dyakonova (2009), then it is possible to argue that in discourse-configurational languages with the EPP, Spec-*v*P also checks the EPP in relation to topic and focus features in parallel to the interaction between CP and TP domains. There are some independent observations in the literature regarding Japanese which provide indirect support to this. Ochi (2009) argues that objects in Japanese always move to Spec-*v*P in overt syntax. Furthermore, Saito (2006) shows that *v*P in Japanese is associated with an EPP feature even in unaccusative and passive constructions. The implication of these two studies is that Spec-*v*P in Japanese always projects a Specifier to the left. Therefore, in relation to the ban on bi-directional Spec formation in discourse-configurational languages, we cannot predict right-adjunction at the *v*P level in Japanese. In Khalkha, Eastern Uzbek, and Osh Kirghiz, too, accusative-marked objects have to appear above the VP-level manner adverbs, as seen in (64a), (64b), and (64c) respectively. This is in parallel to what Ochi (2009) argued for Japanese. In Uyghur and Turkish, on the other hand, accusative marked objects can appear either below or above VP-level adverbs, as illustrated in (64d) and (64e):[16]

---

[16]   Note that in Uyghur, Turkish, and Khalkha it is possible to have objects which are not overtly marked for accusative. The ungrammatical forms in (64a) and (64b) in Khalkha and Osh Kirghiz would become grammatical if the accusative case on the object is dropped. Objects which are not marked for accusative are interpreted as non-specific and non-referential and have to remain VP-internal. Öztürk (2009) argues that these are not true arguments acting as objects but they form a complex predicate along with the lexical verb. See Öztürk (2009) for details.

(64) a. Bulgan   nom-ig   hurdan   hurdan   (*nom-ig)   unsh-san.   (K)
      Bulgan   book-ACC   quick   quick   book-ACC   read-PST
      'Bulgan read the book quickly.'

    b. Zemire   kitab-ni   tez   tez   (*kitab-ni)   oku-duı.   (EU)
      Zemire   book-ACC   quick   quick   book-ACC   read-PST
      'Zemire read the book quickly.'

    c. Zemire   kitap-ti   bat   bat   (*kitap-ti)   oku-duı.   (OK)
      Zemire   book-ACC   quick   quick   book-ACC   read-PST
      'Zemire read the book quickly.'

    c. Zemire   (kitap-nuı)   ittik   ittik   (kitap-nuı)   oqi-di.   (U)
      Zemire   book-ACC   quick   quick   book-ACC   read-PST
      'Zemire read the book quickly.'

    d. Zemire   (kitab-ı)   hızlı   hızlı   (kitab-ı)   oku-du.   (Tk)
      Zemire   book-ACC   quick   quick   book-ACC   read-PST
      'Zemire read the book quickly.'

In the data above, we do not observe obligatory object shift in Turkish and Uyghur, which are languages with no EPP effects at the TP-level. However, there is obligatory object-shift at the *v*P level in Khalkha, Eastern Uzbek, and Osh Kirghiz, which exhibit TP-level EPP effects. The implication of the above data is that in languages with EPP effects at the level of TP, we observe an EPP-like behaviour at the *v*P level as well. Whether we can also argue that Spec-*v*P is associated with an EPP feature in passive and unaccusative constructions in Khalkha, Eastern Uzbek, and Osh Kirghiz in parallel to Japanese requires further investigation, which we leave to a future study.

An obligatory EPP feature for the CP-level in languages like Japanese, Khalkha, Eastern Uzbek, and Osh Kirghiz is harder to motivate and our answer will only remain at a speculative level here. Under Miyagawa's (2005) approach, in such discourse-configurational languages the EPP at the TP-level is related to a topic/focus-related feature which stems from the CP domain. So, one can possibly argue that as the EPP in T is an extension of the features of the CP domain, any XP which checks this feature in Spec-TP also counts as in relation to the CP domain.[17] Thus, having an EPP on T indirectly implies an EPP feature on C. However, this needs to be empirically motivated. One domain to look at to find empirical motivation for an obligatory EPP feature for the C head might be the rich set of sentence-final particles found in Japanese, Eastern Uzbek, Osh Kighiz, and Khalkha. The sentence-final particles found in these languages have specific discourse/pragmatics-related functions, and extensive research has been done on these, especially in Japanese and

---

[17] Note that all the Altaic languages we discuss here are *wh-in-situ*, so hosting wh-elements in Spec-CP is not obligatory in these languages.

Khalkha (Hasegawa 2010; Gang 2010; Davis 2011). It has also been observed that these particles are in close relation with the force and mood/modality of the sentence and as such have an interface with the CP domain. Their co-occurrence is subject to certain ordering restrictions and they exhibit different degrees of embedding properties. In languages like Turkish and Uyghur, the number of such particles is very limited, as opposed to Japanese, Khalkha, Osh Kirghiz, and Eastern Uzbek, which have more developed systems of such particles. This might be one domain to look at for the EPP feature in CP. But as we said before, this is just a speculation and needs to be further investigated.

As seen above, we observe a strong correlation between having EPP effects and having rightward movement. Thus, the EPP has certain implications for the general phrase structure of the language. When the six Altaic languages discussed above are considered, we observe another piece of asymmetry which seems to be related to the presence or absence of EPP effects. Those languages with EPP effects, namely, Khalkha, Japanese, Osh Kirghiz, and Eastern Uzbek, all lack the equivalent of impersonal passive constructions found in Turkish and Uyghur, which have no EPP effects. Example (65) and (66) illustrate impersonal passives for Uyghur and Turkish respectively:

(65) a. Juɣla-n-duɪ.   (U)
         cry-PASS-PST
         '*It was cried.' (People cried)

      b. Ojna-l-duɪ.
         play-PASS-PST
         '*It was played.' (People played)

(66) a. Koş-ul-du.   (Tk)
         run-PASS-PST
         '*It was run.' (People ran)

      b. Gir-il-me-z.
         enter-PASS-NEG-AORIST
         '*It cannot be entered.' (One cannot enter)

Öztürk (2008) argues that there are no null expletives which can occupy Spec-TP in Turkish, based on the evidence from raising constructions and definiteness restriction (DR) effects. First, unlike Italian, there is no obligatory agreement between the subject of the embedded clause and the matrix verb in raising constructions in Turkish, as seen in the asymmetry between (68a) and (68b). The presence of such agreement is taken to be a piece of supporting evidence for expletive *pro* in Italian, which mediates the agreement with the matrix verb (Chomsky 1981; Burzio 1986):

(67) a. *pro*_i sembrano   [t_i [_{VP}   intervenirne   [_{NP}   molti *t*_i]]   (It)
             seem-3PL   to.intervene   many
             (Alexiadou and Anagnostopoulou 1998: 514)

     b. *[_{TP} _____ bana   [_{TP} __   [_{VP} savaş-ta   çocuk-**lar** öl-müş] gibi
                to-me   war-LOC   child-PL   die-PST like
       gel-iyor-(***lar**)]   (Tk)
       come-PROG-3PL
       'It seems to me that children died in the war.'

Second, the lack of DR effects in a language is assumed to indicate the lack of expletive *pro* (Alexiadou and Anagnostopoulou 1998). Turkish also lacks DR effects. Universal quantifiers can occupy VP-internal positions in transitive constructions as shown in (54a) and definites can also remain VP-internal, as seen in (68) in Turkish.

(68) A: Ne   ol-du?
       what happen-PST

     B: [_{TP} [_{VP} Gizlice   adam   kız-ı   öp-tü.]]   (Tk)
              secretly   man   girl-ACC   kiss-PST
       'The man kissed the girl secretly.'

Let us assume that Uyghur, Khalkha, Japanese, Eastern Uzbek, and Osh Kirghiz all pattern with Turkish in terms of the unavailability of null expletives. If there are no null expletives, then in those languages with EPP effects, we predict not to find impersonal passives derived from unergatives. This is what we observe in the case of Khalkha, Japanese, Eastern Uzbek, and Osh Kirghiz, unlike Turkish and Uyghur. Thus, the presence or absence of impersonal passive constructions in these languages again exhibits a correlation to the presence or absence of EPP effects.

Öztürk (2008, 2009) illustrates another construction which is sensitive to the presence or absence of EPP effects in such discourse-configurational languages, namely pseudo-incorporation. While in Turkish, pseudo-incorporation is available for transitives, unergatives, and unaccusatives (69), in Japanese it is restricted to transitives (70):

(69) a. Ali   kitap   oku-du.   (Tk)
       Ali   book   read-PST
       'Ali did book-reading.'

     b. (Ağaç-ta)   <u>kuş öt-üyor.</u>
       tree-LOC   bird sing-PROG
       'There is bird singing in the tree.'

     c. (Ev-e)   <u>misafir gel-di.</u>
       house-DAT   guest   come-PST
       'Guests came to the house.'

(70)　a. Sensei-ga　　　gakusei-ni　　　kin-no-kunsyoo.zyuyo-go.　　　　　(Jp)
　　　　teacher-NOM　　student-DAT　　golden-GEN-decoration.award-after
　　　　'After the teacher golden-decoration awarded the student.'

(Miyagawa 1991: 15)

　　　b. *kodomo.taisoo-tyuu
　　　　child.exercise-while

　　　c. *Hoteru-ni　　kyaku.tootyaku-go
　　　　hotel-DAT　　guest.arrive-after
　　　　'after guest-arriving'　　　　　　　　　　　　　　　(Miyagawa 1991: 16)

If we assume that there are no null expletives to take care of the EPP in Japanese, then it is expected that pseudo-incorporation will not be available in unergatives and unaccusatives, as there will not be any argument available to fill up Spec-TP. But pseudo-incorporation with intransitives will be fine in Turkish, as there are no EPP effects.

The data on impersonal passives and pseudo-incorporation further supports the role of EPP effects for the phrase structure of discourse-configurational Altaic languages and for predicting what kinds of structures are available. Depending on whether a language lacks EPP effects or not, one can predict the type of scope relations and patterns of raising constructions and pseudo-incorporation, as well as the availability of impersonal passives and rightward movement. Whether this effect of the EPP on phrase structure is specific to Altaic or can be extended to other languages outside the Altaic group requires further investigation.

10.8 Conclusion

In the discussion above, we have shown that the PVCs in discourse-configurational languages like Uyghur and in Khalkha require different derivations and cannot be considered a uniform phenomenon. PVCs in Khalkha do not exhibit any evidence of a movement-based derivation. PVCs in Uyghur, on the other hand, are derived via rightward movement. We have further claimed that in discourse-configurational languages rightward movement is subject to parameterization based on EPP effects. The EPP, as a feature interacting with information structure, regulates the projection of specifiers on the left, thereby imposing a degree of configurationality onto the phrase structure, and blocks the projection of specifiers on the right.

11

On the Relevance of the Head
Parameter in a Mixed OV Language*

ARANTZAZU ELORDIETA

11.1 Preliminaries

Since Greenberg (1963) and subsequent typological work on word order (see, for instance, Hawkins 1983; Dryer 1992a, 2007), languages have been classified in two main groups: VO or OV. The reason for this is that the order of object and verb has been shown to be crucial in predicting the order of elements at the clause level as well as within a phrase (see Dryer 2007: 71). Along similar lines, Greenberg used four major criteria to establish his implicational universals:

- (a) the linear order among S(ubject), V(erb), O(bject)
- (b) whether a language has Prep(ositions) or Post(positions)
- (c) the linear order between N(oun) and Adj(ective)
- (d) the linear order between N(oun) and Gen(itive)

From a sample of 30 languages, most fall in either of two types, based on the data he gathered:

(1)   a. VO, Prep, N–Gen, N–Adj

     b. OV, Post, Gen–N, Adj–N

* Part of the material in this chapter was presented at the 2007 Workshop on Antisymmetry at the University of the Basque Country, and a great deal of it at the 2009 Seminar within Theoretical Approaches to Disharmonic Word Orders at Newcastle University. I thank the audiences at both events for lively discussion. The present chapter has greatly benefitted from the constructive comments of two anonymous reviewers, who pointed out some shortcomings in the previous version, as well as from the most valuable comments of the editors, which have been extremely helpful, all of whom I want to acknowledge here. I also thank Bill Haddican for suggestions and comments on an earlier draft. Of course, I take the responsibility for any remaining shortcomings. This research has been supported by funds from the research project FFI2008-05135/FILO (Spanish Ministry of Science), and from funding to the Research Group GIC07/144-IT-210-07 and IT769-13 (granted by the Basque Government).

However, as we will see, many languages display orders that do not easily fit the cluster of properties established in (1a–b). The range of 'disharmony' in these languages will depend on the number and type of properties that escape the generalizations in (1). We denote these languages as *disharmonic languages*.

The typological generalizations stated in (1), except for the relative order N–Adj/ Adj–N, can be accommodated in Principles and Parameters Theory by assuming the existence of a Head Parameter, which determines the linear order of complements with regard to their heads:[1]

(2) a. $X' \rightarrow X$ Comp (head-initial)

b. $X' \rightarrow$ Comp X (head-final)

Therefore, a head-final language will have complements preceding their heads, including PP and DP complements, prenominal genitive complements of nouns, and Aux following V, on the standard assumption that a participial VP is the complement of Aux/T. Nothing else being said, one would expect to find consistent head-initial languages as well as consistent head-final languages. However, this is not generally the case for either type of language (cf. Kroch 2001; Hawkins 1979, 1980). But we do find head-final languages with *many* complements preceding their heads, including PP and DP complements, prenominal genitive complements of nouns, TP preceding C, and Aux following V. This is exemplified in (3) for Basque DPs, relative clauses, and verb clusters:

(3) *Basque*

Julene-n   lagun-a-k   [[$_{\text{RelCP}}$gaur erosi ditu-en] ardo kutxa **handi** bi]
Julene-GEN friend-D-ERG   today buy AUX-C   wine box **big**   two
oparitu   **dizkit**
give   AUX
'Julene's friend has given me two huge wine boxes which she bought today.'

(4) a. Julenen lagunak   = PP–N–D (DP)

b. [gaur erosi ditu-en] = TP–C (CP)

c. kutxa handi bi   = N–Adj–Num (NumP)

d. oparitu dizkit   = V Aux

Given the orderings in (3–4), Basque is usually classified as type (1b), except for the fact that Adj *follows* N, which is not the expected order of Adj and N in rigid OV languages.

---

[1] The relative order of N and Adj is of a different type from OV/VO, if adjectives are non-complements. See the discussion on Basque adjectives further on in this section.

Nevertheless, this property is not problematic per se for the Head Parameter. Note that if, as in traditional analyses, we analyse relative clauses and adjectives as nominal adjuncts, the Head Parameter does not predict any particular ordering with respect to adjuncts, since it is only stated in terms of the linearization of a head and its complement. In this respect, the disharmonic behaviour of N–Adj in Basque does not bear on the directionality parameter.

If we follow Artiagoitia (2006, 2008a,b) and assume Basque attributive adjectives to be head-final, the order in (4c) can easily be derived.[2] This is the structure he proposes for Basque DPs:

(5) $[_{DP} [_{PossP} [_{QP} XP [_{FP}[_{NP} N \ldots Adj] F] Q] Poss] D]$
       (where FP = a functional projection dominating NP, which hosts AdjP).

Notwithstanding the above facts, it is important to point out that this does not mean that clauses are rigidly VAux-final in Basque; in fact, different types of phrases may follow the verbal complex, but given that they mainly occur in contexts of questions and focalizations, under a head-final analysis of Basque those postverbal orders are analysed as derived structures. Specifically, non-V-final orders, such as those in (6) below, arise in negative contexts (6a), in yes/no questions (6b), or after a *wh*-phrase or focused constituent has moved to the left periphery of the clause (6c), which always triggers subsequent [V Aux] movement to the left (see, among others, Ortiz de Urbina 1989, 1999; Elordieta 2001). The fact that the tensed verb (Aux) and the VAux complex appear to the left of TP in (6a) and in (6b–c), respectively, leads to the assumption that negation, interrogative C, and Focus are head-initial:[3]

(6) a. $[_{\Sigma P}$ Ez   du$_m$ $[_{TP}$Jon-ek   liburu-a   erosi t$_m$]] $\Sigma \rightarrow$ head-initial
            NEG   AUX   Jon-ERG   book-D   buy
         'John hasn't bought the book.'

     b. $[_{CPint}$Erosi   du$_v$ $[_{TP}$Jonek   liburu-a t$_v$]]? Interrogative C $\rightarrow$ head-initial
            buy   AUX   Jon-ERG book-D
         'Did Jon buy the book?'

     c. $[_{FocP}$Liburu-a$_m$ erosi   du$_v$ $[_{TP}$Jon-ek t$_m$ t$_v$]]   Foc $\rightarrow$ head-initial
            book-D   buy   AUX   Jon-ERG
         'Jon has bought THE BOOK.'

In fact, Foc° (or C° in pre-cartographic works), as the functional head which Probes focused elements and *wh*-elements, has been exceptionally analysed as initial

---

[2] But see Oyharçabal (2006) for an antisymmetric view of Basque attributive adjectives.

[3] The V2-like properties induced by questions and focus also hold in embedded contexts. I follow Ortiz de Urbina's (1999) cartographic approach to embedded interrogatives in Basque and assume that the suffixal C-heads -*ela*, -*en* (Eng. 'that', 'whether', respectively) are instances of a head-final Finite head, the lowest category in the complementizer cartography, whereas all higher functional heads are initial. See note 9.

by most Basque linguists (see Rebuschi 1983, Ortiz de Urbina 1989, and most literature thereafter). Likewise, there is considerable consensus on the head-initial status of Negation (represented here as Σ (sigma), following Laka 1990).

It is probably not by chance that these three functional heads show a head-initial pattern, whereas head finality is the regular pattern in all other phrases. All three Neg°, Foc°, and interrogative C° (which should be identified with Force° in Rizzi's (1997a) terms) are functional heads pertaining to the left periphery of the clause, which carry scope–discourse interpretation properties and trigger movement ('internal Merge', in Chomsky's 2004, 2008 sense). In this respect, Basque displays a disharmonic behaviour in head directionality with regards to the functional categories of the left periphery. In the following sections, I will argue that a directionality parameter is needed at the base by showing that certain constructions in Basque cannot be derived assuming a basic Head–Complement configuration.

11.2 The universal Spec–Head–Complement approach

The claim that all word orderings are to be derived from a basic universal Spec–Head–Complement order (since Kayne 1994) is a very restrictive theory, which in itself is attractive if it successfully accounts for what is found and what is not found in languages.[4] According to this hypothesis, hierarchical asymmetry corresponds to linear precedence. In the case of Basque, assuming such an approach necessarily implies accounting for surface neutral head-final orders such as those in (3) as a result of massive leftward movements, often involving 'roll-up' remnant movements to specifiers of functional heads, which generally do not leave a phonological trace. Typically the motivation for many of those leftward movements is either lacking or is theory-internal—for example, reducing movement to specifier positions as EPP licensing of a feature of the relevant functional head—in order to account for specific word-order effects (cf. Kayne 1998, 2005a, Biberauer, Holmberg, and Roberts 2008b, and Haddican 2004 for Basque). Still, even in the absence of semantically motivated triggers, or of standard triggers such as case, to motivate displacement, one might accept the existence of successive leftward movements, if such an analysis would account for specific derivations that no other alternative analysis could explain. However, as will be shown in sections 11.4, 11.5, and 11.6, the position of PPs, of manner adverbs, and word order in focus constructions are all problematic for an antisymmetric approach.

---

[4] On the opposite side, Emonds (2000) proposes a universal 'right-headedness' approach, which claims just the opposite to antisymmetry, according to which, in the absence of language-particular properties, heads are always on the right. See also Haider's (2000b) *Binary Branching Constraint* (BBC), which was developed at the same time as Kayne's proposal, but argues that right-branching (OV) structure is more basic than left-branching (VO) structure (see Haider 2000b).

There is, however, a further argument that has been presented against the Head Parameter. It has been argued that the existence of leftward/rightward asymmetries and of unexpected 'gaps', which are not predicted under a strict version of the Head Parameter, constitute evidence in favour of a universal Spec–Head–Comp order (cf. Kayne 1994, 2005a; Cinque 1996). If OV syntax were symmetric, mirroring the type of leftward movement found in VO languages, one would expect to find certain orderings and rightward movement operations in OV languages, such as rightward *wh*-movement. Nevertheless, this type of movement is intriguingly uncommon in OV languages. Despite this generalization, Colarusso (1992) notes that Kabardian has rightward *wh*-movement in cleft interrogatives, and Ndayiragije (1999) has observed that some African languages have it.[5] If we consider other types of 'superficial' rightward movement such as extraposition or heavy NP shift, we find that they do occur in both VO and OV languages. One way of accounting for rightward movement under an antisymmetric approach would be to derive the orderings by remnant predicate movement of the material preceding the 'extraposed' element (cf. Kayne 1994, 2005a). However, the scopal and (Condition C) binding data discussed in Fox and Nissenbaum (1999, 2006) strongly suggest that what seems to be an extraposed adjunct is late-merged to the right edge after the NP associated with the adjunct undergoes rightward QR. In any case, irrespective of the analysis one adopts for extraposition, the question remains why rightward *wh*-movement is so rare—if not missing—across languages.[6] But it is important to note that such a question can be studied independently of the (non-)existence of the Head Parameter. In principle, no linearization with respect to non-complements is predicted by the Head Parameter, and one can think of different possibilities which might account for the lack of rightward *wh*-movement: for instance, that leftward movement and rightward movement are two distinct types of movement operations driven by different mechanisms.[7] For instance, as suggested by an anonymous reviewer, while *wh*-movement involves unvalued feature-checking, the extraposition type of rightward movement does not seem to involve feature-checking, but rather a mechanism related to stress and scopal factors. Alternatively, it might be the case that, unlike leftward A′-movement, rightward movement does not reconstruct, for reasons that are unclear at this stage. Another possibility could be that there is no rightward XP movement,

---

[5] I thank an anonymous reviewer for referring me to Ndayiragije's (1999) work.

[6] In any case, as observed in Bayer (1999), Neidle et al. (1997, 2000) show that American Sign Language (ASL) has movement to the right, which seems to suggest that the universal Spec–Head–Complement linear order should only be applicable to languages that make use of sounds, which must necessarily come into ordered sequences. In languages where hand movements can be simultaneously produced and where scope can be signalled by gestural non-manual elements, such ordering restrictions do not need to apply. In other words, the absence of specifiers to the right in oral languages could be a PF matter.

[7] A possibility that comes to mind is that rightward movement is confined to operations related to background information, which is the opposite of the 'new' information typically associated with *wh*-movement.

but only XP leftward movement (Kayne 1994; Kremers 2009). In such a case, the apparent extraposed elements would be derived as in an antisymmetric approach through remnant movement over the extraposed element, maintaining the directionality parameter. If the functional heads that probe the remnant constituents lack phonological content, one cannot easily discard such a possibility. Maybe there are reasons related to processing and parsing which lead XP movement to be leftwards, since that would mean that the moved element is pronounced or linearized first, while the system continues computing the sentence until it finds the 'source' position of the moved element (cf. Ackema and Neeleman 2002, Abels and Neeleman 2009 for discussion).

In relation to *wh*-movement in OV languages, if V Aux order is to be derived via $[_{FP}$ VP] movement to Spec-T, and complementizer-final CPs are derived via TP movement to Spec-C, one would not expect leftward *wh*-movement to Spec-C to be possible in OV languages because Spec-C would already be occupied by TP (recall that under the LCA, multiple specifiers are disallowed). This seems generally to be the case, but not in Basque, as already observed by Takano (1996):[8]

(7) [nori   eman   dio- la Jon-ek   dirua] esan   duzu?
     to.whom give   AUX-C Jon-ERG money say   AUX
     'To whom did you say that John gave the money?'
     (lit. 'That to whom John gave the money did you say?')

On the other hand, under such an approach the linear order V Aux is the result of VP moving to a position higher than Aux/T, so in order to derive the strict *wh*-V Aux order in (7) one has to make sure that VP and TP movement are remnant movements, with prior extraction of all material internal to VP and TP, stranding V and T. As will be discussed in the following sections, it is unclear where these phrases would be moving to and why.

11.3 Dealing with disharmonic systems while maintaining the directionality parameter

11.3.1 *A split in the directionality parameter*

In the previous section, we saw that Basque shows a superficial head-final pattern as regards VP, TP/AuxP, DP, PP, and declarative CPs. At the same time, Neg, Foc, and interrogative C (Force) are head-initial. The language thus instantiates a mixed or disharmonic system with regards to the Head Parameter. The split involves functional categories associated with properties of scope/discourse semantics. These

---

[8] I thank an anonymous reviewer for pointing out this reference to me.

properties are polarity, force, topic, and focus, which Chomsky (2004, 2008) subsumes under the label 'CP phase', and Rizzi (1997, 2007a,b) associates with so-called 'criterial' positions. All of these are functional categories which cross-linguistically are located rather high in the structure of the clause and whose featural content creates an operator–variable relation with the relevant matching goal. The proposal that the left periphery, unlike lower clausal projections, is head-initial allows us to understand the observed V2 effects, i.e. that there can be no intervening XP between the tensed verb, which has been moved to the head position of one of the CP-related functional projections, and the displaced element in its specifier:

(8)   a. [$_{ForceP}$Nori$_m$ [$_{Force}$[erosi dio]$_v$] [$_{TP}$Jon-ek   t$_m$ liburu-a t$_v$]]? (Interrogative Force)
          to.whom   buy AUX   Jon-ERG   book-D
       'For whom has Jon bought the book?'

      b. *Nori Jonek liburua erosi dio?

      c. [$_{FocP}$ Liburu-a$_m$ [$_{Foc}$[erosi   du]$_v$] [$_{TP}$ Jon-ek t$_m$ t$_v$]]   (Focus)
          book- D   buy   AUX   Jon-ERG
       'Jon has bought THE BOOK.'

      d. *Liburua Jonek erosi du

The idea that left-peripheral functional projections are disharmonic in relation to lower projections with respect to the Head Parameter is not new: the functional domain is the place where parametric cross-linguistic variation related to different surface orderings has been traditionally located and is a common place where disharmony with respect to the Head Parameter arises (see Ouhalla 1991, Chomsky 1995a, among others). Similarly, it has been argued for other head-final languages such as Georgian that focused constituents and interrogative pronouns are placed left-adjacent to the verb, despite the head-final character that Georgian exhibits otherwise in neutral discourse conditions (Nash 1995; McGinnis 1997; Skopeteas, Féry, and Asatiani 2009), and similar facts seem to hold in Turkish (Temürcü 2001). Specifically with regard to Basque, several authors have independently assumed a general head-final pattern, except for one or more functional heads, be it Σ (Laka 1990), Comp (Ortiz de Urbina 1989), Force, Focus, and Topic (Ortiz de Urbina 1999, 2008), or all functional heads related to the left periphery of the clause (Elordieta 2001, 2008). This is the approach I adopt for Basque, namely, that in this language all heads are final except functional heads associated with discourse and scope, which are head-initial.[9]

---

[9] I adopt Ortiz de Urbina's (1999) idea that Fin is the locus of clause-final complementizers like *-ela, -en,* and that it is head-final.

(9)

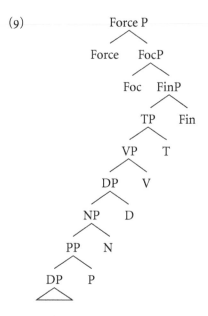

Force P
Force   FocP
Foc   FinP
TP   Fin
VP   T
DP   V
NP   D
PP   N
DP   P

Note that this structure complies with the FOFC (the Final-over-Final Constraint) cross-linguistic generalization formulated in Biberauer, Holmberg, and Roberts (2008a,b, 2010), which states that if α is a head-initial phrase and β is a phrase immediately dominating α, then β must be head-initial. If α is a head-final phrase, and β is a phrase immediately dominating α, then β can be head-initial or head-final. Below I present some illustrative examples:

(10) a. [$_{DP}$[$_{NP}$ [$_{PP}$ ikasle-en]   **bilera]   hau]**   P, N, and D > head-final
          student-GEN   meeting   DEM
       'this student's meeting'

      b. [$_{TP}$Miren [$_{VP}$[$_{PP}$[$_{DP}$ Bilbo]-ra] joan] da]   P, V, T > head-final
          Miren   Bilbao-to go   AUX
       'Miren has gone to Bilbao.'

      c. [$_{ΣP}$Jon-ek ez   du$_m$ [$_{TP}$liburu-a erosi t$_m$]]   Σ/Neg → head-initial
          Jon-ERG NEG AUX   book-D buy
       'John hasn't bought the book.'

      d. [$_{ForceP}$ Non$_m$[erosi du]$_v$ [$_{TP}$ Jon-ek liburu-a t$_m$ t$_v$]]?   Force → head-initial
          where buy AUX   Jon-ERG book-D
       'Where has Jon bought the book?'

      e. [$_{FocP}$ liburu-a$_m$ [erosi du]$_v$ [$_{TP}$Jon-ek t$_m$ t$_v$]]   Foc → head-initial
          book-D   buy AUX   Jon-ERG
       'Jon has bought THE BOOK.'

Despite the absence of a morphological marker expressing force or focus, the occurrence of the tensed verb in a position immediately following the *wh*-word and the focus in (10d) and (10e), respectively, leads to the assumption that Force and Focus are head-initial.

11.3.2 *Evidence from language acquisition*

Data from language acquisition seem to support the view according to which some version of the Head Parameter is at stake while the child is acquiring the language. Early language productions of Basque infants (1;06–3;04) conform to a head-final pattern with respect to N(P)–D, V–Aux, and N–P sequences. They utter expressions such as *liburu hau* (book this), *mahai atzean* (table behind) or *tele ikusi* 'TV watch' rather than *hau liburu* 'this book', *atzean mahai* 'behind table' or *ikusi tele* 'watch TV'. Nevertheless, it should be noted that Basque infants do also produce head-initial sequences, and that they in fact produce equal proportions of OV and VO orders (Barreña 1995; Barreña and Idiazabal 1997; Ezeizabarrena 2003).[10] Concerning VO sequences, Ezeizabarrena (2003: 87) points out that one should take into account the fact that VO orders in Basque, the common order for commands, are relatively frequent in adult–infant communication. The same is true of SVO focus orders, where the subject is focused. Assuming that the child doesn't initially have access to the full range of functional categories—and the particular syntactic and semantic properties associated with them—the occurrence of both OV/VO orders in adult speech may lead the language-acquiring infant to deduce that both orders are possible, despite the predominant head-final pattern in the input data she hears. As for constructions involving questions, unlike what is standard in adult speech, at earlier stages *wh*-elements do not appear in initial position, but rather in frames like XP–*wh*P–Vnonfinite. At later stages (at around 2,04), as soon as more functional material is acquired, they begin to negate sentences, make questions, and build embedded sentences. Mostly this follows the adult pattern, in the sense that they learn that negation is head-initial, and that negation, *wh*-questions, and focalization trigger leftward movement of the finite verb. Those cues lead infants to deduce that the functional categories involved in those structures display a head-initial order, whereas lexical categories follow a head-final system. In principle, the lack of 'errors' (i.e. the exclusive occurrence of head–complement orders) in child production is not predicted by an antisymmetric standpoint; if UG only permits a selecting head and its complement to merge as Head–Complement, one would expect Basque infants, as a consequence of the LCA, to produce head–complement orders at the beginning of their language production, when they are assumed not to have acquired the mech-

---

[10] Barreña (1995) shows that Basque monolinguals produce OV orders slightly more frequently (55% vs 45%) than bilinguals do (50% vs 50%; cf. also Mahlau 1994).

anisms of displacement yet. But head-initial structures such as *hau etxe* 'this house' or *da etorri* 'has come' are not attested. Moreover, given the different VO/OV surface order patterns of Spanish and Basque, the study of acquisition of functional categories in Basque–Spanish bilingual children should be revealing to test whether from the very beginning they are acquiring two different systems, or, instead, whether they use one common system and later on learn the syntactic particularities of each language system. Under a universal basic order approach one might expect to find bilingual children at earlier stages producing head–complement orders that do not occur in adult Basque, such as Aux–V, P–N, or Dem–N orders. However, those sequences do not occur.

Again, this is unexpected if the order Head–Complement is universally given and the derivation of head-final sequences involves several leftward movements induced by a specific feature on the relevant heads. For the language-acquiring child, it seems to me that a Head Parameter approach can guide her in a simpler way. If the Head Parameter is part of UG, and if it is set for Basque in the terms suggested here—all lexical heads are final, left-peripheral functional heads are initial—the learner only has to watch out for cues from the input data to give the relevant value to the word-order parameter and build her grammar accordingly. Thus, at earlier stages she can produce correct head-final structures which have no functional structure in them yet. From the alternative antisymmetric viewpoint, given that many head-final structures—including neutral sequences like Subject–PPcomplement–V–Aux—are argued to involve movement of lower constituents to the Spec of several functional projections (cf. Kayne 1994), if the child hasn't learned those categories yet, one expects that she will produce non-occurring sequences such as Aux–S–V–PP until she learns that the particular heads have a movement trigger. But she doesn't. No such sequences are predicted to occur on a Head Parameter approach. It is in this sense that I consider an analysis of the acquisition data based on the Head Parameter can guide the child in a simpler way.

11.3.3 *Evidence from language processing*

In a similar way, Laka (2008) argues that the type of evidence from language processing investigated so far lends support to a view which conforms to the Head Parameter rather than to the antisymmetric hypothesis (see Erdozia 2006, 2008; Erdozia, Laka, Mestres, and Rodríguez-Fornells 2009; Erdozia, Laka, and Rodríguez-Fornells 2012). In these works a number of experiments based on a self-paced reading task are carried out in order to determine how different word orders affect the processing time of each constituent of a sentence, by comparing how Basque speakers process SOV and OSV orders, in the first place, and verb-medial orders SVO and OVS, in the second. The results derived from the SOV–OSV comparison show that the unmarked SOV order is easier (it takes less time) to process than OSV, where O has been moved leftwards (Erdozia, Laka, Mestres, and Rodríguez-Fornells 2007, 2009). Evidently, this result is predicted given that the OSV order is syntactically complex; it is discourse-marked, resulting in an interpretation in which the object is topicalized, thus one would expect it to be harder to process. The results obtained from the SVO–OVS comparison are more interesting, because they show that they both are equally complex to process, there not being any significant reading time difference between the two orders (Erdozia, Laka, and Rodríguez-Fornells 2012). Moreover, as discussed in Erdozia (2006, 2008), syntactic complexity produces electrophysiological differences (ERPs), which, importantly, do not appear in SOV orders. The crucial point is that in Basque, ERPs differentiate OSV, SVO, and OVS orders, on the one hand, and SOV orders on the other, suggesting that both SVO, OVS, and OSV sentences are syntactically more complex than SOV structures, which have been shown to be the easiest to compute (cf. the references above).

This is not expected if SOV is derived from a basic SVO structure, as postulated by the antisymmetric approach. Rather, the expectation is to find cues which suggest that SOV orders present some grammatical complexity and thus demand significant processing resources. Thus, what these findings show is that SOV orders are processed as 'non-complex' and that SVO orders are syntactically complex, a fact that does not fit well in a frame which claims that head-final languages are the result of several leftward movement operations.

In the next sections, I will discuss a number of syntactic constructions which are more easily accommodated under an analysis which allows for parametric directionality than under an antisymmetric approach. The structures analysed include the derivation of unmarked constituent orders, VP-fronting, idioms, the position of PPs, and the internal and external surface order of finite and non-finite clauses. It will be shown that in order to account for the possible and impossible sequences permitted in a language, a system allowing for the existence of both initial and final heads turns out to be more adequate. Finally, the derivation of focus constructions and the behaviour of evidential particles will be addressed, as their position in the sentence as well as their scope have been a matter of debate in analyses adopting an antisymmetric approach.

11.4 Deriving neutral orders

11.4.1 *Neutral order*

(11a–b) illustrate the unmarked order in Basque ditransitive and unergative sentences (cf. de Rijk 1969; Ortiz de Urbina 1989):

(11) a. Ikasle horre-k   eskutitz bat   idatzi du   email-ez.
         student DEM-ERG   letter   a   write   AUX   email-by
         'That student has written a letter by email.'   *(S–O–V–Aux–PP)*

   b. pro filme horre-kin negar egin dut/* egin negar dut
        film   DEM-with cry   do   AUX do   cry   AUX
        'I cried at that film.'   *(PP N–do$_{lightV}$–Aux)*

    If we follow the standard assumption that DPs raise out of VP for case reasons, the order in (11a) is a *derived* construction and could thus equally be derived from underlying SOV or underlying SVO order. However, deriving neutral affirmative SOVAuxPP from AuxSPPVO involves more movement operations than if the same structure is derived from SPPOVAux.[11] This is the kind of analysis that Haddican (2004) proposes to derive neutral affirmative orders in Basque. According to his antisymmetric analysis, the derivation proceeds as follows: after the DPs have raised out of VP to check Case, the extended VP shell undergoes remnant movement to the specifier of a PolarityP, which he assumes to be always available in the structure:

(12)

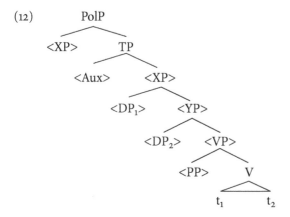

    Leaving aside what the motivation for such a movement would be, this derivation would yield the order SOPPVAux, which is possible in Basque—with a focus interpretation on PP—but is not the intended order in (11a). In order to get the right sequence, one has to make sure that the PP is extracted to a position higher than PolP, so that remnant movement of the extended VP to Spec-Pol is followed by subsequent movement of PolP to, perhaps, PP.

    By contrast, if one does not assume that adjuncts are strictly left-merged, but rather that they are more flexible in the directionality of Merge, the derivation of (11a) easily follows. In any case, the issue of where adjuncts are merged in the structure does not directly bear on the Head Parameter, although it does on a strict view of antisymmetry, according to which adjunctions are always to the left.

    As for (11b), if Laka (1993b) is right that bare NPs like *negar* in the light verb construction in (11b) remain *in situ* because they are not DPs, and thus do not need to

---

[11] I assume that the PP is merged in VP, since it is associated with the VP.

license Case features, one would predict to find the complement following the verb (*egin negar*) when the extended VP moves higher up via roll-up movement. But this order does not occur and renders the sentence ungrammatical. Alternatively, if we take the Head Parameter into account, the sequence in (11b) is easily derived. More generally, with respect to the derivation of neutral orders, economy considerations would lead one to prefer a simpler derivation of a certain construction over another involving more operations. In other words, if two analyses can derive the Basque data but one involves fewer operations than the other, the simpler derivation outranks the other, unless we find evidence showing that postulating more movement operations is necessary to explain the data.

11.4.2 *PP complements*

PP complements precede their heads in the unmarked order (see (13a))—and PP-internally, complements precede P—a result which falls out under a head-final analysis, since no additional assumption has to be made to derive their ordering with respect to V, the selecting head.[12] On the other hand, it requires additional premises under a Head–Complement analysis; (13c) shows that PPs must raise out of VP before VP raises to a position higher than the position where T sits. However, it is not clear why they must do so (see also Haddican 2004: 116).[13] Interestingly, a complement PP can follow VAux, as in (13b), but it is considered to be an instance of subject focalization.[14] In analyses that do not adopt antisymmetry, the structure in (13b) involves focus movement of the subject to Spec-Foc, followed by subsequent V-to-Aux-to-Foc movement (Ortiz de Urbina 1989, 1995, 1999; Elordieta 2001, among others):

(13) a. Abioi   hori   Venezia-ra   joango da   (unmarked)
         plane   DEM   Venice-to   go   AUX
         'That plane will fly to Venice.'

      b. Abioi hori   joango   da   Venezia-ra   (marked, focus on the subject)
         plane DEM   go   AUX   Venezia-to
         'THAT PLANE will fly to Venice.'

      c. *Abioi   hori   joango   Venezia-ra   da
          plane   DEM   go   Venezia-to   AUX

---

[12] This is independent of the fact that at a later stage in the derivation, V or VP raises further up for discourse considerations.

[13] 'The missing pattern ... is a neutral order where the objects appear to the right of the main verb and to the left of the Aux. ... an unacceptable pattern results when the main verb raises without the objects [whatever its syntactic category—AE] extracting.' (Haddican 2004: 116).

[14] This interpretation is not triggered when the postverbal PP is not a complement, like the example (11a) in the text. This is probably related to the different merging site of complements and adjuncts.

Regarding PPs, Kayne (2005a: 227) proposes that we should distinguish between lexical Ps and functional Ps, which include English *to, at, from, by, of, with,* and *for.* He further proposes to analyse functional P-complement sequences not as a constituent [$_{PP}$ P complement], but rather as a more complex structure, like that in (14):

(14) [$_{PP}$P [KP [VP DP]]]

The linear sequence V–P–complement would result after VP-internal O-movement to Spec-K, followed by remnant VP movement to Spec-P:[15]

(15) *First step:*   [$_{VP}$ V DP] → merger of K
      Second step: K [$_{VP}$ V DP] → DP movement to Spec-K
      Third step: [$_{KP}$DP$_i$ K [$_{VP}$ V t$_i$]] → merger of P
      Fourth step: P [$_{KP}$DP$_i$ K [$_{VP}$ V t$_i$]] → VP movement to Spec-P
      Final step: [$_{PP}$[$_{VP}$ V t$_i$]$_m$ P [$_{KP}$DP$_i$ K t$_m$]]

To derive the complement–postposition order typical of OV languages, Kayne proposes to modify the steps in the derivation illustrated in (15) by introducing a silent P′ in the third step, to whose Spec the VP moves; then (a phonological) P is merged and KP moves to its Spec, yielding the order DP K P V:

(16) *Third step:*   [$_{KP}$DP$_i$ K [$_{VP}$ V t$_i$]] → merger of P′
      Fourth step: P′ [$_{KP}$DP$_i$ K [$_{VP}$ V t$_i$]] → VP movement to Spec-P′
      Fifth step: [$_{P'}$P[$_{VP}$ V t$_i$]$_m$ P′ [$_{KP}$DP$_i$ K t$_m$]] → merger of P
      Sixth step: P [$_{P'}$P[$_{VP}$ V t$_i$]$_m$ P′ [$_{KP}$DP$_i$ K t$_m$]] → KP movement to Spec-P
      Final step: [$_{PP}$[$_{KP}$DP$_i$ K t$_m$]$_k$ P [$_{P'}$P[$_{VP}$ V t$_i$]$_m$ P′ t$_k$]]

Leaving aside the stipulative flavour of introducing an extra null P′ in the structure of postpositional phrases in OV languages, what this derivation predicts is that we should not find the sequence V (Aux) DP (K) P, either in VO nor in OV languages, given that V does not move by head movement, but rather by VP movement to Spec-P (in VO languages) or to Spec-P′ (in OV languages). However, we saw above in (13b) that such sequences are found. Below I give another example:

(17) Gaur   ikasle   talde berri bat aurkeztu   digute   eskola-n
      today student   group new one introduce   AUX   school-at
      'Today we were introduced a new group of students at school.'

To derive such orders, one seems to be led to propose that different phrases raise to Spec-T: if a postpositional PP moves to Spec-T, we obtain the order DP K P V P′ Aux; if only the lower P′P moves, the order V P′ Aux DP K P arises. From the perspective

---

[15] The derivation in (15) is only slightly modified from Kayne's (2005a: 228, (15)) own formulation, in that I have abstracted from a real example.

of the motivation for movement, it is unclear what prompts movement to T.[16] Should we conclude that in one case T has a P-feature that attracts PP movement, and in the other case a P′-feature that attracts P′P? What is the motivation behind such a proposal? Note that V P′Aux DP K P is not restricted to focus constructions, since it occurs quite often in unmarked contexts with adverbial PPs, as can be seen in (11a) and (17) above. But if we are dealing with a focus construction, we have to make sure that we end up with a sequence FocusP V Aux...DP P..., where '...' means that a constituent can intervene between V Aux and PP. I do not clearly see how such sequences arise, assuming the derivations in (15) and (16).

If, on the other hand, head directionality is maintained, and thus that heads are final in OV languages, the unmarked orders in (11)–(13a) are predicted, regardless of whether verbal complements are DPs, NPs, or PPs. As for focus constructions, the 'verb-second' effect typically associated with them is accounted for by assuming that functional categories above TP like Foc° are left-headed, and that the complex verb raises to Foc° to satisfy a lexicalization requirement imposed on null functional heads (see Ortiz de Urbina 1995, Costa and Martins 2004, Martins 2006, for a similar proposal).

11.4.3 *Manner adverbs, VP idioms, and VP-fronting*

The syntactic position of manner adverbs is also meaningful for the implications of the universal PP functional structure argued for in Kayne (2005a). On the assumption that manner adverbs mark the boundary of VP (Johnson 1991; Costa 1998, among others), one would expect to find the order Adv V P DP K in VO languages and DP K P Adv V P′ in OV languages.[17] Using English and Basque as testing languages, the latter is found in Basque, but is impossible in English:

(18)   a. *John hard looked at those pictures.

　　　b. John looked hard at those pictures.

(19)   Gure　taldea　aurkari-en　aurka　gogor　lehiatu　da.
　　　our　team　rival-GEN　against　hard　compete　AUX
　　　'Our team has competed hard with its rival.'

The ungrammaticality of (18a) is unexpected if the structure of PPs is as discussed in (15).

---

[16] Balkız Öztürk (in this volume) suggests that in certain OV languages Spec-T is associated with discourse-related properties and that different phrases can merge into that position. However, this cannot be the case in Basque, since moving the remnant PP to Spec-T, yielding a T-final order, renders a neutral sentence. And more generally, Spec-T in Basque is standardly associated with the subject (cf. Ortiz de Urbina 1989 and much literature thereafter).

[17] If one assumes that V raises by head movement, and not by remnant movement, the expected order is one in which the adverb intervenes between V and PP. However, here I am only considering Kayne's proposal—in terms of remnant VP movement—to derive such orders.

Data coming from VP-fronting and VP idioms can also serve as a testing ground to see what the predicted order in those constructions is under a universal Head–Complement pattern. The reason is that these constructions allegedly involve minor functional structure, so one would expect these structures to reflect a more 'basic' pattern of word order. What we find instead is Complement–Head (C–H):

(20)   a. **Autobus-ez   bidaiatu,**   Julene-k   gutxitan   egiten   du.
           bus-by   travel   Julene-ERG   seldom   do   AUX
           'As for travelling by bus, Julene seldom does so.'

       b. **??bidaiatu autobusez,** Julene-k gutxitan egiten du

If what is fronted in (20) is a bare VP, the head-final analysis readily accounts for the PP–V order. If, on the contrary, as discussed earlier in relation to the antisymmetric derivation of PPs, a complex PP is fronted there, it remains unclear how to derive the relevant order, stranding the adverb and the subject behind.

Similarly, VP idioms (in bold) always exhibit the Complement–Head order:

(21)   a. Bere   erantzunak   **ni-re   on-etik   atera**   nau
           his/her   reaction   I-GEN   sense-of   take out   AUX
           'His reaction got on my nerves.' (lit. 'took me out of my sense')

       b. *Bere erantzunak **atera nire onetik** nau

Based on the assumption that non-compositional VP idioms are lexicalized forms, which form a unit and which disallow moving the idiomatic object by itself (cf. Elordieta 2001), one might expect to find the more 'basic' Head–Complement order in these structures under a Kaynean point of view. However, it is never found in idiomatic constructions. These facts strongly suggest a verb-final word order in neutral discourse conditions.

11.4.4 *Complement clauses*

Likewise, the relative order of non-finite complement clauses with respect to the main verb displays the same OV pattern in neutral contexts:

(22)   a. Mikel-ek [xakea-n   jokatzen]   ikasi   du.   *(unmarked)*
           Mikel-ERG [chess-in   play]   learn   AUX   *S CP V Aux*
           'Mikel has learnt to play chess.'

       b. **Mikelek** ikasi du [xakean jokatzen]   *(marked, focus on the subject)*
                                                        S V Aux CP

       b'. Mikelek **ikasi** du [xakean jokatzen]   *(marked, focus on V, S topicalized)*
                                                        S V Aux CP

Not only does the order of non-finite complement clauses and main V show an OV pattern; within a non-finite CP, strict OV order is respected:

(23)   ??/*Mikel-ek [jokatzen xakean] ikasi du

If non-finite complement clauses do not have case features that trigger movement (note that the CP in (22) is not a nominalization), it is not clear why it must move across VP in (22a), rather than remain in its base-generated position to the right of V.

Interestingly, finite complement clauses show a distinct syntactic behaviour. In propositional finite clauses with clause-final complementizers, both S CP V (24a) and S V CP (24b) are available in unmarked contexts:[18]

(24)   a. Amak [$_{CP}$ lagunak gaur   etorri-ko dir-ela] esan dit.   *[S CP VAux]*
           mother   friends today   come-FUT AUX-C   say AUX
           'My mother told me that my friends would come today.'

       b. Amak esan dit [$_{CP}$lagunak gaur etorriko dir-ela]   *[S V Aux CP]*

Putting aside the internal structure of CPs for the moment, the optional S CP V/S V CP order is in fact problematic for both a parametric and a non-parametric approach, given that the CP in (24) lacks case, Agree, or edge features to license movement; more importantly, no syntactic or semantic effect arises as a consequence of the difference in placement. As has already been mentioned, word order in Basque is dependent on the focus/topic interpretation of the sentence, in the sense that foci appear preverbally, left-adjacent to the verb. Thus, one would expect to find some effect associated with focus on the left-hand side of the sentence when CP appears postverbally. Although such an interpretation is available in that order (with focal stress on the subject), (24b) can also be a neutral sentence. Thus, it seems that finite CPs may optionally occur on both sides of the finite verb. In addition, recall from (22) above that the same CP–V/V–CP alternation in non-finite clauses does have a focus effect, unlike the pattern we observe in (24).

For an antisymmetric approach, the existence of two orders CP V and V CP is also problematic, since whatever triggers CP movement to a functional head above V should always apply. One might apply remnant VP movement across CP, yielding V CP:

(25)   [$_{XP}$[$_{VP}$V t $_{CP}$] $_{v}$X [$_{FP}$CP F t$_{v}$]]

But neither the nature of X°, nor the point of the derivation where Aux merges to yield V Aux YP CP—where YP is a constituent that can intervene between V Aux and CP—is immediately clear.[19]

---

[18]   The heavier the CP is, the more likely it is to appear postverbally. This could be related to processing effects.

[19]   YP stands for any VP constituent that can surface between V Aux and CP, like the indirect object in (i):

(i)   Amak   esan   dio   Miren-i   [lagunak   gaur etorriko direla]
       S   V   Aux   Miren-DAT CP

       'Her mother told Miren that her friends will come today.'

One particular context where one could test whether CPs start out to the left of V or to its right is by *wh*-extracting from a preverbal CP (Ormazabal, Uriagereka, and Uribe-Etxebarria 1994, 2008; Vicente 2004, 2008):

(26) a. Zer$_i$ ez duzu entzun [t$_i$ irakurri du-ela Jon-ek]?   [*wh$_i$–main V–CP t$_i$*]
          what NEG AUX hear   read   AUX-C Jon-ERG
          'What didn't you hear that John read?'

     b. *Zer$_i$ ez duzu [t$_i$ irakurri du-ela Jonek] entzun?   [*wh$_i$–CP t$_i$ –main V*]

Some clarification on negative constructions is in order to understand what these examples show. In affirmative sentences, V and Aux are adjacent to each other, and always occur as V Aux. On the other hand, in negative structures the order is Neg Aux V . . . (27a) or Neg Aux . . . V (27b), i.e. the strict adjacency between Aux and V fails to apply:

(27) a. Jon-ek   ez   du   irakurtzen egunkaririk
          Jon-ERG   NEG   AUX   read   paper
          'Jon doesn't read newspapers.'

     b. Jon-ek   ez   du   egunkaririk irakurtzen
          Jon-ERG   NEG   AUX   paper   read

Returning to (26), Ormazabal et al. (1994, 2008) and Vicente (2004, 2008) argue that what rules out (26b) is a freezing effect. According to this idea, freezing effects arise because in (26b) the complement clause has first been moved to the left of V; therefore further extraction from there is disallowed.

However, it seems that the reason for the ungrammaticality of (26b) is not related to freezing effects, and thus does not serve as a good test to determine the base position of complement clauses. Instead, it must have a different source, given that such effects do not arise in other sentences which look very similar:

(28) a. √/?[$_{CP1}$ Nora$_i$ entzun duzu [$_{CP2}$ [$_{CP3}$t$_i$ eramate-ko] eskatu diote-la]]?
              where   hear   AUX   to.bring-c   ask   AUX-C
          'Where did you hear that they asked him to bring?'

     b. [$_{CP1}$Nore-kin$_i$ pentsatu duzu [$_{CP2}$[$_{CP3}$t$_i$ ezkondu behar de-la] agindu diote-la]]?
          who-with think   AUX   marry   must AUX-C ask   AUX-C
          'With whom did you think that they asked him that he should marry?'

That is, if *wh*-extraction from a preverbal CP should be banned due to a restriction of the Left Branch Condition type, (28a,b) ought to be equally bad, contrary to fact. Note that the *wh*-phrase in (28a,b) originates within the most embedded clause (CP$_3$), which, in order to derive the relevant linearization, under an antisymmetric approach would first have been moved to the left of its selecting V (in CP$_2$). But in these cases, further extraction to the Spec of matrix CP$_1$is allowed. I therefore conclude that an LCA account cannot capture the facts illustrated in (26) and (28), given that it yields contradictory results. On the other hand, the question of the ungrammaticality of (26b) remains an open question, even in a non-antisymmetric approach. Regrettably, I do not have any relevant insights to provide with respect to these facts; hence I leave them for further investigation.

11.5 *Evidential particles*

Evidential particles are one of the few elements that can disrupt the otherwise strict adjacency between V and Aux:

(29) Jon   etorri   omen   da.
      Jon   come   EVID   AUX
      'They say that Jon has come.'

In the presence of negation, the evidential particle follows negation (30b), despite the fact that the evidential scopes over negation, as observed by Haddican (2004, 2008):

(30) a. **Ez**   **omen**   da   etorri,   baina   (egiatan)   etorri   da.
         NEG   EVID   AUX   come   but   in.fact   come   AUX
         'They say that he didn't come, but indeed he came.'

      b. *Omen ez da etorri, baina (egiatan) etorri da
         *EVID NEG

      c. *omen (EVID)>ez (NEG)*

Haddican (2004, 2008) adopts an antisymmetric approach and accounts for the scopal facts in (30) by proposing the following hierarchy of the relevant functional categories, à la Cinque (1999):

(31)   PolP[20] > Mood$_{evid}$P > TenseP > Neg/AffP > AspP > VP

In order to derive the order in negative sentences, he proposes that negation, which in his account is a phrase sitting in Spec-Neg, raises all the way up to Spec-Pol, yielding the correct order Neg evid Aux V (see (30a)). As for scope, Haddican proposes that Neg reconstructs to its base position after raising to Spec-Pol across Mood$_{evid}$P, which explains the fact that the evidential takes scope over negation (30c).

Haddican argues that a non-antisymmetric account cannot capture the scopal facts. In fact, on that view, Neg is head-initial, and is structurally higher than TP. But

---

[20] PolP stands for PolarityP, the topmost functional phrase present in unmarked sentences. FocusP and TopP would be higher up, if present. AffP is the affirmative counterpart of NegP.

Mood is head-final in both Ortiz de Urbina's (1989) and Elordieta's (2001) analysis of clause structure:[21]

(32) $[_{\Sigma P}$ neg $[_{TP} [_{MoodevidP} [_{vP} [_{VP}$ O V $]$v $]$ evid$]$ T $]]$

This yields the correct order S O V evid T, for affirmative sentences, and S Neg evid T O V for negatives, provided the assumption that there is evidential-to-T-to-Neg raising by head movement (see references cited for more details on the motivation for such movements). On the other hand, this analysis predicts that the evidential particle will not be able to scope over negation, since it is contained within a complex head.

However, there is an alternative way of accommodating the scopal facts: suppose there are two positions where Neg can surface (see Zanuttini 1997; Cinque 1999), one internal head-final Neg below TP, which is morphologically realized as *ez* 'not', and an external one, above TP, which carries the operator-like semantic properties that negation presents across languages.[22] Thus, if the proposal advocated here is right, the higher NegP will be head-initial, like the other scope- and discourse-related functional heads in Basque. Assume that high Neg is headed by a null element with an Agree [neg] feature which has to be valued by probing a matching goal, and an EPP feature which drives movement. The lower Neg agrees with that feature and hence raises overtly to peripheral Neg to value [neg]. I follow Chomsky (1995a) and Alexiadou and Anagnostopoulou (1998, 2001), who argue that EPP features can be checked either by head or phrasal movement. In its movement to higher Neg, by locality conditions, low Neg pied-pipes evidentials (if any), and T, driven by their morphological clitic status (cf. Ortiz de Urbina 1989, 1992, 1994):

(33) $[_{Neg2P}$ neg+Aux $[_{TP} [_{MoodevidP} [_{Neg1P}[_{vP} [_{VP}$ O V$]$ v$]$ neg$]$ evid$]$ T$]]$

The scopal dominance of the evidential over Neg, illustrated in (30c), would be explained assuming reconstruction of Neg to its low position, as in Haddican's analysis. The idea that head movement can reconstruct is at odds with the general assumption that head movement has no semantic effects (Chomsky 2004). However, as Citko (2008a) points out, Chomsky draws that conclusion based on the lack of semantic differences between raised and non-raised verbs (the prototypical case of head movement), but that does not necessarily imply that head movement is

---

[21] In the clause structure of both Ortiz de Urbina's and Elordieta's analyses, an AspP is represented above lexical VP. The representation in (33) shows a more updated structure in accordance with recent theoretical developments, assuming phase theory (Chomsky 2004, 2008). However, for the purposes of the discussion nothing really hinges on this.

[22] See Laka (1990) for an analysis of negation as one of the values of ΣP, an operator responsible for the emphatic affirmative/negative interpretation of a sentence.

irrelevant for the semantic interface. Nothing precludes the possibility that there could be semantically significant instances of head movement. In fact, Lechner (2005) provides arguments that there are cases of semantically active head movement, based on scope interactions between a modal head and a quantified subject. Given the sequence *subject QP-modal*, he provides arguments that the wide-scope interpretation for the modal cannot be a result of reconstructing the subject to a lower position. Rather, he argues that the modal undergoes LF movement to a position above the position of the subject. Therefore, although Lechner's analysis is different from the proposal I suggest here, what is relevant is that it implies that head movement can have consequences for interpretation, a result that fits well with the idea of having the possibility of reconstruction after head movement.

Clearly, one would expect to find some evidence for the existence of a lower position for Neg in Basque in order to support this proposal. Basque does not show a distinctive morphology for each negation, unlike what holds in some of the Italian dialects discussed by Zanuttini (1997). However, that is not a problem if we find other types of evidence for a lower position for Neg. The syntactic behaviour of negation in relative clauses may provide such evidence for a lower Neg position. Interestingly, relative negative clauses show the opposite syntactic behaviour of main negative clauses:

(34) a. [azterketak gainditu ez ditu-en] ikasle-a etorri da *[O–V–Neg–Aux–C]*
         [exams   pass   NEG AUX-REL] student-D come AUX
         'The student who hasn't passed the exams arrived.'

      b. *[ez ditu-en gainditu azterketak] ikasle-a etorri da   *[*Neg–Aux–C–V–O]*

Compare (34a) to (35a), and (34b) to (35b):

(35) a. *ikasleak   azterketak gainditu ez   ditu   *[*S–O–V–Neg–Aux]*
          student   exams   pass   NEG   AUX

      b. ikasle-a-k   ez   ditu gainditu azterketak   *[S–Neg–Aux–V–O]*
         student-D-ERG   NEG   AUX   pass   exams
         'The student hasn't passed the exams.'

The sentences in (35) show that raising of *ez* to the higher Neg is obligatory in main clauses. In contrast, raising is blocked in relative clauses (34b). The fact that other CPs, such as adjunct clauses and complement clauses, are more flexible than relative clauses in allowing both V–Neg–Aux–C and Neg–Aux–C–V orders, strongly suggests that the asymmetry between (34) and (35) is not a consequence of the fact that all complementizers in Basque are right-headed and are merged above a (head-initial) high Negation:[23]

---

[23] Except for the fact that she does not entertain a lower position for Neg; this is roughly what Laka (1990: 43) proposes to account for the distinct positions of negation in main clauses and relative clauses in Basque.

(36) a. Mikel [azterketak gainditu ez   ditu-elako] haserretu da   *[O–V–Neg–Aux–C]*
         Mikel [exams   pass   NEG AUX-C]   get.angry AUX
         'Mikel got angry because he didn't pass the exams.'

    b. Mikel [azterketak ez ditu-elako gainditu] haserretu da   *[O–Neg–Aux–C–V]*
      (cf. *34b)

Such a proposal would, in addition, violate the FOFC. I therefore conclude that the behaviour of negation in relative clauses must depend on a different factor. There is one possible derivation for the asymmetry if we analyse relative clauses as functional PPs (see Kayne 1994, 2005a), headed by a complementizer-like functional element *-en*, which has the embedded TP in its Spec, and the nominal head of the relative clause in Spec-FinP, as the only remaining phrase in FinP, after TP has evacuated to Spec-PP, driven by the EPP (edge) feature of relative P.[24]

(37) represents the structure I am assuming for relatives like (34), where the higher Neg and relative P are left-headed, as predicted by our analysis, given that they have scopal properties:

(37) [$_{NegP}$ neg [$_{PP}$ P$_{-en}$ [$_{FinP}$ [$_{TP}$ [$_{MoodevidP}$ [$_{NegP}$[$_{vP}$ [$_{VP}$ O V] v] neg] evid] T] Fin]]]

(38)

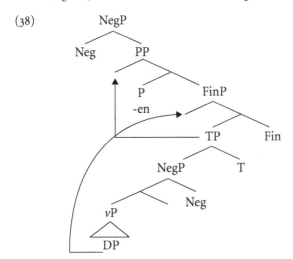

---

[24] There is some evidence that suggests that the material embedded in a relative clause is not a full CP. As an anonymous reviewer points out, topicalization and focalization internal to a relative clause seem deviant in Basque (de Rijk 1972; Elordieta 2010). There may, however, be some dialectal variation involved, given that Oyharçabal (1985) reports that some speakers accept focused constituents within relatives, as the example below illustrates:

(i) [ikusi   egin   dau-en-ak]   esan   daust
    see   AUX   AUX-C-D   say   AUX
    'The (person) who has SEEN it has told me that.' (with narrow focus on V)

As noted above, the construction in (i) is deviant for many speakers. Further investigation on microvariation is required to address this issue properly.

In (38) the DP argument of the embedded clause which functions like the head of the relative clause (*ikaslea* 'the student' in (34)) moves to Spec-FinP, and by remnant movement TP raises to Spec-PP, triggered by the EPP feature of the relative functional P head. Such a derivation accounts for the fact that the complementizer-like element of relatives needs to be strictly left-adjacent to the nominal head of the relative clause. As for the negation facts, I suggest that the higher Neg in relative clauses cannot value its Agree feature in the way that has been described for main clauses, given that lower Neg is in Spec-PP, which is embedded in the entire TP and hence cannot extract in narrow syntax. I therefore propose that the EPP feature of Neg is optional, so that in main clauses it is active and triggers internal Merge of the lower negation, whereas in relative clauses Neg has no EPP feature and hence can value its Agree feature by matching the goal in Spec-PP without triggering overt movement.

If this proposal is on the right track, the scope effects of negation and evidentials find an explanation in an analysis that maintains the directionality parameter.

11.6 Focus structures

The derivation of structures that involve focus is problematic for an antisymmetric analysis, as we will see. Consider the object-focus and the PP-focus sentences in (39a–b):

(39) a. Liburuak$_i$ erosi ditu$_v$ [Mikelek   denda horretan t$_i$t$_v$] *O V Aux S PP*
        books   buy   AUX   Mikel-ERG store DEM.in
        'Mikel has bought BOOKS in that store.'

      b. Denda horretan$_i$ erosi ditu$_v$ [Mikel-ek t$_i$ liburuak t$_v$] *PP V Aux S O*
        store DEM.in   buy   AUX   Mikel-ERG   books
        'Mikel has bought books IN THAT STORE.'

According to Haddican (2004), the derivation of neutral SOVAux orders in Basque proceeds as follows. Given the clause structure in (40):

(40) PolP > Mood$_{evid}$P > TenseP > Neg/AffP > K(ase)P > AspP > VP

he proposes that the entire phrase below TP raises to Spec-Pol, pied-piping all lower phrases with it. Since Pol° is a null head, that yields the neutral SOV order:

(41) [$_{PolP}$ [$_{AffP}$[$_{KP}$DP$_{sub}$ DP$_{obj}$[$_{AspP}$VP$_i$ Asp t$_i$]]]$_m$ [$_{TP}$ T t$_m$]]

The problem is the following: if VAux is to be derived via remnant AffP movement to Spec-Pol, how should the adjacency between a focused constituent and VAux, which is compulsory, be dealt with? Note that in this proposal the focused phrase is contained within a Spec, and secondly, the verb and T do not form a constituent, so it is not clear how the order *Focus V Aux* is derived. As far as I can see, an analysis of

Basque sentence structure in terms of remnant AffP movement fails to account for such orderings in focus constructions.

11.7 Conclusions

In this chapter, I argue that the mixed behaviour in head directionality shown in Basque can be accounted for by adopting a modified version of the Head Parameter. Specifically, I pursue the idea that the clause structure below FinP is head-final, whereas all other functional categories above FinP (i.e. those pertaining to the CP domain associated with the interpretive properties relating to scope and discourse) are head-initial. This captures the fact that 'lower' constructions which do not require CP-related functional projections to value EPP/Agree features systematically show Complement–Head order without requiring additional large-scale movements. This, in turn, leads one to conclude that Complement–Head orders are not always and necessarily the result of ordering rearrangements of an underlying Spec–Head–Complement order.

Evidence drawn from language processing shows that head-final SOV order is costless for processing, whereas SVO order manifests ERP patterns which are induced by syntactic complexity. This result is at odds with the view that SVO is more basic than SOV.

Although an antisymmetric view can derive many of the linear orders found in Basque, I have shown that the derivation of PP complements is problematic, as well as the position of manner adverbs with respect to PPs. In addition, it remains unclear how it deals with *Focus V Aux XP* orders. I therefore argue for an analysis of word-order variation in Basque which assumes a modified version of the Head Parameter, according to which lexical categories are uniformly head-final, whereas functional categories associated to the left periphery are head-initial. From this perspective, one can easily derive the order found in neutral sentences. It also allows us to account for non-neutral orders by assuming that left-peripheral heads bear EPP/Agree features which drive internal Merge to their specifiers, as well as an unvalued V feature which attracts the finite verb to their heads.

Part IV

Novel Alternatives to Antisymmetry

12

Afrikaans Mixed Adposition Orders as a PF-Linearization Effect*

MARK DE VOS

12.1 Introduction

This paper aims to account for the disharmonic word orders evident in the Afrikaans adpositional paradigm. It will be argued that the disharmony is only apparent and is actually a function of bare output conditions at PF. Drawing on Minimalist theory (Chomsky 2000) and Relational theory (Codd 1970/1983; de Vos 2008), the disharmonic effects are analysed as a result of bare output conditions imposed on PF linearization.

The structure of the paper is as follows. First, I will outline the nature of the problem, namely that Afrikaans adpositional constructions seem to display 'mixed' headedness (section 12.2). Since the problem is framed in terms of the Strong Minimalist Hypothesis, I will then zoom out and discuss the nature of the PF interface, claiming that syntactic functional dependencies should be mapped in a one-to-one fashion to linear precedence (section 12.3). Having discussed the general framework, I will then come back to the specifics of the problem and present evidence for feature checking in the adpositional domain (section 12.4). With these building blocks in place, I will then demonstrate how the adpositional word orders may be derived (section 12.5) before concluding with a discussion of the semantics of directed motion and how it relates to syntactic parametric variation (section 12.6).

* I would like to thank Johan Oosthuizen for an early discussion about the data in this article, Alexa Kirsten and Theresa Biberauer for grammaticality judgments, the reviewers for their insight, and the organizers of and the audience at the Theoretical Approaches to Disharmonic Word Orders conference held at Newcastle University, 30 May–1 June 2009, as well as my friends and colleagues at Leiden University who heard a version of the talk on which this paper is based. This paper was partially funded by the NWO and KIC 69593.

12.2 PP word order in Afrikaans

Afrikaans, like Dutch, displays head-initial, head-final, and circumpositional orders in the adpositional domain (1).[1] The central question is whether these contradictory word orders can be derived from deeper principles or whether they must be stipulated lexically. These phenomena have been reported fairly widely: Oosthuizen (2000), Biberauer and Folli (2004), and Biberauer (2007) for Afrikaans, and van Riemsdijk (1990), Koopman (2000/2010), Helmantel (2002), and den Dikken (2010), amongst others, for Dutch.

(1)   Disharmonic word orders in the Afrikaans adpositional domain

    a. Ek   loop   **in**   die   kamer
       I   walk   in   the   room
       'I walk around inside the room.'   [head-initial adposition]

    b. Ek   loop   die   kamer   **in**
       I   walk   the   room   in
       'I walk into the room.'   [head-final adposition]

    c. Ek   loop   **in**   die   kamer   **in**
       I   walk   in   the   room   in
       'I walk into the room.'   [circumpositional adposition]

The generalization seems to be that locative semantics correlates with prepositional, P–DP, orders while directed-motion interpretations correlate with postpositional, (P)–DP–P, orders (see den Dikken 2010 who makes a similar generalization about the Dutch facts). Afrikaans appears to be more systematic in this respect than Dutch: in Afrikaans, P–DP orders are almost always locative in their semantics—with notable exceptions when a prepositional phrase is selected by a verb which itself encodes directed motion (Biberauer 2007: 5, (5)ff.).[2] Although the examples in (1) show that the pre- and postpositions can be identical, they can also exhibit a lexically

---

[1] I will not be dealing with R-words in this paper, i.e. postpositions associated with a *wh*-word (i) or a deictic DP (ii). See Oosthuizen (2000) for examples.

(i)   Watter   kandidaat   moet   ek   voor   stem?
     Which   candidate   must   I   for   vote
     'Which candidate must I vote for?'

(ii) Hy   het   daardie   meisie   mee   ge-praat
     he   have.AUX   that.DISTAL   girl   with   PTCP-speak
     'He spoke with that girl.'

[2] Other exceptions to the generalization that (P)–DP–P orders encode directed motion are for *vir…voor* 'for…for' (i) and *met…mee* 'with…with' (ii).

(i)   Hy   wil   dit   vir   iemand   anders   voor   wys
     He   want   it   for   somebody   else   for   show
     'He wants to show it to somebody else.' (Oosthuizen 2000: 70)

specified morphological alternation (2). In addition, it is possible that the pre- and postpositions are entirely morphologically unrelated (3).

(2) Ek wil   dit **vir** iemand   anders **voor** wys
     I   want it   for somebody else   for   show
     'I want to show it to somebody else.'

(3) Die boot   seil **onder** die brug   **deur**
     the boat   sail under   the bridge   through
     'The boat sails under the bridge and out the other side.'

12.2.1 *Analyses derived by movement*

These data have been fairly widely described. Van Riemsdijk (1990) analyses the circumpositional adposition construction as a head-final *p* head selecting a head-initial PP. From the perspective of disharmonic orders, the problem is quite clear— why have such mixed headedness especially as it relates to a single functional category?

(4) a. Ek   het   hom   met 'n mes   mee   ge-steek
        I   have.AUX   him   with a knife   with   PTCP-stab
        'I stabbed him with a knife.'

     b.

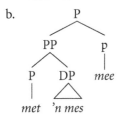

Oosthuizen (2000) reconceptualized the analysis in terms of a universal head-initial base with movement of a PP to a higher specifier of a 'light' *p* as illustrated in (5) (see also Koopman 2000/2010, Biberauer and Folli 2004, den Dikken 2010, Biberauer 2007, and Svenonius 2010 for similar movement-based analyses of languages other than Afrikaans).

(ii) Hy   het   net   met   haar   mee   ge-praat
      he   have.AUX just   with   her   with   PTCP-speak
      'He has just spoken with her.' (Oosthuizen 2000: 70)

A reviewer notes that *vir... voor* can be interpreted as entailing a directed motion in an extended sense (i.e. an act of giving or showing, for example, could be interpreted as involving metaphoric changes in location). This is not unexpected given the strong role location and motion metaphors play in conceptual meaning (cf. Lakoff and Johnson 1980).

(5) a. Ek   het   hom met 'n mes   mee   ge-steek
         I   have.AUX   him with a knife with PTCP-stab
         'I stabbed him with a knife.'

b.

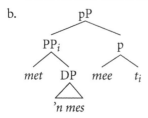

Most recently, Biberauer (2007) and Biberauer and Folli (2004) argue for move-ment to Spec-PDIRP within a pP shell structure motivated by an EPP feature. The constituent that moves can be either PLocP (6a) or the DP (6b), both of which can satisfy the EPP feature. In addition, Biberauer (2007) and Biberauer and Folli (2004) argue for a PF constraint preventing haplology and which derives the correct word orders.

(6) a.

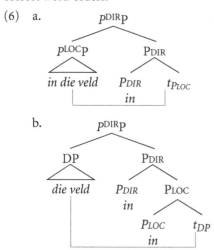

Thus, since van Riemsdijk's (1990) analysis, a consensus seems to have emerged in Kaynian circles about the common analytical core whereby circumpositional PPs are derived by movement of the lower PP to a specifier position in higher P projection; postpositional PPs are derived by moving the DP complement of P into the specifier of a higher P shell (Biberauer and Folli 2004; den Dikken 2010; Koopman 2000/2010; Oosthuizen 2000; Svenonius 2010). The points of difference in these analyses usually relate to the labels of the shell, the constituent that moves, and the motivations for movement, most of which seem to be framed as requirements to obtain the correct word order, leaving room for problematizing the trigger for movement.[3]

In these analyses, the Ps in question are generally not considered members of the same category: the preposition is more likely to be a lexical P (which assigns case) while the postposition *p* is a member of a more functional category. While some authors (Oosthuizen 2000; van Riemsdijk 1990), remain fairly agnostic about the precise label of *p*, others have labelled it descriptively as PathP (Svenonius 2010) and directional P (P^{Dir}) (Biberauer 2007; Biberauer and Folli 2004). Others, such as Koopman (2000/2010) and den Dikken (2010) have expanded the structure into a more articulated set of projections including PathP, DeixisP (den Dikken 2010), and so on. Den Dikken in particular draws an explicit parallel between the projections of the clausal domain and those in the adpositional domain.

Most analyses do not explicitly address the issue of the trigger for movement to Spec-PP. However, den Dikken (2010) frames movement in terms of licensing (drawing on GB theories of movement). Biberauer (2007) and Biberauer and Folli (2004), working in a Minimalist paradigm, argue for an EPP feature to trigger movement to Spec-pP—and this feature must presumably be present in all analyses requiring movement.

In this paper, I would like to problematize the trigger for movement: given an articulated *p*P structure as in (7), there is no a priori need for internal Merge/movement since any φ-features could be checked *in* situ by Agree.[4] The functional head *p* could simply probe the DP in its complement and Agree with it without movement specifically being forced. Consequently, it is only the postulation of EPP that can force movement.

(7)　a.　*Ek loop mee met hom

　　b.

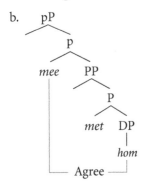

---

[3] There are, of course, numerous differences in the specifics of the particular analyses and I am aware that I have oversimplified the particulars.

[4] I distinguish between the EPP feature and ordinary φ-features since EPP does not come in iEPP/uEPP pairs and is simply a means of ensuring the correct word order.

The objections to EPP are well documented in the literature and there have been numerous attempts to reduce it to other principles (Groat 1995, 1999; Rooryck 1997; Martin 1999; Sabel 2000; Haeberli 2000; Boeckx 2000; Bošković 2002; Epstein and Seely 2006, among many others). One objection to EPP is that it is stipulative in nature. By itself, this is not particularly problematic if one regards EPP as a feature like any other and one which is an expression of Saussurian arbitrariness (see Biberauer, Holmberg, and Roberts 2009 for further discussion this type of view). However, EPP is not a feature like any other insofar as it motivates a particular type of movement: 'overt' movement. For EPP to be satisfied, some constituent must do so in overt syntax, for unlike other movement relations (e.g. *wh*-movement), EPP cannot be satisfied by 'covert' movement or by Agree without Move. As such, EPP appears to interact with PF in ways that have still not been fully explained. In addition, while other feature-checking configurations require a iF/uF pair, the same does not apply to EPP. Another objection to EPP is that it appears to be a purely formal requirement, one which does not have an obvious correlation to an interface condition (as required under the Strong Minimalist Hypothesis).

Thus the central question being addressed is how to motivate movement without the need for a stipulative EPP feature. In most analyses where these mechanisms are appealed to there is an implicit understanding that this device is a necessary evil whose properties will hopefully be explained by later research. One of the aims of this paper will be to motivate these movements as effects of the interfaces (specifically the PF interface). As such, the intention of this paper is not to critique or undermine previous work on the adpositional domain so much as to complement it. However, in order to achieve this, it will be necessary to develop a clearer set of assumptions about the properties of the interfaces. This is the subject of the following section.

12.3 Background assumptions

The proposal in this paper relies on several sets of assumptions: (i) Distributed Morphology, (ii) functional dependencies, (iii) a strong Minimalist view of bare output conditions, and (iv) some reasonable assumptions about the nature of the PF interface.

12.3.1 *Distributed Morphology*

I assume a version of Distributed Morphology (Halle and Marantz 1993; Marantz 1997; Harley and Noyer 1999; Embick and Noyer 2001), where narrow syntax operates through Merge, Move, and Agree on feature bundles. At various points in the derivation these feature bundles are spelled out and sent to the LF and PF interfaces. At the PF interface, the feature bundles are matched to the most highly specified morphological form to which they might be applied. In the absence of there being a more highly specified morpheme available, the elsewhere condition applies (Kiparsky 1973).

12.3.2 *Dependency*

Drawing on a long tradition of dependency in linguistics, the heart of this paper revolves around the notion of a functional dependency (Codd 1970/1983; de Vos 2008), which I take to be a basic relationship in syntactic theory regardless of whether it is instantiated by operations such as Merge or Agree (themselves reflections of features: c-selection, s-selection, φ-features, etc.). A functional dependency is a deterministic, one-to-one mapping between two syntactic constituents.[5]

Although not often explicitly mentioned, functional dependencies follow from basic assumptions about phrase structure. In Minimalist theory, Merge creates structures of the form {A,{A,{B,{B,C}}}} (Chomsky 2001). The structure posited by Chomsky (2001) is, mathematically speaking, by definition a functional dependency and a partially ordered set (Fortuny 2008; Halmos 1960; Kracht 2003; Langendoen 2003; Uriagereka 1999a; Zwart 2011): a set which is reflexive, transitive, and antisymmetric (Devlin 1993; Halmos 1960). This means that Merge cannot just be a pairing of A and B; a mere pairing would yield an unordered set of {A,B}. In fact, it is the notion of projection, central to Merge, that forces an order. Note that the term 'ordered pair' is a technical term used to encode a structured relationship between A and B and does not necessarily imply linear ordering. As Kayne (1994: 4) points out, a linear ordering is a total ordering, while Chomskyan phrase structure entails a partial ordering. In Minimalist conceptions of phrase structure, the mathematically ordered pairs are mapped directly to hierarchical structure.

To illustrate this, consider the following examples. If A selects B and A and B are merged, yielding {A,{A,B}} (8) then this is, by definition, an instantiation of a Functional Dependency. Thus Merge expresses functional dependency. Note that regardless of the directionality of the phrase structure, the Functional Dependency is of the form A → B and can be recovered from the notation of the dependency itself without necessarily looking at the selectional features of the individual categories. Henceforth in this paper, I assume that trees indicate hierarchy and *not* linear precedence; linear precedence is determined at the PF interface.

(8)   

With respect to agreement, in an example like *Peter eats*, there is intuitively a dependency between the φ-features of *Peter* and the uφ-features on *eats* expressed

---

[5] For a more technical definition of a functional dependency as it relates to Relational Theory see Sagiv, Delobel, Parker, and Fagin (1981):

> A functional dependency (abbreviated FD) is a statement of the form X→Y, where both X and Y are sets of attributes. A relation R satisfies the functional dependency X→Y (or X→Y holds in R) if for every pair r1, r2, of tuples of R, if r1[X]= r2[X], then r1[Y]= r2[Y] (Sagiv et al. 1981: 437).

as morphological agreement (Mel'čuk and Polguère 2009). The value of iφ (e.g. Person/Number) features on DP determines the value of uφ on T indicated by morphological agreement on the verb. Correspondingly, iT determines uT on D (Pesetsky and Torrego 2001) which is expressed by Nominative case on the noun. Formally, Agree instantiates a relation between a Goal and a Probe in a c-command domain subject to minimal search (Chomsky 2000). Given these constraints, Agree instantiates a relation between two categories that are ordered in relation to each other i.e. <H,H'> (Chomsky 2004). Furthermore, there exists a dependency between the Goal and the Probe: it is the iF on the Goal that determines the ultimate status of uF on the Probe (whether that be feature valuation, checking, or deletion). Thus, in an example like *Peter eats*, there are *two* functional dependencies: the φ dependency runs from *Peter* to T and the Case dependency runs from T to *Peter*. This proposal differs from standard Probe–Goal theory in three respects. Firstly, it is assumed that for any Agree relation between a particular iF/uF pair, a functional dependency of the form (Goal, Probe) is instantiated; the standard theory is non-committal on this point. Secondly, this dependency is passed to the interface in the form of a set: (Goal, Probe) and it is this set which is interpreted at the interface. Thirdly, I take Agree to be asymmetric as it was originally conceptualized. This is necessitated on empirical grounds which I will discuss in section 12.4.3.

This effectively means that the satisfaction of selection and feature-checking configurations by means of Merge and Agree respectively instantiate functional dependencies. Because functional dependencies are basic in syntax, they do not constitute a stipulation per se, but follow from first principles (de Vos 2008). Moreover, this approach entails that when a structure is passed to the interfaces at Spell-Out, that which is transferred is not merely a set of phrase markers, but a set of functional dependencies.

12.3.3 *The Strong Minimalist Hypothesis*

I will also adopt the Strong Minimalist Hypothesis (Chomsky 2000, *et seq.*) that the properties of narrow syntax are determined by the bare output conditions of the PF and LF interfaces—and nothing else. This guiding principle will inform the analysis which, ultimately, will derive a solution in terms of the PF interface. Naturally, this along with the fact that I will not appeal to EPP to motivate movement will raise the question of how to motivate syntactic movement, or more specifically, displacement. This is the main aim of this paper and is addressed schematically in section 12.3.4 and using Afrikaans adpositional data in section 12.5.[6]

---

[6] This paper only addresses the question of displacement, i.e. 'overt' movement. For a discussion of syntactic movement that is not necessarily directly related to displacement, see de Vos (2008). Unfortunately, space constraints prevent a broader discussion and what would ultimately entail the development of an entirely new theory of syntactic movement.

12.3.3.1 *PF legibility conditions*   Given the commitment to output conditions at the PF interface, it is necessary to entertain some ideas of what such conditions might be. It seems clear that PF bare output conditions must include linearization principles (the LCA of Kayne 1994 was one such principle). Since Functional Dependencies are, by definition, encoded in Merge and Agree, it is the null hypothesis that they should be used for the purposes of linearization. This hypothesis is expressed by Dependency Spell-Out, (9), mapping functional dependency to linear precedence in a one-to-one manner. The result of Dependency Spell-Out, (9), is that if a feature A functionally determines a feature B then A will also precede B in linear order.

(9)   **Dependency Spell-Out:** For any fully normalized relation (A,B) where A $\rightarrow$ B: (A,B) is a PF object and A $>$ B (i.e. if A functionally determines B, then A precedes B).

Dependency Spell-Out, (9), is similar in style to the LCA of Kayne (1994) (but not in content). Like the LCA, it takes a pre-existing syntactic relationship as the input for the linearization component (functional dependencies for Dependency Spell-Out, (9a); asymmetric c-command for the LCA). Also, just as the LCA is axiomatic, the significance of Dependency Spell-Out, (9), depends on the extent to which it allows insight into grammatical phenomena. I wish to point out that the hypothesis does not refute the LCA; it is simply another possible mapping that needs to be investigated. Taken with the results of the previous section, it comes down to a requirement that (i) interpretable features are spelled out preceding their checked, uninterpretable counterparts and (ii) selectors precede selectees.[7]

A reviewer has raised the question of how the interface 'knows' which member of a given Agree relation is the interpretable one, given that there is no way of distinguishing a iF/uF pair once deletion has occurred. The answer to this problem lies in what is passed to the interfaces. I am not suggesting that uninterpretable features are passed to the PF interface (causing the derivation to crash), merely that Agree acts to create a functional dependency between the Goal and Probe namely: (Goal, Probe). Once created, this relation exists as a fact in itself irrespective of the particular features (or their (un)deleted status) on its constituents. It is this relation that is passed to the interface.

Another kind of constraint that might reasonably be present at the PF interface is some restriction on locality, since locality is pervasive in grammatical systems generally. Again, the null hypothesis is that this too can be expressed in terms of

---

[7] It appears that (9) may be too strong expressed in this way. For example, languages with complement–head order such as Japanese seem to contradict it. This ultimately depends on whether a (non-EPP) Agree relation can be justified between a head and its complement in these languages. Just as the head-final nature of Japanese necessitated deeper research into the effects of the LCA, so too with Dependency Spell-Out. In addition, (9) raises questions about long-distance agreement and postverbal agreeing subjects among other things. I leave this research programme to future research.

functional dependencies. This is defined in (10a), which ensures that if A functionally determines B then A should be spelled out as locally as possible to B. Ordinarily this would result in A being strictly linearly adjacent to B. By locality I refer to linear locality with respect to constituents.

(10)   a. *Locality:* a fully normalized relation (A,B) is a PF object and must be spelled out as locally as possible.

   b. *Inclusiveness:* a fully normalized relation (A,B) is a PF object and all components of a syntactic object which is transferred to PF must have an interpretation at PF.

   c. *Chain interpretation:* Chains must be interpreted.

Furthermore, analogous to the LF interface, there should be some version of Inclusiveness, a general interface requirement, presumably applying to any kind of linguistic interface. This prevents spurious insertion and deletions of representations (10b).

Finally, there are requirements on chains, about which I have nothing new to say, and I assume they are independently required. One generalization is that the information content of a chain should typically be spelled out only once within the chain, although this does not necessarily entail that the features are spelled out in the same place (10c). Another is that there is, presumably, some requirement that movement chains are subject to island conditions, etc. See Nunes (1999, 2004) and Bever (2003) for proposals in this regard.

12.3.4 *A schematic example*

In order to understand how this system works, consider a schematic derivation, where X, containing uninterpretable features, has merged with Y(P) and Z(P) is in the specifier of Y(P): X c-selects/subcategorizes for Y; Y s-selects Z. The functional dependencies are indicated on the right-hand side.

(11)

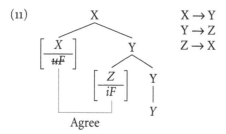

$$X \rightarrow Y$$
$$Y \rightarrow Z$$
$$Z \rightarrow X$$

First, consider only the Agree relation between X and Z.[8] Uninterpretable F-features on X probe for a goal with suitable interpretable F-features which can

---

[8] For ease of explication, let us put aside the relations X→Y and Y→Z for the moment. I will return to them below.

check the uF on X. The goal is Z in Spec-Y and Agree occurs. Traditionally, it was at this point that an EPP feature was postulated to motivate movement to Spec-X. However, this is not necessary given my assumptions above. Given the existence of the agreement dependency (Z^F, X^F), according to Dependency Spell-Out, (9), this yields a linearization pattern where the Z^F precedes X^F (12a,b).[9] Examples (12c,d) both violate Dependency Spell-Out, (9a) (angle brackets indicate strict, immediate precedence; Q is an arbitrary category to illustrate the locality principle).[10]

(12)   PF economy

    a.   <Z, X>   Immediate precedence and optimal solution

    b.   <Z, Q, X>   General precedence but violates (10a)

    c.   <X, Z>   Violation of (9)

    d.   <X, Q, Z>   Violation of (9) and (10a)

Note that the Dependency Spell-Out, (9), by itself does not guarantee immediate precedence. Immediate precedence is enforced by the locality requirement (9b) which requires that Z be as local as possible to X. Within a Minimalist derivational economy approach, (12a) is the optimal solution, conforming to both Dependency Spell-Out, (9), and the locality principle (10a). (12b) conforms to Dependency Spell-Out, (9), but violates Locality and is consequently less optimal than (12a).

Actually, the situation in (11) is more complex because X→Y and Y→Z and Z→X together constitute a linearization paradox. Dependency Spell-Out, (9), thus requires linearization of the following relations (13). A number of potential solutions are listed below.

(13)   (X, Y) (Y, Z) (Z, X) *Linearized as:*

    a.   < X , Y , Z , X >   An optimal solution

    b.   < X , Q , Y , Z , X >   Violates (10a)

    c.   < X , Y , Q , Z , X >   Violates (10a)

    d.   < X , Y , Z , Q , X >   Violates (10a)

Example (13a) is an optimal solution notwithstanding the fact that X is represented twice in the representation; X is part of a chain. Having established the optimal solution, principles of Chain Spell-Out may come into operation and mark the

---

[9] In this example I have assumed that Z is atomic for expository ease. In cases where Z is phrasal, then Z is involved in further dependency relationships. Generally, (10a) would cause a phrasal Z to pied-pipe its complement. However, stranding may be a possibility if the particular feature specification and the morphological resources in a particular language allowed stranding as an optimal solution to the linearization problem.

[10] I have included Q simply to illustrate the locality principle. The example should not be read as: adjuncts cannot ever intervene. The situation for true adjuncts may be different to the schematic example: consider a situation where Q was an adjunct that selected X. Then (12b) would be an optimal solution while (12a) would violate inclusiveness.

highest X for overt Spell-Out, while the lower one is spelled out as a phonetically empty element. Examples (13c,d,e) each violate the Locality requirement because in each case there is an intervening entity that disrupts strict precedence. The following sections explore this mechanism with respect to Afrikaans adpositions.

12.4 Agree in adpositional constructions

Having dispensed with the theoretical preliminaries, I would like to return to the problem at hand. In the earlier discussion of the morphological alternations of the *met–mee* type, I remained agnostic about the relationship between the preposition and the postposition. In this section, I will argue that the relationship is one of agreement. There are theoretical and empirical reasons to think that this may indeed be the case.

12.4.1 *Theoretical motivations*

Den Dikken (2010) posits a specific parallel between the adpositional and clausal domains. In the structures in (14) below, P is analogous to V in that both select DP arguments and mark them for Case and theta roles. These are dominated by projections encoding aspect for space and events respectively. The latter projections, in turn, are dominated by projections encoding spatial and temporal and person deixis. To the extent that the parallels posited by den Dikken (2010) are valid, it follows that since abstract agreement occurs in the clausal domain, the same should be true of the adpositional domain. In fact, the notion of Agree within adpositional phrases is not necessarily new: Biberauer (2007) and Kayne (2005a)—not to mention any analysis requiring movement within an extended PP projection—all argue for probe–goal checking by Agree, although the precise nature of the features involved is not necessarily clear.

(14)   Parallels between the adpositional and clausal domains
   a. $[C^{Space} [Deixis_{Space} [Aspect_{Space} [P DP]]]]$ [Adpositional functional projections]
   b. $[C^{Force} [Deixis^{Tense} [Aspect^{Event} [V DP]]]]$ [Clausal functional projections]

12.4.2 *Morphological alternations*

There is also suggestive morphological evidence for agreement projections within the adpositional domain because with DP–P orders, a subset of adpositions display a morphological change in a restricted fashion, as illustrated in (2) and (15) below. However, since these alternations are not productive (they do not correlate with singular/plural agreement for example) and given the general paucity of inflectional agreement on verbs in Afrikaans, it is understandable to be sceptical that these alternations by themselves are evidence of abstract agreement. For this reason, it is necessary to bolster this evidence with cross-linguistic support.

(15)   Ek   het   hom   met 'n mes mee   /*met   ge-steek
       I   have.AUX   him   with a knife with.AGR /with   PTCP-stabbed
       'I stabbed him with a knife.'

12.4.3 Wh-*extraction*

From a comparative perspective, there are languages with overt P-agreement. For example, in Kilega (Baker 2008) P-agreement occurs only under extraction from the PP (16b). In fact, Anikó Lipták (p.c.) suggests that this may be a strong correlation across many languages with P-agreement, including Hungarian. Note that I am not proposing an analysis of this phenomenon, I am only using it as an indicator. Interestingly, Afrikaans exhibits exactly the same pattern: extraction from a PP is only possible if the adposition evidences a morphological change (16b).[11] The fact that Afrikaans patterns identically in this respect to a language which uncontroversially displays P-agreement strongly suggests that Afrikaans has P-agreement too.

(16)   *wh*-extraction occurs only in the presence of agreement on P.

a. Aba-syakulu b-o   Kambale a-ka-kanay-a   na-bo
   2-old.people 2-FOC   Kambale 1S-PRES-speak-FV   with-2
   'It's old people that Kambale is speaking with.' ([Kilega] Kinyalolo 1991, cited in Baker 2008: 192)

b. Watter kandidaat   moet   ek   voor   /*vir   stem
   which candidate   must   I   for.AGR   /*for   vote
   'Which candidate must I vote for?' (Oosthuizen 2000: 72)

At this point a problem arises. Under standard Minimalist approaches Agree is bidirectional and can therefore only operate when both heads in an Agree relation have uninterpretable features. This poses difficulties for case assignment in PPs since the only way Case can be assigned is if DP agrees with P, presumably with respect to a ɸ-feature. This entails that all languages have agreeing PPs. However, since languages diverge empirically with respect to PP agreement (e.g. the *wh*-extraction asymmetry in (16)), it follows that not all languages do have P agreement. Consequently, it seems that the bidirectional condition on Agree may need to be revisited. For this reason, I assume an earlier version of Agree which is asymmetric and need not be bidirectional.

---

[11] This applies only when a morphological alternate exists. However with adpositions such as *in*, which has no morphological alternate, this does not apply.

12.4.4 *The feature specification of P*

There is thus theoretical and empirical evidence for the presence of feature agreement in the adpositional domain. Given the previous discussion, I would like to be more explicit about what I take the feature specification of the various P heads to be. Ps which appear as prepositions only (i.e. typical Locative Ps) have the canonical feature specification: they subcategorize for a DP and assign theta roles and Case and establish a single, locative relationship between Figure and Ground (17a). Ps which appear in postpositional and circumpositional constructions (typical of Afrikaans Path Ps) also include uF-features in their specification (17b).[12]

(17)   Feature specifications of P

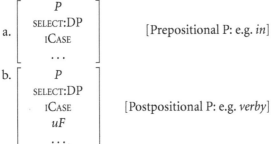

This yields an elegant parallelism with the specifications of prepositional P, postpositional P, and V, T respectively. The V+v feature bundle selects arguments and assigns theta roles and Case, just as prepositional P does. Similarly, T includes uninterpretable features in the same way that postpositional P does. In both cases, Agree checks uninterpretable features against the equivalent interpretable ones on DP resulting in a morphological change on the head: T is spelled out as being inflected for person, number, etc., while postpositional P is spelled out as the 'agreeing' form of the preposition if the suppletive, Agreeing form is available in the lexicon. To complete the parallel, just as T mediates between Reference Time and Speech/Utterance Time to create a complex tense, postpositional P mediates between Figure and Ground to create a complex spatial configuration. The proposal is briefly outlined below and will be explained in section 12.5.

---

[12] Marjo van Koppen (p.c.) suggests that (16) may be evidence that the agreement in question is *wh*-agreement. While this is a distinct possibility, the presence of the morphologically restricted forms *mee*, *toe*, etc. in non-*wh*-contexts suggests that the feature may not be restricted to *wh*-contexts. Furthermore, in languages like Kilega, agreement is with the noun class (i.e. gender agreement). For these reasons I will remain agnostic about the precise nature of the feature, merely referring to it as an F-feature. However, if adpositional clauses evidence deictic features, as suggested by den Dikken (2010), and given the work by Ritter and Wiltschko (2010), which argues for the reconceptualization of various ϕ-features in terms of spatial, temporal, and person deixis, it may well be the case that the F-features in question are ϕ-features. This remains for future research.

(18)   a. Prepositional P has no uF-features.

b. Postpositional P (represented here as P^F) has uF-features.

c. Prepositional P is spelled out as 'non-agreeing' forms: *met, vir, tot, in*, etc.

d. P^F is spelled out by the highest specified suppletive/'agreeing' forms: *mee, voor, toe.*

e. The Elsewhere Condition (Kiparsky 1973) applies: i.e. if no 'agreeing' form is available, then the feature matrix is spelled out by the most applicable non-agreeing form, e.g. *in*.

In terms of morphology, a prepositional P feature bundle (17a) is spelled out with default adpositions such as *met, vir, tot, in*, etc. while a postpositional P (17b) with uF-features is spelled out by the highest-specified lexical forms, namely *mee, voor, toe*, etc. if such forms are available in the lexicon. In cases where there is no 'agreeing' form, such as for the preposition *in*, then the feature bundle is simply matched to the default form.

12.5 Derivations

In the previous two sections I have argued that linearization as a PF output condition can be expressed in terms of functional dependencies and that there is uF-feature checking in the postpositional structures of Afrikaans. With these building blocks in place, we can now proceed to deriving the attested prepositional, postpositional, and circumpositional structures illustrated in (1).

12.5.1 *Prepositional P*

Prepositional P, with the feature specification in (17a), is merged with a DP (19a). Since P selects DP there is a functional dependency such that P→DP. By Dependency Spell-Out, (9), this yields a linearization pattern where the P feature bundle precedes the DP feature bundle (19b). The feature bundles are matched to their respective morphological specifications: P is matched to *in* (or a similar preposition) while the DP is matched to *die kamer* (or whatever it corresponds to) (19c). This derives a prepositional phrase with P–DP order such as the one in (1a).

(19)   Deriving precedence relations for a prepositional P: *in die kamer.*

a.

b. Precedence: P > DP

c. Feature Bundles:

$$\begin{bmatrix} \text{P} \\ \text{SELECT:DP} \\ \text{ICASE} \\ \cdots \end{bmatrix} > \begin{bmatrix} \text{DP} \\ \text{DEF} \\ \text{N:}\cdots \end{bmatrix}$$

d. Spelled out as:
   in die kamer (1a)

12.5.2 *Postpositional P*

Postpositions have the feature specification (17b). P is merged with a DP to satisfy its selectional requirements (20a). Thus, there is a functional dependency such that P→ DP. However, DP also checks uF-features on P, instantiating a functional dependency where DP→PF. This yields a linearization paradox where P both precedes and follows DP (20b). According to Dependency Spell-Out, (9), this can be linearized in two different ways: one with doubled DPs (20b) and another with doubled adpositions (21a).

(20)   Deriving precedence relations for postpositional P

a.   PP

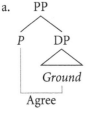

b. Option 1: DP > P^F > DP

c. Feature Bundles:

$$\begin{bmatrix} \text{DP} \\ \text{DEF} \\ \text{N:}\cdots \end{bmatrix} > \begin{bmatrix} \text{P} \\ \text{SELECT:DP} \\ \text{ICASE} \\ \textit{u}\text{F} \\ \cdots \end{bmatrix} > \begin{bmatrix} \text{DP} \\ \text{DEF} \\ \text{N:}\cdots \end{bmatrix}$$

d. Spelled out as:
   Die kamer in t (1b)

With respect to (20b), the feature bundles are sent to the interface where they are matched to their respective morphological forms. The preposition feature bundle is matched to the minimal feature set which can both (a) assign Case and select DP and (b) agree with DP. This is the postpositional feature bundle in (17b). Note that it is not possible to simply match the P feature bundle to a non-agreeing adposition because, firstly, a more highly specified morphological form (i.e. the agreeing form exists) and secondly, this would result in the F-features not being spelled out—a violation of Full Interpretation (10b). Since both DP feature bundles are formally identical they constitute a chain and are spelled out according to the independent principles governing the Spell-Out of chains (10c). Typically this involves pronunciation of only the first constituent, while the tail of the chain is spelled out as being phonetically empty.

(21) a. *Option 2:* P > DP > P^F

b. Feature Bundles:

$$
\begin{bmatrix} P \\ \text{SELECT:DP} \\ \text{ICASE} \\ \ldots \end{bmatrix} > \begin{bmatrix} DP \\ \text{DEF} \\ \text{N:} \ldots \end{bmatrix} > \begin{bmatrix} P \\ \text{SELECT:DP} \\ \text{ICASE} \\ \text{uF} \\ \ldots \end{bmatrix}
$$

c. Spelled out as:
in die kamer in (1c)

The same set of relations can also be spelled out as in (21), but the logic of Spell-Out remains the same. In this representation P is represented twice, not necessarily in the syntactic structure but in the PF linearization. In effect, the features within a single P feature bundle are spelled out in distributed positions. The leftmost P represents the features of P that assign Case to and select DP. The minimal feature set which matches these properties is (17a). Consequently the leftmost preposition is spelled out as a prepositional, non-agreeing form. The rightmost adposition represents the (uF)-features of P which are determined by agreement with DP. The minimal feature set matching these properties is (17b). Thus, the rightmost P is spelled out as an 'agreeing' form of the adposition if such exists in the lexicon. If there is no 'agreeing' form in the lexicon (as for the Afrikaans adposition *in*), then the most highly specified morphological form is inserted. This accounts for the data in (1c).

Importantly, the Spell-Out forms (20b) and (21b) are equally optimal linearizations of the same numeration and the same syntactic structure. Both forms are therefore predicted to be optional and have identical semantics, which is indeed the case.

Just as importantly, the analysis can account for the ungrammaticality of certain patterns.

(22) Some ungrammatical patterns

	P >	DP >	P^F
a. Cannot be spelled out as:	*mee	die mes	met
b. Cannot be spelled out as:	*met	die mes	met

The structure in (21a) cannot be spelled out as (22a) because if DP^F→P^F then the agreeing form of the adposition must follow the DP, not precede it. Thus the agreeing form will always be to the right of the DP. In addition, examples like (22b) are ruled out if there exists a more highly specified form in the lexicon (e.g. *mee*) which matches the P^F feature bundle. If no such highly specified form exists in the lexicon, as is the case for most adpositions, then the best match is achieved by spelling out P^F as the base adposition.[13]

12.5.3 *Deriving disjoint Ps and blocking effects*

The analysis can also account for circumpositional structures where the preposition and the postposition are morphophonologically unrelated; cf. (3) above, reprinted here as (23).

(23) a. Die boot seil *onder* die brug *deur*
          the boat sail under the bridge through
          'The boat sails under the bridge and out the other side.'

   b. Option 2: P > DP > P^F

   c. Feature Bundles:

$$
\begin{bmatrix} P \\ \text{SELECT:DP} \\ \text{ICASE} \\ \dots \end{bmatrix} >
\begin{bmatrix} DP \\ \text{DEF} \\ \text{N:}\dots \end{bmatrix} >
\begin{bmatrix} P \\ \text{SELECT:DP} \\ \text{ICASE} \\ \text{uF} \\ \dots \end{bmatrix}
$$

These constructions are circumpositional and so will have uF-features and the derivation of an example like (23) would proceed as in (20), yielding an underlying linearization pattern similar to 'Option 2' in (21b). Each feature bundle is matched to adpositions which are consistent with the semantics of the construction. A reviewer points out that in this type of construction it is almost always obligatory to spell out both Ps and that Option 1 (20) is not available as a linearization strategy. A reason for this may be due to the recoverability of the semantics. Option 1 would yield examples like (24) with anomalous pragmatics. The semantics of *deur* encode a path meaning, and it is in the nature of bridges that one can only sail beneath them, not through

---

[13] R-words can be accommodated within this analysis under the assumption that movement of the DP is triggered by a deictic or *wh*-feature (as opposed to an F-feature), yielding the same linearization dynamics as described above. (An R-word is the term used to refer to a type of word common in Germanic languages which contains an incorporated deictic or question element such as *daarmee* 'there-with' or *waarmee* 'where-with'.) It is also worth pointing out that the current analysis cannot easily explain why 'Option 2' is not productively available with the adposition pair *tot* 'until' and *toe* 'to' in Afrikaans (although it exists in Dutch); instead *toe* appears as a postposition (as is predicted under 'Option 1'). However, I suspect this is also a problem for other analyses. A reviewer suggests that this option may be ruled out by lexical blocking: the existence of *na...toe* blocks the *tot...toe* pattern.

(i) *Ek loop tot   die brug   toe
       I   walk until the bridge to
       'I walk to the bridge.'

(ii) Ek loop skool   toe
       I   walk school to
       'I walk to school.'

them. This can be contrasted with (25) where the preposition can be dropped, presumably because towns are more likely than bridges to allow thoroughfare.[14]

(24)   #Die   boot   seil   die   brug   deur
       the   boat   sail   the   bridge   through
       'The boat sails through the bridge.'

(25)   Hy   is (by)   die   dorp   deur
       he   is   by   the   town   through
       'He went through the town.'

Since doubling of this type (i.e. when the two adpositions are non-identical) only occurs in contexts where there is no more highly specified, 'agreeing' form in the lexicon, the current analysis predicts the existence of 'blocking effects': if the leftmost adposition in a doubling construction is *vir* 'for' or *met* 'with', then the rightmost adposition must be *voor* and *mee* respectively. The inverse does not apply. This prediction is supported by the comprehensive data collected by Helmantel (2002: 178–9) who mapped the co-occurence of various adpositions in Dutch. In her list, there are no examples of doubling with *tot* or *met* followed by anything other than *toe* or *mee* respectively.[15] This also seems to be borne out in Afrikaans.[16]

---

[14] I would like to thank an anonymous reviewer for alerting me to this example.

[15] Dutch does not distinguish between *vir* 'for' and *voor* 'for.AGR'/'in front of', so patterns for this adposition cannot be tested in Dutch, although they can be for Afrikaans.

[16] In some varieties of Afrikaans, the preposition *met* can be doubled by a morphologically unrelated form *saam* 'together'.

(i)   Ek   wil   met   haar   saam   gesels
     I   want   with   her   together   talk
     'I want to talk with her.'

Prima facie, this appears to contradict the claim about blocking effects. However, *saam* may not actually be identical to an agreeing postposition in all dialects since it appears in contexts where an agreeing postposition cannot.

(ii)   Hoe   gaan   dit   saam   met   jou?
     How   go   it   together   with   you
     'How are you?' (Colloquial North Cape Afrikaans)

(iii)   *Hoe   gaan   dit   mee   met   jou?
      How   go   it   with.AGR   with   you
      'How are you?'

It is also worth noting that in fieldwork in the Northern and Eastern Cape, I often found that speakers who used *saam* resisted the use of *mee*. This indicates that for at least some speakers, *saam* may itself be an agreeing form which blocks the use of *mee* entirely. Although these two explanations are mutually exclusive, they both strongly suggest that the use of *saam* may not be counter-evidence to blocking effects.

(26)   Blocking effects

    a. Ek   wil   dit   vir   iemand   anders   voor   wys
       I   want   it   for   somebody   else   for   show
      'I want to show it to somebody else.'

    b. Vir   iemand   anders   voor,   wil   ek   dit   wys
       For   somebody   else   for,   want I   it   show
      'To somebody else, I want to show it.'

(27)   a. *Ek   wil   dit   vir   iemand   anders   aan   wys
       I   want   it   for   somebody   else   to   show
      Intended: 'I want to show it to somebody else.'

    b. *Vir   iemand   anders   aan,   wil   ek   dit   wys
       for   somebody   else   to,   want   I   it   show
      Intended: 'I want to show it to somebody else.'

(28)   a. *Ek   wil   dit   vir   iemand   anders   toe   wys
       I   want   it   for   somebody   else   to   show
      Intended: 'I want to show it to somebody else.'

    b. *Vir   iemand   anders   toe,   wil   ek   dit   wys
       For   somebody   else   to,   want   I   it   show
      Intended: 'I want to show it to somebody else.'

Example (26a) is a grammatical sentence showing the alternation between *vir* and the more highly specified form *voor*. Fronting as in the (b) examples demonstrates that the fronted PP is a constituent and that the final adposition is not a verbal particle.

Example (27b) substitutes *aan* and the sentence is ungrammatical. It is important to note that the use of *aan* is semantically plausible because it can also be used to encode an indirect object as in (29). The ungrammaticality of (27b), despite semantic plausibility points to a structural cause—in this case, morphological blocking: the existence of the more highly specified *voor* in the lexicon prevents *aan* from ever being used as a postposition.

(29)   Ek   wil   dit   aan   iemand   wys
       I   want   it   to   somebody   show
      'I want to show it to somebody.'

Example (28b) substitutes *toe* and the sentence is ungrammatical. However, while *vir* typically encodes a Receiver (Dative), *toe* typically encodes path semantics. Consequently, the existence of *voor*, which is more highly specified, will block insertion of *toe*.

Similar effects can be seen with the adposition pair *met* and *mee*.[17] Example (30a) is ungrammatical as a doubling structure, but some speakers accept it if *deur* is a verbal particle. Topicalization in (30b) removes this reading and it is demonstrated that it is ungrammatical in a doubling construction, i.e. it is not possible to Merge *deur* as a postposition when the preposition is *met*. This can be contrasted with (23) where *deur* can indeed be used as a postposition when another preposition, which does not have a highly specified agreeing form, is used. In fact, the apparent grammaticality (for some speakers) of the verbal particle construction shows that this example is semantically plausible. The ungrammaticality of (30b) then must follow from a structural property—in this case a morphological blocking effect. The same logic applies to examples (31) and (32).

(30) a. %Ek   steek   Jan   met   die   mes   deur
           I   stab   Jan   with   the   knife   through
           Intended: 'I stabbed John through with the knife.'

      b. *Met   die   mes   deur,   steek   ek   Jan
           with   the   knife   through,   stab   I   Jan
           Intended: 'I stabbed John through with the knife.'

(31) a. *Ek   loop   met   my   vriende   aan
           I   walk   with   my   friends   on
           Intended: 'I walked with my friends.'

      b. *Met   my   vriende   aan,   loop   ek
           with   my   friends   on   walk   I
           Intended: 'With my friends, I walked.'

(32) a. *Ek   loop   met   my   vriende   af
           I   walk   with   my   friends   down
           Intended: 'I walked down with my friends.'

      b. *Met   my   vriende   af,   loop   ek
           With   my   friends   down,   walk   I
           Intended: 'I walked down with my friends.'

12.6 Semantics and parametric variation

Thus far, I have argued on empirical and theoretical grounds for the existence of some feature, uF on P which triggers agreement with the DP bearing the corresponding F-feature and thereby motivates overt movement of the DP. The following section is somewhat more speculative in character, outlining the possible semantic implications of a research programme along the lines suggested in this paper.

---

[17] Note that the distribution of these adpositions seems to be a bit more restricted, as not all Afrikaans speakers accept *mee* being used outside an R-word context.

Generally, prepositions encode location while postpositions encode directed motion semantics (den Dikken 2010). Semantically, P heads mediate between Figure and Ground. A simple, locative relation between Figure and Ground can be handled by a single P head. Thus in an example like *the cat is in the box*, locative P encodes a relation of containment between the Figure, *the cat*, and the Ground, *the box*. However, a directed motion eventuality is a complex spatial situation.

Evidence that directed motion PPs are more complex than locative PPs is provided by the different ways in which they are mapped to the *Aktionsarten* of events. Complex adpositions are sensitive to the *Aktionsart* of the verbal predicate with which they are associated. Directed motion PPs are mapped to internally complex *Aktionsarten* (activities and accomplishments) but not to internally simplex *Aktionsarten* (states and achievements).

(33)   PPs are sensitive to *Aktionsarten*
   a.   I walked (on/onto) the grass   [Activity]
   b.   I walked 10 kilometers (on/?onto) the beach   [Accomplishment]
   c.   I was (on/*onto) the mountain   [State]
   d.   The rocket failed (on/*onto) the launch pad   [Achievement]

(34)   PPs are sensitive to *Aktionsarten*
   a.   I walked along the path   [Activity]
   b.   I walked 10 kilometers along the path   [Accomplishment]
   c.   *I was intelligent along the path   [State]
   d.   *I fainted along the path   [Achievement]
        Ungrammatical on a directed-motion reading[18]

Examples (33a–d) show that simple, locative prepositions can be associated with all event types (accomplishments, activities, states, and achievements). However, directed-motion prepositions such as *onto* and *along* are only compatible with activities and accomplishments (34a–d). Given that only activities and accomplishments involve complex internal event structure (states have no internal event structure, and achievements are punctual), it is unsurprising that only these event types can support complex prepositional semantics. The conclusion, then, is that directed motion semantics is mapped to internal event semantics and that directed motion semantics are internally complex.

The next question that arises is how to instantiate the relationship between the Figure and the Ground. It is useful to make an analogy with successive frames of a movie viewed individually. In an example like *the cat jumped into the box*, the directed motion semantics can be mapped from two simple locative situations: (a) a

---

[18] Example (34d) is only grammatical on a locative reading where the fainting event (an achievement) occurs somewhere on a footpath.

situation where the cat is outside the box and (b) a subsequent situation where the cat is inside the box.

(35)   Directed Motion requires at least two syntactic relations

Given that there are two 'frames' it follows that the relationship between Figure and Ground must be specified twice.[19] The strongest, and null hypothesis, is that syntactic relations are mapped directly to semantic relations in a one-to-one manner. There are a couple of ways in which this may occur, each yielding typologically different adpositional patterns: (i) by selection: P selects a specifier and a complement (i.e. two syntactic relations between P and a DP), and (ii) by agreement: P selects a complement and P agrees with the complement (two syntactic relations between P and a DP).

Structure (36) illustrates option (i) where P selects a complement representing 'Ground' and a specifier also representing 'Ground'.[20] There are therefore two syntactic relationships which satisfy the requirement, imposed by the 'frames' view of the semantics that there be two relationships between P and 'Ground'. In this structure, P selects DP (complement) and P selects DP (specifier). Thus, according to the analysis developed in this paper, P > DP. This accounts for English- and Norwegian-type directed-motion PPs which are prepositional in nature (Mai Tungseth, p.c.).

(36)   The English-type structure

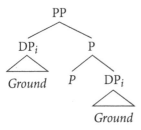

---

[19] I would like to remain agnostic about whether having two Figure–Ground relations always necessarily results in a directed-motion reading; having two Figure–Ground 'frames' could also possibly be mapped to other complex semantics, without necessarily implying directed motion per se. For example, *Charlemagne built a wall around the castle* encodes a path of some sort but not motion (den Dikken 2010: 91) while *Stella burped into my ear* encodes some kind of directionality and bringing into existence, but again there is no motion implied. It may be that these types of examples are metaphoric extensions, but it is still the job of the semantics to explain them.

[20] I assume that the relationship between P and the DP representing the 'Figure' is established in another way, perhaps by binding of a Figure variable on P.

Structure (37) illustrates option (ii) where P selects a DP complement representing 'Ground' and an agreement relationship exists between uF on P and F on the DP. This configuration is identical to (21) and derives Afrikaans- and Dutch-type postpositions and circumpositions.

(37)   Two dependencies instantiated by Merge and Agree

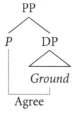

In this structure, there are also two dependencies (Merge with a complement and Agree with a complement) which may, by hypothesis, be mapped to the two semantic relations required for the 'frames' semantics of directed motion to be realized. The linearization options for this structure have already been discussed in this paper and account for the Afrikaans- and Dutch-type adpositional paradigms.

This section has outlined an informal view of the semantics of directed-motion adpositions which, along with a strong hypothesis about the nature of the syntax–LF interface, accounts for some of the parametric variation occurring in adpositional, directed-motion constructions.[21] For languages like Afrikaans, Dutch, and German, uF-features are included in the feature bundle; for languages like English and Norwegian, there are no uF-features in the feature bundle—for these languages the relationship between Figure and Ground is arguably instantiated by selection.

12.7 Conclusion

The proposed analysis provides a solution to the problem posed in section 12.2.1: how can one derive movement without the need to stipulate an EPP feature to motivate it? The proposed analysis derives the disharmonic word orders characteristic of the Afrikaans adpositional domain without EPP: movement of the EPP type in a sense

---

[21] Thus far in the paper, I have simply argued, on empirical and theoretical grounds, for the existence of some uF/F-feature pair. It is interesting to speculate about the possibility that these features may actually be φ-features. To the extent that φ-features express deictic relations (Cowper 2005; Harley and Ritter 2002; Sigurðsson 2007), they could also, plausibly, be used to express the deictic relationships between the Figure and Ground—in exactly the same way that they serve the purpose of relating the Speaker and Hearer; as well as Speech Time, Reference Time, and Event Time in the clausal domain. Thus, in a way, yet to be determined, the φ-feature checking could possibly result in the appropriate directed-motion semantics.

does not exist, but the effect of displacement is an artefact of the linearization requirements imposed at the PF interface. Moreover, the analysis explains various empirical effects such as optionality, the identical semantics of circumpositional and postpositional phrases, and, finally, to the extent that this analysis is correct, it offers support for the Strong Minimalist Hypothesis.

13

Traversal Parameter at the PF Interface: Graph-Theoretical Linearization of Bare Phrase Structure*

TAKASHI TOYOSHIMA

13.1 Introduction

Intra- or cross-linguistic variations and differences in word orders have long been, and still are, the major concerns in linguistic studies. Classic typology of sentence word orders deals with the relative ordering among the verb (V) and its argument constituents, the subject (S) and the direct object (O) (Greenberg 1963). Another typology classifies the languages of the world into harmonic and disharmonic (Hawkins 1983), looking at the word orders at the phrase level; consistently head-initial or head-final harmonic languages, and disharmonic or mixed-order languages with head-initial and head-final phrases depending on their categories.

* Parts of the material in this work have been presented at BCGL III (University College Brussels, May 2008), Conference on Theoretical Approaches to Disharmonic Word Orders (Newcastle University, May–June 2009), GLOW in Asia VII (The EFL University, Hyderabad, February 2009), Philosophy, Mathematics, Linguistics: International Conference (St Petersburg Department of V. A. Steklov Mathematical Institute, November 2009), and DGfS 32 (Humboldt-Universität zu Berlin, February 2010). I thank the audiences at these conferences for clarifying questions, comments, and criticisms, in particular, Alastair Appleton, Theresa Biberauer, Cedric Boeckx, Andrew Carnie, Guglielmo Cinque, Joe Emonds, Hans-Martin Gärtner, Richie Kayne, Tommi Leung, Ian Roberts, Michelle Sheehan, Peter Svenonius, Mark De Vries, and Hedde Zeijlstra, among others. I am also indebted to two reviewers for extensive critiques that helped to reshape the contents, to whom I hope I have not failed to do justice. Any errors or inadequacies that may still persist are mine alone. This work has been partially supported by the Grants-in-Aid for Exploratory Research (#19652044) and for Scientific Research (C) (#22520401) from the Japan Society for the Promotion of Science, which I gratefully acknowledge here.

In generative syntax, the harmonic languages are traditionally accounted for with the across-the-board settings of the head directionality parameter for all the categories in a given language, and the disharmonic ones with a parameter setting for each category within a single language (Koster 1975). The latter possibility should in principle allow a multitude of combinations of the head directionality in a given language, but empirical attestations are not balanced in their distributions. Observing that there is virtually no configuration where a head-final phrase immediately dominates a head-initial phrase, Holmberg (2000) makes a descriptive generalization called the Final-over-Final Constraint (FOFC). Biberauer, Holmberg, and Roberts (2008a, *et seq.*) give an account for it, in terms of phase-cyclic Spell-Out (Chomsky 2000, *et seq.*) and the Linear Correspondence Axiom (LCA) of Kayne's (1994) theory of antisymmetry.

Although the LCA has often been adopted for linearization (i.a. Chomsky 1995a,b; Fox and Pesetsky 2005), it is not quite suited for such a purpose in its original form. The LCA was proposed to explain some basic properties of phrase structures, restricting the possible structures, in particular, of X'-theoretic structures. It was not a procedure or operation to yield linear strings of words from hierarchical structures but an axiomatic statement that specifies a mapping relation from a linear order of terminal words into the asymmetric c-command relation in the hierarchical structures.

The oft-adopted inverse mapping from the asymmetric c-command to the linear order is not one-to-one, and the LCA does not logically entail that the linear order in question must be precedence, as Kayne (1994: 35ff.) acknowledges. Kayne claims that by the LCA, the specifier–head–complement order is the universal base order. This implies that any other orders are to be derived by movement, which can be massive, in particular for the SOV languages. Some movement, if not most, appears to be self-serving, and a number of functional projections need to be postulated that often appear to play no other role than supplying the landing-sites.

Yet, the thesis of the universal specifier–head–complement order is not a genuine theorem logically deduced from the LCA but rather an empirical generalization that the specifier element appears overwhelmingly to the left of the head–complement structure. That is, the complement–head–specifier order is not logically excluded, but by some obscure stipulation about the timing in linearization, with an 'abstract' node adjoined to the root, which in turn dominates an abstract terminal with no phonetic content (Kayne 1994: 37).[1,2]

---

[1] As Chomsky (1995b: 437, note 32) notes, attributing to Sam Epstein in their personal communication, Kayne's indirect formulation of linear order as a transitive, asymmetric, total relation among terminals in terms of dominance and asymmetric c-command allows, in principle, any interchange of sister nodes if a class of phrase markers satisfies the LCA, not only the complement–head–specifier order but also the specifier–complement–head order as well as the head–complement–specifier order.

[2] Uriagereka (1999a) speculates that in the course of human evolution, both precedence-based and subsequence-based grammars may have existed, but only the former has survived through natural selection, either by an adaptive advantage or by chance. A reviewer also suggests a possibility that precedence/subsequence may be a parameter and we may have been failing to recognize the latter type.

Technically, the LCA employs an unorthodox notion of c-command, based on the first category node, not on the conventional first branching node. A head–complement structure is thus necessarily an XP, which can be segmented only once by adjunction of a specifier. That is, there is no intermediate X′ projection level for head–complement structures, and an XP with its head alone without a complement (or an adjunct) requires a non-branching unary projection. A specifier is a species of adjunct, and specifiers and adjuncts are not distinguished in structural terms (Sternefeld 1994). As such, contrary to what everyone is led to believe, the following types of structures are permitted in principle, with Kayne's (1994) original formulation of the LCA, as Guimarães (2008) points out: (i) n-ary branching ($n > 0$); (ii) heads adjoined to non-heads; (iii) non-heads adjoined to heads; (iv) multiple specifiers; (v) multiple adjunction to heads. They are possible only in limited contexts, and it is an empirical issue whether they are realized or what kinds of structures are desirable. Yet, it clearly undermines the rudimentary goal of antisymmetry theory to restrict the possible syntactic structures.

Taking stock of these predicaments of the LCA, this paper proposes an alternative, developing a linearization procedure for the Minimalist theory of Bare Phrase Structure as advanced in Chomsky (1995a,b), based on a graph-theoretical approach (i.a. Yasui 2003; Kural 2005). I submit that the graph-theoretical linearization procedure is a viable alternative to LCA-based analyses, which deserves serious attention. It is a promising approach, in that it derives the three cross-linguistically common variations in word order (VSO, SVO, SOV) from a single structure without self-serving movement, and accounts for the rarity of the other three logically possible variations (VOS, OVS, OSV). It also accounts for the disharmonic word-order patterns in Vata and German, the latter by stipulating a parametric feature on phase categories that kicks in at the PF interface when syntactic structures are converted into a linear sequence of words.

The following section appraises the tree traversal linearization that Kural (2005) proposes for the traditional X′-tree structures, and points out the empirical and theoretical problems that arise from the head-adjunction structure and the branching directions of the X′-trees. Section 13.3 briefly reviews Chomsky's (1995a,b) theory of Bare Phrase Structure (BPS), focusing on the innovations from the traditional X′-theory, and the problems of head-to-head adjunction. In section 13.4, I propose a linearization procedure, incorporating Kural's (2005) proposal into BPS, with head-to-specifier movement as it should avail itself in BPS. In section 13.5, I will demonstrate how the proposed BPS traversal linearization derives the disharmonic word-order patterns in the Vata *wh*-question, compound tense, and relative clause, reported in Koopman (1984), as well as the disharmonic patterns in German, respecting the stipulated parameter at the PF interface. Section 13.6 discusses the general predictions of the proposal and some theoretical implications, comparing them with Fukui and Takano's (1998) proposal of linearization. Finally, section 13.7 concludes the paper with some remarks.

13.2 Linearization by tree traversal: Kural (2005)

13.2.1 *Tree traversal in graph theory*

Tree structures are not exclusive to linguistics, and they are widely used to represent a hierarchical organization of information, from a folk family tree, bibliographical cataloguing, and organizational management structures, to evolutionary relationships in biology, for example, constituting types of mathematical objects.

As such, tree structures find a wide variety of uses in various fields. In computer science, for example, data structures are often modelled on trees. For data manipulation in such tree structures, systematic ways of visiting every node, where each datum is stored, have been developed, known as tree traversals. There are three types: preorder, inorder, and postorder traversals. They all start from the root node, visiting nodes as deep as possible along one branch before visiting nodes in other branches. They are classified by the order of steps: performing an action on the current node (conventionally called a 'visit'), or repeating the traversal process with the subtree rooted at its child nodes. These can be effectively implemented in a recursive algorithm.

Assuming a binary tree, the three traversal methods can be described as follows:[3]

(1) Tree traversals
     Starting from the root, at a given node *N*:
     a. Preorder: Visit the node.
        i. Recursively traverse the left subtree.
     b. Inorder: Visit the node.
        ii. Recursively traverse the right subtree.
     c. Postorder: Visit the node.

The common traversal steps are (i, ii), and the three traversal methods differ in whether the 'visit' is called upon, before the traversal steps (a. preorder), between the two (b. inorder), or after them (c. postorder). Informally put, when the traversal finds no child to traverse deeper, it backtracks to its parent and looks for other children. The preorder traversal first visits a parent node, the left child/subtree second, and then the right child/subtree last. The inorder traversal visits the left child/subtree first, the parent node second, and then the right child/subtree last. The postorder traversal visits the left child/subtree first, the right child/subtree second, and finally the parent node.

---

[3] Trees need not be binary, and the standard convention is to traverse children/subtrees from left to right. Also, there is another class of traversal methods known as the breadth-first level-order traversal, which does not seem to give us any linguistically significant insights.

13.2.2 *Kural's (2005) proposal*

Assuming the traditional two-dimensional X′-theoretic trees (Chomsky 1970; Jackendoff 1977), Kural (2005) proposes to apply the tree traversal methods for linearization of syntactic trees, and argues that it eliminates the need to posit structures (as specified with the head parameter) or derivations (with/without movement as entailed in Kayne's LCA) that vary greatly across languages.

Applied to a syntactic tree such as (2), the preorder traversal (1a) yields the sequence (3a); the inorder traversal (1b), the sequence (3b); and the postorder traversal (1c), the sequence (3c); respectively.

(2)

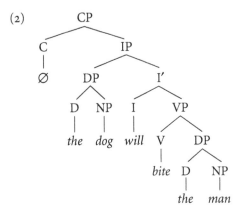

(3)   a. {CP, C, Ø, IP, DP, D, *the*, NP, *dog*, I′, I, *will*, VP, V, *bite*, DP, D, *the*, NP, *man*}

b. {Ø, C, CP, *the*, D, DP, *dog*, NP, IP, *will*, I, I′, *bite*, V, VP, *the*, D, DP, *man*, NP}

c. {Ø, C, *the*, D, *dog*, NP, DP, *will*, I, *bite*, V, *the*, D, *man*, NP, DP, VP, I′, IP, CP}

Simply collecting the terminal words from (3a–c) produces exactly the same sequence as (4), which is good enough for English but not particularly illuminating.

(4)   {Ø, *the*, *dog*, *will*, *bite*, *the*, *man*}

Kural observes, however, that there are linguistically significant patterns in (3a–c), in the relative ordering of phrasal nodes (5a–c), respectively.

(5)   a. Preorder: {CP, IP, DP, NP, VP, DP, NP}

b. Inorder: {CP, DP, NP, IP, VP, DP, NP}

c. Postorder: {NP, DP, NP, DP, VP, IP, CP}

Replacing the phrasal nodes (5a–c) with the category symbol of their heads yields (6a–c), which coincide with the three typologically common word orders, VSO, SVO, and SOV, respectively, assuming the V-to-I head movement in the preorder traversal (6a).

(6) a. Preorder: {C, I, D, N, V, D, N}   (C)(I)SVO → (C)V(+I)S(t_V)O

    b. Inorder: {C, D, N, I, V, D, N}   (C)S(I)VO

    c. Postorder: {N, D, N, D, V, I, C}   SOV(I)(C)

Proposing a terminal-extraction algorithm embedded in the traversal algorithm, Kural argues that tree traversal linearization can produce cross-linguistic variations in basic word orders without recourse to excessive movements as entailed in the LCA-based linearization approach that sometimes appear to be motivated only for obtaining the desired word orders.

2.3 Problems with Kural's traversal linearization

Ingenious as it is, however, there are two major problems in Kural's proposal of tree traversal linearization, one empirical and the other theoretical. The empirical problem is concerned with a certain type of movement, *wh*-movement and head movement in particular, as in (7).

(7)

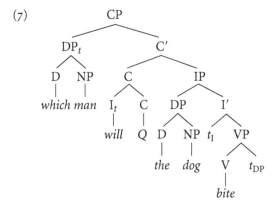

The preorder traversal, i.e. for VSO languages, yields the sequence (8a), only maximal projections of which is (8b), and its categorical reduction (8c), with the trace positions included for expository convenience.

(8) a. {CP, DP, D, *which*, NP, *man*, C′, [C, I, *will*, C, Q], IP, DP, D, *the*, NP, *dog*, I′, t_{will}, VP, V, *bite*, t_{wh}}

    b. {CP, DP, NP, IP, DP, NP, (t_{will}) VP, (t_{wh})}

    c. {C, D, N, I, D, N, (t_{will}) V, (t_{wh})}

An English gloss rendition will be (9).

(9) {[*will* + Q], *which*, *man*, *the*, *dog*, (t_{will}) *bite*, (t_{wh})}

As Kural's head-extraction algorithm spells out the [*will* + Q] complex as the head of CP, the moved *wh*-phrase follows it, which does not seem to be attested in any VSO languages. That is, if there is I-to-C movement, the moved I inevitably precedes the fronted *wh*-phrase in the preorder traversal for VSO languages.

The theoretical problem has to do with the directionality (left/right subtrees) referred to in the traversal algorithms (1a–c), and the assumption that syntactic structures are two-dimensional X′-theoretic trees with some fixed branching directions. Graph-theoretically, trees can be unordered, meaning that an ordering direction is not specified for the children of each node, and the reference to the left/right subtrees is only possible in an ordered tree. A tree is necessarily a *planar graph*; that is, it *can be* drawn on a two-dimensional Euclidean plane without any crossing of branches, but need not be a *plane graph*, meaning that it need not actually be so cast onto a two-dimensional plane.

The concern for the directionality in the traversal algorithms and in branching of trees is acknowledged and discussed in Kural (2005: 385ff.), but his argument falls short of any further insights. As Kural correctly points out, it is just a convention to traverse a tree from left to right, and nothing theoretically prohibits traversals from right to left. Kural demonstrates that reversing the traversal order does not affect the results if the branching in the tree is also reversed.

The preorder, inorder, and postorder traversals of the following tree (10) yield the respective sequences in (11a–c) with the conventional left-to-right traversal.

(10)

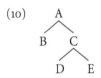

(11) a. Preorder: {A, B, C, D, E}

  b. Inorder: {B, A, D, C, E}

  c. Postorder: {B, D, E, C, A}

The tree in (12) is the mirror image of (10), branching right to left. Applying the reverse traversals from right to left yield exactly the same sequences as in (13a–c).

(12)

(13) a. Reverse Preorder: {A, B, C, D, E}

  b. Reverse Inorder: {B, A, D, C, E}

  c. Reverse Postorder: {B, D, E, C, A}

Kural claims that once a grammar sets the branching direction of the trees, it 'feeds into the traversal algorithms'. That is, if the branching direction of the trees is set as left to right for a given language, then the order in the traversal algorithms will also be set as left to right. However, it is not at all clear why the branching direction of the trees should covary with the traversal direction of the algorithms. The branching direction of trees and the traversal direction of the algorithms are logically independent, and nothing seems to impose the same directionality in both.

Further, Kural argues paradoxically that the reportedly rare VOS, OVS, and OSV orders can readily be derived by countering the traversal direction against the branching direction, without demonstrating the actual processes of traversal linearization, leaving their verification to the reader.

Let us see, then, how they work out, with the same X′-tree (2), applying the reverse traversals. The respective reverse traversals yield the sequences in (14).

(14) a. {CP, IP, I′, VP, DP, NP, *man*, D, *the*, V, *bite*, I, *will*, DP, NP, *dog*, D, *the*, C, Ø}

   b. {*man*, NP, DP, *the*, D, VP, *bite*, V, I′, *will*, I, IP, *dog*, NP, DP, *the*, D, CP, C, Ø}

   c. {*man*, NP, *the*, D, DP, *bite*, V, VP, *will*, I, I′, *dog*, NP, *the*, D, DP, IP, Ø, C, CP}

Extracting only the phrasal nodes produces the following sequences, respectively.

(15) a. Reverse Preorder: {CP, IP, VP, DP, NP, DP, NP}

   b. Reverse Inorder: {NP, DP, VP, IP, NP, DP, CP}

   c. Reverse Postorder: {NP, DP, VP, NP, DP, IP, CP}

And their categorial reductions are the following:

(16) a. Reverse Preorder: {C, I, V, D, N, D, N}   (C)(I)VOS

   b. Reverse Inorder: {N, D, V, I, N, D, C}   OV(I)S(C)

   c. Reverse Postorder: {N, D, V, N, D, I, C}   OVS(I)(C) → O(t_V)SV(+I)(C)

Assuming the V-to-I movement, the reverse postorder (16c) instantiates the OSV word order, one of the three rare cases.

Kural seems to be taking the fact that these typologically rare word orders can readily be derived with the same mechanism, to be one of the theoretical advantages over the analyses of word-order variations in terms of movement. Yet, it strikes me as not at all desirable. The virtue of Kural's tree traversal linearization is the fact that the typologically common word orders of VSO, SVO, and SOV can be obtained from the same single structure without excessive self-serving movement.[4] If the rare orders of VOS, OVS, and OSV can be just as easily derived as

---

[4] Modulo the V-to-I movement for the VSO order.

underlying orders, we would not be surprised to find that all the word orders are more or less equally prevalent. If VOS, OVS, and OSV orders are indeed rare, they should not be equally derivable as the other three cross-linguistically common word orders VSO, SVO, and SOV. They ought to be derived by some movements that the majority of the world's languages do not employ, not as underlying orders; hence, typologically rare.

Furthermore, as a reviewer points out, Kural simply takes for granted the specifier–head–complement order (or its mirror image) in the X′-theoretic trees. Kayne (1994), on the other hand, partly derives it as a sort of a theorem from the LCA. Despite their initial appearances to the contrary, Kural's linearization procedure by tree traversal is in a way similar to the LCA-based linearization procedure in spirit; the latter takes the partial orders in asymmetric c-command whereas Kural's takes them in mutual c-command with the left–right ordering: the left subtree, the parent, and the right subtree. After all, they are both extracting a linear order of terminal words from (strict) partial orders that preexist in the hierarchical structures.

13.3 Bare Phrase Structure

The empirical problem for Kural's (2005) tree traversal linearization derives from the head-adjunction structure, and the theoretical problem from the branching directions in the phrase structure trees and the references to them in the algorithms. In order to resolve the problem of the branching directions of syntactic structures, let us adopt the Minimalist theory of Bare Phrase Structure (BPS) as advanced in Chomsky (1995a,b), which assumes no directions of branching, and consider how head movement should be treated in BPS.

Chomsky (1995a,b) supplants the representational schemata of the X′-theory with BPS, subjecting various concepts and hidden assumptions in the X′-theory to Minimalist scrutiny. Following Muysken (1982), levels of projections in BPS are taken to be relational properties, contextually determined in derivations.

(17)   Given a phrase marker, a category that does not project any further is a maximal projection XP, and one that is not a projection at all is a minimal projection X^0; any other is an X′, invisible at the interface and for computation.

(Chomsky 1995b: 396)

Thus, there is no non-branching unary projection, and a minimal projection, equivalent to X^0 in the traditional X′-theoretic sense, can be maximal at the same time, equivalent to a non-branching XP in the traditional X′-theory.

(18)

Bare Phrase Structure projections	traditional X′ projections
[+ maximal, + minimal] (X^{0max})	XP (non-branching)
[+ maximal, − minimal] (XP)	XP (branching)
[− maximal, + minimal] (X^0)	X^0
[− maximal, − minimal] (X′)	X′

Syntactic objects are lexical items or phrasal constituents already formed out of them. BPS is built up incrementally step-by-step in the course of the derivation, with the operations Merge and Move.[5] Merge is a recursive operation that applies to two syntactic objects α and β, projecting either α or β.[6] The syntactic object so formed is a labelled set $\gamma = \{\delta, \{\alpha, \beta\}\}$, where δ is the label of γ, indicating the head of γ, either $\delta =$ H(α) or H(β), the head of α or β. A typical structure of specifier–head–complement can be informally represented in a familiar tree diagram as in the following.

(19) $\zeta = \{\eta, \{\varepsilon, \gamma\}\}$ ($= \{\eta, \{\varepsilon, \{\gamma, \{\alpha, \beta\}\}\}\}$)
$= \{\alpha, \{\varepsilon, \{\alpha, \beta\}\}\}$ if α, the head of γ, projects)

ε $\gamma = \{\delta, \{\alpha, \beta\}\}$ ($= \{\alpha, \{\alpha, \beta\}\}$ if α projects)

α β

The nodes, i.e. syntactic objects, are labelled directly with a lexical item that heads the projection, dispensing with category labels or projection levels, such as P, N′, VP, etc.

Multiple specifiers are allowed in principle, and it is assumed that there is no linear ordering among nodes in narrow syntax.[7] For linearization, Chomsky (1995a,b) partly incorporates the LCA into BPS, assuming that ordering applies to the output of the morphological subcomponent in the phonological component, assigning a temporal left-to-right linear order to the output elements of the morphology subcomponent.

The problem for BPS to fully embrace Kayne's (1994) original version of the LCA is the fact that no linear order can be determined when the complement is a simplex terminal, as the complement and its head mutually c-command each other. As possible solutions, Chomsky (1995a,b) suggests that either the LCA is to be weakened

---

[5] The operation Move was taken to be the combination of Merge + Feature-Checking (+ Generalized Pied-Piping, if overt) in Chomsky (1995a,b), and later as Merge + Agree + Pied-Piping in Chomsky (2004), where Move is reconceptualized as *internal Merge* (IM) with the original Merge as *external Merge* (EM).

[6] For possibilities of projecting both α and β, or neither α nor β, see i.a. Citko (2008a,b).

[7] Chomsky (2000) further suggests that adjunct modifiers may belong to a dimension distinct from the ones for the core structure of predicate-arguments, implicating dimensions higher than two. For possible deployments of adjunct modifiers in such another dimension, see i.a. Pietroski and Uriagereka (2001); Irurtzun and Gallego (to appear).

to admit non-total orderings, or to optionally ignore or delete traces of symmetry-breaking movement in mutual c-command relations.[8]

Segment projections are distinguished from category projections by labelling. The label of a segment projection is an ordered pair of the lexical item that heads the projection. Thus, in the following representation, α is the head of the structure, β the complement, δ a specifier, and ϵ an adjunct, and ζ_1 and ζ_2 are segments of the category ζ, the maximal projection of α.

(20) $\zeta_1 = \{\langle\alpha, \alpha\rangle, \{\{\{\alpha, \beta\}, \delta\}, \epsilon\}\} = \{\langle\alpha, \alpha\rangle, \{\{\gamma, \delta\}, \epsilon\}\} = \{\langle\alpha, \alpha\rangle, \{\zeta_2, \epsilon\}\}$

ϵ $\zeta_2 = \{\alpha, \{\{\alpha, \beta\}, \delta\}\} = \{\alpha, \{\gamma, \delta\}\}$

δ $\gamma = \{\alpha, \{\alpha, \beta\}\}$

α β

When we consider a segmented structure with head-to-head adjunction, it is not clear how its projections should be labelled.

(21) $\zeta = \{?, \{\{\{\epsilon, \alpha\}, \beta\}, \delta\}\} = \{?, \{\{\alpha, \beta\}, \delta\}\} = \{?, \{\gamma, \delta\}\}$

δ $\gamma = \{?, \{\{\epsilon, \alpha\}, \beta\}\} = \{?, \{\alpha, \beta\}\}$

$\{\langle\alpha, \alpha\rangle, \{\epsilon, \alpha\}\} = \alpha$ β

ϵ α

Here, α is the head of the maximal projection ζ, to which another head ϵ is adjoined, β is the complement, and δ is the specifier. Chomsky (1995a,b) does not elucidate how γ and ζ are labelled; whether they should be labelled as $\langle\alpha, \alpha\rangle$ since they are projecting from the upper segment of α whose label is $\langle\alpha, \alpha\rangle$, or simply as α, since their head is α and $\langle\alpha, \alpha\rangle$ is not their head but the label of only the upper segment of their head α.[9]

Recall that the empirical problem, in Kural's (2005) tree traversal linearization with head-extraction upon visiting a maximal projection, has to do with the fact that the I-to-C adjoined auxiliary precedes the fronted *wh*-phrase in the preorder traversal for VSO languages. Not only for Kural, head-to-head adjunction has been a

---

[8] For various solutions to reconcile the LCA with BPS, see i.a. Moro (1997b, 2000), Guimarães (2000), and Fortuny (2008).

[9] In Chomsky (2000), segments and categories are distinguished, not by labels but with an order in the constituent as $\{\gamma, \langle\alpha, \beta\rangle\}$ and $\{\gamma, \{\alpha, \beta\}\}$, respectively formed by two subtypes of the Merge operation, *Pair*-Merge and *Set*-Merge. In such a system, the upper segment of the head α in (21) should be $\{a, \langle\epsilon, \alpha\rangle\}$, $\gamma = \{a, \{\langle\epsilon, \alpha\rangle, \beta\}\} = \{a, \{\alpha, \beta\}\}$, and $\zeta = \{a, \{\{\langle\epsilon, \alpha\rangle, \beta\}, \delta\}\} = \{a, \{\gamma, \delta\}\}$, respectively. Nevertheless, the congenital problems of the head-to-head adjunction discussed below are not solved by these innovations.

perennial troublemaker since the inception of the X′-theory, and it still is in BPS. The adjoined head does not c-command its trace in the strict first-branching definition of c-command. It is a counter-cyclic operation, violating the Extension Requirement of Chomsky (1993: 22ff.); head-to-head adjunction does not create a new root node that extends the whole structure.

Furthermore, as Gärtner (1995) points out, the upper segment $\{\langle a, a \rangle, \{\epsilon, a\}\} = a$ of a complex head in (21) should count as a non-minimal non-maximal projection, since it 'projects' to γ and further to ζ while it 'is a projection' of the lower segment a, the original head that hosts the adjunction of ϵ. Then, the whole complex head should be 'invisible' to any further operations, just as X′ projections are; see (17). A consequence would be that no head-adjoined complex head can ever be further moved, contrary to the standard assumption of successive cyclic head-to-head adjunction, such as V-to-I-to-C movement, for example.

In an attempt to maintain the structure-preserving hypothesis (Emonds 1976), Chomsky (1995b: 406, (14)) stipulates the following condition:

(22) A chain is uniform with regard to phrase structure status [i.e. projection levels—TT].

By (22), X^0-to-XP adjunction in the traditional sense is ruled out (*pace* Carnie 2000). If a non-maximal X^0 adjoins to an XP, the X^0 will become maximal, by definition.

In the same vein, however, (22) prevents any movement of a non-maximal X^0 category. In the standard case of head-to-head adjunction, V^0-to-I^0 movement, for instance, a non-uniform chain is created: V^0 projects VP at its base position. After adjoining to I^0, the moved V^0 does not project VP there. Therefore, it is non-maximal at its base position while maximal at the landing-site.

Recognizing this problem, Chomsky (1995b: 405, (12), 409, (21)) stipulates the further provisos for head-to-head adjunction.

(23) Morphology gives no output (so the derivation crashes) if presented with an element that is not an X^0.

(24) At LF, X^0 is submitted to independent word-interpretation processes WI, where WI ignores principles of C_{HL} [computational system for human language: TT], within X^0.

This state of affairs has prompted various proposals. One approach is to relegate head movement to the PF component (i.a. Chomsky 2000, 2001; Boeckx and Stjepanović 2001; cf. Zwart 2001; Lechner 2006), and another is by interarboreal movement (i.a. Bobaljik 1995, Bobaljik and Brown 1997; cf. Nunes 2001, 2004). Other approaches include the elimination of head movement altogether, in terms of remnant movement (i.a. Koopman and Szabolcsi 2000; Mahajan 2003), or reprojection of the moved head (i.a. Koeneman 2000; Bury 2003; cf.

Hornstein and Uriagereka 2002). There is another approach pursued in Toyoshima (1997, *et seq.*) and by many others since (i.a. Fukui and Takano 1998; Landau 2006; Matushansky 2006; Vicente 2007) that a head moves into one of multiple specifiers, head-to-specifier movement, which I will adopt here.[10]

In BPS, there is no structure that can be preserved in the traditional sense (Emonds 1976), as structures are built up incrementally, and projection levels are derivatives of structure-building processes, changing in the course of derivation. Thus, (22) is not a tenable condition, and hence its further provisos (23) and (24) are either spurious or redundant.

13.4 BPS traversals: proposal

Adopting head-to-specifier movement into BPS, I propose several modifications to Kural's (2005) tree traversal linearization. As BPS is an unordered tree without fixed directions of branching, possibly multi-dimensional, we need some ways of referring to its unordered children/subtrees. Thus, I define the two distinct relations in domination and the non-distinctness of labels as follows:

(25)   **Domination Relations**

　　a. A child/subtree is ***consanguineous*** if its label is *non-distinct* from that of its parent.

　　b. A child/subtree is ***adopted*** if its label is distinct from that of its parent.

(26)   **Label Non-distinctness**
　　Labels are ***non-distinct*** iff they are of the projections of the same token of the same lexical item.

Instead of left or right, we refer to the children/subtrees as ***consanguineous*** or ***adopted***, dispensing with the ordering direction. Assuming the binary branching of BPS, the ***consanguineous*** children/subtrees inherit the same label of their parent node, modulo the projection levels.[11] The ***consanguineous*** relation picks out a head projection, while the ***adopted*** relations are of a specifier, a complement, or an adjunct.

Then, I modify the traversal algorithms as below, making the action performed by 'visit' more explicit.

---

[10] Perhaps, the earliest precursor of the idea that a head moves into a specifier may be traced back to Maling (1980) for stylistic fronting in Icelandic, where a head category competes for the subject position. Others include Koopman's (1984) analysis of predicate cleft in Vata, where a V head is moved to Spec-CP in current terms, and Källgren and Prince (1989) and Holmberg (1999) for verb topicalization in Yiddish and in Mainland Scandinavian, respectively.

[11] The inheritance of the label is from the perspective of the dominance relations in a tree. From the perspective of projection, the parent node inherits the label from a child/subtree. The projection levels are always distinct, but they are not annotated. They are determined in the structural contexts at a given point in derivation.

(27)   BPS traversals
　　　 Starting from the root, at a given node *N*:
　　　 a. Preorder:　　Spell out the label if maximal.
　　　　　 i. If a child is consanguineous but childless, traverse that child. Otherwise, recursively traverse its adopted subtree/child.
　　　 b. Inorder:　　Spell out the label if maximal.
　　　　　 ii. Recursively traverse the other subtree/child that has not been traversed.
　　　 c. Postorder:　Spell out the label if maximal.

By the maximal label, I mean the label of a maximal projection, which can readily be read off in the structural contexts. The projection levels need not to be indicated on their labels (see note 11). If the parent of a given node bears a distinct label, the label of that node is maximal; otherwise, non-maximal. To put it another way, if the parent is *consanguineous*, the given node bears a non-maximal label; otherwise, maximal.

　　With these, let us see now how the problematic case of *wh*-movement in (7) can be dealt with. The BPS tree representation of the X′-tree (7), with head-to-specifier movement, would be something like the following, with irrelevant details omitted for ease of exposition.

(28)

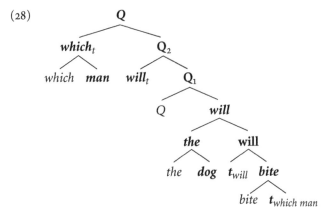

Hereafter, the **bold italic** indicates maximal projections; the *plain italic*, minimal projections; and the **plain bold**, intermediate projections, i.e. [–maximal, –minimal], for ease of expository distinction.

　　The BPS traversal in preorder (27a) of the BPS tree (28) yields the sequence (29).

(29)　{Q, *which*$_t$, which, *man*, **Q$_2$**, *will*$_t$, **Q$_1$**, Q, *will*, **the**, *the*, *dog*, *will*, *t*$_{will}$, **bite**, *bite*, *t*$_{which\ man}$}

Starting from the root **Q** of the entire tree, its child node **Q$_2$** is consanguineous but with children. Thus, the traversal proceeds to the adopted subtree of **Q**, which is the subtree rooted at **which**$_t$. Recursively starting from the node **which**$_t$ as the root, the child *which* is consanguineous and childless, so it is visited next. Then, the other child *man*, which has not been traversed, is traversed. As there is no more subtree/child to be traversed deeper, the traversal backtracks to the parent Q, and proceeds to the other subtree rooted at Q_2. Starting from Q_2 as the root, the traversal next visits the adopted child *will$_t$*, as the consanguineous child Q_1 is not childless. Then, the traversal backtracks to Q_2, and visits the other subtree rooted at Q_1, and so on.

Note, in passing, that the I-to-Spec-CP moved head *will$_t$* is a maximal projection as well as a minimal projection; it does not project any further at its landing site (Spec-CP), nor is it a projection of any other category.

Categorial reduction of (29) by the action step 'spell out the label if maximal' in the preorder traversal (27a) yields the following sequence, with expository annotations of the relevant trace positions for ease of discussion:

(30)   {Q, *which$_t$*, *man*, *will$_t$*, *will*, *the*, *dog*, (t_{will}) *bite*, ($t_{which\ man}$)}

Here, there are two *will*s. The first *will$_t$* on the left was originally a non-maximal projection, that is, the I head of the IP projection, moved to Spec-CP, and became maximal; its virtual trace position is indicated as t_{will} in (30). The second *will* on the right is the spelled-out maximal label of the IP projection, registering the otherwise *in situ* position of the head *will* if it had not moved. In other words, the second *will* on the right *is* the trace copy of the I-to-Spec-CP moved *will$_t$* in this system. Thus, if movement is overt, the second *will* on the right will not be phonetically realized by whatever conditions block the phonetic realization of the trace copies for overt movement. Then, the final sequence produced is the following:

(31)   {Q, *which$_t$*, *man*, *will$_t$*, *the*, *dog*, *bite*}

Unlike Kural's (2005) tree traversal with head extraction, the moved I-head *will$_t$* correctly follows the moved *wh*-phrase **which man**. And yet, it still follows the complementizer, the question morpheme Q. Nevertheless, Q does not have any phonetic content, so the same problem (9) with Kural's (2005) does not arise.

What if the complementizer Q is phonetically overt? Such appears to be the case in Irish, perhaps the best studied VSO language in the generative literature. Consider the following *wh*-question in Irish (McCloskey 1979: 52, (2a)).

(32)   Cén   fear   a^N bhfaigheann tú   an   t-airgead uaidh?
        which   man   COMP   get   you   the   money   from.him
        'Which man do you get the money from?'

The *wh*-phrase *cén fear* 'which man' precedes the overt particle *a^N* that McCloskey (1979) identifies as a complementizer, which appears to be a problem for the present proposal.

However, there is a reason to believe that the overt particle is not in the C-head position. There are embedded topicalization-like constructions in Irish, in which the fronted material precedes the embedded 'complementizer' particle (McCloskey 1996).

(33) a. Deiridís   [an chéad Nollaig   eile   **go**   dtiocfadh   sé aníos].
      they.used.to.say the first   Christmas other COMP would.come he up
      'They used to say [that next Christmas, he would come up].'

   b. Fuair   muid amach [na mic léinn   ar   éirigh go maith leo
      found   we   out   the students COMP rose   well   with.them
      go   raibh siad   dall].
      COMP   were they   blind
      'We discovered [that the students who had done well were blind].'

   c. Tá sé   ráite ariamh má   cháineann tú   sagart [maithiúnas
      is   it   said   ever   if   censure   you   priest forgiveness
      nach   bhfaighidh   tú].
      COMP.NEG   will.get   you
      'It has always been said that if you criticize a priest, [you will never be forgiven].'

Assuming that adjunction to an argument is barred (Chomsky 1986), McCloskey (1996) claims that the fronted constituents are adjoined to IP and the 'complementizer' particle lowers to the I-head position. Syntactic lowering is generally problematic for the bottom-up theories, and McCloskey contends that it takes place in PF.

   In the present proposal, a syntactic account for these facts is possible without head lowering, even in PF; the 'complementizer' particle is, in fact, an I-head, which needs to be licensed in the CP projection, by moving into Spec-CP. The example (32) has the following kind of structure:

(34)

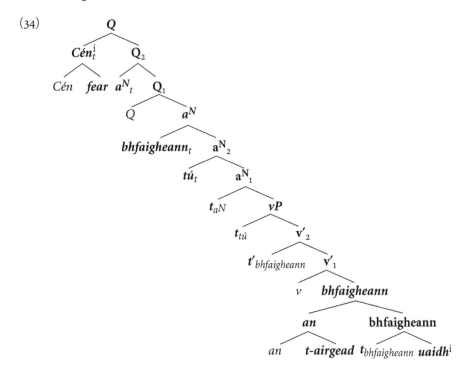

The *wh*-phrase *cén fear* 'which man' is in the outer specifier of Q, binding *uaidh* 'from him', a resumptive pronoun syncretized with a preposition, whereas the 'complementizer' particle a^N moves to the inner specifier of Q.[12]

Kural's (2005) approach in head-to-head adjunction, on the other hand, either ends up with a wrong order as in (9) or has to resort to head lowering before linearization.

13.5 Disharmonic word order and the Traversal Parameter

13.5.1 Wh-*movement and verb raising in Vata*

Given the BPS traversals I have proposed, the inorder and postorder traversals in the BPS tree (28) yield the following sequences after categorial reduction, respectively, again with trace positions annotated, including the maximal label *qua* the trace copy of head-to-specifier movement, with ~~double strikethrough~~.

(35)   a.   {which$_t$, man, Q, will$_t$, the, dog, ~~will~~, (t_{will_t}) *bite*(, $t_{which\ man}$)}

   b.   {man, which$_t$, will$_t$, dog, the, (t_{will_t}) ($t_{man\ which_t}$) *bite*, ~~will~~, Q}

A plain English *wh*-question is instantiated in (35a) as the object *wh*-question in SVO languages. The postorder traversal is for SOV languages as in Kural's (2005) original proposal, and (35b) may be instantiating the object *wh*-question in Vata, as reported in Koopman (1984). Categorially, (35b) has the following sequence:

(36)   {N, D$_{wh}$, I$_t$, N, D, (t_{I_t}) ($t_{N,\ Dwh_t}$) V, ~~I~~, C$_Q$}

The first N–D$_{wh}$ sequence is the *wh*-moved object and the second N–D sequence is the subject. The first I$_t$ is the moved head of the IP projection while the second ~~I~~ reflects its *in situ* position. Were there no auxiliary inversion, the sequence would have been the following:

(37)   {N, D$_{wh}$, N, D, ($t_{N,\ Dwh_t}$) V, I, C$_Q$}

This appears to correspond to a simple object *wh*-question in Vata such as the following:

(38)   àlÓ   Kòfí   yÉ̀ t_{wh} t_v yé   lá
       who   Kofi   saw   PRT   Q
       'Who did Kofi see?'

---

[12] Irish employs a resumptive strategy for *wh*-questions that differs from relativization and other A′-dependencies. See McCloskey (1979) for details. Note also that here, the finite verb moves to the outer Spec-IP and the subject to the inner Spec-IP, a theoretical possibility opened up with the head-to-specifier movement. See Fukui and Takano (1998) and Toyoshima (2000, 2001), for such analyses of the Irish VSO word order and discussion in section 13.6.1.

For determining the relative ordering among multiple specifiers in terms of an economy condition, see Toyoshima (2000, 2009).

Assuming that the particle *yé* is an auxiliary at the I-head and the verb *yÉ`* 'saw' moves to Spec-IP, its BPS tree representation with an English gloss will be (39), with the branching directions appropriated for SOV languages in the manner of the more familiar X′-theoretic representation for ease of illustration.

(39)

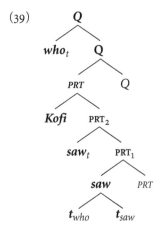

The postorder traversal in BPS tree (39) yields the sequence (40) whose categorial reduction is (41), which in turn is translated into the Vata lexical items in (42).

(40) {*who$_t$*, Q, *Kofi*, *saw$_t$*, PRT, (*t$_{saw}$*) (*t$_{who}$*) ~~saw~~, PRT$_1$, PRT$_2$, PRT, Q, Q}

(41) {*who*, *Kofi*, *saw*, (*t$_{saw}$*) (*t$_{who}$*) ~~saw~~, PRT, Q}

(42) {àlÓ, Kòfí, yÉ`, (*t$_{saw}$*) (*t$_{who}$*) ~~yÉ`~~, yé, lá}

According to Koopman, Vata is a head-final language, but exhibits a mixed ordering: the SVO order in simple tenses (43a) and S(Aux)OV order in compound tenses (43b).

(43) a. à   lì   sàká
         we   ate   rice
         'We ate rice.'

      b. à   lā   sàká   lī
         we   have   rice   eaten
         'We have eaten rice.'

Koopman argues that in simplex tenses, the verb raises to I from the underlying S(I) OV structure, where the perfect auxiliary resides. Assuming that the perfect auxiliary *lā* is *v* that raises to Spec-IP, (43a,b) in the present proposal have the respective BPS tree representations as in (44a,b), shown in English gloss, omitting irrelevant details.

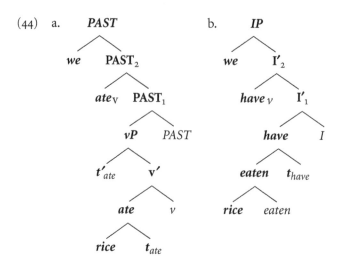

(44)   a.   **PAST**   b.   **IP**

The postorder traversal in the BPS tree representations (44a,b) yields the following sequences, respectively.

(45)   a.   {*we, ate*ᵥ, *PAST*, (*t′*ₐₜₑ₎) *v*, (*t*ₐₜₑ₎) *rice*, ~~*ate*~~, *v′*, *vP*, *PAST*₁, *PAST*₂, *PAST*}
       b.   {*we, have*ᵥ, *I*, (*t*ₕₐᵥₑ₎) *eaten*, *rice*, *eaten*, ~~*have*~~, *I′*₁, *I′*₂, *IP*}

And their respective reduction as below:

(46)   a.   {*we, ate, rice, PAST*}
       b.   {*we, have, rice, eaten, IP*}

In essence, the verb or the auxiliary, whichever is finite, moves to Spec-IP for its finiteness to be licensed.[13]

In these perspectives, an apparent problem of the word order in Vata relative clauses falls into places, where the object follows the past tense particle and the relative marker, as in the following (Koopman 1984: 61, (46)):

(47)   kÖ (mÖmÖ̀) Ò̀   lī -dā-ɓÖ̀   zué   sàká,...
       man HIM-HIM he-R eat-PT-REL yesterday rice
       'the man who was eating rice yesterday,...'

The lexical verb *lī* follows the resumptive pronoun *Ò̀*, obligatory for subject relativization, which in turn follows the optional relative pronoun *mÖmÖ̀*.

I would claim that the past tense particle *-dā* and the relative marker *-ɓÖ̀* are suffixed/encliticized to the lexical verb, forming a single unit as a V head, before they

---

[13] Whether we treat the perfect auxiliary *lā* (*have*ᵥ in 44b) as the base-generated I-head or the *v*-head adjoined to I, it will surface in clause-final position, indicated with *IP* in (46b), in Kural's (2005) head-extraction approach with head-to-head adjunction, the verification of which I leave to the reader, for the reason of space.

enter into syntactic computation (the lexicalist hypothesis), and the complex *overtly* raises to Spec-IP for the past tense to be licensed, and *covertly* onto Spec-CP for relativization, yielding the traversed sequence (48) from the structure as in (49), with covert parts of structure indicated with *outline italics*.

(48) {*man*^{i}, (HIM-HIM^i,) C, *he*-R^i, eat-PT-REL$_t$, I, ($t'$$_{eat-PT-REL}$,) v, *yesterday*, ($t_{eat-PT-REL}$,) *rice*, eat-PT-REL$'$, ~~eat-PT-REL~~, v$'$, ~~vP~~, I$'_1$, I$'_2$, ~~IP~~, C$'_1$, ~~CP~~, ~~D/NP~~}

(49)

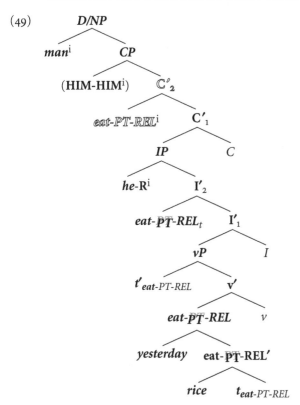

In otherwise well-behaved head-final nature in Vata, another disharmonic pattern appears in the position of the tensed complement clauses as below (Koopman 1984: 89, (110c)):

(50) ń   nÍ   gblì   nā   Ò   yì
      I   NEG-A   know   NA   he   came
      'I did not know that he arrived.' *or* 'I did not know whether he arrived.'

Tensed complement clauses are introduced by *nā*, following the selecting verb. From the literal translation in (50), it would appear that *nā* is a *bona fide* complementizer, just like *that* or *whether* in English. Koopman argues, however, that it is a kind of verb of saying, formalized and deprived of its semantic content, and it can be selected only by a certain class of verbs. In turn, *nā* selects a tensed complement clause whose head is phonetically empty, and the tensed complement clause is obligatorily extraposed to the right.

In the present proposal, the matrix verb 'know' selects, as its complement, a bare VP headed by *nā* as a verb that in turn selects a tensed CP whose head is phonetically empty Ø, and *nā* moves to Spec-VP headed by the matrix verb 'know,' perhaps for licensing its selection property, which in turn raises to Spec-*v*P, headed by a negative auxiliary that moves to Spec-IP as a finite auxiliary, as in the following kind of structure, with irrelevant details omitted for ease of exposition:

(51)

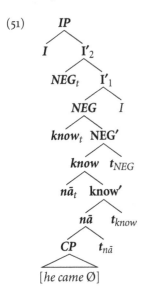

The postorder BPS traversal will yield the following sequence:

(52)   {*I, NEG$_t$, I, know$_t$, (t$_{NEG}$), nā$_t$, (t$_{know}$) (t$_{nā}$) CP, ~~nā~~, know', ~~know~~, NEG', ~~NEG~~, I'$_1$, I'$_2$, IP*}

Reducing to the maximal labels will be following:

(53)   {*I, NEG$_t$, know$_t$, nā$_t$, CP, ~~nā~~, ~~know~~, ~~NEG~~, IP*}

Cleaning up the maximal labels qua traces, and filling the material of the complement CP will yield the final string as follows:

(54)   {*I, NEG$_t$, know$_t$, nā$_t$, [he came Ø], IP*}

In this analysis, neither the embedded complementizer Ø nor **IP** has phonetic content.

As can be seen, the tensed complementation can be accounted for without (rightward) extraposition of the tensed complement CP.

13.5.2 *Root vs embedded clauses in German*

Unlike in Vata, embedded clauses in German always follow their embedding verbs, and within embedded clauses, a verb follows its non-clausal objects. In root clauses, non-finite verbs also follow their non-clausal objects, and the highest finite (auxiliary) verb appears as the 'second' constituent, which is known as the verb-second phenomenon. If there is no auxiliary and the lexical verb is finite, the word order in the root clause is SVO.[14]

Given the facts that the tensed embedded clauses always follow their embedding verbs, that the determiners precede nouns, and that adpositions are generally prepositional, I assume that German is underlyingly an SVO language like English, so the traversal method employed for German is the inorder (27b).

Let us consider the following kind of embedded clause.

(55) …daß der Hund den Mann gebissen haben wird
      …that the dog the man bitten have will
      '…that the dog will have bitten the man'

Assuming that the perfect auxiliary *haben* 'have' is *v*, I stipulate that in German, *v* as a phase head projects a [postorder] feature to its maximal projection and the C-head of the selected CP as a phase assigns its complement IP with a [postorder] feature. The BPS tree representation of (55) would be something like (56) below.

(56)

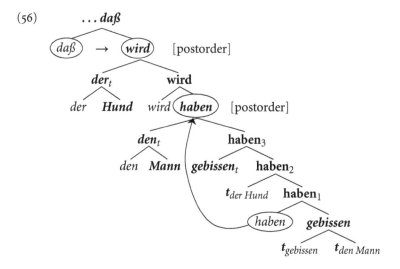

Starting from the CP-node *daß* as the root, the inorder traversal first visits its consanguineous child with no children of itself, the C-head *daß*, then back onto its parent, the CP-node *daß*, spelling it out as it bears a maximal label, and then traverses to the other subtree rooted at the IP-node *wird*. Then, starting from the IP-node *wird* as the root, the inorder traversal first visits the subject DP *der Hund* as the adopted subtree since the consanguineous child node I′ *wird* is not childless.

After spelling out *der Hund*, the inorder traversal comes back to the parent node IP *wird*, but by stipulation, it is marked with a [postorder] feature from the C-head *daß*, so it will be skipped until the postorder visit. The inorder traversal then goes onto the other subtree rooted at I′ *wird*. Then, the inorder traversal restarts from the I′-node *wird*, visiting its consanguineous and childless node, the I-head *wird*, and then back to the I′-node *wird*, without spelling them out, as they are not maximal. Then, the inorder traversal moves onto the other subtree *v*P rooted at *haben*.

Starting from the *v*P-node *haben* as the root, the inorder traversal first visits its adopted subtree *den Mann*, the object DP, shifted perhaps for the reasons of Case and/or agreement. After spelling out *den Mann*, the inorder traversal returns to the parent *v*P-node *haben*, but again by stipulation, it is marked with a [postorder] feature so the traversal skips it to the other subtree rooted at the *v*′-node $\mathbf{haben_3}$.

From the *v*′ node $\mathbf{haben_3}$, the inorder traversal first visits its adopted child *gebissen*, the moved V-head, and spells it out. Then, the inorder traversal visits its parent *v*′ node $\mathbf{haben_3}$ without spelling it out, as it is not a maximal projection. Then, the inorder traversal moves on to the other subtree rooted at another *v*′ node $\mathbf{haben_2}$.

Starting from the *v*′ node $\mathbf{haben_2}$, the inorder traversal first visits its adopted subtree rooted at $t_{der\ Hund}$, but as it is a trace copy of the moved subject, it is not spelled out. Then, the inorder traversal visits its parent *v*′-node $\mathbf{haben_2}$, again without spelling it out. Then, it goes down on to the other subtree rooted at another *v*′-node $\mathbf{haben_1}$.

Starting from the *v*′-node $\mathbf{haben_1}$, the inorder traversal first visits its childless consanguineous child, the *v*-head *haben*, then back on to the *v*′ node $\mathbf{haben_1}$, and then down onto the other subtree rooted at the VP-node *gebissen*. The inorder traversal starts from the VP-node *gebissen*, going down to its consanguineous child $t_{gebissen}$, and visits back the VP-node *gebissen*, and then down to the other child $t_{den\ Mann}$.

As the bottom of the tree is reached and there are no more branches to be traversed deeper, the inorder traversal comes back to the root CP node *daß* of the entire tree. On its way back, it traverses the *v*P-node *haben* and the IP-node *wird*, spelling them out in that order, as both are marked with a [postorder] feature by stipulation, and the traversal order is now the same as the postorder.

To summarize, the inorder traversal of the BPS tree (56) yields the following sequence:

(57) {*daß, daß, der, der, Hund, wird,* **wird, den, Mann, gebissen, haben₃,** ($t_{der\ Hund}$),
      haben₂, *haben,* **haben₁,** ($t_{gebissen}$) ~~gebissen~~, ($t_{den\ Mann}$) **haben, wird**}

Reducing it to the maximal labels that are spelled out, would be as follows:

(58) {*daß, der, Hund, den, Mann, gebissen, haben, wird*}

Assuming further that the finiteness of the perfect auxiliary does not need to be overtly licensed in the IP domain (see note 15 below), an embedded clause without a modal auxiliary, such as (59), would have a structure like (60).

(59) ...daß   der   Hund   den   Mann   gebissen   hat
      ...that   the   dog   the   man   bitten   has
      '...that the dog has bitten the man'

(60)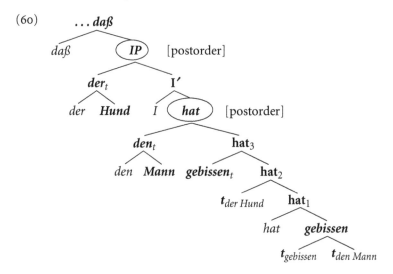

And the final yield will be the following:

(61) {*daß, der, Hund, den, Mann, gebissen, hat, IP*}

In root clauses, finite (auxiliary) verbs moves to Spec-CP for the verb-second effect, via Spec-IP, I assume, as in the following.[15]

---

[15] Vikner (1995) observes that in Mainland Scandinavian VO languages in the Germanic family, a finite (auxiliary) verb in root clauses never surfaces in the IP domain though it can in the CP domain. German perhaps shares this property. See also Kayne (1989) for participle agreement in Romance that manifests only when the direct object moves past the participle but the object never surfaces at its intermediate landing-site.

(62) Gestern   hat   der   Hund   den   Mann   gebissen.
     yesterday has   the   dog   the   man   bitten
     'Yesterday, the dog bit the man.'

As a root clause, CP is not selected, and hence by stipulation, it does not have a [postorder] feature to assign to its complement IP. Even though the *v*P-node *hat* is still marked with a [postorder] feature, it has no effect on the final Spell-Out as its head has moved out.

(63)

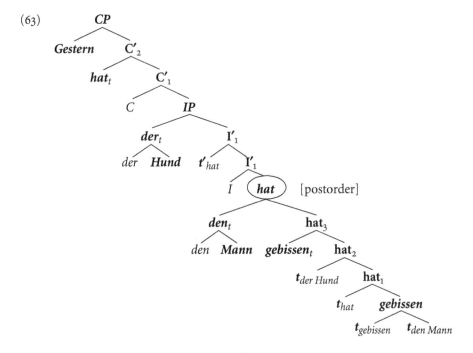

The sequence produced from (63) is the following:

(64)   {*Gestern, CP, hat, der, Hund, IP, den, Mann, gebissen, ~~hat~~*}

Finally, consider a root clause that takes a CP complement, such as the following:

(65) Wir   sollten   gedacht   haben   [cp daß...]
      we   should   thought   have   that
      'We should have thought that...'

The structure of (65) would be something like the following:

(66)

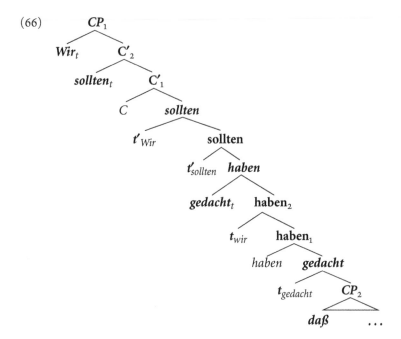

Unlike a DP object, the CP complement does not shift into the *v*P domain, perhaps as CP does not need Case. Suppose, for some reason, that the *v*-head *haben* does not project any [postorder] feature to its maximal projection *v*P, perhaps because it does not license Case.

Then, the traversal is just the inorder, and when it reaches the *v*P-node *haben*, it first visits the adopted child, the moved V-head *gedacht*ₜ, then back to its parent *v*P-node *haben*, and down onto the other subtree rooted at the *v*′-node *haben*₂, and further down to the complement clause CP₂.

The traversed sequence is as follows:

(67)   {*Wir*ₜ, *CP*₁, *sollten*ₜ, *C*′₂, *C*, *C*′₁, (*t*′_*Wir*) ~~*sollten*~~, (*t*_*sollten*) *sollten*, *gedacht*ₜ, *haben*,
          (*t*_*Wir*) **haben**₂, *haben*, **haben**₁, (*t*_*gedacht*) ~~*gedacht*~~, *CP*₂}

The assumption that the DP objects shift and the lexical verbs move into the *v*P projection is not uncontroversial but not particularly unreasonable or peculiar to our analyses. Although the analyses are tentative and speculative, with the stipulations of the [postorder] features, together with the absence of such features in the root clauses that take a CP complement, the BPS traversal linearization can, as the first approximation, give an account for the basic disharmonic patterns in German that invites further improvements.

13.6 Predictions and implications

13.6.1 (Non-)adjacency and long-distance head movement

The present proposal makes interesting and perhaps surprising predictions about the correspondence between linear ordering and movement. Consider the following schematic structures.

(68)   a.   b.

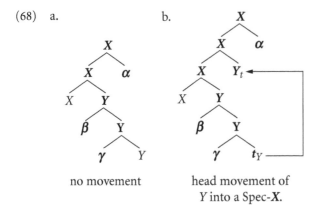

no movement   head movement of
                           Y into a Spec-**X**.

Here, I have taken the liberty of representing the structures with arbitrary directions of branching in accord with the assumption of unordered trees in BPS. As before, maximal projections are indicated in ***bold italics***, minimal projections in *plain italics*, and intermediate projections in **plain bold**. *Y* is the complement of *X*, α a specifier of *X*, β the specifier of *Y*, and γ the complement of *Y*. (68a) is the base structure without any movement. In (68b), the head *Y* is moved into the inner specifier of the higher projection of **X**. Bear in mind that in this system, there is no leftward or rightward movement. There is only upward movement into a specifier, which consequently surfaces to the left.

The three orders of the BPS traversal produce the following: (a)-sequences without any movement and (b)-sequences with head-to-specifier movement of *Y*.

(69)   Preorder: a. *X* α *Y* β γ b. *X* α Y_t *Y* β γ

(70)   Inorder: a. α *X* β *Y* γ b. α *X* Y_t β *Y* γ

(71)   Postorder: a. α β γ *Y* *X*   b. α Y_t β γ *Y* *X*

In the preorder traversal (69b), the single-step movement of *Y* into the immediately dominating projection has no effect on linear order, as a reviewer points out. That is, the preorder traversal in BPS generally yields the head–specifier–complement order with or without head movement. Thus, the VSO order obtains without V movement if the subject remains in Spec-VP. If the subject moves out of VP, the V-head must move higher than the subject, and it can be to the outer Spec-IP even if the subject is already in Spec-IP, as discussed in section 13.4 (see note 12). The present proposal as is will be proven untenable, if in a preorder language, i.e. a VSO language, a specifier constituent of some projection precedes the unmoved overt head of that projection, say, a *wh*-phrase preceding an overt complementizer, as we have already discussed.

When the head Y is moved to the outer Spec-X and α is the inner Spec-X, the produced sequences are the following, again (a)-sequences without movement and (b)-sequences with head movement of Y to the outer Spec-X.

(72) Preorder: a. $X \, \alpha \, Y \, \beta \, \gamma$ b. $X \, Y_t \, \alpha \, Y \, \beta \, \gamma$

(73) Inorder: a. $\alpha \, X \, \beta \, Y \, \gamma$ b. $Y_t \, \alpha \, X \, \beta \, Y \, \gamma$

(74) Postorder: a. $\alpha \, \beta \, \gamma \, Y \, X$ b. $Y_t \, \alpha \, \beta \, \gamma \, Y \, X$

As can be seen, head movement is not always string-vacuous. In the inorder traversal, the moved head Y_t may appear to the immediate right of the attracting 'head' qua maximal projection X (70b), but to the left of the intervening inner specifier α (73b), depending on whether the movement is to the inner or outer specifier. That is, the head-to-specifier movement does not necessarily result in linear adjacency between the moved head and the attracting 'head', and the BPS traversals do not necessarily linearize the moved head to the left of the attracting 'head', contrary to the standard assumption in head-to-head adjunction analyses.[16]

In the lexicalist approach for inflectional morphology taken in the Minimalist Program (Chomsky 1993: 27ff.), the linear adjacency or direction of an inflectional head does not matter for feature-checking/valuation. In general, head-to-head adjunction to the left works straightforwardly for suffixal inflections, but not for other affixations—prefixal, infixal, or circumfixal—not to mention for suppletion, vowel alternation, reduplication, or suprasegmental inflections. Other than the affixal ones, attracting heads are phonetically empty in general (i.a. van Riemsdijk 1998; Fukui and Takano 1998); for the traditional I-to-C movement in subject–auxiliary inversion, the C-head is never overt, for instance. The complementarity of the overt C-head and the moved I-head has been explained in terms of head-to-head 'substitution' (den Besten 1976, *pace* den Besten 1983), which is no longer available in BPS (Chomsky 1995a,b).[17]

In the postorder traversal, the left-adjacent lower 'head' Y in the base order (71a, 74a) moves far away to the left from the higher attracting 'head' X on the right, unlike the standard string-vacuous successive cyclic 'roll-up' head-to-head adjunction in the

[16] Kayne (1994) derives the right-headedness of complex heads from his theorem that movement is always to the left, including head-to-head adjunction. Yet, it is a curious fact that morphology is head-final while syntax is universally head-initial, if Kayne is correct.

[17] For a lexicalist analysis of incorporation in terms of head-to-specifier movement, see Toyoshima (2001).

head-final configuration. We have witnessed this situation in section 13.5.1 with verb movement in Vata, which supports the present proposal. It implies that in the strict head-final languages, such as Japanese and Korean, the verbal complex is not derived by head movement, but rather by morphophonological concatenation after linearization, reflecting the base order.

6.2 *Linearization by Demerge: Fukui and Takano (1998)*

The implication that the verbal complex in the strict head-final languages is not derived by head movement is shared in Fukui and Takano (1998), in which another type of BPS linearization is proposed that is in a way similar to the present proposal, as a reviewer points out. Assuming the unordered BPS, Fukui and Takano propose a top-down process of linearization as follows:

(75) Applied to Σ, *Demerge* yields $\{a, \{\Sigma - a\}\}$, a an X^{max} constituent of Σ, and *Concatenate* turns $\{a, \{\Sigma - a\}\}$ into $a + (\Sigma - a)$.

Demerge is a sort of reverse operation of Merge, recursively breaking down the structures already formed by the bottom-up structure-building by Merge (including Move as internal Merge). *Concatenate* is an associative, non-commutative binary operation that recursively maps the demerged constituent a in the precedence relation to the residue $(\Sigma - a)$.

As a is specified to be an X^{max} constituent of Σ, the problem with the simplex complement does not arise, as in the LCA-based linearization. Suppose, Σ is a projection of the head σ, and a its complement. When Demerge applies to Σ, the complement a is already maximal, whether simplex or complex. If simplex, it is minimal at the same time. On the other hand, the head σ is minimal only, projecting to Σ. It becomes maximal only after Demerge breaks down Σ. Thus, Concatenate maps the complement a first, followed by the head σ. In our terms, it amounts to linearizing the adopted child/subtree before any of the consanguineous children/subtrees, whether childless or not, which can simplify the first traversal step (27i) with the following non-conditional one.

(76) Recursively traverse its adopted subtree.

It is tempting to adopt (76) as our first traversal step for (27i), but it forces us to adopt Fukui and Takano's view that overt 'heads' in VSO and SVO languages are either moved into, or merged as, a specifier. The former is the head-to-specifier movement, which we are adopting, and hence no problem. The latter may be true, but it deprives us of the very virtue of yielding the three typologically salient word orders without excessive self-serving movement.

Unlike the present proposal, Fukui and Takano's system linearizes the terminal words, and it yields the specifier–complement–head order as the universal base order, as opposed to the LCA. In essence, the VSO and SVO orders are derived from the underlying SOV order by some movement, on a par with the LCA-based linearization. Fukui and Takano claim that all the agreement-inducing functional heads are phonetically empty, and in English, an SVO language, i.e. an inorder language in our terms, what we see as overt functional 'heads', such as determiners and complementizers, are the elements directly merged as a specifier. This extends to prepositions, which they claim are pseudo-functional, forming a closed class.

13.7 Concluding remarks

As I have shown, the proposed BPS traversals overcome the empirical as well as the theoretical problems in Kural's (2005) tree traversal linearization. Dispensing with the directionality both in branching of the trees and in the traversal algorithms, word orders for *wh*-movement in VSO languages were accounted for, and typologically rare VOS, OVS, and OSV word orders are made impossible to be derived without movement. In addition, seemingly mixed orderings in Vata are accounted for.

By stipulating a parametric feature, the disharmonic word orders in German are also accounted for. Yet, the analyses are speculative and tentative, and they await further improvements. The stipulations of the [postorder] feature are not innocent; an immediate question is why it is [postorder], not [preorder] or anything else. This is a question for future research, but it should be pointed out that their loci are related to the phase categories, which I think is significant.

The proposal shares an important insight from Kural (2005): it is the order of maximal projections that is reflected in surface word orders. In other words, the word orders are the 'images' of the hierarchical relations of the maximal projections. It is almost the same intuition behind Kayne's (1994) LCA. For that, our proposal makes a crucial reference to labels. If labels are eliminable from syntax as argued in Collins (2002), we may think of labels as phonological, functioning at the PF interface for linearization of syntactic structures, with possible specifications of parametric features for the disharmonic languages.

The proposal also keeps the two empirical insights that Kayne's (1994) theory of antisymmetry implies: specifiers are on the left, and movement should be always to the left. The BPS traversals capture these insights without fixing the branching directions in phrase structures. Yet, the BPS traversal linearization does not inherit what is perhaps Kayne's most important inference that specifier–head–complement is the universal underlying order. Roughly speaking, this amounts to saying that all languages are underlyingly SVO. It does not seem to be reflected in typological distributions, however; although it is not easy to determine, the SOV languages perhaps outnumber the SVO languages. The number of VSO languages is much smaller, but still significant, compared to the other three exceptionally rare word orders that are logically possible. Meanwhile, Kayne's LCA does not logically preclude the mirror image, namely the OVS order. Given the possibility of massive pied-piping and remnant movement, it may not be too much to expect to find SVO and OVS to be the two dominant majorities and the other four more or less equally distributed. I do not think it is a mere coincidence that there are three depth-oriented tree traversal methods, and VSO, SVO, and SOV are the three typologically common word orders out of the six logically possible ones.

Tacitly, I have been assuming that the BPS traversal linearization applies at the PF interface, as understood in the traditional Y-model, after all the (narrow) syntactic derivations have completed. It is a topic of future research whether and how it can be implemented under the multiple Spell-Out hypothesis, though I remain agnostic about it. It can be true that it reduces memory load in the narrow syntax, as is often claimed (Chomsky 2000, *et seq.*), but the burden is simply shifted to PF. In fact, the overall memory requirement may increase for the computational system as a whole; PF needs to keep track of multiply spelled-out chunks to be strung together in the correct order, not just holding them in memory.

Although the proposed BPS traversal linearization awaits further development with wider empirical coverage, I believe it is a viable alternative to the LCA-based linearization that merits serious attention. It is a promising approach, in that its formal aspects are well-studied and it is domain-independent. Tree traversals are readily available to the human language faculty by natural laws as one of the third factors in the sense of Chomsky (2005), and it is a matter of finding a good tree to traverse.

Part V

The Final-over-Final Constraint

14

Disharmonic Word Orders from a Processing-Efficiency Perspective

JOHN A. HAWKINS

14.1 Introduction

When a phrase XP immediately contains another phrase YP we have the following four ordering possibilities for the heads X and Y within each:

(1)　　**XP**　　　(2)　　　**XP**　　(3)　　**XP**　　(4)　　　**XP**
　　　　/ \　　　　　　　　/ \　　　　　　　/ \　　　　　　　　/ \
　　　X　YP　　　　　**YP　X**　　　　**X　YP**　　　　　**YP　X**
　　　　　/ \　　　　　　　/ \　　　　　　　/ \　　　　　　　/ \
　　　　Y　ZP　　　　**ZP　Y**　　　　**ZP　Y**　　　　**Y　ZP**

　　　Head-initial　　　　Head-final　　　　Mixed　　　　　Mixed

(3) and (4) are 'inconsistent' or 'disharmonic' word orders in the language typology research tradition (Greenberg 1963; Hawkins 1983; Dryer 1992a), (1) and (2) are consistently and harmonically head-initial and head-final respectively. Within formal grammar a proposal has been made for a different partitioning that distinguishes the mixed type in (4) from the other three (Holmberg 2000):

(5)　　The Final-over-Final Constraint (FOFC)
　　　　If α is a head-initial phrase and β is a phrase immediately dominating α, then β must be head-initial. If α is a head-final phrase, and β is a phrase immediately dominating α, then β can be head-initial or head-final.

This rules out (4), and permits (1–3). The precise formulation of FOFC that has been proposed by Biberauer, Holmberg, and Roberts in refinements made over the years (see Biberauer, Holmberg, and Roberts 2008a,b, 2009, 2010) incorporates principles of Minimalist Syntax (Chomsky 2000; Kayne 1994) and has, in effect, limited the applicability of FOFC to those instances of type (4) in which YP and XP are of the same or similar syntactic type, e.g. both verbal heads of some kind, as opposed to different syntactic types such as a PP within a VP. Only the former are now excluded as impossible. In what follows I shall examine typological data and their processing correlates for all of (1–4) and for the different subtypes of (4), whether they fall under the current limitations of FOFC or not, since the perspective to be pursued here, and the type of explanation to be given, is different.

These patterns will be examined from the processing-efficiency perspective of Hawkins (1994, 2004, to appear). Formal grammarians may (or may not) wish to make use of the principles presented here in order to account for disharmonic word-order data that are not covered by FOFC, while reserving this latter as a grammatical and ultimately innate UG explanation for a set of absolute universals. The interesting research question then becomes whether the kinds of efficiency principles I propose, which account for many statistical typological patterns involving harmonic and disharmonic word orders, as well as for some apparently exceptionless patterns, can also subsume the data for which FOFC has been proposed. Lack of comparability between available typological data and many of the detailed syntactic analyses illustrated in the papers of this volume makes it difficult for a definitive answer to be given to this question at the moment. Hence I shall try to give the best possible support for the alternative approach advocated here and leave it to others to adjudicate whether, and to what extent, the principles proposed here can also generalize to subsume the effects of FOFC.

From a general typological perspective FOFC looks, prima facie, like it is not quite right: languages with (4) are generally dispreferred, occasionally unattested (i.e. it appears to be too strong); while languages with (3) appear to be similarly dispreferred, occasionally unattested (i.e. it is too weak). Types (1) and (2) are always fully productive. This can be seen in some illustrative 'Greenbergian' correlations for word orders in which a prepositional or postpositional phrase (PP) is immediately dominated by a verb phrase (VP) (Greenberg 1963). The four orderings possibilities (1–4) are exemplified using English words in (6). Language quantities for each are shown in (6′), using data from Hawkins (1994: 257) provided by Matthew Dryer and taken from his (1992a) typological sample (measuring languages here rather than groups of related languages or 'genera'):

(6) a. vp[went pp[to the movies]]   (1)   b. vp[pp[the movies to] went]   (2)

     c. vp[went pp[the movies to]]   (3)   d. vp[pp[to the movies] went]   (4)

(6′) a. vp[V pp[P NP]] = 161 (41%)   b. vp[pp[NP P] V] = 204 (52%)

     c. vp[V pp[NP P]] = 18 (5%)   d. vp[pp[P NP] V] = 6 (2%)
        (6a)+(b) = 365/389 (94%)

The consistently head-initial and head-final types, found in English and Japanese respectively, account for the vast majority of languages, 94%. The disharmonic (3) (exemplified by Kru) is found in 5%, and disharmonic (4) (exemplified by Persian) in 2%. A very similar distribution can be seen in the other Greenbergian correlations, for example when an NP containing a head noun and a possessive phrase sister is contained within a PP in phrases corresponding to pp{with, np{soldiers, possp{of [the king]}}}:

(7)   a. pp[P np[N Possp]] = 134 (40%) (1)   b. pp[np[Possp N] P] = 177 (53%) (2)

    c. pp[P np[Possp N]] = 14 (4%)   (3)   d. pp[np[N Possp] P] = 11 (3%)   (4)

    (7a) + (b) = 311/336 (93%) (data from Hawkins 1983)

It is clear from these data why the original formulation of FOFC in (5) needs to be revised and why its applicability would need to be restricted to a proper subset of the configurations in (4) that are genuinely unattested.

Instead, the typological distributions of (6') and (7) support the traditional generalization of head-ordering consistency (or Cross Category Harmony, cf. Hawkins 1983), whereby (1) and (2) are preferred over both (3) and (4). They do not support a generalization in which (4) is singled out for special treatment. The processing approach to typology advocated here provides an explanation for this, and it can also account for the different levels of infrequency for different combinations of phrases of types (3) and (4), ranging from limited occurrence to what appears to be complete absence. Seen from this perspective, a purely grammatical explanation for FOFC may not be necessary, therefore. Whether it is or not will depend crucially on certain data sets that can potentially decide between alternative explanations, and also on the range of data and the generality of competing theories. Whatever the outcome of this, I have argued in Hawkins (1985), and will reiterate here, that typologists and formal grammarians need to work together in areas such as this in order to identify the precise cross-linguistic patterns. The formal grammarian gives depth to the syntactic analysis, the typologist gives breadth, while a psycholinguistic approach to typology gives a new type of explanation that can potentially account for the productive patterns, including absolute universals, and also for the minority types and exceptions. I turn first to this general research programme (section 14.2), before working out its consequences for the different word-order types of (1)–(4) in subsequent sections.

14.2 The processing-efficiency research programme and linear ordering

The research programme presented here examines cross-linguistic patterns and compares them with the patterns and preferences found in performance in languages with several structures of a given type (word orders, relative clauses, etc.). It tests the 'Performance–Grammar Correspondence Hypothesis' (PGCH) of Hawkins (2004) which asserts that the same principles underlie both sets of patterns and that performance and processing can help us better understand grammatical variation and language universals.

For example, relative clauses may exhibit a 'gap' or a 'resumptive pronoun' strategy (as in Hebrew in which there are relatives corresponding to *the students [that I teach (them)]*), or a strategy with and without a relative pronoun (as in English, cf. *the students [(whom) I teach]*). One of these strategies may be 'fixed' or 'conventionalized' in certain environments, e.g. the relative pronoun is generally obligatory in English when it functions as a subject within its clause, while there can be optionality and variation in others.

The selection from the variants in performance exhibits patterns. The retention of the relative pronoun in English is correlated inter alia with the degree of separation of the relative from its head (Quirk 1957): the bigger the separation, the more relative pronouns are retained (Hawkins 2004). The Hebrew gap is favoured with smaller distances between filler and gap, the resumptive pronouns with larger and more complex relativization domains (Ariel 1999). Correlating with these distance and processing-complexity effects we find corresponding patterns in grammars: the distribution of gaps to pronouns follows the Keenan–Comrie (1977) Accessibility Hierarchy (AH), and Keenan and Comrie argued that their hierarchy was explainable in terms of declining ease of processing. This argument has been extended and generalized within the processing typology programme. What is of immediate relevance in this paper is that the preferred word orders in structures and languages with freedom appear to be those that are grammaticalized in languages with less freedom and with more fixed and basic orderings (Hawkins 1994, 2004).

The PGCH is defined in (8):

(8) **Performance–Grammar Correspondence Hypothesis** (PGCH)
     Grammars have conventionalized syntactic structures in proportion to their degree of preference in performance, as evidenced by patterns of selection in corpora and by ease of processing in psycholinguistic experiments.

This makes predictions for occurring and non-occurring language types, and for frequent and less frequent ones. It can also motivate many of the stipulated principles of formal grammar and it accounts for numerous exceptions to proposed universals (Newmeyer 2005b; Hawkins 2004).

As a preliminary to the head-ordering discussion of subsequent sections notice that grammatical heads (cf. Corbett, Fraser, and McGlashen 1993) are a subset of what are called 'mother node constructing categories' in Hawkins (1994: ch. 6) to which the parsing principle of Mother Node Construction applies, which builds on Kimball's (1973) New Nodes:

(9) **Mother Node Construction** (Hawkins 1994: 62)
     In the left-to-right parsing of a sentence, if any word of syntactic category C uniquely determines a phrasal mother node M, in accordance with the PS rules of the grammar, then M is immediately constructed over C.

A second parsing principle proposed for non-heads in Hawkins is Immediate Constituent Attachment:

(10) **Immediate Constituent Attachment** (Hawkins 1994: 62)
      In the left-to-right parsing of a sentence, if an IC does not construct, but can be attached to, a given mother node M, in accordance with the PS rules of the grammar, then attach it, as rapidly as possible. Such ICs may be encountered *after* the category that constructs M, or *before* it, in which case they are placed in a look-ahead buffer.

Why is it then that certain linear orderings of words are preferred over others in performance and in grammars? In the theory of Hawkins (1994, 2004) this is because there are principles of processing efficiency that motivate the preferences. For example, the adjacency of the categories V and P in (6a,b) guarantees the smallest possible string of words for the construction of VP and of PP, and for the attachment of V and PP to VP as sister ICs. Non-adjacency of heads in (6c,d) is less efficient for phrase structure processing.

Specifically I have argued that the smallest possible string of connected words is preferred for the construction of phrases and for recognition of the combinatorial and dependency relations within them. This was referred to as the principle of Early Immediate Constituents (EIC) in Hawkins (1994), which was then generalized to a similar preference for 'minimal domains' in the processing of all syntactic and semantic relations in Hawkins (2004); cf. also Gibson's (1998) 'locality' principle. Minimize Domains is defined in (11):

(11) **Minimize Domains** (MiD) (Hawkins 2004: 31)
      The human processor prefers to minimize the connected sequences of linguistic forms and their conventionally associated syntactic and semantic properties in which relations of combination and/or dependency are processed. The degree of this preference is proportional to the number of relations whose domains can be minimized in competing sequences or structures, and to the extent of the minimization difference in each domain.

Linear orderings (1) and (2) above (the consistently head-initial and head-final ones) are optimal by MiD: two adjacent words suffice for the construction of the mother XP (projected from X) and for construction of the mother YP (projected from Y) and its attachment to XP as a sister of X. Structures (3) and (4) are less efficient: more words must be processed for construction and attachment because of the intervening ZP.

MiD can be argued to motivate the grammatical principle of Head Adjacency and the Head-Ordering Parameter (cf. Newmeyer 2005b: 43). One and the same principle explains both the preferred conventions of grammars and also the preferred structural selections in performance in languages and structures in which speakers have a choice. See Hawkins (1994, 2004, 2009) for a detailed summary of these performance data from many languages (which cannot be reproduced here on account of space limitations and which are in any case readily available in this published work).

MiD can also explain why there are two highly productive mirror-image language types, the head-initial and the head-final one, i.e. (1) and (2). Heads can be adjacent in both orders and the processing domains for phrase structure recognition and production can be minimal in both, i.e. these two are equally efficient. Structures (3) and (4) are not as efficient and both are significantly less productive.

A second interacting principle proposed in Hawkins (2004) is Maximize Online Processing, which I shall simply define here and comment on below.

(12) **Maximize Online Processing** (MaOP) (Hawkins 2004: 51)
The human processor prefers to maximize the set of properties that are assignable to each item X as X is processed, thereby increasing O(nline) P(roperty) to U(ltimate) P(roperty) ratios. The maximization difference between competing orders and structures will be a function of the number of properties that are unassigned or misassigned to X in a structure/sequence S, compared with the number in an alternative.

14.3 Structures (1–4) and the timing of phrasal constructions and attachments

When parsing principles (9) Mother Node Construction and (10) Immediate Constituent Attachment apply to terminal elements of the structures (1–4) they result in very different online timing patterns for the construction and attachment of these phrases. The trees are repeated here for convenience:

(1)	XP	(2)	XP	(3)	XP	(4)	XP
	/ \		/ \		/ \		/ \
	X YP		YP X		X YP		YP X
	/ \		/ \		/ \		/ \
	Y ZP		ZP Y		ZP Y		Y ZP
	Head-initial		Head-final		Mixed		Mixed

In tree number (1), X first constructs XP, then Y constructs YP at the next word, and YP is immediately attached left as a daughter to the mother XP. The processing of ZP then follows.

In (2), ZP is processed first, Y then constructs YP, and X constructs XP at the next word. YP is immediately attached right as daughter to the mother XP. Note that the attachment of YP follows its construction by one word here, a point that will be of some interest and that I shall return to in section 14.6 below.

In (3), X first constructs XP, then after processing ZP Y constructs YP and this YP is attached left to the mother XP, possibly several words after the construction of XP. The result is delayed assignment of the daughter YP to XP.

TABLE 14.1 **The optimality of harmonic and disharmonic word orders in relation to MiD and MaOP**

	MiD	MaOP
Structure (1)	optimal	adjacent words for XP & YP construction & attachments
Structure (2)	optimal	adjacent words for XP & YP construction & attachments (Mother XP assignment to YP delayed by one word)
Structure (3)	non-optimal	non-adjacent...Delayed Daughter YP assignment to XP
Structure (4)	non-optimal	non-adjacent...Delayed Mother XP assignment to YP

In (4), Y constructs YP first, then after processing ZP X constructs XP and YP is attached right to the mother XP, possibly several words after the construction of YP. This results in delayed assignment of the mother XP to YP.

Structures (1) and (2) are optimal from the perspective of Minimize Domains; therefore, both (3) and (4) are non-optimal. For Maximize Online Processing construction and attachment proceed on the basis of adjacent words in (1) and (2), though I pointed out that both construction and attachment are simultaneous for (1), whereas the attachment of ZP to XP follows the actual construction of YP by one word in (2). (3) involves a significant delay in the assignment of the daughter YP to the mother XP following construction of the latter, while (4) involves a significant delay in the assignment of the mother XP to the daughter YP following construction of this latter. This can be summarized in Table 14.1.

14.4 Processing-efficiency predictions for structure (4)

The inefficiency of structure (4), repeated here, is that it involves the delayed assignment of a mother XP to a head-initial daughter YP, i.e. there is no mother to attach YP to for several words of online processing, which goes against both Minimize Domains (11) and Maximize Online Processing (12).

```
(4)      XP
        /  \
      YP   X
     / \
     Y  ZP
```

By the Performance–Grammar Correspondence Hypothesis (8) we expect that structures of type (4) will be limited as basic word orders in grammars in comparison to structure (2) (which keeps X final) and to structure (1) (which keeps Y initial). This is shown in (13) and (14) respectively, using data mainly from Dryer (1992a) and counting 'genera' rather than languages (i.e. groups of genetically related languages at a time depth corresponding roughly to the subgroupings of Indo-European). The phrases corresponding to YP and XP are (i) an NP within a VP where the NP consists of a head noun plus Possessive Phrase (Dryer's Noun and Genitive orders, 1992a: 91), (ii) a PP within a VP (Dryer 1992a: 83), (iii) a VP within a TP (headed by a Tense or Aspect Auxiliary Verb with a VP sister, Dryer 1992a: 100), and (iv) a CP within an NP (where CP is represented by a relative clause structure; cf. Lehmann 1984):

(13) **Limited productivity of (4) compared with (2) as basic orders** (keeping X final)
   (i) vp[np[N Possp] V] vs vp[np[Possp N] V] = 9.7% genera (12/124) Dryer (1992a)
   (ii) vp[pp[P NP] V] vs vp[pp[NP P] V] = 6.1% genera (7/114) Dryer (1992a)
   (iii) tp[vp[V NP] T] vs tp[vp[NP V] T] = 10% genera (4/40) Dryer (1992a)
   (iv) np[cp[C S] N] vs np[cp[S C] N]   = 0   Lehmann (1984)

(14) **Limited productivity of (4) compared with (1) as basic orders** (keeping Y initial)
   (i) vp[np[N Possp] V] vs vp[V np[N Possp]] =16% genera (12/75) Dryer (1992a)
   (ii) vp[pp[P NP] V] vs vp[V pp[P NP]]   =9.1% genera (7/77) Dryer (1992a)
   (iii) tp[vp[V NP] T] vs tp[T vp[V NP]] =12.5% genera (4/32) Dryer (1992a)
   (iv) np[cp[C S] N] vs np[N cp[C S]]   = 0   Lehmann (1984)

These figures clearly show that structure (4) is unproductive, compared with (1) and (2). It is not exceptionless for the combinations (i)–(iii), but it is for (iv) involving a CP within an NP. This absolute universal is not predicted under current formulations of FOFC, while structures of type tp[vp[V NP] T] which it excludes seem to be attested (Biberauer, Holmberg, and Roberts 2008a,b). Clearly the potentially offending language types in Dryer's sample need to be investigated more closely syntactically, in order to see whether they are genuine violations.

From a processing perspective we make a different prediction: the more structurally complex YP is, the more it should be dispreferred in (4). For example, a CP as YP should be worse than an NP or PP. This appears to be the case. This prediction can be made because domains for phrase structure processing are least minimal when YP is complex, offending Minimize Domains (11), and the more they delay the assignment of the mother XP to YP, offending Maximize Online Processing (12). Whether a more fine-tuned ranking and prediction can be made between the less complex YP categories, NP, PP, and VP-based on their aggregate weights and complexities remains to be investigated. This is more complicated because there are cross-linguistic differences between PPs, for example, which can involve single-word adpositions or affixes (see Hawkins 2008), and differences between languages with regard to the very existence of a VP. But certainly a sentence-like CP should be more complex on aggregate than these other phrases, and it is the np[cp[C S] N] configuration that is unattested typologically (and at the same time a potential FOFC violation that is not currently subsumed under the definition of FOFC).

14.4.1 *Non-rigid OV vs rigid OV languages*

The term 'non-rigid' OV languages comes from Greenberg (1963). They are languages with basic OV order that have certain complements and/or adjuncts of V to the right of V. Configurationally we might say that they combine pre- and post-verbal phrases in VP.

Such languages are predicted here to be those that combine a Y-initial YP with an X-final XP, i.e. languages of type (4), and they are further predicted to postpose YP to the right of V, in proportion to the complexity of YP, creating alternations with structure (1). This can be seen in the obligatory extraposition rules of Persian, German, and other non-rigid OV languages converting vp[cp[C S] V] into vp[V cp [C S]] (cf. Dryer 1980; Hawkins 1990), as in the following Persian example from Dryer (1980):

(15) a. *An   zan   cp[ke   an   mard   sangi   partab kard]   mi   danat
          the   woman   that   the   man   rock   threw   CONT   knows
          'The woman knows that the man threw a rock'

      b. An zan mi danat cp[ke an mard sangi partab kard]

Data from the *World Atlas of Language Structures* (*WALS*) confirm this prediction (see Dryer and Gensler 2005; Haspelmath, Dryer, Gil, and Comrie 2005). 78% (7/9) of OV genera in *WALS* with prepositions (rather than postpositions) are non-rigid OV rather than rigid, i.e. these are potential combinations of type (4), and PPs regularly follow V in these languages converting (4) into (1), see (14ii) above (cf. Hawkins 2008). Similarly, 73% (8/11) of OV genera in *WALS* with np[N Possp] (i.e. postnominal rather than prenominal genitives) are non-rigid OV rather than rigid, and NPs regularly follow V in these languages; see (14i) (Dryer and Gensler 2005; Haspelmath et al. 2005; Hawkins 2008).

Rigid OV languages, by contrast, are those with basic OV in which V is final in VP and sisters precede. Such languages are predicted here to combine an X-final XP (i.e. OV) with a Y-final YP. And indeed 96% (47/49) of rigid OV genera in *WALS* have postpositions (rather than prepositions), i.e. vp[pp[NP P] V] (Dryer and Gensler 2005; Haspelmath et al. 2005; Hawkins 2008). 94% (46/49) of rigid OV genera in *WALS* also have vp[np[Possp N] V] (i.e. prenominal rather than postnominal genitives) (Dryer and Gensler 2005; Haspelmath et al. 2005; Hawkins 2008).

14.4.2 *Shortening YP in (4)*

Another solution for relieving the inefficiency of type (4) structures involves keeping the YP *in situ* in (4), but shortening it by extraposing items within it. This is very productive in German, for example, in which the initial head noun of an NP remains *in situ* within a verb-final VP while a relative clause CP is extraposed to the right of V, as shown in (16):

(16)   a. Ich habe vp [np[den Lehrer cp[der das Buch geschrieben hat]] gesehen]
           I   have   the   teacher who   the book written   has   seen
           'I have seen the teacher who wrote the book.'

       b. I habe vp[np[den Lehrer] gesehen] cp[der das Buch geschrieben hat]

Detailed predictions for when Extraposition from NP will apply, based on the competing efficiencies for NP and VP processing domains, are illustrated and supported in Hawkins (1994: 198–210, 2004: 142–6) using corpus data from Shannon (1992) and Uszkoreit et al. (1998).

14.5 Processing-efficiency predictions for structure (3)

The inefficiency of structure (3), repeated here, is that it involves the delayed assignment of a daughter YP to a constructed mother XP, i.e. no clear daughter can be assigned online to XP for several words of processing during which terminal material is processed that is contained within ZP. This goes against both Minimize Domains (11) and Maximize Online Processing (12):

(3)   **XP**
       / \
       X YP
          / \
        ZP Y

As with structure (4), the PGCH (8) leads to the prediction that structures of type (3) will be limited as basic word orders in grammars in comparison to structure (1) (keeping X initial) and to structure (2) (keeping Y final). This is tested in (17) and (18) respectively using data mainly from Dryer (in terms of genera), but also data from Lehmann (1984) and Hawkins (1983). The phrases corresponding to YP and XP are (i) an NP within a VP where the NP consists of a head noun plus Possessive Phrase (Dryer's Noun and Genitive orders, 1992a: 91), (ii) a PP within a VP (Dryer 1992a: 83), (iii) a VP within a TP (headed by a Tense or Aspect Auxiliary Verb with a VP sister, Dryer 1992a: 100), (iv) a CP within an NP (where CP is represented by a relative clause structure; cf. Lehmann 1984); and (v) a CP within a VP where CP is a sentence complement structure with a complementizer C (Hawkins 1990):

(17) **Limited productivity of (3) compared with (1) as basic orders** (keeping X initial)
  (i) vp[V np[Possp N]] vs vp[V np[N Possp]] = 32% (30/93) genera Dryer (1992a)
  (ii) vp[V pp[NP P]] vs vp[V pp[P NP]] = 14.6% (12/82) genera Dryer (1992a)
  (iii) tp[T vp[NP V]] vs tp[T vp[V NP]] = 9.7% (3/31) genera Dryer (1992a)
  (iv) np[N cp[S C]] vs np[N cp[C S]] = very few, if any Lehmann (1984)
  (v) vp[V cp[S C]] vs vp[V cp[C S]]   = 0   Hawkins (1990)

(18) **Limited productivity of (3) compared with (2) as basic orders** (keeping Y final)
  (i) vp[V np[Possp N]] vs vp[np[Possp N] V] = 21.1% (30/142) genera Dryer (1992a)
  (ii) vp[V pp[NP P]] vs vp[pp[NP P] V] = 10.1% (12/119) genera Dryer (1992a)
  (iii) vp[T vp[NP V]] vs tp[vp[NP V] T] = 7.7% (3/39) genera Dryer (1992a)
  (iv) np[N cp[S C] vs np[cp[S C] N]   = very few, if any Lehmann (1984)
  (v) vp[V cp[S C]] vs vp[cp[S C] V]   = 0   Hawkins (1990)

As with structure (4), these figures clearly show that (3) is unproductive compared with (1) and (2). The dispreference figures here are not that different from those in (13) and (14), which violate FOFC, supporting the point made in section 14.1 that the correct partitioning seems to be structures (1) and (2) (productive) versus (3) and (4) (unproductive), and that FOFC seems to be both too weak and too strong. Notice that the combination vp[V cp[S C]] in (v) appears to be unattested, making its absence a possible absolute universal, yet FOFC does not apply to structures of this type (i.e. (3)). Structures of the type np[N cp[S C]] in (iv) may also be unattested, depending on what counts as a category C across languages.

The more general prediction that we make for structure (3) from a processing perspective is that the more complex the (centre-embedded) ZP is, the more it will be dispreferred. For example, a centre-embedded S in (iv) and (v) is worse than an NP or Possp in (i)–(iii). The typological frequency data support this prediction.

14.5.1 *Construct YP early in advance of Y through alternative constructors in ZP*

One way in which structures of type (3) can be made more efficient is by positioning items in ZP early that can construct YP by the parsing principle of Grandmother Node Construction (Hawkins 1994: 361). In this way YP can be constructed early, in accordance with Minimize Domains (11), and attached to XP without having to wait for category Y, making the processing domain for XP and its immediate constituents minimal.

This may be at least part of the explanation for why non-nominative case-marked pronouns are preposed in the German VP and for why case-marked full NPs precede PPs and other non-case marked categories. Non-nominative case marking can construct a VP by Grandmother Node Construction in this language in structures such as tp[T vp[NP . . . V]], see (19) (Hawkins 1994: 393–402):

(19) Ich   tp[habe   vp[ihn   [noch einmal]   gesehen]
      I   have   him (+ACC)   once again   seen
      'I have seen him once again.'

14.5.2 *Avoid online ambiguity between YP and ZP or nodes dominated by ZP*

A major source of inefficiency in structure (3) involves the potential for online structural misassignments or garden paths (Hawkins 2004), whereby what will eventually be parsed as ZP or a phrase within ZP is initially parsed as YP, the sister of X. Misassignments are inefficient for Maximize Online Processing (12). This may explain the non-occurrence of vp[V cp[S C]] structures in (v), in addition to its inefficiency by MiD, since different phrases within S could be readily attached immediately to VP unless C precedes and constructs CP at the outset, marking a clear clausal boundary for CP-dominated material. When complementizers are optionally deleted in English there are garden paths of this sort in structures like *I believe the clever student wrote . . .*, which is disambiguated only at *wrote*. There is clear performance evidence in English corpora showing that complementizers are not deleted when the misanalysis would persist over more than a few words, and they are not deleted even when there would be no garden path (e.g. when *realize* replaces *believe* in the example just given) if the 'unassignment' of CP persists for more than a couple of words (see Hawkins 2004: 49–61 for discussion and relevant data).

Similarly this may contribute to the explanation for the relative infrequency of vp[V pp[NP P]] in (ii) and vp[V np[Possp N]] in (i). It would be advantageous for grammars to distinguish NP arguments of V from pp[NP P] or np[Possp N] in such cases, perhaps through case marking for the former and not for the latter, or through different case marking. In the event that the grammar permits a genuine garden path here, as in English *I* vp[*met* np[possp[*the king's*] *daughter*]], in which *the king* can first be assigned as a direct object to *met*, we expect certain consequences, such as a limitation on the length of these prenominal genitives in performance. Biber, Johansson, Leech, Conrad, and Finegan (1999: 597) point out that 70–80% of pre-modified noun phrases in English are limited to single-word premodifiers, including prenominal genitives. The cliticization of the genitive case marking is also interesting here since it distinguishes the genitive NP from other NPs within the genitive phrase itself.

14.6 Processing-efficiency predictions for structure (2) (Head Finality)

Structure (2), repeated here, like structure (1), is optimal for MiD (11) since heads are consistently adjacent. There is one small respect, however, in which it is not optimal for MaOP (12). YP is constructed at Y and the parser must then wait one word until X has constructed XP for the attachment of YP to this latter, i.e. for one word of online processing there is no mother to attach YP to. In the mirror-image (1), by contrast, XP is constructed first and YP can then be constructed by Y and attached immediately to XP with no processing delay.

(2)

There are some typological patterns in SOV languages that are as yet unexplained grammatically, as far as I am aware, which suggest that this small processing delay between the construction and attachment of YP does have certain grammatical consequences. I shall briefly consider two such (sections 14.6.1 and 14.6.2) and then draw attention to a more general characteristic of left-branching structures like (2) that is also relevant here.

14.6.1 *Fewer free-standing X words follow Y*

When X precedes YP, for example when a preposition precedes NP as in English, the preposition is typically a free-standing word. But when P follows NP as a postposition there are many fewer free-standing postpositions. More generally, when X follows Y there are many more X affixes on Y, e.g. derivational and inflectional suffixes on nouns and on verbs, and these X affixes can construct YP and XP simultaneously at Y, the former through Mother Node Construction (9), the latter through Grandmother Node Construction (Hawkins 1994: 361–6). This is an efficient solution to the one-word processing delay for YP since construction and attachment can now take place at one and the same word, Y, just as they do in the head-initial structure (1).

Postpositions are not as productive in head-final languages as prepositions are in head-initial. Many head-final languages have very limited postpositions, sometimes just one or two. Many languages with strong head-final characteristics even have no free-standing postpositions at all, but only suffixes with adposition-type meanings and a larger class of NPs bearing rich case features. Tsunoda, Ueda, and Itoh (1995: 757) attempt to quantify the number of such head-final languages with suffixes and without postpositions and in their sample this number is almost 30% (19/66). Head-initial languages, by contrast, retain free-standing prepositions productively (cf. Hall 1992).

Consider also sentence complementizers, which in head-initial languages are typically free-standing words that construct subordinate clauses. In head-final languages these correspond more commonly to participial and other subordinate clause indicators affixed to verbs, and they are much less productive as independent words. Dryer (2009) gives some relevant figures from his typological sample. Of the languages that have free-standing complementizers, 74% (140) occur initially in CP within VO languages, i.e. in structure (1). Just 14% (27) occur finally in CP within OV languages, i.e. in structure (2). The remaining 12% (22) occur initially in CP within OV in basic orders corresponding to structure (4). By contrast, adding affixes to verbs that indicate subordinate clause status in OV languages means that both S and its subordinate status are constructed simultaneously on the last word of the subordinate clause (see Hawkins 1994: 387–93 for exemplification of different types of subordinating affixes in grammars and their corresponding parsing routines).

14.6.2 *Avoid additional constructors of phrasal nodes in OV languages*

In the kind of classical syntax model assumed in Hawkins (1994, 2004), which is close in spirit to the Simpler Syntax of Culicover and Jackendoff (2005), trees are flatter than in other models and there can be more than one daughter category that constructs a given phrase (in accordance with Mother Node Construction (9)), i.e. the set of constructing categories for phrases is not just limited to syntactic heads (see Hawkins 1993, 1994). If we adopt such a perspective, an interesting difference emerges between VO and OV languages. Assume (controversially given the DP theory; see Abney 1987; Payne 1993) that definite articles construct NP, just like N or Pro and other categories uniquely dominated by NP (see Hawkins 2004: 82–93, 2011). If so then either N or Art can construct NP immediately on its left periphery and provide efficient and minimal 'phrasal combination domains' (PCDs) in VO languages. Art-initial will be especially favoured when N is not initial in the NP, see (20):

(20)   vp[V np[N ... Art ...]
        vp[V np[Art ... N ...]
            |-------|

In OV languages, on the other hand, any additional constructor of NP will lengthen these processing domains, whether it follows or precedes N, by constructing the NP early and extending the processing time from the construction of NP to the processing of V. Additional constructors of NP are therefore inefficient in OV orders, as shown in (21):

(21)   [[... N ... Art]np V]vp
        [[... Art ... N]np V]vp
            |--------------|

It is significant, therefore, that definite articles, which typically emerge historically out of demonstrative determiners (Lyons 1999), are found predominantly in VO rather than OV languages. The data of (22) are taken from *WALS* (Dryer 2005e) and compare language quantities for VO and (rigid) OV languages in which there is a separate definite article word from a demonstrative determiner.

(22)	Def word distinct from Dem	No definite article	[*WALS* data]
Rigid OV	19% (6)	81% (26)	
VO	58% (62)	42% (44)	

This same consideration provides a further motivation for the absence of free-standing complementizers in head-final languages (in addition to the point made in the last section 14.6.1). Complementizers can shorten PCDs when they precede V in VO languages, by constructing subordinate clauses on their left peripheries (*John knows [**that** he is sick]*), but they will lengthen PCDs in OV languages, compared with projections from V alone, whether they are clause-initial or clause-final.

14.6.3 *Reduce left-branching YP and ZP phrases*

Finally in this section let me make a brief observation about a typological asymmetry for which there appears to be no clear grammatical explanation but which may be explainable in terms of MaOP (12). Left-branching phrases like YP and ZP in (2) are often more reduced and constrained in comparison with their right-branching counterparts in (1). For example, Lehmann (1984: 168–73) observes that prenominal relative clauses are significantly more restricted in their syntax and semantics than postnominal relatives. They often involve greater nominalization (i.e. more non-sentential properties); restrictions on tense, aspect, and modal forms; more non-finite rather than finite verbs; fewer syntactic embedding possibilities; the conversion of an underlying subject to a genitive; and less tolerance of appositive interpretations. The effect of these limitations is to make a left-branching relative clause recognizably different from a main clause, thereby signalling its subordinate status early and avoiding a structural misassignment or garden path in online processing, in accord-ance with MaOP's preference (Hawkins 2004: 205–10).

14.7 Conclusions

The typological patterns presented in this paper suggest that the FOFC (as formu-lated in (5)) is not capturing the right generalization: it is too strong (structure (4) is generally dispreferred, occasionally unattested), and too weak (structure (3) is also dispreferred, occasionally unattested). There are also apparent exceptions in typo-logical samples such as Dryer (1992a) to the more recent formulations of FOFC in Biberauer, Holmberg, and Roberts (2008a,b); see (13iii) and (14iii) in section 14.4, and these need to be subjected to careful syntactic analysis. A processing approach, on the other hand, appears to provide a more general account of all these disharmonic word orders and of their relative frequencies.

Typologists need to take account of the more precise and in-depth analysis of their languages that formal syntax can provide, however, in order to determine what exactly the cross-linguistic patterns are, how best to formulate them, and what the relevant syntactic categories are. Apparent exceptions to FOFC may not be genuine counterexamples, depending on the best syntactic analysis. Conversely, formal syntacticians need to take note of the fact that structure (3) looks almost as bad in these typological correlations as (4). It is misleading of them to suggest that all of (1)–(3) are common, while (4) is the only violation.

Typologists also need a more sophisticated theoretical basis, and more explanatory theories, for their cross-linguistic correlations. The goal of the processing-efficiency research programme outlined in section 14.2 is to provide one: it brings an independent body of evidence from language performance and psycholinguistics (especially processing) to bear on cross-linguistic grammatical conventions and parameters. The central hypothesis is the PGCH (8): grammars have conventionalized syntactic structures in proportion to their degree of preference in performance.

It is important to try to integrate insights from different branches of the language sciences in this way when examining cross-linguistic variation. The rich theoretical apparatus of generative syntax is subtle and its principles and parameters are an important source of insight in the present context. But much of this apparatus is stipulated, and the appeal to an innate UG is largely speculation and is increasingly controversial (cf. the papers in Christiansen, Collins, and Edelman 2009). Independent evidence from performance in diverse languages is growing meanwhile, and the preferences and dispreferences in structural selections in performance (in languages with choices) are being shown to correlate with preferences and dispreferences in the grammatical conventions themselves, supporting the PGCH (Hawkins 1994, 2004). The stipulations of formal models can become less stipulative by shifting their ultimate motivation away from an innate UG towards (ultimately innate and neurally predetermined) processing mechanisms.

The PGCH defines an alternative research programme and explanation for the cross-linguistic patterns that have ultimately led to the FOFC. I suggest that typologists, formal syntacticians, and psycholinguists work more closely together, in order to get the facts right and in order to pursue and compare different explanatory ideas. More individual languages need to be analysed, and more phrasal combinations of types (1)–(4) need to be investigated, in order to determine whether the PGCH is supported more generally, and whether it can eventually subsume and replace the purely grammatical FOFC. I thank the editors of this volume for permitting me to present this explanatory alternative for disharmonic word orders here.

15

Explaining the Final-over-Final Constraint: Formal and Functional Approaches*

MICHELLE SHEEHAN

15.1 Introduction: harmony and disharmony in natural language

Typologists have long noted a preference for 'harmony' in the linear alignment of certain heads and modifying dependents (cf. Greenberg 1963; Vennemann 1974a; Hawkins 1983, this volume; Dryer 1992a; see the introduction to this volume). In X-bar Theory, this trend was attributed to a parameter governing the order of a syntactic head X and its complement/sister, which can be informally stated as follows:[1]

(1)   The sister of X precedes/follows X

Unfortunately, the neatness of the Head Parameter is empirically challenged by the fact that many languages are not fully harmonic, as has often been noted. In fact, as Jackendoff (1977: 84–5) noted, even English has some degree of disharmony.[2]

* A previous (quite different) version of this paper was published in *Newcastle Working Papers in Linguistics* (*NWP*). I would like to thank two anonymous reviewers from *NWP* as well as two equally anonymous reviewers from this volume for forcing me to clarify my ideas. I would also like to acknowledge the AHRC and members of the projects 'Structure and Linearization in Disharmonic Word Orders' (Universities of Cambridge and Newcastle) and 'Un-Cartesian Linguistics' (University of Durham) for their comments and critiques: Laura Bailey, Wolfram Hinzen, Anders Holmberg, Ulrich Reichard, Ian Roberts, and particularly Theresa Biberauer. Finally, I also benefitted greatly from a brief discussion with Jack Hawkins while writing this paper as well as from email correspondence with him. All errors are, as ever, my own.

[1] As Dryer (1992a: 88, note 6) notes, the Head Parameter does not regulate the order of heads and adjuncts, and distinct mechanisms are often assumed to regulate the linear positioning of the latter (cf. Ernst 2003; Haider 2004).

[2] Dryer (1992a: 109, fn. 17) notes, for example, that there are few languages which consistently branch in the same direction, though he includes non-complements in his correlation pairs such as the order of subject and verb. As such, it cannot be inferred from this that few languages are consistently head-initial or head-final. Nonetheless, the existence of languages with mixed word orders does indicate that there is more to word order than the Head Parameter. See also note 4.

A starker example is German, which has what appear to be head-final VPs in non-V2 contexts, head-initial CPs and DPs, and both head-initial and head-final PPs, as well as circumpositions. This is further complicated by the fact that certain matrix and embedded clauses in German display the V2 property, giving rise to surface VO order.[3] As such, it seems clear that the word order of a given language cannot be straightforwardly determined by a single parameter like that in (1).[4]

A similar point emerges from the fact that word-order change proceeds on a category-sensitive basis rather than in 'one fell swoop' (cf. Li and Thompson 1974; Biberauer, Newton, and Sheehan 2009). The implication is that there can be no across-the-board 'Head Parameter', but rather the basic order of a head and its complement must be relativized to subsets of categories (cf. Huang 1994), and regulated either by a series of head parameters or in some other way (cf. Kayne 1994, Cinque 2005b for movement-based theories of word order).

In some cases, there is even evidence that two heads of the same category are specified differently for directionality within a single language. Thus, Bengali has both phrase-initial and phrase-final complementizers with synchronically equivalent subordinating functions, as Bayer (1999, 2001) shows. Such cases indicate that surface disharmony is a very real phenomenon in natural language, and one that any theory of word order must allow for. Even if the Head Parameter exists at some abstract level, at the very least there must be other forces interacting with it to give rise to disharmony.

15.2 Degrees of disharmony and the Final-over-Final Constraint

The implication of all this disharmony is that word order at least *can* simply be acquired on a case-by-case basis (relative to (subsets of) categories or even individual lexical items). Indeed, evidence from acquisition suggests that children acquire the word order of their native language very early, even in languages such as German with complex disharmony and V2 effects (Clahsen and Muysken 1986). But if word order is simply acquired on a category-by-category basis, then the fact that certain pairs of categories display a strong cross-linguistic preference for harmony is mysterious. In a sense, in weakening the Head Parameter to render it empirically adequate, we lose the GB explanation for harmony altogether. The apparent prediction is that any harmonic/disharmonic combination should be equally syntactically viable, as Biberauer, Holmberg, and Roberts (2008a) note.[5]

---

[3] Of course it is possible to posit an underlyingly head-initial system and derive head-final orders via movement, as Zwart (1997a) proposes for Dutch.

[4] This point was noted by Koopman (1984) and Travis (1984), who proposed an interaction between theta-marking and Case-marking parameters to account for these more complex word-order systems.

[5] Of course, harmony may well lie beyond the remit of syntax, deriving from patterns of diachronic change/acquisition (cf. Bybee 1988; Roberts 2007b) or functional pressures (Hawkins 1994, 2004, this volume). We return to Hawkins' approach shortly, as well as to a potential explanation in terms of economy.

In actual fact, though, it appears that certain disharmonic orders are fairly common, whereas others are unattested in many syntactic domains. Examples (2a–b) represent harmonic structures, well-known to occur most frequently in natural languages. Holmberg (2000) claims, however, that between the two possible disharmonic combinations, (2c) is fairly common, whereas (2d) is unattested or extremely rare:

(2)   Harmonic and disharmonic combinations

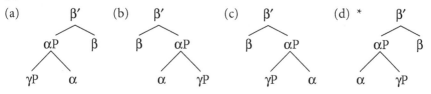

Biberauer, Holmberg, and Roberts (BHR) (2008a,b, 2010) term this effect the *Final-over-Final Constraint* (henceforth FOFC):[6]

(3)   The Final-over-Final Constraint (FOFC)
      If α is a head-initial phrase and β is a phrase immediately dominating α, then β must be head-initial. If α is a head-final phrase, and β is a phrase immediately dominating α, then β can be head-initial or head-final.

I will term the disharmonic order in (2c) the 'inverse-FOFC order' and that in (2d) the 'FOFC-violating order' for ease of reference, but no theoretical implications should be read into these terms. Section 15.3 briefly introduces some of the empirical support for FOFC, drawing on work by BHR (2008a,b, 2010), Biberauer, Newton, and Sheehan (BNS) (2009), Biberauer, Sheehan, and Newton (BSN) (2010), and Biberauer and Sheehan (2012). Section 15.4 introduces two different accounts of FOFC: one 'formal', the other 'functional'. The discussion puts aside certain apparent counterexamples to FOFC until section 15.5, when they are used to compare the two approaches. Section 15.5 shows that while some evidence arguably goes in favour of an account stated in terms of Hawkins' (1994) Performance–Grammar Correspondence Hypothesis (PGCH), other evidence raises some serious problems for an explanation along these lines. The implication is that the PF interface account is a more promising line of explanation for FOFC, despite remaining challenges. Section 15.6 addresses the problematic status of particles in relation to the two accounts, and proposes that the PF interface account can provide a new perspective on this problem. Finally, section 15.7 reconsiders the 'formal' status of the PF interface account, arguing that it might actually have a functional underpinning, before section 15.8 concludes.

---

[6] The version of FOFC given here is the first version offered by BHR, and it subsequently undergoes revisions, to accommodate apparent counterexamples. As these counterexamples will be discussed in section 15.5.2, I use the maximally general version of the constraint here. A full discussion of BHR's formal account of FOFC is beyond the scope of this paper.

15.3 Empirical evidence for FOFC

15.3.1 *Inflected auxiliary placement and the verb phrase*

It is well known from the typological literature that inflected auxiliaries are verb patterners, meaning that they are more commonly preverbal in VO languages and postverbal in OV languages (Dryer 1992a).[7] It is, however, less well known that the two potential disharmonic orders between an auxiliary, verb and object are not equally well attested. BHR (2008a,b, 2010) show that, surprisingly, all possible combinations of verb, object, and inflected auxiliary (even discontinuous ones) are attested in diachronic and synchronic stages of Germanic with one exception, *V–O–Aux:

(4) a. **O–V–Aux** German and dialects of German, Dutch and its dialects, Afrikaans; Old English, Old Norse

   b. **O–Aux–V** or so-called *verb-raising/VR* structures: Swiss German dialects, Dutch and its dialects, Afrikaans; Old English, Old Norse

   c. **Aux–O–V** or so-called *verb-projection raising/VPR* structures which involves a head-initial TP and a head-final VP: Swiss German dialects, Dutch dialects, spoken Afrikaans; Middle Dutch, Old High German, Old English, Old Norse

   d. **V–Aux–O**: required for CP complements in German, Dutch, Afrikaans, and their dialects; possible with PP complements in Dutch and Afrikaans and, to a lesser extent, German; possible with DPs in Old English and Old Norse

   e. **Aux–V–O**: English, Mainland Scandinavian, Icelandic; Old English

   f. ***V–O–Aux**: unattested[8] (summary based on BHR 2008a: 97)

Note crucially that the effects in (4) go beyond a simple preference for harmony (contra Hawkins, this volume). The inverse-FOFC order, Aux–O–V in (4c), is actually very common in Germanic and beyond, notably in Niger-Congo and Cushitic languages (cf. Koopman 1984, on Vata; Creissels 2005, on Mande; and

---

[7] Auxiliary and modal verbs are usually taken to be base-generated in or to move to some functional head between *v*P and CP (e.g. I, Agr, Asp, or T; cf. Roberts 1985; Pollock 1989). Ultimately the categorial status of auxiliaries, while undeniably important, does not affect FOFC as an empirical generalization in its most basic form. This is because FOFC holds transitively through the clause and thus, in a VO language, the possibility of any higher head-final phrase is ruled out. As such, as long as an auxiliary c-commands VP, its position with respect to VP is potentially evidence for/against FOFC.

[8] A reviewer points out that sentences involving A-bar VP-fronting are a superficial exception to this otherwise robust gap:

(i) I asked him to pay the bill, and pay the bill he did.

Given that these structures involve non-local A-bar movement of VP (past the subject) they fall outside the constraint as described in (3) because VP is not dominated by AuxP in its derived position (cf. BHR 2008b, 2010).

Mous 1993, on Iraqw).[9] The V–O–Aux order, on the other hand is systematically banned in languages with inflected auxiliaries, even those with variable word orders which permit all other permutations of verb, object, and auxiliary (see BHR 2008a, b, 2010, citing Holmberg 2000 on Finnish and Haddican 2004 on Basque). In a model of word order in which directionality is free, there is nothing to rule out the base generation of the order V–O–Aux as per (2d). BHR thus posit (3), initially as a descriptive constraint, to capture this gap. Hawkins (this volume) points out that uninflected tense markers (particles) do not adhere to FOFC (as BHR also note). I return to this complication in section 15.6.

15.3.1 *Polarity question particles and complementizers*

BSN (2010) argue that the presence of an initial polarity question head has blocked the development/borrowing of a final complementizer in a number of Indo-Aryan languages. Drawing on work by Bayer (1999, 2001) and Davison (2007), they show that South Asian languages show great variation in the placement of complementizers and question particles (henceforth Pol(arity) heads) (cf. Masica 1989; Bayer 1999, 2001; Davison 2007). Sanskrit had a final complementizer *iti,* lost in Modern Indo-Aryan. Conversely, all Mainland Modern Indic languages have initial complementizers. The variation in the area concerns the borrowing/development of a final complementizer from either a quotative or demonstrative source. While some Indo-Aryan languages have developed a final C (possibly under influence from Dravidian or other contact languages), others have not (Davison 2007).

Interestingly, the split appears to be syntactically determined: all languages with an initial Pol head have failed to develop/borrow a final C (Marlow 1997; Davison 2007). As an illustration, compare Hindi-Urdu and Marathi. Hindi-Urdu has an (optional) initial Pol head *kyaa* (homophonous with the word meaning 'what') and lacks any kind of final complementizer from either a verbal or demonstrative root:

---

[9] Aux–O–V is relatively common as a surface order, though this does not mean that all surface strings have the same underlying syntax. In Germanic, Aux–O–V arises as a result of V2, which by hypothesis involves movement of the finite auxiliary to C, or verb projection raising in embedded clauses (den Besten 1981). The fact that the basic word order in some Niger-Congo languages is S–Aux–DO–V–IO strongly suggests that OV is derived by A-movement of the object, in an otherwise head-initial clause. This is because all constituents except DO occur in a head-initial order (cf. Kandybowicz and Baker 2003 on Nupe). A similar argument might be made for Iraqw, which actually has a number of different object positions with different case and agreement properties (cf. Mous 1993). As the PGCH is concerned with surface strings and how they serve to construct hierarchical structure, the varying derivations of disharmonic orders are of limited relevance, though, as dominance plays a role, syntactic structure is not completely irrelevant. From a formal syntactic perspective, however, any analysis will have to rule out a number of possible ways of deriving the FOFC-violating order. Sheehan (in press) discusses this issue and argues that the PF interface account of FOFC given here extends to rule out instances of V–O–Aux derived by A-movement.

(5) a. kyaa   aap   wahaaN   aaeeNgii?
      POL   you   there   go.FUT.2PL
      'Are you going there?'

    b. *usee   [[vee aa   rahee   haiN]   **yah/ kah-kar**]   maaluum   hai
       3SG.DAT   3PL come   PROG   are   this/ say-PTCP   known   is
      'He/she knows [that they are coming].'   [Hindi-Urdu, Davison 2007: 182]

Marathi, on the other hand, has a final Pol head *kaa(y)* which can co-occur with either a final or initial C:

(6) a. [[to kal parat   aalaa   **kaa(y)**]   mhaaNun/asa] raam malaa
      he yesterday   back come.PST.3MSG   POL   Quot/such   Ram I.DAT
      witSaarat   hotaa
      ask.PROG   be.PST.3MSG
      'Ram was asking me [whether/if he came back yesterday].'

    b. raam   maalaa   witSaarat   hotaa   [**ki**   to   kal   parat
      Ram   I.DAT   ask.PROG   be.PST.3MSG   that   he   yesterday   back
      aalaa   **kaa(y)**
      come.PST.3MSG POL
    'Ram was asking me [whether/if he came back yesterday].'
    [Marathi, Davison 2007: 184, attributed to R. Pandharipande]

Assuming that C is higher than Pol (as argued by Laka 1994, Rizzi 2001, and Holmberg 2003) and that polarity question particles are Pol heads in Indo-Aryan, BSN propose that this gap is again an effect of FOFC. Interestingly, data from the *World Atlas of Language Structures (WALS)* suggest that this gap holds more generally, also outside Indo-Aryan (Dryer 2005e/2011g, 2005f/2011e), as shown in Table 15.1 (see also BSN):

TABLE 15.1 **Typological positioning of Polarity heads and complementizers**

Type	Position of Pol	Position of C	Number of Language: genera: families[10]
A	Initial	Initial	72: 35: 13 (78)[11]
B	Final	Final	45: 33: 20 (46)
C	Final	Initial	74: 40: 16 (82)
D	Initial	Final	4: 3: 3 (4)

[10] Where genera denote groups of languages whose 'relatedness is fairly obvious without systematic comparative analysis' with a time depth no greater than 3500–4000 years (Dryer 2011f: 584). For example, '[t]he standard subfamilies of Indo-European (e.g. Germanic, Slavic, Celtic) are fairly clearly examples of genera...'.

[11] The numbers in brackets are the updated versions from Dryer (2011e,g). The breakdown into genera and language families is not provided in the online resource.

Once again, we see that the two harmonic possibilities as well as the inverse FOFC order are common, whereas the FOFC-violating order (D) is virtually unattested.[12]

15.3.3 *Clausal complements*

Biberauer and Sheehan (2012) discuss the placement of CP complements in OV languages, arguing that this area of grammar is also regulated by FOFC. While there are many head-initial languages in which a head-initial CP follows the verb, giving a harmonic head-initial sequence, there seem to be no languages in which a head-initial CP precedes the verb, giving rise to the FOFC-violating order *C–TP–V (cf. Hawkins 1994, this volume; Dryer 2009). This is true of familiar OV Germanic languages and of Persian, but also of unrelated languages such as Mangarrayi, Iraqw, Neo-Aramaic, Sorbian, Anywa, and Päri (cf. Dryer 2009 for further evidence).[13] That this is a FOFC effect is most obvious in languages like Turkish in which the canonical position for embedded clauses, both nominalized (7a) and 'direct' (7b), is preverbal, but where C-initial embedded clauses are obligatorily extraposed (7c):

(7) a. (Ben)   siz-in   Ankara-ya   git-tiğ-iniz]   -i
     I   you-GEN   Ankara-DAT   go-NOM-POSS.2PL   -ACC
     duy-du-m
     head-PST-1SG
     'I heard that you went to Ankara.'   [Turkish, Özsoy 2001: 216]

   b. Biz   [sen-   Ø   Ankara-ya   git   -ti-n]
      we   you-   NOM   Ankara-DAT   go   -PST-2SG
      san   -dı   -k
      consider -PST -1PL
      'We consider you to have gone to Ankara.'   [Turkish, Özsoy 2001: 217]

   c. Anla   -dı -m   [$_{CP}$ **ki**   onun   bir
      understand   -PST-1SG   that   3SG.GEN   one
      derdi   var
      problem.POSS.3SG   exists
      'I realized that he had a problem.'   [Turkish, Haig 2001: 201]

---

[12] The four counterexamples are Tacana and Ese Ejja (Tacanan), Gavião (Tupi), and Resígaro (Arawakan). These languages appear to nominalize embedded clauses (cf. Ottaviano 1980 on Tacana; Moore 1989 on Gavião; and Allin 1976 on Resígaro). If nominalization triggers atomization as Sheehan (2010) suggests then these counterexamples might be classified as particles and analysed in the manner proposed in section 15.6.

[13] Dryer (2009) finds only one language with initial Cs in which the unmarked position for embedded clauses is preverbal (Harar Oromo). To this, we must add Akkadian at a certain stage of development (cf. Deutscher 2000). These languages require further investigation.

Hawkins (this volume) claims that the inverse-FOFC combination V–TP–C is also virtually unattested, calling into question the relevance of FOFC as an empirical generalization in this domain. This objection is unfair, though, as FOFC independently rules out V–TP–C as a basic word order, as Biberauer and Sheehan (2012) show. As BHR note, FOFC rules out the possibility of a head-final CP in a VO language, by transitivity. VO order rules out the possibility of a final T (*[[V–O]–T]), and T–VP order in turn rules out the possibility of a final C (*[[T–VP]–C]). If we assume that, all else being equal, CP and DP arguments will surface in the same position in a given language, it follows that wherever a language has a final complementizer, it will also be an OV language and so the clause in question will surface preverbally.

Of course, the assumption that CP and DP arguments should, all else being equal, surface in the same position might be queried, given empirical evidence from languages like Dutch, German, Persian, and Hindi, and Stowell's (1981) influential Case Resistance Principle (CRP). Nonetheless, Biberauer and Sheehan claim that if obligatory 'extraposition' of CP complements in these languages is actually a FOFC effect, then we can maintain the simpler idea that CP/DP complements are base-generated in the same position, and that extraposition is an FOFC compliance strategy. In an OV language, it follows that there is no motivation to obligatorily extrapose a head-final CP. The data from languages such as Turkish, above, strongly support the claim that extraposition in such contexts is tied to directionality (cf. Hawkins 1994 for a processing account of the same empirical phenomenon). Note also that languages with greater word-order flexibility do display surface V–TP–C order (cf. Uriagereka 1999b on Basque):

(8) Nork esan   du   [ardoa   bidali   dio-la]?
     who said   have-   wine   sent   that
     'Who has he/she said has sent (*the) wine?'   [Basque, Uriagereka 1999b: 409]

Hawkins (this volume) raises a further, more challenging objection relating to the apparent absence of the order *C–TP–N. As he notes, according to the specific formulation of FOFC in BHR (2010), which relativizes FOFC to heads within an extended projection, the *C–TP–N gap falls beyond the remit of the generalization. Given that the order *C–TP–N appears to be unattested and also appears to be an instance of 'final over initial' it is arguably problematic that it falls outside the empirical scope of the generalization. The two accounts of FOFC presented here differ from that in BHR (2010) in several respects and predict clausal complements of N to fall within their remit, and thus sidestep one of Hawkins' objections.[14]

---

[14] BHR (2008a,b) add a category proviso to their formal account of FOFC to allow for the fact that head-initial DPs and PPs are possible in OV languages. In BHR (2010), this is reformulated as a restriction to extended projections, though this requires a CP complement and its selecting verb to be in the same extended projection. The rationale behind such a move is questioned in section 15.5 below.

An additional problem remains, though, as the order *N–TP–C is, according to Hawkins, also unattested, and this inverse-FOFC order is not ruled out by transitivity; in fact, in many cases the order of categories in DP operates completely independently of those in VP (cf. section 15.5.2 below). As such, the lack of *C–TP–V can be taken as straightforward empirical evidence for FOFC, but the lack of *C–TP–N is more controversial.

15.3.3 *Summary*

In this section, I have considered three syntactic contexts in which something akin to FOFC appears to hold. The reader is referred to BHR (2008a,b, 2010), BNS (2009), BSN (2010), and Biberauer and Sheehan (2012) for further discussion. The status of FOFC as a true empirical generalization is challenged by Hawkins (this volume) on a number of counts. On the one hand, Hawkins claims, FOFC is too strong, as it seems to face certain potential counterexamples. On the other hand, he claims, FOFC is too weak, because the other disharmonic order is also not widely attested. The data in sections 15.3.1–15.3.4 partly confirm Hawkins' suspicions and partly allay them.

On the one hand, it is true that there are a small number of counterexamples to FOFC. There are four languages from four genera, for example, which display the surface word order *Pol–TP–C, though there may be an independent explanation for their behaviour. It is not true, however, that the other disharmonic combination is equally rare in the cases discussed, as there are 70 languages from 16 genera with the combination C–TP–Pol. In fact, in the above discussion we have seen that the inverse-FOFC order is in fact widely attested in the first two contexts (Aux–O–V, C–TP–Pol). In the third context, where both disharmonic orders are virtually unattested (*V–TP–C, *C–TP–V), FOFC provides an independent explanation for the lack of the first order at least. Of course, this is not to say that these data are sufficient to prove that FOFC holds universally across all categories in all languages. Clearly substantial, careful cross-linguistic investigation is required to ascertain whether this is the case, and there are already clear classes of FOFC exceptions, to be discussed in sections 15.5.2 and 15.6. Nonetheless, the fact that FOFC holds in the three domains discussed above is sufficient to make it an interesting potential generalization, worthy of theoretically informed investigation.

Ultimately, FOFC remains open to falsification, based on a careful consideration of potential counterexamples. As a methodological point, though, it seems fair to begin with the hypothesis that it is a hard universal and investigate it as such. One might equally begin with the even stronger hypothesis that the other disharmonic order is equally dispreferred, as Hawkins (this volume) suggests, and indeed this was the working hypothesis under the Head Parameter. The data discussed in this section, however, suggest that there is more at stake than a preference for harmony. In fact, in many ways, as Hawkins points out, more problematic than the few counterexamples to FOFC are the unattested orders which appear similar to the FOFC gap, but which do not involve complementation, and so would fall outside the remit of BHR's general approach.[15] It is possible that these gaps may fall within the remit of the two approaches discussed here, though a full discussion of these facts is left for future work.

The fact that Hawkins (this volume) rejects FOFC as an empirical generalization is, in a sense, surprising, as an elegant account of (a statistical version of) the asymmetry emerges from one version of the Performance–Grammar Correspondence Hypothesis (PGCH) (Hawkins 1994).[16] In the remainder of this paper I describe the 'functional' account of FOFC emerging from the PGCH and contrast it with a 'formal' approach based on a version of Kayne's (1994) Linear Correspondence Axiom (cf. Sheehan in press). Interestingly, the two approaches make many similar predictions, but they also differ in certain respects, as discussed in section 15.5.

15.4 Explaining the Final-over-Final Constraint

15.4.1 *Performance–Grammar Correspondence Hypothesis (PGCH)*

It is often claimed that word-order universals lie beyond the remit of generative grammar and stem ultimately from parsing/processing principles or patterns of diachronic change (cf. Newmeyer 2005a; Whitman 2008; Abels and Neeleman 2009).[17] One highly articulated processing-based theory of word order is that proposed by Hawkins (1994, 2004, this volume), which provides a potential explanation for the tendency for cross-categorial harmony discussed in section 15.1, as well many other online word-order tendencies (heavy NP shift and other kinds of 'rightward' displacement). As mentioned above, Hawkins (this volume) rejects FOFC as an empirical generalization, and claims that all that is observed cross-linguistically is a

---

[15] Theresa Biberauer (p.c.) reminds me that the distinction between complements and adjuncts is murky territory. She claims that from a Cinquean perspective, adjuncts form part of the clausal/nominal spine and so are expected to be subject to a version of FOFC stated in terms of complementation. To me this appears to be true only inasmuch as adjuncts are themselves construed as functional heads (as suggested by Abney 1987 for adjectives). If adverbs are specifiers of functional heads then they should not be affected by roll-up movement. In fact, Cinque's roll-up approach to adverb and adjective ordering specifically requires the presence of null functional heads, which give rise to FOFC violations (cf. Cinque 2005b).

[16] I focus here on Hawkins (1994) rather than Hawkins (2004) because the earlier version of the theory makes clear predictions in relation to FOFC. Hawkins (this volume) implies that this is no accident, as he now rejects the empirical basis of the FOFC asymmetry. In personal communication, he notes that his 2004 approach could explain the asymmetry only if there were some preference for mother attachment rather than daughter attachment. Interestingly, this is reminiscent of the core idea behind the Linear Correspondence Axiom, whereby there is a requirement for higher categories to precede lower categories. One might say, then, that Hawkins' (2004) approach leads us irrevocably back to the LCA as an explanation of FOFC. See Walkden (2009) for further discussion of Hawkins (2004) in relation to FOFC.

[17] In section 15.7, I propose a partial endorsement of this position.

tendency towards harmony in the order of grammatical categories and their respective complements. Interestingly, though, the PGCH, when applied to disharmonic structures, appears to predict a statistical version of FOFC without further stipulation.

Hawkins (1994) proposes a theory of Early Immediate Constituents (EIC), which favours harmony over disharmony for processing/parsing reasons:

(9) Early Immediate Constituents (EIC) (Hawkins 1994: 77)
    The human parser prefers linear orders that maximize the I[mmediate]C[onstituents]-to-non-I[mmediate]C[onstituents] ratios of Constituent Recognition Domains.

Immediate constituents (ICs) are the constituents required to identify a certain grammatical category. For example, a transitive VP consists of two ICs: the category V, which is constructed by the verb and the category NP, constructed by the determiner or noun whose presence indicates that it is a transitive VP. *Constituent Recognition Domain* and *IC-to-non-IC ratio* are defined in the following ways by Hawkins:

(10) Constituent Recognition Domain (CRD) (Hawkins 1994: 58–9)
    The CRD for a phrasal mother node M consists of the set of terminal and non-terminal nodes that must be parsed in order to recognize M and all ICs of M, proceeding from the terminal node in the parse string that constructs the first IC on the left, to the terminal node that constructs the last IC on the right, and including all intervening terminal nodes and the non-terminal nodes they construct.

(11) IC-to-non-IC ratio = $\dfrac{\text{Number of ICs in domain}}{\text{Number of non-IC nodes in domain}}$

Obviously, as Hawkins acknowledges, the number of non-IC nodes in a given structure will vary depending on a number of independent syntactic assumptions (i.e. binary vs ternary branching, heads and movements posited, and more pertinently nowadays X-bar theory vs Bare Phrase Structure, *v*P-internal subject hypothesis, etc.). Hawkins ignores null functional structure and allows ternary branching, meaning that his trees look very different from standard trees in the current literature. Aware of such issues, he also provides a simplified IC-to-word ratio, which factors out syntactic assumptions and gives results broadly similar to the IC-to-non-IC ratio:[18]

---

[18] Theresa Biberauer (p.c.) asks me to clarify what is meant by a word. As far as I can see, Hawkins gives no definition, and rather uses the term in an informal sense. This may, of course, prove problematic, especially if Julien (2002) is right, and words have no syntactic status. One might plausibly reformulate his proposal, nonetheless, substituting 'morpheme' for 'word', as an anonymous reviewer suggests.

(12)   IC-to-word ratio = $\dfrac{\text{Number of ICs in domain}}{\text{Number of words in domain}}$

Finally, he proposes that the ratio for a CRD is the average of the scores for all IC-to-word ratios calculated left to right.

(13)   Calculating left-to-right IC-to-non-IC ratios

The L-to-R IC-to-non-IC ratio for a non-optimal CRD is measured by first counting the ICs in the domain from left to right (starting from 1), and then counting the non-ICs (or words alone) in the domain (again starting from 1). The first IC is then divided by the total number of non-ICs that it dominates (e.g. 1/2); the second IC is divided by the highest total for the non-ICs that it dominates (e.g. if this IC dominates the third through seventh non-IC in the domain, then 2/7 is the ratio for the second IC); and so on for all subsequent ICs. The ratio for each IC is expressed as a percentage, and these percentages are then aggregated to achieve a score for the whole CRD.

(adapted from Hawkins 1994: 82)

According to Hawkins, these processing principles predict that harmonic head-initial and head-final constructions should be most common cross-linguistically as these kinds of structures are optimal in terms of processing, with CRD and ratios as small as possible. Consider, by way of illustration, the harmonic orders for VPs containing an adpositional complement and a verb (Hawkins 1994: 96–7, this volume):

(14)   [$_{VP}$ [$_V$ **go**] [$_{PP}$ [$_P$ **to**] [$_{NP}$ school]]]   IC-to-word ratio = 1/1, 2/2, average = 100%[19]
               1   2

(15)   [$_{VP}$ [$_{PP}$ [$_{NP}$ school] [$_P$ **to**]] [$_V$ **go**]]   IC-to-word ratio = 1/1, 2/2, average = 100%
                     1   2

In both (14) and (15) the NP complement of P is not included in the CRD of VP as NP is an IC of PP but not of VP. In (14), the IC-to-word ratio of V (the first IC) is 1/1, as the word *go* serves to construct it (though at this point it remains unclear whether the V is transitive, intransitive, ditransitive, etc.). The IC-to-word ratio of PP is 2/2, as the second IC (PP) dominates only the second word contained in the CRD of VP, namely *to* (recall that NP falls outside the CRD of PP). The average IC-to-word ratio is therefore 100%, as the number of words is exactly equal to the number of ICs constructed. In (15) a similar effect holds, except that this time, the head-final language is constructed 'bottom-up'. Once again, the NP is not included in the CRD of VP. As such, the CRD begins with *to*, which constructs the first IC of VP,

---

[19]   I use Hawkins' labels here for consistency.

namely PP. Because NP is outside the CRD of VP, PP dominates only one word in the CRD (namely *to*), giving it an optimal 1/1 IC-to-word ratio. The word *go*, similarly, serves to construct the second IC of VP, and V also dominates the second word in the CRD (namely *go*). Once again the average of these two IC-to-word ratios gives a perfect 100% as two adjacent words serve to construct the two ICs of VP. As such, Hawkins' approach means that harmonically head-final and harmonically head-initial languages are equally optimal in processing terms. Assuming that frequency correlates with processing efficiency, Hawkins' EIC theory predicts that harmonic structures will be most frequent in the world's languages, as appears to be the case.

Hawkins (1994: 255) also discusses the two disharmonic combinations, where NP complements of P are necessarily included in the CRD of VP. He gives the following IC-to-word ratios, assuming that V and P are single words and that NP comprises a determiner and a noun:

(16)   [$_{VP}$ [$_V$ go]   [$_{PP}$ [$_{DP}$ the shops]   [$_P$ to]]]
　　　　　　 1　　　　 　 2　 3　　　　　 4　　 IC-to-word-ratio = 1/1, 2/4 = 75%

(17)   [$_{VP}$ [$_{PP}$ [$_P$ to]   [$_{DP}$ the shops]]   [$_V$ go]]
　　　　　　　　 1　　 　 2　 3　　　　　 4　　 IC-to-word ratio = 1/3, 2/4 = 42%

In (16), the first word *go* serves to construct the first IC of VP, V, giving an IC-to-word ratio of 100%. The second IC of VP (PP) is constructed by *to*. Now PP dominates the second through fourth words in the CRD, and so the IC-to-word ratio of PP is 2/4. The aggregate IC-to-word ratio is thus 75% for this word order. In (17) on the other hand, the first IC which is constructed is PP. In this case, PP dominates the first through third words in the CRD of VP (i.e. *to, the*, and *shops*). According to the definition in (13), then, the first IC-to-word ratio in (17) is 1/3. The IC-to-word ratio of the second IC, namely V, is 2/4 because the IC V dominates the fourth word in the CRD (i.e. *go*). As such, (17) has a substantially lower efficiency rate of 42%. Moreover, the greater the number of words in the intervening DP constituent, the larger the difference in efficiency between the two disharmonic word orders will be. In effect, the NP complement of P is parsed twice in (17), once in the construction of the first IC (PP), and again in the construction of the second IC (V). Crucially, this makes the prediction that structures/orders like (17) will be more difficult to process, and hence less frequent than those in (16). As (17) is the FOFC-violating order, this version of the PGCH thus appears to derive a statistical FOFC from independently justifiable principles of efficient processing.[20]

---

[20] It should be made clear that in the final cut, DP and PP complements to V are beyond the remit of FOFC for BHR (2008b, 2010) because of a category or extended projection proviso. Nonetheless, as discussed below, there is a sense in which a kind of FOFC asymmetry is observed with PP complements of V, suggesting that PP complements of V should perhaps not be ruled out of FOFC.

In these terms, FOFC reduces to the fact that (i) CRDs are constructed left to right and (ii) higher heads are privileged in constructing more independent ICs. Another way to think of this is that where a phrase appears sandwiched between two heads, the most economical way to parse it is if it forms a constituent with the second head. The prediction, then, is that this parsing preference will be reflected in the linear orders of the world's languages.[21]

Note crucially that the PGCH does not necessarily rule out completely the possibility of FOFC-violating orders. Rather it predicts that they will be infrequent and certainly less frequent than harmonic or inverse-FOFC orders. IC-to-word ratios are also influenced by the relative 'heaviness' of the constituents involved and the implication is that average relative weights might affect grammaticalization trends (cf. Hawkins, this volume, for discussion).[22] As such, it is predicted that FOFC effects may be (i) directly sensitive to heaviness or (ii) category-sensitive, where different categories have different tendencies towards heaviness. For example, the FOFC-violating order should surface more frequently with the lightest categories like DP and less frequently with heavy categories like CP. We will see below that these predictions seem to hold, though the numbers of exceptions are very small in all cases. However, the PGCH also makes other predictions, which are not so well supported. Crucially it predicts that where two categories display a typological preference for harmony they will also display an FOFC effect and vice versa.[23] This is because the same principle which gives rise to the preference for harmony (i.e. EIC) also gives rise to FOFC. While there might be additional (historical/sociolinguistic) factors which skew the typological sample away from harmony, where this happens, these same factors should also serve to rule *in* an FOFC-violating order. The prediction of EIC is therefore biconditional:

Cross-linguistic preference for harmony between X and Y iff FOFC holds between X and Y.

---

[21] Interestingly, a similar processing effect appears to apply in phonology if we assume that vowels/ nuclei are equivalent to syntactic heads. The Maximal Onset Principle prefers consonants to be parsed with a following rather than preceding nucleus (as an onset rather than a coda, subject to partially language-specific phonotactic constraints) (Blevins 1995: 230):

(i) */ ... VC–V ... /   / ... V–CV ... /

A full consideration of these facts is beyond the scope of this paper. When discussing potential FOFC effects in morphology, BHR (2010) note that Hawkins' theory stops at the word level. As such, if a unified processing account of both onset maximization and FOFC is possible, it will look different from the PGCH in its current form. An anonymous reviewer claims, though, that there is nothing per se to prevent an extension of Hawkins' approach to the morphemic and even phonemic level. This is an important area for future research.

[22] As Theresa Biberauer (p.c.) points out, some light categories such as R-pronouns in West Germanic very frequently extrapose whereas heavier PPs do not, raising some problems for the heaviness constraint.

[23] I am not concerned here with conceptual objections to Hawkins' general approach, but rather with teasing out its empirical predictions. For a critique of the PGCH see Mobbs (2008).

I will argue below that there is suggestive evidence against such a biconditional relation, hence against an account of FOFC based on the PGCH.

15.4.2 *A Phonological Form–interface account*

There is strong empirical evidence that specifiers uniformly precede the head/complement in their containing phrase (e.g. from the preference for leftwards movement and initial subjects and the lack of verb-penultimate orders; cf. Kayne 1994, 2004). This is often taken as evidence for the Linear Correspondence Axiom (LCA), a linearization mechanism which maps asymmetric c-command to linear precedence.[24] In relation to the order of head and complement, however, there is less empirical evidence for any such asymmetry. Both VO and OV are equally frequent, for example (Dryer 2005c/2011b), and the asymmetries cited by Kayne do not relate to the order of head and complement. The lack of verb-penultimate, for example, is evidence only of the lack of final specifiers (Richards 2008: 280). Based on observations of this kind, Abels and Neeleman (2009) propose that the empirical asymmetries usually taken as evidence for the LCA actually reduce to a ban on rightward movement. FOFC is of particular interest in this respect as it provides crucial evidence of a cross-linguistic asymmetry in the ordering of heads. If the linear order of heads displays the same kind of asymmetry observed with specifiers, then word-order asymmetries cannot be reduced to a ban on rightward movement. FOFC can thus be taken as crucial empirical evidence in favour of the LCA and against efforts to reduce it to a ban on rightward movement.

Previous formal accounts of FOFC have capitalized on this fact and relied upon the idea that head finality is derived via very local comp-to-spec movement, following the ideas in Kayne (1994) (cf. Holmberg 2000; BHR 2008a,b, 2010; BNS 2009; Sheehan 2009a,b). In these terms, a harmonically head-final TP is derived in the following way: the object of the verb first moves locally to Spec-VP, then the whole VP, complement of T, 'rolls up' to Spec-TP:

(18)

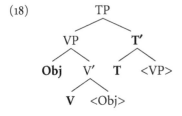

---

[24] As an anonymous reviewer notes, strictly speaking the LCA at its most basic is the proposal that asymmetric c-command maps to order (Kayne 1994: 6). The claim that the relevant order is precedence rather than subsequence is separate and is justified independently by Kayne (1994: 33), partly on an empirical basis. I return to this issue in section 15.7.

If it is assumed that internal Merge is costless, in some sense then, head finality arises in those cases where a head simply merges twice with its complement. According to Kayne's (1994) category-based definition of c-command, the complex specifier VP asymmetrically c-commands the head T and so must precede it, giving a head-final order. BHR (2010) provide an account of FOFC in these terms, claiming that movement in such cases is triggered by a caret feature ^ which is optionally associated with c-selection features. In their terms, FOFC stems from certain restrictions in the distribution of ^, which serve to ban local comp-to-spec movement of a head-initial phrase. Sheehan (2009a,b) provides an alternative account whereby this kind of movement is permitted at the narrow syntactic level, but gives rise to discontinuous linearization at PF (as developed in different terms below).

There are several potential objections to these kinds of accounts. Firstly, Kayne's same-category-based definition of c-command which ensures that a specifier (VP) asymmetrically c-commands a head (T) also means that multiple specifiers of T are ruled out (cf. Kayne 1994). If the LCA holds at the narrow syntactic level, then it follows that any phrase containing an externally merged specifier cannot be the target of roll-up movement (cf. Julien 2002). This creates considerable problems for FOFC, as vP, assuming that it introduces the external argument, will necessarily be head-initial. This in turn implies that there will be no phrase-final auxiliaries or complementizers in any languages (contrary to fact). There is an escape from this problem in the form of Chomsky's (1995b) reconceptualization of the LCA as, essentially, a linearization algorithm. If this is the status of the LCA, then the ban on multiple specifiers holds only at the mapping to PF and not at the narrow syntactic level (cf. Moro 2000). From this perspective, a strong prediction is that in languages with roll-up movement of VP to Spec-vP the subject should vacate vP by the point of Spell-Out, moving to some (possibly null) head which is (i) not the target of roll-up movement, and (ii) higher than the highest head-final phrase. Interestingly, evidence suggests that this does *not* happen in some well-studied head-final languages, as Julien (2002: 130–6) notes. Thus, in Japanese and Turkish, evidence from the licensing of NPIs and scope interactions has been taken as evidence that the subject remains inside vP.[25] Given that heads above vP are final in both languages (e.g. negation, question particles, certain complementizers), these facts raise a serious empirical challenge for accounts of FOFC relying on comp-to-spec movement. Altering the definition of c-command so that it allows multiple specifiers to be linearized is a potential solution to this problem, though this is no simple task, as the basic spec–head–comp order

---

[25] In Turkish, for example, NPIs are licensed in subject position (Julien 2002: 132, citing Kural 1997: 502):

(i)   Kimse   uyu-ma-dı
       anyone   sleep-NEG-PST
       'No one slept.'

itself relies crucially on a category-based definition of c-command, and multiple specifiers of a single category by definition do not differ in relative 'height'.

A second objection to roll-up movement concerns Abels' (2003) anti-locality condition, which blocks movement which cannot result in feature-checking. His argument is that the head–complement relationship is the closest syntactic dependency possible and so comp-to-spec movement cannot possibly be motivated by feature-checking. Strong empirical support for the ban on comp-to-spec movement comes from evidence that extraction of the complement of a phase head is generally banned. Of course, it is possible to make the feature triggering comp-to-spec movement distinct from other features and immune to anti-locality, but this in turn weakens the main conceptual argument for deriving head finality via movement, namely that the mechanisms required to do so are independently needed by the grammar.[26]

Thirdly, as Richards (2008) notes, roll-up movement of this kind creates massive redundant structure, which strongly suggests that head finality should be marked. This is particularly true because, as Abels and Neeleman (2009) and Richards (2008) note, the antisymmetry hypothesis is not as restrictive as it first appears. Given the availability of (and need for) remnant movement, it is actually eminently possible to derive spec-final or inverse V2 orders. As such, the LCA can only explain typological asymmetries if some notion of markedness is associated with movement. If this is the case then spec-final orders cannot be categorically ruled out by the LCA, but can only be predicted to be rare. The implication of this move, though, implies that head finality will also be marked, and as noted above, there is no evidence that, for example, OV order is rarer than VO order. In fact, the only evidence that head finality is more restricted than head initiality comes from FOFC. It follows that if FOFC can be explained without the need for comp-to-spec movement then the only evidence that head finality is movement-derived also disappears.

The traditional alternative to (18) is to assume that the order of head and complement is regulated by a parameter, applying either in the Narrow Syntax or at the mapping to Phonological Form (PF). If we take the latter option then head-initial and head-final phrases have potentially identical syntax but different PF forms. Moreover, as Richards (2004, 2008) has shown, approaches assuming a PF Head Parameter are actually more successful in accounting for certain VO/OV asymmetries than analyses which assume all head finality to be derived via narrow syntactic movement.[27] All in

---

[26] An alternative to this very local movement is what Aboh (2004) terms 'snowballing', where null functional heads lacking phonetic/semantic content are present to attract the complement of a given phrase past its selecting head (cf. Kayne 1998). While these kinds of approaches get around the anti-locality problem, they introduce further problems, notably the positing of functional heads illegible at both the PF and LF interface.

[27] Richards takes the LCA to rely on c-command rather than asymmetric c-command. For this reason, a phrasal complement and its selecting head will always stand in a relation of mutual c-command, replicating the bottom pair problem and forcing the need for a PF Head Parameter. As a result it is true that Richards derives the need for a Head Parameter from the version of the LCA he posits, and the same is not true of the

all, then, it is worth considering to what extent it is possible to state previous analyses of FOFC without the need for local comp-to-spec movement. In this section, I argue that this is eminently possible. More specifically, I propose a simple restatement of Sheehan's (2009a,b) analysis of FOFC in Head-Parameter-based terms, whereby the LCA regulates word order only where it remains underspecified by the settings of c-selection-based PF parameters. This analysis, it will emerge, makes many similar predictions to Hawkins' account, but some differences nonetheless emerge, as discussed in section 15.5.

Assuming that language acquires linear order only at the PF interface, it follows that in a minimalist system, PF will rely on independently necessary syntactic asymmetries in order to impose this order. A number of potential candidates exist. Most locally, c-selection creates an immediate asymmetry between heads.[28] Non-locally, other asymmetric relations hold, all of which seem to be parasitic on asymmetric c-command (Probe–Goal, copy–trace). Kayne (1994) proposes that only the latter, non-local asymmetry is used to determine word order, but the weight of empirical evidence suggests that both kinds of dependencies are used. More specifically, local c-selectional dependencies regulate head–complement orders and then non-local c-command relations order the remaining categories. The result is a system in which something akin to the LCA regulates the order of disharmonic orders and specifiers.

Assume that where two categories stand in a relation of c-selection, a PF parameter of the following kind exists:

(19)   If a category A c-selects a category B, then A precedes/follows B at PF.

Following Richards (2004), if phase-internal movement must respect this ordering command at least in some languages, then (19) serves to derive Holmberg's Generalization.[29] I further propose, following Sheehan (in press), that a head and its (label) projections form a single category, so that projection is effectively reconceptualized as copying, and all arguments/adjuncts are formally merged via adjunction. The key implication of this proposal is that there is a one-to-one mapping between terminal nodes and categories so that a terminal, its projected 'labels', and any copies of it

---

account put forth here, as an anonymous reviewer asks me to clarify. However, while Richards' approach is undeniably elegant, it remains unclear why a symmetric relation would be the crucial determiner of linear order, when syntax is otherwise full of asymmetries.

[28] Theresa Biberauer (p.c.) suggests that some specifiers are also selected. If we limit our attention to c-selection, then evidence suggests that this is not the case (cf. Svenonius 1994). Of course externally merged subjects are thematically selected, and this too appears to be a very local asymmetrical relation, suggesting that *in situ* subjects might also be ordered by a PF parameter. This provides the potential for a novel account of VS orders in Romance, which will be explored elsewhere.

[29] Richards (2004) shows that this allows a simple account of Holmberg's Generalization, stating that an object can shift out of VP in a VO language, only if V also leaves VP. The Head Movement Constraint is arguably a more general case of Holmberg's Generalization, in these terms.

generated by movement constitute a single multi-segment category.[30] Combined with a minimally revised category-based definition of c-command, based on Kayne (1994), this notion of copying effectively derives FOFC.

The following definitions reformulate Kayne's definitions of c-command/inclusion/exclusion in a manner compatible with the copy theory of labelling:

(20)   Complete Dominance: A category X completely dominates a category Y iff $X \neq Y$ and the shortest path from every copy of Y to the root of the tree includes all non-terminal copies of X.

(21)   Partial category dominance: A category X partially dominates a category Y iff $X \neq Y$, and the shortest path from every copy of Y to the root of the tree includes a copy of X, but X does not completely dominate Y.

(22)   C-command: A c-commands B iff A and B are categories, $A \neq B$, A does not partially dominate B, and any category which completely dominates A also completely dominates B.[31]

The outcomes of these definitions are that a specifier asymmetrically c-commands a head and a head asymmetrically c-commands its complement. The one-to-one correlation between categories and terminals simplifies the linearization process substantially. Firstly, where an atomic (non-branching) category moves, no deletion is necessary in order for the resultant two-segment category to be linearized (cf. X in the following example):

(23)

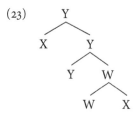

In (23), the category X will simply c-command Y and W without the need for deletion, because both Y and W partially dominate X. This serves to derive the hitherto poorly understood fact that moved phrases are (generally) spelled out in

---

[30] A reviewer objects to this idea as 'methodologically and ontologically non-minimalist'. I disagree. Sheehan (in press) argues that representational headedness is, at our current level of understanding, ineliminable from Narrow Syntax. Given this fact, labels, or some notational variant thereof are required, and copying is the most Minimalist method available to generate them. The unification of 'labelling' and 'movement' has considerably Minimalist ontological implications, and in conjunction with a reformulation of Kayne's category-based definition of c-command, makes well-supported empirical predictions (cf. Sheehan in press for discussion).

[31] Note that under these definitions a given category can both dominate and c-command another.

their derived position at PF.[32] It has the further implication that problematic non-terminal (X-bar) categories can be dispensed with and c-selection reduced to a category–category relation.

Putting aside specifiers/adjuncts and the added complications they introduce here, for reasons of space, let us consider how this kind of system works where a structure is harmonically head-initial.[33] In such a structure, all categories are specified to precede the category which they select (at PF) as indicated by subscript P. Crucially, the copy theory of labelling clarifies the fact that it is only the order of the selecting and selected *categories* which is specified by this parameter. Just because W in (24) must precede X, for example, this implies nothing about the order between W and Y or W and Z.[34] Nonetheless, the sum of all the PF parameters in a harmonic system does serve to provide a single unambiguous order of categories by transitivity:

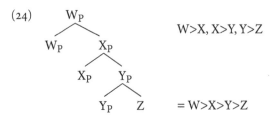

(24) W_P W>X, X>Y, Y>Z

W_P X_P

X_P Y_P

Y_P Z   = W>X>Y>Z

In such cases, W c-commands Y and Z and also precedes them but this information is not, by hypothesis, required to linearize the categories in (24). If X>Y and Y>Z then it follows, by transitivity, that X>Z, irrespective of any direct c-command relation between X and Z (see Fox and Pesetsky 2005 for discussion). As such, we can assume that only very local c-selection based PF parameters are used to linearize harmonic structures such as (24).[35] This issue becomes more salient when we consider harmonically head-final orders such as that in (25), where all categories are specified to follow their selected complement at PF, as indicated by subscript F:

---

[32] Nunes (1995, 2004) provides an alternative account of this relying on the idea that lower copies have more unchecked features than higher copies. It is not clear whether this account can be maintained in a system without spec–head agreement, however (cf. Fernández-Salgueiro 2008).

[33] Theresa Biberauer raises many interesting questions concerning specifiers and adjuncts which I take up elsewhere (cf. Sheehan in press).

[34] Recall that if projection is copying then there is no head/category distinction. All the copies of a given head/terminal form a single category.

[35] Note that if this holds then there is a sense in which harmonic structures are actually more economical to linearize than disharmonic structure.

(25)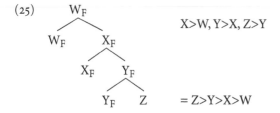

In (25), once again, we obtain a total linear order of categories by the sum of locally defined PF parameters. In such cases, despite the fact that W still (asymmetrically) c-commands Y and Z, it fails to precede them. As such, the LCA fails to hold in such cases.[36] In our terms, this is because it is never invoked. The fact that W c-commands Y and Z is irrelevant, as local PF parameters based on c-selectional asymmetries are sufficient to order all the categories in (25).

Local c-selection asymmetries between categories will not, however, always be sufficient to impose an unambiguous linear order on a hierarchical structure. In disharmonic contexts, for example, linear order will be underdetermined by the sum of PF parameters.[37] In such cases, I propose that non-local syntactic asymmetries between categories, in the form of asymmetric c-command, are also used. In short, a revised LCA is proposed whereby linear order between categories is first determined as far as possible based on local c-selection relations and only as a last resort by non-local asymmetric c-command relations:

(26)   Revised LCA
    (i)   If a category A c-selects a category B, then A precedes/follows B at PF.
    (ii) If no order is specified between A and B by the sum of all precedence pairs defined by (i), then A precedes B at PF if A asymmetrically c-commands B.[38]

In these terms, asymmetric c-command is a last-resort linearization aid, necessary only where no linear order between two categories is determined by the sum of all locally determined PF parameters.

Before continuing, it is necessary to consider certain objections raised by an anonymous reviewer to (26). His/her main objection runs as follows: by Occam's razor, a linearization algorithm which relies only on asymmetric c-command (strong

---

[36] Note that this problem arises also for Richards (2008), who is also forced to accept that the LCA is overridden in such circumstances.

[37] This provides the rationale for using both local and non-local asymmetries to determine linear order: local asymmetries are not sufficient to establish an unambiguous order between all categories. Of course, it would be possible to use only non-local asymmetries, as Kayne suggests, bypassing more local asymmetries. I return to this objection shortly.

[38] This raises the question why (ii) is not parameterized as (i) is. In section 15.7 I propose that it is at the level of UG, but that third-factor pressures so strongly prefer precedence that it has the appearance of a principle (cf. Biberauer, Holmberg, Roberts, and Sheehan 2010).

LCA) should be favoured over one which relies on both c-selection and asymmetric c-command (revised LCA). Note, first of all, that this objection is valid only if both approaches are empirically equivalent. As mentioned above, strong LCA-based approaches to head finality face certain empirical and conceptual challenges which render them independently problematic, making an appeal to Occam's razor irrelevant. Even if both approaches were directly comparable, though, the above characterization of the difference between the approaches is misleading. Head finality exists, in descriptive terms, in that languages like Japanese have essentially the opposite linear order of spine categories to English-type languages. As noted above, even deriving these orders under the strong LCA gives rise to certain amounts of redundant structure. It might be that the apparent simplicity of the strong LCA option is somewhat illusory.

As such, while conceptual considerations of 'methodological and ontological minimalism' must be taken seriously, explanatory adequacy must also be achieved. One could just as easily observe, for example, that Agree has the capacity to value features at a distance and so it is methodologically and ontologically un-Minimalist for thematic roles to be determined only by external (and more controversially internal) Merge. Nonetheless, it is still generally accepted that thematic roles cannot be assigned/valued via Agree, based on empirical evidence. Likewise, Agree is able to establish non-local dependencies between categories, precluding the conceptual need for movement; nonetheless it is generally accepted that movement exists in addition to Agree. In short, theories are also constrained by empirical considerations. In this case, the analysis proposed represents an attempt to salvage the crucial insights of the LCA from certain serious empirical and conceptual challenges. To the extent that it succeeds, the apparent departure from the Strong Minimalist Thesis (SMT) may be justified. Alternatively, it may even turn out that there is some more principled reason why the linearization algorithm favours local over non-local asymmetries.

Now let us consider how this version of the LCA serves to derive FOFC. Assume that individual heads/categories can be freely specified to precede or follow the categories they select, as appears to be empirically necessary (see sections 15.1–15.2 above). It follows that in such cases, part (ii) of the revised LCA in (26) will be required to aid the linearization of these heads.[39] Consider first a structure where W_P selects X_F (the inverse-FOFC order):[40]

---

[39] The linear position of specifiers will always be regulated by asymmetric c-command, hence the robust tendency for them to surface on the left, and hence for movement to be leftwards (cf. Kayne 1994; Cinque 2005b).

[40] From now on, PF parameter settings will be represented in tree diagrams. No theoretical implications should be read into this move, which is for ease of reference only.

(27)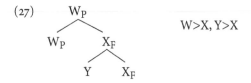

$$W>X, Y>X$$

The sum of locally determined PF parameters here leaves the order of terminals underspecified for (27). Both W and Y must precede X, but the order between W and Y themselves is simply not specified. In such cases, linearization appeals to less local asymmetries between categories. As such, it is necessary also to consider the c-command relations between W and Y, as per (26 (ii)). In (27), W asymmetrically c-commands Y and so must precede it (according to (26 (ii))), giving the total linear order W>Y>X. The inverse-FOFC order is therefore straightforwardly linearizable by the revised LCA in (26).

Crucially, the same is not true of the 'FOFC-violating' order in (28):

(28)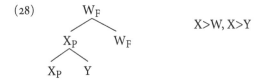

$$X>W, X>Y$$

In (28), the sum of locally determined PF parameters once again leaves the linear order of categories underspecified. This time it is known that both W and Y must follow X, but again no order is specified between W and Y themselves. In this case, too, W asymmetrically c-commands Y and so via (ii) of the revised LCA the additional precedence pair W>Y is added. This gives rise to the surprising word order X>W>Y, for (28), rather than the FOFC-violating order *X>Y>W. Crucially, the surface order *X>Y>W cannot be derived from such a structure by the revised LCA unless the constituent [X Y] is spelled out separately (an option which I return to in section 15.6).[41] This raises the question whether orders of the X>W>Y kind are indeed attested. In the case of verb, object, and auxiliary, V–Aux–O is possible in Old English, Finnish, and Basque:

(29) þæt   ænig   mon atellan   mæge   ealne   þone   demm
      that   any   man   relate   can   all   the   misery
      '... that any man can relate all the misery...'
                    [Old English, Pintzuk 2005: 13 (coorosiu,Or_2:8.52.6.1011)]

---

[41] In actual fact, as Sheehan (in press) notes, FOFC also appears to hold where a disharmonic word order is derived via movement rather than via non-harmonic head parameters. In such cases, she argues, the copy theory of labelling predicts that FOFC will hold for similar reasons to those outlined here.

In Old English, V–Aux–O order is attested where O is *not* a negative object, pronominal object, or particle, as Pintzuk (2005) notes. Interestingly, the latter often raise out of VP in Old English, making it plausible that (29) involves an *in situ* object. In all three languages, it is unlikely that such word orders are base-generated, and rather all seem to involve phrasal movement of VP (a point to which I return below). Plausibly, when V–Aux–O occurs as a basic word order Aux is reanalysed as a verbal suffix.[42]

15.5 Contrasting the approaches

Many of the predictions made by the two approaches are very similar. Both attach a certain cost to disharmony and both predict that the inverse-FOFC order will be more frequent than the FOFC-violating order. In what follows I outline both the similarities and differences between the two accounts. Data which are equally problematic for both accounts are discussed in section 15.6.

15.5.1 *The core cases*

Both approaches account for the core cases of FOFC described in section 15.3. *V–O–Aux is predicted by Hawkins (1994) to be rarer than Aux–O–V for exactly the same reasons that *P–DP–V is predicted to be rarer than V–DP–P. Consider the following example:

(30)   [$_{TP}$ [$_{VP}$ [$_{V}$ eaten] [$_{NP}$ the cake]][$_{T}$ has]]   1/3, 2/4 = 42%

The first IC of the TP (namely VP) will be constructed by *eaten*. VP dominates the first through third word in the CRD and so its IC-to-word ratio will be 1/3. The second IC is T, which is constructed by *has*. T dominates the fourth word in the CRD, so its ratio is 2/4. Once again, the inverse-FOFC order has a higher efficiency rating:

(31)   [$_{TP}$ [$_{T}$ has] [$_{VP}$ [$_{NP}$ the cake] [$_{V}$ eaten]]]   1/1, 2/4 = 75%

In this case the first IC of TP, namely T, is constructed by *has*. As T dominates only the first word in the CRD, it has a maximally efficient IC-to-word ratio 1/1. The second IC, namely VP is constructed by *eaten*. VP dominates the second through fourth words in the CRD and so has a ratio of 2/4. The case of polarity question markers and complementizers works in the same way, as long as Pol serves to construct PolP and C constructs CP.

The PF interface account explains the first two cases in exactly the manner outlined in section 15.4.2:

---

[42] As Sheehan (in press) shows, the PF account also serves to account for these FOFC effects.

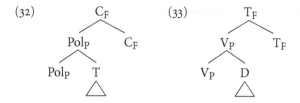

(32) C_F (33) T_F
       Pol$_P$ C_F V_P T_F
    Pol$_P$ T V_P D

In both (32) and (33), PF parameters alone fail to provide an unambiguous linear order of categories. In (32), no order is specified between T and C, and in (33) the same is true between D and T. Crucially, in both cases the FOFC-violating orders are predicted never to surface.[43]

15.5.2 *Exceptions to FOFC*

Thus far we have focused on the empirical support in favour of FOFC. It must be noted, however, that BHR (2008a,b, 2010) also discuss certain apparent counter-examples to the generalization in its most abstract form and actually present a rather different version of FOFC, in order to accommodate these counterexamples. They propose, for example, that FOFC holds only within extended projections, and that particles, being acategorial, are not subject to the generalization (cf. BHR 2010). Hawkins (this volume) raises some objections to limiting the scope of FOFC in this way, as it appears to rule out of the scope of the generalization some apparent FOFC effects. The two approaches to FOFC explored here actually make slightly different predictions about which [[head–complement]–head] surface orders will be permitted. These overlap only partially with the kinds of exceptions allowed by BHR's account. This section explores which surface FOFC violations are attested and which of the two approaches discussed above fares better in accounting for these exceptions.[44]

The first apparent exception comes from DP complements of V, which surface in a preverbal position:

(34) Johann hat   das/ein Buch   ausgeliehen
      John   has   the/a book   borrowed
      'John has borrowed the/a book.'

---

[43] An anonymous reviewer asks whether Pol–C–T and C–V–TP are attested as predicted. A potential example of Pol–C–TP occurs in Mecayapan Nahuatl, assuming that the conditional marker occupies the same position as question particles, which often have the same form:

(i) Si iga quijliisquej iga quena, huel monaamictij.
     'If that he gets permission, he can marry.'   [Mecayapan Nahuatl, Gutiérrez-Morales 2008: 181]

Si iga alternates with a fused form siga. Note that iga always surfaces in a clause-initial position, but this is as predicted if all clauses contain an optionally covert polarity head, triggering 'extraposition' of TP to the right of C. C–V–TP appears to be unattested, but full CP extraposition in such contexts is common (see Biberauer and Sheehan 2012 on the connection between CP extraposition and FOFC).

[44] It is beyond the scope of this paper to provide a critical discussion of BHR's account.

In actual fact, there are relatively few OV languages with clear determiners which allow a FOFC-violating configuration between DP and V. Most OV languages either (i) lack determiners distinct from demonstratives (which are plausibly specifiers) or (ii) have final determiners (cf. Dryer 1992a: 104). Moreover, OV languages with initial articles are no less common (taking into account areal and genetic factors) than VO languages with final articles. For this reason, there is no evidence for a FOFC asymmetry in this domain. A relevant question, then, is whether either approach can account for this fact.

Interestingly, the PGCH appears to have a ready explanation. Recall that the PGCH is sensitive to the relative heaviness of phrases. It follows, therefore, that DPs, tending to be the lightest phrases, might allow FOFC violations more often than other categories from a cross-linguistic perspective, unlike heavier phrases such as PP and CP.[45] The lack of a skewing between the two disharmonic combinations of article, NP, and V is therefore not an immediate problem for Hawkins' approach. In fact, given the status of articles in Hawkins' theory, it is not clear that there should actually be any difference between the inverse-FOFC order and the FOFC-violating order in terms of EIC. Hawkins rejects Abney's (1987) DP hypothesis and assumes that NPs comprise Det and N, with either being sufficient to construct an NP. As such, N-initial and Det-initial nominals are equally efficient in processing terms. It follows that in the absence of other material, the order of constituents in the NP will have no effect on processing efficiency, and thus is expected to be irrelevant. A potential problem for Hawkins, however, is Dryer's (1992a: 103) claim that articles are nonetheless verb patterners, as this means that we have a context in which there is a preference for harmony but no evidence of a FOFC effect. Hawkins (1994, this volume), however, offers an alternative account of the distribution of articles, which potentially overcomes this problem.

The PF interface account also has a potential account of the lack of FOFC effects between V and DP. Firstly, note that specific DPs arguably fall outside the purview of FOFC, if Kayne (2004: 10) is correct and, in all OV languages, specific DPs scramble outside VP.[46] In these terms, then, we might even say that the existence of obligatory scrambling predicts that no FOFC asymmetry will be observed between specific DP and V. Whatever triggers scrambling, then, plausibly serves to render specific DPs

---

[45] Theresa Biberauer (p.c.) asks how heaviness is determined. Heaviness equates to number of words for the purposes of online reordering processes. According to the PGCH, though, grammars can develop categorical rules stemming from heaviness tendencies. Thus, the fact that PP always contains DP makes PP heavier than DP in general terms, even though both can have different heaviness values in different contexts. As such, an extraposition rule might be grammaticalized to apply only to PP and not DP irrespective of their relative online heaviness.

[46] Thanks to Theresa Biberaer (p.c.) for reminding me of this point. Sheehan (2010), however, suggests that some kinds of A- and A-bar movement also display FOFC effects and so more must still be said about these specific DPs. We leave these matters to one side here for reasons of space and refer the reader to Sheehan (2009a,b) for an account based on multiple Spell-Out, in the sense of Uriagereka (1999a).

immune to FOFC. Non-specific nominals, however, can clearly remain inside VP in OV scrambling languages, meaning that they nonetheless constitute an apparent FOFC violation. If the indefinite article were a projecting head in such cases then the following discontinuous word order would be predicted to surface, contrary to fact:

(35) *Johann hat ein ausgeliehen Buch
     John has a borrowed book

Interestingly, these non-specific representational nominals permit subextraction, whereas specific scrambled DPs do not (Müller 1996: 401–2, citing Webelhuth 1992, Fanselow 1991):[47]

(36) Worüber hat Antje ein/*das Buch gelesen?
     what.about has Antje a/the book read
     'What has Antje read a/*the book about?'   [German Müller 1996: 402]

Even in languages without scrambling, however, subextraction from specific representational DPs is severely degraded (cf. Fiengo and Higginbotham 1981; Davies and Dubinsky 2003):

(37) Which topic did you borrow a/*the/*my book about?

As such, the effect in (36) does not reduce to a complement/specifier distinction as per Huang's (1982) Condition on Extraction Domain (contra Mahajan 1992). Sheehan (2010) proposes, following an idea in Bowers (1987), that non-specific indefinites are not full DPs, but rather truncated NumPs. As such, *ein* is not a projecting head in (34) hence the ungrammaticality of (35). Rather the structure of (34) is a projection of a head-final (at PF) Num as follows:

(38)

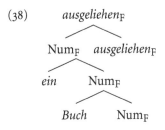

(i) *Buch* > Num, Num > *ausgeliehen*,
    = *Buch* > Num > *ausgeliehen*
(ii) *ein* > *Buch*, *ein* > Num[48]
    = *ein* > *Buch* > Num > *ausgeliehen*

---

[47] Thanks to Theresa Biberauer (p.c.) for asking me to clarify this point.

[48] If order is computed online we might assume that once an unambiguous order of all categories has been calculated, no further asymmetric c-command relations are used. If this is the case then either *ein*>*Buch* or *ein*>Num would be sufficient here. This becomes more pertinent in relation to (40) below, where *ein* asymmetrically c-commands four categories.

Evidence in favour of this structure comes from instances of 'extraposition' from indefinite non-specific NumPs in German:[49]

(39) a. Er   hat   ein/*das   Buch   ausgeliehen   über Syntax.
          he   has   a/the   book   borrowed   about syntax
          'He has borrowed a book about syntax.'

      b. *Er   hat   ein   Buch doch   ausgeliehen   über Syntax.
          he   has   a   book already   borrowed   about syntax
          'He has already borrowed a (specific) book about syntax.'

As (39) shows, 'extraposition' is only possible from non-specific unscrambled nominals. This is as predicted if *Buch* projects to a head-initial (at PF) phrase, giving rise to discontinuous linearization as described in section 15.4.2:[50]

(40)

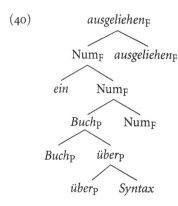

(i) *Buch* > Num, Num > *ausgeliehen*,
        Buch > *über*, *über* > *Syntax*
     = *Buch* > Num > *ausgeliehen*, *Buch* >
        über > *Syntax*
(ii) *ein* > *Buch*, *ein* > Num . . .
        Num > *über*, Num > *Syntax*
        ausgeliehen > *über*, *ausgeliehen* > *Syntax*
     = *ein* > *Buch* > Num > *ausgeliehen* >
        über > *Syntax*

In these terms, the claim is that NumP is not immune to FOFC, but rather that a FOFC effect does obtain where N has the relevant kind of complement.

BHR (2008a,b) also discuss another kind of exception to FOFC involving prepositional phrases in OV languages. Once again, German provides a relevant example:

(41) Sie   ist   [VP [PP nach   Berlin]   gefahren]
       she   is   to   Berlin   driven
       'She went to Berlin.'

As Hawkins (this volume) notes, it appears, nonetheless, that despite a small number of robust counterexamples, there is cross-linguistic evidence of a FOFC effect between PP complements and V. Firstly, the raw data from Dryer (2005b/2011b, 2005d/2011c) indicate that there are more inverse FOFC languages than FOFC-violating languages,

<hr>

[49] Some speakers seem to allow PP extraposition from definite DPs, suggesting that they are construing them as reduced relative clauses (cf. Sheehan 2010).

[50] As Theresa Biberauer notes, this looks like a FOFC violation in BHR's terms. For the account of FOFC presented here, however, FOFC is not a narrow syntactic constraint but rather a PF effect deriving from linearization. As such, the head-final Num dominating a head-initial NP simply gives rise to a discontinuous Spell-Out of NP, as detailed.

TABLE 15.2 **Languages with disharmony between the ordering of VP and PP**

	FOFC-violating P–NP and OV	Inverse-FOFC NP–P and VO
N of language	12[51]	38
N of macro areas	3	5
Language families	5	16
Genera	8	22

and that these languages occur in more macro-areas and represent a more genetically diverse group than the small number of FOFC-violating languages:

These data seem to be consistent with the spirit of the PGCH, whereby FOFC is a statistical rather than a categorical effect, as there appear to be a number of languages which allow the FOFC-violating combination. Note, however, that *WALS* contains data about the directionality of PP and VP, but it does not consider the actual placement of head-initial and head-final PPs in otherwise OV and VO languages. An examination of the problematic languages reveals that many of the 12 languages, despite being OV, actually require PPs to be obligatorily postverbal, meaning that the surface FOFC-violating construction *P>DP>V does not actually occur (as Hawkins also notes).

Of the 12 languages, only the Indo-European languages (German, Dutch, Persian, Tajik, Kurdish, and Sorbian) and Tigré (Semitic) allow structures of the kind P>DP>V. The other languages all either lack true adpositions or are languages in which PPs appear in a postverbal position. Mangarrayi (Australian, Mangarrayi, Northern Territories) lacks true prepositions according to Merlan (1989: 26); instead it has 'prepositional-like phrases consisting of an adverb followed by a noun appropriately case-marked to complement the combined meaning of the adverb and verb in the clause'. Moreover, the order of the adverb and its complement is not fixed, both adv>comp and comp>adv are possible. As such, it is not clear that Mangarrayi is a true exception to FOFC.[52] In Päri (Nilo-Saharan, Nilotic, Sudan), Tobelo (West Papuan, North Halmaheran, Indonesia), Iraqw (Afro-Asiatic, Southern Cushitic, Tanzania), and Neo-Aramaic (Afro-Asiatic, Semitic, Israel) PP complements to V seem to surface in a postverbal position, as the following examples illustrate:

(42) á- lw'ʌʌr'   kí   kwàc   [Päri, Anderson 1988: 303]
      1SG-fear   PREP   leopard
      'I am afraid of leopards.'

(43) lăbulmunne   [ta-Bagdàd]   [Neo-Aramaic, Khan 1999: 338]
      take.me   to-Bagdad
      'Take me to Bagdad!'

---

[51] I have added German and Dutch to this category although they are categorized as having mixed order of verb and object on *WALS* because of their V2 property.

[52] As such, it seems that Mangarrayi is wrongly classified on *WALS*.

(44) i-na   ta'<a'>ín   [ay dí-r   konkomo] [Iraqw, Mous 1993: 100]
      S.3-PST   run<HAB>3SGM   to place.F-CON cock
      'He ran to the cock.'

In Päri, this is obligatory (Anderson 1988: 303), as it is in all dialects of Neo-Aramaic (Geoffrey Khan, p.c.). There is insufficient information to say the same for Iraqw, though all examples suggest it to be the case. Matters are slightly less clear in Tobelo.[53] Following Kandybowicz and Baker's (2003) analysis of Nupe, we might take the position of PP as evidence that these languages are basically head-initial with DP–V order derived via A-movement of a DP object. This means that the number of languages displaying FOFC violations of this type is extremely small so that P>DP>V is far rarer than the inverse-FOFC order [V–[DP–P]]. If this were not a FOFC effect, but merely a preference for harmony then there would be no explanation for the fact that postpositional phrases in VO languages are rarely preposed (cf. Dryer 1992a: 92).

These data can be accommodated by the PGCH, if they are taken to indicate a statistical FOFC effect. PP is a relatively 'light' IC, so FOFC violations between V and PP are predicted to be typologically rare but not impossible. In these terms, Germanic, Iranian, AND Tigré are not optimal for processing purposes, but not ruled out by UG. Moreover, optional PP extraposition is available to varying degrees in the languages in question, meaning that the problematic surface order P>NP>V may be avoided to a certain extent in usage. This raises the question, though, pointed out by Theresa Biberauer (p.c.), why German has not lost preverbal PPs over time. One might also question why there are so few counterexamples to FOFC in this domain, given that, for Hawkins, PP is a fairly light category.

The small number of well-studied exceptions are more problematic for the PF interface account.[54] There is no obvious reason why PPs should fail to be subject to

---

[53] The vast majority of the examples show PPs to be extraposed:

(i) ngohi-o   to-modeke   de   o-Matias
     I-also   1-agree   PREP   NM-Matias
     'I also agreed with Matias.'   [Tobelo, Holton 2003: 30]

However, Holton (2003: 55) explicitly states that oblique arguments can occur 'either before or after the verb'. Unfortunately, he uses the term 'oblique arguments' to refer to both PPs and DPs marked with a locative or directional case suffix. The only example with PP–V order which he gives involves an instrumental PP which may be a topic in the CP layer:

(ii) de   ma-kakatama   n-a-lye-ino   [Tobelo, Holton 2003: 55]
      PREP   NM-tongs   2-3-roll-ALL
      'Roll it up with the tongs.'

In the absence of further data is it impossible to say for certain whether Tobelo PPs adhere to FOFC or not.
[54] It is worth reiterating, though, that in the hard sciences analyses are rarely required to explain 100% of a data set (cf. Johnson 2007).

FOFC only in this particular subset of Indo-European and Semitic languages.[55] In relation to the Indo-European counterexamples, one possible approach might be to exploit the idea that P is parameterized as to whether or not it is a phase-head (Abels 2003). In languages allowing P>DP>V, PPs would constitute separate Spell-Out domains or phases and would therefore behave like atoms for the purposes of linearization. In this respect, it is initially suggestive that all Germanic VO languages allow preposition stranding, whereas most Germanic OV languages disallow it (as does Persian).[56] This suggests that in standard German, Dutch, and the relevant Iranian languages PPs are phases and preposition stranding is ruled out by anti-locality (Abels 2003). As expected, non-local subextraction from PPs in German is possible, as Abels shows:

(45) [über welches Thema]$_i$ hast du mich noch mal[$_{PP}$ nach einem Buch t$_i$] gefragt?
      over which subject have you me again   after a   book   asked
      'Which topic did you ask me for a book on again?'

This is not a satisfactory solution to the problem, though, as FOFC effects are observed across phasal barriers and this is as expected if Spell-Out leaves the edge of the phase active in the derivation. Note that CP complements of V are presumably phasal but nonetheless display a FOFC asymmetry (as discussed above). At present then, the existence of a non-categorical FOFC effect between PP and VP remains problematic for the PF interface account.[57] Ultimately, the behaviour of PPs in these languages should be attributed to some independent property of their grammar.[58] Unfortunately, this property remains elusive at present.

As such, it must be conceded that the fact that a statistical FOFC asymmetry appears to be attested between PP and VP is suggestive evidence against the PF interface approach and in favour of the PGCH-based analysis of FOFC.[59] In the

---

[55] Baker and Kramer (2011) argue that Amharic, another Semitic language which also allows the FOFC-violating order, may not be a true counterexample to FOFC as the adpositions in question are not actually prepositions but rather clitics which are ordered via independent PF rules.

[56] Though, as Theresa Biberauer (p.c.) notes, colloquial Afrikaans and some dialects of Dutch and German allow preposition stranding, so this correlation is not perfect.

[57] BHR (2010) and a caveat to their formulation of FOFC so that it holds only within extended projections. This is also unsatisfactory, though, as only a small number of closely related languages permit the order [[P–DP]–V].

[58] Potentially related phenomena, though, include the availability of circumpositions in Iranian/Germanic, which are in themselves problematic for FOFC, and the positioning of head-initial adjuncts. Note also that unlike many languages, which have few or even a single preposition, Iranian and Germanic are notable for their rich inventory of Ps. A full consideration of these structures is beyond the scope of the present paper.

[59] Theresa Biberauer raises a further potential FOFC exception in Germanic verb clusters:

(iv) ... dat hy   die boek moes   koop het   [2, 3, 1] (Afrikaans)
          that he   the book must.PST buy   have
      '... that he should have bought the book'

These raise problems for both the accounts proposed here as well as for other accounts of FOFC and I put them to one side here.

following section, however, I raise a potentially more serious problem with the PGCH-based approach.

15.5.3 *The relation to harmony*

According to the PGCH, harmony and FOFC are two effects of the same processing principle (EIC). The clear prediction is that if two categories show a preference for harmony then they should also show a FOFC skewing and vice versa. The PF interface account makes no such prediction. The preference for harmony may be neutralized for some independent reason, but FOFC will always hold as long as the two categories in question are linearized in the same application of Spell-Out. This is because on the PF interface account, the effect results from basic facts about asymmetric c-command and linearization.

Some categories display both a preference for harmony and an FOFC effect. This is the case for Aux and VP, V and PP, C and VP, and V and CP (cf. Dryer 1992a). As such, these pairs of categories are well-behaved by the standards of EIC. More problematic for the PGCH is the fact that, according to Dryer (1992a), articles are also verb patterners, but not subject to FOFC effects cross-linguistically (see the discussion in the previous section).

Polar question particles, on the other hand, seem to display the opposite situation. From a functional perspective, question particles (Pol) arguably serve the function of identifying a clause as a polar question, and C serves to construct an embedded clause. For this reason, it is surprising that, according to the data in table 15.1 from Dryer (2005e/2011g, 2005f/2011e) repeated here as Table 15.3, the disharmonic inverse FOFC combination initial C and final Pol is more common than the harmonic combinations in terms of languages and genera and almost as common in terms of language families.

TABLE 15.3 **Typological positioning of Polarity heads and complementizers**

Type	Position of Pol	Position of C	Number of languages (genera: families)
A	Initial	Initial	72: 35: 13 (78)
B	Final	Final	45: 33: 20 (46)
C	Final	Initial	74: 40: 16 (82)
D	Initial	Final	4: 3: 3 (4)

There is thus no evidence of a preference for harmony between C and Pol. Crucially, though, FOFC appears to hold in this domain (as discussed in section 15.3.2). It therefore appears to be the case that one and the same category displays an FOFC effect but no preference for harmony. This is highly problematic for the PGCH, which attributes both FOFC and the preference for harmony to the same principle, namely EIC. Of course, it remains an open question why there is no harmonic preference between Pol and C.[60] Under both approaches this fact can be accommodated as an effect of grammaticalization (cf. Bailey 2010). A difference emerges in relation to whether the approaches can deal with an FOFC effect in such contexts. From a formal perspective, even if two heads are shown not to display a cross-linguistic tendency towards harmony, they are still expected to be subject to FOFC, as FOFC is an unavoidable fact about linearization. From a processing perspective, on the other hand, once two heads fail to display a cross-linguistic tendency towards harmony, they fail to be subject to EIC and as such any adherence to FOFC cannot be attributed to the processing principle. In such cases, then, FOFC effects simply cannot be explained by EIC.

15.6 *The problem of particles*

The final type of exception to FOFC, also discussed by BHR (2008a,b, 2010) comes from particles. It is well known from the typological literature that tense/aspect particles, unlike inflected auxiliaries, are not verb patterners (cf. Dryer 1992a: 114–15; Hawkins this volume). Interestingly, they also fail to be subject to FOFC:

(46) Wo-men daoda shan- ding **le** [Mandarin Chinese]
      1SG-PL   reach   mountain-top PART
      'We have reached the top of the mountain.'   [BHR, citing Soh and Gao 2004]

Mandarin Chinese also has a plethora of final discourse particles, limited to matrix clauses, which appear to violate FOFC (cf. Paul to appear). BHR (2008a,b) note that these kinds of structures tend to cluster in a given language with languages allowing many different C particles in the same VO . . . PART structure.

The first thing to observe is that there is no clear independent diagnostic for particlehood and this potentially challenges the validity of FOFC as a generalization. Particles are often claimed to be 'deficient' in some sense. In empirical terms, this equates to at least the following properties:

i. lack of inflection/morphologically invariance (cf. Greenberg 1963; Dryer 1992a; Cinque 1999);
ii. phonological deficiency (but cf. Cardinaletti 2011);
iii. immobility;
iv. lack of category (BHR 2010);
v. inability to c-select (BHR 2010).

---

[60] Ultimately this might also shed light on the reason why final Q is so frequent in VO languages (cf. Dryer 2005c/2011b, 2005e/2011g).

Note that while (i) may be a necessary condition for particlehood, it is arguably not sufficient. Lack of inflection is the norm for many categories and indeed in isolating languages such as Mandarin, it is the norm across all categories. Diagnostics (ii) and (iii), likewise, are necessary but not sufficient conditions for particlehood, as they are more general properties of functional heads (cf. Roberts and Roussou 2003). Diagnostics (iv) and (v) are theoretically interesting but empirically ill-defined. It is not clear what the empirical diagnostic for lack of categoryhood is, for example. In conjunction with (v), though, (iv) suggests that particles should be fairly free in their distribution, able to merge with a number of different complements and be invisible to selection. Indeed there are 'particles' with this behaviour. So-called focus-related particles such as *only* are a case in point as they can be associated with any kind of phrase, suggesting that they do not have a place in the functional sequence (cf. Cinque 1999 for this conclusion). The particles which fail to be subject to FOFC in many cases fail to have these properties, though. Final high particles in Mandarin and Cantonese occur in a rigid sequence for example. Even this diagnostic then is not sufficient to determine the class of heads which are immune to FOFC.

As a result, it is impossible even to add a stipulation to FOFC stating that it does not apply to particles, as at present the only diagnostic for particlehood is insensitivity to FOFC. This problem is compounded by the fact that some categories appear to be subject to FOFC in one direction but not the other. Final question particles, for example, are frequently attested in VO languages and also fail to harmonize with the order of verb and object (Dryer 2005c/2011b, 2005e/2011g). However, this does not render question particles immune to FOFC per se. As discussed in section 15.3.2, evidence suggests that FOFC rules out the order *Pol–TP–C, suggesting that it is not possible to simply classify question markers as particles and rule them out of the FOFC generalization altogether.

This problem, in a sense, extends to the PGCH. On the one hand, the PGCH allows that a pair of categories might fail to display a cross-linguistic tendency for harmony, and in such cases makes the prediction that these categories will also fail to be subject to FOFC. On the other hand it offers no real explanation as to why certain categories fall outside its remit in this way.[61] In the absence of an independent definition/diagnostic of particlehood, the account again risks circularity.

The PF interface account potentially avoids this problem by simply avoiding any reference to the term 'particle'. More specifically, it makes a strong prediction regarding surface orders which appear to be FOFC violations: the phrase preceding a final particle must be an atomic strong island, unless it is harmonically head-final. This stems from the fact that as long as the complement of a 'particle' is a hierarchical head-

---

[61] An anonymous reviewer suggests that particles might be non-projecting elements which therefore fail to head a projection and hence do not construct a category. Again, although this is an interesting theoretical characterization, it provides no independent diagnostic for particlehood.

initial phrase (at PF), the particle will fail to appear in final position. If the complement of the 'particle' is already spelled out, though, and hence atomized in the sense of Uriagereka (1999a), then its internal hierarchy is obliterated and it is rendered immune to FOFC. Interestingly, there is some initial evidence that the prediction holds with certain final particles in Mandarin Chinese (a VO language). Lin (2006) observes that the presence of certain final particles indeed correlates with the strong islandhood of the preceding phrase. More specifically, he observes that the presence of the final aspectual particle *le* blocks extraction of manner adverbials from VP:

(47)   a. Zhangsan   zenmeyang   xiu   che __?
          Zhangsan   how   repair   car
          'How does Zhangsan repair the car?'

       b. *Zhangsan   zenmeyang   xiu   che   le?
          Zhangsan   how   repair   car   SFP
          'How did Zhangsan repair the car?'   [Mandarin, Lin 2006: 4]

Adopting a Kaynean position, Lin attributes this to Huang's (1982) Condition on Extraction Domain, whereby specifiers, as they are ungoverned, are strong islands, unlike complements, which are governed and hence permit subextraction. The idea is that (47b), unlike (47a), involves movement of vP to a specifier position above Asp.

In relation to FOFC, this explanation of the facts is problematic, though, as it overgenerates, and would allow us to derive any number of surface FOFC-violating orders with final inflected heads *V–O–Aux, *Pol–TP–C, etc. In fact, as Sheehan (in press) observes, even languages which appear to derive a head-final order via this kind of movement still appear to adhere to FOFC. Thus, Finnish allows both VO and OV orders (depending on information structure) and both Aux–V and V–Aux orders. Moreover, Holmberg (2001) argues at length that Finnish V-Aux orders are derived via VP movement, and this is consistent with the fact that they are optional. Nonetheless, *V–O–Aux order is still ungrammatical in Finnish, suggesting that the FOFC generalization applies even where phrasal movement is involved. This is especially suggested by the grammaticality of (49), which is arguably the linear order resulting from movement of a head-initial VP:

(48)   *Milloin   Jussi   *kirjoittanut*   romaanin   olisi?   *[V–O–Aux]
         when   Jussi   written   novel   would.have
                                                          [Finnish, Holmberg 2000]

(49)   Milloin   Jussi   kirjoittanut   olisi   romaanin?
        when   Jussi   written   would.have   novel
        'When would Jussi have written a novel?'   [Finnish, Anders Holmberg p.c.]

So what is the explanation for Lin's observation then, and how does it solve the particle problem? It must be the case that the islandhood of vP in (47b) is not caused by movement to a specifier position, but rather that the surface violation of FOFC is possible because the phrase which is selected happens to be atomic. Let us further capitalize on one of the necessary properties of particles and assume that only heads that lack uninterpretable features other than a c-selection specification can select for an atomized complement.[62] This is because the presence of uninterpretable features on a given category requires that head to probe some other category in its c-command domain. If the complement of a head is atomized, it follows that the categories inside that domain are closed off to probing. In these terms, we can define 'particle' as a functional head without uninterpretable features (other than c-selection features) which merges with an atomized phrase. This, at least, yields falsifiable predictions about where (and how) surface FOFC violations will arise. The implication is that FOFC does hold absolutely as a condition on the linearization of structures: all superficial exceptions involve a reduced structure in which the head-initial phrase has been atomized for independent reasons.[63]

15.7 Formal or functional?

Up to this point, the PF interface account has been characterized as a 'formal' account of the FOFC asymmetry essentially because it takes the constraint to be categorical rather than statistical, and to derive from I-language rather than E-language principles. This formal/functional divide is, however, misleading in the context of the Minimalist Program which attempts to declutter the biological component of UG by assigning some core properties of language to second and third factors (cf. Chomsky 2005). As such, the PF interface account is formal only in as far as the LCA is a formal principle of first-factor UG (the genetic endowment). In recent work, Biberauer, Holmberg, Roberts, and Sheehan (2010) question this assumption, and argue rather that the LCA might actually emerge from the inexorable need for linear order in externalization. Note that, in these terms, parameters are defined as points of underspecification in UG (Biberauer and Richards 2006; Richards 2009; Roberts and Holmberg 2010). As such, then, there would actually be a parameter setting in both part (i) and (ii) of the revised LCA:

---

[62] If accusative Case is assigned by v, rather than V, then verbs selecting an atomized complement also fall into this category.

[63] Theresa Biberauer (p.c.) raises some potential empirical problems for this prediction which warrant close attention, notably from the presence of final particles in clauses with *wh*-movement in Singaporean English. Given that *wh*-movement in Singaporean English is optional, one possibility is that *wh*-movement is to a Focus position below the position occupied by Pol. The fact that extraction from circumpositions in Dutch and German is also possible remains problematic.

(50)   Revised LCA

    (i)   If a category A c-selects a category B, then A **precedes/follows** B at PF

    (ii) If no order is specified between A and B by the sum of all precedence pairs defined by (i), then A **precedes/follows** B at PF if A asymmetrically c-commands B.

The idea is that linearization is parasitic on Narrow Syntactic asymmetries (which are part of the biological endowment) because this is the simplest way to translate a hierarchical structure into linear order. However, the linearization algorithm is free to map the relevant asymmetries to either precedence or subsequence, the two logical possibilities arising from linearity. This raises the question why asymmetries of the FOFC kind exist at all.

The answer provided by Biberauer, Holmberg, Roberts, and Sheehan (2010) is that spoken languages unanimously set the parameter in (ii) to 'precedence' rather than 'subsequence' so that (ii) essentially constitutes a 'no-choice parameter'. Interestingly, the reason why non-local asymmetries in Narrow Syntax preferentially map onto precedence might plausibly stem from processing preferences of the kind which Hawkins has also discussed. First, note that filler-gap dependencies are easier to parse if the filler precedes the gap (Hawkins 2001; Abels and Neeleman 2009). This is reflected by experimental evidence which suggests that subjects look for a gap once they have heard/read a filler (cf. Crain and Fodor 1985, Wagers and Phillips 2009 for a recent overview). The hypothesis is that this exerts a strong pressure favouring the precedence setting of (ii) above. Why then, doesn't the same thing happen with (i)? Arguably this is because there is no such parsing pressure affecting (i). As Hawkins argues, head-final and head-initial orders are equally optimal in parsing terms.

Crucially, then, as Biberauer, Holmberg, Roberts, and Sheehan (2010) note, once (ii) has been set to precedence it may have further more arbitrary implications for word order which do not afford any direct processing advantage: hence FOFC. In these terms, the PF interface account of FOFC, while not functional, has a functional basis of sorts. The linear order of natural languages is derived from Narrow Syntactic asymmetries which exist in all natural languages, but the basic asymmetry which ultimately gives rise to FOFC (as a side effect) actually stems from processing pressures.

15.8 Conclusions and unresolved issues

In conclusion, there is some evidence that something akin to FOFC seems to hold of natural language, despite a small number of counterexamples. However, it seems to be the case that FOFC is independent of any preference for cross-categorial harmony. This renders the PGCH problematic as it predicts harmony and FOFC to be inextricably linked. As such, the PF interface account remains the more plausible account at present, subject to further investigation (notably of the problematic PP structures in Germanic/Iranian). Characterizing the PF interface account as a purely formal account might, however, be misleading as the LCA plausibly reduces to an emergent 'no-choice parameter', which means that where non-local dependencies are concerned higher categories preferably precede lower categories for processing reasons.

16

Sentence-Final Particles, Complementizers, Antisymmetry, and the Final-over-Final Constraint*

BRIAN HOK-SHING CHAN

16.1 Introduction: sentence-final particles in Chinese varieties[1]

Sentence-final particles (henceforth SFPs) are an integral feature of different Chinese varieties, as illustrated by the following examples in Mandarin Chinese (1), Taiwanese Southern Min (2), Cantonese (3), and Classical Chinese (4):

(1) a. ni-men zou **ba**
       2-PL   go   SFP (order)
       'You leave (now).'

$$\hfill \text{(Mandarin; Huang, Li, and Li 2009: 35)}$$

   b. ta   qu   guo **ma**
      3   go   ASP SFP/Q
      'Has he (or she) been there (before)?'

$$\hfill \text{(Mandarin, Huang, Li, and Li 2009: 35)}$$

---

* This chapter developed from an earlier paper entitled 'Two types of disharmonic word order in Cantonese: A view from bilingual code-switching'. The paper was presented in the Workshop of Theoretical Approaches to Disharmonic Word Order (TADWO) at Newcastle University and I have been immensely grateful for helpful remarks and encouragement from many audiences. Thanks also go to three anonymous reviewers and the editors whose insightful comments have been most helpful in improving earlier drafts. Any errors and inadequacies are mine.

[1] The term 'variety' or 'varieties' is used here to avoid the ideologically loaded labels of 'language' and 'dialect' as so often discussed in sociolinguistics. Being a native speaker of Cantonese, I shall pay most attention to Cantonese data in this chapter.

(2)   a. A-sin u   khiau   **bo**
         A-sin AUX   clever   SFP/Q
         'Is A-sin clever?'

                              (Taiwanese Southern Min, Simpson and Wu 2002: 71)

      b. i   ma   bo   huantui   **ma**   **honn**
         3   too   NEG   objection   SFP   SFP
         '(You know), he (or she) did not have any objection either, right?'

                              (Taiwanese Southern Min, Hsieh and Sybesma 2007: 7)

(3)   a. nei5   gin3   gwo3   keoi5   **me1**
         2   see   ASP   3   SFP/Q
         'Have you seen him (or her)?'

                                                              (Cantonese)

      b. bi4bi1   neoi2   hou2   leng3   **aa3**
         baby   girl   EMPH   pretty   SFP
         'The baby girl is so pretty!'

                                                              (Cantonese)

      c. nei5   sik6-zo2   faan6   **mei6**
         you   eat-ASP   rice   SFP/NEG/Q
         'Have you eaten rice? (i.e. Did you have your meal?)'

                                                              (Cantonese)

      d. hou2   fan3-gaau3   **ge3**   **lo3**   **bo3**
         good   sleep   SFP   SFP   SFP (reminder)
         'You'd better go to sleep now.'

                                                 (particle cluster, Cantonese)

(4)   you   guo   wo   zhe   **wu**
      have   surpass   me   person   SFP/NEG/Q
      'Is there anyone who surpasses me?'

                                              (Classical Chinese, Aldridge 2011)

These particles express a wide range of modal and pragmatic meanings such as directive (e.g. order in (1a), reminder in (3d)), question (e.g. (1b), (2a), (3a)), and assertion (e.g. (3b)). The meaning of some particles is complex; for instance, *mei6* in (3c) and *wu* in (4) are negation markers which mark 'negative questions', a special type of disjunctive question (Huang, Li, and Li 2009: 259). Many particles also convey information about the stance or presupposition of the speaker. In (3a), for instance, the particle *me1* implies that the speaker does not believe in the proposition; that is, in this case, the speaker presupposes that 'you have NOT seen him (or her)'. Question particles similar to those in (1b), (2a), (3a), (3c), and (4) are fairly common in different languages, including VO and OV languages, and they may be sentence-final or sentence-initial (Dryer 2007: 91–3; Dryer and Haspelmath 2011).

In addition to *illocutionary force* such as assertion of a statement, question, and directive, SFPs in Chinese also convey the likelihood of the proposition expressed in the clause as the speaker sees it, or the speaker's commitment to the truth of the proposition. Lee and Law (2001) discuss the acquisition of some of these particles in Cantonese which they consider to be markers of *epistemic modality* and *evidentiality*, respectively, including *ge3*, *gwaa3*, and *wo5*. The following are some examples:

(5) a. keoi5 m4   wui5 aak1 ngo5 **ge3**
        3   NEG   MOD   cheat me   SFP (assertion: certainty)
       'He (or she) doesn't cheat me.'

    b. keoi5 m4   wui5 aak1 ngo5 **gwaa3 (or ge2)**
        3   NEG   MOD   cheat me   SFP (assertion: less certain)
       'He (or she) doesn't cheat me, I guess.'

    c. keoi5 m4   wui5 aak1 ngo5 **wo5**
        3   NEG   MOD   cheat me   SFP (hearsay)
       'He (or she) doesn't cheat me (he (or she) said).'

In (5a), the speaker is sure that '*he (or she) doesn't cheat me*', but in (5b) the speaker is less certain. In (5c), the speaker merely reports what he has heard, but the speaker shows no commitment to the truth of the sentence. Lee and Law (2001) note that markers of epistemic modality are also found in Tibetan, Uighur, and Turkish, although in these languages the markers are verb suffixes rather than SFPs.[2] Evidential markers are widely attested in different languages, some of which appear to be SFPs too (i.e. see the examples from Tariana and Cherokee cited in Aikhenvald 2004). In other languages evidential markers are suffixes (e.g. Quechua, see examples in Muysken 2008: 18–19).

Having examined thirty Cantonese SFPs, Sybesma and Li (2007) conclude that the meaning of these particles can be characterized systematically by dissecting their phonology. More specifically, the initial (or onset), the rhyme, the coda, and the tone are each associated with a particular meaning, and an SFP is a combination of these meanings. On top of this, SFPs in Chinese are often polysemous, and their meaning varies in different contexts. For instance, the Cantonese particle *lo1* may indicate the speaker's assumption that the proposition is obvious to the listener (Lee and Law 2001), or it may function as a hedge which makes a statement less blunt (Sybesma and

---

[2] These verb suffixes are always incorporated with their associated verbs (see examples in Lee and Law 2001: 2–3). In contrast, the evidentiality markers in (5) are SFPs which are not attached to the verb *aak1* (cheat).

Li 2007). The rich variety of meanings, their complexities and context sensitivity have rendered pragmatics the natural focus in linguistic research on Chinese SFPs (e.g. Luke 1990; Wu 2004).

The syntax of SFPs in Chinese has also received some attention. Most linguists who work within generative grammar have assumed that SFPs are a functional category, specifically, a C-head (T.-C. Tang 1989; S.-P. Law 1990; Cheng 1991; Gasde and Paul 1996; S.-W. Tang 1998; A. Law 2002; Cheung 2008, 2009; Sybesma and Li 2007; Hsieh and Sybesma 2007, 2008).[3] More recently, it has been suggested that this C-head is actually in a position preceding the sentence, with the sentence (or IP[4]) undergoing leftward movement to the specifier position of C, resulting in the sentence-final order of the particles (Simpson and Wu 2002; Cheung 2008, 2009). This derivational account of SFPs has the advantage of being consistent with the influential Antisymmetry thesis in generative grammar; in brief, phrase structure is underlyingly head-initial, and head-final orders are derived from movement (Kayne 1994, 2003a, 2005b). This is illustrated for SFPs in (6):

(6)

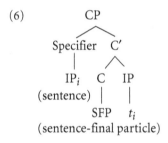

Cheung (2008, 2009) adds that this account is empirically supported by the Dislocation Focus Construction in Cantonese, and that, in addition, it provides a unified

---

[3] Law (1990) actually proposes that non-question-marking particles are realized in C whereas the question particles are in the right-branching specifier of C. However, the C-specifier analysis of question particles seems to receive little support from other linguists. Tang (1998) distinguishes two types of particles. Inner particles are related to time (such as *le* in Mandarin, which expresses perfective aspect) or focalization (such as *zaa3* in Cantonese), whereas outer particles are those 'clause-typing' particles which express mood or illocutionary force (e.g. the question particle *ne* in Mandarin). Tang (1989) suggests that the inner particles instantiate T in Chinese, and that they move to C. On the other hand, the outer particles are base-generated in a C-head above TP. Most recently, Cheung (2009) suggests that SFPs occupy a functional head position in the C-domain below a Focus Phrase. See details in section 16.4.

[4] The term IP is still used by some linguists working on Chinese (e.g. Simpson and Wu 2002; Cheung 2008, 2009) not so much because they subscribe to pre-Minimalist frameworks, but because linguists are still divided as to whether there are tense morphemes and hence TPs in Chinese. Tang (1998) suggests that some aspectual markers realize T in Chinese (see footnote 3 above) and hence there is TP in Chinese, while others assume that TP in Chinese is AspP (i.e. Aspect Phrase) precisely because of the behaviour of these aspect markers (Cheng 1991). See recent discussion in Huang, Li, and Li (2009), J.-W. Lin (2010), and Jonah Lin (2012). I will consistently use IP in this paper.

account of the derivation of the Dislocation Focus Construction and Canonical Word Order (i.e. sentences without dislocation) in Cantonese.

In spite of these advantages, such a derivational account of SFPs faces a number of problems. First and foremost, more evidence has been uncovered which indicates that SFPs are very different from complementizers in terms of syntactic, semantic, and pragmatic properties, and so if complementizers are C-heads, SFPs are most probably not C-heads. Concerning dislocation in Cantonese, the whole range of word-order variations in Cantonese (with or without dislocation) is not necessarily better explained by positing that SFPs are based-generated in a head-initial C position (see Cheung 2008, 2009).

There is another related issue. Irrespective of whether IP undergoes movement, the configuration of [$_{CP}$ IP C] in Chinese presents a counterexample to the Final-over-Final Constraint or FOFC (Biberauer, Holmberg, and Roberts 2008a,b, 2009, 2010, Biberauer, Newton and Sheehan 2009; Biberauer and Sheehan 2012), if it is assumed that SFPs are C-heads. Motivated by gaps in constituent order gleaned from various languages, the constraint rules out a head-final phrase immediately dominating a head-initial phrase within the same extended projection. For instance, a head-final IP cannot dominate a head-initial VP, and VOI (or VOAux) order is indeed absent in various languages (Biberauer, Holmberg, and Roberts 2010; Biberauer and Sheehan 2012).

(7)   *A FOFC-violating structure*

In the generative literature, Chinese is widely assumed to be verb-initial (i.e. a VO language; Mulder and Sybesma 1992),[5] with I also being initial.[6] If an SFP were indeed a C-head, a head-final CP would dominate a head-initial IP and a head-initial VP, presenting a counterexample to FOFC, regardless of whether there is IP movement (8a) or no IP movement (8b).

---

[5] Many linguists of a more functional orientation have suggested that Chinese is in fact an OV language because it shows many properties typically found in OV languages, for instance, a prenominal relative clause (see discussion in Li and Thompson 1981; Comrie 2008; and Yip and Matthews 2007).

[6] See footnote 4 above.

(8)   a.

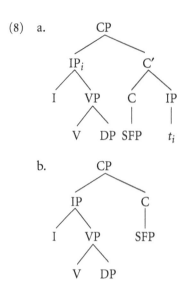

b.

Recent works on FOFC (Biberauer, Holmberg, and Roberts 2010; Biberauer, Newton, and Sheehan 2009; Biberauer and Sheehan 2012) have cast doubt on whether SFPs are genuinely C-elements in the same way that subordinating conjunctions such as *that* in English (see Huddleston 2002; Huddleston and Pullum 2006) are. Focusing on SFPs in Chinese varieties, this chapter argues that SFPs in these varieties are better treated as a category of their own, and that only complementizers (in the sense of subordinating conjunctions) are C-heads which may trigger IP movement. Furthermore, SFPs are argued to be merged with clauses in sentence-final position, and they do not induce IP movement. The remainder of this chapter is organized as follows. Section 16.2 provides the background of the C-head analysis of Chinese SFPs. Section 16.3 presents arguments for the proposal that SFPs are not C-heads. Section 16.4 examines the Dislocation Focus Construction in Cantonese in which SFPs function as focus markers and hence look like a species of C-head. However, it is suggested here that SFPs are affixes attached to the focused constituent, and that this constituent moves to the specifier position of a Focus head which is phonetically null. This account then derives the canonical word order of SFPs and the order of SFPs (no longer sentence-final) in various types of dislocated constructions. Section 16.5 concludes. As a native speaker of Cantonese, my primary focus throughout will be on Cantonese data.

16.2 The C-head analysis of sentence-final particles in Chinese

In the generative literature on Chinese, an SFP has been widely assumed to be a C-head (T.-C. Tang 1989; S.-P. Law 1990; Cheng 1991; Gasde and Paul 1996; S.-W. Tang

1998; A. Law 2002; Sybesma and Li 2007; Hsieh and Sybesma 2007, 2008; Cheung 2008, 2009). But what exactly is a C-head?

In the Principles and Parameters framework, C refers to the head position of a functional projection which is a sister of IP. Complementizers, which mark an embedded clause as the complement of a higher verb, are analysed as C-heads (cf. English *that* and *for*, C-heads whose complements are a finite clause and a non-finite clause respectively). Moreover, C may be the landing site of movement. For instance, auxiliary verbs or modal verbs in English raise to C in questions or other kinds of inversion. In German and Dutch, finite verbs raise to C in matrix clauses, resulting in V2 order (den Besten 1983; Zwart 1997b). According to Rizzi (1997), the C-domain contains various projections which relate to information or discourse structure. For Rizzi (1997), CP is split into different layers above IP, including the Force phrase, the Topic phrase, the Focus phrase, and the Finite phrase. The heads of these phrases may be phonetically null in some languages, or they may be overtly realized by markers of Topic or Focus in others. The various forms in which C-heads are realized are summarized in (9):

(9)   *What are C elements?*

    a. Complementizers marking embedded clauses.

    b. Verbs, modal verbs, or auxiliary verbs which move to C from IP via head movement.

    c. Markers of Topic, Focus, or heads of other functional projections above IP.

SFPs generally fit into the class of elements generativists call 'function words' or 'functional categories' (cf. i.a. Abney 1987: 64–5; Muysken 2008: 61–5).[7] The list of properties given below summarizes the motivations for this classification:

(10)   *Chinese SFPs as function words*

    a. 'Functional elements are generally phonologically and morphologically dependent. They are generally stressless, often clitics or affixes, and sometimes even phonologically null' (Abney 1987: 64–5). SFPs do not appear as

---

[7] The open-class vs closed-class distinction as a diagnostic criterion for lexical vs functional categories (Abney 1987) has remained controversial. This distinction might be better conceived as a continuum, as becomes clear when one compares different word classes within a language (e.g. articles vs prepositions) or the same category across languages (e.g. prepositions in Chinese and prepositions in English). A well-known case is the preposition, putatively a type of function word, but this category does not look so 'closed' in that it has quite a lot of members, at least in some languages (e.g. English or Dutch, see Muysken 2008). In our case, we may note that Cantonese has around forty particles (Sybesma and Li 2007), whereas Mandarin Chinese has much fewer (Li and Thompson 1981 list only six). SFPs in Cantonese thus look more 'open' than those in Mandarin Chinese.

single words (e.g. as in sentence fragments); they have to appear with a
sentence to their left.[8] SFPs usually do not receive stress.[9]

b. 'Functional elements permit only a single type of complement. [...]
(Abney 1987: 65). An SFP appears to select only IP as its complement
(Muysken 2008).

c. 'Functional elements are inseparable from their complements' (Abney 1987:
65). SFPs cannot be separated from the sentences they follow by any word or
phrase (e.g. adverb/adjunct), and also not by an intonation break.[10] This
differentiates SFPs from discourse markers (e.g. *right, okay, huh* in English),
which also appear to the right of a sentence, albeit after an intonation break.

d. 'Functional elements lack what I will call "descriptive content". Their
semantic contribution is second order, regulating, or contributing to the
interpretation of their complement' (Abney 1987: 65). Whereas SFPs are
not meaningless, the pragmatic meanings they convey (e.g. likelihood,

---

[8] An apparent exception is *laa4* in Cantonese, which may be uttered on its own without a sentence. But
then it conveys a meaning roughly equivalent to 'Look!' in English (e.g. when the speaker is showing
something to the listener). It may also imply a mild warning (e.g. 'Stop that!'). In sentence-final position,
laa4 marks a question and does not carry these meanings.

(i) faan1   uk1-kei2   **laa4**
     go   home   SFP/Q
     '(Are you) going home?'

[9] It is possible to stress a few SFPs, for instance, the hearsay particle *wo5* (see (5c)):

(i) keoi5   hou2   leng3-zai2   **WO5**
     3   EMPH   handsome   SFP (hearsay)
     'He is very handsome (somebody said) (*but I don't think so*).'

Stressing the hearsay particle conveys the inference that the speaker totally disagrees with what is said.

[10] This can be illustrated by the dislocation constructions in Cantonese. In these constructions, an
adverb which is usually preverbal may appear at the end of a sentence. The adverb has to follow the SFP. In
example (iii) below, the adverb *ji5-ging1* (already) separates a clause (i.e. *ngo5 zou6-zo2 gong1-fo3* ('I have
done homework')) and an SFP (i.e. *laa3*), and the sequence is ungrammatical. The dot '·' in the examples
indicates an intonation break.

(i) ngo5   **ji5-ging1**   zou6-zo2   gong1-fo3   (*·)   laa3 ·
     1   already   do-ASP   homework   SFP
     'I have already done homework.'

                                                          (Canonical Word Order)

(ii) ngo5   zou6-zo2   gong1-fo3   (* ·)   laa3   **ji5-ging1**
     1   do-ASP   homework   SFP   already
     'I have done homework already.'

                                                          (Dislocation)

(iii) *ngo5   zou6-zo2   gong1-fo3   **ji5-ging1**   laa3
      1   do-ASP   homework   already   SFP

                                                          (Ungrammatical)

There is more discussion of dislocation constructions such as (ii) in section 16.4 below.

evidentiality, presupposition—see examples (1) to (5) above) pragmatically refines the interpretation of the sentence.[11]

It also appears that SFPs have scope over whole sentences at their right edge, not just a part of a sentence; for instance, a question particle turns the whole sentence into a question (Gasde and Paul 1996). In the context of generative grammar where function words or bound morphemes are widely considered to project functional heads, it therefore seems reasonable to analyse these particles as C-heads taking an IP complement.

There is, however, still room for discussion as to whether SFPs are C-heads of the type instantiated by complementizers. Earlier works on Chinese syntax consider SFPs to be C-heads, largely because the analysis enables us to make straightforward cross-linguistic generalizations that can be attributed to parametric variation in the Principles-and-Parameters framework. For instance, if SFPs in Chinese were C-elements, we could conclude that C is head-initial in English or other European languages whereas it is head-final in Chinese (Tang 1989; Law 1990; Cheng 1991). In the light of more recent discussion, however, this generalization does not appear to be correct. In particular, Chappell (2008) and Yeung (2006) have observed that a complementizer seems to have evolved in some Chinese varieties and this word surfaces at the beginning of the clause with which it is associated (see section 16.3 below). Tang (1989) suggests that C in Chinese (i.e. SFPs) appears in main/root clauses only, whereas C in English (i.e. *that*) appears in embedded clauses only, but the former statement is probably not entirely true (see section 16.3 below). Cheng (1991) proposes that natural languages either invoke movement or a particle in marking *wh*-questions, and both strategies involve the C-domain; for instance, a *wh*-phrase moves to Spec-CP and a SFP is instantiated in C. However, SFPs are not obligatory in Chinese *wh*-questions.

(11) a. ni   xi-huan   shei   (**ne**)?
          2   like   who   SFP/Q
          'Who(m) do you like?'

(Mandarin Chinese)

      b. nei5   zong1-ji3   bin1-go3   (**le1**)?
          2   like   who   SFP/Q
          'Who(m) do you like?'

(Cantonese)

---

[11] As for the case of particle clusters, it has been suggested that the SFPs are located in fixed order in various C-heads preceding IP (Li 2006). The IP may then undergo successive movements to the specifiers of these heads, resulting in the fixed sentence-final order of these particles (Sybesma and Li 2007; Cheung 2009: 217, note 15). Upon closer scrutiny, there are still a lot of problems that remain unsolved in this account. For instance, Li (2006) remains neutral as to whether SFPs are based-generated in a head-initial or head-final C-position. Cheung (2009) actually suggests that IP movement is triggered by a functional head higher than the C-heads hosting the SFPs, and supposedly they do not really pass through the specifiers of all these C-heads. See details in section 16.4.

Huang, Li, and Li (2009: 260–82) argue that in Chinese *wh*-questions (with or without an overt SFP), the *wh*-phrase undergoes covert movement to Spec-CP, with C carrying an interrogative Q-feature. Alternatively, the *wh*-phrase is bound by a Q-operator in C or Spec-CP. In either of these proposals, the C-head is phonetically null and precedes the sentence, but the SFP is not the C-head.

In yes–no questions, it is clearer that the C-domain may or may not be invoked. Whereas an I-element (modal or auxiliary verb) moves to C in English, an A-not-A question in Chinese is apparently marked in the I-domain rather than the C-domain. The following is an example in Cantonese.

(12)   nei5   **sik6-m4-sik6**   faan6?
      you   eat-NEG-eat   rice
      'Would you like to dine out (with us)?'

(Cantonese, A-not-A question)

Huang, Li, and Li (2009: 253) suggest that A-not-A questions realize an interrogative functional head Q in a position where we also find the negation head, in other words, an I-position between subject and VP. In sum, it is inconclusive whether SFPs are C-heads because some of them mark questions and the C-domain is usually (but not obligatorily) invoked in question marking across languages.

Pollock (1989), Rizzi (1997), and subsequent works envisage that the I-domain and the C-domain may well be split into many functional projections. Inspired by these approaches, Li (2006) and Sybesma and Li (2007) locate various Cantonese particles in functional heads whose order is fixed in a richly articulated C-domain, which apparently accounts for the combinatory restrictions of SFPs in particle clusters (e.g. (3d)). Despite these strengths, we may still have some reservations about the proposal, not least those often levelled against the cartographic approach (e.g. Are these functional heads always projected in every sentence even though the corresponding SFPs are absent?). Furthermore, we may notice that some of these putative functional heads, for instance those which host markers of evidentiality or epistemic modality (e.g. (5)), are most probably instantiated in the I-domain in other languages where these markers are realized as suffixes (see section 16.1 above) or modal verbs (such as those in English). It still makes sense, however, to analyse these particles as some kind of C-head because of their sentence-peripheral position, but their modal meaning (i.e. evidentiality, likelihood, presupposition, etc., especially those in Cantonese, such as (3) and (5)) does not map naturally onto the discourse-related heads proposed by Rizzi (1997), namely, Topic, Focus, Finite, or Force.

There is another way to interpret the split-C analysis: while complementizers spell out an 'unscattered' CP, other elements may only spell out parts of this articulated domain, including, potentially, individual heads (cf. Biberauer and Sheehan 2011 for discussion). This seems to be the approach of Huang, Li, and Li (2009), although we do not find much elaboration there. Huang, Li and Li (2009: 34–5) briefly suggest that SFPs in Chinese are not exactly C, but Clause-Typers (CT), apparently extending Cheng's (1991) theory of clause-typing. They observe that Korean has both a complementizer which links a verb and a clause (i.e. *ko*) and other morphemes which indicate mood (e.g. *ta* for declarative mood and *nya* for interrogative mood). In this proposal, *if* in the following English sentence has dual functions in being a clause-typer and a complementizer:

(13)   I wonder if he was the killer.

Assuming that SFPs are indeed clause-typers, they look similar to Force proposed by Rizzi (1997), and one may still argue that they are a species of C-head. Whereas some SFPs do encode the illocutionary force of a sentence (e.g. *ba* and *ma* mark an imperative and a question in (1a) and (1b) respectively), this analysis is problematic for many other Chinese SFPs whose meaning is related to modality (e.g. (5)) rather than mood or illocutionary force. These particles do not seem to fit into the category of Clause-Typers or Force. What is more, many SFPs have multiple meanings (e.g. *me1* in (3a), *mei6* in (3c), see above), of a kind which does not seem compatible with the idea that they realize a single functional head (e.g. Force, Attitude, or Polarity).

16.3 Sentence-final particles and complementizers in Chinese varieties

In the above section, we have seen that there are some reasons for analysing SFPs as C-heads; more specifically, SFPs are function words and they seem to take IP as their complement in a projection above IP. However, some controversy remains as to whether SFPs are really C-heads as conceived in generative grammar. This chapter argues for the case that SFPs are *not* C-heads. The main argument is that SFPs systematically exhibit vastly different properties from those of complementizers (in the sense of 'subordinating conjunction' of the English *that*-type). Therefore, if complementizers are C-heads (i.e. (9a) above), SFPs cannot be. Additionally, there are emergent complementizers in Chinese varieties which seem to be more appropriately analysed as C-heads.

As noted in section 16.1, an SFP signals rich pragmatic meaning, including speakers' presuppositions and attitude (e.g. (1) to (5)), but a complementizer conveys little pragmatic meaning. There is also a difference in the number of complementizers and SFPs: there are few complementizers in a single language (e.g. *that*, *if*, and *for* in English), but there may be many different particles in one language, expressing a wide range of pragmatic meanings; for instance, Sybesma and Li (2007: 1739) suggest that there are at least forty SFPs in Cantonese. Whereas complementizers link a clause with a higher verb which selects the clause, SFPs mostly appear with root clauses (e.g. (1) to (5); see below). In addition, there is only one complementizer marking an embedded clause (e.g. *I think [cthat [IP he is the killer]]*), but there may be a cluster of SFPs attached to a single clause (see (3d)).

The analysis of SFPs in Chinese as C becomes even less plausible in the light of emerging complementizers in Chinese varieties. Interestingly, some words have been recognized as clause-initial complementizers (Chappell 2008; Yeung 2006). The following are some examples in Beijing Mandarin, Taiwanese Southern Min, and Cantonese respectively:

(14) a. wo   zongshi juede **shuo** shenghuo-li queshao le   dian shenme
       1   always feel say/C life-in   lack PART little something
       'I've always felt that there is something lacking in my life.'

                          (Beijing Mandarin, Fang 2006, as cited in Chappell 2008: 84)

      b. A-hui   siong **kong** A-sin m   lai
         A-hui   think say/C   A-sin NEG come
         'A-hui thought that A-sin was not coming.'

                          (Taiwanese Southern Min, Simpson and Wu 2002: 77)

      c. keoi5 gong2- gwo3 **waa6** nei5 wui5 lai4
         3   say   ASP   say/C   you   will come
         'He (or she) said that you would come.'   (Cantonese, Yeung 2006: 13)

These complementizers show many properties of *that* in English (as listed above), although in terms of etymology, these Chinese complementizers evolve from verbs of saying (that is, *verba dicendi*; Chappell 2008).[12] In contrast, SFPs in Chinese seem to have grammaticalized from various sources and via different routes (Yap, Matthews, and Horie 2004; Yap and Wang 2009). The coexistence of complementizers and SFPs within the same language variety with radical differences strongly suggests that the two are different word classes and that they should not be treated as the same category (that is, C). We return to this point below. For the moment, Table 16.1 summarizes the differences between SFPs and complementizers in Chinese (based on Yap, Matthews, and Horie 2004; Yeung 2006; Chappell 2008; Yap and Wang 2009).

---

[12] Actually, there are similarities and differences between Chinese complementizers and the English complementizer *that*. Apart from the similarities I have been alluding to, the use of Chinese complementizers is, like the English one, optional when introducing a clause. But there are also differences. For instance, *waa6* in Cantonese can be used to introduce a clause which is direct speech, but *that* in English does not serve this function. Note that *waa6* co-occurs with SFP in this example (also see example (23) below).

(i)   keoi5 gin3 dou2 ngo5 gin3 dou2 keoi5, zung6 daai6 seng1 giu3 **waa6**
       3   see   PART 1   see   PART 3   even   big   voice shout C
       aa3-fun1   nei5   mai5   soeng5   lai4   **aa3**
       Ah-Fun   2   NEG   up   come   SFP
       'When he (or she) saw me see him (or her), he (or she) actually shouted (*that),
       "Ah-Fun, don't come forward."'

                          (Yeung 2006: 41)

Secondly, *waa6* may appear after a connective, such as '*jyu4 gwo2 waa6* . . . (if *waa6* . . .)'. Further research is needed to probe into the properties of *waa6* as a complementizer in Cantonese and also into the complementizers in other Chinese varieties.

TABLE 16.1 Differences between sentence-final particles and clause-initial complementizers in Chinese

Sentence-final particles	Complementizers
Signal rich pragmatic meaning in terms of speakers' attitude and presuppositions	Convey little pragmatic meaning
Appear in root clauses and some may appear in embedded clauses, but in the latter case they do not mark their 'subordinate' status	Link an embedded clause to a higher verb which selects the clause
Clause-final	Clause-initial
More than one particle is possible, that is, a particle cluster	Only one complementizer is possible
Grammaticalized from various sources via different routes	Grammaticalized from verbs of saying (verba dicendi)
Have existed for a long time, found in Classical Chinese	Have evolved much more recently, grammaticalized in different degrees across Chinese varieties

From a cross-linguistic perspective, SFPs diverge from complementizers in their distribution in sentences. Complementizers always appear in a position between the verb and the embedded clause, and so there are two basic word orders of a complex sentence which contains a complementizer. Many languages have only one of these orders (e.g. V–C–IP for English, IP–C–V for Japanese, Korean). Some languages show both orders, such as the South Asian languages (Bayer 1999, 2001); however, in either order, the complementizer lies adjacent to the verb. The order V–IP–C is unattested across languages (Dryer 1992a, 2007, 2009; Kayne 2005b).[13] The order C–IP–V is very rare, and Biberauer and Sheehan (2012) have an in-depth discussion of this issue in relation to Antisymmetry and FOFC.[14]

(15)   Complementizer placement in relation to the clauses they select

    a. V C IP (clause-initial complementizers, such as *that* in English)

    b. IP C V (clause-final complementizers, such as *to* in Japanese or *ko* in Korean)

    c. V IP C (extremely rare)

    d. (*)C IP V (extremely rare)

---

[13] Dryer (2009: 200) actually lists Khoekhoe (also known as Nama), an OV language with a postverbal complement clause and a final complementizer, in other words, a sequence of V–IP–C. There are not sufficient data for us to draw any meaningful speculation. In the light of our discussion here, however, it is possible that the so-called 'complementizer' might be some element similar to the Cantonese SFPs.

[14] Biberauer and Sheehan (2012) note that Harar Oromo (Dryer 2009) and Akkadian (Deutscher 2006) present exceptions to this generalization. See Biberauer and Sheehan (2012) for more discussion.

Tang (1989) observes that an SFP cannot appear in embedded classes in Mandarin Chinese:

(16) a. ta   lai-bu-lai   **ne?**   (A-not-A)
         3   come-NEG-COME   SFP/Q
         'Is he (or she) coming)?'

      b. [ta   lai-bu-lai   (***ne**)]   gen   wo   mei   guanxi
         3   come-NEG-come   SFP   with   1   NEG   relationship
         'Whether he (or she) comes does not bother me.'
                            (Mandarin Chinese, slightly modified from Tang 1998: 542, (5.63))

Law (2002), however, observes examples of Cantonese sentences in which SFPs appear in complex sentences. Strikingly, though, when SFPs occur in complex sentences (i.e. a matrix clause containing one or more embedded clauses), their placement is after the embedded clause or IP, as indicated in (17b):

(17) a. keoi5   ci4-zo2   zik1   **me1**
         3   quit-ASP   job   SFP/Q
         'Did he (or she) quit his (or her) job?'

      b. nei5 m4   zi1-dou3   keoi5   ci4-zo2   zik1   **me1**
         2   NEG   know   3   quit-ASP   job   SFP/Q
                V   IP   SFP
         'Didn't you know he (or she) quit his (or her) job?'

As (17) shows, when an SFP appears with an embedded clause, the word order of these sentences is consistently V–IP–SFP. If SFPs were complementizer-type C-elements, it is puzzling why they are not adjacent to the verb as in (15a) or (15b). SFPs, then, exhibit a very different distribution to what we observe cross-linguistically in relation to the relative placement of complementizers and V (cf. (15) above).

Importantly, where an SFP appears in a complex sentence in Cantonese, it can only be interpreted as being attached to the higher clause, as in (17b) above (also see examples (28) and (29) in Law 2002: 386). The reading derived from SFP being attached to the lower clause is simply not available (i.e. the reading in (18) marked with #, following the conventions in Law 2002):

(18) nei5   m4   zi1-dou3   keoi5   ci4-zo2   zik1   **me1**
      2   NEG   know   3   quit-ASP   job   SFP/Q
      'Didn't you know that he (or she) has quit his (or her) job?'
      #'You do not know whether he (or she) has quit his (or her) job.'

However, SFPs can also be attached to the lower clause (i.e. the embedded clause) in complex sentences in Cantonese. In the following examples, it is reasonable to assume that they are attached to the lower embedded clause. The readings in which an SFP scopes over the matrix clause seem extremely unnatural:

(19) a. nei5   sik6-zo2   faan6   **mei6**
          2   eat-ASP   rice   SFP/NEG/Q
          'Have you eaten rice (i.e. Have you eaten/Have you had your meal)?'

                                                              (SFP in root clause)

      b. keoi5   **man6**   [nei5   sik6-zo2   faan6   **mei6**]
          3   ask   2   eat-ASP   rice   SFP/NEG/POL
          V   [IP   SFP]
          'He (or she) asks whether you have eaten rice (i.e. had a meal).'
          #'Has he (or she) asked whether you've eaten rice (i.e. had a meal)?'

                                                          (SFP in embedded clause)

(20) a. keoi5   hou2   lek1   **gaa3**
          3   very   smart   SFP (assertion)
          'He (or she) is really very smart!'

                                                              (SFP in root clause)

      b. ngo5   **gok3-dak1**   [keoi5   hou2   lek1   **gaa3**]
          1   feel-PART   3   very   smart   SFP (assertion)
          V   [IP   SFP]
          'I feel (i.e. think) that he (or she) is really very smart.'
          #'I really think that he (or she) is very smart.'

                                                          (SFP in embedded clause)

(21) a. keoi5   hou2   leng3-zai2   **wo5**
          3   very   handsome   SFP (hearsay)
          'He is very handsome, somebody said.'

                                                              (SFP in root clause)

      b. keoi5   **waa6**   [keoi5   hou2   leng3-zai2   **wo5**]
          3   say   3   very   handsome   SFP (hearsay)
          V   [IP   SFP]
          'He says he is very handsome.'
          #'Somebody says that he says that he is very handsome.'

                                                          (SFP in embedded clause)

As pointed out by a reviewer, strong evidence of SFPs not being complementizer-type C-heads is provided by data in which a Chinese clause-initial complementizer co-occurs with an SFP (cf. the discussion of (14) above). As far as Cantonese is concerned, Yeung's (2006) corpus data do show some examples in which the complementizer *waa6* coexists with an SFP in a complex sentence. However, it is not crystal-clear whether the SFP is attached to the lower embedded clause. In my intuition, a complementizer can coexist with an SFP attached to an embedded clause, as illustrated in the following example:

(22) a. nei5   siki-daki   keoi5   **gaa1**   **maa3**
        2   know-PART   3   SFP   SFP (presupposition)
        'You know him (or her), don't you?'
        (i.e. So I assumed you wouldn't have problems getting along with him (or her).)
                                                       (SFP in root clause)

      b. ngo5   lam2-zyu6 **waa6** [nei5 siki-daki   keoi5 **gaa1 maa3**]
        1   think-ASP C   2   know-PART 3   SFP SFP (presupposition)
        'I was supposing that you knew him (or her).'
        (i.e. So I assumed you wouldn't have problems getting along with him (or her).)
        #'I suppose I think that you knew him (or her).'
                                        (SFP in embedded clause)

The particle cluster *gaa1 maa3* here implies that the speaker presupposed that 'you know him (or her)', but it turns out that the listener does not, or the listener did not behave as if he or she knows somebody being referred to here. In (22b) the meaning of the particle(s) echoes that of the higher verb (i.e. *lam2-zyu6* (think/suppose)), similar to (19b) to (21b) above. If the particle cluster *gaa1 maa3* is attached to the lower clause in (22b), then the complementizer *waa6* is higher than the lower clause and the SFP.

(23) [$_{IP}$ V C [IP SFP]]

Why is there a difference of canonical word orders between V–C–IP-(SFP) and V–IP–SFP? What exactly are the properties of complementizers and SFPs which contribute to this difference? Before investigating these questions further, we need to examine the Dislocation Focus Constructions in Cantonese, where SFPs do appear to be a C-element, namely a focus marker (i.e. (9c)). Based on these constructions, Cheung (2009) proposes that SFPs are base-generated in a functional head preceding the sentence in the C-domain. The sentence-final order of an SFP is derived from movement of IP to the left of the SFP to give Canonical Word Order (i.e. sentences without dislocation); Dislocation Focus Constructions, by contrast, are derived by the fronting of focused constituents within IP.

16.4 The Dislocation Focus Constructions in Cantonese

As noted above, it has previously been proposed that SFPs are base-generated in a C-head position, with their sentence-final order being derived from IP movement (cf. i.a. Simpson and Wu 2002; Hsieh and Sybesma 2007, 2008). Cheung (2009: 209) notes that these accounts of SFPs are based on either certain question particles or specific constructions in one Chinese variety (e.g. *kong* in Taiwanese Southern Min), which limits the generalizability of these analyses. He suggests that the Dislocated Focus Construction (DFC) in Cantonese, which co-occurs with many different SFPs, provides convincing evidence of the underlying head initiality of C. Example (24a) below is an instance of the unmarked word order (what Cheung (2009) calls the 'Canonical Word Order'), whereas (24b) is the corresponding sentence in Dislocation Focus Construction:

(24) a. keoi5 zau2 zo2 loeng5 go3 zung1-tau4 **laa3**
       3   go   ASP two   CLF hour   SFP
       'He (or she) has left for two hours.'   (Canonical Word Order)

     b. **loeng5 go3 zung1-tau4 laa3** keoi5 zau2 zo2
        two   CLF hour   SFP 3   go   ASP
        'He (or she) has left for two hours.'
             (Dislocation Focus Construction, Cheung 2009: 198)

In a sentence such as (24b) the SFP (no longer sentence-final here) appears to be a focus marker marking a focused constituent (in **bold** letters in (24b) above). In Cheung's (2009) analysis, both (24a) and (24b) are derived from the same underlying structure in which the SFP is a functional head F in the C-domain selecting an IP complement, and there is another Focus phrase FocP above FP, as illustrated in (25):

(25) [$_{FocP}$ [$_{Foc}$ Ø][$_{FP}$ [$_F$ laa3] [$_{IP}$ keoi5 zau2 zo2 [$_{DP}$ loeng5 go3 zung1-tau4]]]]
               (Corresponding to (48) in Cheung 2009: 218)

The Dislocation Focus Construction in (24a) is derived by DP moving to the specifier of FocP, checking off a focus feature in the Focus head which is phonetically null. This is shown in (26):

(26) [$_{FocP}$ [$_{DP}$loeng5 go3 zung1-tau4]$_i$[$_{Foc}$ Ø] [$_{FP}$[$_F$ **laa3**] [$_{IP}$ keoi5 zau2 zo2 [$_{DP}$ t_i]]]]
        two CLF hour   SFP   3   go ASP
     'He has gone for two hours.'
                    (Dislocation Focus Construction)

Cheung (2009) argues that this analysis also provides an account of the Canonical Word Order in (24a): it is derived by IP moving to the left of the SFP. A problem with this analysis is that the IP does not usually receive a focused interpretation[15] and in

---

[15] Cheung (2009: 229) adds that IP can receive a focused interpretation in Canonical Word Order, for instance, the 'out of the blue cases', but he does not elaborate on these cases. In my opinion, some assertion SFPs do seem to assign a focused interpretation to the IP, as shown in the following pair of sentences.

(i) Keoi5   zau2-   zo2
    3   go-   ASP
    'He (or she) has gone.'

these cases it should not be Focus which drives the movement. Cheung (2009: 229) acknowledges the problem. He assumes that IP is moved to the specifier of a functional projection YP, but he remains open as to what kind of phrase YP is.[16] The analysis he assumes is given in (27):

(27) $[_{YP} [_{IP}$ keoi5 zau2 zo2 loeng5 go3 zung1-tau4$]_i$ $[_{YP} [_Y \emptyset]$ $[_{FP} [_F$ laa3$]$ $[_{IP} t_i$ $]]]]$
               3   go   ASP two   CLF hour   SFP
       'He has left for two hours'

(Canonical Word Order)

Cheung (2009) schematizes various parts in the Dislocation Focus Construction using the notations of α, β, and SFP which stand for the remnant, the fronted constituent and the SFP respectively. The underlying order is hence 'SFP α β' as in (28a); the Dislocation Focus Construction is then 'β SFP α' (i.e. (28b)). Finally, the Canonical Word Order is 'α β SFP' (i.e. (28c)):

(28)   a. $[_{CP}$ SFP $[_{IP} \alpha \beta]]$ (Underlying Word Order, as in (25))

       b. $[_{CP} \beta_i$ SFP $[_{IP} \alpha t_i]]$ (Dislocation Focus Construction, as in (26))

       c. $[_{CP} [_{IP} \alpha \beta]_i$ SFP $t_i]$ (Canonical Word Order, as in (27))

Cheung's account has obvious strengths. For one, Dislocation Focus Constructions such as (24b) are most likely derived by the fronting of the focused constituent β (as illustrated in (26)) instead of rightward movement of α, since the fronting is subject to locality constraints (Law 2003; Cheung 2008, 2009). Another point is related to the position of SFPs. In earlier work, Cheung (2008) actually assumed that the SFP is in the Focus head, which triggers movement. Cheung (2009) revises the idea and proposes instead that the Focus head is phonetically null and located above the SFP. This new analysis appears to cope better with the fact that the Dislocation Focus Construction does not always contain an overt SFP, as illustrated in (29):

(29)   a. ngo5   ji4-gaai   heoi3   ci3-so2
          I   now   go   toilet
       'I'm going to the toilet now.'

(Canonical Word Order)

(ii) $[_{IP}$ Keoi5   zau2- zo2$]$ laa3
              3   go-   ASP   SFP
       'He (or she) has gone!'

The assertion particle *laa3* in (ii) calls for additional attention paid to the proposition of the sentence, and it looks as if the whole IP is focused. Sentence (i), on the other hand, does not have this effect without the particle.

[16] Cheung (2009: 229) tentatively suggests that IP movement in Canonical Word Order is due to defocalization, following the proposal of Simpson and Wu (2002) and Zubizarreta (1998). However, we are not sure which functional head (i.e. What is Y?) is responsible for defocalization. Moreover, IP in Canonical Word Order sometimes carries a focused interpretation (see footnote 15 above), and these cases do not seem to be explained satisfactorily by defocalization.

b. **ci3-so2** ngo5 ji4-gaa1 heoi3
toilet I now go
'I'm going to the toilet now.'

(Dislocation Focus Construction)

Two issues remain unresolved on this proposal, however. Firstly, the identity of the functional head, F, which hosts the SFP is unclear. As mentioned above, Chinese SFPs, especially those in Cantonese, are often polysemous, which seems to make it even more difficult to assign an SFP to a specific functional head. The second issue, also mentioned above, is that obligatory IP-raising in sentences featuring Canonical Word Order (as illustrated in (27) above) seems problematic. Since the raised IP usually does not receive a focused interpretation, it remains obscure as to what the motivation for the movement is. In other words, the identity of Y and YP stays unclear.

Other kinds of dislocation constructions in Cantonese (other than (24b)) further cast doubt over the analysis that SFPs are underlyingly head-initial. In what I will refer to as 'Clause-Internal Dislocation', a focused constituent appears to move to an IP-internal position. This type of dislocation has hitherto been seldom studied, Liang (2002), who has some similar examples, being an exception. In (30) below, the focused constituent which introduces new information is evidently in clause-medial position:

(30) a. di1 pou4-zap1   *hou2*   *ci5*   **gei2**   hou2-mei6   wo3
      the Portuguese-sauce   EMPH   seem   quite   tasty   SFP
      α β γ
      'The Portuguese sauce does seem quite tasty.'

(Canonical Word Order)

     b. di1 pou4-zap1   **gei2**   hou2-mei6   wo3   *hou2*   *ci5*
      the Portuguese-sauce   quite   tasty   SFP   EMPH   seem
      α γ β
      'The Portuguese sauce does seem quite tasty.'

(Clause-Internal Dislocation)

As with Dislocation Focus Constructions (e.g. (29)), Clause-Internal Dislocation does not necessarily appear with an overt SFP:

(31) a. ngo5 dei6 *ji4-gaa1* *zung6* *hai6* **mou5** **syu1**
     1   PL   now   still   COP   lack   book
     'We still don't have the (text)book by now.'

(Canonical Word Order)

     b. ngo5 dei6 **mou5** **syu1** *ji4-gaa1* *zung6* *hai6*
     1   PL   lack   book   now   still   COP
     'We still don't have the (text)book now.'

(Clause-Internal Dislocation)

In keeping with the spirit of Antisymmetry and the insight that what looks like right-dislocation in Cantonese actually involves leftward movement (Law 2003; Cheung 2008, 2009), we might assume these sentences are also derived from some kind of leftward movement. However, there is apparently no satisfactory way in which they may be derived from an underlying CP structure with a head-initial C-element hosting an SFP (such as (25); Cheung 2008, 2009). According to this account, movement would have to apply to discontinuous constituents, which is generally forbidden:

(32)   a. di1   pou4-zap1   gei2   hou2-mei6   wo3   hou2   ci5
         the   Portuguese-sauce   quite   tasty   SFP   EMPH   seem
         'The Portuguese sauce does seem quite tasty.'   (Repeated from (31a))

   b. ?[_FocP di1 pou4-zap1___gei2 hou2-mei6][_Foc∅][_FP[_Fwo3][_IP___hou2 ci5___]]

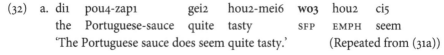

It is possible that (30b) is due to two separate movement operations rather than one movement of a discontinuous constituent. Accordingly, the focused constituent *gei2 hou2-mei6* (quite tasty) is fronted and the movement is triggered by Focus. Nonetheless, it is not clear what functional head drives the movement of the other fronted constituent, namely, *di1 pou4-zap1* (the Portuguese sauce), which is *not* focused. There is little evidence that this phrase moves to the specifier of a Topic Phrase above Focus (Rizzi 1997). That is, there is an intonation break after the topic which is optionally marked with a topic marker (e.g. *le1* or *aa3* in Cantonese, Matthews and Yip 2011). Neither an intonation break nor a topic marker is possible after the subject (i.e. *di pou4-zap1* 'the Portuguese sauce') in (30b), however.

(33)   di1   pou4-zap1   (?aa3/le1/·)   **gei2**   **hou2-mei6**   **wo3**   *hou2*   *ci5*
         the   Portuguese-sauce   quite   tasty   SFP   EMPH   seem
         'The Portuguese sauce does seem quite tasty.'

It seems implausible to derive both the Canonical Word Order and IP-internal focus by positing that an SFP is base-generated in a functional head above IP in the C-domain.[17]

---

[17]   In addition to IP-internal focus, some naturalistic data suggest that there may be a Focus within DP in Cantonese, which has hitherto not, to my knowledge, been documented or discussed. Sentence (ii) is an example in Cantonese which I observed and find grammatical.

(i)   [_IP [_DP   aa3-maan1   ji4-gaai   go3   lou2-po4]   hai6   ou3-mun2   jan4   lai4   gaa3]
                  Aman   now   CLF   wife   COP   Macau   person   SFP   SFP
       'Aman's wife now (i.e. his second wife) is a Macau Chinese.'

                                                                       (Canonical Word Order)

Three generalizations emerge from the above discussion of various kinds of dislocation in Cantonese:

(34)   Dislocation in Cantonese

    a. Dislocation is not necessarily associated with the presence of an overt SFP.

    b. In Canonical Word Order, the IP usually does not receive a focused interpretation.

    c. In Clause-Internal Dislocation, a focused constituent is preposed to a clause-medial position rather than a clause-initial position.

The following is a proposal which seeks to incorporate the facts in (34). Crucially, an SFP is not base-generated as a functional head in a head-initial phrase (Simpson and Wu 2002; Cheung 2008, 2009); instead, it is an affix attached to the right of an IP. Assuming that it is not a 'fully-fledged' head and it does *not* project its own phrase (e.g. CP or PrtP), an SFP can merge with an IP in its surface sentence-final position.

(35)   Dislocation in Cantonese: an alternative account

    a. The Focus head is always phonetically null in Cantonese.

    b. The Focus head attracts the focused constituent XP to its specifier position.

    c. An SFP is lowered and affixed to a focused constituent [XP SFP] before movement.

    d. There is a Focus projection above IP and within IP.

Let us now see how these ideas are applied. A sentence in Canonical Word Order is derived from IP merging with an SFP. The SFP does not project its own phrase, and the Merge of IP and SFP consequently results in another IP. This is shown below:

(ii) [$_{IP}$[$_{DP}$ aa3-maan1 ji4-gaa1 [hai6 ou3-mun2 jan4 lai4 gaa3] go3 lou2-po4]]
       Aman   now   COP   Macau   person SFP SFP CLF wife

   'Aman's wife now (i.e. his second wife) is a Macau Chinese.'

                              (Clausal-Internal Dislocation, DP-internal focus)

Sentence (iv) below is another instance of DP-internal focus without an overt SFP.

(iii) [$_{IP}$ [$_{DP}$ ngo5-dei6 go3 sat6-lik6] tung4 maa2-loi4-sai1-aa3 caa1-m4-do1]]
        1-   PL CLF strength   with   Malaysia   similar

   'The strength (of our team) is similar to that of the Malaysian (team).'

                                    (Canonical Word Order)

(iv) [$_{DP}$ ngo5-dei6 [tung4 maa2-loi4-sai1-aa3 caa1-m4-do1] go3 sat6-lik6]
        1-   PL   with   Malaysia   similar   CLF strength

   'The strength of (our team) is similar to that of the Malaysian (team).'

                            (Clausal-Internal Dislocation, DP-internal focus)

DP-internal focus has been discussed recently in Laenzlinger (2005), who assumes a Focus projection in DP in French. But examples such as (ii) and (iv) involve movement of a focused constituent from outside the DP which seems uncommon and seldom discussed. I leave aside a more detailed analysis of this phenomenon for further research.

(36) a. [IP [IP zek3 gai1   jik6 siu1   dak1 hou2 leng3] [SFP wo3]]
          CLF chicken wing barbecue PART EMPH fine   SFP
     'The chicken-wing is barbecued so nicely!'

                        (Repeated from (30a), Canonical Word Order)

     b.   IP

   In a Dislocation Focus Construction, the SFP is affixed to the focused constituent,
as shown below:

(37) a. [IP [IP zek3 gai1   jik6 siu1   dak1 [XP hou2 leng3 wo3]] [SFP w̶o̶3̶]]
          CLF chicken wing barbecue PART   EMPH fine SFP
     'The chicken-wing is barbecued so nicely!'

     b.   IP
         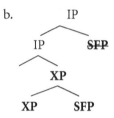

                 (SFP lowers and is affixed to the focused constituent XP)

Afterwards, this constituent moves to the specifier of FocusP:

(38) a. [Spec-Foc[XPhou2 leng3 wo3]i [Foc Ø] [IP zek3 gai1   jik6 siu1   dak1 [XPti]]]
          EMPH fine SFP   CLF chicken wing barbecue PART
     'The chicken-wing is barbecued so nicely!'

                        (Dislocation Focus Construction deriving from (37a))

     b.   FocP
         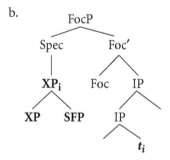

                 (XP moves to the specifier of Focus)

   The derivations for Clause-Internal Dislocation are similar. The SFP is first affixed
to the focused constituent XP:

(39) a. [$_{IP}$ di1 pou4-zap1   hou2 ci5   [$_{XP}$ **gei2 hou2-mei6 wo3**] [$_{SFP}$ ~~wo3~~]]
the Portuguese-sauce EMPH seem   quite tasty   SFP
'The Portuguese sauce does seem quite tasty.'

b.

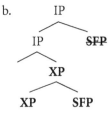

(SFP lowers and is affixed to the focused constituent XP)

The focused constituent XP then moves to an IP-internal focus, following proposals of Belletti (2004) and Jayaseelan (2001):

(40) a. [$_{IP}$ di1 pou4-zap1 [$_{FocP}$[$_{XP}$**gei2 hou2-mei6wo3**]$_i$ [$_{Foc}$Ø] [$_{VP}$hou2 ci5 [$_{XP}$ t_i]]]] [$_{SFP}$**wo3**]]
the   Portuguese-sauce quitetasty   SFP   EMPH seem
'The Portuguese sauce does seem quite tasty.'

b.

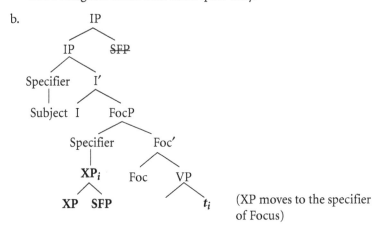

(XP moves to the specifier of Focus)

In sum, this alternative analysis proposes that an SFP is an affix attached to an IP. Since an SFP is not a 'fully-fledged' functional head, we do not need to assume that it must precede the sentence in the underlying structure, and IP movement is not necessary to derive the Canonical Word Order. If there is no IP movement, the question of what drives the IP movement in Canonical Word Order does not arise. If an SFP is not a functional head preceding IP in underlying order, not only clause-initial dislocation (i.e. the Dislocation Focus Construction in terms of Cheung 2008, 2009, for example, (24b)) but also Clause-internal Dislocation (for example, (30b)) can be explained. Moreover, there is an account of SFPs behaving as focus markers (i.e. they are affixed to the focused constituents) even though they are not in Focus or any other head position in the C-domain.

16.5 Conclusions

The mainstream view that SFPs in Chinese varieties are some kind of C-head has raised various issues concerning word order and phrase structure in Chinese varieties, which have been the focus of this paper. Under this view, SFPs are, in accordance with Antisymmetry (Kayne 1994, 2003a, 2005b), base-generated in IP-initial position, with IP movement resulting in their sentence finality. However, IP movement does not seem to be well motivated, and some dislocation constructions (i.e. Clause-internal Dislocation) indicate that SFPs may not be underlyingly sentence-initial. Irrespective of whether IP undergoes movement and whether SFPs are underlyingly head-initial/head-final, SFPs present an apparent counterexample to FOFC, which bars a head-final phrase immediately dominating a head-initial phrase. FOFC is able to explain many word-order restrictions in typologically different languages (Biberauer, Newton, and Sheehan 2009; Biberauer, Holmberg, and Roberts 2010; Biberauer and Sheehan 2012), and the exceptional behaviour of SFPs therefore needs to be accounted for.

This chapter re-examines the basis and rationale of the C-head analysis of SFPs, and evaluates various proposals of how sentences with these particles are derived. The key idea is that complementizers and SFPs show vastly different properties in terms of semantics, pragmatics, and syntax; accordingly, if complementizers are C-heads, SFPs cannot be. Furthermore, if SFPs are not really 'full' functional heads, they may not need to appear sentence-initially in the underlying structure; nor is there a need for IP movement. Their exceptional behavior with regard to FOFC can then be understood as a consequence of the syntactic deficiency of SFPs. In section 16.4, I suggest that this account is also compatible with a range of word-order variations due to focus and dislocation in Cantonese. The crucial assumption is that SFPs do not project their own phrase (e.g. a particle phrase or PrtP). There are obviously many issues awaiting further exploration, such as various types of dislocation constructions and their constraints in Cantonese, the nature of SFPs and particle clusters, the properties of the Chinese emergent complementizers, and the diachronic emergence of CP more generally. What we have seen here, however, is that Chinese presents particularly fertile ground for future research on disharmonic word orders.

References

Abe, Jun (2004). On directionality of movement: a case of Japanese right dislocation. *Proceedings of the 58th Conference: The Tohoku English Literary Society*. Sendai: Tohoku English Literary Society, 54–61.

Abels, Klaus (2003). *Successive Cyclicity, Anti-locality, and Adposition Stranding*. PhD dissertation, University of Connecticut.

Abels, Klaus (2007). Towards a restrictive theory of (remnant) movement. *Linguistic Variation Yearbook* 7: 57–120.

Abels, Klaus, and Ad Neeleman (2006). Universal 20 without the LCA. Unpublished manuscript, University of Tromsø/University College London. Extended version at <http://ling.auf.net/lingbuzz/000279>, last accessed 11 January 2013.

Abels, Klaus, and Ad Neeleman (2009). Universal 20 without the LCA. In J. Brucart, A. Gavarro, and J. Solá (eds.), *Merging Features: Computation, Interpretation, and Acquisition*. Oxford: Oxford University Press, 60–79.

Abels, Klaus, and Ad Neeleman (2012). Linear Asymmetries and the LCA. *Syntax* 15(1): 25–74.

Abney, Steven (1987). *The English Noun Phrase in its Sentential Aspect*. PhD dissertation, MIT.

Aboh, Enoch (2004). *The Morphosyntax of Complement–Head Sequences*. New York: Oxford University Press.

Ackema, Peter, and Ad Neeleman (2002). Effects of short-term storage in processing rightward movement. *Studies in Theoretical Psycholinguistics* 30: 219–56.

Aghaei, Behrad (2006). *The Syntax of ke-clauses and Clausal Extraposition in Modern Persian*. PhD dissertation, University of Texas.

Aikhenvald, Alexandra, Y. (2004). *Evidentiality*. Oxford: Oxford University Press.

Ajíbóyè, Ọládiípọ̀ Jacob (2005). *Topics in Yoruba Nominal Expressions*. PhD dissertation, University of British Columbia.

Alber, Birgit (2010). Past Participle in Mòcheno: allomorphy, alignment and the distribution of obstruents. In M. Putnam (ed.), *German-Language Speech Islands: Generative and Structural Approaches*. Amsterdam/Philadelphia: John Benjamins, 33–4.

Alboiu, Gabriela (2006). Feature-inheritance and Case values in Nominative–Accusative systems. Unpublished manuscript, York University.

Aldridge, Edith (2006). The heterogeneity of VOS and extraction in Austronesian languages. Unpublished manuscript, Northwestern University. Available online at <http://faculty.washington.edu/ecai/pdf/VOS.pdf>, last accessed 7 January 2013.

Aldridge, Edith (2011). Neg-to-Q: the historical development of one clause-final particle in Chinese. *The Linguistic Review* 28(4): 411–47.

Alexiadou, Artemis (2001). *Functional Structure in Nominals: Nominalizations and Ergativity*. Amsterdam: John Benjamins.

Alexiadou, Artemis, and Elena Anagnostopoulou (1998). Parameterizing AGR: word order, V-movement and EPP checking. *Natural Language and Linguistic Theory* 16: 491–539.

Alexiadou, Artemis, and Elena Anagnostopoulou (2001). The Subject-in-Situ Generalization and the role of Case in driving computations. *Linguistic Inquiry* 32: 193–231.

Alexiadou, Artemis, and Elena Anagnostopoulou (2007). The Subject-in-Situ Generalisation revisited. In H.-M. Gärtner and U. Sauerland (eds.), *Interfaces + Recursion = Language?* Berlin: Mouton de Gruyter, 31–60.

Alexiadou, Artemis, Liliane Haegeman, and Melita Stavrou (2007). *The Noun Phrase in Generative Perspective*. Berlin: Mouton de Gruyter.

Allan, Robin, Philip Holmes, and Tom Lundskaer-Nielsen (1995). *Danish: A Comprehensive Grammar*. London: Routledge.

Allin, Trevor R. (1976). *A Grammar of Resígaro*. Horsleys Green, Buckinghamshire: SIL.

Anagnostopoulou, Elena (2005). Holmberg's Generalization and cyclic linearization: remarks on Fox and Pesetsky. *Theoretical Linguistics* 31: 95–110.

Anderson, Torben (1988). Ergativity in Päri, a Nilotic OVS language. *Lingua* 75: 289–324.

Antinucci, Francesco (1977). *Fondamenti di una teoria tipologica del linguaggio*. Bologna: Il Mulino.

Antinucci, Francesco, and Guglielmo Cinque (1977). Sull'ordine delle parole in italiano: l'emarginazione. *Studi di Grammatica Italiana* 6: 121–46.

Aoun, Joseph E., Elabbas Benmamoun, and Lina Choueiri (2010). *The Syntax of Arabic*. Cambridge: Cambridge University Press.

Ariel, Mira (1999). Cognitive universals and linguistic conventions: the case of resumptive pronouns. *Studies in Language* 23: 217–69.

Aronoff, Mark (1976). *Morphology by Itself*. Cambridge, MA: MIT Press.

Artiagoitia, Xabier (2006). *Euskarazko izen-sintagma: arkitektura eta egitura funtzionala* [Noun phrase in Basque: architecture and functional structure]. Bilbao: University of the Basque Country Professorship Report.

Artiagoitia, Xabier (2008a). Izen sintagmaren hurrenkera: osagarriak aurretik, buruak gero [NP order: complements precede heads]. In I. Arteatx, X. Artiagoitia, and A. Elordieta (eds.), *Antisimetriaren hipotesia vs. buru parametroa: euskararen oinarrizko hurrenkera ezbaian* [The Antisymmetry Hypothesis vs. the Head Parameter: the basic word order in Basque]. Bilbao: University of the Basque Country Publications, 157–98.

Artiagoitia, Xabier (2008b). Some arguments for complement–head order in Basque DPs. In X. Artiagoitia and J. A. Lakarra (eds.), *Gramatika Jaietan. Patxi Goenagaren omenez*. Bilbao: Supplements of ASJU, 71–92.

Aygen, Gulsat (2002). *Finiteness, Case and Clausal Architecture*. PhD dissertation, Harvard University.

Bailey, Laura (2010). Sentential word order and the syntax of question particles. *Newcastle Working Papers in Linguistics* 16: 23–43.

Baker, Mark C. (1985). The Mirror Principle and morphosyntactic explanation. *Linguistic Inquiry* 16(3): 373–416.

Baker, Mark C. (1988). *Incorporation: A Theory of Grammatical Function Changing*. Chicago: University of Chicago Press.

Baker, Mark C. (2003). *Lexical Categories: Verbs, Nouns, and Adjectives*. Cambridge: Cambridge University Press.

Baker, Mark C. (2005). On verb-initial and verb-final word orders in Lokaa. *Journal of African Languages and Linguistics* 26: 125–64.

Baker, Mark C. (2008). *The Syntax of Agreement and Concord*. Cambridge: Cambridge University Press.

Baker, Mark C. (2009). Language universals: abstract not mythological. *Behavior and Brain Sciences* 32: 448–9.

Baker, Mark C. (2010). Formal Generative Typology. In B. Heine and H. Narrog (eds.), *The Oxford Handbook of Linguistic Analysis*. Oxford: Oxford University Press, 285–312.

Baker, Mark C., and Ruth Kramer (2011). 'Prepositions' as case morphemes inserted at PF in Amharic. To appear in D. Jaspers (ed.), *Case at the Interfaces*. Bingley: Emerald. Available online at <http://www.rci.rutgers.edu/~mabaker/Amharic-Ps-as-case-paper-posted.pdf>, last accessed 6 January 2013.

Barbiers, Sjef (1995). *The Syntax of Interpretation*. The Hague: Holland Academic Graphics.

Barbiers, Sjef (2000). The right periphery in SOV languages: English and Dutch. In P. Svenonius (ed.), *The Derivation of VO and OV*. Amsterdam/Philadelphia: John Benjamins, 181–218.

Barbiers, Sjef (2010). Syntactic Doubling and Deletion as a Source of Variation. Unpublished manuscript, Meertens Instituut. Available online at <https://www.meertens.knaw.nl/cms/files/Syntactic%20Doubling%20and%20Variation-paper.pdf>, last accessed 5 March 2012.

Barreña, Andoni (1995). *Gramatikaren jabekuntza-garapena eta haur euskaldunak* [Grammar-acquisition development and Basque infants]. Leioa: University of the Basque Country.

Barreña, Andoni, and Itziar Idiazabal (1997). Diferenciación bilingüe precoz de códigos: los objetos en español y euskera. In L. Díaz and C. Pérez (eds.), *Views on the Acquisition and Use of a Second Language. EUROSLA'7*. Barcelona: University of Pompeu Fabra, 157–70.

Barrie, Michael (2006a). *Dynamic Antisymmetry and the Syntax of Noun Incorporation*. PhD dissertation, University of Toronto.

Barrie, Michael (2006b). On unifying antisymmetry and bare phrase structure. In L. Bateman and C. Ussery (eds.), *Proceedings of the 35th Meeting of the North East Linguistic Society*. Amherst, MA: GLSA Publications, 103–14.

Barrie, Michael (2009). Clausal temporal adjuncts: against late adjunction. Paper given at 83rd Annual Meeting of the Linguistic Society of America, San Francisco, CA.

Bartsch, Renate, and Theo Vennemann (1972). *Semantic Structures*. Frankfurt: Athenäum.

Bates, Dawn (1988). *Prominence Relations and Structure in English Compound Morphology*. PhD dissertation, University of Washington.

Bayer, Josef (1996). *Directionality and Logical Form*. Dordrecht: Kluwer.

Bayer, Josef (1999). Final complementizers in hybrid languages. *Journal of Linguistics* 35: 233–71.

Bayer, Josef (2001). Two grammars in one: sentential complements and complementizers in Bengali and other South-Asian languages. In P. Bhaskararao and K. Subbarao (eds.), *The Yearbook of South Asian Languages 2001*. New Delhi: Sage Publications, 11–36.

Bayer, Josef, and Hans-Georg Obenauer (2011). Discourse particles, clause structure, and question types. *The Linguistic Review* 28: 449–91.

Beckman, Mary E. (1986). *Stress and Non-Stress Accent*. Dordrecht: Foris.

Behaghel, Otto (1932). *Deutsche Syntax*. Heidelberg: Carl Winters Universitätsbuchhandlung.

Belletti, Adriana (1981). Frasi ridotte assolute. *Rivista di Grammatica Generativa* 6: 3–32.

Belletti, Adriana (2001). Inversion as focalization. In A. Hulk and J. Y. Pollock (eds.), *Inversion in Romance and the Theory of Universal Grammar*. New York/Oxford: Oxford University Press, 60–90.

Belletti, Adriana (2004). Aspects of the low IP area. In L. Rizzi (ed.), *The Structure of CP and IP: The Cartography of Syntactic Structures*. New York: Oxford University Press, 16–51.

Belletti, Adriana (2006). (Past) participle agreement. In M. Everaert and H. van Riemsdijk (eds.), *The Blackwell Companion to Syntax*. Oxford: Blackwell, 493–521.

Belletti, Adriana, and Luigi Rizzi (1988). Psych-verbs and Theta-Theory. *Natural Language and Linguistic Theory* 6: 291–352.

Belletti, Adriana, and Luigi Rizzi (2002). Editors' introduction: some concepts and issues in linguistic theory. In A. Belletti and L. Rizzi (eds.), *Noam Chomsky: On Nature and Language*. Cambridge: Cambridge University Press, 1–44.

Bender, Emily M. (2002). Number names in Japanese: a head-medial construction in a head-final language. Manuscript, Stanford University. Available online at <http://faculty.washington.edu/ebender/papers/jnn.pdf>, last accessed 7 January 2013.

Benincà, Paola (1988). L'ordine degli elementi della frase e le costruzioni marcate. In L. Renzi (ed.), *Grande Grammatica Italiana di Consultazione*, vol. 1. Bologna: Il Mulino, 115–94.

Benincà, Paola (2001). The position of Topic and Focus in the left periphery. In G. Cinque and G. Salvi (eds.), *Current Studies in Italian Syntax: Essays Offered to Lorenzo Renzi*. Amsterdam: Elsevier, 39–64.

Benincà, Paola (2006). A detailed map of the left periphery of medieval Romance. In R. Zanuttini, H. Campos, E. Herburger, and P. Portner (eds.), *Crosslinguistic Research in Syntax and Semantics: Negation, Tense and Clausal Architecture*. Washington: Georgetown University Press, 53–86.

Benincà, Paola, and Nicola Munaro (2010). *Mapping CPs: The Cartography of Syntactic Structures*. New York/Oxford: Oxford University Press.

Benincà, Paola, and Cecilia Poletto (2004). Topic, Focus and V2: defining the CP sublayers. In L. Rizzi (ed.), *The Structure of CP and IP. The Cartography of Syntactic Structures*. New York: Oxford University Press, 52–75.

Bennett, Paul A. (1979). On Universal 23. *Linguistic Inquiry* 10: 510–11.

Bernstein, Judy (1991). DPs in French and Walloon: evidence for parametric variation in nominal head movement. *Probus* 3: 101–26.

Bernstein, Judy (1997). Demonstratives and reinforcers in Romance and Germanic languages. *Lingua* 102: 87–113.

Bernstein, Judy (2008). Reformulating the Determiner Phrase analysis. *Language and Linguistics Compass* 2: 1–25.

Berwick, Robert, and Noam Chomsky (2011). The Biolinguistic Program: the current state of its evolution and development. In A.-M. Di Sciullo and C. Boeckx (eds.), *The Biolinguistic Enterprise*. Oxford: Oxford University Press, 19–41.

Besten, Hans den (1976). Het Kiezen van Lexicale Delenda. *Spektator* 5: 415–32.

Besten, Hans den (1977). On the interaction of Root Transformations and lexical deletive rules. Unpublished manuscript: University of Amsterdam. Published as: Hans den Besten (1983). On the interaction of root transformations and lexical deletive rules. In Werner Abraham (ed.), *On the Formal Syntax of the West Germania*. Amsterdam: Benjamins, 74–131.

Besten, Hans den (1981). On the interaction of root transformations and lexical deletive rules. *Groninger Arbeiten zur Germanistischen Linguistik* 20: 1–78.

Besten, Hans den (1983). On the interaction of Root Transformations and Lexical Deletive Rules. In Werner Abraham (ed.), *On the Formal Syntax of the West Germania*. Amsterdam: John Benjamins, 47–131.

Bever, Tom (2003). Deconstructing functionalist explanations of linguistic universals. In A. Carnie, H. Harley, and M. Willie (eds.), *Formal Approaches to Function in Grammar*. Amsterdam: John Benjamins, 333–52.

Bianchi, Valentina (1999). *Consequences of Antisymmetry: Headed Relative Clauses*. Berlin: Mouton de Gruyter.

Biber, Douglas, Stig Johansson, Geoffrey Leech, Susan Conrad, and Edward Finegan (1999). *Longman Grammar of Spoken and Written English*. London: Longman.

Biberauer, Theresa (2003). *Verb Second (V2) in Afrikaans: A Minimalist Investigation*. PhD dissertation, University of Cambridge.

Biberauer, Theresa (2007). 'Doubling and Omission: Insights from Afrikaans'. In *Papers from the Workshop on Doubling in the Dialects of Europe*. Amsterdam: Meertens online Publications. Available online at <http://www.meertens.knaw.nl/projecten/edisyn/>.

Biberauer, Theresa. (2008a). Doubling vs. omission: insights from Afrikaans negation. In S. Barbiers, M. Lekakou, M. van der Ham, and O. Koeneman (eds.), *Microvariation in Syntactic Doubling* (Syntax and Semantics, vol. 36). Bingley: Emerald Group Publishing Limited, 103–40.

Biberauer, Theresa (2008b). A 'third factor'-imposed typology of (dis)harmonic languages? Paper presented at the Cambridge–Delhi–Hyderabad–Nanzan Workshop, Hyderabad, January 2008.

Biberauer, Theresa, and Raffaella Folli (2004). Goals of motion in Afrikaans. *Journées d'Études Linguistiques* (*Actes des JEL 2004/Proceedings of JEL 2004—[DOMAIN$_{[E]}$S]*), 19–26.

Biberauer, Theresa, Anders Holmberg, and Ian Roberts (2008a). Disharmonic word-order systems and the Final-over-Final-Constraint (FOFC). In A. Bisetto and F. E. Barbieri (eds.), *Proceedings of the XXXIII Incontro di Grammatica Generativa*. Bologna: Università di Bologna, 86–105. Available online at <http://amsacta.cib.unibo.it/archive/00002397/>, last accessed 7 January 2013.

Biberauer, Theresa, Anders Holmberg, and Ian Roberts (2008b). Structure and linearization in disharmonic word orders. In C. B. Chang and H. J. Haynie (eds.), *Proceedings of the 26th West Coast Conference on Formal Linguistics*. Somerville: Cascadilla Press, 96–104. Available online at <http://www.lingref.com/cpp/wccfl/26/paper1660.pdf>, last accessed 7 January 2013.

Biberauer, Theresa, Anders Holmberg, and Ian Roberts (2009). Linearization and the architecture of grammar: a view from the Final-over-Final Constraint. In V. Moscati and E. Servidio (eds.), *Proceedings of the XXXV Incontro di Grammatica Generativa*. Studies in Linguistics 3, 77–89. Available online at <http://research.ncl.ac.uk/linearization/BHR_IGG35_Proceedings_paper.pdf>, last accessed 7 January 2013.

Biberauer, Theresa, Anders Holmberg, and Ian Roberts (2010). A syntactic universal and its consequences. Unpublished manuscript: Universities of Cambridge and Newcastle.

Biberauer, Theresa, Anders Holmberg, and Ian Roberts (in press). A syntactic universal and its consequences. To appear in *Linguistic Inquiry*.

Biberauer, Theresa, Anders Holmberg, Ian Roberts, and Michelle Sheehan (2010). Reconciling formalism and functionalism: a minimalist perspective. Paper presented at Linguistics Association of Great Britain Annual Conference (Leeds).

Biberauer, Theresa, Glenda Newton, and Michelle Sheehan (2009). Limiting synchronic and diachronic variation and change: the Final-over-Final Constraint. *Language and Linguistics* 10: 701–43.

Biberauer, Theresa, and Marc Richards (2006). True optionality: when the grammar doesn't mind. In C. Boeckx (ed.), *Minimalist Essays*. Amsterdam: John Benjamins, 35–67.

Biberauer, Theresa, and Ian Roberts (2008). Phases, word order and types of clausal complements in West Germanic languages. Paper presented at the 23rd Comparative Germanic Syntax Workshop (Edinburgh).

Biberauer, Theresa, Ian Roberts, and Michelle Sheehan (2013). No-choice parameters and the limits of syntactic variation. To appear in N. Danton, D. Nostadinovska, and R. Santana-LaBarge (eds.), *Proceedings of the 31st West Coast Conference on Formal Linguistics (WCCFL 31)*. Somerville, MA: Cascadilla Press.

Biberauer, Theresa, and Michelle Sheehan (2011). Introduction: particles through a modern syntactic lens. *The Linguistic Review* 28: 387–410.

Biberauer, Theresa, and Michelle Sheehan (2012). Disharmony, Antisymmetry, and the Final-over-Final Constraint. In M. Uribe-Etxebarria and V. Valmala (eds.), *Ways of Structure Building*. Oxford: Oxford University Press, 206–44.

Biberauer, Theresa, Michelle Sheehan, and Glenda Newton (2010). Impossible changes and impossible borrowings: the Final-over-Final Constraint. In Anne Breitbarth, Christopher Lucas, Sheila Watts, and David Willis (eds.), *Continuity and Change in Grammar*. Amsterdam: John Benjamins, 35–60.

Bidese, Ermenegildo (2008). *Die diachronische Syntax des Zimbrischen*. Tübingen: Günther Narr Verlag.

Bion, Ricardo, Barbara Höhle, and Michaela Schmitz (2007). The role of prosody on the perception of word-order differences by 14-month-old German infants. *Proceedings of ICPhS 2007* (Saarbrücken, Germany), 1537–40.

Björverud, Susanna (1998). *A Grammar of Lalo*. PhD dissertation, University of Lund.

Blevins, Juliette (1995). The syllable in phonological theory. In J. Goldsmith (ed.), *Handbook of Phonological Theory*. Oxford: Blackwell, 206–44.

Bloom, Lois (1970). *Language Development: Form and Function in Emerging Grammars*. Cambridge, MA: MIT Press.

Bloomfield, Leonard (1933). *Language*. New York: Henry Holt and Co.

Bloomfield, Leonard (1934). Review of *Handbuch der erklärenden Syntax* by Wilhelm Havers (Heidelberg: Winters, 1931). *Language* 10: 32–9.

Bobaljik, Jonathan D. (1995). In terms of Merge: Copy and head movement. *Papers on Minimalist Syntax. MIT Working Papers in Linguistics* 27: 41–64.

Bobaljik, Jonathan D. (2005). Re: CycLin and the role of PF in object shift. *Theoretical Linguistics* 31: 111–25.

Bobaljik, Jonathan, and Samuel Brown (1997). Interarboreal operations: head movement and the extension requirement. *Linguistic Inquiry* 2: 345–56.

Boeckx, Cedric (2000). EPP eliminated. Unpublished manuscript, University of Connecticut, Storrs. Available online at <http://www.sinc.sunysb.edu/Clubs/nels/jbailyn/EPPELIMINATED.pdf>, last accessed 5 January 2013.

Boeckx, Cedric (2010). What Principles and Parameters got wrong. Manuscript, ICREA/UAB. Available online at <http://ling.auf.net/lingbuzz/001118>, last accessed 14 December 2012.

Boeckx, Cedric, and Sandra Stjepanović (2001). Head-ing toward PF. *Linguistic Inquiry* 32(2): 345–55.

Boisson, Claude (1981). Hiérarchie universelle des spécifications de temps, de lieu, et de manière. *Confluents* 7: 69–124.

Borer, Hagit (1984). *Parametric Syntax*. Dordrecht: Foris.

Bošković, Zjelko (2002). A-movement and the EPP. *Syntax* 5(3): 167–218.

Bowers, John. (1987). Extended X-bar theory, the ECP and the left-branch condition. *Proceedings of the 6th West Coast Conference on Formal Linguistics*. Stanford: Stanford Linguistics Association, 47–62.

Brattico, Pauli, and Alina Leinonen (2009). Case distribution and nominalization: evidence from Finnish. *Syntax* 12: 1–31.

Bresnan, Joan (1972). Sentence stress and transformations. *Language* 47: 237–97.

Bresnan, Joan (1973). Syntax of the comparative clause construction in English. *Linguistic Inquiry* 4(3): 275–343.

Broadwell, George Aaron (2005). It ain't necessarily S(V)O: two kinds of VSO languages. In M. Butt and T. Holloway King (eds.), *Proceedings of the LFG05 Conference*. Stanford: CSLI, 87–106.

Brown, Roger (1973). *A First Language: The Early Stages*. Cambridge, MA: Harvard University Press.

Bury, Dirk (2003). *Phrase Structure and Derived Heads*. PhD dissertation, University College London.

Burzio, Luigi (1986). *Italian Syntax*. Dordrecht: Foris.

Bybee, Joan (1988). The diachronic dimension in explanation. In J. Hawkins (ed.), *Explaining Language Universals*. Oxford: Blackwell, 350–79.

Cable, Seth (2010). *The Grammar of Q: Q-Particles, Wh-Movement, and Pied-Piping*. New York: Oxford University Press.

Cabredo Hofherr, Patricia (2010). Adjectives: an introduction. In Patricia Cabredo Hofherr and Ora Matushansky (eds.), *Adjectives: Formal Analyses in Syntax and Semantics*. Amsterdam: John Benjamins, 1–28.

Calabrese, Andrea (1982). Alcune ipotesi sulla struttura informazionale della frase in italiano e sul suo rapporto con la struttura fonologica. *Rivista di Grammatica Generativa* 5: 65–115.

Campbell, Lyle, Vit Bubenik, and Leslie Saxon (1988). Word order universals: refinements and clarifications. *Canadian Journal of Linguistics* 33: 209–30.

Cardinaletti, Anna (2002). Against optional and zero clitics: right dislocation versus marginalization. *Studia Linguistica* 56(1): 29–57.

Cardinaletti, Anna (2011). German and Italian modal particles and clause structure. *The Linguistic Review* 28(4): 493–532.

Cardinaletti, Anna, and Michal Starke (1999). The typology of structural deficiency: a case study of three classes of pronouns. In H. van Riemsdijk (ed.), *Clitics in the Languages of Europe: Empirical Approaches to Language Typology*. Berlin: Mouton de Gruyter, 145–233.

Carnie, Andrew (1995). *Non-Verbal Predication and Head-Movement*. PhD dissertation, MIT.

Carnie, Andrew (2000). On the notions XP and X⁰. *Syntax* 3: 59–106.

Carnie, Andrew, and Eithne Guilfoyle (eds.) (2000a). *The Syntax of Verb Initial Languages*. New York: Oxford University Press.

Carnie, Andrew, and Eithne Guilfoyle (2000b). Introduction. In A. Carnie and E. Guilfoyle (eds.), *The Syntax of Verb Initial Languages*. New York: Oxford University Press, 3–11.

Carstens, Vicki (2002). Antisymmetry and word order in serial verb constructions. *Language* 78: 3–50.

Casad, Eugene H. (1984). Cora. In R. Langacker (ed.), *Studies in Uto-Aztecan Grammar*. Arlington: SIL and University of Texas, 151–459.

Cecchetto, Carlo (1999). A comparative analysis of left and right dislocation in Romance. *Studia Linguistica* 53(1): 40–67.

Chang, Henry Yungli (2006). The guest playing host: modifiers as matrix verbs in Kavalan. In H.-M. Gärtner, P. Law, and J. Sabel (eds.), *Clause Structure and Adjuncts in Austronesian Languages*. Berlin: Mouton de Gruyter, 43–82.

Chang, Henry Yungli (2009). Adverbial verbs and adverbial compounds in Tsou: a syntactic analysis. *Oceanic Linguistics* 48: 339–76.

Chappell, Hilary (2008). Variation in the grammaticalization of verba *dicendi* in Taiwanese Southern Min and other Sinitic languages. *Linguistic Typology* 12(1): 45–98.

Cheng, Lisa Lai-Shen (1986). *De* in Mandarin. *Canadian Journal of Linguistics* 31: 313–26.

Cheng, Lisa Lai-Shen (1991). *On the Typology of Wh-Questions*. PhD dissertation, MIT.

Cheng, Lisa, and Rint Sybesma (2009). *De* as an underspecified classifier: first explorations. *Yǔyánxué Lùncóng* [Essays on Linguistics] 39: 123–56.

Cheung, Lawrence Y. L. (2008). Obligatory XP raising in Chinese. *Toronto Working Papers in Linguistics* 28: 15–28.

Cheung, Lawrence Y. L. (2009). Dislocation focus construction in Chinese. *Journal of East Asian Linguistics* 18: 197–232.

Choi, Inji (2005). The internal structure of the Korean DP: evidence from prenominal and postnominal classifiers. *Oxford Working Papers in Linguistics, Philology and Phonetics* 10: 19–38.

Chomsky, Noam (1964). On the notion 'rule of grammar'. In J. Fodor, and J. Katz (eds.), *The Structure of Language: Readings in the Philosophy of Language*. Englewood Cliffs, NJ: Prentice Hall, 119–36.

Chomsky, Noam (1965). *Aspects of the Theory of Syntax*. Cambridge, MA: MIT Press.

Chomsky, Noam (1970). Remarks on nominalization. In R. A. Jacobs and P. S. Rosenbaum (eds.), *Readings in English Transformational Grammar*. Waltham, MA: Ginn, 184–221.

Chomsky, Noam (1973). Conditions on transformations. In S. R. Anderson and P. Kiparsky (eds.), *A Festschrift for Morris Halle*. New York: Holt, Rinehart, and Winston, 232–86.

Chomsky, Noam (1981). *Lectures on Government and Binding*. Dordrecht: Foris.

Chomsky, Noam (1986). *Barriers*. Cambridge, MA: MIT Press.

Chomsky, Noam (1993). A minimalist program for linguistic theory. In K. Hale and S. J. Keyser (eds.), *A View from Building 20: Essays in Honor of Sylvain Bromberger*. Cambridge, MA: MIT Press, 1–52.

Chomsky, Noam (1995a). *The Minimalist Program*. Cambridge, MA: MIT Press.

Chomsky, Noam (1995b). Bare Phrase Structure. In G. Webelhuth (ed.), *Government and Binding Theory and the Minimalist Program: Principles and Parameters in Syntactic Theory*. Cambridge, MA: Blackwell, 383–439.

Chomsky, Noam (2000). Minimalist inquiries. In R. Martin, D. Michaels, and J. Uriagereka (eds.), *Step by Step: Essays on Minimalist Syntax in Honor of Howard Lasnik*. Cambridge, MA: MIT Press, 89–155.

Chomsky, Noam (2001). Derivation by phase. In M. Kenstowicz (ed.), *Ken Hale: A Life in Language*. Cambridge, MA: MIT Press, 1–54.

Chomsky, Noam (2004). Beyond explanatory adequacy. In A. Belletti (ed.), *Structures and Beyond: The Cartography of Syntactic Structure*. New York: Oxford University Press, 104–31.

Chomsky, Noam (2005). Three factors in language design. *Linguistic Inquiry* 36: 1–22.

Chomsky, Noam (2007). Approaching UG from below. In U. Sauerland and H.-M. Gärtner (eds.), *Interfaces + Recursion = Language? Chomsky's Minimalism and the View from Syntax-Semantics*. Berlin: Mouton de Gruyter, 1–29.

Chomsky, Noam (2008). On phases. In R. Freidin, C. P. Otero, and M. L. Zubizarreta (eds.), *Foundational Issues in Linguistic Theory: Essays in Honor of Jean-Roger Vergnaud*. Cambridge, MA: MIT Press, 291–321.

Chomsky, Noam (2013). Problems of projection. *Lingua* 130: 33–49.

Chomsky, Noam, and Morris Halle (1968). *The Sound Pattern of English*. New York: Harper and Row.

Chomsky, Noam, and Howard Lasnik (1993). Principles and Parameters Theory. In J. Jacobs, A. von Stechow, W. Sternefeld, and T. Vennemann (eds.), *Syntax: An International Handbook of Contemporary Research*. Berlin: Walter de Gruyter, 13–127. Reprinted as chapter 1 of Chomsky (1995a).

Christiansen, Morten Christopher Collins, and Shimo Edelman (eds.) (2009). *Language Universals*. Oxford: Oxford University Press.

Christophe, Anne, Marina Nespor, Maria-Teresa Guasti, and Brit van Ooyen (2003). Prosodic structure and syntactic acquisition: the case of the Head-Direction Parameter. *Developmental Science* 6: 211–20.

Cinque, Guglielmo (1977). The movement nature of Left Dislocation. *Linguistic Inquiry* 8: 397–412.

Cinque, Guglielmo (1990). *Types of A' Dependencies*. Cambridge, MA: MIT Press.

Cinque, Guglielmo (1993). A null theory of phrase and compound stress. *Linguistic Inquiry* 24: 239–98.

Cinque, Guglielmo (1994). On the evidence for partial N-movement in the Romance DP. In G. Cinque, J. Koster, J.-Y. Pollock, L. Rizzi, and R. Zanuttini (eds.), *Paths Towards Universal Grammar: Studies in Honor of Richard S. Kayne*. Washington DC: Georgetown University Press, 85–110.

Cinque, Guglielmo (1995). *Italian Syntax and Universal Grammar*. Cambridge: Cambridge University Press.

Cinque, Guglielmo (1996). The 'antisymmetric' programme: theoretical and typological implications. *Journal of Linguistics* 32: 447–64. Also in Cinque (2013b: 34–46).

Cinque, Guglielmo (1999). *Adverbs and Functional Heads: A Cross-linguistic Perspective*. New York: Oxford University Press.

Cinque, Guglielmo (2002). Complement and adverbial PPs: implications for clause structure. Paper presented at the 25th GLOW Colloquium (Amsterdam, published as Cinque 2006b).

Cinque, Guglielmo (2003). The prenominal origin of relative clauses. Paper presented at the Workshop on Antisymmetry and Remnant Movement (NYU, 31 Oct–1 Nov).

Cinque, Guglielmo (2004). Issues in adverbial syntax. *Lingua* 114: 683–710.

Cinque, Guglielmo (2005a). A note on verb/object order and head/relative clause order. In M. Vulchanova, and T.A. Åfarli (eds.), *Grammar and Beyond: Essays in honour of Lars Hellan*. Oslo: Novus Press, 69–89. Also in Cinque (2013b: 129–58).

Cinque, Guglielmo (2005b). Deriving Greenberg's Universal 20 and its exceptions. *Linguistic Inquiry* 36: 315–32. Also in Cinque (2013b: 57–67).

Cinque, Guglielmo (2006a). *Restructuring and Functional Heads: The Cartography of Syntactic Structures*. New York: Oxford University Press.

Cinque, Guglielmo (2006b). Complement and adverbial PPs: implications for clause structure. In G. Cinque (ed.), *Restructuring and Functional Heads. The Cartography of Syntactic Structures*. New York: Oxford University Press, 145–66.

Cinque, Guglielmo (2008). Two types of nonrestrictive relatives. In O. Bonami and P. Cabredo Hofherr (eds.), *Empirical Issues in Syntax and Semantics 7*. Paris: CSSP, 99–137. Also in Cinque (2013b: 181–207).

Cinque, Guglielmo (2009a). The fundamental left-right asymmetry of natural languages. In S. Scalise, E. Magni, and A. Bisetto (eds.), *Universals of Language Today*. Dordrecht: Springer, 165–84. Also in Cinque (2013b: 99–106).

Cinque, Guglielmo (2009b). Greenberg's Universal 23 and SVO languages. *University of Venice Working Papers in Linguistics* 19: 29–34. Also in Cinque (2013b: 110–13).

Cinque, Guglielmo (2010). *The Syntax of Adjectives: A Comparative Study*. Cambridge, MA: MIT Press.

Cinque, Guglielmo (2013a). Lognition, typological generalizations, and Universal Grammar. *Lingua* 130: 50–65.

Cinque, Guglielmo (2013b). *Typological Studies: Word Order and Relative Clauses*. London: Routledge.

Cinque, Guglielmo (to appear). Again on Tense, Aspect, Mood morpheme order and the 'Mirror Principle'. In P. Svenonius (ed.), *From Top to Toe: A Festschrift for Tarald Taraldsen*. New York: Oxford University Press.

Cinque, Guglielmo, and Luigi Rizzi (2010a). The cartography of syntactic structures. In B. Heine and H. Narrog (eds.), *The Oxford Handbook of Linguistic Analysis*. Oxford: Oxford University Press, 51–65.

Cinque, Guglielmo, and Luigi Rizzi (eds.) (2010b). *Mapping Spatial PPs: The Cartography of Syntactic Structures*. New York: Oxford University Press.

Citko, Barbara (2008a). Missing labels: head movement as *Project Both*. In C. Chang and H. Haynie (eds.), *Proceedings of the 26th West Coast Conference on Formal Linguistics*. Somerville, MA: Cascadilla Press, 121–28.

Citko, Barbara (2008b). Missing labels. *Lingua* 118: 907–44.

Clahsen, Harald, and Pieter Muysken (1986). The availability of Universal Grammar to adult and child learners: a study of the acquisition of German word order. *Second Language Research* 9: 93–119.

Codd, Edgar F. (1970). A relational model of data for large shared data banks. *Communications of the ACM* 13: 377–87. Reprinted as Edgar F. Codd (1983). A relational model of data for large shared data banks. *Communications of the ACM* 26: 64–9.

Cognola, Federica (2008). OV/VO word orders in Mocheno main declarative clauses. In P. Benincà, F. Damonte, and N. Penello (eds.), *Selected Proceedings of the XXXIV Incontro di Grammatica Generativa*. Special Issue of the *Rivista di Grammatica Generativa* 33, 83–97.

Cognola, Federica (2010). *Word Order and Clause Structure in a German Dialect of Northern Italy: On the Interaction between High and Low Left Periphery*. PhD dissertation, University of Padua.

Cognola, Federica (2013a). *Syntactic Variation and Verb Sound: A German Dialect in Northern Italy*. Amsterdam/Philadelphia John Benjamins.

Cognola, Federica (2013b). Scrambling as verum focus in Mòcheno. Ms. University of Trento.

Colarusso, John (1992). *A Grammar of the Kabardian Language*. Calgary, Alberta: University of Calgary Press.

Cole, Peter, and Gabriella Hermon (2008). VP raising in a VOS language. *Syntax* 11: 144–97.

Collins, Chris (1997). *Local Economy*. Cambridge, MA: MIT Press.

Collins, Chris (2002). Eliminating labels. In S. D. Epstein and T. D. Seely (eds.), *Derivation and Explanation in the Minimalist Program*. Malden, MA: Blackwell, 42–64.

Collins, Chris (2004). The absence of the linker in double object constructions in N|uu. *Studies in African Linguistics* 33: 163–98.

Collins, Chris (2005). A smuggling approach to the passive in English. *Syntax* 8: 85–120.

Collins, Chris, and Paul M. Postal (2010). Imposters. Unpublished manuscript: NYU. Available online at <https://files.nyu.edu/cc116/public/Manuscript%20August%202%20%28dist%29.pdf>, last accessed 8 January 2013.

Collins, Chris, and Ed Stabler (2012). A formalization of Minimalist Syntax. Unpublished manuscript, NYU/UCLA. Available online at <http://ling.auf.net/lingbuzz/001691>, last accessed 8 January 2013.

Compton, Richard (2006). Phasal words and inverse morpheme order in Inuktitut. Generals paper, University of Toronto. Available online at <http://individual.utoronto.ca/richardcompton/Education_ files/ComptonGP1.pdf>, last accessed 2 January 2013.

Comrie, Bernard (2008). Prenominal relative clauses in VO Languages. *Language and Linguistics* 9(4): 723–33.

Coon, Jessica (2010). VOS as predicate fronting in Chol. *Lingua* 120: 354–78.

Cooper, William, and John R. Ross (1975). Word order. In Robin E. Grossman, L. James San, and Timothy J. Vance (eds.), *Chicago Linguistic Society: Papers from the Parasession on Functionalism*. Chicago: Chicago Linguistic Society, 63–111.

Corbett, Greville, Norman M. Fraser, and Scott McGlashan (eds.) (1993). *Heads in Grammatical Theory*. Cambridge: Cambridge University Press.

Corver, Norbert (1997). The internal syntax of the Dutch extended Adjectival Projection. *Natural Language and Linguistic Theory* 15: 289–368.

Costa, João (1998). *Word Order Variation*. PhD dissertation, Leiden.

Costa, João, and Ana Maria Martins (2004). What is a strong functional head? Paper delivered at the Lisbon Workshop on Alternative Views on the Functional Domain (Lisbon).

Cowper, Elizabeth (2005). The geometry of interpretable features: INFL in English and Spanish. *Language*: 81: 10–46.

Craig, Colette G. (1977). *The Structure of Jacaltec*. Austin: University of Texas Press.

Crain, Stephen, and Janet D. Fodor (1985). How can grammars help parsers? In D. Dowty, L. Karttunen, and A. Zwicky (eds.), *Natural Language Parsing*. Cambridge: Cambridge University Press, 94–128.

Crain, Stephen, and Mineharu Nakayama (1987). Structure dependence in grammar formation. *Language* 6: 522–43.

Creissels, Denis (2005). SOVX constituent order and constituent order alternations in West African languages. *Proceedings of the 31st Annual Meeting of the Berkeley Linguistics Society*. Berkeley: Berkeley Linguistics Society, 1–15.

Cruschina, Silvio (2006). Informational focus in Sicilian and the left periphery. In M. Frascarelli (ed.), *Phases of Interpretation*. Berlin: Mouton de Gruyter, 363–85.

Cruschina, Silvio (2010). Syntactic extraposition and clitic resumption in Italian. *Lingua* 120: 50–73.

Culicover, Peter, and Ray Jackendoff (2005). *Simpler Syntax*. Oxford: Oxford University Press.

Cysouw, Michael (2008). Linear order as a predictor of word order regularities. *Advances in Complex Systems* 11: 415–20.

Dahl, Östen (1979). Typology of sentence negation. *Linguistics* 17: 79–106.

Daly, John P. (1973). *A Generative Syntax of Peñoles Mixtec*. Norman, OK: SIL and University of Oklahoma.

Davidson, Donald (1967). The logical form of action sentences. In N. Rescher (ed.), *The Logic of Decision and Action*. Pittsburgh: University of Pittsburgh Press, 104–12.

Davies, William, and Stanley Dubinsky (2003). On extraction from NPs. *Natural Language and Linguistic Theory* 21: 1–37.

Davis, Christopher (2011). *Constraining Interpretation: Sentence-Final Particles in Japanese*. PhD dissertation, University of Masachussetts, Amherst.

Davison, Alice (2007). Word order, parameters, and the extended COMP projection. In J. Bayer, T. Bhattacharya, and M. T. Hany Babu (eds.), *Linguistic Theory and South Asian Languages: Essays in Honour of K. A. Jayaseelan*. Amsterdam: John Benjamins, 175–98.

Dean, O. C. Jr. (1974). Verb position and the order of adverbials in German. Unpublished manuscript, University of Georgia. Available online at <http://www.eric.ed.gov/ERICDocs/data/ericdocs2sql/content_storage_01/0000019b/80/36/bd/e7.pdf>, last accessed 8 January 2013; URL no longer active.

Déchaine, Rose-Marie, and Mireille Tremblay (1998). On category features. Paper presented at GLOW 21 (Tilburg).

Déchaine, Rose-Marie, and Martina Wiltschko (2002). Decomposing pronouns. *Linguistic Inquiry* 33(3): 409–42.

Dejean, Yves (1993). *Manifestations en créole haïtien du principe d'adjacence stricte*. Port-au-Prince: Revue de l'Institut de Linguistique Appliquée.

DeLancey, Scott (2001). On functionalism. Lecture 1 handout. LSA Institute (Santa Barbara). Available online at <http://pages.uoregon.edu/delancey/sb/LECT01.htm>, last accessed 14 December 2012.

Delsing, Lars-Olof (1992). On attributive adjectives in Scandinavian and other languages. *Studia Linguistica* 47: 105–25.

Delsing, Lars-Olof. (2000). From OV in a VO in Swedish. In S. Pintzuk, G. Tsoulas, and A. Warner (eds.), *Diachronic Syntax: Models and Mechanisms*. Oxford: Oxford University Press, 255–74.

Déprez, Viviane (1998). Semantic effects of agreement: the case of French participle agreement. *Probus* 10: 1–67.

Derbyshire, Desmond C. (1977). Word order universals and the existence of OVS languages. *Linguistic Inquiry* 8(3): 590–99.

Derbyshire, Desmond C. (1979). *Hixkaryana*. Amsterdam: North Holland Publishing Company.

Derbyshire, Desmond C. (1985). *Hixkaryana and Linguistic Typology*. Dallas, TX: SIL and University of Texas at Arlington.

Deutscher, Guy (2000). *Syntactic Change in Akkadian: The Evolution of Sentential Complementation*. Oxford: Oxford University Press.

Deutscher, Guy (2006). Complement clause types and complementation strategies in Akkadian. In R. M. W. Dixon, and A. Y. Aikhenvald (eds.), *Complementation*. Oxford: Oxford University Press, 159–77.

Devlin, Keith (1993). *The Joy of Sets: Fundamentals of Contemporary Set Theory*. New York: Springer.

Diesing, Molly (1992). *Indefiniteness*. Cambridge, MA: MIT Press.

Diesing, Molly (1997). Yiddish VP order and the typology of object movement in Germanic. *Natural Language and Linguistic Theory* 15: 369–427.

Diessel, Holger (2001). The ordering distribution of main and adverbial clauses: a typological study. *Language* 77: 433–55.

Dikken, Marcel den (2003). On the syntax of locative and directional adpositional phrases. MS, CUNY. Available online at <http://web.gc.cuny.edu/dept/lingu/dendikken/docs/syntax_of_pp.pdf>.

Dikken, Marcel den (2006). On the syntax of locative and directional adpositional phrases. Unpublished manuscript, CUNY. Available online at <http://www.gc.cuny.edu/CUNY_GC/media/CUNY-Graduate-Center/PDF/Programs/Linguistics/Dikken/pp_cinqueandschweikert.pdf>, last accessed 8 January 2013.

Dikken, Marcel den (2010). On the functional structure of locative and directional PPs. In G. Cinque and L. Rizzi (eds.), *Mapping Spatial PPs: The Cartography of Syntactic Structures*, vol. 6. Oxford: Oxford University Press, 74–126.

Djamouri, Redouane (1999). Evolution of *zhi* in Archaic Chinese. In A. Peyraube and S. Chaofen (eds.), *In Honor of Mei Tsu-lin: Studies on Chinese Historical Syntax and Morphology*. Paris: CRLAO, EHESS, 33–48.

Djamouri, Redouane, Barbara Meisterernst, and Waltraud Paul (2009). Particles in Classical Chinese: complementisers and topic markers. Paper presented at the 29th International Conference on Historical Linguistics (Nijmegen).

Djamouri, Redouane, and Waltraud Paul (1997). Les syntagmes prépositionnels en *yu* 于 et *zai* 在 en chinois archaïque. *Cahiers de Linguistique Asie Orientale* 26(2): 221–48.

Djamouri, Redouane, and Waltraud Paul (2009). Verb-to-preposition reanalysis in Chinese. In P. Crisma and G. Longobardi (eds.), *Historical Syntax and Linguistic Theory*. Oxford: Oxford University Press, 194–211.

Downing, Bruce T. (1978). Some universals of relative clause structure. In J. Greenberg (ed.), *Universals of Human Language*. Stanford: Stanford University Press, 375–418.

Dryer, Matthew (1980). The positional tendencies of sentential noun phrases in universal grammar. *Canadian Journal of Linguistics* 25: 123–95.

Dryer, Matthew (1988a). Object–verb order and adjective–noun order: dispelling a myth. *Lingua* 74: 77–109.

Dryer, Matthew (1988b). Universals of negative positions. In M. Hammond, E. A. Moravcsik, and J. R. Wirth (eds.), *Studies in Syntactic Typology*. Amsterdam: John Benjamins, 93–124.

Dryer, Matthew (1989a). Plural words. *Linguistics* 27: 865–95.

Dryer, Matthew (1989b). Article–Noun order. In C. Wiltshire, R. Graczyk, and B. Music (eds.), *Papers from the 25th Regional Meeting of the Chicago Linguistic Society*. Chicago: Chicago Linguistic Society, 83–97.

Dryer, Matthew (1989c). Large linguistic areas and language sampling. *Studies in Language* 13: 257–92.

Dryer, Matthew (1991). SVO languages and the OV:VO typology. *Journal of Linguistics* 27: 443–82.

Dryer, Matthew (1992a). The Greenbergian word order correlations. *Language* 68: 81–138.

Dryer, Matthew (1992b). Adverbial subordinators and word order asymmetries. In J. A. Hawkins and A. Siewierska (eds.), *Performance Principles of Word Order*. European Science Foundation: EUROTYP Working Papers, 50–67.

Dryer, Matthew (1996). Word order typology. In J. Jacobs (ed.), *Handbook of Syntax*, vol. 2. Berlin: Mouton de Gruyter, 1050–65.

Dryer, Matthew (1998). Why statistical universals are better than absolute universals. In K. Singer, R. Eggert, and G. Anderson (eds.), *Proceedings of the 33rd Regional Meeting of the Chicago Linguistic Society (The Panels)*. Chicago: Chicago Linguistic Society, 123–45.

Dryer, Matthew (2001). Mon-Khmer word order from a crosslinguistic perspective. In K. L. Adams, and T. J. Hudak (eds.), *Papers from the 6th Annual Meeting of the Southeast Asian Linguistics Society*. Tempe: Arizona State University Program for Southeast Asian Studies, 83–99.

Dryer, Matthew (2005a). Relationship between the order of object and verb and the order of relative clause and noun. In M. Haspelmath, M. Dryer, D. Gil, and B. Comrie (eds.), *World Atlas of Language Structures*. Oxford: Oxford University Press, 390–93.

Dryer, Matthew (2005b). Relationship between the order of object and verb and the order of adjective and noun. In M. Haspelmath, M. Dryer, D. Gil, and B. Comrie (eds.), *World Atlas of Language Structures*. Oxford: Oxford University Press, 394–97.

Dryer, Matthew (2005c). Order of in verb object. In M. Haspelmath, M. Dryer, D. Gil, and B. Comrie (eds.), *The World Atlas of Language Structures*. Oxford: Oxford University Press, 338–41. Reissued as: Dryer, Matthew (2011b). Order of object and verb. In M. Dryer and M. Haspelmath (eds.), *The World Atlas of Language Structures Online*. Munich: Max Planck Digital Library, ch. 83, available online at <http://wals.info/chapter/83>, last accessed 5 September 2011.

Dryer, Matthew (2005d). Order of adposition and noun phrase. In M. Haspelmath, M. Dryer, D. Gil, and B. Comrie (eds.), *The World Atlas of Language Structures*. Oxford: Oxford University Press, 346–9. Reissued as: Dryer, Matthew (2011). Order of Adposition and noun phrase. In M. Dryer and M. Haspelmath (eds.), *The World Atlas of Language Structures Online*. Munich: Max Planck Digital Library, ch. 85, available online at <http://wals.info/chapter/85>, last accessed 5 September 2011.

Dryer, Matthew (2005e). Position of polar question particles. In M. Haspelmath, M. Dryer, D. Gil, and B. Comrie (eds.), *The World Atlas of Language Structures*. Oxford: Oxford University Press, 374–7. Reissued as Dryer, Matthew (2011g), Position of polar question particles. In M. Dryer and M. Haspelmath (eds.), *The World Atlas of Language Structures Online*. Munich: Max Planck Digital Library, ch. 92, available online at <http://wals.info/chapter/92>, last accessed 5 September 2011.

Dryer, Matthew (2005f). Order of adverbial subordinator and clause. In M. Haspelmath, M. Dryer, D. Gil, and B. Comrie (eds.), *The World Atlas of Language Structures*. Oxford: Oxford University Press, 382–5. Reissued as Dryer, Matthew (2011e). Order of adverbial subordinator and clause. In M. Dryer and M. Haspelmath (eds.), *The World Atlas of Language Structures Online*. Munich: Max Planck Digital Library, ch. 94, available online at <http://wals.info/chapter/94>, last accessed 5 September 2011.

Dryer, Matthew (2005g). Definite articles. In M. Haspelmath, M. Dryer, D. Gil, and B. Comrie (eds.), *The World Atlas of Language Structures (WALS)*. Oxford: Oxford University Press, 154–7.

Dryer, Matthew (2007). Word order. In T. Shopen (ed.), *Language Typology and Syntactic Description*, vol. 1. Cambridge: Cambridge University Press, 61–131.

Dryer, Matthew (2008). Word order in Tibeto-Burman languages. *Linguistics of the Tibeto-Burman Area* 31: 1–88.

Dryer, Matthew (2009). The branching direction theory of word order correlations revisited. In S. Scalise, E. Magni, and A.Bisetto (eds.), *Universals of Language Today*. Dordrecht: Springer, 185–207.

Dryer, Matthew (2011a). Prefixing vs. suffixing in inflectional morphology. In M. Dryer and M. Haspelmath (eds.), *The world Atlas of Language Structures Online*. Munich: Max Planck Digital Library, ch. 26. Available online at <http://wals.info/chapter/26>, last accessed on 3 October 2011.

Dryer, Matthew S. (2011b). Order of object and verb. In M. Dryer and M. Haspelmath (eds.), *The World Atlas of Language Structures Online*. Munich: Max Planck Digital Library, ch. 83. Available online at <http://wals.info/chapter/83>, last accessed on 3 October 2011.

Dryer, Matthew (2011c). Order of adposition and noun phrase. In M. Dryer and M. Haspelmath (eds.), *The World Atlas of Language Structures Online*. Munich: Max Planck Digital Library, ch. 85. Available online at <http://wals.info/chapter/85>, last accessed on 3 October 2011.

Dryer, Matthew (2011d). Order of genitive and noun. In M. Dryer and M. Haspelmath (eds.), *The World Atlas of Language Structures Online*. Munich: Max Planck Digital Library, ch. 86. Available online at <http://wals.info/chapter/86>, last accessed on 3 October 2011.

Dryer, Matthew (2011e). Order of adverbial subordinator and clause. In M. Dryer and M. Haspelmath (eds.), *The World Atlas of Language Structures Online*. Munich: Max Planck Digital Library, ch. 94. Available online at <http://wals.info/chapter/94>, last accessed on 3 October 2011.

Dryer, Matthew (2011f). Genealogical language list. In M. Dryer and M. Haspelmath (eds.), *The World Atlas of Language Structures Online*. Munich: Max Planck Digital Library. Available online at <http://wals.info/languoid/genealogy>, last accessed 17 December 2012.

Dryer, Matthew (2011g). Position of polar question particles. In M. Dryer and M. Haspelmath (eds.), *The World Atlas of Language Structures Online*. Munich: Maz Planch Digital Library, chapter 92. Available online at <http://wals.info/chapter/92>, last accessed on 3 October 2011.

Dryer, Matthew, with Orin Gensler (2005). 'Order of object, oblique, and verb'. In M. Haspelmath, M. S. Dryer, D. Gil, and B. Comrie (eds.), *The World Atlas of Language Structures*. Oxford: Oxford University Press, 342–5.

Dryer, Matthew, and Orin Gensler (2008). Order of object, oblique and verb. In M. Dryer and M. Haspelmath (eds.), *The World Atlas of Language Structures Online*. Munich: Max Planck Digital Library, ch. 84. Available online at <http://wals.info/chapter/84>, last accessed on 3 October 2011.

Dryer, Matthew, and Martin Haspelmath (eds.) (2011). *The World Atlas of Language Structures Online*. Oxford: Oxford University Press.

Duffield, Nigel (1998). Auxiliary placement and interpretation in Vietnamese. In M. C. Gruber, D. Higgins, K. S. Olson, and T. Wysocki (eds.), *Proceedings of the 34th Regional Meeting of the Chicago Linguistic Society*. Chicago: Chicago Linguistic Society, 95–109.

Dyakonova, Marina (2009). *A Phase-based Approach to Russian Free Word Order*. PhD dissertation: Universiteit Amsterdam.

Elordieta, Arantzazu (2001). *Verb Movement and Constituent Permutation in Basque*. Utrecht: LOT series 47.

Elordieta, Arantzazu (2008). OA hizkuntzak: oinarrizko hurrenkeraz eta hurrenkera eratorriez [OV languages: on basic order and derived orders]. In I. Arteatx, X. Artiagoitia, and A. Elordieta (eds.), *Antisimetriaren hipotesia vs. buru parametroa: euskararen oinarrizko hurrenkera ezbaian* [The Antisymmetry Hypothesis vs. the Head Parameter: the Basic Word Order in Basque]. Bilbao: University of the Basque Country Publications, 97–130.

Elordieta, Arantzazu (2010). Aditzaren bikoizketa foku–topikoa denean [Verb doubling in focus–topic contexts]. In B. Fernandez, P. Albizu, and R. Etxepare (eds.), *Euskara eta euskarak: aldakortasun sintaktikoa aztergai* [The syntax of Basque varieties: dialectal variation in syntax]. Bilbao: Supplements of ASJU LII, 37–54.

Embick, David, and Ralph Noyer (2001). Movement operations after syntax. *Linguistic Inquiry* 32(4): 555–95.

Emonds, Joseph E. (1976). *A Transformational Approach to English Syntax: Root, Structure-Preserving and Local Transformations*. New York: Academic Press.

Emonds, Joseph E. (2000). *Lexicon and Grammar: The English Syntacticon*. Berlin: Mouton de Gruyter.

Emonds, Joseph E. (2001). The flat structure economy of semi-lexical heads. In N. Corver and H. van Riemsdijk (eds.), *Semi-Lexical Categories: The Function of Content Words and the Content of Function Words*. Berlin: Mouton de Gruyter, 23–66.

Emonds, Joseph E. (2008). Q: the one and only functional head. In R. Kawashima, G. Phillippe, and T. Sowley (eds.), *Phrases Fantômes: Festschrift for Ann Banfield*. Pieterlen: Peter Lang, 193–226.

Emonds, Joseph E. (2009). Universal default right headedness and how stress determines word order. *Lingue e Linguaggio* 8(1): 1–30.

Emonds, Joseph E. (2010). Little words don't lie: X′ have initial X⁰. In M. de Vries and J.-W. Zwart (eds.), *Structure Preserved: Syntactic Squibs for Jan Koster*. Amsterdam: John Benjamins, 109–24.

Epstein, Samuel D., and T. Daniel Seely (2006). *Derivations in Minimalism*. Cambridge: Cambridge University Press.

Epstein, Samuel D., Eric Groat, Ruriko Kawashima, and Hisatsagu Kitahara (1998). *A Derivational Approach to Syntactic Relations*. New York: Oxford University Press.

Erdozia, Kepa (2006). *Euskal Hitz hurrenkerak azterketa psikolinguistiko eta neurolinguistikoen bidez*, [A psycholinguistic and neurolinguistic analysis of Basque word order]. PhD dissertation, University of the Basque Country.

Erdozia, Kepa (2008). Processing canonical and derived word orders in Basque: evidence from native and non-native bilinguals. Paper presented at the I Brainglot Workshop (Barcelona).

Erdozia, Kepa, Itziar Laka, Anna Mestres, and Antoni Rodríguez-Fornells (2007). Word order and ambiguity resolution in Basque: behavioral and electrophysiological evidences. Paper presented at the workshop 'Case, Word Order and Prominence in Argument Structure', Nijmegen, The Netherlands.

Erdozia, Kepa, Itziar Laka, Anna Mestres, and Antoni Rodríguez-Fornells (2009). Syntactic complexity and ambiguity resolution in a free word order language: behavioural and electrophysiological evidences from Basque. *Brain and Language* 109(1): 1–17.

Erdozia, Kepa, Itziar Laka, and Antoni Rodríguez-Fornells (2012). Processing verb medial word orders in a verb final language. In M. Lamers and P. de Swart (eds.), *Case, Word Order and Prominence: Interacting Cues in Language Production and Comprehension*. Dordrecht: Springer, 217–38.

Ernestus, Mirjam, and Anneke Neijt (2008). Word length and the location of primary word stress in Dutch, German, and English. *Linguistics* 46: 507–40.

Ernst, Thomas (1988). Chinese postpositions—again. *Journal of Chinese Linguistics* 16(2): 219–44.

Ernst, Thomas (2002). *The Syntax of Adjuncts*. Cambridge: Cambridge University Press.

Ernst, Thomas (2003). Adjuncts and word order asymmetries. In A. M. di Sciullo (ed.), *Asymmetry in Grammar*. Amsterdam: John Benjamins, 187–208.

Etxepare, Ricardo (2006). Number long-distance agreement in (substandard) Basque. In J. A. Lakarra, and J. I. Hualde (eds.), *Studies in Basque and Historical Linguistics in memory of R. L. Trask: Supplements of the Anuario del Seminario de Filología Vasca 'Julio de Urquijo'* XL 1–2. Donostia: Diputación Foral de Gipuzkoa, 303–50.

Etxepare, Ricardo (2009). Case, person and number in Basque long-distance agreement. Paper presented at the 19th Colloquium on Generative Grammar (Bilbao).

Ezeizabarrena, Maria Jose (2003). Teoría paramétrica en el estudio de la sintaxis del bilingüe. In I. Dova and M. Pérez R. (eds.), *Adquisición, enseñanza y contraste de lenguas, bilingüismo y traducción*. Vigo: Servicio de Publicaciones de la Universidad de Vigo, 81–90.

Fang, Xujun (2006). Particle *ba le* and *er yi. Yuyan Kexue* 5(3): 49–54.

Fanselow, Gisbert (1991). *Minimale Syntax.* Habilitation dissertation, Universitat Passau.

Fernández-Salgueiro, Gerardo (2008). The case-F valuation parameter in Romance. In T. Biberauer (ed.), *The Limits of Syntactic Variation.* Amsterdam: John Benjamins, 295–310.

Fiengo, Robert, and James Higginbotham (1981). Opacity in NP. *Linguistic Analysis* 7: 395–422.

Firbas, Jan (1957). On the problem of non-thematic subjects in contemporary English. *Časopis pro moderní Filologii* 39: 171–3.

Fitch, Tecumseh (2010). *The Evolution of Language.* Cambridge: Cambridge University Press.

Fowlie, Meaghan (2013). Multiple multiple spellout. In Theresa Biberauer and Ian Roberts (eds.), *Challenges to Linearization.* Berlin: Mouton de Gruyter, 129–69.

Fortuny, Jordi (2008). *The Emergence of Structure in Syntax.* Amsterdam: John Benjamins.

Fox, Danny, and David Pesetsky (2005). Cyclic linearization of syntactic structure. *Theoretical Linguistics* 31: 1–45.

Fox, Danny, and Jon Nissenbaum (1999). Extraposition and scope: A case for overt QR*. In S. Bird, A. Carnie, J. Haugen, and P. Norquest (eds.), *Proceedings of the 18th West Coast Conference on Formal Linguistics.* Somerville, MA: Cascadilla Press, 132–44.

Fox, Danny, and Jon Nissenbaum (2006). Extraposition and scope: a case for overt QR. In R. Freidin and H. Lasnik (eds.), *Syntax: Critical Concepts in Linguistics.* London: Routledge, 51–64.

Frascarelli, Mara (2000). *The Syntax-Phonology Interface in Topic and Focus Constructions in Italian.* Dordrecht: Kluwer.

Frascarelli, Mara, and Roland Hinterhölzl (2007). Types of Topics in German and Italian. In S. Winkler and K. Schwabe (eds.), *On Information Structure, Meaning and Form.* Amsterdam/Philadelphia: John Benjamins, 87–116.

Freidin, R., and H. Lasnik (eds.), *Syntax: Critical Concepts in Linguistics,* vol. III. London: Routledge, 51–64.

Fukui, Naoki, and Margaret Speas (1986). Specifiers and projection. *MIT Working Papers in Linguistics* 8: 128–72.

Fukui, Naoki, and Yuji Takano (1998). Symmetry in syntax: Merge and Demerge. *Journal of East Asian Linguistics* 7: 27–86.

Gang, Jin (2010). *Modality in the Mongolian Language: A Descriptive Study Based on Corpus Data.* PhD dissertation, Tokyo University Foreign Studies.

Gärtner, Hans-Martin (1995). Has Bare Phrase Structure theory superseded X-bar Theory? *Forschungsschwerpunkt Allgemeine Sprachwissenschaft Papers in Linguistics* 4: 22–35.

Gasde, Horst-Dieter, and Waltraud Paul (1996). Functional categories, topic prominence, and complex sentences in Mandarin Chinese. *Linguistics* 34: 263–94.

Gervain, Judit, Marina Nespor, Reiko Mazuka, Ryota Horie, and Jacques Mehler (2008). Bootstrapping word order in prelexical infants: a Japanese-Italian cross-linguistic study. *Cognitive Psychology* 57: 56–74.

Gibson, Edward (1998). Linguistic complexity: locality of syntactic dependencies. *Cognition* 68: 1–76.

Giridhar, Puttushetra Puttuswamy (1980). *Angami Grammar.* Mysore: Central Institute of Indian Languages.

Giusti, Giuliana (2002). The functional structure of noun phrases: a Bare Phrase Structure approach. In Guglielmo Cinque (ed.), *Functional Structure in DP and IP*. Oxford: Oxford University Press, 54–90.

Goedemans, Rob, and Harry van der Hulst (2005a). Fixed stress locations. In M. Haspelmath, M. Dryer, D. Gil, and B. Comrie (eds.), *The World Atlas of Language Structures*. Oxford: Oxford University Press, 62–5.

Goedemans, Rob, and Harry van der Hulst (2005b). Weight-sensitive stress. In M. Haspelmath, M. Dryer, D. Gil, and B. Comrie (eds.), *The World Atlas of Language Structures*. Oxford: Oxford University Press, 66–9.

Goedemans, Rob, and Harry van der Hulst (2011a). Fixed stress locations. In M. Dryer and M. Haspelmath (eds.), *The World Atlas of Language Structures Online*. Munich: Max Planck Digital Library, ch. 14. Available online at <http://wals.info/chapter/14>, last accessed on 3 October 2011.

Goedemans, Rob, and Harry van der Hulst (2011b). Weight-sensitive stress. In M. Dryer and M. Haspelmath (eds.), *The World Atlas of Language Structures Online*. Munich: Max Planck Digital Library, ch. 15. Available online at <http://wals.info/chapter/15>, last accessed on 3 October 2011.

Göksel, Aslı (2011). A phono-syntactic template for Turkish: base-generating free word order. In A. Nolda and O. Teuber (eds.), *Syntax and Morphology Multidimensional*. Berlin: Mouton de Gruyter, 45–76.

Göksel, Aslı, and Sumru Özsoy (2000). Is there a focus position in Turkish? In A. Göksel and C. Kerslake (eds.), *Studies on Turkish and Turkic Languages: Proceedings of the 9th International Conference on Turkish Linguistics*. Wiesbaden: Harrassowitz Verlag, 219–28.

Gowda, K. S. Gurubasave (1975). *Ao Grammar*. Manasagangotri: Central Institute of Indian Languages.

Graffi, Giorgio (2001). *200 Years of Syntax: A Critical Survey*. Amsterdam: John Benjamins.

Greenberg, Joseph (1963). Some universals of grammar with particular reference to the order of meaningful elements. In J. Greenberg (ed.), *Universals of Language*. Cambridge MA: MIT Press, 73–113.

Grewendorf, Günther, and Cecilia, Poletto (2010). Hidden verb second: the case of Cimbrian. In M. Putnam (ed.), *German-Language Speech Islands: Generative and Structural Approaches*. Amsterdam/Philadelphia: John Benjamins, 301–46.

Grimshaw, Jane (1991). Extended projection. Unpublished manuscript, Brandeis University.

Groat, Eric (1995). English expletives: a Minimalist approach. *Linguistic Inquiry* 26: 354–65.

Groat, Eric (1999). Raising the Case of expletives. In S. D. Epstein and N. Hornstein (eds.), *Working Minimalism*. Cambridge, MA: MIT Press, 27–43.

Guasti, Maria-Teresa (2000). An excursion into interrogatives in early English and Italian. In M. A. Friedemann and L. Rizzi (eds.), *The Acquisition of Syntax*. London: Longman, 105–28.

Guimarães, Maximiliano (2000). In defense of vacuous projections in Bare Phrase Structure. *University of Maryland Working Papers in Linguistics* 9: 90–115.

Guimarães, Maximiliano (2004). *Derivation and Representation of Syntactic Amalgams*. PhD dissertation, University of Maryland.

Guimarães, Maximiliano (2008). A note on the strong generative capacity of standard Antisymmetry theory. *Snippets* 18: 5–7.

Güldemann, Tom (2004). Linear order as a basic morphosyntactic factor in Non-Khoe Khoisan. Paper given at the Syntax of the World's Languages Conference (Leipzig).

Gundel, Jeanette K. (1989). *The Role of Topic and Comment in Linguistic Theory*. New York: Garland.

Gutiérrez-Morales, Salomé (2008). *Borrowing and Grammaticalization in Sierra Popoluca: The Influence of Nahuatl and Spanish*. PhD dissertation: University of California at Santa Barbara.

Haddican, William (2004). Sentence polarity and word order in Basque. *The Linguistic Review* 21(2): 81–124.

Haddican, William (2008). Euskal perpausaren oinarrizko *espez-buru-osagarri* hurrenkeraren aldeko argudio batzuk [Some evidence for a basic Spec-head-complement order in Basque]. In I. Arteatx, X. Artiagoitia, and A. Elordieta (eds.), *Antisimetriaren hipotesia vs. buru parametroa: euskararen oinarrizko hurrenkera ezbaian* [The Antisymmetry Hypothesis vs. the Head Parameter: the Basic Word Order in Basque]. Bilbao: University of the Basque Country Publications, 69–96.

Haeberli, Eric (2000). Towards deriving the EPP and abstract Case. *Generative Grammar @ Geneva* 1: 105–39.

Haegeman, Liliane (1997). Verb second, the split CP and null subjects in early Dutch. *GenGen* 4(2): 133–75.

Haegeman, Liliane (1998). V-positions and the Middle Field in West Flemish. *Syntax* 1: 259–99.

Haegeman, Liliane (2000). Remnant Movement and OV Order. In P. Svenonius (ed.), *The Derivation of VO and OV*. Amsterdam: John Benjamins, 69–96.

Haegeman, Liliane (2004). Topicalization, CLLD and the left periphery. In B. Shaer, W. Frey, and C. Maienborn (eds.), *Proceedings of the Dislocated Elements Workshop*. ZAS Berlin: ZAS Papers in Linguistics 35(1): 157–92.

Haider, Hubert (1993). *Deutsche Syntax, generative: Vorstudien zur Theorie einer projektiven Grammatik*. Tübingen: Narr.

Haider, Hubert (1997). Precedence among predicates. *Journal of Comparative Germanic Linguistics* 1: 3–41.

Haider, Hubert (2000a). Adverb placement-convergence of structure and licensing. *Theoretical Linguistics* 26: 95–134.

Haider, Hubert (2000b). OV is more basic than VO. In P. Svenonius (ed.), *The Derivation of VO and OV*. Amsterdam: John Benjamins, 45–67.

Haider, Hubert (2004). Pre- and postverbal adverbials in OV and VO. *Lingua* 114: 779–807.

Haig, Geoffrey (2001). Linguistic diffusion in present-day Easter Anatolia: from top to bottom. In A. Y. Aikhenvald and R. M. W. Dixon (eds.), *Areal Diffusion and Genetic Inheritance: Problems in Comparative Linguistics*. Oxford: Oxford University Press, 195–224.

Hale, Ken (2002). On the Dagur object relative: some comparative notes. *Journal of East Asian Linguistics* 11: 109–22.

Hale, Ken, and Samuel J. Keyser (2002). *Prolegomenon to a Theory of Argument Structure*. Cambridge, MA: MIT Press.

Hall, Christopher (1992). *Morphology and Mind*. London: Routledge.

Halle, Morris, and Alec Marantz (1993). Derivational Morphology and the pieces of inflection. In K. Hale and S. J. Keyser (eds.), *The View from Building 20: Essays in Linguistics in Honor of Sylvain Bromberger*. Cambridge, MA: MIT Press, 111–76.

Halle, Morris, and Karuvannur P. Mohanan (1985). Segmental phonology of Modern English. *Linguistic Inquiry* 16: 57–116.

Halmos, Paul R. (1960). *Naive Set Theory*. Princeton: Van Norstrand.

Han, Eunjoo (1994). *Prosodic Structure in Compounds*. PhD dissertation, Stanford University.

Harbour, Daniel (2008). Discontinuous agreement and the syntax–morphology interface. In D. Harbour, D. Adger, and S. Béjar (eds.), *Phi Theory. Phi-Features across Modules and Interfaces*. Oxford: Oxford University Press, 185–220.

Harley, Heidi, and Elizabeth Ritter (2002). Person and Number in pronouns: a feature-geometric analysis. *Language* 78: 482–526.

Harley, Heidi, and Rolf Noyer (1999). Distributed Morphology. *GLOT International* 4: 3–9.

Hasegawa, Yoko (2010). The sentence-final particles *ne* and *yo* in soliloquial Japanese. *Pragmatics* 20(1): 71–89.

Haspelmath, Martin (2008a). Coordination. In T. Shopen (ed.), *Language Typology and Syntactic Description*, vol. 2: *Complex Constructions*. Cambridge: Cambridge University Press, 1–51.

Haspelmath, Martin (2008b). Parametric versus functional explanations of syntactic universals. In T. Biberauer (ed.), *The Limits of Syntactic Variation*. Amsterdam: Benjamins, 75–107.

Haspelmath, Martin, Matthew S. Dryer, David Gil, and Bernard Comrie (eds.) (2005). *The World Atlas of Language Structures*. Oxford: Oxford University Press.

Hawkins, John A. (1979). Implicational universals as predictors of word order change. *Language* 55: 618–48.

Hawkins, John A. (1980). On implicational and distributional universals of word order. *Journal of Linguistics* 16: 193–235.

Hawkins, John A. (1982). Cross-category harmony, X-bar and the predictions of markedness. *Journal of Linguistics* 18: 1–35.

Hawkins, John A. (1983). *Word Order Universals*. New York: Academic Press.

Hawkins, John A. (1985). Complementary methods in Universal Grammar: a reply to Coopmans. *Language* 61: 569–87.

Hawkins, John A. (1990). A parsing theory of word order universals. *Linguistic Inquiry* 21: 223–62.

Hawkins, John A. (1993). Heads, parsing and word-order universals. In G. Corbett, N. M. Fraser, and S. McGlashen (eds.), *Heads in Grammatical Theory*. Cambridge: Cambridge University Press, 231–65.

Hawkins, John A. (1994). *A Performance Theory of Order and Constituency*. Cambridge/New York: Cambridge University Press.

Hawkins, John A. (2001). Why are categories adjacent? *Journal of Linguistics* 37: 1–34.

Hawkins, John A. (2004). *Efficiency and Complexity in Grammar*. Oxford: Oxford University Press.

Hawkins, John A. (2008). An asymmetry between VO and OV languages: the ordering of obliques. In G. Corbett and M. Noonan (eds.), *Case and Grammatical Relations: Essays in Honour of Bernard Comrie*. Amsterdam: John Benjamins, 167–90.

Hawkins, John A. (2009). Language universals and the Performance–Grammar Correspondence Hypothesis. In M. H. Christiansen, C. Collins, and S. Edelman (eds.), *Language Universals*. Oxford: Oxford University Press, 54–78.

Hawkins, John A. (2011). A processing approach to the typology of noun phrases. *Italian Journal of Linguistics (Rivista di Linguistica)* 23(1): 59–78.

Hawkins, John A. (to appear). *Cross-linguistic Variation and Efficiency*. Oxford: Oxford University Press.

Heine, Bernd (1981). Determination in some East African Languages. In G. Brettschneider and C. Lehmann (eds.), *Wege zur Universalienforschung: sprachwissenschaftliche Beiträge zum 60. Geburtstag von Hansjakob Seiler*. Tübingen: Gunter Narr, 180–6.

Heine, Bernd (1993). *Auxiliaries: Cognitive Forces and Grammaticalization*. Oxford: Oxford University Press.

Hellenthal, Anne-Christie (2007). Modality properties of sentence type markers in Sheko. *Leiden Working Papers in Linguistics* 4(2): 17–32.

Heller, Katrin (1979). Alcuni problemi linguistici del dialetto dei mocheni sulla base di testi dialettali. In G. B. Pellegrini (ed.), *La valle del Fersina e le isole linguistiche tedesche del Trentino: Atti del convegno di S. Orsola, 1–3 settembre 1978*. San Michele all'Adige: Museo degli Usi e Costumi della Gente Trentina, 113–20.

Helmantel, Marjon (2002). *Interactions in the Dutch Adpositional Domain*. PhD dissertation, University of Leiden.

Hendrick, Randall (2000). Celtic initials. In A. Carnie and E. Guilfoyle (eds.), *The Syntax of Verb Initial Languages*. New York: Oxford University Press, 13–37.

Hetzron, Robert (1978). On the relative order of adjectives. In H. Seiler (ed.), *Language Universals*. Tübingen: Narr, 165–84.

Higginbotham, James (1985). On Semantics. *Linguistic Inquiry* 16: 547–631.

Hinterhölzl, Roland (2000). Licensing movement and stranding in the West Germanic OV languages. In P. Svenonius (ed.), *The Derivation of VO and OV*. Amsterdam: John Benjamins, 293–314.

Hinterhölzl, Roland (2001). Event-related adjuncts and the OV/VO distinction. In K. Megerdoomian and Leora Bar-el (eds.), *WCCFL 20 Proceedings*. Somerville, MA: Cascadilla Press, 276–89.

Hinterhölzl, Roland (2002). Parametric variation and scrambling in English. In W. Abraham and J. W. Zwart (eds.), *Studies in Comparative Germanic Syntax*. Amsterdam: John Benjamins, 131–51.

Hinterhölzl, Roland (2004a). Scrambling, optionality and non-lexical triggers. In A. Breitbarth and H. van Riemsdijk (eds.), *Triggers*. Berlin: Mouton de Gruyter, 173–205.

Hinterhölzl, Roland (2004b). Language change versus grammar change: what diachronic data reveal about the distinction between core grammar and periphery. In E. Fuss and C. Trips (eds.), *Diachronic Clues to Synchronic Grammar*. Amsterdam: John Benjamins, 131–60.

Hinterhölzl, Roland (2006). *Scrambling, Remnant Movement and Restructuring in West Germanic*. New York: Oxford University Press.

Hinterhölzl, Roland (2009a). A phase-based comparative approach to modification and word order in Germanic. *Syntax* 12(3) 242–84.

Hinterhölzl, Roland (2009b). Information structure and unmarked word order in (Older) Germanic. In C. Fery, and M. Zimmermann (eds.), *Information Structure from Different Perspectives*. Oxford: Oxford University Press, 282–304.

Hinterhölzl, Roland (2009c). The role of information structure in word order variation and word order change. In R. Hinterhölzl and S. Petrova (eds.), *Information Structure and Language Change: New Approaches to Word Order Variation in Germanic*. Berlin: Mouton de Gruyter, 45–66.

Hinterhölzl, Roland (2011). How prosody restricts the syntax. In M. Frascarelli (ed.), *Structures and Meanings: Cross-Theoretical Perspectives*. Paris: L'Harmattan, 81–100.

Hoeksema, Jack (1985). *Categorial Morphology*. New York: Garland Press.

Hoeksema, Jack (1992). The Head Parameter in morphology and Syntax. In Dicky Gilbers and Sietze Looyenga (eds.), *Language and Cognition* 2 Groningen: University of Groningen, 119–32.

Holmberg, Anders (1986). *Word Order and Syntactic Features in the Scandinavian Languages and English*. PhD dissertation, University of Stockholm.

Holmberg, Anders (1999). Remarks on Holmberg's Generalization. *Studia Lingustica* 63: 1–39.

Holmberg, Anders (2000). Deriving OV order in Finnish. In P. Svenonius (ed.), *The Derivation of VO and OV*. Amsterdam: John Benjamins, 123–52.

Holmberg, Anders (2001). The syntax of yes and no in Finnish. *Studia Linguistica* 55: 140–74.

Holmberg, Anders (2003). Yes/no questions and the relation between tense and polarity in English and Finnish. *Linguistic Variation Yearbook* 3: 45–70.

Holmberg, Anders, and Christer Platzack (1995). *The Role of Inflection in Scandinavian Syntax*. New York: Oxford University Press.

Holmer, Arthur (1996). *A Parametric Grammar of Seediq*. Lund: Lund University Press.

Holmer, Arthur (2005). Antisymmetry and final particles in a Formosan VOS languages. In A. Carnie, H. Harley, and S. A. Dooley (eds.), *Verb First: On the Syntax of Verb-Initial Languages*. Amsterdam: John Benjamins, 175–201.

Holmer, Arthur (2006). Seediq-adverbial heads in a Formosan language. In H.-M. Gärtner, P. Law, and J. Sabel (eds.), *Clause Structure and Adjuncts in Austronesian Languages*. Berlin: Mouton de Gruyter, 83–123.

Holton, Gary (2003). *Tobelo*. Munich: Lincom Europa.

Hornstein, Norbert (1999). Movement and Control. *Linguistic Inquiry* 30: 69–96.

Hornstein, Norbert, and Juan Uriagereka (2002). Reprojections. In S. D. Epstein and T. D. Seely (eds.), *Derivation and Explanation in the Minimalist Program*. Malden, MA: Blackwell, 106–32.

Hróarsdóttir, Thorbjorg (2000a). *Word Order Change in Icelandic: From OV to VO*. Amsterdam: John Benjamins.

Hróarsdóttir, Thorbjorg (2000b). Parameter Change in Icelandic. In P. Svenonius (ed.), *The Derivation of VO and OV*. Amsterdam: John Benjamins, 153–79.

Hsiao, Stella I-Ling (2004). *Adverbials in Squliq Atayal*. MA thesis, National Tsing Hua University.

Hsieh, Feng-fan, and Rint Sybesma (2007). On the linearization of Chinese sentence-particles: Max Spell Out and why CP moves. Unpublished manuscript, MIT and Leiden University.

Hsieh, Feng-fan, and Rint Sybesma (2008). Generative syntax and sentence-final particles in Chinese. In Y. Shen and S. Feng (eds.), *Contemporary Linguistic Theories and Related Studies in Chinese*. Beijing: Commercial Press, 364–74.

Huang, C. T. James (1982). *Logical Relations in Chinese and the Theory of Grammar*. PhD dissertation, MIT. Published in 1998 by Garland.

Huang, C. T. James (1994). More on Chinese word order and parametric theory. In B. Lust, M. Suñer, J. Whitman, G. Hermon, J. Kornfilt, and S. Flynn (eds.), *Syntactic Theory and First Language Acquisition: Cross-Linguistic Perspectives*. Hillsdale, NJ: Lawrence Erlbaum Associates, 15–35.

Huang, C. T. James, Y. H. Audrey Li, and Yafei Li (2009). *The Syntax of Chinese*. Cambridge: Cambridge University Press.

Huddleston, Rodney (2002). Content clauses and reported speech. In R. Huddleston, and G. Pullum (eds.), *The Cambridge Grammar of the English Language*. Cambridge: Cambridge University Press.

Huddleston, Rodney, and Geoffrey Pullum (2006). Co-ordination and sub-ordination. In B. Aarts, and A. McMahon (eds.), *The Handbook of English Linguistics*. Oxford: Blackwell, 198–219.

Hulst, Harry, van der, Rob Goedemans, and Ellen van Zanten (eds.), (2010). *A Survey of Word Accentual Patterns in the Languages of the World*. Berlin: Mouton de Gruyter.

Hyman, Larry M. (2008). Directional asymmetry in the morphology and phonology of words, with special reference to Bantu. *Linguistics* 46, 309–50.

Irurtzun, Artiz, and Ángel Gallego (to appear). Consequences of pair-Merge (at the Interfaces). *Proceedings of Bilbao-Deusto Conference in Linguistics BIDE05*. Available online at <http://www.ehu.es/ojs/index.php/ASJU/article/viewFile/3896/3510>, last accessed 6 January 2013.

Ishihara, Shinchiro (2001). Stress, focus, and scrambling in Japanese. *A Few from Building E39. MIT Working Papers in Linguistics* 39: 151–85.

Itoh, Yoshiaki, and Sumie Ueda. (2004). The Ising model for changes in word ordering rules in natural languages. *Physica D* 198: 333–9.

Ivana, Adrian, and Hiromu Sakai (2007). Honorification and light verbs in Japanese. *Journal of East Asian Linguistics* 16: 171–91.

Jackendoff, Ray (1977). *X-bar Syntax: A Study of Phrase Structure*. Cambridge, MA: MIT Press.

Jayaseelan, Karattuparambil (1991). The pronominal system of Malayalam. *CIEFL Occasional Papers in Linguistics* 3: 68–107.

Jayaseelan, Karattuparambil (2001). IP-internal Topic and Focus Phrases. *Studia Linguistica* 55(1): 39–75.

Jayaseelan, Karattuparambil (2010a). On two types of movement. Paper presented at GLOW in Asia 2010 (Beijing).

Jayaseelan, Karattuparambil (2010b). Stacking, stranding and pied-piping: a proposal about word order. *Syntax* 13: 298–330.

Jellinek, Max (1913–14). *Geschichte der neuhochdeutschen Grammatik von den Anfängen bis auf Adelung*. Heidelberg: Carl Winter.

Johnson, Kent (2007). The legacy of methodological dualism. *Mind and Language* 22: 366–401.

Johnson, Kyle (1991). Object positions. *Natural Language and Linguistic Theory* 9(4): 577–636.

Johnson, Kyle (2002). Towards an etiology of adjunct islands. Unpublished manuscript, University of Massachussetts. Available online at <http://people.umass.edu/kbj/homepage/Content/Etiology.pdf>, last accessed 17 February 2013.

Jónsson, Johannes G. (1996). *Clausal Architecture and Case in Icelandic.* PhD dissertation, University of Massachusetts, Amherst.

Joseph, John (2012). *Saussure.* Oxford: Oxford University Press.

Julien, Marit (2002). *Syntactic Heads and Word Formation.* Oxford: Oxford University Press.

Julien, Marit (2003). Word order type and syntactic structure. In J. Rooryck and P. Pica (eds.), *Linguistic Variation Yearbook 1.* Amsterdam: John Benjamins, 19–61.

Källgren, Gunnel, and Ellen F. Prince (1989). Swedish VP-topicalization and Yiddish verb-topicalization. *Nordic Journal of Linguistics* 12: 47–58.

Kandybowicz, Jason, and Mark C. Baker (2003). On directionality and the structure of the verb phrase: evidence from Nupe. *Syntax* 6: 115–55.

Kanerva, Jonni (1989). *Focus and Phrasing in Chichewa Phonology.* PhD dissertation, Stanford University.

Kaplan, Tami (1991). A classification of VSO languages. In G. F. Westphal, B. Ao, and H. R. Chae (eds.), *Proceedings of ESCOL '91.* Ohio: Ohio State University, 198–209.

Karimi, Simin (2005). *A Minimalist Approach to Scrambling: Evidence from Persian.* Berlin: Mouton de Gruyter.

Kastenholz, Raimund (2003). Auxiliaries, grammaticalization and word order in Mande. *Journal of African Languages and Linguistics* 24: 31–53.

Kato, Takaomi (2007). On the nature of the Left Branch Condition: syntactic or phonological? Paper presented at the 9th Seoul International Conference on Generative Grammar.

Kayne, Richard (1975). *French Syntax: The Transformational Cycle.* Cambridge, MA: MIT Press.

Kayne, Richard (1981a). Unambiguous Paths. In R. May and J. Koster (eds.), *Levels of Syntactic Representation.* Dordrecht: Foris, 143–83. Reprinted in Kayne (1984).

Kayne, Richard (1981b). Binding, quantifiers, clitics and control. In F. Heny (ed.), *Binding and Filtering.* London: Croom Helm, 191–211. Reprinted in Kayne (1984).

Kayne, Richard (1984). *Connectedness and Binary Branching.* Dordrecht: Foris.

Kayne, Richard (1985). L'accord du participe passé en français et en italien. *Modèles Linguistiques* VII: 73–90. English translation in Kayne (2000a: ch. 2).

Kayne, Richard (1989). Facets of Romance past participle agreement. In P. Benincà (ed.), *Dialect Variation and the Theory of Grammar.* Dordrecht: Foris, 85–103. Reprinted in Kayne (2000a).

Kayne, Richard (1994). *The Antisymmetry of Syntax.* Cambridge, MA: MIT Press.

Kayne, Richard (1998). Overt vs. covert movement. *Syntax* 1: 128–91.

Kayne, Richard (2000a). *Parameters and Universals.* New York: Oxford University Press.

Kayne, Richard (2000b). A note on prepositions, complementizers and word order universals. In R. Kayne, *Parameters and Universals.* New York: Oxford University Press, 314–26.

Kayne, Richard (2002). Pronouns and their antecedents. In S. Epstein and D. Seely (eds.), *Derivation and Explanation in the Minimalist Program.* Malden, MA: Blackwell, 133–66. Reprinted in Kayne (2005a).

Kayne, Richard (2003a). Antisymmetry and Japanese. *English Linguistics* 20: 1–40. Reprinted in Kayne (2005a).

Kayne, Richard (2003b). Some remarks on agreement and on heavy-NP-shift. In M. Ukaji, M. Ike-Uchi, and Y. Nishimara (eds.), *Current Issues in English Linguistics.* Tokyo: Kaita-kusha, 67–86. Reprinted in Kayne (2005a).

Kayne, Richard (2003c). Silent years, silent hours. In L.-O. Delsing, C. Falk, G. Josefsson, and H. Sigurðsson (eds.), *Grammar in Focus: Festschrift for Christer Platzack*, vol. 2. Lund: Wallin and Dalholm. Reprinted in Kayne (2005a).

Kayne, Richard (2004). Prepositons as Probes. In A. Belletti (ed.), *Structures and Beyond*. New York: Oxford University Press, 192–212. Reprinted in Kayne (2005a).

Kayne, Richard (2005a). *Movement and Silence*. New York: Oxford University Press.

Kayne, Richard (2005b). Antisymmetry and Japanese. In R. Kayne. *Movement and Silence*. New York: Oxford University Press, 215–40.

Kayne, Richard (2005c). Prepositions as Probes. In R. Kayne, *Movement and Silence*. New York: Oxford University Press, 85–104.

Kayne, Richard (2005d). Some notes on comparative syntax, with special reference to English and French. In G. Cinque and R. Kayne (eds.), *The Oxford Handbook of Comparative Syntax*. New York: Oxford University Press, 3–69.

Kayne, Richard (2007). On the syntax of quantity in English. In J. Bayer, T. Bhattacharya, and M. T. Hany Babu (eds.), *Linguistic Theory and South Asian Languages: Essays in Honour of K. A. Jayaseelan*. Amsterdam: John Benjamins, 73–105. Reprinted in Kayne (2005a).

Kayne, Richard (2008). Expletives, datives, and the tension between morphology and syntax. In T. Biberauer (ed.), *The Limits of Syntactic Variation*. Amsterdam: John Benjamins, 175–217. Reprinted in Kayne (2010).

Kayne, Richard (2009a). A note on auxiliary alternations and silent causation. In L. Baronian and F. Martineau (eds.), *Le français d'un continent à l'autre: mélanges offerts à Yves Charles Morin*. Québec: Presses de l'Université Laval 211–35. Reprinted in Kayne (2010).

Kayne, Richard (2009b). Antisymmetry and the lexicon. In J. van Craenenbroeck and J. Rooryck (eds.), *Linguistic Variation Yearbook*. Amsterdam: John Benjamins, 1–31.

Kayne, Richard (2010a). *Comparisons and Contrasts*. New York: Oxford University Press.

Kayne, Richard (2010b). Why isn't *this* a complementizer? In Kayne (2010a, 190–227).

Kayne, Richard (to appear). Why isn't *this* a complementizer? In P. Svenonius (ed.), *Functional Structure from Top to Toe: A Festschrift for Tarald Taraldsen*. New York: Oxford University Press.

Kayne, Richard, and Jean-Yves Pollock (2012). Toward an analysis of French hyper-complex inversion. In L. Brugè, A. Cardinaletti, G. Giusti, N. Munaro, and C. Poletto (eds.), *Functional Heads*. New York: Oxford University Press, 150–167. Also in Kayne (2010a, 228–44).

Keenan, Edward (1978a). The syntax of subject-final languages. In W. P. Lehmann (ed.), *Syntactic Typology: Studies in the Phenomenology of Language*. Austin: University of Texas Press, 267–327.

Keenan, Edward (1978b). On surface form and logical form. In B.B. Kachru (ed.), *Linguistics in the Seventies: Directions and Prospects. Studies in the Linguistic Sciences* 8(2): 163–204.

Keenan, Edward (1985). Relative clauses. In T. Shopen (ed.), *Language Typology and Syntactic Description*, vol. II: *Complex Constructions*. Cambridge: Cambridge University Press, 141–70.

Keenan, Edward, and Bernard Comrie (1977). Noun Phrase accessibility and Universal Grammar. *Linguistic Inquiry* 8: 63–99.

Kelepir, Meltem (2001). *Topics in Turkish Syntax: Clausal Structure and Scope*. PhD dissertation, MIT.

Kemenade, Ans van, and Bettelou Los (2006). Discourse adverbs and clausal syntax in Old and Middle English. In A. van Kemenade and B. Los (eds.), *The Handbook of the History of English*. Oxford: Blackwell, 224–48.

Khan, Geoffrey (1999). *A Grammar of Neo-Aramaic: The Dialect of the Jews of Arbel*. Leiden: Brill.

Kimball, John (1973). Seven principles of surface structure parsing in natural language. *Cognition* 2: 15–47.

Kinyalolo, Kasangati (1991). *Syntactic Dependencies and the Spec-Head Agreement Hypothesis in KiLega*. PhD dissertation, UCLA.

Kiparsky, Paul (1973). Elsewhere in phonology. In S. Anderson and P. Kiparsky (eds.), *A Festschrift for Morris Halle*. New York: Holt, Rinehart, and Winston, 96–106.

Kiparsky, Paul (2008). Universals constrain change: change results in typological generalizations. In J. Good (ed.), *Language Universals and Language Change*. Oxford: Oxford University Press, 23–53.

Kiss, Katalin É. (1987). *Configurationality in Hungarian*. Dordrecht: Kluwer.

Kiss, Katalin É. (2008). Free word order, (non)configurationality, and phases. *Linguistic Inquiry* 39: 441–75.

Ko, Heejong (2005). *Syntactic Edges and Linearization*. PhD dissertation, MIT.

Koeneman, Olaf (2000). *The Flexible Nature of Verb Movement*. PhD dissertation, Utrecht.

Koizumi, Masatoshi (1994). Secondary predicates. *Journal of East Asian Linguistics* 3: 25–79.

Koizumi, Masatoshi (1995). *Phrase Structure in Minimalist Syntax*. PhD dissertation, MIT.

Koopman, Hilda (1984). *The Syntax of Verbs: From Verb Movement Rules in the Kru Languages to Universal Grammar*. Dordrecht: Foris.

Koopman, Hilda (2000). Prepositions, postpositions, circumpositions, and particles: the structure of Dutch PPs. In H. Koopman, *The Syntax of Specifiers and Heads: Collected Essays of Hilda J. Koopman*. London: Routledge, 204–60. Reprinted in G. Cinque and L. Rizzi (eds.) (2010), *Mapping Spatial PPs: The Cartography of Syntactic Structures*. New York: Oxford University Press, 26–73.

Koopman, Hilda (2003). The locality of agreement and the structure of the DP in Maasai. In W. E. Griffin (ed.), *The Role of Agreement in Natural Language: TLS 5 Proceedings*. Austin: Texas Linguistic Forum, 206–27.

Koopman, Hilda (2005a). On the parallelism of DPs and clauses: Evidence from Kisongo Maasai. In A. Carnie, H. Harley, and S. Dooley (eds.), *Verb First: On the Syntax of Verb-initial Languages*. Amsterdam: John Benjamins, 281–302.

Koopman, Hilda (2005b). Korean (and Japanese) morphology from a syntactic perspective. *Linguistic Inquiry* 36: 601–33.

Koopman, Hilda (2010). Prepositions, postpositions, circumpositions, and particles. In G. Cinque and L. Rizzi (eds.), *Mapping Spatial PPs: The Cartography of Syntactic Structures*, vol. 6. New York: Oxford University Press, 26–73.

Koopman, Hilda, and Anna Szabolcsi (2000). *Verbal Complexes*. Cambridge, MA: MIT Press.

Koopman, Hilda, and Dominique Sportiche (1991). The position of subjects. *Lingua* 85: 211–58.

Kornfilt, Jaklin (2000). Locating relative agreement in Turkish and Turkic. In A. Göksel and C. Kerslake (eds.), *Studies on Turkish and Turkic Languages*. Wiesbaden: Harrassowitz Verlag, 189–96.

Kornfilt, Jaklin (2005). Asymmetries between pre-verbal and post-verbal scrambling in Turkish. In J. Sabel and M. Saito (eds.), *The Free Word Order Phenomenon*. Berlin: Mouton de Gruyter, 163–79.

Kornfilt, Jaklin (2007). Agr in Turkish as an expression of categorial features. In M. Kelepir and B. Öztürk (eds.), *Proceedings of the 4th Workshop on Altaic Formal Linguistics*. MIT Working Papers in Linguistics 54. Cambridge, MA: MITWPL, 21–46.

Koster, Jan (1975). Dutch as an SOV language. *Linguistic Analysis* 1: 111–36.

Kracht, Marcus (2003). *The Mathematics of Language*. Berlin: Mouton de Gruyter.

Krapova, Iliyana, and Guglielmo Cinque. 2008. On the order of *wh*-phrases in Bulgarian multiple *wh*-fronting. In G. Zybatow, L. Szucsich, U. Junghanns, and R. Meyer (eds.), *Formal Description of Slavic Languages: The Fifth Conference, Leipzig 2003*. Frankfurt: Peter Lang, 318–36.

Kratzer, Angelika (1995). Stage-level and individual-level predicates. In G. Carlson and J. Pelletier (eds.), *The Generic Book*. Chicago: Chicago University Press, 125–75.

Kratzer, Angelika (1996). Severing the external argument from its verb. In J. Rooryck and L. Zaring (eds.), *Phrase Structure and the Lexicon*. Dordrecht: Kluwer, 109–38.

Kratzer, Angelika (1998). More structural analogies between pronouns and tenses. In D. Strolovitch and A. Lawson (eds.), *Proceedings of SALT VIII*. Cornell University: eLanguage, 92–110.

Kremers, Joost (2009). Recursive linearization. *The Linguistic Review* 26: 135–66.

Kroch, Anthony (1989). Reflexes of grammar in patterns of language change. *Language Variation and Change* 1: 199–244.

Kroch, Anthony (2001). Syntactic change. In M. Baltin and C. Collins (eds.), *The Handbook of Contemporary Syntactic Theory*. Oxford: Blackwell, 699–729.

Krott, Andrea, Gary Libben, Gonia Jarema, Wolfgang Dressler, Robert Schreuder, and Harald Baaven (2004). Probability in the grammar of German and Dutch: interfixation in triconstituent compounds. *Language and Speech* 47: 83–106.

Kuiper, Albertha, and Joy Oram (1991). A syntactic sketch of Diuxi-Tilantongo Mixtec. In C. H. Bradley and B. Hollenbach (eds.), *Studies in the Syntax of Mixtecan Languages*, vol. 3. Arlington: SIL and University of Texas, 179–408.

Kuno, Susumo (1978). Japanese: a characteristic OV language. In W. Lehmann (ed.), *Syntactic Typology*. Austin: University of Texas Press, 57–138.

Kural, Murat (1997). Postverbal constituents in Turkish and the Linear Correspondence Axiom. *Linguistic Inquiry* 28: 498–519.

Kural, Murat (2005). Tree traversal and word order. *Linguistic Inquiry* 36: 367–88.

Kuwana, Yasutomo, and Hisao Tokizaki (2009). The co-variation of head–complement order and the position of word stress. Paper presented at the 8th International Conference of the Association for Linguistic Typology (University of California, Berkeley).

Ladd, D. Robert (1986). Intonational phrasing: the case for recursive prosodic structure. *Phonology* 3: 311–40.

Laenzlinger, Christopher (2005). French adjective ordering: perspectives on DP-internal movement types. *Lingua* 115: 649–89.

Lahiri, Aditi, and Frans Plank (2009). What linguistic universals can be true of. In S. Scalise, E. Magni, and A. Bisetto (eds.), *Universals of Language Today*. Dordrecht: Springer, 31–58.

Laka, Itziar (1990). *Negation in Syntax: On the Nature of Functional Categories and Projections.* PhD dissertation, MIT.

Laka, Itziar (1993a). The structure of inflection: a case study in X^0 syntax. In J. I. Hualde and J. Ortiz de Urbina (eds.), *Generative Studies in Basque Linguistics.* Amsterdam: John Benjamins, 21–70.

Laka, Itziar (1993b). Unergatives that assign ergative, unaccusatives that assign accusative. In J. Bobaljik and C. Phillips (eds.), *Papers on Case and Agreement I.* MIT Working Papers in Linguistics 18. Cambridge, MA: MITWPL, 149–72.

Laka, Itziar (1994). *On the Syntax of Negation.* New York: Garland Press.

Laka, Itziar (2008). Simetria ala Simetria eza? Hitzordenaz hausnarrean [Symmetry or Asymmetry? Some reflections on word order]. In I. Arteatx, X. Artiagoitia, and A. Elordieta (eds.), *Antisimetriaren hipotesia vs. buru parametroa: euskararen oinarrizko hurrenkera ezbaian* [The Antisymmetry Hypothesis vs. the Head Parameter: the Basic Word Order in Basque]. Bilbao: University of the Basque Country Publications, 199–219.

Lakoff, George, and Mark Johnson (1980). *Metaphors We Live By.* Chicago: University of Chicago Press.

Lancioni, Giuliano (1995). Intrinsic VSO languages: the generalized expletive hypothesis. *Proceedings of ConSOLE III* Leiden: Leiden University Centre for Linguistics, 189–210.

Landau, Idan (2003). Movement out of control. *Linguistic Inquiry* 34: 471–98.

Landau, Idan (2006). Chain resolution in Hebrew V(P) fronting. *Syntax* 9: 32–66.

Landau, Idan (2007). EPP extensions. *Linguistic Inquiry* 38: 485–523.

Langendoen, Terence D. (2003). Merge. In A. Carnie, H. Harley, and M. Willie (eds.), *Formal Approaches to Function in Grammar: In Honor of Eloise Jelinek.* Amsterdam: John Benjamins, 307–18.

LaPolla, Randy J. (2002). Problems of methodology and explanation in word order universals research. In P. Wuyun, (ed.), *Dongfang Yuyan yu Wenhua (Languages and Cultures of the East).* Shanghai: Dongfang Chuban Zhongxin, 204–37.

Larson, Richard (1985). Bare-NP adverbs. *Linguistic Inquiry* 16: 595–621.

Larson, Richard (1988). On the Double Object Construction. *Linguistic Inquiry* 19: 335–91.

Larson, Richard (1990). Double objects revisited: reply to Jackendoff. *Linguistic Inquiry* 21: 589–632.

Lasnik, Howard (1976). Remarks on coreference. *Linguistic Analysis* 2: 1–22.

Lasnik, Howard (2001). Subjects, objects and the EPP. In W. Davies and S. Dubinsky (eds.), *Objects and Other Subjects.* Dordrecht: Kluwer, 103–21.

Law, Ann (2002). Cantonese sentence-final particles and the CP domain. *UCL Working Papers in Linguistics* 14: 375–98.

Law, Ann (2003). Right dislocation in Cantonese as a focus-marking device. *UCL Working Papers in Linguistics* 15: 243–75.

Law, Sam-Po (1990). *The Syntax and Phonology of Cantonese Sentence-final Particles.* PhD dissertation, Boston University.

Lechner, Winfried (2005). Interpretive effects of head movement. Unpublished manuscript, University of Tübingen.

Lechner, Winfried (2006). An interpretive effect of head movement. In M. Farascarelli (ed.), *Phases of Interpretation.* Berlin: Mouton de Gruyter, 45–70.

Lee, Felicia Ann (2000a). VP remnant movement and VSO in Quiaviní Zapotec. In A. Carnie and E. Guilfoyle (eds.), *The Syntax of Verb Initial Languages*. New York: Oxford University Press, 143–62.

Lee, Felicia Ann (2000b). *Antisymmetry and the Syntax of San Lucas Quiavini Zapotec*. PhD dissertation, UCLA.

Lee, Thomas Hun-Tak (1986). *Studies on Quantification in Chinese*. PhD dissertation, UCLA.

Lee, Thomas Hun-Tak, and Ann Law (2001). Epistemic modality and the acquisition of Cantonese final particles. In M. Nakayama (ed.), *Issues in East Asian Language Acquisition*. Tokyo: Kuroshio Publishers, 67–128.

Legate, Julie A. (2001). The configurational structure of a nonconfigurational language. In P. Pica (ed.), *Linguistic Variation Yearbook 3*. Amsterdam: John Benajmins, 61–104.

Legate, Julie A. (2003). Reconstructing nonconfigurationality. In A. M. Di Sciullo (ed.), *Asymmetry in Grammar*. Philadelphia: John Benjamins, 99–116.

Lehmann, Christian (1984). *Der Relativsatz*. Tübingen: Narr.

Lehmann, Winfred P. (1973). A structural principle of language and its implications. *Language* 49: 47–66.

Lehmann, Winfred P. (1978a). The great underlying ground-plans. In W. P. Lehmann (ed.), *Syntactic Typology: Studies in the Phenomenology of Language*. Austin: University of Texas Press, 3–55.

Lehmann, Winfred P. (1978b). Conclusion: toward an understanding of the profound unity underlying languages. In W. P. Lehmann (ed.), *Syntactic Typology: Studies in the Phenomenology of Language*. Austin: University of Texas Press, 395–432.

Li, Boya (2006). *Chinese Final Particles and the Syntax of the Periphery*. PhD dissertation, Leiden.

Li, Chao-Lin (2007). Adverbial verbs and argument attraction in Puyuma. *Nanzan Linguistics*, Special Issue 3, vol. 1, 165–201.

Li, Charles N., and Sandra A. Thompson (1974). An explanation of word order change SVO→SOV. *Foundations of Language* 12: 201–14.

Li, Charles, N., and Sandra A. Thompson (1981). *Mandarin Chinese: A Functional Reference Grammar*. California: University of California Press.

Li, Yen-hui Audrey (1990). *Order and Constituency in Mandarin Chinese*. Dordrecht: Kluwer.

Li, Yen-hui Audrey (2007). De: adjunction and conjunction. Paper presented at the Joint Conference of IACL-15/NACCL-19 (Columbia University, New York).

Liang, Yuan (2002). *Dislocation in Cantonese: Sentence Form, Information Structure, and Discourse Function*. PhD dissertation, University of Hong Kong.

Lieber, Rochelle (1980). *On the Organization of the Lexicon*. PhD dissertation, MIT.

Lieber, Rochelle (1992). *Deconstructing Morphology*. Chicago: University of Chicago Press.

Lightfoot, David (1979). *Principles of Diachronic Syntax*. Cambridge: Cambridge University Press.

Lin, Hsiu-hsu (2005). The grammaticalization of Tense/Aspect auxiliaries in Seediq. *Concentric: Studies in Linguistics* 31: 111–32.

Lin, T. H. Jonah (2006). *Complement-to-Specifier Movement in Mandarin Chinese*. Unpublished manuscript, National Tsing Hua University.

Lin, T. H. Jonah (2012). Multiple-modal constructions in Mandarin Chinese and their finiteness properties. *Journal of Linguistics* 48(1): 151–86.

Lin, Jo-Wang (2009). Chinese comparatives and their implicational parameters. *Journal of Natural Language Semantics* 17: 1–27.

Lin, Jo-Wang (2010). A tenseless analysis of Mandarin Chinese revisited: a reply to Sybesma 2007. *Linguistic Inquiry* 41(2): 305–29.

Liu, En-Hsing (2003). *Conjunction and Modification in Amis*. MA dissertation, National Tsing Hua University.

Liu, Feng-Hsi (1998). A clitic analysis of locative particles. *Journal of Chinese Linguistics* 26(1): 48–70.

Lojenga, Constance K. (1994). *Ngiti: A Central-Sudanic Language of Zaire*. Köln: Rüdiger Köppe Verlag.

López, Luis (2009). *A Derivational Syntax for Information Structure*. New York: Oxford University Press.

Lounsbury, Floyd G. (1949). *Iroquoian Morphology*. PhD dissertation, Yale University.

Lounsbury, Floyd G. (1953). *Oneida Verb Morphology*. New Haven, CT: Yale University.

Lü, Shuxiang (ed.) (2000). *Xiàndài hànyǔ bābǎ icí* [Eight hundred words of Modern Chinese]. Beijing: Shangwu.

Luhtala, Anneli (1994). Early medieval grammar. *The Encyclopedia of Language and Lingusitics I*. Oxford: Pergamon Press, 1461–8.

Luke, Kang Kwong (1990). *Utterance-Final Particles in Cantonese*. Amsterdam: John Benjamins.

Lyons, Christopher (1999). *Definiteness*. Cambridge: Cambridge University Press.

Macaulay, Monica (2005). The syntax of Chalcatongo Mixtec: preverbal and postverbal. In A. Carnie, H. Harley, and S. Dooley (eds.), *Verb First: On the Syntax of Verb-Initial Languages*. Amsterdam: John Benjamins, 341–66.

Magni, Elisabetta (2000). L'ordine delle parole nel latino pompeiano: sulle tracce di una deriva. *Archivio Glottologico Italiano* 85: 3–37.

Mahajan, Anoop (1989). Agreement and agreement phrases. *MIT Working Papers in Linguistics* 10: 217–52.

Mahajan, Anoop (1990). *The A/A-bar Movement Distinction and Movement Theory*. PhD dissertation, MIT.

Mahajan, Anoop (1992). Specificity Condition and the CED. *Linguistic Inquiry* 23: 510–16.

Mahajan, Anoop (2003). Word order and (remnant) VP movement. In S. Karimi (ed.), *Word Order and Scrambling*. Cambridge, MA: Wiley-Blackwell, 217–37.

Mahlau, Axel (1994). Orden de palabras y estructura oracional en los niños bilingües. In J. Meisel (ed.), *La adquisición del vasco y del castellano en niños bilingües* [Basque and Spanish acquisition in bilingual children]. Frankfurt: Vervuert, 69–112.

Maling, Joan (1980). Inversion in embedded clauses in modern Icelandic. *Íslenskt Mál og Almenn Málfæði* 2: 175–93.

Mallinson, Graham, and Barry Blake (1981). *Language Typology: Cross-Linguistic Studies in Syntax*. Amsterdam: North Holland.

Marantz, Alec (1997). No escape from syntax: don't try morphological analysis in the privacy of your own lexicon. In A. Dimitriadis, L. Siegel, C. Surek-Clark, and A. Williams (eds.), *Proceedings of the 21st Annual Penn Linguistics Colloquium: Penn Working Papers in Linguistics* 4(2): 201–25.

Marcus, Gary, Ursula Brinkmann, Harald Clahsen, Richard Wiese, and Steven Pinker (1995). German inflection: the exception that proves the rule. *Cognitive Psychology* 29: 189–256.

Marlow, Patrick E. (1997). *Origin and Development of the Indo-Aryan Quotatives and Complementizers: An Areal Approach*. PhD dissertation, University of Illinois.

Martin, Roger (1999). Case, the Extended Projection Principle and Minimalism. In S. D. Epstein and N. Hornstein (eds.), *Working Minimalism*. Cambridge, MA: MIT Press, 1–25.

Martins, Ana Maria (2006). Emphatic verb reduplication in European Portuguese. In S. Barbiers, O. Koeneman, M. Lekakou, and M. van der Ham (eds.), *Papers from the Workshop on Doubling in the Dialects of Europe*. Amsterdam: Meertens Online Publications. Available online at <http://www.meertens.knaw.nl/projecten/edisyn/Online_proceedings/Paper_Martins.pdf>, last accessed 5 January 2013.

Masaryk, Tomáš (1885). *Základovékonkretní logiky: trídení a soustava ved* [Foundations of concrete logic: classification and system of the sciences]. Prague: Bursík a Kohout, 69–80.

Masica, Colin P. (1989). *The Indo-Aryan Languages*. Cambridge: Cambridge University Press.

Massam, Diane (2000). VSO and VOS: aspects of Niuean word order. In A. Carnie and E. Guilfoyle (eds.), *The Syntax of Verb-Initial Languages*. New York: Oxford University Press, 97–116.

Massam, Diane (2001). On predication and the status of subjects in Niuean. In W. Davies and S. Dubinsky (eds.), *Objects and Other Subjects*. Amsterdam: Kluwer, 225–46.

Massam, Diane (2005). Predicate fronting and lexical category in Niuean. In Andrew Carnie, Heidi Harley, and Sheila Dooley-Colburg (eds.), *Verb First: Studies in Predicate-Initial Languages*. Amsterdam: John Benjamins, 227–42.

Mathesius, Vilém (1911). O potenciálnosti jevů jazykových [On the potentiality of language phenomena]. *Věstník Královské české společnosti nauk*: 1–24.

Mathesius, Vilém (1927/1983). Functional linguistics. In Josef Vachek (ed.), *Praguiana: Some Basic and Less-known Aspects of the Prague Linguistics School*. Amsterdam: John Benjamins, 121–42.

Mathesius, Vilém (1928). On linguistic characterology with illustration from modern English. *Actes du Premier congrès international de linguistes à la Haye du 10–15 avril 1928*. Leiden: A. W. Sijthoff, 56–63.

Matthews, Stephen, and Virginia Yip (1994). *Cantonese: A Comprehensive Grammar*. London: Routledge.

Matthews, Stephen, and Virginia Yip (2011). *Cantonese: A Comprehensive Grammar*, 2nd edition. London: Routledge.

Matushansky, Ora (2006). Head-movement in linguistic theory. *Linguistic Inquiry* 37: 69–107.

May, Lillian, Krista Byers-Heinlein, Judit Gervain, and Janet Werker (2011). Language and the newborn brain: does prenatal language experience shape the neonate neural response to speech? *Frontiers in Psychology* 2: 222.

May, Robert (1985). *Logical Form: Its Structure and Derivation*. Cambridge, MA: MIT Press.

Maylor, B. Roger (2002). *Lexical Template Morphology: Change of State and the Verbal Prefixes of German*. Amsterdam: John Benjamins.

McCarthy, John, and Alan Prince (1994). The emergence of the unmarked: optimality in prosodic morphology. In Mercè Gonzàlez (ed.), *Proceedings of NELS 24*. Amherst, MA: GLSA, 333–79.

McCawley, James D. (1992). Justifying part-of-speech assignments in Mandarin Chinese. *Journal of Chinese Linguistics* 20(2): 211–45.

McCloskey, James (1979). *Transformational Syntax and Model Theoretic Semantics*. Dordrecht: D. Reidel.

McCloskey, James (1996). On the scope of verb movement in Irish. *Natural Language and Linguistic Theory* 14: 49–104.

McGinnis, Martha (1997). Case and locality in L-Syntax: evidence from Georgian. In H. Harley (ed.), *The UPenn/MIT Roundtable on Argument Structure and Aspect*. MIT Working Papers in Linguistics 32. Cambridge, MA: MITWPL, 139–58.

Mchombo, Sam (2004). *The Syntax of Chichewa*. Cambridge: Cambridge University Press.

Meillet, Antoine (1903). *Introduction à l'étude comparative des langues indoeuropéennes*. Paris: Hachette. Reprint: 1964, Alabama, University of Alabama Press.

Meinunger, André (2000). *Syntactic Aspects of Topic and Comment*. Amsterdam: John Benjamins.

Mel'čuk, Igor, and Alain Polguère (2009). *Dependency in Linguistic Description*. Amsterdam: John Benjamins.

Merlan, Francesca (1989). *Mangarrayi*. London: Routledge.

Miyagawa, Shigeru (1991). *Case Realisation and Scrambling*. Unpublished manuscript, Ohio State University. Available online at <http://web.mit.edu/miyagawa/www/pdfs/Case_Realization_Scrambling.pdf>, last accessed 4 January 2013.

Miyagawa, Shigeru (2001). EPP, scrambling, and wh-in-situ. In M. Kenstowicz (ed.), *Ken Hale: A Life in Language*. Cambridge, MA: MIT Press, 293–338.

Miyagawa, Shigeru (2003). A-movement scrambling and options without optionality. In S. Karimi (ed.), *Word Order and Scrambling*. Cambridge, MA: Wiley-Blackwell, 177–200.

Miyagawa, Shigeru (2005). On the EPP. In N. Richards and M. McGinnis (eds.), *Perspectives on Phases*. MIT Working Papers in Linguistics 49. Cambridge, MA: MITWPL, 201–36.

Mobbs, Iain (2008). *'Functionalism', the Design of The Language Faculty, and (Disharmonic) Typology*. MPhil dissertation, University of Cambridge.

Mobbs, Iain (in progress). *Minimalism and the Design of the Language Faculty*. PhD dissertation, University of Cambridge.

Moore, Denny (1989). Gavião nominalizations as relative clause and sentential complement equivalents. *International Journal of American Linguistics* 55: 309–25.

Moro, Andrea (1997a). *The Raising of Predicates: Predicative Noun Phrases and the Theory of Clause Structure*. Cambridge: Cambridge University Press.

Moro, Andrea (1997b). Dynamic Antisymmetry: movement as a symmetry-breaking phenomenon. *Studia Linguistica* 52: 50–76.

Moro, Andrea (2000). *Dynamic Antisymmetry*. Cambridge, MA: MIT Press.

Mous, Marten (1993). *A Grammar of Iraqw*. Hamburg: H. Buske.

Moyse-Faurie, Claire (1995). *Le Xârâcùù, langue de Thio-Canala (Nouvelle-Calédonie): éléments de syntaxe*. Paris: Peeters.

Mulder, René, and Rint Sybesma (1992). Chinese is a VO Language. *Natural Language and Linguistic Theory* 10(3): 439–76.

Müller, Gereon (1996). A constraint on remnant movement. *Natural Language and Linguistic Theory* 14: 355–407.

Müller, Gereon (2000). Shape conservation and remnant movement. In M. Hirotani, A. Coetzee, N. Hall, and J. Y. Kim (eds.), *Proceedings of the 30th Northeastern Linguistics Society*. Amherst, MA: GLSA, 525–39.

Munn, Alan B. (1993). *Topics in the Syntax and Semantics of Coordinate Structures*. PhD dissertation, University of Maryland.

Muriungi, Peter (2006). Categorizing adpositions in Kîîtharaka. *Nordlyd: Tromsø Working Papers in Linguistics* 33(1): 26–48.

Muysken, Pieter (1982). Parametrizing the notion 'head'. *Journal of Linguistic Research* 2(3): 57–75.

Muysken, Pieter (2008). *Functional Categories*. Cambridge: Cambridge University Press.

Myler, Neil (2009). Linearization and post-syntactic operations in the Quechua DP. *Cambridge Occasional Papers in Linguistics* 5: 46–66.

Nash, Léa (1995). *Portée argumentale at marquage casuel dans les langues SOV et dans les langues ergatives: l'exemple du géorgien*. PhD dissertation, Université de Paris VIII.

Nash, Lea, and Alain Rouveret (2002). Cliticization as unselective Attract. *Catalan Journal of Linguistics* 1: 157–99.

Ndayiragije, Juvénal (1999). Checking economy. *Linguistic Inquiry* 30(3): 399–444.

Neidle, Carol, Judy Kegl, Benjamin Bahan, Debra Aarons, and Dawn MacLaughlin (1997). Rightward wh-movement in American Sign Language. In D. Beerman, D. LeBlanc, and H. van Riemsdijk (eds.), *Rightward Movement*. Amsterdam: John Benjamins, 247–78.

Neidle, Carol, Judy Kegl, Dawn Maclaughlin, Benjamin Bahan, and Robert G. Lee (2000). *The Syntax of American Sign Language: Functional Categories and Hierarchical Structure*. Cambridge, MA: MIT Press.

Nespor, Marina, and Irene Vogel (1982). Prosodic domains of external sandhi rules. In H. van der Hulst and N. Smith (eds.), *The Structure of Phonological Representations*. Dordrecht: Foris, 225–56.

Nespor, Marina, and Irene Vogel (1986). *Prosodic Phonology*. Dordrecht: Foris.

Nespor, Marina, Maria-Teresa Guasti, and Anne Christophe (1996). Selecting word order: the rhythmic activation principle. In Ursula Kleinhenz (ed.), *Interfaces in Phonology*. Berlin: Akademie Verlag, 1–26.

Nespor, Marina, Ruben van de Vijver, Hanna Schraudolf, Mohinish Shukla, Cinzia Avesani, and Caterina Donati (2008). Different phrasal prominence realizations in VO and OV languages, *Lingue e Linguaggio* VII(2): 1–29.

Newmeyer, Frederick J. (2003). Grammar is grammar and usage is usage. *Language* 79: 682–707.

Newmeyer, Frederick J. (2005a). A reply to the critiques of 'Grammar is grammar and usage is usage'. *Language* 81: 229–36.

Newmeyer, Frederick J. (2005b). *Possible and Probable Languages: A Generative Perspective on Linguistic Typology*. Oxford: Oxford University Press.

Newton, Glenda (2007). Complementizers and C particles. Unpublished manuscript: Cambridge University. Available online at <http://research.ncl.ac.uk/linearization/Final_C_elements.pdf>.

Nikitina, Tatiana (2009). The syntax of postpositional phrases in Wan, an 'SOVX' language. *Studies in Language* 33: 910–33.

Nilsen, Øystein (2003). *Eliminating Positions: The Syntax and Semantics of Sentence Modification*. PhD dissertation, Utrecht.

Nilsen, Øystein (2005). Some notes on cyclic linearization. *Theoretical Linguistics* 31: 173–83.

Nkemnji, Michael A. (1992). *Issues in the Syntax of Negation in Nweh*. MA dissertation, UCLA.

Nkemnji, Michael A. (1995). *Heavy Pied-Piping in Nweh*. PhD dissertation, UCLA.

Nunes, Jairo (1995). *The Copy Theory of Movement and Linearization of Chains in the Minimalist Program*. PhD dissertation, University of Maryland.

Nunes, Jairo (1999). Linearization of chains and phonetic realization of chain links. In S. Epstein and N. Hornstein (eds.), *Working Minimalism*. Cambridge, MA: MIT Press, 217–50.

Nunes, Jairo (2001). Sideward movement. *Linguistic Inquiry* 32: 303–44.

Nunes, Jairo (2004). *Linearization of Chains and Sideward Movement*. Cambridge, MA: MIT Press.

O'Neil, John (1995). Out of control. In J. N. Beckman (ed.), *Proceedings of the 25th Northeastern Linguistics Society*. University of Massachusetts, Amherst: GLSA, 361–71.

O'Neil, John (1997). *Means of Control. Deriving the Properties of PRO in the Minimalist Program*. PhD dissertation, Harvard University.

Ochi, Masao (2009). Overt object shift in Japanese. *Syntax* 12(4): 324–62.

Odden, David. (1988). Antigemination and the OCP. *Linguistic Inquiry* 19: 451–75.

Oishi, Masayuki (2003). When linearity meets Bare Phrase Structure. *Current Issues in English Linguistics* 2: 18–41.

Olawsky, Knut J. (2006). *A Grammar of Urarina*. Berlin: Mouton de Gruyter.

Olawsky, Knut J. (2007). ObViouS OVS in Urarina syntax. In P. K. Austin and A. Simpson (eds.), *Endangered Languages*. Hamburg: Helmult Buske, 45–72.

Oosthuizen, Johan. (2000). Prepositions left and right in Afrikaans. *Stellenbosch Papers in Linguistics (SPiL)* 33: 67–90.

Ordóñez, Francisco (1998). Post-Verbal Asymmetries in Spanish. *Natural Language and Linguistic Theory* 16: 313–46.

Ormazabal, Javier, Juan Uriagereka, and Myriam Uribe-Etxebarria (1994). *Word Order and Wh-movement: Towards a Parametric Account*. Unpublished manuscript, University of Connecticut/UPV-EHU, University of Maryland, and MIT.

Ormazabal, Javier, Juan Uriagereka, and Myriam Uribe-Etxebarria (2008). Hitz hurrenkera eta NZ-mugida: azalpen parametriko baten bila (A slightly revised Basque version of the 1994 paper). In I. Arteatx, X. Artiagoitia, and A. Elordieta (eds.), *Antisimetriaren hipotesia vs. buru parametroa: euskararen oinarrizko hurrenkera ezbaian* [The Antisymmetry Hypothesis vs. the Head Parameter: the Basic Word Order in Basque]. Bilbao: University of the Basque Country Publications, 25–48.

Ortiz de Urbina, Jon (1989). *Parameters in the Grammar of Basque*. Dordrecht: Foris.

Ortiz de Urbina, Jon (1992). Interrogative discharge and the Wh-criterion in Basque. In J. Lakarra and J. Ortiz de Urbina (eds.), *Syntactic Theory and Basque Syntax*. Donostia: Supplements of *ASJU* 27, 295–308.

Ortiz de Urbina, Jon (1994). Verb-initial patterns in Basque and Breton. *Lingua* 94: 125–53.

Ortiz de Urbina, Jon (1995). Residual verb second and verb first in Basque. In K. É. Kiss (ed.), *Discourse-Configurational Languages*. Oxford: Oxford University Press, 99–121.

Ortiz de Urbina, Jon (1999). Force Phrases, Focus Phrases and left heads in Basque. In J. Franco and A. Landa (eds.), *Grammatical Analysis of Romance and Basque*. Amsterdam: John Benjamins, 179–94.

Ortiz de Urbina, Jon (2002). Focus of correction and remnant movement in Basque. In X. Artiagoitia, P. Goenaga, and J. A. Lakarra (eds.), *Erramu Boneta: Festschrift for Rudolf P. G. de Rijk*. Bilbao: Universidad del País Vasco/Euskal Herriko Unibertsitatea, 511–24.

Ortiz de Urbina, Jon (2008). Indar Sintagmak, Foku Sintagmak eta ezkerraldeko buruak Euskaran [Basque revised version of Ortiz de Urbina 1999]. In I. Arteatx, X. Artiagoitia, and A. Elordieta (eds.), *Antisimetriaren hipotesia vs. buru parametroa: euskararen oinar-rizko hurrenkera ezbaian* [The Antisymmetry Hypothesis vs. the Head Parameter: the Basic Word Order in Basque]. Bilbao: University of the Basque Country Publications, 51–67.

Osumi, Midori (1995). *Tinrin Grammar*. Honolulu: University of Hawai'i Press.

Otsu, Yukio (1980). Some aspects of *Rendaku* in Japanese and related problems. *Theoretical Issues in Japanese Linguistics*. MIT Working Papers in Linguistics, 2. Cambridge, MA: MIT Press, 207–27.

Otsuka, Yuko (2005). Two derivations of VSO: a comparative study of Niuean and Tongan. In A. Carnie, H. Harley, and S. Dooley (eds.), *Verb First: On the Syntax of Verb-Initial Languages*. Amsterdam: John Benjamins, 65–90.

Ottaviano, Ida de (1980). *Textos Tacana*. Riberalta, Bolivia: Instituto Lingüístico de Verano, en colaboración con el Ministerio de Educación y Cultura.

Ouhalla, Jamal (1991). *Functional Categories and Parametric Variation*. London: Routledge.

Oyharçabal, Bernard (1985). *Les relatives en Basque*. Paris: Université de París.

Oyharçabal, Bernard (2006). DSaren barneko zenbait ordena kontu. [Some word order issues inside DP]. In B. Fernández and I. Laka (eds.), *Andolin Eguzkitza Gogoan: Essays in Honour of Professor Eguzkitza*. Bilbao: University of the Basque Country, 741–55.

Özsoy, Sumru (2001). On 'small' clauses, other 'bare' verbal complements and feature checking in Turkish. In Erguvanlı E. Taylan (ed.), *The Verb in Turkish*. Amsterdam: John Benjamins, 213–37.

Öztürk, Balkız (2001). Turkish as a non-pro-drop language. In Erguvanlı E. Taylan (ed.), *The Verb in Turkish*. Amsterdam: John Benjamins, 239–59.

Öztürk, Balkız (2004). *Case, Referentiality and Phrase Structure*. PhD dissertation: Harvard.

Öztürk, Balkız (2005). *Case, Referentiality and Phrase Structure*. Amsterdam: John Benjamins.

Öztürk, Balkız (2008). Relativization strategies in Turkish. In M. Kelepir and B. Öztürk (eds.), *Proceedings of the Fourth Workshop of Altaic Formal Linguistics*. MIT Working Papers in Linguistics 56. Cambridge, MA: MIT Press, 241–54.

Öztürk, Balkız (2009). Incorporating Agents. *Lingua* 119(2): 334–58.

Öztürk, Balkız (2013). Rightward movement, EPP and specifiers: evidence from Uyghur and Khalkha. In Gert Webelhuth, Manfred Sailer, and Heike Walker (eds.), *Rightward Movement in a Comparative Perspective*. Amsterdam: John Benjamins, 175–210.

Padovan, Andrea (2010). Diachronic clues to grammaticalization phenomena in the Cimbrian CP. In M. Putnam (ed.), *German-Language Speech Islands: Generative and Structural Approaches*. Amsterdam/Philadelphia: John Benjamins, 279–99.

Parsons, Terence (1990). *Events in the Semantics of English: A Study in Subatomic Semantics*. Cambridge, MA: MIT Press.

Patnaik, Manideepa (1996). A BDT-approach to Angami word orders. In V. S. Lakshmi and A. Mukherjee (eds.), *Word Order in Indian Languages*. Hyderabad Center for Advanced Study in Linguistics: Osmania University and Booklinks Corporation, 61–72.

Paul, Waltraud (2002). Sentence-internal topics in Mandarin Chinese: the case of object preposing. *Language and Linguistics* 3(4): 695–714.

Paul, Waltraud (2005). Low IP area and left periphery in Mandarin Chinese. *Recherches linguistiques de Vincennes* 33: 111–34. Available online at http://crlao.ehess.fr/document.php?id=177.

Paul, Waltraud (2009). Consistent disharmony: sentence-final particles in Chinese. Unpublished manuscript, CRLAO, Paris. Available online at http://crlao.ehess.fr/document.php?id=177.

Paul, Waltraud (2012). Why Chinese *de* is not like French *de*: A critical analysis of the predicational approach to nominal modification. *Studies in Chinese Linguistics* [The Chinese University of Hong Kong] 33(3): 183–210.

Paul, Waltraud (to appear). Why particles are not particular: sentence-final particles in Chinese as heads of a split CP. *Studia Linguistica* 68, 1 (Special issue on particles, edited by Liliane Haegeman and Ans van Kemenade).

Payne, Doris L. (1985). Review of J. A. Hawkins, *Word Order Universals*. New York: Academic Press 1983. *Language* 61: 462–66.

Payne, John (1993). The headedness of noun phrases: slaying the nominal hydra. In G. Corbett, N. M. Fraser, and S. McGlashen (eds.), *Heads in Grammatical Theory*. Cambridge: Cambridge University Press, 114–39.

Pearson, Matt (2000). Two types of VO languages. In P. Svenonius (ed.), *The Derivation of VO and OV*. Amsterdam: John Benjamins, 327–63.

Peperkamp, Sharon (1997). *Prosodic Words*. PhD dissertation, University of Amsterdam.

Pesetsky, David (1987). Wh-in-situ: movement and unselective binding. In E. Reuland and A. Meulen (eds.), *The Representation of (In)definiteness*. Cambridge MA: MIT Press, 98–129.

Pesetsky, David, and Esther Torrego (2001). T-to-C movement: causes and consequences. In M. Kenstowicz (ed.), *Ken Hale: A Life in Language*. Cambridge, MA: MIT Press, 355–426.

Petronio, Karen, and Diane Lillo-Martin (1997). WH-movement and the position of spec-CP: evidence from American Sign Language. *Language* 73(1): 18–57.

Peyraube, Alain (1980). *Les constructions locatives en chinois moderne*. Paris: Editions Langages Croisés.

Pickett, Velma B. (1983). Mexican Indian Languages and Greenberg's 'Universals of Grammar ...'. In F. Agard, G. Kelley, A. Makkai, and V. Becker Makkai (eds.), *Essays in Honor of Charles F. Hockett*. Leiden: Brill, 530–51.

Pietroski, Paul, and Juan Uriagereka (2001). Dimensions of natural language. *University of Maryland Working Papers in Linguistics* 11: 192–219.

Pinker, Steven, and Paul Bloom (1990). Natural language and natural selection. *Behavioral and Brain Sciences* 13(4): 707–84.

Pinker, Steven, and Alan Prince (1991). Regular and irregular morphology and the psychological status of the rules of grammar. In Laurel Sutton, Christopher Johnson, and Ruth Shields (eds.), *Proceedings of the 17th Annual Meeting of the Berkeley Linguistics Society*. Berkeley, CA: Berkeley Linguistics Society, 230–51.

Pinker, Steven, and Alan Prince (1994). Regular and irregular morphology and the psychological status of rules of grammar. In Susan Lima, Roberta Corrigan, and Gregory Iverson (eds.), *The Reality of Linguistic Rules*. Amsterdam: John Benjamins, 321–51.

Pintzuk, Susan (1999). *Phrase Structures in Competition: Variation and Change in Old English Word Order*. New York: Garland Press.

Pintzuk, Susan (2005). Arguments against a universal base: evidence from Old English. *English Language and Linguistics* 9: 115–38.

Plank, Frans (2006). Canonical and non-canonical order in noun phrases (and where is information structure?). Paper presented at the workshop DP-Internal Information Structure: Topic, Focus and Other Illocutionary Forces (University of Utrecht).

Poletto, Cecilia (2002). The left periphery of a V2-Rhaetoromance dialect: a new perspective on V2 and V3. In S. Barbiers, L. Cornips, and S. van der Kleij (eds.), *Syntactic Microvariation*. Amsterdam: Meertens Institute, 214–42.

Poletto, Cecilia (2006). Parallel phases: a study of the high and low left periphery of Old Italian. In M. Frascarelli (ed.), *Phases of Interpretation*. Berlin: Mouton de Gruyter, 261–94.

Poletto, Cecilia, and Jean-Yves Pollock (2004). On the Left Periphery of some Romance Wh-questions. In L. Rizzi (ed.), *The Structure of CP and IP. The Cartography of Syntactic Structures*. New York: Oxford University Press, 251–96.

Polinsky, Maria (1997). Dominance in precedence: SO/OS languages. In K. Singer, R. Eggert, and G. Anderson (eds.), *Proceedings of the 33rd Regional Meeting of the Chicago Linguistic Society (The Panels)*. Chicago: Chicago Linguistic Society, 253–69.

Pollock, Jean-Yves (1989). Verb movement, Universal Grammar, and the structure of IP. *Linguistic Inquiry* 20: 365–424.

Polo, Chiara (2004). *Word Order Between Morphology and Syntax*. Padova: Unipress.

Preminger, Omer (2009). Breaking agreements: distinguishing agreement and clitic doubling by their failures. *Linguistic Inquiry* 40: 619–66.

Pylkkänen, Liina (2008). *Introducing Arguments*. Cambridge, MA: MIT Press.

Quirk, Randolph (1957). Relative clauses in educated spoken English. *English Studies* 38: 97–109.

Rackowski, Andrea, and Lisa Travis (2000). V-initial languages: X or XP movement and adverbial placement. In A. Carnie and E. Guilfoyle (eds.), *The Syntax of Verb-Initial Languages*. New York: Oxford University Press, 117–41.

Rebuschi, Georges (1983). A note on focalization in Basque. *ASJU* 4(2): 29–42. Reprinted in G. Rebuschi (1997). *Essais de linguistique basque. ASJU XXXV*. Donostia: EHU-Gipuzkoako Foru Aldundia, 31–41.

Rezac, Milan (2006). The interaction of Th/Ex and Locative Inversion. *Linguistic Inquiry* 37(4): 685–97.

Rhodes, Richard A. (1998). *Clause Structure, Core Arguments, and the Algonquian Relative Root Construction*. The 1998 Belcourt Lecture. Winnipeg: Voices of Rupert's Land.

Richards, Marc (2004). *Object Shift and Scrambling in North and West Germanic: A Case Study in Symmetrical Syntax*. PhD dissertation, University of Cambridge.

Richards, Marc (2007). On feature-inheritance: an argument from the Phase Impenetrability Condition. *Linguistic Inquiry* 38: 563–72.

Richards, Marc (2008). Desymmetrization: parametric variation at the PF-interface. *The Canadian Journal of Linguistics/La revue canadienne de linguistique* 53: 275–300.

Richards, Marc (2009). Two kinds of variation in a Minimalist system. In F. Heck, G. Müller, and J. Trommer (eds.), *Varieties of Competition*. Linguistische Arbeitsberichte. Leipzig: Leipzig University, 87: 133–62.

Richards, Norvin (2001). A Distinctness Condition on linearization. In K. Megerdoomian and L. A. Bar-el (eds.), *Proceedings of the 20th West Coast Conference on Formal Linguistics*. Somerville, MA: Cascadilla Press, 470–83.

Riemsdijk, Henk van (1990). Functional prepositions. In H. Pinkster and I. Genee (eds.), *Unity in Diversity: Papers Presented to Simon C. Dik on his Fiftieth Birthday*. Dordrecht: Foris, 229–41.

Riemsdijk, Henk van (1998). Head movement and adjacency. *Natural Language and Linguistic Theory* 16: 633–79.

Rijk, Rudolf P. de (1969). Is Basque S.O.V.? *Fontes Linguae Vasconum* 1: 319–51.

Rijk, Rudolf P. de (1972). *Studies in Basque Syntax: Relative Clauses*. PhD dissertation, MIT.

Ritter, Elizabeth, and Martina Wiltschko. (2010). The composition of INFL: an exploration of tense, tenseless languages, and tenseless constructions. Unpublished manuscript, University of British Columbia. Available online at <http://ling.auf.net/lingbuzz/001078>, last accessed 9 January 2013.

Rizzi, Luigi (1990). *Relativized Minimality*. Cambridge, MA: MIT Press.

Rizzi, Luigi (1993/1994). Some notes on linguistic theory and language development: the case of root infinitives. *Language Acquisition* 3: 341–93.

Rizzi, Luigi (1997). The fine structure of the left periphery. In L. Haegeman (ed.). *Elements of Grammar*. Dordrecht: Kluwer, 281–337.

Rizzi, Luigi (2001). On the position 'Int(errogative)' in the left periphery of the clause. In G. Cinque and G. Salvi (eds.), *Current Studies in Italian Syntax. Essays Offered to Lorenzo Renzi*. Amsterdam: Elsevier, 287–96.

Rizzi, Luigi (2004a). Locality and left periphery. In A. Belletti (ed.), *Structures and Beyond: The Cartography of Syntactic Structures*. New York: Oxford University Press, 223–51.

Rizzi, Luigi (ed.), (2004b). *The Structure of CP and IP: The Cartography of Syntactic Structures*. New York: Oxford University Press.

Rizzi, Luigi (2007a). On the form of chains: criterial positions and ECP effects. In Lisa L.-S. Cheng and Norbert Corver (eds.) (2006). *Wh Movement: Moving On*. Cambridge, MA: MIT Press, 97–133.

Rizzi, Luigi (2007b). On some properties of Criterial freezing. *CISCL Working Papers on Language and Cognition* 1: 145–58.

Rizzi, Luigi (2010). On the elements of syntactic variation. Paper presented at the Workshop on Linguistic Variation in the Minimalist Framework (Universitat Autònoma de Barcelona).

Rizzi, Luigi, and Ur Shlonsky (2007). Strategies of subject extraction. In H.-M. Gärtner and U. Sauerland (eds.), *Interfaces + Recursion = Language? Chomsky's Minimalism and the View from Syntax-Semantics*. Berlin: Mouton de Gruyter, 115–60.

Roberts, Ian G. (1985). Agreement parameters and the development of English modal auxiliaries. *Natural Language and Linguistic Theory* 3: 21–58.

Roberts, Ian G. (1996). Remarks of the Old English C-system and the diachrony of V2. In E. Brandner and G. Ferraresi (eds.), *Language Change and Generative Grammar*, Linguistische Berichte, Sonderheft 7. Opladen: Westdeutscher Verlag, 154–67.

Roberts, Ian G. (1997). Directionality and word order change in the history of English. In A. van Kemenade and N. Vincent (eds.), *Parameters of Morphosyntactic Change*. Cambridge: Cambridge University Press, 423–60.

Roberts, Ian G. (2004). The C-System in Brythonic Celtic Languages, V2 and the EPP. In L. Rizzi (ed.), *The Structure of CP and IP: The Cartography of Syntactic Structures*. New York: Oxford University Press, 125–55.

Roberts, Ian G. (2005). *Principles and Parameters in a VSO Language: A Case Study in Welsh*. New York: Oxford University Press.

Roberts, Ian G. (2007a). Introduction. In I. Roberts (ed.), *Comparative Grammar: Critical Concepts in Linguistics*, vol. III. London: Routledge, 1–40.

Roberts, Ian G. (2007b). *Diachronic Syntax*. Oxford: Oxford University Press.

Roberts, Ian G., and Anders Holmberg. (2010). Introduction: parameters in minimalist theory. In T. Biberauer, A. Holmberg, I. Roberts, and M. Sheehan. *Parametric Variation: Null Subjects in Minimalist Theory*. Cambridge: Cambridge University Press, 1–57.

Roberts, Ian, and Anna Roussou (2003). *Syntactic Change: A Minimalist Approach to Grammaticaliaion*. Cambridge: Cambridge University Press.

Rogger, Igino (1979). Dati storici sui mocheni e i loro stanziamenti. In G. B. Pellegrini (ed.), *La valle del Fersina e le isole linguistiche tedesche del Trentino: Atti del convegno di S. Orsola, 1–3 settembre 1978*. San Michele all'Adige: Museo degli Usi e Costumi della Gente Trentina, 153–73.

Rooryck, Johan (1997). On the interaction between raising and focus in sentential complementation. *Studia Linguistica* 51: 1–49.

Rosenbach, Anette (2002). *Genitive Variation in English: Conceptual Factors in Synchronic and Diachronic Studies*. Berlin: Mouton de Gruyter.

Rosenbaum, Peter S. (1967). *The Grammar of English Predicate Complement Constructions*. Cambridge, MA: MIT Press.

Ross, John R. (1967). *Constraints on Variables in Syntax*. PhD dissertation, MIT.

Rowley, Anthony (2003). *Liacht as de sproch: grammatica della lingua mòchena*. Palù del Fersina: Pubblicazioni dell'Istituto Culturale Mòcheno-Cimbro.

Ruhlen, Merritt (1975). *A Guide to the Languages of the World*. Stanford: Language Universals Project, Stanford University.

Sabel, Joachim (2000). Expletives as Features. In R. Billerey, and B. D. Lillehaugen (eds.), *Proceedings of the 19th West Coast Conference on Formal Linguistics*. Somerville, MA: Cascadilla Press, 411–24.

Sagiv, Yehoshua, Claude Delobel, D. Stott Parker, and Ronald Fagin (1981). An equivalence between relational database dependencies and a fragment of propositional logic. *Journal of the Association for Computing Machinery* 28: 435–53.

Saito, Mamuro (2006). Optional A-scrambling. Paper presented at the 16th Japanese/Korean Linguistics Conference (Kyoto University).

Sanders, Gerald (1975). On the explanation of constituent order universals. In C. N. Li (ed.), *Word Order and Word Order Change*. Austin: University of Texas Press, 389–36.

Sapir, Edward (1921). *Language*. New York: Harcourt Brace and Co.

Sapir, Edward (1929). Central and North American languages. *Encyclopaedia Britannica* (14th edition), vol. 5: 138–41.

Sapir, Edward (1949). *Language: An Introduction to the Study of Speech*, 2nd edn. New York: Harcourt, Brace and Co.

Saussure, Ferdinand de (1916). *Cours de linguistique générale*. Lausanne-Paris: Payot.

Saxton, Dean (1982). Papago. In R. W. Langacker (ed.), *Studies in Uto-Aztecan Grammar*, vol. 3. Arlington: SIL and University of Texas, 93–266.

Scalise, Sergio (1984). *Generative Morphonology*. Dordrecht: Foris.

Scalise, Sergio (1988). Inflection and derivation. *Linguistics* 26: 561–81.

Schaeffer, Jeanette (1997). *Direct Object Scrambling in Dutch and Italian Child Language*. PhD dissertation, UCLA.

Schaeffer, Jeanette (2000). *The Acquisition of Direct Object Scrambling and Clitic Placement: Syntax and Pragmatics*. Amsterdam: John Benjamins.

Schmidt, Wilhelm (1926). *Die Sprachfamilien und Sprachenkreise der Erde*. Heidelberg: C. Winter.

Schweikert, Walter (2005a). *The Order of Prepositional Phrases in the Structure of the Clause*. Amsterdam: John Benjamins.

Schweikert, Walter (2005b). The position of prepositional modifiers in the adverbial space. *Rivista di Grammatica Generativa* 30: 115–34.

Scott, Gary-John (2002). Stacked adjectival modification and the structure of nominal phrases. In G. Cinque (ed.), *Functional Structure in DP and IP: The Cartography of Syntactic Structures*. New York: Oxford University Press, 91–120.

Selkirk, Elisabeth O. (1984). *Phonology and Syntax: The Relation between Sound and Structure*. Cambridge, MA: MIT Press.

Selkirk, Elisabeth O. (1995). The prosodic structure of function words. In Jill Beerman et al. (eds.), *Papers in Optimality Theory*. University of Massachusetts Occasional Papers 18. Amherst: GLSA, 439–69.

Sells, Peter (1999). Postposing in Japanese. Unpublished manuscript, Stanford. Available online at <http://www-csli.stanford.edu/~sells/jp-www.pdf>, last accessed 4 January 2013.

Sells, Peter (2000). Raising and the order of clausal constituents in the Philippine languages. In I. Paul, V. Phillips, and L. Travis (eds.), *Formal Issues in Austronesian Linguistics*. Dordrecht: Kluwer, 117–43.

Şener, Serkan (2005). Postverbal constituents in Turkish: they are still high! Paper presented at ConSole XIV (EHU-University of the Basque Country).

Seuren, Pieter (1998). *Western Linguistics: An Historical Introduction*. Oxford: Blackwell.

Shannon, Thomas F. (1992). Toward an adequate characterization of relative clause extraposition in Modern German. In I. Rauch, G. F. Carr, and R. L. Kyes (eds.), *On Germanic Linguistics: Issues and Methods*. Berlin: Mouton de Gruyter, 253–81.

Sheehan, Michelle (2009a). The Final-over-Final Constraint as an effect of complement stranding. *Newcastle Working Papers in Linguistics* 15: 104–25.

Sheehan, Michelle (2009b). Labelling, Multiple Spell-Out and the Final-over-Final Constraint. In V. Moscati and E. Servidio (eds.), *StiL—Studies in Linguistics Proceedings of XXXV Incontro di Grammatica Generativa*. Siena: Università di Siena, 231–43.

Sheehan, Michelle (2010). Extraposition and Antisymmetry. In Jeroen van Craenenbroeck (ed.), *Linguistic Variation Yearbook*. Amsterdam: John Benjamins, 203–25.

Sheehan, Michelle (2012). FOFC and the Head-Final Filter. To appear in Theresa Biberauer, Anders Holmberg, Ian Roberts, and Michelle Sheehan. *The Final-over-Final Constraint: A Word-Order Universal and its Implications for Linguistic Theory*. Cambridge, MA: MIT Press.

Sheehan, Michelle (in press). Some implications of a copy theory of labeling. To appear in *Syntax*.

Shlonsky, Ur (1989). The hierarchical representation of subject verb agreement. Unpublished manuscript, University of Geneva. Available online at <http://lear.unive.it/bitstream/10278/1628/1/Shlonsky.agreement.pdf>, last accessed 9 January 2013.

Shlonsky, Ur (2004). The form of Semitic noun phrases: an Antisymmetric, non N-movement account. *Lingua* 114: 1465–526.

Siegel, Melanie, and Emily M. Bender (2004). 'Head-initial' constructions in Japanese. In S. Müller (ed.), *Proceedings of the HPSG04 Conference*. Stanford: CSLI, 243–59. Available online at <http://cslipublications.stanford.edu/HPSG/5/siegel-bender.pdf>, last accessed 9 January 2013.

Siewierska, Anna (1988). *Word Order Rules*. London: Croom Helm.

Sigurðsson, Halldor (2007). Argument features, clausal structure and the computation. In E. Reuland, T. Bhattacharya, and G. Spathas (eds.), *Argument Structure*. Amsterdam: John Benjamins, 121–55.

Simpson, Andrew (2001). Definiteness agreement and the Chinese DP. *Language and Linguistics* 2(1): 125–56.

Simpson, Andrew, and Zoe Wu (2002). IP-raising, tone sandhi and the creation of S-final particles: evidence for cyclic spell-out. *Journal of East Asian Linguistics* 11: 67–99.

Simpson, Jane (1983). Resultatives. In B. Levin, M. Rappaport, and A. Zaenen (eds.), *Papers in Lexical-Functional Grammar*. Bloomington: Indiana University Linguistics Club, 143–57.

Skopeteas, Stavros, Caroline Féry, and Rusudan Asatiani. (2009). Word order and intonation in Georgian. *Lingua* 119(1): 102–27.

Smith, Carlota S. (1991). *The Parameter of Aspect*. Dordrecht: Kluwer.

Smith, Neil V. (1981). Consistency, markedness and language change: on the notion 'consistent language'. *Journal of Linguistics* 17: 39–54.

Soh, Hooi Ling, and Meijia Gao (2004). Perfective aspect and transition in Mandarin Chinese: an analysis of double *le* sentences. In L. P. Denis, E. McCready, A. Palmer, and B. Reese (eds.), *Proceedings of the 2004 Texas Linguistics Society Conference: Issues at the Semantics-Pragmatics Interface*. Somerville, MA: Cascadilla Press, 107–22.

Sohn, Ho-Min (1999). *The Korean Language*. Cambridge: Cambridge University Press.

Song, Jae Sung (2012). *Word Order*. Cambridge: Cambridge University Press.

Steele, Susan (1978). The category AUX as a language universal. In J. Greenberg (ed.) *Universals of Human Language*, vol. 3. Stanford: Stanford University Press, 7–46.

Sternefeld, Wolfgang (1994). Subjects, adjuncts, and SOV-order in Antisymmetric syntax. *Groninger Arbeiten zur Gerministischen Linguistik* 37: 227–46.

Stowell, Timothy (1981). *Origins of Phrase Structure*. PhD dissertation, MIT.

Stowell, Timothy (1996). The phrase structure of tense. In J. Rooryck and L. Zaring (eds.), *Phrase Structure and the Lexicon*. Dordrecht: Kluwer, 271–86.

Subbarao, K. V. (1984). *Complementation in Hindi Syntax*. Delhi: Academic Publications.

Subbarao, K. V. (2008). Typological characteristics of South Asian languages. In B. B. Kachru, Y. Kachru, and S. N. Sridhar (eds.), *Language in South Asia*. Cambridge: Cambridge University Press, 49–78.

Svenonius, Peter (1993). Selection, adjunction, and concord in the DP. *Studia Linguistica* 47: 198–220.

Svenonius, Peter (1994). C-selection as feature-checking, *Studia Linguistica* 58: 133–55.

Svenonius, Peter (ed.) (2000a). *The Derivation of VO and OV*. Amsterdam: John Benjamins.

Svenonius, Peter (2000b). Quantifier movement in Icelandic. In P. Svenonius (ed.), *The Derivation of OV and VO*. Amsterdam/Philadelphia: John Benjamins, 255–91.

Svenonius, Peter (2006). The emergence of axial parts. In P. Svenonius and M. Pantcheva (eds.), *Tromsø Working Papers in Language and Linguistics, 33.1: Special Issue on Adpositions*. Tromsø: University of Tromsø, 49–77.

Svenonius, Peter (2007). Adpositions, particles and the arguments they introduce. In E. Reuland, T. Bhattacharya, and G. Spathas (eds.), *Argument Structure*. Amsterdam: John Benjamins, 71–110.

Svenonius, Peter (2008). The position of adjectives and other phrasal modifiers in the decomposition of DP. In L. McNally and C. Kennedy (eds.), *Adjectives and Adverbs: Syntax, Semantics, and Discourse*. Oxford: Oxford University Press, 16–42.

Svenonius, Peter (2010). Spatial P in English. In G. Cinque and L. Rizzi (eds.), *Mapping Spatial PPs: The Cartography of Syntactic Structures*. New York: Oxford University Press, 127–60.

Sybesma, Rint, and Boya Li (2007). The dissection and structural mapping of Cantonese sentence-final particles. *Lingua* 117: 1739–83.

Takamine, Kaori (2010). *The Postpositional Hierarchy and its Mapping to Clause Structure in Japanese*. PhD dissertation, University of Tromsø.

Takano, Yuji (1996). *Movement and Parametric Variation in Syntax*. PhD dissertation, UC Irvine.

Tallerman, Maggie (1998a). Word order in Celtic. In A. Siewierska (ed.), *Constituent Order in the Languages of Europe*. Berlin: Mouton de Gruyter, 21–45.

Tallerman, Maggie (1998b). Celtic word order: some theoretical issues. In A. Siewierska (ed.), *Constituent Order in the Languages of Europe*. Berlin: Mouton de Gruyter, 599–647.

Tanaka, Hideo (2001). Right-dislocation as scrambling. *Journal of Linguistics* 37: 551–79.

Tang, C.-C. Jane (2007). Modifier licensing and the Chinese DP: a feature analysis. *Language and Linguistics* 8(4): 967–1024.

Tang, Sze-Wing (1998). *Parametrizations of Features in Syntax*. PhD dissertation, University of California, Irvine.

Tang, Ting-Chi (1989). *Studies on Chinese Morphology and Syntax 2*. Taipei: Student Book Co. Ltd.

Taraldsen, Knut Tarald (2000). V-movement and VP-movement in derivations leading to VO-order. In P. Svenonius (ed.), *The Derivation of VO and OV*. Amsterdam: John Benjamins, 97–122.

Taylan, Erguvanlı E. (1984). *The Function of Word Order in Turkish Grammar*. Berkeley: University of California Press.

Taylor, Ann, and Susan Pintzuk (2012). The effect of Information Structure on object position in the history of English. In A. Meurman-Solin, M. J. López-Couso, and B. Los (eds.), *Information Structure and Syntactic Change*. Oxford Studies in the History of English, vol. 1. New York: Oxford University Press, 47–65.

Taylor, Douglas (1952). The principal grammatical formatives of Island Carib (C. A. Dialect). *International Journal of American Linguistics* 18: 150–65.

Temürcü, Ceyhan (2001). *Word Order Variations in Turkish: Evidence from Binding and Scope*. MS dissertation, Middle East Technical University.

Thackston, W. M. (2006a). *Kurmanji Kurdish: A Reference Grammar with Selected Readings*. Unpublished manuscript, Harvard University: Available online at <http://www.fas.harvard.edu/~iranian/Kurmanji/index.html>, last accessed 9 January 2013.

Thackston, W. M. (2006b). *Sorani Kurdish: A Reference Grammar with Selected Readings*. Unpublished manuscript, Harvard University: Available online at <http://www.fas.harvard.edu/~iranian/Sorani/sorani_ complete.pdf>, last accessed 9 January 2013.

Thráinsson, Höskuldur, Hjalmar P. Petersen, Jógvan í Lon Jacobsen, and Zakaris Svabo Hansen (2004). *Faroese: An Overview and Reference Grammar*. Tórshavn: Foroya Frodskaparfelag.

Togni, Lucia (1990). Per un'analisi di alcuni fenomeni linguistici del dialetto della valle del Fersina: un confronto con la sintassi tedesca. MA thesis, University of Trento.

Tokizaki, Hisao (1999). Prosodic phrasing and bare phrase structure. In P. Tamanji, M. Hirotani, and N. Hall (eds.), *Proceedings of the 29th North East Linguistic Society*, (NELS 29). Amherst MA: GLSA, 381–95.

Tokizaki, Hisao (2008). Symmetry and asymmetry in the syntax–phonology interface. *Phonological Studies* 11: 123–30.

Tokizaki, Hisao (2011). The nature of linear information in the morphosyntax–PF interface. *English Linguistics* 28: 227–57.

Tokizaki, Hisao, and Yasutomo Kuwana (2013). Unattested word orders and left-branching structure. In T. Biberauer and I. Roberts (eds.), *Challenges to Linearization*. Berlin: Mouton de Gruyter, 211–34.

Tomaselli, Alessandra (1990). *La sintassi del verbo finito nelle lingue germaniche*. Padova: Unipress.

Tomlin, Russell (1979). *An Explanation of the Distribution of Basic Constituent Orders*. PhD dissertation, University of Michigan.

Tomlin, Russell (1986). *Basic Word Order: Functional Principles*. London: Croom Helm.

Tonhauser, Judith (2006). *The Temporal Semantics of Noun Phrases: Evidence from Guaraní*. PhD dissertation, Stanford University.

Torrego, Esther (1998). *The Dependencies of Objects*. Cambridge, MA: MIT Press.

Torrence, Harold (2005). *On the Distribution of Complementizers in Wolof.* PhD dissertation, UCLA.

Toyoshima, Takashi (1997). 'Long' head movement, or wrong 'head movement'? *Proceedings from the Main Session of the Chicago Linguistic Society's 33rd Meeting.* Chicago: Chicago Linguistic Society, 401–16.

Toyoshima, Takashi (2000). *Head-to-Spec Movement and Dynamic Economy.* PhD dissertation, Cornell University.

Toyoshima, Takashi (2001). A neo-Lexicalist movement analysis of incorporation. In K. Megerdoomian and L. A. Bar-el (eds.), *Proceedings of the 20th West Coast Conference on Formal Linguistics.* Somerville, MA: Cascadilla Press, 579–92.

Toyoshima, Takashi (2009). Dynamic economy of derivation. In K. Grohmann (ed.), *Explorations of Phase Theory.* Berlin: Mouton de Gruyter, 211–51.

Traill, Anthony (1994). *A !Xóõ Dictionary.* Köln: Rüdiger Köppe.

Travis, Lisa D. (1984). *Parameters and Effects of Word Order Variation.* PhD dissertation, MIT.

Travis, Lisa D. (1989). Parameters of phrase structure. In A. Kroch and M. Baltin (eds.), *Alternative Conceptions of Phrase Structure.* Chicago: University of Chicago Press, 263–79.

Travis, Lisa de Mena (1991). Inner aspect and the structure of VP. Paper given at the 22nd Meeting of the Northeast Linguistics Society (University of Delaware).

Truckenbrodt, Hubert (1999). On the relation between syntactic phrases and phonological phrases. *Linguistic Inquiry* 30: 219–55.

Tryon, Darrell T. (1970). *An Introduction to Maranungku (Northern Australia).* Canberra: Pacific Linguistics.

Tsai, Wei-Tien Dylan, and Melody Yayin Chang (2003). Two types of Wh-adverbials: a typological study of *how* and *why* in Tsou. In P. Pica and J. Rooyck (eds.), *The Linguistic Variation Yearbook III.* Amsterdam: John Benjamins, 213–36.

Tsunoda, Tasaku (1990). Typological study of word order in languages of the Pacific region (6) Korean. *Studies in Language and Literature* 18: 1–13.

Tsunoda, Tasaku (1992). Typological study of word order (10) Swedish and (11) Q'eqchi. *Studies in Language and Literature* 21: 121–56.

Tsunoda, Tasaku, Sumie Ueda, and Yoshiaki Itoh (1995). Adpositions in word order typology. *Linguistics* 33: 741–61.

Ueda, Sumie, and Yoshiaki Itoh (2002). Classification of natural languages by word ordering rule. In O. Opitz and M. Schwaiger (eds.), *Explanatory Data Analysis in Empirical Research.* Dordrecht: Springer, 180–7.

Uhmann, Susanne (1993). *Fokusphonologie des Deutschen.* Tübingen: Niemeyer.

Uriagereka, Juan (1999a). Multiple spell-out. In S. D. Epstein and N. Hornstein (eds.), *Working Minimalism.* Cambridge, MA: MIT Press, 251–82.

Uriagereka, Juan (1999b). Minimal restrictions on Basque movements. *Natural Language and Linguistic Theory* 17: 403–44.

Uszkoreit, Hans, Thorsten Brants, Denys Duchier, Brigitte Krenn, Lars Konieczny, Stefan Oepen, and Wojciech Skut (1998). Studien zur Performanzorientierten Linguistik: Aspekte der Relativsatzextraposition im Deutschen. *Kognitionswissenschaft* 7: 129–33.

Uygun, Dilek (2006). Scrambling bare singular nominal objects in Turkish. Paper presented at the 13th International Conference on Turkish Linguistics (Uppsala).

Vendler, Zeno (1967). Verbs and times. In Z. Vendler (ed.), *Linguistics in Philosophy*. Ithaca: Cornell University Press, 97–121.

Vennemann, Theo (1972). Analogy in generative grammar: the origin of word order. Paper presented at the 11th Congress of Linguists (Bologna). Published in: Luigi Heilmann (ed.), *Proceedings of the Eleventh International Congress of Linguistics, Bologna-Florence, Aug. 28–Sept. 2, 1972*, vol. II. Bologna: Mulino, 79–83.

Vennemann, Theo (1973). Explanation in syntax. In J. P. Kimball (ed.), *Syntax and Semantics*, vol. 2. New York: Seminar Press, 1–50.

Vennemann, Theo (1974a). Topics, subjects, and word order: from SXV to SVX via TVX. In John Anderson and Charles Jones (eds.), *Historical Linguistics*. Edinburgh: North-Holland, 339–76.

Vennemann, Theo (1974b). Theoretical word order studies: results and problems. *Papiere zur Linguistik* 7: 5–25.

Vennemann, Theo (1975). An explanation of drift. In Charles Li and Sandra Thompson (eds.), *Word Order and Word Order Change*. Austin: University of Texas Press, 269–305.

Vennemann, Theo (1976). Categorial Grammar and the order of meaningful elements. In A. Juilland (ed.), *Linguistic Studies Offered to Joseph Greenberg on the Occasion of his Sixtieth Birthday*, vol. 3. Saratoga, CA: Anma Libri, 615–34.

Vennemann, Theo and Ray Harlow (1977). Categorial grammar and consistent basic VX serialization. *Theoretical Linguistics* 4: 227–54.

Vicente, Luis (2004). Derived vs base-generated OV. *Leiden Working Papers in Linguistics* 1(1): 83–96.

Vicente, Luis (2007). *The Syntax of Heads and Phrases*. PhD dissertation, Leiden University.

Vicente, Luis (2008). El movimiento del verbo en un análisis antisimétrico del euskera. In I. Arteatx, X. Artiagoitia, and A. Elordieta (eds.), *Antisimetriaren hipotesia vs. buru parametroa: euskararen oinarrizko hurrenkera ezbaian* [The Antisymmetry Hypothesis vs the Head Parameter: the basic word order in Basque]. Bilbao: University of the Basque Country Publications, 131–55.

Vikner, Sten (1995). *Verb Movement and Expletive Subjects in the Germanic Languages*. New York: Oxford University Press.

Vilkuna, Maria (1995). Discourse configurationality in Finnish. In K. É. Kiss (ed.), *Discourse Configurational Languages*. Oxford: Oxford University Press, 244–68.

Vilkuna, Maria (1998). Word order in European Uralic. In A. Siewierska (ed.), *Constituent Order in the Languages of Europe*. Berlin: Mouton de Gruyter, 173–233.

Villalba, Xavier (1999). Right Dislocation is not Right Dislocation. In O. Fullana and F. Roca (eds.), *Studies on the Syntax of Central Romance Languages: Proceedings of the III Symposium on the Syntax of Central Romance Languages*. Girona: Universitat de Girona, 227–41.

Villalba, Xavier, and Anna Bartra-Kaufmann (2010). Predicate focus fronting in the Spanish Determiner Phrase. *Lingua* 120(4): 819–49.

Vos, Mark de (2008). Deriving Narrow Syntax from principles of lexical organization. *Lingua* 118: 1864–99.

Wagers, Matthew, and Colin Phillips (2009). Multiple dependencies and the role of the grammar in real-time comprehension. *Journal of Linguistics* 45: 395–433.

Wagner, Michael (2005). Asymmetries in prosodic domain formation. In N. Richards and M. Mcginnis (eds.), *Perspectives on Phases*. Cambridge, MA: MIT Press, 329–67.

Walinska de Hackbeil, Hanna (1985). *En*-prefixation and the syntactic domain of zero derivation. In M. Niepokej et al. (eds.), *Proceedings of the 11th Annual Meeting of the Berkeley Linguistics Society*. Berkeley: University of California Linguistics Department, 337–57.

Walinska de Hackbeil, Hanna (1986). *The Roots of Phrase Structure: The Syntactic Basis of English Morphology*. PhD dissertation, University of Washington.

Walkden, George (2009). Deriving the Final-over-Final Constraint from third-factor considerations. *Cambridge Occasional Papers in Linguistics* 5: 67–72.

Watters, John R. (2003). Grassfields Bantu. In D. Nurse and G. Philippson (eds.), *The Bantu Languages*. London: Routledge, 225–56.

Webelhuth, Gert (1992). *Principles and Parameters of Syntactic Saturation*. New York: Oxford University Press.

Weerman, Fred (1997). On the relation between morphological and syntactic case. In A. van Kemenade and N. Vincent (eds.), *Parameters of Morphosyntactic Change*. Cambridge: Cambridge University Press, 427–59.

Weil, Henri (1879). *De l'ordre des mots dans les langues anciennes comparées aux langues modernes*: Paris: Joubert, Libraire-Éditeur.

Weinberg, Steven (1976). The forces of nature. *Bulletin of the American Academy of Arts and Sciences* 29: 13–29.

Welmers, William E. (1946). *A Descriptive Grammar of Fanti*. Baltimore: Linguistic Society of America.

Westergaard, Marit (2009a). *The Acquisition of Word Order: Input Cues, Information Structure and Economy*. Amsterdam: John Benjamins.

Westergaard, Marit (2009b). The development of word order in Old and Middle English: the role of Information Structure and first language acquisition. *Diachronica* 26(1): 65–102.

Wexler, Ken (1998). Very early parameter setting and the Unique Checking Constraint: a new explanation of the optional infinitive stage. *Lingua* 106: 23–79.

Whitman, John (2001). Kayne 1994: p. 143, fn. 3. In G. M. Alexandrova and O. Arnaudova (eds.), *The Minimalist Parameter*. Amsterdam: John Benjamins, 77–100.

Whitman, John (2005). Preverbal elements in Korean and Japanese. In G. Cinque and R. Kayne (eds.), *Handbook of Comparative Syntax*. New York: Oxford University Press, 880–902.

Whitman, John (2008). The classification of constituent order generalizations and diachronic explanation. In J. Good (ed.), *Linguistic Universals and Language Change*. Oxford: Oxford University Press, 233–52.

Williams, Alexander (2008). Word order in resultatives. In C. B. Chang and H. J. Haynie (eds.), *Proceedings of the 26th West Coast Conference on Formal Linguistics*. Somerville, MA: Cascadilla Press, 507–15.

Williams, Edwin (1981). On the notions 'lexically related' and 'head of a word'. *Linguistic Inquiry* 12: 245–74.

Williams, Edwin (1982). Another argument that passive is transformational. *Linguistic Inquiry* 13(1): 203–38.

Willis, David (2006). Against N-raising and NP-raising analyses of Welsh noun phrases. *Lingua* 116: 1807–39.

Wu, Chunming (2006). Adverbials in Paiwan. Paper presented at Tenth International Conference on Austronesian Linguistics (Puerto Princesa City, Palawan, Philippines).

Wu, Regina R. J. (2004). *Stance in Talk: A Conversational Analysis of Mandarin Final Particles.* Amsterdam: John Benjamins.

Wurmbrand, Susanne (2001). *Infinitives: Restructuring and Clause Structure.* Berlin: Mouton de Gruyter.

Wurmbrand, Susanne (2005). Verb clusters, verb raising, and restructuring. In M. Everaert and H. van Riemsdijk (eds.), *The Blackwell Companion to Syntax.* Oxford: Blackwell, 227–341.

Yap Foong-Ha, Stephen Matthews, and Kaoru Horie (2004). From pronominalizer to pragmatic marker: implications for unidirectionality from a crosslinguistic perspective. In O. Fisher, M. Norde, and H. Parridon (eds.), *Up and Down the Cline: The Nature of Grammaticalization.* Amsterdam: John Benjamins, 137–68.

Yap, Foong-Ha, and Jiao Wang (2009). Clausal integration and the emergence of sentence-final particles. Paper presented at the 17th Conference of the International Association of Chinese Linguistics (IACL-17) (Paris).

Yasui, Miyoko (2003). A graph-theoretical reanalysis of Bare Phrase Structure theory and its implications on parametric variation. Unpublished manuscript, Dokkyo University. Available online at <http://myasui81.s3-website-ap-northeast-1.amazonaws.com/publications/Yasui_2002.pdf>, last accessed 6 January 2013.

Yeung, Ka-Wai (2006). On the status of *Waa6* in Cantonese. *Taiwan Journal of Linguistics* 4(1): 1–48.

Yip, Virginia, and Stephen Matthews (2007). Relative clauses in Cantonese-English bilingual children: typological challenges and processing motivations. *Studies in Second Language Acquisition* 29(2): 277–300.

Young, Phil D., and Talmy Givón (1990). The puzzle of Ngäbére auxiliaries: grammatical reconstruction in Chibchan and Misumalpan. In W. Croft, K. Denning, and S. Kemmer (eds.), *Studies in Typology and Diachrony: For Joseph H. Greenberg.* Amsterdam: John Benjamins, 209–43.

Yu, Xin-Xian Rex (2008). Two types of adverbials in Mayrinax Atayal. *Nanzan Linguistics* (Special Issue 5), 125–37.

Zamboni, Alberto (1979). Fenomeni di interferenza nelle isole linguistiche tedesche del Trentino (con particolare riguardo all'area mochena). In G. B. Pellegrini (ed.), *La valle del Fersina e le isole linguistiche tedesche del Trentino: Atti del convegno di S. Orsola, 1–3 settembre 1978.* San Michele all'Adige: Museo degli Usi e Costumi della Gente Trentina, 83–111.

Zanuttini, Raffaella (1997). *Negation and Clausal Structure: A Comparative Study of Romance Languages.* New York: Oxford University Press.

Zhang, Niina Ning (2002). Movement within a spatial phrase. In Hubert Cuyckens and Günther Radden (eds.), *Perspectives on Prepositions.* Tübingen: Max Niemeyer Verlag, 47–63.

Zhang, Niina Ning (2010). *Coordination in Syntax.* Cambridge: Cambridge University Press.

Zubizarreta, Maria-Luisa (1998). *Prosody, Focus and Word Order.* Cambridge, MA: MIT Press.

Zwart, Jan-Wouter (1996). Verb clusters in Continental West-Germanic dialects. In J. R. Black and V. Motapanyane (eds.), *Microparametric Syntax and Dialect Variation.* Amsterdam: John Benjamins, 229–58.

Zwart, Jan-Wouter (1997a). *Morphosyntax of Verb Movement: A Minimalist Approach to the Syntax of Dutch*. Dordrecht: Kluwer.

Zwart, Jan-Wouter (1997b). The Germanic SOV languages and the Universal Base Hypothesis. In L. Haegeman (ed.), *The New Comparative Syntax*. London: Longman, 246–67.

Zwart, Jan-Wouter (2001). Syntactic and phonological verb movement. *Syntax* 4: 34–62.

Zwart, Jan-Wouter (2002). The antisymmetry of Turkish. *Generative Grammar @ Geneva* 3: 23–36.

Zwart, Jan-Wouter (2003). Agreement and remnant movement in the domain of West-Germanic verb movement. In J. Koster and H. van Riemsdijk (eds.), *Germania et Alia: A Linguistic Webschrift for Hans den Besten*. Department of Linguistics, University of Groningen. Available online at <http://www.let.rug.nl/~koster/DenBesten/contents.htm>, last accessed 9 January 2013.

Zwart, Jan-Wouter (2005). A note on functional adpositions. In Hans Broekhuis, N. Corver, R. Huybregts, U. Kleinhenz, and J. Koster (eds.), *Organizing Grammar: Linguistic Studies in Honor of Henk van Riemsdijk*. Berlin: Mouton de Gruyter, 689–95.

Zwart, Jan-Wouter (2007). Some notes on the origin and distribution of the IPP-effect. *Groninger Arbeiten zur Germanistischen Linguistik* 45: 77–99.

Zwart, Jan-Wouter (2009a). Relevance of typology to minimalist inquiry. *Lingua* 119: 1589–606.

Zwart, Jan-Wouter (2009b). The FOFC asymmetry: a layered derivation perspective. Paper presented at the Theoretical Approaches to Disharmonic Word Order conference (Newcastle). Available online at <http://www.let.rug.nl/zwart/>, see *Presentations*; last accessed 17 December 2012.

Zwart, Jan-Wouter (2011). Structure and order: Asymmetric Merge. In C. Boeckx (ed.), *Oxford Handbook of Linguistic Minimalism*. Oxford: Oxford University Press, 96–118.

Index of Languages

Index of Subjects